Advance Praise for *Head First JavaScript*

"So practical and useful, and so well explained. This book does a great job of introducing a complete newbie to JavaScript, and it's another testament to Head First's teaching style. Out of the other JavaScript books, *Head First JavaScript* is great for learning, compared to other reference books the size of a phone book."

> — **Alex Lee, Student, University of Houston**

"An excellent choice for the beginning JavaScript developer."

> — **Fletcher Moore, Web Developer & Designer, Georgia Institute of Technology**

"Yet another great book in the classic 'Head First' style."

> — **TW Scannell**

"JavaScript has long been the client-side engine that drives pages on the Web, but it has also long been misunderstood and misused. With *Head First JavaScript*, Michael Morrison gives a straightforward and easy-to-understand introduction of this language, removing any misunderstanding that ever existed and showing how to most effectively use it to enhance your web pages."

> — **Anthony T. Holdener III, Web applications developer, and the author of *Ajax: The Definitive Guide*.**

"A web page has three parts—content (HTML), appearance (CSS), and behaviour (JavaScript). *Head First HTML* introduced the first two, and this book uses the same fun but practical approach to introduce JavaScript. The fun way in which this book introduces JavaScript and the many ways in which it reinforces the information so that you will not forget it makes this a perfect book for beginners to use to start them on the road to making their web pages interactive."

> — **Stephen Chapman, Owner Felgall Pty Ltd., JavaScript editor, *about.com***

"This is the book I've been looking for to recommend to my readers. It is simple enough for complete beginners but includes enough depth to be useful to more advanced users. And it makes the process of learning fun. This might just be the only JavaScript book you ever need."

> — **Julie L Baumler, JavaScript Editor, *BellaOnline.com***

Praise for *Head First HTML with CSS & XHTML*

If you haven't read this book yet, and you're new to JavaScript, we recommed that you do.

"Eric and Elisabeth Freeman clearly know their stuff. As the Internet becomes more complex, inspired construction of web pages becomes increasingly critical. Elegant design is at the core of every chapter here, each concept conveyed with equal doses of pragmatism and wit."

— Ken Goldstein, Executive Vice President & Managing Director, Disney Online

"The Web would be a much better place if every HTML author started off by reading this book."

— L. David Baron, Technical Lead, Layout & CSS, Mozilla Corporation
http://dbaron.org/

"I've been writing HTML and CSS for ten years now, and what used to be a long trial and error learning process has now been reduced neatly into an engaging paperback. HTML used to be something you could just hack away at until things looked okay on screen, but with the advent of web standards and the movement towards accessibility, sloppy coding practice is not acceptable anymore... from a business standpoint or a social responsibility standpoint. *Head First HTML with CSS & XHTML* teaches you how to do things right from the beginning without making the whole process seem overwhelming. HTML, when properly explained, is no more complicated than plain English, and the Freemans do an excellent job of keeping every concept at eye-level."

— Mike Davidson, President & CEO, Newsvine, Inc.

"Oh, great. You made an XHTML book simple enough a CEO can understand it. What will you do next? Accounting simple enough my developer can understand it? Next thing you know we'll be collaborating as a team or something."

—Janice Fraser, CEO, Adaptive Path

"This book has humor, and charm, but most importantly, it has heart. I know that sounds ridiculous to say about a technical book, but I really sense that at its core, this book (or at least its authors) really care that the reader learn the material. This comes across in the style, the language, and the techniques. Learning – real understanding and comprehension – on the part of the reader is clearly top most in the minds of the Freemans. And thank you, thank you, thank you, for the book's strong, and sensible advocacy of standards compliance. It's great to see an entry level book, that I think will be widely read and studied, campaign so eloquently and persuasively on behalf of the value of standards compliance in web page code. I even found in here a few great arguments I had not thought of – ones I can remember and use when I am asked – as I still am – 'what's the deal with compliance and why should we care?' I'll have more ammo now! I also liked that the book sprinkles in some basics about the mechanics of actually getting a web page live - FTP, web server basics, file structures, etc."

—Robert Neer, Director of Product Development, Movies.com

""Freeman's *Head First HTML with CSS & XHTML* is a most entertaining book for learning how to build a great web page. It not only covers everything you need to know about HTML, CSS, and XHTML, it also excels in explaining everything in layman's terms with a lot of great examples. I found the book truly enjoyable to read, and I learned something new!"

> — **Newton Lee, Editor-in-Chief, ACM Computers in Entertainment,**
> ***http://www.acmcie.org***

"My wife stole the book. She's never done any web design, so she needed a book like *Head First HTML with CSS & XHTML* to take her from beginning to end. She now has a list of web sites she wants to build – for our son's class, our family, ... If I'm lucky, I'll get the book back when she's done."

> — **David Kaminsky, Master Inventor, IBM**

"Beware. If you're someone who reads at night before falling asleep, you'll have to restrict *Head First HTML with CSS & XHTML* to daytime reading. This book wakes up your brain."

> — **Pauline McNamara, Center for New Technologies and Education,**
> **Fribourg University, Switzerland**

"The information covered in this book is the same material the pros know, but taught in an educational and humorous manner that doesn't ever make you think the material is impossible to learn or you are out of your element."

> —**Christopher Schmitt, Author of *The CSS Cookbook* and *Professional CSS*,**
> ***schmitt@christopher.org***

"*Head First HTML with CSS & XHTML* is a thoroughly modern introduction to forward-looking practices in Web page markup and presentation. It correctly anticipates readers' puzzlements and handles them just in time. The highly graphic and incremental approach precisely mimics the best way to learn this stuff: make a small change and see it in the browser to understand what each new item means."

> —**Danny Goodman, author of *Dynamic HTML: The Definitive Guide***

Other related books from O'Reilly

JavaScript: The Definitive Guide

JavaScript Pocket Reference

Learning JavaScript

JavaScript & DHTML Cookbook

Other books in O'Reilly's *Head First* series

Head First Java

Head First Object-Oriented Analysis and Design (OOA&D)

Head First HTML with CSS and XHTML

Head First Design Patterns

Head First Servlets and JSP

Head First EJB

Head First PMP

Head First SQL

Head First Software Development

Head First C#

Head First Ajax

Head First Physics

Head First Statistics

Head First Rails

Head First PHP & MySQL

Head First Algebra

Head First Web Design

Head First Networking (2009)

Head First JavaScript

Wouldn't it be dreamy if there was a way to learn JavaScript from a book without wanting to set fire to it halfway through and swearing off the Web forever? I know, it's probably just a fantasy...

Michael Morrison

O'REILLY®

Beijing · Cambridge · Köln · Sebastopol · Taipei · Tokyo

Head First JavaScript

by Michael Morrison

Published by O'Reilly Media, Inc., 1005 Gravenstein Highway North, Sebastopol, CA 95472.

O'Reilly Media books may be purchased for educational, business, or sales promotional use. Online editions are also available for most titles (*safari.oreilly.com*). For more information, contact our corporate/institutional sales department: (800) 998-9938 or *corporate@oreilly.com*.

Series Creators:	Kathy Sierra, Bert Bates
Series Editor:	Brett D. McLaughlin
Editor:	Catherine Nolan
Design Editor:	Louise Barr
Cover Designers:	Louise Barr, Steve Fehler
Production Editor:	Sanders Kleinfeld
Proofreader:	Colleen Gorman
Indexer:	Julie Hawks
Page Viewers:	Masheed Morrison (wife), family, and pet fish

...but my koi fish couldn't care less.

Printing History:

December 2007: First Edition.

My family knows how to celebrate a book release...

No rocks, stick figures, cube puzzles, or macho moviegoers were harmed in the making of this book. Just me, but I can handle it...I'm wiry.

RepKover.™ This book uses RepKover,™ a durable and flexible lay-flat binding.

ISBN: 978-0-596-52774-7

To the folks at Netscape who, way back in the last century, dreamed that the Web could be much more than a big online book with a bunch of linked pages that don't **do** anything.

Of course, they also dreamed up that horrific `<blink>` tag...dare to dream, just don't get too carried away!

Author of Head First JavaScript

Michael Morrison, child JavaScript prodigy.

Michael Morrison, full-size nerd who refuses to grow up.

Michael Morrison has been tinkering with computers since his first PC, a TI-99/4A, complete with its supremely ergonomic keyboard, state of the art black and white TV "monitor," and sweet cassette tape storage system. He has owned and tinkered with a few more computers since then, but still longs for the days of playing Parsec on that TI in between epic Nerf football games in the backyard.

Now Michael is all grown up and has moved on to much more mature interests, such as creating interactive web applications...and skateboarding. Cut, bruised, and often limping, he approaches tech challenges with the same reckless intensity as high-risk sports. After developing a few video games, inventing a couple of toys, writing dozens of computer books, and creating numerous online courses, Michael finally felt ready to tackle *Head First JavaScript*. He no longer trusts his feelings.

As it turns out, you're never really ready to write a *Head First* book. The best you can be is ready to pop the red pill and enter the Matrix that is *Head First*. Having emerged from the other side with a few intellectual bruises to add to his real ones, Michael will never look at learning (or teaching) the same again. And he's thrilled about that fact. Right about now he's with his wife next to their koi pond reflecting on the wonders of the interactive Web.

Table of Contents (Summary)

Table of Contents (the real thing)

Intro

Your brain on JavaScript. You're sitting around trying to *learn* something, but your *brain* keeps telling you all that learning *isn't important*. Your brain's saying, "Better leave room for more important things, like which wild animals to avoid and whether naked water skiing is a bad idea." So how *do* you trick your brain into thinking that your life really depends on learning JavaScript?

the interactive web

Reacting to the Virtual World

1

Tired of thinking of the Web in terms of passive pages?

Been there, done that. They're called books. And they're good for reading, learning... lots of good things. But they're not **interactive**. And neither is the Web without a little help from JavaScript. Sure, you can submit a form and maybe do a trick here and there with some crafty HTML and CSS coding, but you're really just playing *Weekend at Bernie's* propping up a lifeless web page. Real live **interactivity** requires **a bit more smarts** and a **little more work**... but it has a *much bigger payoff*.

2

storing data

Everything Has Its Place

In the real world, people often overlook the importance of having a place to store all their stuff. Not so in JavaScript. You simply don't have the luxury of walk-in closets and three-car garages. In JavaScript, **everything has its place**, and it's your job to make sure of it. The issue is **data**—how to *represent it*, how to *store it*, and how to *find it* once you've put it somewhere. As a JavaScript storage specialist, you'll be able to take a cluttered room of JavaScript data and impose your will on it with a flurry of virtual labels and storage bins.

exploring the client
Browser Spelunking

3

Sometimes JavaScript needs to know what's going on in the world around it. Your scripts may begin as code in web pages but they ultimately live in a world created by the browser, or client. **Smart scripts** often need to know more about the world they live in, in which case they can **communicate with the browser** to find out more about it. Whether it's finding out the screen size or accessing the browser's snooze button, scripts have an awful lot to gain by cultivating their browser relationship.

Start here!

Finish!

decision making

If There's a Fork in the Road, Take It

4

Life is all about making decisions. Stop or go, shake or bake, plea bargain or go to trial... without the ability to make decisions, nothing would ever get done. It works the same in JavaScript—**decisions allow scripts to decide between different possible outcomes**. *Decision-making drives the "story" of your scripts*, and even the most mundane scripts involve a story of some sort. Do you trust what the user entered and book her a trip on a Sasquatch expedition or do you double-check that maybe she really just wanted to ride a bus to Saskatchewan? The choice is yours to make!

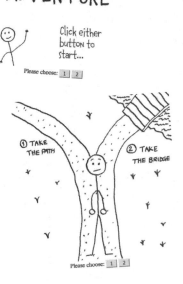

looping

At the Risk of Repeating Myself

5

Some say repetition is the spice of life. Sure, doing something new and interesting is certainly exciting, but it's the little repetitive things that really make it possible to get through the day. Compulsive hand sanitizing, a nervous tick, clicking Reply To All to every freaking message you receive! Okay, maybe repetition isn't always such a great thing in the real world. However, it can be extremely handy in the world of JavaScript. You'd be surprised how often you need a script to *run a piece of code several times*. Without **loops**, you'd be wasting a lot of time cutting and pasting a bunch of wasteful code.

Available

seat_avail.png

Unavailable

seat_unavail.png

Select

seat_select.png

functions

Reduce, Reuse, Recycle

6

If there was an environmental movement within JavaScript, it would be led by functions. Functions allow you to make JavaScript code more efficient, and yes, more reusable. Functions are also task-oriented, good at code organization, and excellent problem solvers. Sounds like the makings of a good resume! In reality, all but the simplest of scripts stand to benefit from a functional reorganization. While it's hard to put a number on the carbon footprint of the average function, let's just say they do their part in making scripts as eco-friendly as possible.

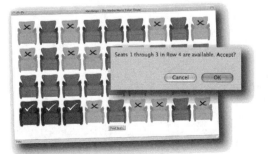

forms and validation

Getting the User to Tell All

7

You don't have to be suave or sneaky to successfully get information from users with JavaScript. But you do have to be careful. Humans have this strange tendency to make mistakes, which means *you can't* always count on the data provided in online forms being *accurate*. Enter JavaScript. By **passing form data through the right JavaScript code** as it is being entered, you can **make web applications much more reliable**, and also **take some load off of the server**. We need to *save that precious bandwidth for important things* like stunt videos and cute pet pictures.

Bannerocity...banner ads in the sky!

wrangling the page

8

Slicing and Dicing HTML with the DOM

Taking control of web page content with JavaScript is a lot like baking. Well, without the mess... and unfortunately, also without the edible reward afterward. However; you get *full access to the HTML* ingredients that go into a web page, and more importantly, you have the ability to *alter* the recipe of the page. So **JavaScript makes it possible to manipulate the HTML code within a web page** to your heart's desire, which opens up all kinds of interesting opportunities all made possible by a *collection of standard objects* called **the DOM** (Document Object Model).

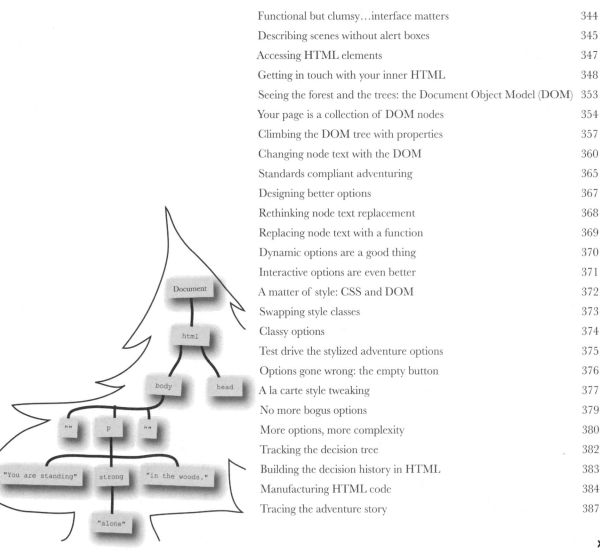

9

bringing data to life

Objects as Frankendata

JavaScript objects aren't nearly as gruesome as the good doctor might have you think. But they are interesting in that they combine pieces and parts of the JavaScript language together so that they're more powerful together. **Objects combine data with actions** to create a new data type that is much more "alive" than data you've seen thus far. You end up with *arrays that can sort themselves*, *strings that can search themselves*, and scripts that can grow fur and howl at the moon! OK, maybe not that last one but you get the idea...

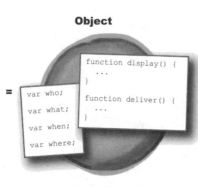

Data

```
var who;
var what;
var when;
var where;
```

Actions

```
function display(what, when, where) {
    ...
}
function deliver(who) {
    ...
}
```

+

Object

```
function display() {
    ...
}
function deliver() {
    ...
}
var who;
var what;
var when;
var where;
```

=

creating custom objects

Having It Your Way with Custom Objects

If it was only that easy, we'd surely have it made. JavaScript doesn't have a money-back guarantee, but you can definitely have it your way. Custom objects are the JavaScript equivalent of a decaf triple shot grande extra hot no whip extra drizzle no foam marble mocha macchiato. That is one custom cup of coffee! And with custom JavaScript objects, you can brew up some code that does exactly what you want, while taking advantage of the benefits of properties and methods. The end result is reusable code that effectively extends the JavaScript language...just for you!

10

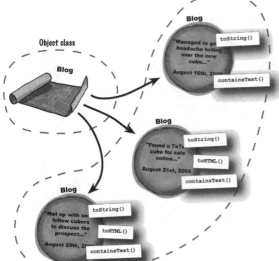

Object instances

Object class

11

kill bugs dead

Good Scripts Gone Wrong

Even the best laid JavaScript plans sometimes fail. When this happens, and it will, your job is not to panic. The best JavaScript developers are not the ones who never create bugs - those people are called liars. No, the best JavaScript developers are those who are able to **successfully hunt down and eradicate** the **bugs** they create. More importantly, top notch JavaScript bug exterminators **develop good coding habits** that minimize the sneakiest and nastiest of bugs. *A little prevention can go a long way.* But bugs happen, and you'll need an arsenal of weapons to combat them...

dynamic data
Touchy-Feely Web Applications

12

The modern Web is a very responsive place where pages are expected to react to the user's every whim. Or at least that's the dream of many web users and developers. JavaScript plays a vital role in this dream through a programming technique known as **Ajax** that provides a mechanism for dramatically changing the "feel" of web pages. With Ajax, web pages act much more like full-blown applications since they are able to **quickly load and save data dynamically** while **responding to the user in real time** without any page refreshes or browser trickery.

youcube.html   blog.xml

Intro

In this section we answer the burning question:
"So why DID they put that in a JavaScript book?"

Who is this book for?

If you can answer "yes" to all of these:

 Do you have access to a computer with a web browser, a text editor, and an Internet connection?

 Do you want to **learn**, **understand**, and **remember how to create web pages that are alive with energy, turning the Web into a truly interactive experience?**

 Do you prefer **stimulating dinner party conversation** to **dry**, **dull**, **academic lectures**?

We'll help you learn how to write JavaScript code that makes web pages do all kinds of cool things that are impossible with HTML alone.

this book is for you.

Who should probably back away from this book?

If you can answer "yes" to any of these:

 Are you **completely new** to creating web pages?

(You don't need to be an HTML guru, but you should understand the basics of how web pages go together with HTML and CSS, and how to post them online.)

 Do you hold a ninth degree black belt in Script Fu, and are really looking for a JavaScript **reference book**?

 Are you **afraid to try something different**? Would you rather have a root canal than mix stripes with plaid? Do you believe that a technical book can't be serious if JavaScript code is anthropomorphized?

This book makes a great sequel to Head First HTML with CSS & XHTML, so definitely check it out if you want to brush up on your HTML.

this book is not for you.

[Note from marketing: this book is for anyone with a credit card.]

We know what you're thinking

"How can *this* be a serious JavaScript book?"

"What's with all the graphics?"

"Can I actually *learn* it this way?"

We know what your *brain* is thinking

Your brain craves novelty. It's always searching, scanning, *waiting* for something unusual. It was built that way, and it helps you stay alive.

So what does your brain do with all the routine, ordinary, normal things you encounter? Everything it *can* to stop them from interfering with the brain's *real* job—recording things that *matter*. It doesn't bother saving the boring things; they never make it past the "this is obviously not important" filter.

How does your brain *know* what's important? Suppose you're out for a day hike and a tiger jumps in front of you, what happens inside your head and body?

Neurons fire. Emotions crank up. *Chemicals surge.*

And that's how your brain knows...

This must be important! Don't forget it!

But imagine you're at home, or in a library. It's a safe, warm, tiger-free zone. You're studying. Getting ready for an exam. Or trying to learn some tough technical topic your boss thinks will take a week, ten days at the most.

Just one problem. Your brain's trying to do you a big favor. It's trying to make sure that this *obviously* non-important content doesn't clutter up scarce resources. Resources that are better spent storing the really *big* things. Like tigers. Like the danger of fire. Like how you should never have agreed to house sit for your friend with the pet anaconda.

And there's no simple way to tell your brain, "Hey brain, thank you very much, but no matter how dull this book is, and how little I'm registering on the emotional Richter scale right now, I really *do* want you to keep this stuff around."

Your brain thinks THIS is important.

Your brain thinks THIS isn't worth saving.

Great. Only 600 more dull, dry, boring pages.

We think of a "Head First" reader as a <u>learner</u>.

So what does it take to *learn* something? First, you have to *get* it, then make sure you don't *forget* it. It's not about pushing facts into your head. Based on the latest research in cognitive science, neurobiology, and educational psychology, *learning* takes a lot more than text on a page. We know what turns your brain on.

Some of the Head First learning principles:

Make it visual. Images are far more memorable than words alone, and make learning much more effective (up to 89% improvement in recall and transfer studies). It also makes things more understandable. **Put the words within or near the graphics** they relate to, rather than on the bottom or on another page, and learners will be up to *twice* as likely to solve problems related to the content.

Use a conversational and personalized style. In recent studies, students performed up to 40% better on post-learning tests if the content spoke directly to the reader, using a first-person, conversational style rather than taking a formal tone. Tell stories instead of lecturing. Use casual language. Don't take yourself too seriously. Which would *you* pay more attention to: a stimulating dinner party companion, or a lecture?

on focus!

on blur!

Get the learner to think more deeply. In other words, unless you actively flex your neurons, nothing much happens in your head. A reader has to be motivated, engaged, curious, and inspired to solve problems, draw conclusions, and generate new knowledge. And for that, you need challenges, exercises, and thought-provoking questions, and activities that involve both sides of the brain and multiple senses.

Get—and keep—the reader's attention. We've all had the "I really want to learn this but I can't stay awake past page one" experience. Your brain pays attention to things that are out of the ordinary, interesting, strange, eye-catching, unexpected. Learning a new, tough, technical topic doesn't have to be boring. Your brain will learn much more quickly if it's not.

Touch their emotions. We now know that your ability to remember something is largely dependent on its emotional content. You remember what you care about. You remember when you *feel* something. No, we're not talking heart-wrenching stories about a boy and his dog. We're talking emotions like surprise, curiosity, fun, "what the...?", and the feeling of "I Rule!" that comes when you solve a puzzle, learn something everybody else thinks is hard, or realize you know something that "I'm more technical than thou" Bob from engineering *doesn't*.

I'm burning up! Please turn the heater off. Or am I feeling the effects of local warming?

Metacognition: thinking about thinking

If you really want to learn, and you want to learn more quickly and more deeply, pay attention to how you pay attention. Think about how you think. Learn how you learn.

Most of us did not take courses on metacognition or learning theory when we were growing up. We were *expected* to learn, but rarely *taught* to learn.

But we assume that if you're holding this book, you really want to learn how to create interactive web pages that sizzle. And you probably don't want to spend a lot of time. If you want to use what you read in this book, you need to *remember* what you read. And for that, you've got to *understand* it. To get the most from this book, or *any* book or learning experience, take responsibility for your brain. Your brain on *this* content.

The trick is to get your brain to see the new material you're learning as Really Important. Crucial to your well-being. As important as a tiger. Otherwise, you're in for a constant battle, with your brain doing its best to keep the new content from sticking.

I wonder how I can trick my brain into remembering this stuff...

So just how *DO* you get your brain to treat JavaScript like it was a hungry tiger?

There's the slow, tedious way, or the faster, more effective way. The slow way is about sheer repetition. You obviously know that you *are* able to learn and remember even the dullest of topics if you keep pounding the same thing into your brain. With enough repetition, your brain says, "This doesn't *feel* important to him, but he keeps looking at the same thing *over* and *over* and *over*, so I suppose it must be."

The faster way is to do ***anything that increases brain activity,*** especially different *types* of brain activity. The things on the previous page are a big part of the solution, and they're all things that have been proven to help your brain work in your favor. For example, studies show that putting words *within* the pictures they describe (as opposed to somewhere else in the page, like a caption or in the body text) causes your brain to try to makes sense of how the words and picture relate, and this causes more neurons to fire. More neurons firing = more chances for your brain to *get* that this is something worth paying attention to, and possibly recording.

A conversational style helps because people tend to pay more attention when they perceive that they're in a conversation, since they're expected to follow along and hold up their end. The amazing thing is, your brain doesn't necessarily *care* that the "conversation" is between you and a book! On the other hand, if the writing style is formal and dry, your brain perceives it the same way you experience being lectured to while sitting in a roomful of passive attendees. No need to stay awake.

But pictures and conversational style are just the beginning…

Here's what WE did:

We used *pictures*, because your brain is tuned for visuals, not text. As far as your brain's concerned, a picture really *is* worth a thousand words. And when text and pictures work together, we embedded the text *in* the pictures because your brain works more effectively when the text is *within* the thing the text refers to, as opposed to in a caption or buried in the text somewhere.

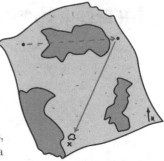

We used *redundancy*, saying the same thing in *different* ways and with different media types, and *multiple senses*, to increase the chance that the content gets coded into more than one area of your brain.

We used concepts and pictures in *unexpected* ways because your brain is tuned for novelty, and we used pictures and ideas with at least *some emotional* content, because your brain is tuned to pay attention to the biochemistry of emotions. That which causes you to *feel* something is more likely to be remembered, even if that feeling is nothing more than a little *humor*, *surprise*, or *interest.*

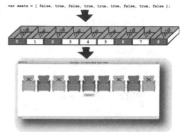

We used a personalized, *conversational style*, because your brain is tuned to pay more attention when it believes you're in a conversation than if it thinks you're passively listening to a presentation. Your brain does this even when you're *reading*.

We included more than 80 *activities*, because your brain is tuned to learn and remember more when you *do* things than when you *read* about things. And we made the exercises challenging-yet-do-able, because that's what most people prefer.

We used *multiple learning styles*, because *you* might prefer step-by-step procedures, while someone else wants to understand the big picture first, and someone else just wants to see an example. But regardless of your own learning preference, *everyone* benefits from seeing the same content represented in multiple ways.

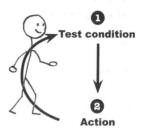

1 Test condition

2 Action

We include content for *both sides of your brain*, because the more of your brain you engage, the more likely you are to learn and remember, and the longer you can stay focused. Since working one side of the brain often means giving the other side a chance to rest, you can be more productive at learning for a longer period of time.

And we included *stories* and exercises that present *more than one point of view,* because your brain is tuned to learn more deeply when it's forced to make evaluations and judgments.

BRAIN POWER

We included *challenges*, with exercises, and by asking *questions* that don't always have a straight answer, because your brain is tuned to learn and remember when it has to *work* at something. Think about it—you can't get your *body* in shape just by *watching* people at the gym. But we did our best to make sure that when you're working hard, it's on the *right* things. That *you're not spending one extra dendrite* processing a hard-to-understand example, or parsing difficult, jargon-laden, or overly terse text.

We used *people*. In stories, examples, pictures, etc., because, well, because *you're* a person. And your brain pays more attention to *people* than it does to *things*.

Cut this out and stick it on your refrigerator.

Here's what YOU can do to bend your brain into submission

So, we did our part. The rest is up to you. These tips are a starting point; listen to your brain and figure out what works for you and what doesn't. Try new things.

---

(1) Slow down. The more you understand, the less you have to memorize.

Don't just *read*. Stop and think. When the book asks you a question, don't just skip to the answer. Imagine that someone really *is* asking the question. The more deeply you force your brain to think, the better chance you have of learning and remembering.

(2) Do the exercises. Write your own notes.

We put them in, but if we did them for you, that would be like having someone else do your workouts for you. And don't just *look* at the exercises. **Use a pencil.** There's plenty of evidence that physical activity *while* learning can increase the learning.

(3) Read the "There are No Dumb Questions"

That means all of them. They're not optional sidebars—*they're part of the core content!* Don't skip them.

(4) Make this the last thing you read before bed. Or at least the last challenging thing.

Part of the learning (especially the transfer to long-term memory) happens *after* you put the book down. Your brain needs time on its own, to do more processing. If you put in something new during that processing time, some of what you just learned will be lost.

(5) Drink water. Lots of it.

Your brain works best in a nice bath of fluid. Dehydration (which can happen before you ever feel thirsty) decreases cognitive function.

(6) Talk about it. Out loud.

Speaking activates a different part of the brain. If you're trying to understand something, or increase your chance of remembering it later, say it out loud. Better still, try to explain it out loud to someone else. You'll learn more quickly, and you might uncover ideas you hadn't known were there when you were reading about it.

(7) Listen to your brain.

Pay attention to whether your brain is getting overloaded. If you find yourself starting to skim the surface or forget what you just read, it's time for a break. Once you go past a certain point, you won't learn faster by trying to shove more in, and you might even hurt the process.

(8) Keep it real!

Your brain needs to know that this *matters*. Get involved with the stories. Make up your own captions for the photos. Groaning over a bad joke is *still* better than feeling nothing at all.

(9) Just do it!

There's only one way to learn JavaScript: **writing a lot of JavaScript code**. And that's what you're going to do throughout this book. Don't just skip over the JavaScript exercises—a lot of the learning happens when you solve problems, even unusual ones like Stick Figure Adventure, the Mandango macho movie seat finder, and the YouCube blog. And definitely stick with an exercise and get it working before you move on to the next part of the book. Oh, and if you have an interactive web project you've been dreaming about, don't be afraid to build it as you work through the book and add to your shiny new bag of JavaScript programming tricks.

Read Me

This is a learning experience, not a reference book. We deliberately stripped out everything that might get in the way of learning whatever it is we're working on at that point in the book. And the first time through, you need to begin at the beginning, because the book makes assumptions about what you've already seen and learned.

We teach JavaScript on a "need to know" basis.

If you're looking for a history of JavaScript, keep on looking because this book won't help. The goal here is to teach you how to do cool, practical things in JavaScript to amp up the interactivity of web pages, turning them into responsive web **applications** that people will want to **experience**. We forego formalities, and only teach the JavaScript concepts you need to know to do real things, in real time. Really.

We don't cover every hidden nuance of the JavaScript language.

While we could have put every single JavaScript statement, object, event, and keyword in this book, we thought you'd prefer a reasonably portable book that doesn't require a forklift to carry from your desk to the gym. Oh yeah, it's a great workout read, but you might want to invest in a sweat-proof pencil! We focus on the parts of JavaScript you need to know, the ones you'll use 95 percent of the time. And when you're done with this book, you'll have the confidence to go look up that elusive method you need to finish off that killer script you just dreamed up in the shower.

Since JavaScript includes a huge built-in library of reusable code, it's important to understand when you're dealing with standard JavaScript code, as opposed to custom code that you create. Any time you see the word "custom," that means the code is custom built by you, and not a built-in part of JavaScript.

We encourage you to use more than one browser with this book.

Even though all modern web browsers support JavaScript, there are sometimes subtle differences in how they handle certain JavaScript code. So, we encourage you to pick at least two up-to-date browsers and test your scripts using them. We've found Firefox to currently be a superior browser for helping track down JavaScript coding errors, but your scripts will ultimately need to run consistently on a variety of different browsers. Don't hesitate to get your friends, family members, co-workers, and highly trained pets to help test out your scripts in their browsers.

The activities are NOT optional.

The exercises and activities are not add-ons; they're part of the core content of the book. Some of them are to help with memory, some are for understanding, and some will help you apply what you've learned. ***Don't skip the exercises.*** The crossword puzzles are the only thing you don't *have* to do, but they're good for giving your brain a chance to think about the words and terms you've been learning in a different context. And the Page Benders, well those are optional too if you hate the thought of creasing these beautiful pages. But you'll miss out on some fun.

The redundancy is intentional and important.

One distinct difference in a *Head First* book is that we want you to *really* get it. And we want you to finish the book remembering what you've learned. Most reference books don't have retention and recall as a goal, but this book is about *learning*, so you'll see some of the same concepts come up more than once.

The examples are as lean as possible.

Our readers tell us that it's frustrating to wade through 200 lines of an example looking for the two lines they need to understand. Most examples in this book are shown within the smallest possible context, so that the part you're trying to learn is clear and simple. Don't expect all of the examples to be robust, or even complete—they are written specifically for learning, and aren't always fully-functional.

We've placed the complete code for all of the examples on the Web so you can copy and paste it into your text editor and explore. You can also play around with the finished scripts online. You'll find them at:

http://www.headfirstlabs.com/books/hfjs/

The Brain Power exercises don't have answers.

For some of them, there is no right answer, and for others, part of the learning experience of the Brain Power activities is for you to decide if and when your answers are right. In some of the Brain Power exercises, you will find hints to point you in the right direction. It's your brain...feel its power!

The technical review team

TW Scannell Fletcher Moore Elaine Norman Stephen Tallent Alex Lee

Katherine St. John Zachary Kessin Anthony T. Holdener III

Technical Reviewers:

Alex Lee is a student at the University of Houston majoring in Management Information Systems. Enjoys running, video games and staying up late learning new programming languages.

TW Scannell of Sisters, Oregon has been tweaking the bits since 1995 and is currently a Ruby on Rails developer.

Elaine Nelson has been designing websites for nearly 10 years. As she tells her mother, an English degree comes in handy everywhere. Elaine's current musings and obsessions can be found at elainenelson.org.

Fletcher Moore is a web developer and designer at Georgia Tech. In his spare time he's an avid cyclist, musician, gardener, and Red Sox fan. He resides in Atlanta with his wife Katherine, daughter Sailor, and son Satchel.

Anthony T. Holdener III is a web applications developer and the author of *Ajax: The Definitive Guide* (O'Reilly).

Zachary Kessin has been programming on the Web since rocks were soft and dirt was a fresh new idea, which is to say about 15 years. He lives in Israel with his wife and 3 children.

Katherine St. John is an associate professor of computer science and mathematics at the City University of New York, and her research focuses on computational biology and random structures.

Stephen Tallent lives and works in Nashville, Tennessee primarily developing sports applications and coping with the chaos that is parenting small children. When not all consumed with the aforementioned tasks, he enjoys skateboarding and preparing for a second career as a short order cook.

Acknowledgments

My editor:

Remember in elementary school when you were assigned some kid across the country (or world) to become your pen pal, and then you got to share stuff about your life with them through letters? Well, **Catherine Nolan** became my *Head First* pen pal when we started this project. But we communicate with telephones, chat clients, emails, fax machines, and anything else that accepts OMG, LOL, and my personal favorite, BHH (Bless Her Heart). In the process, Catherine became much more than my JavaScript cognitive learning online collaborator. She became my friend. It's not every day that a "business" call meanders from JavaScript to jam bands to home remodeling, and back. It was a pleasure going through the ups and downs of this crazy process with a consummate pro. Thanks, Catherine! I owe you a few martinis.

Catherine Nolan, fellow Phish and Dewey Decimal afficionado.

The O'Reilly team:

Wow, it's hard to say enough glowing things about the *Head First* team. But I'll try.

Brett McLaughlin initially fed me to the educational psych wolves in the *Head First* boot camp I attended, and hasn't backed down since. The guy is as serious about reverse-engineering the learning process as he is about guitars. I'm fairly convinced he doesn't go to sleep without first posing the question, "what's my motivation?" But his undying commitment is what makes these books so awesome. Thanks, Brett!

Lou Barr, design goddess.

Lou Barr became my other virtual pen pal during this project, as well as my cultural guide to navigating the subtle differences between the U.S. and England (her home). I think she's really just on loan to us from the gods of design. The layout of this book would've simply been impossible without her magic.

Sanders Kleinfeld operates a bit more stealthily but his presence is always felt, keeping production running smoothly and offering that elusive "big idea" just when you need it most.

Brett McLaughlin, Head First expedition leader and blues man.

The rest of the O'Reilly team is also not forgotten in the thank-you department. **Laurie Petrycki** trusted me enough to green light the project, **Caitrin McCullough** manages a killer support site (*www.headfirstlabs.com*), and **Keith McNamara** fills in the gaps with military precision. Thanks, guys!

Finally, **Kathy Sierra** and **Bert Bates** deserve perhaps the biggest thanks of all for their incredible vision with the *Head First* series. It's truly a privilege to be a part of it...

Safari® Books Online

 When you see a Safari® icon on the cover of your favorite technology book that means the book is available online through the O'Reilly Network Safari Bookshelf.

Safari offers a solution that's better than e-books. It's a virtual library that lets you easily search thousands of top tech books, cut and paste code samples, download chapters, and find quick answers when you need the most accurate, current information. Try it for free at *http://safari.oreilly.com*.

1 the interactive web

Reacting to the Virtual World

> Oh my stars! I didn't realize the Web could be so "feely." Does it know what I'm thinking right now?

Tired of thinking of the Web in terms of passive pages?

Been there, done that. They're called books. And they're good for reading, learning... lots of good things. But they're not **interactive**. And neither is the Web without a little help from JavaScript. Sure, you can submit a form and maybe do a trick here and there with some crafty HTML and CSS coding, but you're really just playing *Weekend at Bernie's* propping up a lifeless web page. Real live **interactivity** requires **a bit more smarts** and a **little more work**... but it has a *much bigger payoff*.

(Online) people have needs

All right, we know the Web is virtual, but the people on the Web are real people, with real world needs. Needs like searching for a killer meatloaf recipe, downloading their favorite song by Meatloaf, or something even as huge as shopping for a new home. Fortunately, the Web differentiates when it comes to prioritizing your needs!

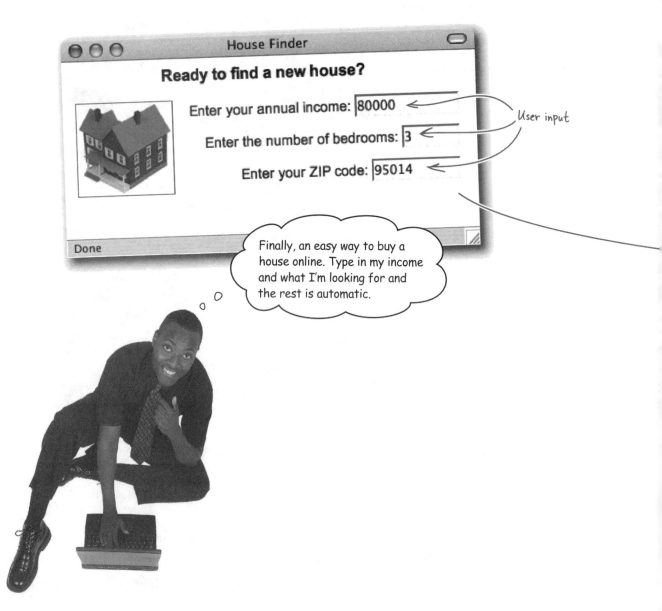

Like talking to a brick wall... nothing happens

The Web isn't always as responsive as it could be. In fact, it can sometimes feel downright cold and unfeeling, detached from the outside world and unresponsive to the needs of its many users. You would expect that entering data like this would generate some sort of response...but nothing happened. Don't take it personally; the static Web just doesn't know better.

But JavaScript talks back

JavaScript flips the switch that turns a web page into an interactive experience. It powers things that can listen to your needs, process your input, and respond to your deepest desires. OK, perhaps that's a stretch, but JavaScript can turn a web page into an interactive application as opposed to a static, lifeless page, and that's a good thing!

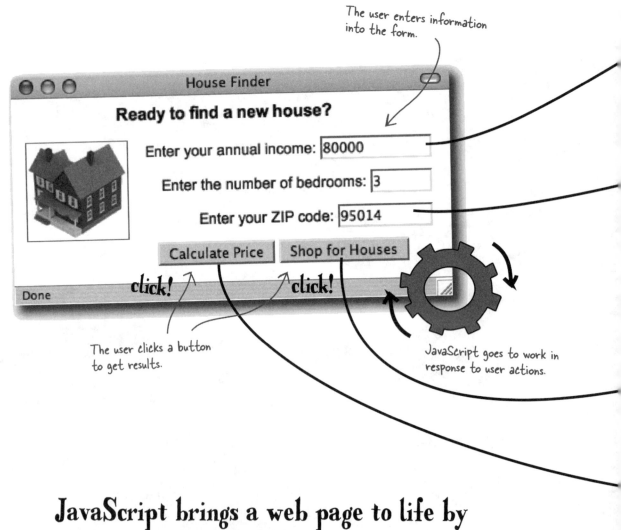

The user enters information into the form.

The user clicks a button to get results.

JavaScript goes to work in response to user actions.

JavaScript brings a web page to life by allowing it to respond to a user's input.

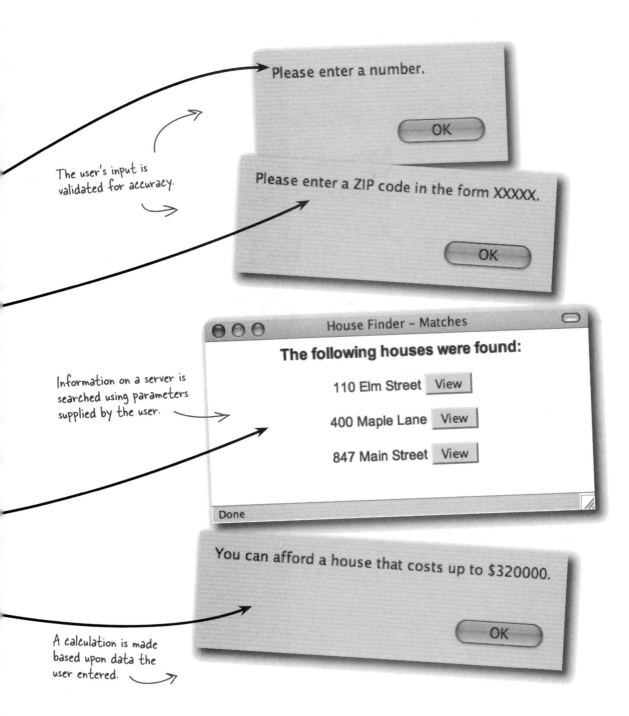

Please enter a number.

OK

The user's input is validated for accuracy.

Please enter a ZIP code in the form XXXXX.

OK

Information on a server is searched using parameters supplied by the user.

House Finder – Matches

The following houses were found:

110 Elm Street View

400 Maple Lane View

847 Main Street View

Done

You can afford a house that costs up to $320000.

OK

A calculation is made based upon data the user entered.

Lights, camera, ^inter action!

JavaScript sits with HTML and CSS as one of the three pieces of modern Web page construction. HTML provides the structure, CSS adds the style, and JavaScript puts the rubber to the road and makes things happen. To find the path to an interactive web page, you must follow the trail of **structure** (HTML) to **style** (CSS), and then to **action** (JavaScript). Similar to CSS, JavaScript code often resides right there in the web page.

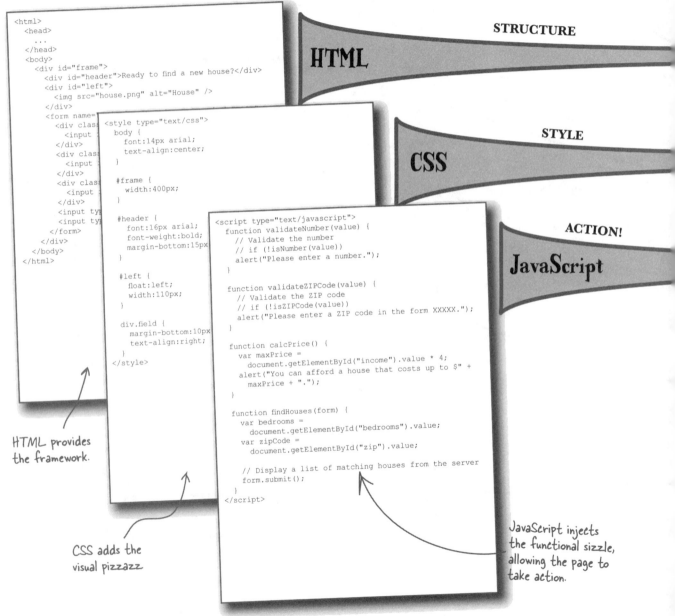

STRUCTURE

HTML

```
<html>
  <head>
    ...
  </head>
  <body>
    <div id="frame">
      <div id="header">Ready to find a new house?</div>
      <div id="left">
        <img src="house.png" alt="House" />
      </div>
      <form name=
        <div clas
          <input
        </div>
        <div clas
          <input
        </div>
        <div clas
          <input
        </div>
        <input typ
        <input typ
      </form>
    </div>
  </body>
</html>
```

HTML provides the framework.

STYLE

CSS

```
<style type="text/css">
  body {
    font:14px arial;
    text-align:center;
  }

  #frame {
    width:400px;
  }

  #header {
    font:16px arial;
    font-weight:bold;
    margin-bottom:15px
  }

  #left {
    float:left;
    width:110px;
  }

  div.field {
    margin-bottom:10px
    text-align:right;
  }
</style>
```

CSS adds the visual pizzazz

ACTION!

JavaScript

```
<script type="text/javascript">
  function validateNumber(value) {
    // Validate the number
    // if (!isNumber(value))
    alert("Please enter a number.");
  }
  function validateZIPCode(value) {
    // Validate the ZIP code
    // if (!isZIPCode(value))
    alert("Please enter a ZIP code in the form XXXXX.");
  }

  function calcPrice() {
    var maxPrice =
      document.getElementById("income").value * 4;
    alert("You can afford a house that costs up to $" +
      maxPrice + ".");
  }

  function findHouses(form) {
    var bedrooms =
      document.getElementById("bedrooms").value;
    var zipCode =
      document.getElementById("zip").value;

    // Display a list of matching houses from the server
    form.submit();
  }
</script>
```

JavaScript injects the functional sizzle, allowing the page to take action.

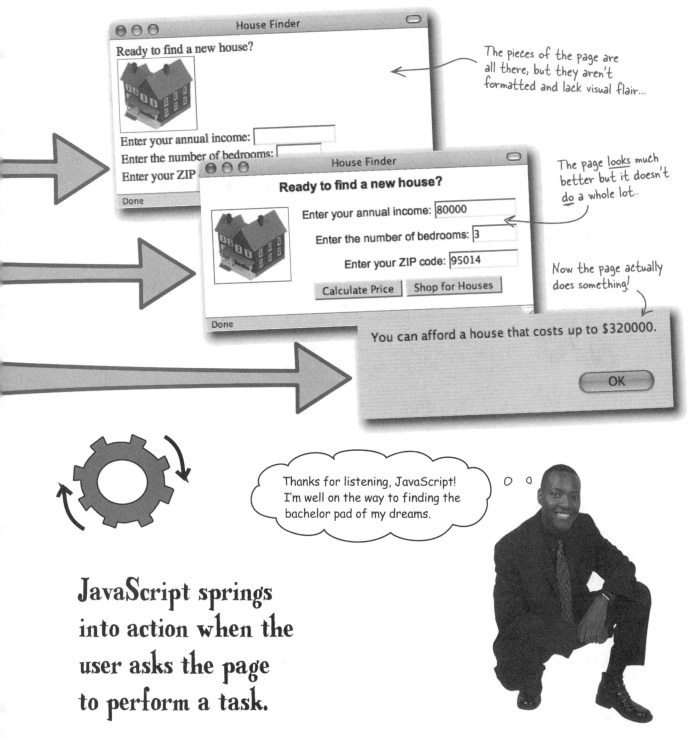

The pieces of the page are all there, but they aren't formatted and lack visual flair...

The page looks much better but it doesn't do a whole lot..

Now the page actually does something!

Thanks for listening, JavaScript! I'm well on the way to finding the bachelor pad of my dreams.

JavaScript springs into action when the user asks the page to perform a task.

Can't you do all the same stuff with HTML and CSS? The Web was still pretty cool **before** JavaScript, you know.

HTML and CSS aren't really interactive

The problem is that HTML and CSS aren't really interactive. There certainly are CSS tricks you can use to manipulate styles in very specific situations, such as mouse hovers over links, but your options are fairly limited if you're using just HTML and CSS.

JavaScript allows you to detect just about anything that takes place in a web page, like a user clicking buttons, resizing the browser window, or entering data into a text field. And since JavaScript is a scripting programming language, you can learn to write code to respond to these user interactions, like performing a calculation, dynamically swapping images on the page, or even validating data.

Don't sweat the JavaScript details, at least not yet.

Although JavaScript is capable of doing all sorts of things, We know you're at the beginning of your journey. Rest assured that events, functions, and many other pieces of the JavaScript puzzle will come together in time. Besides, you're probably further ahead of the game than you realize.

HTML + CSS + JavaScript = REAL Interactivity

Sharpen your pencil

You already know more than you think. Look at the code for the House Finder web page, and write down what you think each circled chunk of JavaScript code is doing. It's okay to guess.

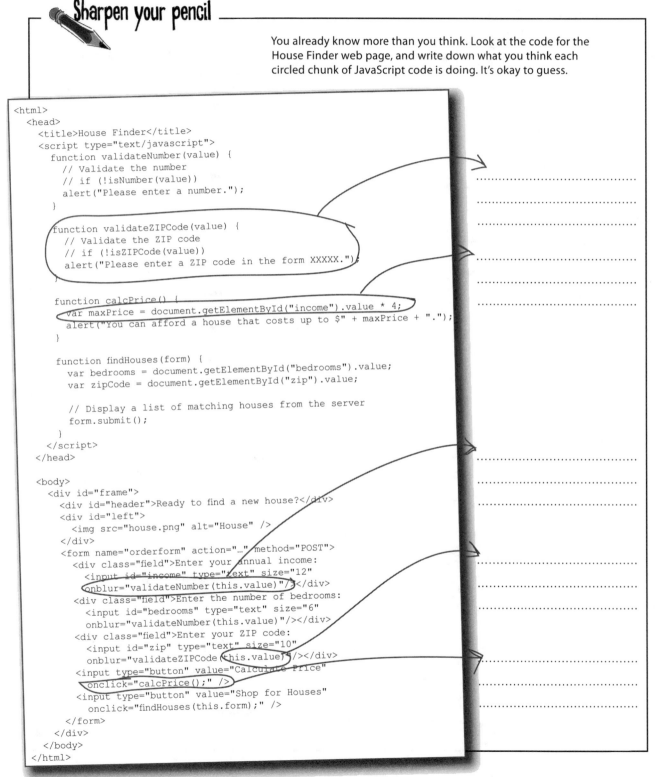

```html
<html>
  <head>
    <title>House Finder</title>
    <script type="text/javascript">
      function validateNumber(value) {
        // Validate the number
        // if (!isNumber(value))
        alert("Please enter a number.");
      }

      function validateZIPCode(value) {
        // Validate the ZIP code
        // if (!isZIPCode(value))
        alert("Please enter a ZIP code in the form XXXXX.");
      }

      function calcPrice() {
        var maxPrice = document.getElementById("income").value * 4;
        alert("You can afford a house that costs up to $" + maxPrice + ".");
      }

      function findHouses(form) {
        var bedrooms = document.getElementById("bedrooms").value;
        var zipCode = document.getElementById("zip").value;

        // Display a list of matching houses from the server
        form.submit();
      }
    </script>
  </head>

  <body>
    <div id="frame">
      <div id="header">Ready to find a new house?</div>
      <div id="left">
        <img src="house.png" alt="House" />
      </div>
      <form name="orderform" action="…" method="POST">
        <div class="field">Enter your annual income:
          <input id="income" type="text" size="12"
            onblur="validateNumber(this.value)" /></div>
        <div class="field">Enter the number of bedrooms:
          <input id="bedrooms" type="text" size="6"
            onblur="validateNumber(this.value)" /></div>
        <div class="field">Enter your ZIP code:
          <input id="zip" type="text" size="10"
            onblur="validateZIPCode(this.value)" /></div>
        <input type="button" value="Calculate Price"
          onclick="calcPrice();" />
        <input type="button" value="Shop for Houses"
          onclick="findHouses(this.form);" />
      </form>
    </div>
  </body>
</html>
```

Sharpen your pencil
Solution

You already know more than you think. Take a look at the code for the House Finder web page, and write down what you think each circled chunk of JavaScript code is doing. It's okay to guess.

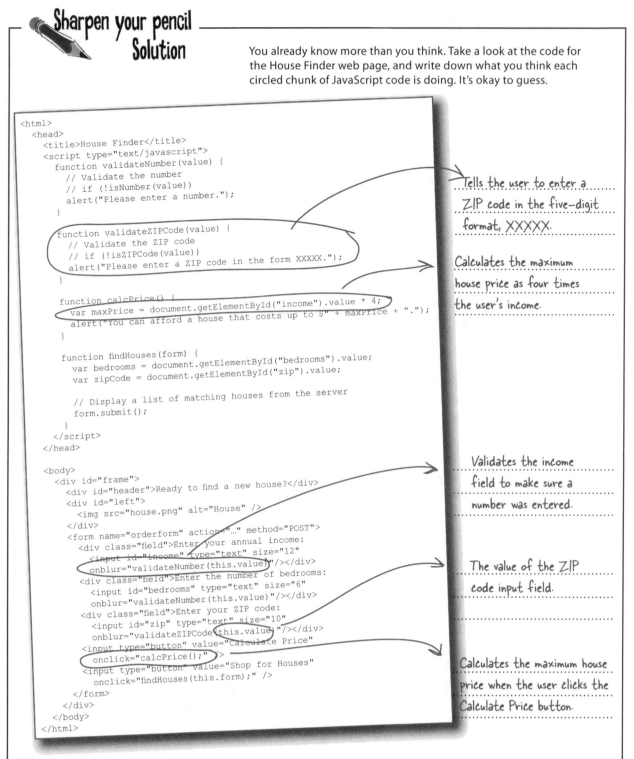

```
<html>
  <head>
    <title>House Finder</title>
    <script type="text/javascript">
      function validateNumber(value) {
        // Validate the number
        // if (!isNumber(value))
        alert("Please enter a number.");
      }

      function validateZIPCode(value) {
        // Validate the ZIP code
        // if (!isZIPCode(value))
        alert("Please enter a ZIP code in the form XXXXX.");
      }

      function calcPrice() {
        var maxPrice = document.getElementById("income").value * 4;
        alert("You can afford a house that costs up to $" + maxPrice + ".");
      }

      function findHouses(form) {
        var bedrooms = document.getElementById("bedrooms").value;
        var zipCode = document.getElementById("zip").value;

        // Display a list of matching houses from the server
        form.submit();
      }
    </script>
  </head>

  <body>
    <div id="frame">
      <div id="header">Ready to find a new house?</div>
      <div id="left">
        <img src="house.png" alt="House" />
      </div>
      <form name="orderform" action="…" method="POST">
        <div class="field">Enter your annual income:
          <input id="income" type="text" size="12"
          onblur="validateNumber(this.value)"/></div>
        <div class="field">Enter the number of bedrooms:
          <input id="bedrooms" type="text" size="6"
          onblur="validateNumber(this.value)"/></div>
        <div class="field">Enter your ZIP code:
          <input id="zip" type="text" size="10"
          onblur="validateZIPCode(this.value)"/></div>
        <input type="button" value="Calculate Price"
          onclick="calcPrice();" />
        <input type="button" value="Shop for Houses"
          onclick="findHouses(this.form);" />
      </form>
    </div>
  </body>
</html>
```

Tells the user to enter a ZIP code in the five-digit format, XXXXX.

Calculates the maximum house price as four times the user's income.

Validates the income field to make sure a number was entered.

The value of the ZIP code input field.

Calculates the maximum house price when the user clicks the Calculate Price button.

Use the <script> tag to tell the browser you're writing JavaScript

For now, we're going to put JavaScript directly into an HTML web page, just like you saw on the last page. The first thing you have to do is let the web browser know that we're about to give it JavaScript, instead of HTML... and that's where the <script> tag comes in.

You can add a <script> tag anywhere in your HTML, but it's usually best to put it in the <head> of our web page, like this:

```
<html>
  <head>
    <title>House Finder</title>

    <script type="text/javascript">

      function validateNumber(value) {
        // Validate the number
        // if (!isNumber(value))
        alert("Please enter a number.");
      }

    </script>
  </head>

  <body>
    <!-- All the rest of your HTML -->
  </body>
</html>
```

This script tag says that anything after it is a scripting language...

...and in this case, the type of the scripting language is JavaScript.

Everything between the opening and closing script tags is JavaScript... the browser knows to treat this as a scripting language, and not HTML.

You can put the script tag into a normal HTML page, usually in the head section.

The closing script tag tells the browser that normal HTML is continuing now.

there are no Dumb Questions

Q: So anything I put inside the <script> tag is JavaScript?

A: Not necessarily... the <script> tag tells the browser that a scripting language is coming, but it doesn't have to be JavaScript. The type part, type="text/ javascript", is what lets the browser know you're about to give it JavaScript specifically.

Q: So are there other scripting languages I can use?

A: Absolutely. Microsoft has a couple of varieties like VBScript (a scripting version of Visual Basic) and their flavor of Ajax, called ASP.NET AJAX. We'll talk more about Ajax in Chapter 12, too. And there are several other scripting languages you can use. But for our purposes, we'll always use text/ javascript in this book.

Q: Do my <script> elements have to be in the <head> part of my HTML page?

A: That's a good catch. You can put <script> elements anywhere in your web page... but it's generally considered bad practice to put them anywhere but the <head> of your web page. It's kind of like putting CSS in the middle of a web page... it's usually better to separate the JavaScript out, and the <head> of your page is a perfect place to do that.

Your web browser can handle HTML, CSS, <u>AND</u> JavaScript

You already know that a web browser knows how to take your HTML and display it. And you've used CSS to tell the browser how to show different parts of your HTML. Think of JavaScript as just another way to talk to the browser... but instead of telling the browser how to display something (like in HTML or CSS), you're giving the browser some commands to follow.

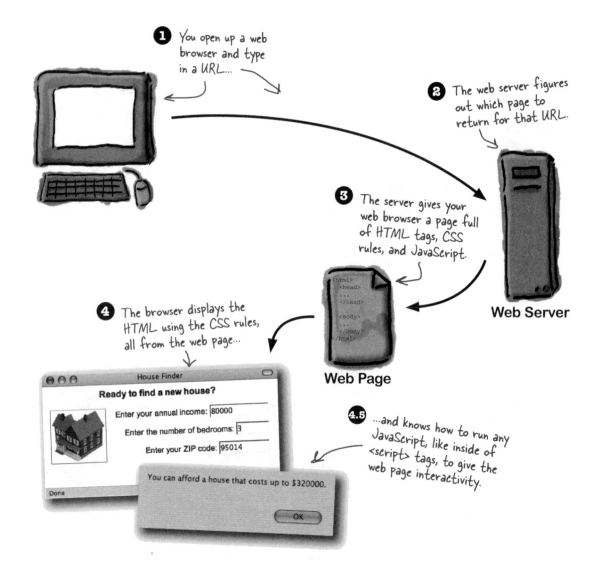

1 You open up a web browser and type in a URL...

2 The web server figures out which page to return for that URL.

3 The server gives your web browser a page full of HTML tags, CSS rules, and JavaScript.

Web Server

4 The browser displays the HTML using the CSS rules, all from the web page...

Web Page

4.5 ...and knows how to run any JavaScript, like inside of <script> tags, to give the web page interactivity.

House Finder

Ready to find a new house?

Enter your annual income: 80000

Enter the number of bedrooms: 3

Enter your ZIP code: 95014

Done

You can afford a house that costs up to $320000.

OK

there are no
Dumb Questions

Q: **How do web browsers run JavaScript code?**

A: Web browsers have a special piece of software inside them called a JavaScript interpreter, and its job is to run JavaScript code that appears within a page. This is why you might have heard JavaScript described as an *interpreted* language, as opposed to a *compiled* language. Compiled languages, such as C++ or C#, must be converted by a tool called a compiler into an executable program file. It isn't necessary to compile JavaScript programs because JavaScript code is interpreted directly by the browser.

Q: **How do I tell a web page to start running JavaScript code?**

A: Most JavaScript code is run when something takes place within the page, such as the page being loaded or the user clicking a button. A JavaScript mechanism known as an "event" allows you to trigger a piece of JavaScript code when something of interest happens to the page.

Q: **Considering the Web's security problems, is JavaScript safe?**

A: Yes, for the most part. JavaScript is designed from the ground up to prevent malicious code from causing problems. For example, JavaScript doesn't allow you to read or write files on the user's hard drive. This limitation wipes out the potential for a lot of viruses and similarly evil code. Of course, this doesn't mean you can't write buggy JavaScript code that makes web pages a pain to use, it just means you're unlikely to put users in serious jeopardy with JavaScript. And for the record, browser bugs and crafty hackers have figured out ways to breach JavaScript security in the past, so it's certainly not bulletproof.

Q: **So about that `<script>` tag in the House Finder code... Is it HTML or JavaScript?**

A: The `<script>` tag itself is HTML, and its purpose is to provide a way to blend script code with the HTML code. The code appearing **inside** the `<script>` tag is JavaScript code. Since the `<script>` tag is designed to support multiple script languages, you indicate that the code is JavaScript code by using its `type` attribute.

Q: **I've seen web pages that have interactivity, such as forms that check to make sure a date is entered correctly, and they seem to do it without JavaScript. Is this possible?**

A: Yes. It's possible to get interactivity in web pages without JavaScript, but in many cases it's inefficient and clunky. For example, data validation on forms can be handled on the web server when you submit the form. However, this means you have to submit the entire form and then wait for the server to do the validating and return the results as a new page. You might as well validate the form with paper and pencil! JavaScript interactivity occurs entirely within the browser without loading a new page, eliminating the unnecessary passing of data back and forth to a server. Not only that, but a great deal of what JavaScript has to offer in terms of interactivity cannot be done any other way without third party browser add-ons.

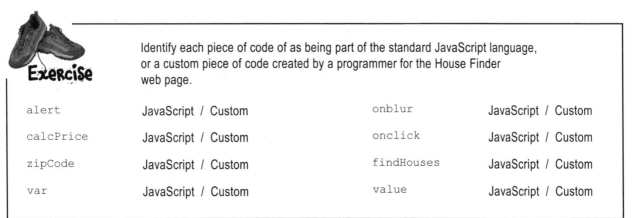

Exercise

Identify each piece of code of as being part of the standard JavaScript language, or a custom piece of code created by a programmer for the House Finder web page.

`alert`	JavaScript / Custom		`onblur`	JavaScript / Custom
`calcPrice`	JavaScript / Custom		`onclick`	JavaScript / Custom
`zipCode`	JavaScript / Custom		`findHouses`	JavaScript / Custom
`var`	JavaScript / Custom		`value`	JavaScript / Custom

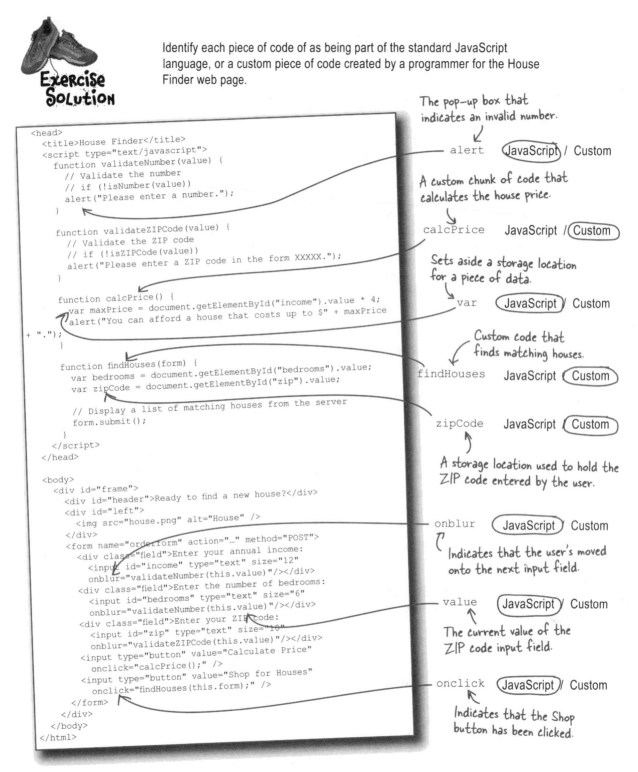

Exercise Solution

Identify each piece of code of as being part of the standard JavaScript language, or a custom piece of code created by a programmer for the House Finder web page.

```
<head>
  <title>House Finder</title>
  <script type="text/javascript">
    function validateNumber(value) {
      // Validate the number
      // if (!isNumber(value))
      alert("Please enter a number.");
    }

    function validateZIPCode(value) {
      // Validate the ZIP code
      // if (!isZIPCode(value))
      alert("Please enter a ZIP code in the form XXXXX.");
    }

    function calcPrice() {
      var maxPrice = document.getElementById("income").value * 4;
      alert("You can afford a house that costs up to $" + maxPrice
+ ".");
    }

    function findHouses(form) {
      var bedrooms = document.getElementById("bedrooms").value;
      var zipCode = document.getElementById("zip").value;

      // Display a list of matching houses from the server
      form.submit();
    }
  </script>
</head>

<body>
  <div id="frame">
    <div id="header">Ready to find a new house?</div>
    <div id="left">
      <img src="house.png" alt="House" />
    </div>
    <form name="orderform" action="…" method="POST">
      <div class="field">Enter your annual income:
        <input id="income" type="text" size="12"
        onblur="validateNumber(this.value)"/></div>
      <div class="field">Enter the number of bedrooms:
        <input id="bedrooms" type="text" size="6"
        onblur="validateNumber(this.value)"/></div>
      <div class="field">Enter your ZIP code:
        <input id="zip" type="text" size="10"
        onblur="validateZIPCode(this.value)"/></div>
      <input type="button" value="Calculate Price"
        onclick="calcPrice();" />
      <input type="button" value="Shop for Houses"
        onclick="findHouses(this.form);" />
    </form>
  </div>
</body>
</html>
```

The pop-up box that indicates an invalid number.

alert (JavaScript) / Custom

A custom chunk of code that calculates the house price.

calcPrice JavaScript / (Custom)

Sets aside a storage location for a piece of data.

var (JavaScript) / Custom

Custom code that finds matching houses.

findHouses JavaScript (Custom)

zipCode JavaScript (Custom)

A storage location used to hold the ZIP code entered by the user.

onblur (JavaScript) Custom

Indicates that the user's moved onto the next input field.

value (JavaScript) Custom

The current value of the ZIP code input field.

onclick (JavaScript) Custom

Indicates that the Shop button has been clicked.

Man's virtual best friend... needs <u>YOUR</u> help

Fresh off of a successful gig writing HTML and CSS pages, you've been called into your boss's office to see his latest online invention: the iRock. The virtual pet is making waves at all the toy conferences, but beta users are really unhappy with the online pet.

Apparently, the users are clicking on the rock, and expecting something cool to happen...but your boss never thought about that. Now, it's up to you to **make the iRock interactive**, and get the glory...or go down in flames with the iRock.

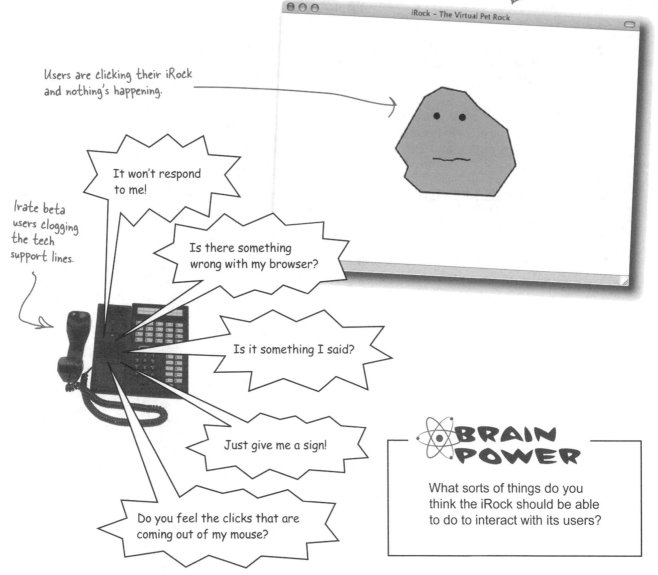

Here's the iRock so far... just some HTML and CSS. And that means no interaction with the user.

iRock – The Virtual Pet Rock

Users are clicking their iRock and nothing's happening.

Irate beta users clogging the tech support lines.

It won't respond to me!

Is there something wrong with my browser?

Is it something I said?

Just give me a sign!

Do you feel the clicks that are coming out of my mouse?

⚛BRAIN POWER

What sorts of things do you think the iRock should be able to do to interact with its users?

Making iRock interactive

Not only is it up to you to make the iRock interactive, but you're going to have to learn some JavaScript along the way. That's okay, though, you'll have that pet rock saying hello in no time.

Here's what you're going to do in the rest of this chapter:

 Create the iRock HTML web page. *You already know how to do this.*

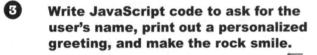 **Add a JavaScript <u>alert</u> to make the rock greet users when the iRock web page is loaded.** *An alert is JavaScript's way of popping up a simple message box.*

❸ **Write JavaScript code to ask for the user's name, print out a personalized greeting, and make the rock smile.** *You're connecting something the user does, like clicking the virtual pet rock...*

❹ **Add an <u>event</u> <u>handler</u> so that when users click on the rock, the code you wrote in step 3 runs.** *...with activity that you design.*

❺ **Win the admiration and lavish gratitude of your boss.**

Create the iRock web page

You couldn't find a much simpler HTML page than the iRock. Go ahead and type this HTML into your favorite editor, and save it as iRock.html. You can download the pet rock images from the Head First Labs web site, at http://www.headfirstlabs.com.

The pet rock's HTML page is about as boring as the rock itself... no wonder your boss needs your help.

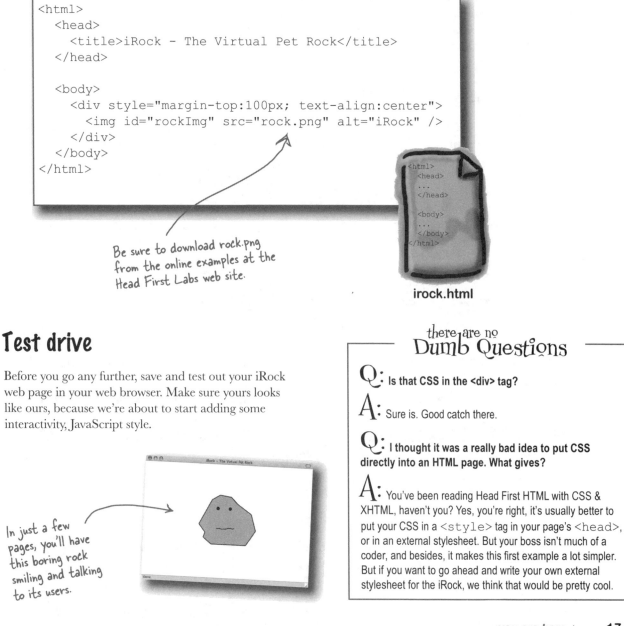

```html
<html>
  <head>
    <title>iRock - The Virtual Pet Rock</title>
  </head>

  <body>
    <div style="margin-top:100px; text-align:center">
      <img id="rockImg" src="rock.png" alt="iRock" />
    </div>
  </body>
</html>
```

Be sure to download rock.png from the online examples at the Head First Labs web site.

irock.html

Test drive

Before you go any further, save and test out your iRock web page in your web browser. Make sure yours looks like ours, because we're about to start adding some interactivity, JavaScript style.

In just a few pages, you'll have this boring rock smiling and talking to its users.

there are no Dumb Questions

Q: Is that CSS in the <div> tag?

A: Sure is. Good catch there.

Q: I thought it was a really bad idea to put CSS directly into an HTML page. What gives?

A: You've been reading Head First HTML with CSS & XHTML, haven't you? Yes, you're right, it's usually better to put your CSS in a <style> tag in your page's <head>, or in an external stylesheet. But your boss isn't much of a coder, and besides, it makes this first example a lot simpler. But if you want to go ahead and write your own external stylesheet for the iRock, we think that would be pretty cool.

JavaScript events: giving the iRock a voice

To use JavaScript to greet the user when the page first loads, we'll have to solve two main JavaScript-related problems: knowing when the page finishes loading and knowing how to display a greeting so that the user can see it.

The first problem involves responding to an event (the page load event), while the second problem involves using a built-in JavaScript feature, the "alert" box. *Events* are JavaScript notifications that let you know when something of interest has happened, such as a page loading (onload) or a button getting clicked (onclick). You can respond to events with your own custom JavaScript code.

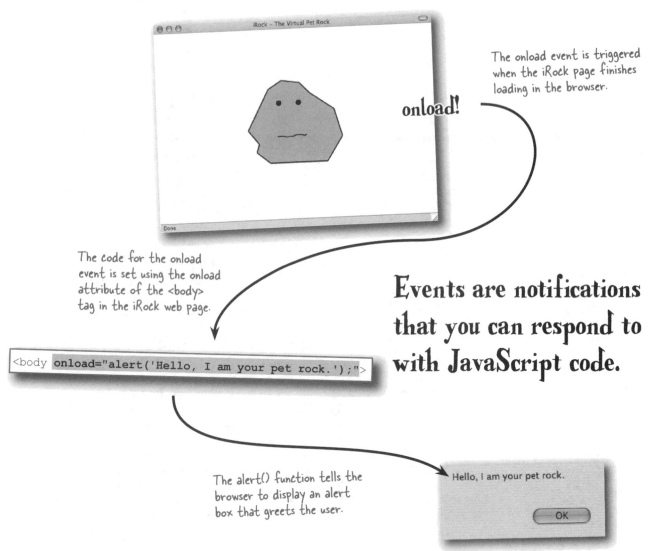

The onload event is triggered when the iRock page finishes loading in the browser.

onload!

The code for the onload event is set using the onload attribute of the <body> tag in the iRock web page.

```
<body onload="alert('Hello, I am your pet rock.');">
```

Events are notifications that you can respond to with JavaScript code.

The alert() function tells the browser to display an alert box that greets the user.

Hello, I am your pet rock.

OK

Alerting the user with a function

A JavaScript **alert** is a pop-up window, or box, that you can use to display information to the user. Displaying an alert box involves writing code to call the JavaScript `alert()` function and passing it the text you want to display. *Functions* are reusable chunks of JavaScript code that perform common tasks, such as displaying information in a pop-up window.

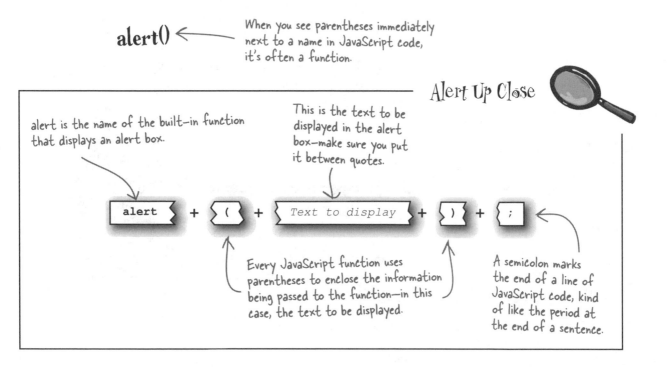

alert() ←

When you see parentheses immediately next to a name in JavaScript code, it's often a function.

Alert Up Close

alert is the name of the built-in function that displays an alert box.

This is the text to be displayed in the alert box—make sure you put it between quotes.

```
alert  +  (  +  Text to display  +  )  +  ;
```

Every JavaScript function uses parentheses to enclose the information being passed to the function—in this case, the text to be displayed.

A semicolon marks the end of a line of JavaScript code, kind of like the period at the end of a sentence.

When you pull it all together, you get a complete line of JavaScript code that calls a function to display greeting text in an alert box:

```
alert('Hello, I am your pet rock.');
```

Functions are reusable pieces of code that perform common tasks.

The text to be displayed is placed within a pair of apostrophes or quotes.

Don't stress over events.

If all this event stuff seems like a buzz kill, don't worry about it because events will continue to unfold (and make more sense) as you work through the book.

Add the iRock greeting

So to greet users when they load the iRock page, you need to add an `onload` event handler, and a greeting by using JavaScript's `alert()` function. Add this line of JavaScript into your `irock.html` page:

```html
<html>
  <head>
    <title>iRock - The Virtual Pet Rock</title>
  </head>

  <body onload="alert('Hello, I am your pet rock.');">
    <div style="margin-top:100px; text-align:center">
      <img id="rockImg" src="rock.png" alt="iRock" />
    </div>
  </body>
</html>
```

Even though the onload event applies to the entire page, you set it as an attribute of the `<body>` tag because the body of a page is the part that is visible in a browser.

Remember, your JavaScript goes right in your web page. The web browser knows how to handle JavaScript, just like it does HTML and CSS.

irock.html

Test drive your interactive rock

The iRock page is now a touch more interactive thanks to an alert box greeting that is displayed in response to the `onload` event. Load up irock. html in your web browser, and see what happens:

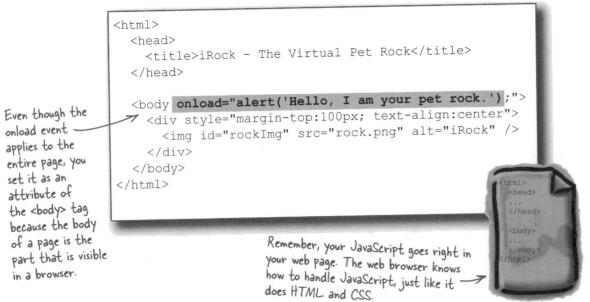

As soon as the page loads, an alert box should pop up on your screen with a greeting.

Hello, I am your pet rock.

OK

Q: Where do events come from?

A: Although events are initiated by a user, they ultimately come from the browser. For example: a "key press" is an event triggered by the user but the browser must package up information about the event (like which key was pressed) and then pass it along to a function that has been designated to respond to the event.

Q: What happens to events that don't have code tied to them?

A: If a tree falls and no one is around to hear it, does it make a sound? Same deal with events. If you don't respond to an event, the browser goes about its business and no one is the wiser. In other words, responding or not responding to `onload` has no bearing on the page actually loading.

Q: Didn't you say that JavaScript code belonged in <script> tags?

A: It usually does. But you can also put it directly in an event handler, like we did with the `onload` event. And, when you need to run just a single line of JavaScript, like for the iRock, that's often a simpler approach.

Q: Are there other built-in functions like the alert() function?

A: Yes, lots of them. `alert()` is just the tip of the iceberg when it comes to built-in reusable JavaScript code. We'll cover a lot of the standard functions as we journey through the features of JavaScript. By the end of the book you'll even be creating your own custom functions.

Q: Why does the iRock `onload` code mix quotes and apostrophes?

A: HTML and JavaScript require you to close a sequence of text before starting another one... unless you use a different delimiter (quote or apostrophe). So in cases where JavaScript code appears in an HTML attribute (text within text), you have to mix quotes and apostrophes to work around this problem. It doesn't matter which ones you use for the attribute or the JavaScript text, but whatever you choose—you'll have to be consistent. Maybe an example of quotes and apostrophes in language will clear things up...according to the iRock, "The user clicked and said, 'Hello there.'"

WHO DOES WHAT?

Match each piece of JavaScript code to what it does.

onload   Display a text message in a pop-up window

()   Terminate a line of JavaScript code

alert   Indicate that the web page has finished loading

;   Enclose the information passed into a function

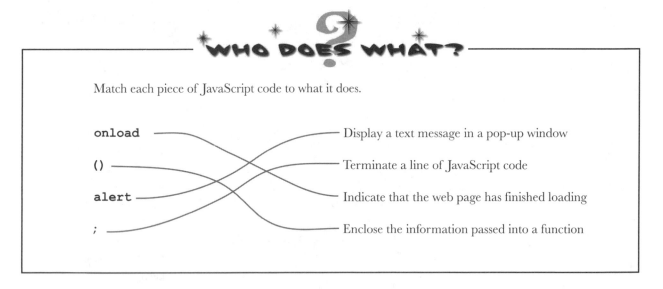

WHO DOES WHAT?

Match each piece of JavaScript code to what it does.

onload — Display a text message in a pop-up window

() — Terminate a line of JavaScript code

alert — Indicate that the web page has finished loading

; — Enclose the information passed into a function

Now let's make the iRock really <u>interactive</u>

You're making some progress toward a more interactive iRock, but there's still more to do before the virtual pet rock is going to win over any customers... remember our check list?

1 ~~Create the iRock HTML web page.~~ ← *Done!*

2 ~~Add a JavaScript alert to make the rock greet users when the iRock web page is loaded.~~ ← *Got this one finished, too.*

3 **Write JavaScript code to ask for the user's name, print out a personalized greeting, and make the rock smile.**

4 **Add an <u>event</u> <u>handler</u> so that when users click on the rock, the code you wrote in step 3 runs.**

5 **Win the admiration and lavish gratitude of your boss.**

Interaction is <u>TWO</u>-way communication

Right now, our rock says hi, but doesn't let the user do much with it. We really want the rock to *respond* to users. With help from a little JavaScript, though, the iRock can be turned into an engaging pet that is surprisingly sociable and downright friendly by changing its facial expression and greeting the owner by name...

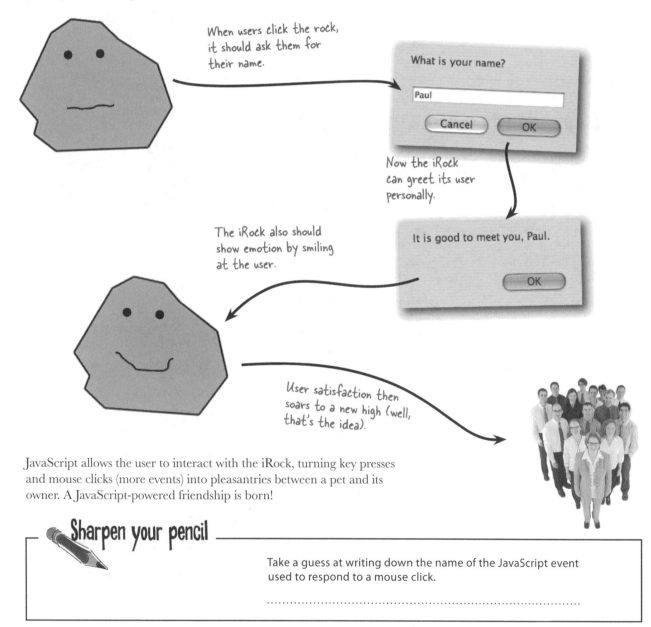

When users click the rock, it should ask them for their name.

What is your name?

Paul

Cancel   OK

Now the iRock can greet its user personally.

The iRock also should show emotion by smiling at the user.

It is good to meet you, Paul.

OK

User satisfaction then soars to a new high (well, that's the idea).

JavaScript allows the user to interact with the iRock, turning key presses and mouse clicks (more events) into pleasantries between a pet and its owner. A JavaScript-powered friendship is born!

Sharpen your pencil

Take a guess at writing down the name of the JavaScript event used to respond to a mouse click.

....

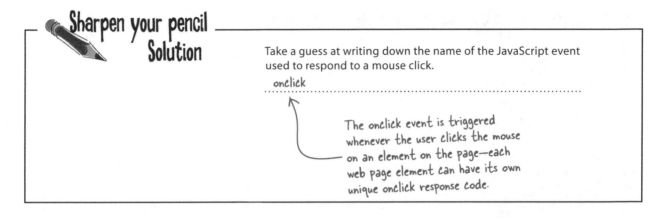

Sharpen your pencil Solution

Take a guess at writing down the name of the JavaScript event used to respond to a mouse click.

onclick

The onclick event is triggered whenever the user clicks the mouse on an element on the page—each web page element can have its own unique onclick response code.

Add a function to get the user's name

Here's a JavaScript function, all baked up and ready to go. Whenever you see Ready Bake JavaScript, that means you should just type the code in, as-is. But trust us, you'll learn everything about this code before long, and be writing your own functions.

Ready Bake JavaScript

This code is for a custom function called `touchRock()`, which prompts the user to enter their name, and then displays a personalized greeting in an alert box. The function also changes the rock image to a smiling iRock. It's all you need to add personalization to the iRock.

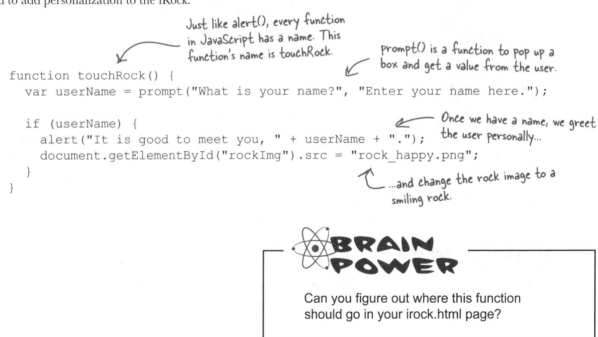

Just like alert(), every function in JavaScript has a name. This function's name is touchRock.

prompt() is a function to pop up a box and get a value from the user.

```javascript
function touchRock() {
    var userName = prompt("What is your name?", "Enter your name here.");

    if (userName) {
        alert("It is good to meet you, " + userName + ".");
        document.getElementById("rockImg").src = "rock_happy.png";
    }
}
```

Once we have a name, we greet the user personally...

...and change the rock image to a smiling rock.

⚛ BRAIN POWER

Can you figure out where this function should go in your irock.html page?

JavaScript Magnets

The user-friendly iRock code is missing a few key code pieces.
Can you fill in the missing pieces to make the page whole?

Hint: Not sure about your answers? Test out your answers by typing them into your irock.html page.

```html
<html>
  <head>
    <title>iRock - The Virtual Pet Rock</title>

    < ............... type="text/javascript">
      function touchRock() {
        var userName = prompt("What is your name?", "Enter your name here.");

        if (userName) {
          alert("It is good to meet you, " + userName + ".");
          document.getElementById("rockImg").src = "rock_happy.png";
        }
      }
    </script>
  </head>

  <body ............="" ............ ( ...................................................... );">
    <div style="margin-top:100px; text-align:center">

      <img id="rockImg" src="rock.png" alt="iRock" style="cursor:pointer"
           ...............="" ........................;" />
    </div>
  </body>
</html>
```

touchRock()   '

alert

onload

script

onclick

'Hello, I am your pet rock.'

JavaScript Magnets Solution

The user-friendly iRock code is missing a few key code pieces.
Your job was to use the magnets to fill in those missing pieces.

JavaScript functions are placed in a special <script> tag that goes in the <head> of the page.

The type attribute of the <script> tag is used to identify the type of the script language, in this case JavaScript.

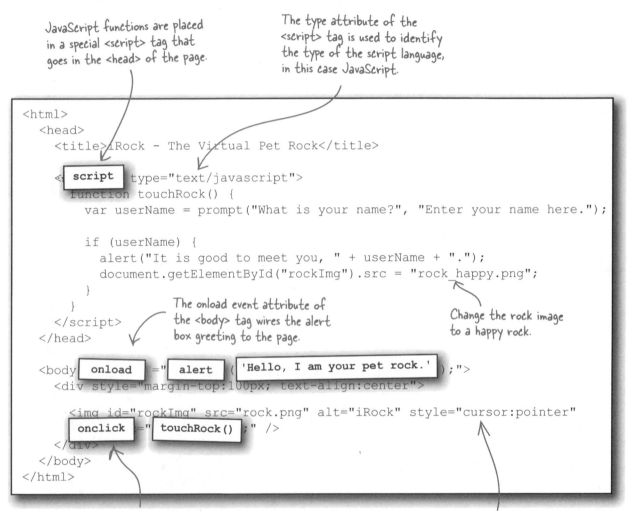

```html
<html>
  <head>
    <title>iRock - The Virtual Pet Rock</title>
    <script type="text/javascript">
      function touchRock() {
        var userName = prompt("What is your name?", "Enter your name here.");

        if (userName) {
          alert("It is good to meet you, " + userName + ".");
          document.getElementById("rockImg").src = "rock_happy.png";
        }
      }
    </script>
  </head>

  <body onload=" alert ('Hello, I am your pet rock.' );">
    <div style="margin-top:100px; text-align:center">

      <img id="rockImg" src="rock.png" alt="iRock" style="cursor:pointer"
        onclick=" touchRock() ;" />
    </div>
  </body>
</html>
```

The onload event attribute of the <body> tag wires the alert box greeting to the page.

Change the rock image to a happy rock.

The onclick event attribute of the rock image causes the touchRock() function to get called when the rock is clicked.

Change the mouse cursor to a hand when hovering over the rock.

Instant replay: what just happened?

A little bit of JavaScript triggered a lot of changes, resulting in a more endearing version of the iRock. Let's view an instant replay of what changes were made and how they impact the page.

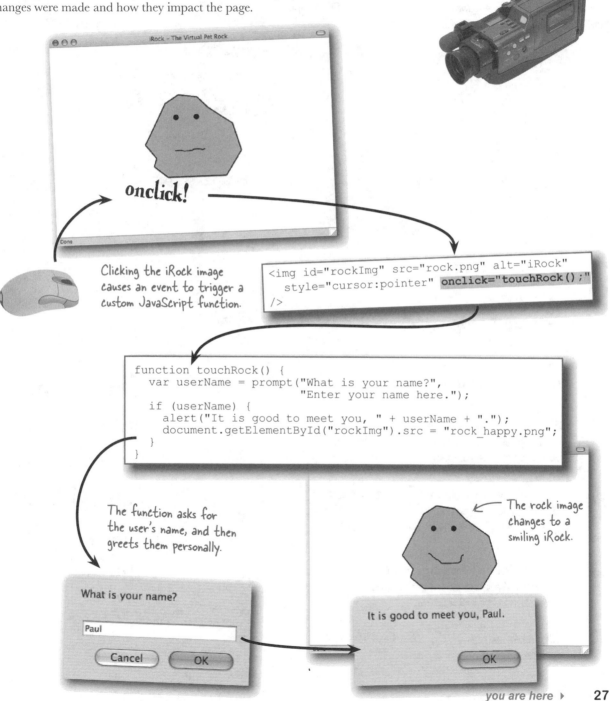

onclick!

Clicking the iRock image causes an event to trigger a custom JavaScript function.

```
<img id="rockImg" src="rock.png" alt="iRock"
   style="cursor:pointer" onclick="touchRock();"
/>
```

```
function touchRock() {
  var userName = prompt("What is your name?",
                        "Enter your name here.");
  if (userName) {
    alert("It is good to meet you, " + userName + ".");
    document.getElementById("rockImg").src = "rock_happy.png";
  }
}
```

The function asks for the user's name, and then greets them personally.

The rock image changes to a smiling iRock.

What is your name?

Paul

Cancel   OK

It is good to meet you, Paul.

OK

Test drive iRock 1.0

Make sure you've made your version of `irock.html` look like the one on page 26, and that you've downloaded both rock images from Head First Labs (*http://www.headfirstlabs.com/books/hfjs/*). Then, open up your web page, and give the rock a spin:

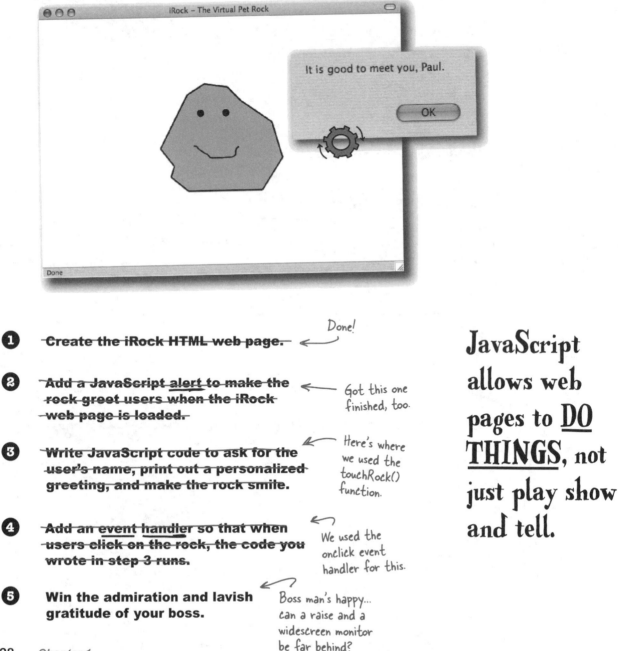

1 ~~Create the iRock HTML web page.~~ ← *Done!*

2 ~~Add a JavaScript alert to make the rock greet users when the iRock web page is loaded.~~ ← *Got this one finished, too.*

3 ~~Write JavaScript code to ask for the user's name, print out a personalized greeting, and make the rock smile.~~ ← *Here's where we used the touchRock() function.*

4 ~~Add an event handler so that when users click on the rock, the code you wrote in step 3 runs.~~ ← *We used the onclick event handler for this.*

5 **Win the admiration and lavish gratitude of your boss.** ← *Boss man's happy... can a raise and a widescreen monitor be far behind?*

JavaScript allows web pages to <u>DO</u> <u>THINGS</u>, not just play show and tell.

JavaScriptcross

Take some time to sit back and give your right brain something to do. It's your standard crossword; all of the solution words are from this chapter.

Across

2. The name of a chunk of code that provides the iRock with a personalized greeting,
4. To respond to a mouse click, just set some JavaScript code to the .... attribute of an HTML element.
7. Without this, you might as well just stick with HTML and CSS.
8. To display text to the user, just call the ..... function.

Down

1. A reusable piece of JavaScript code that performs a common task.
3. Something just happened and the browser is trying to let you know.
5. "The feel good online toy of the season."
6. Lets you know that a Web page has finished loading.

 JavaScriptcross Solution

Page Bender

Fold the page vertically to line up the two brains and solve the riddle.

What does JavaScript add to web pages?

It's a meeting of the minds!

There are cold rocks...

... and there are warm rocks.

onclick!

But they all crave the same thing!

Woof!

Hey, how's it going?

Meow...

Now the iRock has something in common with these real, non-virtual pets. What is it?

Searching the Internet for this answer is an action that probably won't help you very much. You should just spend time with users instead. All web pages want it.

2 storing data

Everything Has Its Place

> Every lady needs a special place to store treasured belongings...not to mention some petty cash and a bogus passport for a quick getaway.

In the real world, people often overlook the importance of having a place to store all their stuff. Not so in JavaScript. You simply don't have the luxury of walk-in closets and three-car garages. In JavaScript, **everything has its place**, and it's your job to make sure of it. The issue is **data**—how to *represent it*, how to *store it*, and how to *find it* once you've put it somewhere. As a JavaScript storage specialist, you'll be able to take a cluttered room of JavaScript data and impose your will on it with a flurry of virtual labels and storage bins.

Your scripts can store data

Just about every script has to deal with data in one way or another, and that usually means storing data in memory. The JavaScript interpreter that lives in web browsers is responsible for setting aside little areas of storage for JavaScript data. It's your job, however, to spell out exactly **what the data is** and **how you intend to use it**.

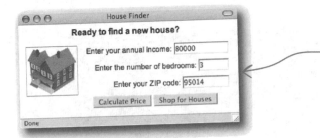

The information associated with a house search must all be stored within the script that performs the calculations.

Scripts use stored data to carry out calculations and **remember** information about the user. Without the ability to store data, you'd never find that new house or really get to know your iRock.

The user's name entered into the iRock page is stored away so that the script can show you a personalized greeting.

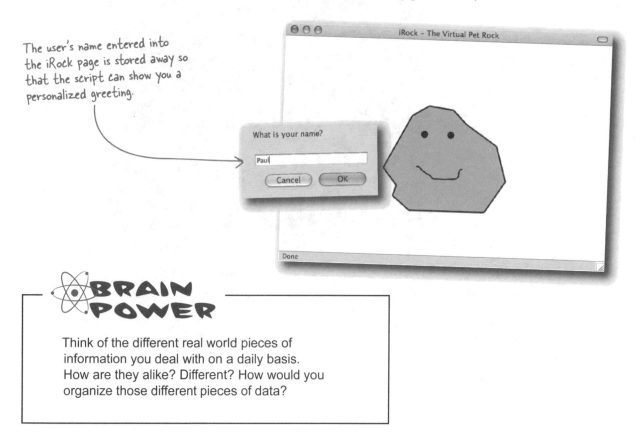

⚛**BRAIN POWER**

Think of the different real world pieces of information you deal with on a daily basis. How are they alike? Different? How would you organize those different pieces of data?

Scripts think in <u>data types</u>

You organize and categorize real world data into types without even thinking about it: names, numbers, sounds, and so on. JavaScript also categorizes script data into **data types**. Data types are the key to mapping information from your brain to JavaScript.

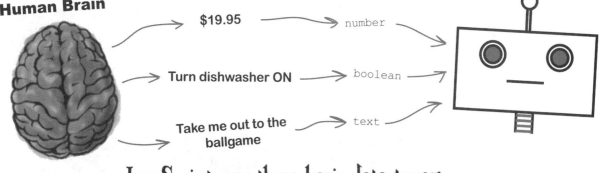

Human Brain

$19.95 → number

Turn dishwasher ON → boolean

Take me out to the ballgame → text

JavaScript

JavaScript uses three basic data types: text, number, and boolean.

Number

Numbers are used to store numeric data like the weights and quantities of things. JavaScript numbers can be either integer/whole numbers (2 pounds) or decimals (2.5 pounds).

Boolean

Boolean data is always in one of two possible states—**true** or **false**. So you can use a boolean to represent anything that has two possible settings, like a toaster with an On/Off switch. Booleans show up all the time and you can use them to help in making decisions. We'll talk more about that in Chapter 4.

Text

Text data is really just a sequence of characters, like the name of your favorite breakfast cereal. Text is usually words or sentences, but it doesn't have to be. Also known as **strings**, JavaScript text always appears within quotes ("") or apostrophes (' ').

Data types **directly affect** how you work with data in JavaScript code. For example, alert boxes only display text, not numbers. So numbers are converted to text behind the scenes before they're displayed.

Sharpen your pencil

Find everything that could be represented by a JavaScript data type, and write down what type that thing should be.

Sharpen your pencil Solution

Your job was to find everything that JavaScript could represent, and figure out the type JavaScript would use.

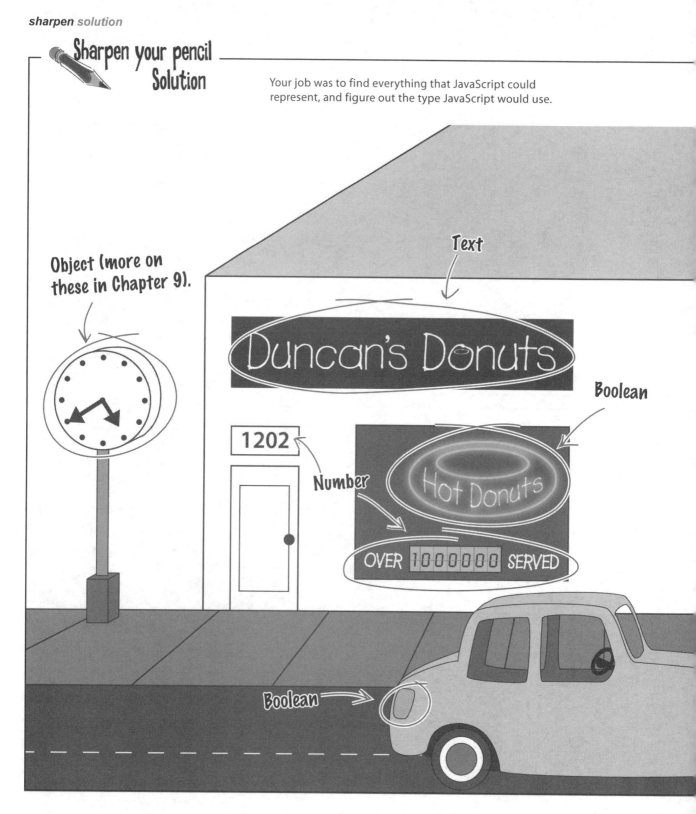

Object (more on these in Chapter 9).

Text

Duncan's Donuts

Boolean

1202

Number

Hot Donuts

OVER 1000000 SERVED

Boolean

Constants stay the <u>SAME</u>, variables can <u>CHANGE</u>

Storing data in JavaScript isn't just about **type**, it's also about **purpose**. What do you want to do with the data? Or more specifically, will the data **change** throughout the course of your script? The answers determine whether you code your data type in JavaScript as a *variable* or a *constant*. *A variable changes throughout the course of a script*, while *a constant never changes its value*.

Variable data can change—constant data is fixed.

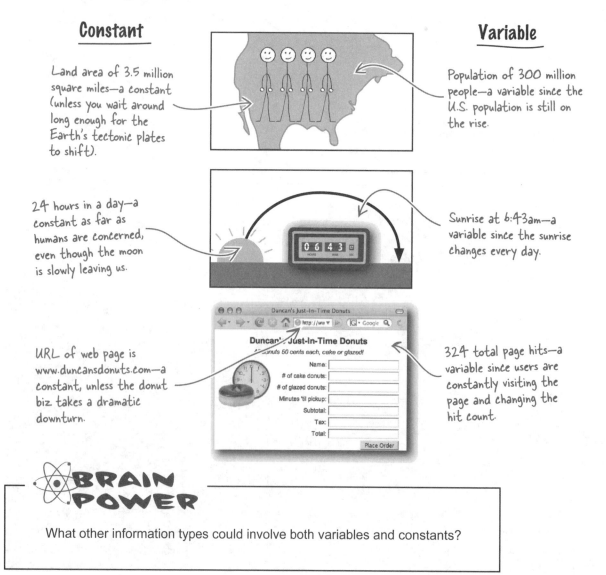

Constant

Land area of 3.5 million square miles—a constant (unless you wait around long enough for the Earth's tectonic plates to shift).

24 hours in a day—a constant as far as humans are concerned, even though the moon is slowly leaving us.

URL of web page is www.duncansdonuts.com—a constant, unless the donut biz takes a dramatic downturn.

Variable

Population of 300 million people—a variable since the U.S. population is still on the rise.

Sunrise at 6:43am—a variable since the sunrise changes every day.

324 total page hits—a variable since users are constantly visiting the page and changing the hit count.

⚛ BRAIN POWER

What other information types could involve both variables and constants?

Sharpen your pencil

Circle all of the data at Duncan's Donuts, and then identify each thing you circled as being either a variable or a constant.

Sharpen your pencil
Solution

Your job was to find all the variables and constants.

Fireside Chats

Variable:

When it comes to storing data, I offer the most in flexibility. You can change my value all you want. I can be set to one value now and some other value later—that's what I call freedom.

Constant:

And I call that flip-flopping! I say pick a value and stick to it. It's my ruthless consistency that makes me so valuable to scripters...they appreciate the predictability of data that always stays the course.

Sure, but your mule-headed resistance to change just won't work in situations where data has to take on different values over time. For example, a rocket launch countdown has to change as it counts down from 10 to 1. Deal with that!

Oh, so you think *you're* the only data storage option for mission critical applications, huh? Wrong! How do you think that rocket ever got to the launch pad? Because someone was smart enough to make the launch date a constant. Show me a deadline that's a variable and I'll show you a project behind schedule.

Yeah, sure, whatever. How do you get off calling variation a bad thing. Don't you realize that change can be a good thing, especially when you've got to to store information entered by the user, perform calculations, anything like that?

I say the more things change, the more they stay the same. And really, why change in the first place? Settle on a good value from the start and leave it alone. Think about the comfort in knowing that a value can never be changed, accidentally or otherwise.

I suppose we'll just have to agree to disagree.

Actually, I've disagreed with you all along.

Variables start out without a value

A variable is a **storage location** in memory with a **unique name**, like a label on a box that's used to store things. You create a variable using a special JavaScript keyword called var, and the name of the new variable. A **keyword** is a word set aside in JavaScript to perform a particular task, like creating a variable.

The var keyword indicates that you're creating a new variable.

The semicolon ends this line of JavaScript code.

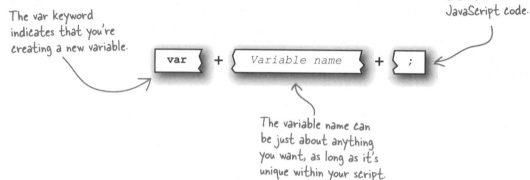

The variable name can be just about anything you want, as long as it's unique within your script.

When you create a variable using the var keyword, that variable's initially empty.... it has no value. It's fine for a variable to start off being empty as long as you don't attempt to read its value before assigning it a value. It'd be like trying to play a song on your MP3 player before loading it with music.

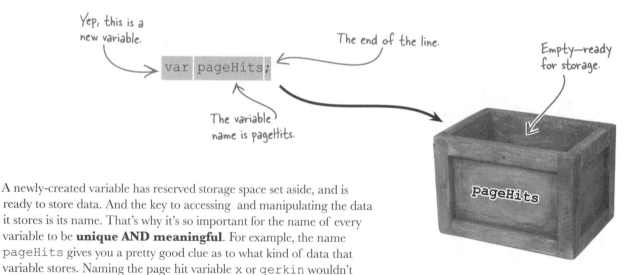

Yep, this is a new variable.

The end of the line.

Empty—ready for storage.

The variable name is pageHits.

A newly-created variable has reserved storage space set aside, and is ready to store data. And the key to accessing and manipulating the data it stores is its name. That's why it's so important for the name of every variable to be **unique AND meaningful**. For example, the name pageHits gives you a pretty good clue as to what kind of data that variable stores. Naming the page hit variable x or gerkin wouldn't have been nearly as descriptive.

Initialize a variable with "="

You don't have to create variables without an initial value. In fact, it's usually a pretty good idea to give a variable a value when you first create it. That's called **initializing** a variable. That's just a matter of adding a tiny bit of extra code to the normal variable creation routine:

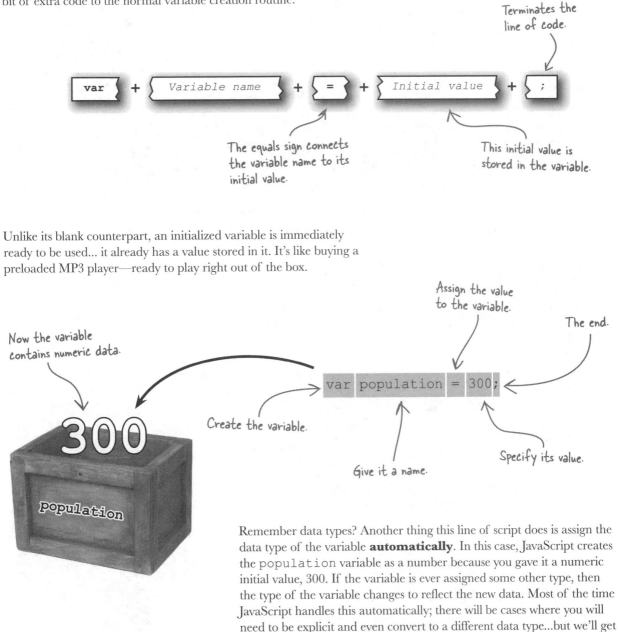

Terminates the line of code.

| var | + | *Variable name* | + | = | + | *Initial value* | + | ; |

The equals sign connects the variable name to its initial value.

This initial value is stored in the variable.

Unlike its blank counterpart, an initialized variable is immediately ready to be used... it already has a value stored in it. It's like buying a preloaded MP3 player—ready to play right out of the box.

Now the variable contains numeric data.

Assign the value to the variable.

The end.

```
var population = 300;
```

Create the variable.

Give it a name.

Specify its value.

300

population

Remember data types? Another thing this line of script does is assign the data type of the variable **automatically**. In this case, JavaScript creates the `population` variable as a number because you gave it a numeric initial value, 300. If the variable is ever assigned some other type, then the type of the variable changes to reflect the new data. Most of the time JavaScript handles this automatically; there will be cases where you will need to be explicit and even convert to a different data type...but we'll get to all that a bit later.

Constants are resistant to change

Initializing a variable is all about setting its **first** value—there's nothing stopping that value from being changed **later**. To store a piece of data that can never change, you need a constant. Constants are created just like initialized variables, but you use the const keyword instead of var. And the "initial" value becomes a **permanent** value...constants play for keeps!

Watch it!

Not all browsers support the const keyword.

The const *keyword is fairly new to JavaScript, and not all browsers support it. Be sure to double check your target browsers before releasing JavaScript code that uses const.*

This creates a constant that can't be changed.

Assign a value to the constant.

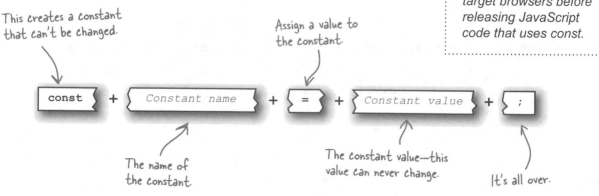

const + *Constant name* + = + *Constant value* + ;

The name of the constant.

The constant value—this value can never change.

It's all over.

The biggest difference between creating a constant and a variable is you have to use the const keyword instead of var. The syntax is the same as when you're initializing a variable. But, constants are often named using all capital letters to make them **STANDOUT** from variables in your code.

This data will never, ever, ever change...ever!

The value the constant will have throughout all eternity.

This data <u>cannot</u> change.

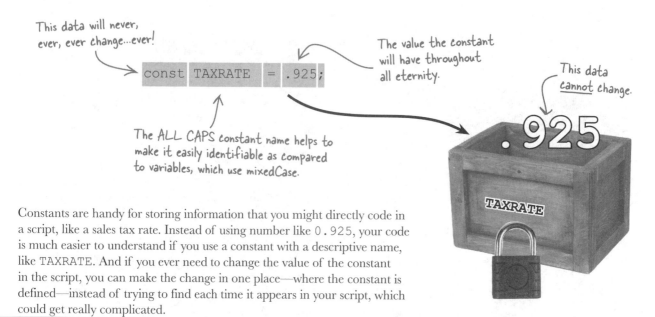

```
const TAXRATE = .925;
```

The ALL CAPS constant name helps to make it easily identifiable as compared to variables, which use mixedCase.

.925

TAXRATE

Constants are handy for storing information that you might directly code in a script, like a sales tax rate. Instead of using number like 0.925, your code is much easier to understand if you use a constant with a descriptive name, like TAXRATE. And if you ever need to change the value of the constant in the script, you can make the change in one place—where the constant is defined—instead of trying to find each time it appears in your script, which could get really complicated.

Hang on, I thought constants couldn't change.

Constants can't change, at least not without a text editor.

It's true that constants can't change while a script is **running**...but there's nothing stopping *you* from changing the value of a constant where it's first created. So from your script's perspective, a constant is absolutely fixed, but from your perspective, it can be changed by going back to the point where you created the constant. So a tax rate constant can't change while the script is running, but you can change the rate in your initialization code, and the new constant value will be reflected in the script from then on out.

Exercise

Decide whether each of the following pieces of information should be a variable or a constant, and then write the code to create each, and initialize them (if that's appropriate).

 The current temperature, which is initially unknown

 The conversion unit from human years to dog years (1 human year = 7 dog years)

 The countdown for a rocket launch (from 10 to 0)

 The price of a tasty donut (50 cents)

....

....

....

....

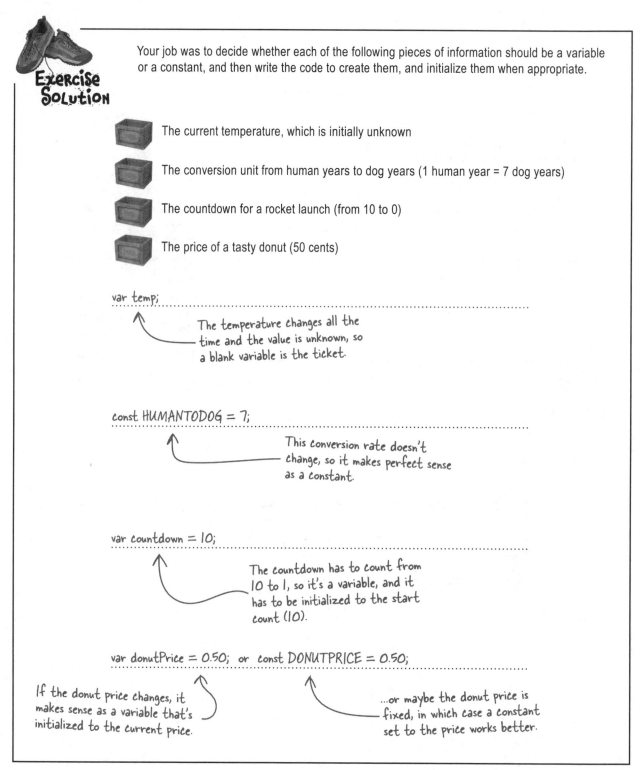

Exercise
Solution

Your job was to decide whether each of the following pieces of information should be a variable or a constant, and then write the code to create them, and initialize them when appropriate.

The current temperature, which is initially unknown

The conversion unit from human years to dog years (1 human year = 7 dog years)

The countdown for a rocket launch (from 10 to 0)

The price of a tasty donut (50 cents)

```
var temp;
```

The temperature changes all the time and the value is unknown, so a blank variable is the ticket.

```
const HUMANTODOG = 7;
```

This conversion rate doesn't change, so it makes perfect sense as a constant.

```
var countdown = 10;
```

The countdown has to count from 10 to 1, so it's a variable, and it has to be initialized to the start count (10).

```
var donutPrice = 0.50;   or   const DONUTPRICE = 0.50;
```

If the donut price changes, it makes sense as a variable that's initialized to the current price.

...or maybe the donut price is fixed, in which case a constant set to the price works better.

there are no
Dumb Questions

Q: If I don't specify the data type of JavaScript data, how does it ever know what the type is?

A: Unlike some programming languages, JavaScript doesn't allow you to explicitly set the type of a constant or variable. Instead, the type is **implied** when you set the value of the data. This allows JavaScript variables a lot of flexibility since their data types can change when different values are assigned to them. For example: if you assign the number 17 to a variable named x, the variable is a number. But if you turn around and assign x the text "seventeen", the variable type changes to string.

Q: If the data type of JavaScript data is taken care of automatically, why should I even care about data types?

A: Because there are plenty of situations where you can't rely solely on JavaScript's automatic data type handling. For example, you may have a number stored as text that you want to use in a calculation. You have to convert the text type to the number type in order to do any math calculations with the number. The reverse is true when displaying a number in an alert box—it must first be converted to text. JavaScript will perform the number-to-text conversion automatically, but it may not convert exactly like you want it to.

Q: Is it OK to leave a variable uninitialized if I don't know what it's value is up front?

A: Absolutely. The idea behind initialization is to try to head off problems where you might try to access a variable when it doesn't have a value. But, there are also times where there's no way to know the value of a variable when you first create it. If that happens, just make sure that the variable gets set before you try to use it. And keep in mind that you can always initialize a variable to a "nothing" value, such as " " for text, 0 for numbers, or `false` for booleans. This helps eliminate the risk of accidentally accessing uninitialized data.

Q: Is there any trick to knowing when to use a variable and when to use a constant?

A: While it's easy to just say constants can't change and variables can, there's a bit more to it than that. In many cases you'll start out using variables for everything, and only realize that there are opportunities to make some of those variables into constants later. Even then, it's rare that you'll be able to turn a variable into a constant. More likely, you'll have a fixed piece of text or number that is used in several places, like a repetitive greeting or conversion rate.

Instead of duplicating the text or number over and over, create a constant for it and use that instead. Then if you ever need to adjust or change the value, you can do it in one place in your code.

Q: What happens to script data when a web page is reloaded?

A: Script data gets reset to its initial values, as if the script had never been run before. In other words, refreshing a web page has the same effect on the script as if the script was being run for the first time.

Data types are established when variable's and constant's values are set.

BULLET POINTS

- Script data can usually be represented by one of the three basic data types: **text**, **number**, or **boolean**.

- A **variable** is a piece of data that can **change** over the course of a script.

- A **constant** is a piece of information that **cannot change**.

- The `var` keyword is used to **create variables**, while `const` is used to **create constants**.

- The **data type** of a piece of JavaScript data is established when you **set the data** to a certain value, and for variables the type can change.

What's in a name?

Variables, constants, and other JavaScript syntax constructs are identified in scripts using unique names known as **identifiers**. JavaScript identifiers are like the names of people in the real world, except they aren't as flexible (people can have the same name, but JavaScript variables can't). In addition to being unique within a script, identifiers must abide by a few naming laws laid down by JavaScript:

An identifier must be at least one character in length.

The first character in an identifier must be a letter, an underscore (_), or a dollar sign ($).

Each character after the first character can be a letter, an underscore (_), a dollar sign ($), or a number.

Spaces and special characters other than _ and $ are not allowed in any part of an identifier.

When you create a JavaScript identifier for a variable or constant, you're naming a piece of information that typically has **meaning** within a script. So, it's not enough to simply abide by the laws of identifier naming. You should definitely try to add context to the names of your data pieces so that they are immediately **identifiable**.

Of course, there are times when a simple x does the job—not every piece of data in a script has a purpose that is easily described.

> I'm not going to tolerate law breakers when it comes to identifiers.

Sheriff J.S. Justice, dedicated lawman.

Identifiers should be descriptive so that data is easily identifiable, not to mention legal...

Legal and illegal variable and constant names

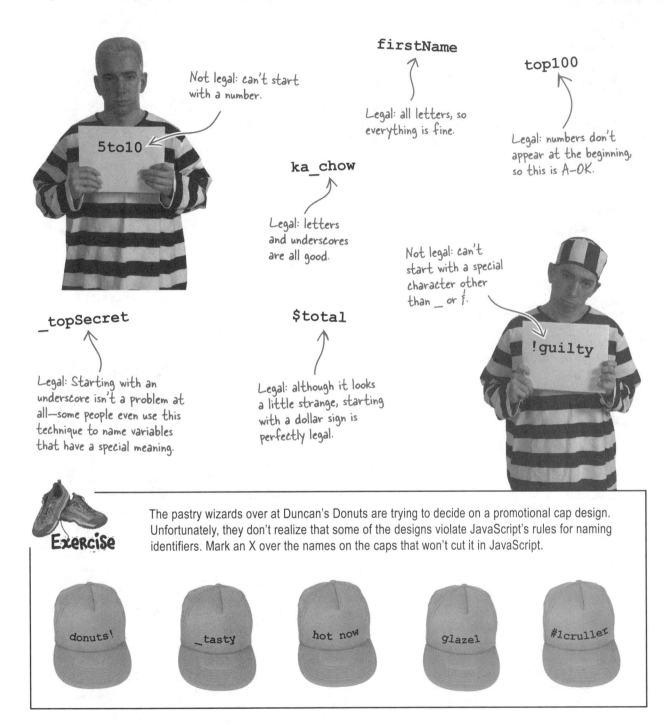

Not legal: can't start with a number.

5to10

firstName

Legal: all letters, so everything is fine.

top100

Legal: numbers don't appear at the beginning, so this is A-OK.

ka_chow

Legal: letters and underscores are all good.

Not legal: can't start with a special character other than _ or $.

!guilty

_topSecret

Legal: Starting with an underscore isn't a problem at all—some people even use this technique to name variables that have a special meaning.

$total

Legal: although it looks a little strange, starting with a dollar sign is perfectly legal.

Exercise

The pastry wizards over at Duncan's Donuts are trying to decide on a promotional cap design. Unfortunately, they don't realize that some of the designs violate JavaScript's rules for naming identifiers. Mark an X over the names on the caps that won't cut it in JavaScript.

donuts!

_tasty

hot now

glaze1

#1cruller

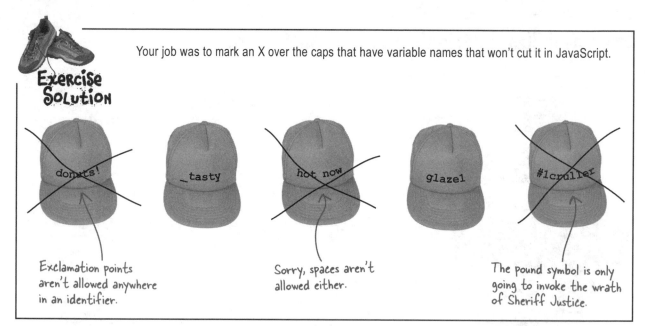

Your job was to mark an X over the caps that have variable names that won't cut it in JavaScript.

Exercise Solution

donuts!

_tasty

hot now

glaze1

#1cruller

Exclamation points aren't allowed anywhere in an identifier.

Sorry, spaces aren't allowed either.

The pound symbol is only going to invoke the wrath of Sheriff Justice.

Variable names often use CamelCase

Although there aren't any JavaScript laws governing how you style identifier names, the JavaScript community has some **unofficial** standards. One of these standards is using **CamelCase**, which means mixing case within identifiers that consist of more than one word (remember, you can't have spaces in a variable name). Variables usually use **lower** camel case, in which the first word is all lowercase, but additional words are mixed-case.

`num_cake_donuts`

Separating multiple words with an underscore in a variable identifier isn't illegal, but there's a better way.

The first letter of each word is capitalized.

`NumCakeDonuts`

Better... this style is known as camel case, but it still isn't quite right for variables.

The first letter of each word <u>except</u> the <u>first</u> is capitalized.

`numCakeDonuts`

Ah, there it is—lower camel case is perfect for naming variables with multiple words.

lowerCamelCase is used to name <u>multiWord</u> variables.

JavaScript Magnets

The identifier magnets have gotten separated from the variables and constants they identify at Duncan's Donuts. Match up the correct magnet to each variable/constant, and make sure you avoid magnets with illegal names. Bonus points: identify each data type.

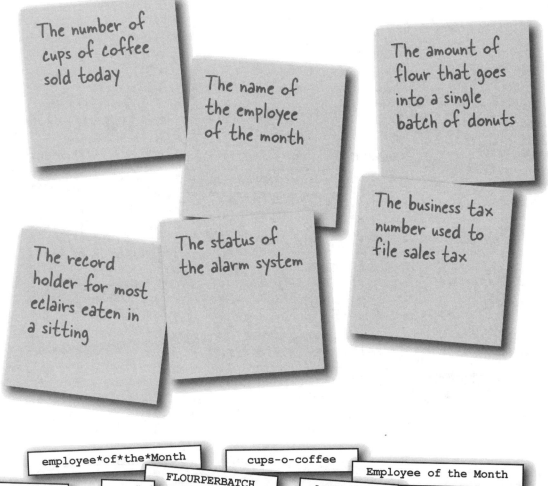

The number of cups of coffee sold today

The name of the employee of the month

The amount of flour that goes into a single batch of donuts

The business tax number used to file sales tax

The record holder for most eclairs eaten in a sitting

The status of the alarm system

```
employee*of*the*Month          cups-o-coffee
                    FLOURPERBATCH          Employee of the Month
alarmStatus       Tax#                  alarm_status
                    eclairRECORDHOLDER          TAXNUM
                                  numCups          eclairRecord
eclairWinner!
    employeeOfMonth    ALARM-STATUS      flour quantity    #OfCups
```

JavaScript Magnets Solution

The identifier magnets have gotten separated from the variables and constants they identify at Duncan's Donuts. Match up the correct magnet to each variable/constant, and make sure you avoid magnets with illegal names. Bonus points: identify each data type.

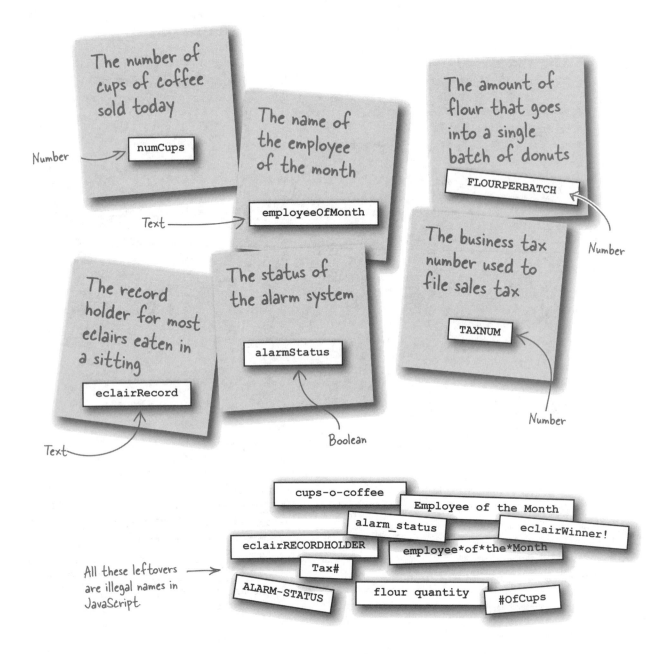

The number of cups of coffee sold today

Number → `numCups`

The name of the employee of the month

Text → `employeeOfMonth`

The amount of flour that goes into a single batch of donuts

`FLOURPERBATCH` ← Number

The business tax number used to file sales tax

`TAXNUM`

Number

The record holder for most eclairs eaten in a sitting

`eclairRecord`

Text

The status of the alarm system

`alarmStatus`

Boolean

All these leftovers are illegal names in JavaScript. →

`cups-o-coffee`
`Employee of the Month`
`alarm_status`
`eclairWinner!`
`eclairRECORDHOLDER`
`employee*of*the*Month`
`Tax#`
`ALARM-STATUS`
`flour quantity`
`#OfCups`

The next big thing (in donuts)

You may know about Duncan's Donuts, but you haven't met Duncan or heard about his big plan to shake up the donut market. Duncan wants to take the "Hot Donuts" business to the next level...he wants to put it online! His idea is **just-in-time donuts**, where you place an order online and enter a specific pick-up time, and have a **hot** order of donuts waiting for you at the precise pick-up time. **Your job is to make sure the user enters the required data, as well as calculate the tax and order total.**

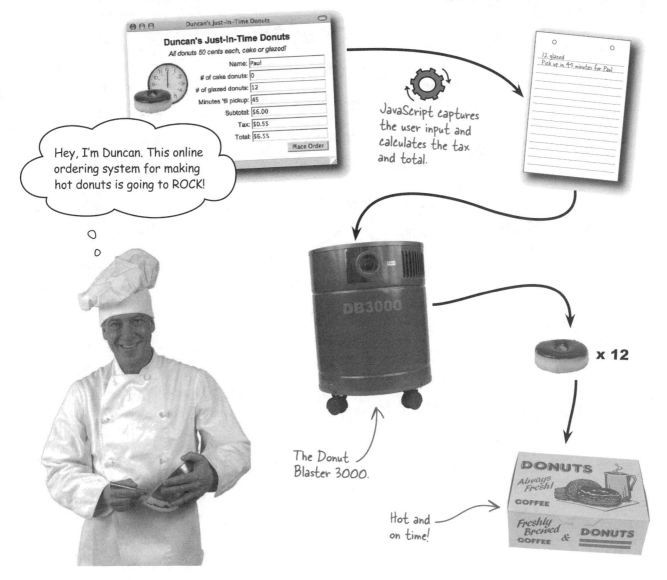

Hey, I'm Duncan. This online ordering system for making hot donuts is going to ROCK!

JavaScript captures the user input and calculates the tax and total.

The Donut Blaster 3000.

Hot and on time!

Plan the Duncan's Donuts web page

Processing a just-in-time donut order involves both checking (or validating) the order form for required data, and calculating the order total based upon that data. The subtotal and total are calculated **on the fly** as the data is entered so that the user gets **immediate feedback** on the total price. The Place Order button is for submitting the final order, which isn't really a JavaScript issue...we're not worrying about that here.

This information is required for the order, and so it should be validated by JavaScript.

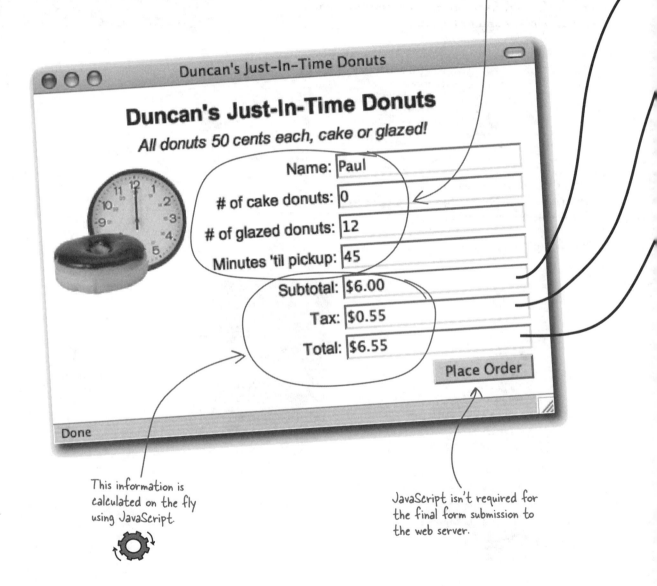

This information is calculated on the fly using JavaScript.

JavaScript isn't required for the final form submission to the web server.

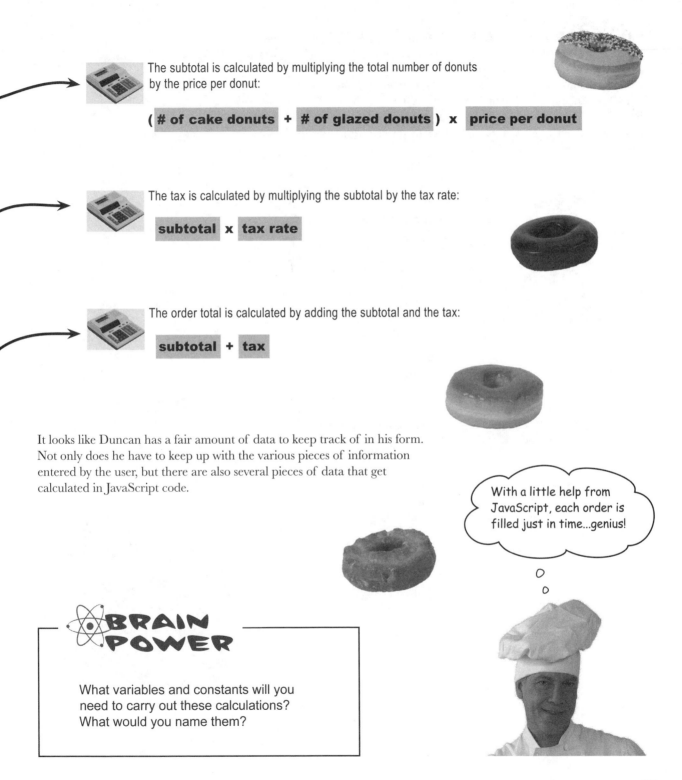

The subtotal is calculated by multiplying the total number of donuts by the price per donut:

(**# of cake donuts** + **# of glazed donuts**) x **price per donut**

The tax is calculated by multiplying the subtotal by the tax rate:

subtotal x **tax rate**

The order total is calculated by adding the subtotal and the tax:

subtotal + **tax**

It looks like Duncan has a fair amount of data to keep track of in his form. Not only does he have to keep up with the various pieces of information entered by the user, but there are also several pieces of data that get calculated in JavaScript code.

With a little help from JavaScript, each order is filled just in time...genius!

BRAIN POWER

What variables and constants will you need to carry out these calculations? What would you name them?

A first take at the donut calculations

Duncan tried to write the JavaScript for the calculations himself, but ran into problems. As soon as a user enters a number of donuts, the on-the-fly calculations immediately go haywire. They're coming up with values of $NaN, which doesn't make much sense. Even worse, orders aren't getting filled and customers aren't exactly thrilled with Duncan's technological "advancements."

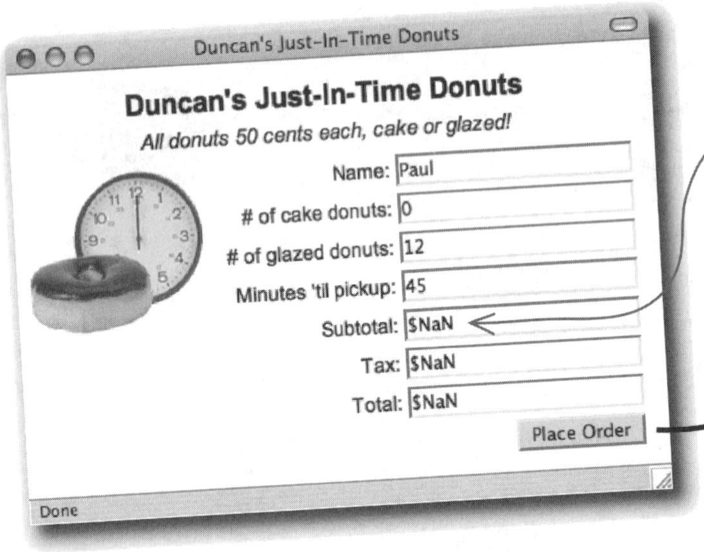

Duncan's Just-In-Time Donuts

Duncan's Just-In-Time Donuts
All donuts 50 cents each, cake or glazed!

Name: Paul
# of cake donuts: 0
# of glazed donuts: 12
Minutes 'til pickup: 45
Subtotal: $NaN
Tax: $NaN
Total: $NaN

Place Order

Done

$NaN, is that code for something terribly bad?

That's not good!

x 0

It's time to take a look at the code for the donut script and see exactly what's going on. Look over on the next page (or at the code samples you can download from *http://www.headfirstlabs.com/books/hfjs/*), and see if you can figure out what happened.

Freshly Brewed & DONUTS
COFFEE

No donuts = big problem.

This code is called to update the order by calculating the subtotal and total on the fly.

Since the data entered by the user looks OK, there must be something wrong with the constants.

This code submits the order to the server and confirms the order with the user.

The order is updated when either number of donuts changes.

The order is submitted when the Place Order button is clicked.

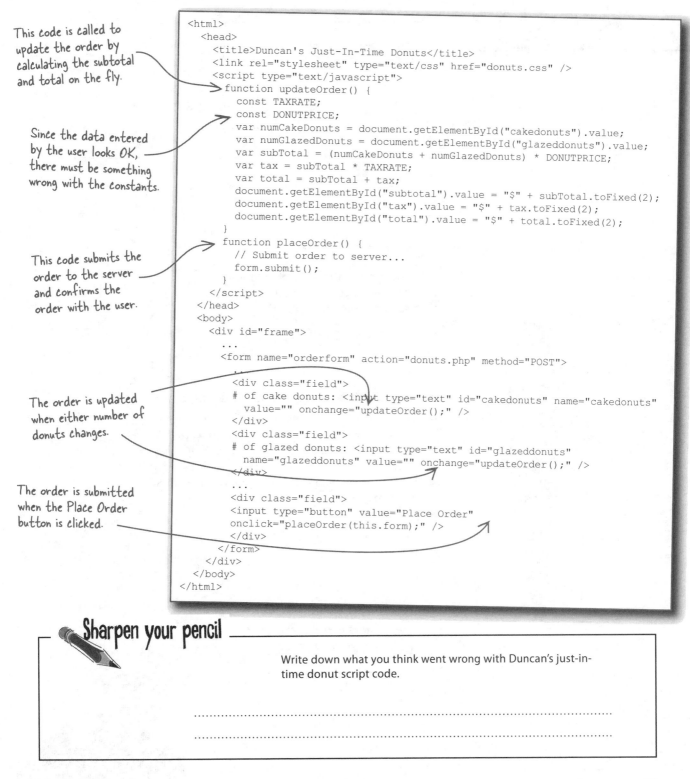

```html
<html>
  <head>
    <title>Duncan's Just-In-Time Donuts</title>
    <link rel="stylesheet" type="text/css" href="donuts.css" />
    <script type="text/javascript">
    function updateOrder() {
      const TAXRATE;
      const DONUTPRICE;
      var numCakeDonuts = document.getElementById("cakedonuts").value;
      var numGlazedDonuts = document.getElementById("glazeddonuts").value;
      var subTotal = (numCakeDonuts + numGlazedDonuts) * DONUTPRICE;
      var tax = subTotal * TAXRATE;
      var total = subTotal + tax;
      document.getElementById("subtotal").value = "$" + subTotal.toFixed(2);
      document.getElementById("tax").value = "$" + tax.toFixed(2);
      document.getElementById("total").value = "$" + total.toFixed(2);
    }
    function placeOrder() {
      // Submit order to server...
      form.submit();
    }
    </script>
  </head>
  <body>
    <div id="frame">
      ...
      <form name="orderform" action="donuts.php" method="POST">
        ...
        <div class="field">
        # of cake donuts: <input type="text" id="cakedonuts" name="cakedonuts"
          value="" onchange="updateOrder();" />
        </div>
        <div class="field">
        # of glazed donuts: <input type="text" id="glazeddonuts"
          name="glazeddonuts" value="" onchange="updateOrder();" />
        </div>
        ...
        <div class="field">
        <input type="button" value="Place Order"
        onclick="placeOrder(this.form);" />
        </div>
      </form>
    </div>
  </body>
</html>
```

Sharpen your pencil

Write down what you think went wrong with Duncan's just-in-time donut script code.

....

....

Sharpen your pencil Solution

Write down what you think went wrong with Duncan's just-in-time donut script code.

The two constants, TAXRATE and DONUTPRICE, aren't initialized, which means the calculations that depend on them can't be completed.

OK, I understand that a constant always has the same value, but if that's the case then how can it be uninitialized?

You shouldn't ever <u>uninitialize</u> a constant.

You can uninitialize a constant by never giving it a value, but it's **a very bad idea**. When you don't initialize a constant when you create it, that constant ends up in no man's land—it has no value, and even worse, **it can't be given one**. An uninitialized constant is essentially a **coding error**, even though browsers don't usually let you know about it.

Always initialize constants when you create them.

Initialize your data...or else

When you don't initialize a piece of data, it's considered *undefined*,
which is a fancy way of saying it has no value. That doesn't mean it
isn't worth anything, it just means it doesn't contain any information...
yet. The problem shows up when you try to use variables or constants
that haven't been initialized.

Uninitialized

```
const DONUTPRICE;
```

Initialized

```
var numCakeDonuts = 0;
```

```
var numGlazedDonuts = 12;
```

In JavaScript you
multiply numbers
using * instead of x

```
var subTotal = (numCakeDonuts + numGlazedDonuts) * DONUTPRICE;
```

0   12   ?

subtotal = (0 + 12) * ?

This is a
big problem.

The `DONUTPRICE` constant is **uninitialized**, which means it has **no
value**. Actually JavaScript has a special value just for this "non-value"
state: `undefined`. It's sort of like how your phone's voice mail will
report "no messages" when you don't have any messages—"no messages"
is technically still a message but it's purpose is to represent the **lack of
messages**. Same deal with `undefined`—it indicates a **lack of data**.

You have no
messages.

No data
here, so it's
undefined.

**A piece of data
is <u>undefined</u>
when it has
<u>no value</u>.**

DONUTPRICE

NaN is <u>NOT</u> a number

Just as `undefined` represents a special data **condition**, there's another important value used to indicate a special case with JavaScript variables: NaN. NaN means **Not a Number**, and it's what the `subTotal` variable gets set to since there isn't enough information to carry out the calculation. In other words, you treated a missing value as a number... and got NaN.

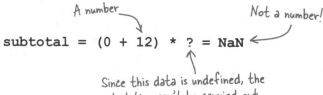

A number

Not a number!

$$subtotal = (0 + 12) * ? = NaN$$

Since this data is undefined, the calculation can't be carried out.

So solving the NaN problem requires initializing the DONUTPRICE constant when you create it:

```
const DONUTPRICE = 0.50;
```

> <u>NaN</u> is a value that <u>isn't a</u> <u>number</u> even though you're expecting the value to be one.

there are no Dumb Questions

Q: What does it mean that identifiers must be unique within a script?

A: The whole point of identifiers is to serve as a unique name that you can use to *identify* a piece of information in a script. In the real world, it isn't all that uncommon for people to have the same name... but then again, people have the ability to deal with such "name clashes" and figure out who is who. JavaScript isn't equipped to deal with ambiguity, so it needs you to carefully distinguish different pieces of information by using *different* names. You do this by making sure identifiers within your script code are all unique.

Q: Does every identifier I create have to be unique, or unique only in a specific script?

A: Identifier uniqueness is really only important within a **single** script, and in some cases only within certain portions of a single script. However, keep in mind that scripts for big web applications can get quite large, spread across lots of files. In this case, it becomes more challenging to ensure uniqueness among all identifiers. The good news it that it isn't terribly difficult to maintain identifier uniqueness in scripts of your own, provided you're as descriptive as possible when naming them.

Q: I still don't quite understand when to use camel case and lower camel case. What gives?

A: Camel case (with the first word capitalized) only applies to naming JavaScript objects, which we'll talk about in Chapter 9. Lower camel case applies to variables and functions, and is the same as camel case, except the first letter in the identifier is lowercase. So camel case means you would name an object `Donut`, while lower camel case means you would name a function `getDonut()` and a variable `numDonuts`. There isn't a cute name for constants—they're just all caps.

Q: Are text and boolean data considered NaN?

A: Theoretically, yes, since they definitely aren't numbers. But in reality, no. The purpose of NaN is to indicate that a number isn't what you think it is. In other words, NaN isn't so much a description of JavaScript data in general as it is an error indicator for number data types. You typically only encounter NaN when performing calculations that expect numbers but for some reason are given non-numeric data to work with.

Meanwhile, back at Duncan's...

Back at Duncan's Donuts, things have gone from bad to worse.
Instead of empty boxes, now there are donuts everywhere—every
order is somehow getting overcalculated. Duncan is getting
overwhelmed with complaints of donut overload and pastry gouging.

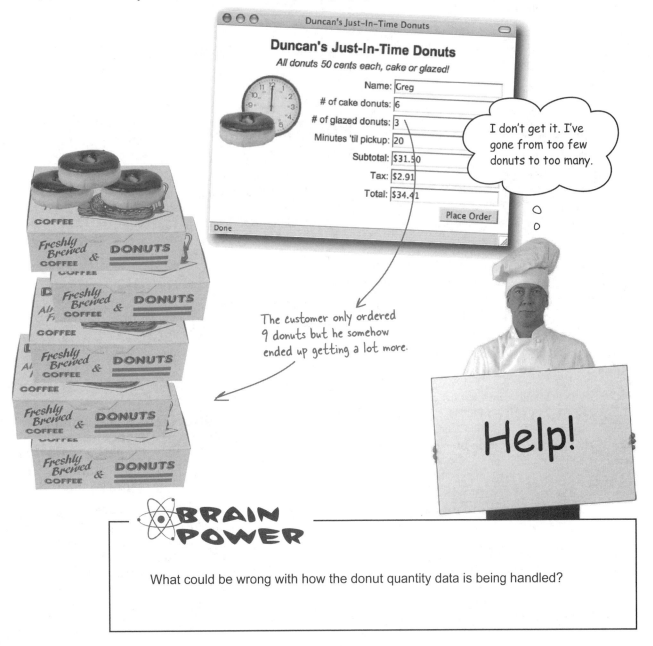

Duncan's Just-In-Time Donuts

All donuts 50 cents each, cake or glazed!

Name:	Greg
# of cake donuts:	6
# of glazed donuts:	3
Minutes 'til pickup:	20
Subtotal:	$31.90
Tax:	$2.91
Total:	$34.41

Place Order

Done

I don't get it. I've gone from too few donuts to too many.

The customer only ordered 9 donuts but he somehow ended up getting a lot more.

Help!

What could be wrong with how the donut quantity data is being handled?

You can add more than numbers

In JavaScript, **context** is everything. Specifically, it matters what **kind** of data you're manipulating in a given piece of code, not just what you're **doing** with the data. Even something as simple as adding two pieces of information can yield very different results depending upon the **type** of data involved.

$$1 + 2 = 3$$

$$\text{"do"} + \text{"nuts"} = \text{"donuts"}$$

Fancy word for "stick these things together".

Numeric Addition

Adding two numbers does what you might expect—it produces a result that is the **mathematical** addition of the two values.

String Concatenation

Adding two strings also does what you might expect but it's very different than mathematical addition—here the strings are attached **end-to-end.**

Knowing that strings of text are added differently than numbers, what do you think happens when an attempt is made to add two textual numbers?

$$\text{"1"} + \text{"2"} = ?$$

Addition, concatenation, what gives?

JavaScript doesn't really care what's in a string of text—it's all characters to JavaScript. So the fact that the strings hold numeric characters makes no difference... string concatenation is still performed, resulting in an **unexpected** result if the **intent** was numeric addition.

$$\text{"1"} + \text{"2"} = \text{"12"}$$

The result is a string that doesn't look like mathematical addition at all.

Since these are strings and not numbers, they are "added" using string concatenation.

Always make sure you're adding what you think you're adding.

Accidentally concatenating strings when you intend to add numbers is a common JavaScript mistake. Be sure to convert strings to numbers before adding them if your intent is numeric addition.

parseInt() and parseFloat(): converts text to a number

Despite the addition/concatenation problem, there are legitimate situations where you need to perform a mathematical operation on a number that you've got stored as a string. In these cases, you need to **convert** the string to a number **before** performing any numeric operations on it. JavaScript provides two handy functions for carrying out this type of conversion:

| parseInt() |

Give this function a string and it converts the string to an integer

| parseFloat() |

Give this function a string and it converts the string to a floating point (decimal) number

Each of these built-in functions accepts a string and returns a number after carrying out the conversion:

parseInt() turns "1" into 1.

This time the result is the <u>mathematical</u> addition of 1 and 2.

$$parseInt("1") + parseInt("2") = 3$$

The string "2" is converted to the number 2.

Keep in mind that the parseInt() and parseFloat() functions **aren't guaranteed** to always work. They're only as good as the information you provide them. They'll do their best at converting strings to numbers, but the idea is that you should be providing them with strings that **only** contain numeric characters.

$$parseFloat("\$31.50") = NaN$$

This code is a problem because the $ character confuses the function.

Surprise, surprise, the result is *Not a Number.*

Don't worry if this function stuff is still a little confusing.

You'll get the formal lowdown on functions a little later—for now all you really need to know is that functions allow you pass them information and then give you back something in return.

Why are extra donuts being ordered?

Take a closer look at the just-in-time donut order form. We should be able to figure out why so many donuts are being accidentally ordered...

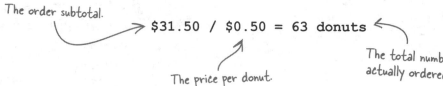

We can divide the subtotal by the price for each donut...and the answer is how many donuts are getting ordered.

The order subtotal.

$$\$31.50 \; / \; \$0.50 = 63 \text{ donuts}$$

The price per donut.

The total number of donuts actually ordered... hmmm.

Remember "1" + "2" = "12"? Looks kind of like that, doesn't it?

This looks a whole lot like the numeric string addition problem, especially when you consider that form data is always stored as strings regardless of what it is. Even though numbers are entered into the form fields, from a JavaScript perspective, they're really just text. So we just need to convert the strings to actual numbers to prevent a numeric addition from being misinterpreted as a string concatenation.

Sharpen your pencil

Using the pieces of code below to grab the contents of the donut quantity form fields, write the missing lines of code in Duncan's `updateOrder()` function so that the donut quantities are converted from strings to numbers.

```
document.getElementById("cakedonuts").value
```

This code gets the number of cake donuts entered by the user in the donut form.

This code grabs the number of glazed donuts entered into the donut form.

```
document.getElementById("glazeddonuts").value
```

```
function updateOrder() {
  const TAXRATE = 0.0925;
  const DONUTPRICE = 0.50;
  var numCakeDonuts =

  ....................................................................................................................
  var numGlazedDonuts =

  ....................................................................................................................
  if (isNaN(numCakeDonuts))
    numCakeDonuts = 0;
  if (isNaN(numGlazedDonuts))
    numGlazedDonuts = 0;
  var subTotal = (numCakeDonuts + numGlazedDonuts) * DONUTPRICE;
  var tax = subTotal * TAXRATE;
  var total = subTotal + tax;
  document.getElementById("subtotal").value = "$" + subTotal.toFixed(2);
  document.getElementById("tax").value = "$" + tax.toFixed(2);
  document.getElementById("total").value = "$" + total.toFixed(2);
}
```

Sharpen your pencil
Solution

Using the pieces of code below to grab the contents of the donut quantity form fields, write the missing lines of code in Duncan's `updateOrder()` function so that the donut quantities are converted from strings to numbers.

```
document.getElementById("cakedonuts").value
```

```
document.getElementById("glazeddonuts").value
```

Since both numbers are integers, parseInt() is used for the conversion.

```
function updateOrder() {
  const TAXRATE = 0.0925;
  const DONUTPRICE = 0.50;
  var numCakeDonuts =

    parseInt(document.getElementById("cakedonuts").value);

  var numGlazedDonuts =

    parseInt(document.getElementById("glazeddonuts").value);

  if (isNaN(numCakeDonuts))
    numCakeDonuts = 0;
  if (isNaN(numGlazedDonuts))
    numGlazedDonuts = 0;
  var subTotal = (numCakeDonuts + numGlazedDonuts) * DONUTPRICE;
  var tax = subTotal * TAXRATE;
  var total = subTotal + tax;
  document.getElementById("subtotal").value = "$" + subTotal.toFixed(2);
  document.getElementById("tax").value = "$" + tax.toFixed(2);
  document.getElementById("total").value = "$" + total.toFixed(2);
}
```

The toFixed() function rounds the dollar values to two decimal places.

BULLET POINTS

- Although not a strict JavaScript requirement, it's a good coding convention to name **constants** in **ALL UPPERCASE** and **variables** in **lowerCamelCase**.

- **Always initialize constants** when you create them, and initialize variables whenever possible.

- When a variable isn't initialized, it remains **undefined** until a value is eventually assigned to it.

- NaN stands for **Not a Number**, and is used to indicate that a piece of data is not a number when the expectation is that it should be.

- String concatenation is very different from mathematical addition, even though both use the familiar plus sign (+).

- The built-in `parseInt()` and `parseFloat()` functions are used to **convert strings to numbers**.

You figured out the problem...

Duncan is thrilled with the JavaScript code fixes you made. He's finally receiving orders that are accurate.... and business is booming.

Duncan's Just-In-Time Donuts

All donuts 50 cents each, cake or glazed!

Name:	Greg
# of cake donuts:	6
# of glazed donuts:	3
Minutes 'til pickup:	20
Subtotal:	$4.50
Tax:	$0.42
Total:	$4.92

Place Order

6 cake
3 glazed
Pick up in 20 minutes for Greg

> Great, you got the online order system working perfectly!.

Of course, it's risky to assume that a few quick fixes here and there will solve your problems for all eternity. In fact, sometimes the peskiest problems are exposed by unexpected outside forces...

Duncan discovers donut espionage

Duncan's got a new problem: a weasel competitor named Frankie. Frankie runs the hotdog business across the street from Duncan, and is now offering a Breakfast Hound. Problem is, Frankie's playing dirty and submitting bogus donut orders with no names. So now we have orders with no customers—and that's not good.

Duncan's Just-In-Time Donuts

All donuts 50 cents each, cake or glazed!

Name:
\# of cake donuts: 18
\# of glazed donuts: 30
Minutes 'til pickup: 15
Subtotal: $24.00
Tax: $2.22
Total: $26.22

Place Order

Even though no name has been entered, the order is still accepted.

I'm not worried about my competitors, I just need to make the donut code smarter about how it accepts data.

18 cake
30 glazed
Pick up in 15 minutes for ?

Duncan is wasting precious time, energy, and donuts filling bogus orders... and he needs you to make sure all the form data has been entered before allowing an order to go through.

Use getElementById() to grab form data

In order to check the validity of form data, you need a way to grab the data from your Web page. The key to to accessing a web page element with JavaScript is the `id` attribute of the HTML tag:

```
<input type="text" id="cakedonuts" name="cakedonuts" />
```

The id attribute is what you use to access the form field in JavaScript code.

The cake donut quantity HTML input element.

# of cake donuts: 18

JavaScript allows you to retrieve a web page element with its ID using a function called `getElementById()`. This function doesn't grab an element's data directly, but instead provides you with the HTML field itself, as a JavaScript object. You then access the data through the field's `value` property.

Technically, getElementById() is a method on the document object, and not a function.

```
document.getElementById()
```

Give this method the ID of an element on a web page and it gives you back the element itself, which can then be used to access web data

The getElementById() method belongs to the document object.

Don't sweat objects, properties, and methods right now.

JavaScript supports an advanced data type called an object that allows you to do some really cool things. In fact, the JavaScript language itself is really just a bunch of objects. We'll talk a lot more about objects later in the book—for now, just know that a method is a lot like a function, and a property is a lot like a variable.

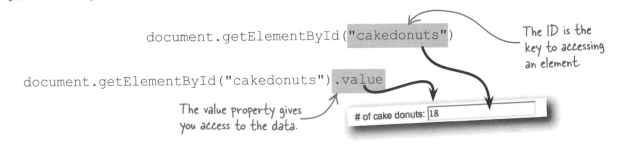

```
document.getElementById("cakedonuts")
```

The ID is the key to accessing an element.

```
document.getElementById("cakedonuts").value
```

The value property gives you access to the data.

# of cake donuts: 18

With this code in hand, you're now ready to check Duncan's form data to make sure the fields aren't empty before accepting an order.

Validate the web form's data

You need to check to make sure a name is entered into the donut form. Not entering the number of minutes until pick-up could also be a problem, since the whole point is to provide hot donuts just in time. So, best case, you want to ensure both pieces of data are filled-in and valid.

Checking for empty data in a form field is a matter of checking to see if the form field value is an empty string ("").

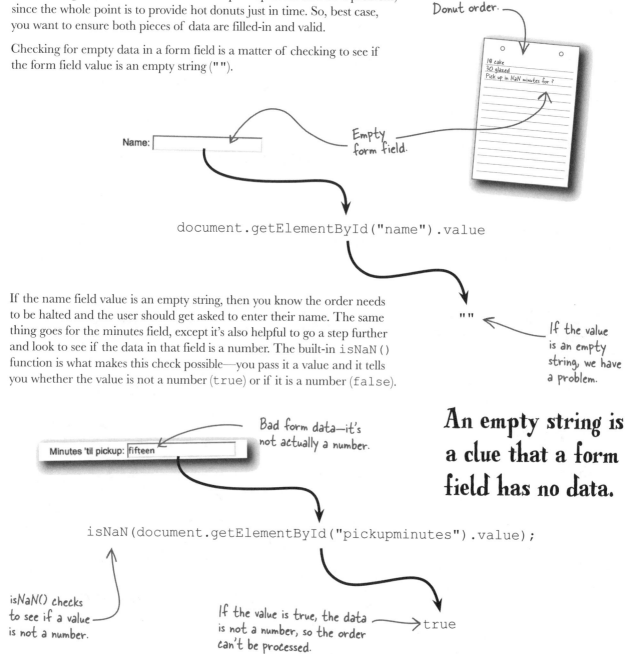

Donut order.

18 cake
30 glazed
Pick up in NaN minutes for ?

Name:

Empty
form field.

document.getElementById("name").value

If the name field value is an empty string, then you know the order needs to be halted and the user should get asked to enter their name. The same thing goes for the minutes field, except it's also helpful to go a step further and look to see if the data in that field is a number. The built-in isNaN() function is what makes this check possible—you pass it a value and it tells you whether the value is not a number (true) or if it is a number (false).

""

If the value
is an empty
string, we have
a problem.

An empty string is a clue that a form field has no data.

Bad form data—it's
not actually a number.

Minutes 'til pickup: fifteen

isNaN(document.getElementById("pickupminutes").value);

isNaN() checks
to see if a value
is not a number.

If the value is true, the data
is not a number, so the order
can't be processed.

→ true

JavaScript Magnets

The `placeOrder()` function is where the name and pick-up minutes data validation takes place. Use the magnets to finish writing the code that checks for the existence of name and pick-up minutes data, along with making sure that the pick-up minutes entered is a number. You'll need to use each magnet, and some magnets more than once.

"if" is used to test for a condition and then take action accordingly—if this, then do something.

This is an equality test—is one thing equal to another thing?

This means one of two conditions can result in the action—if this OR that, then do something.

```
function placeOrder() {
  if (.............................................................................................................==..........)
    alert("I'm sorry but you must provide your name before submitting an order.");
                                                                            ==..........||
  else if (........................................................................................
    ..............................................................................................................)
    .......................................
    alert("I'm sorry but you must provide the number of minutes until pick-up" +
      " before submitting an order.");
  else
    // Submit the order to the server
    form.submit();
}
```

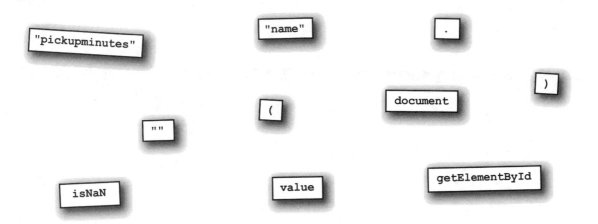

`"pickupminutes"`   `"name"`   `.`

`(`   `document`   `)`

`""`

`isNaN`   `value`   `getElementById`

JavaScript Magnets Solution

The `placeOrder()` function is where the name and pick-up minutes data validation takes place. Use the magnets to finish writing the code that checks for the existence of name and pick-up minutes data, along with making sure that the pick-up minutes entered is a number. All of the magnets are used, and some are used several times.

This says, if the name value is empty, then pop up an alert...else do something different.

This checks the value of the name field to see if it's equals to "".

Here, we're saying if the value is empty, OR if the value is not a number.

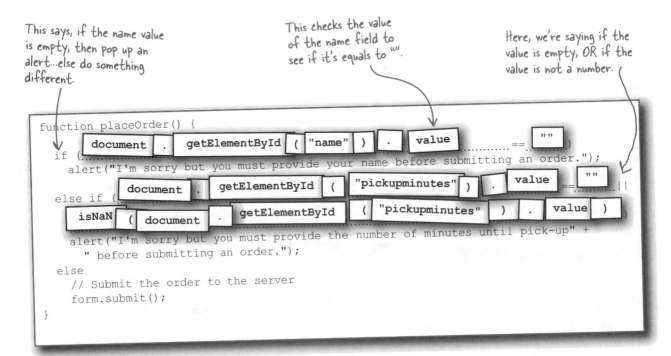

```
function placeOrder() {
  if (document . getElementById ( "name" ) . value ............. == .. "" )
    alert("I'm sorry but you must provide your name before submitting an order.");
  else if (document . getElementById ( "pickupminutes" ) . value ==........ ||
    isNaN ( document . getElementById ( "pickupminutes" ) . value ) )
    alert("I'm sorry but you must provide the number of minutes until pick-up" +
      " before submitting an order.");
  else
    // Submit the order to the server
    form.submit();
}
```

You saved Duncan's Donuts... again!

The new and improved just-in-time donut form with data validation has put an end to Frankie's pastry espionage, and also made the page more robust for real customers. Using JavaScript to protect the integrity of data entered by the user is a win-win, especially in the cutthroat breakfast biz!

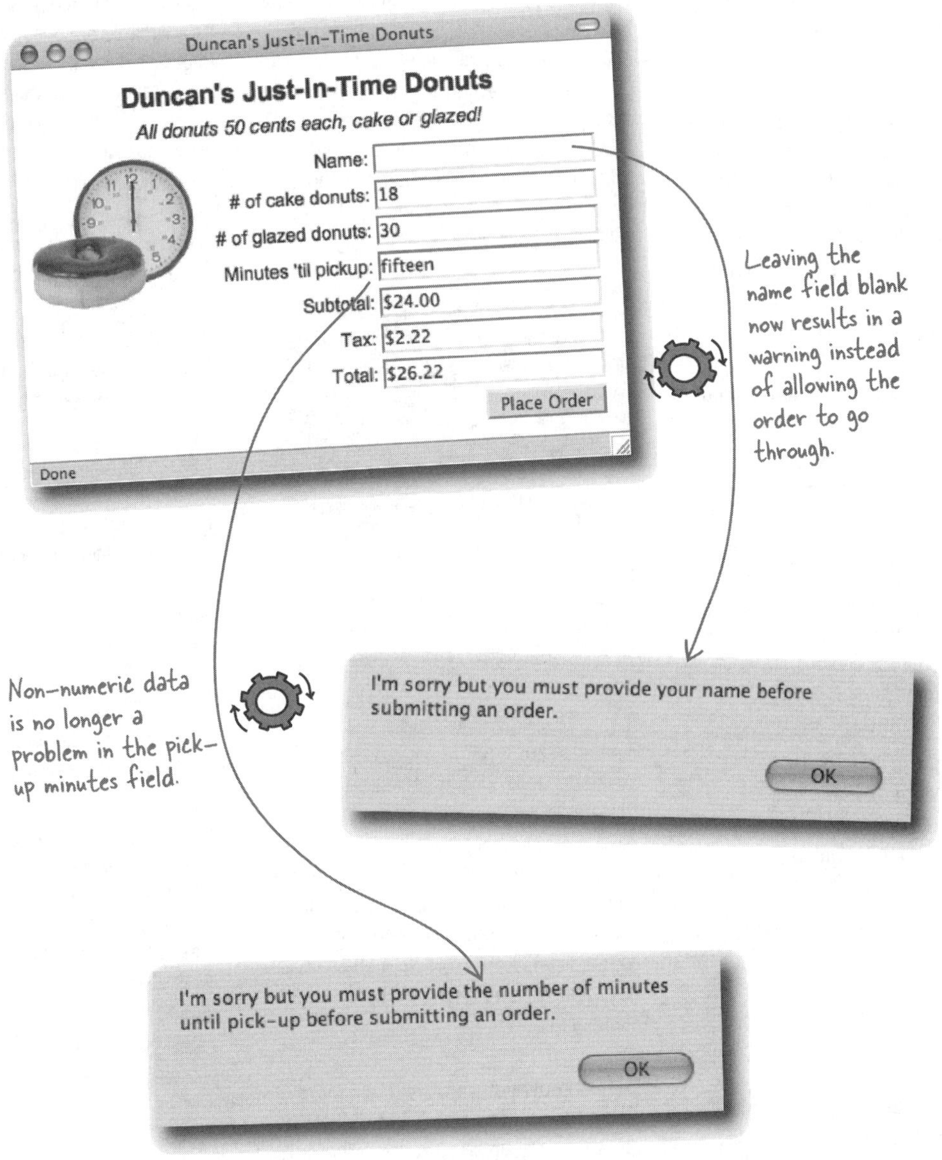

Leaving the name field blank now results in a warning instead of allowing the order to go through.

Non-numeric data is no longer a problem in the pick-up minutes field.

I'm sorry but you must provide your name before submitting an order.

OK

I'm sorry but you must provide the number of minutes until pick-up before submitting an order.

OK

Q: How does the plus sign (+) know to add or concatenate?

A: Like many things in JavaScript, functionality is determined by context. This means the plus sign takes a look at the two things being "added" and decides whether to numerically add them or concatenate them as text based upon their data types. You already know that "adding" two words means sticking them end-to-end. But problems can occur when you mistakenly assume that you're working with one type of data when it's actually another. That's another reason why it's always a good idea to check to make sure you provide numeric data when you intend numeric addition, and text for text.

Q: What happens when you attempt to add a string to a number?

A: Since number-to-string conversion is automatic in JavaScript, mixing the two data types in an addition always results in a string concatenation. So, the number first gets converted to a string, and then the two strings get concatenated. If you intended to add the two numbers, you need to explicitly convert the string to a number using `parseInt()` or `parseFloat()`.

Q: What happens if you use `parseInt()` to convert a string containing a decimal number?

A: Don't worry, nothing catches on fire. All that happens is that JavaScript assumes you don't care about the fractional part of the number, so it returns only the integer portion of the number.

Q: How does the `id` HTML attribute tie web elements to JavaScript code?

A: Think of the `id` attribute as the portal through which JavaScript code accesses HTML content. When people say JavaScript code runs on a web page, they don't literally mean the web page itself—they mean the browser. In reality, JavaScript code is fairly insulated from HTML code, and can only access it through very specific mechanisms. One of these mechanisms involves the `id` attribute, which lets JavaScript retrieve an HTML element. Tagging a web element with an ID allows the element to be found by JavaScript code, opening up all kinds of scripting possibilities.

Q: That's pretty vague. How specifically does JavaScript code access an HTML element?

A: The `getElementById()` method of the `document` object is the key to accessing an HTML element from JavaScript, and this method uses the `id` attribute of the element to find it on the page. HTML IDs are like JavaScript identifiers in that they should be unique within a given page. Otherwise, the `getElementById()` method would have a tough time knowing what web element to return.

Q: I know you said we'll talk more about them in Chapter 9, but objects have already come up a few times. What are they?

A: We're jumping ahead a little here, so don't tell anyone. Objects are an advanced JavaScript data type that can combine functions, constants, and variables into one logical entity. A method is just a function that is part of an object, while a property is a variable or constant in an object. On a practical level, JavaScript uses objects to represent just about everything—the browser window is an object, as is the web page document. That's why the `getElementById()` method must be called through the `document` object—it's a part of the object, which represents the entire web page. OK, back to Chapter 2...

Q: I still don't understand the difference between a web page element and its value. What gives?

A: Web page elements are exposed to JavaScript as objects, which means they have properties and methods you can use to manipulate them. One of these properties is `value`, which holds the value stored in the element. As an example, the *value* of a form field is the data entered into the field.

Q: Why is it necessary to know if a value is *not* a number? Wouldn't it make more sense to see if it *is* a number?

A: Good question. What it boils down to is why you care about a value being a number or not. In most cases the assumption is that you're dealing with a number, so it makes sense to check for the exception (the unexpected). By checking for `NaN`, you're able to make number-handling script code more robust, and hopefully alleviate a weird computation involving a non-number.

Strive for intuitive user input

Now that Duncan is no longer putting out fires, he really wants to improve the user experience of the just-in-time donut form. Just as the "hot donuts" sign is **intuitive** to people passing by his storefront, he wants the online form to be similarly intuitive. Duncan knows that donuts are typically ordered and served in dozens. Very few people order 12 or 24 donuts—they order 1 or 2 dozen donuts. He thinks the donut form should allow users to enter data in the most natural way possible.

Problem is, the current script doesn't take into account the user entering the word "dozen" when specifying the quantity of donuts.

```
○○○            Duncan's Just-In-Time Donuts         ○

           Duncan's Just-In-Time Donuts
            All donuts 50 cents each, cake or glazed!

                           Name: Dierdre
                # of cake donuts: 3 dozen
              # of glazed donuts:
              Minutes 'til pickup: 60
                        Subtotal: $1.50
                             Tax: $0.14
                           Total: $1.64
                                       Place Order

Done
```

"3 dozen" donuts gets converted into the number 3 thanks to the parseInt() function.

`parseInt("3 dozen")`

3

This is a number, not a string.

The script doesn't complain when the user enters the word "dozen" alongside a number... the parseInt() function ignores any text present after a number in a string. So, the word "dozen" is just discarded, and all that's kept is the number.

BRAIN POWER

Is it possible for the donut script to allow users to enter either a number or a number **and** the word "dozen" for ordering by the dozen? How?

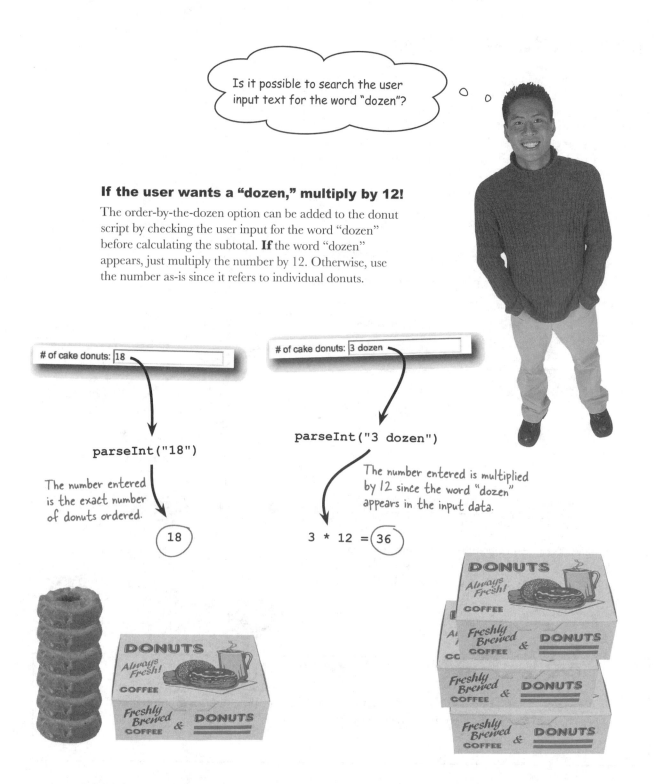

Is it possible to search the user input text for the word "dozen"?

If the user wants a "dozen," multiply by 12!

The order-by-the-dozen option can be added to the donut script by checking the user input for the word "dozen" before calculating the subtotal. **If** the word "dozen" appears, just multiply the number by 12. Otherwise, use the number as-is since it refers to individual donuts.

# of cake donuts: 18

# of cake donuts: 3 dozen

`parseInt("18")`

`parseInt("3 dozen")`

The number entered is the exact number of donuts ordered.

The number entered is multiplied by 12 since the word "dozen" appears in the input data.

18

3 * 12 = 36

Ready Bake JavaScript

The custom `parseDonuts()` function is responsible for processing donut quantity input data. It first converts the data to a number, and then checks for the appearance of the word "dozen" in the input data. If "dozen" appears, the number of donuts is multiplied by 12. Get this recipe at *http://www. headfirstlabs.com/books/hfjs/*.

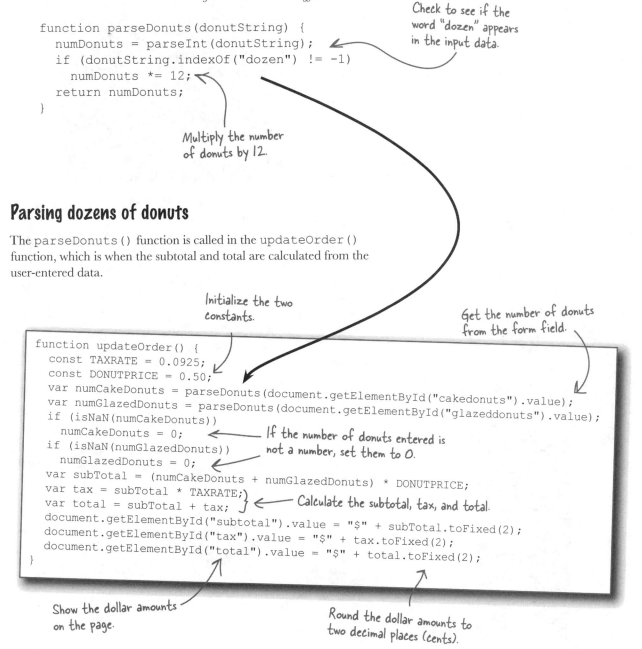

```javascript
function parseDonuts(donutString) {
  numDonuts = parseInt(donutString);
  if (donutString.indexOf("dozen") != -1)
    numDonuts *= 12;
  return numDonuts;
}
```

Check to see if the word "dozen" appears in the input data.

Multiply the number of donuts by 12.

Parsing dozens of donuts

The `parseDonuts()` function is called in the `updateOrder()` function, which is when the subtotal and total are calculated from the user-entered data.

Initialize the two constants.

Get the number of donuts from the form field.

```javascript
function updateOrder() {
  const TAXRATE = 0.0925;
  const DONUTPRICE = 0.50;
  var numCakeDonuts = parseDonuts(document.getElementById("cakedonuts").value);
  var numGlazedDonuts = parseDonuts(document.getElementById("glazeddonuts").value);
  if (isNaN(numCakeDonuts))
    numCakeDonuts = 0;
  if (isNaN(numGlazedDonuts))
    numGlazedDonuts = 0;
  var subTotal = (numCakeDonuts + numGlazedDonuts) * DONUTPRICE;
  var tax = subTotal * TAXRATE;
  var total = subTotal + tax;
  document.getElementById("subtotal").value = "$" + subTotal.toFixed(2);
  document.getElementById("tax").value = "$" + tax.toFixed(2);
  document.getElementById("total").value = "$" + total.toFixed(2);
}
```

If the number of donuts entered is not a number, set them to 0.

Calculate the subtotal, tax, and total.

Show the dollar amounts on the page.

Round the dollar amounts to two decimal places (cents).

Just-in-time donuts a smashing success!

Life is good now that Duncan and his just-in-time hot donut idea has been fully realized in a JavaScript-powered page that carefully validates orders entered by the user.

Now donut lovers can order their piping hot donuts online **and** just in time.

OVER 1000000 SERVED

Hot Donuts

Just in time!

Duncan's Just-In-Time Donuts

All donuts 50 cents each, cake or glazed!

Name:	Alan
# of cake donuts:	15
# of glazed donuts:	4 dozen
Minutes 'til pickup:	10
Subtotal:	$31.50
Tax:	$2.91
Total:	$34.41

Place Order

JavaScriptcross

Data isn't always stored in JavaScript code. Sometimes it gets stored in the rows and columns of a crossword puzzle, where it waits patiently for you to uncover it.

Across

4. When you set the value of a piece of data upon creating it, you .... it.
6. The unique name used to reference a piece of data.
7. The JavaScript keyword used to create a variable.
9. 3.14, 11, and 5280 are all this data type.
10. A coding convention that involves naming identifiers with mixed case, as in ThisIsMyName.
11. It's not a num-bah.
12. A piece of information whose value can change.
13. An piece of data with an on/off value would be stored as this data type.

Down

1. A piece of data whose value cannot change.
2. The data type used to store characters, words, and phrases.
3. When a value isn't set for a variable or constant, the data is considered ....
5. The built-in JavaScript function used to convert a string to an integer.
8. The process of checking to make sure user-entered data is accurate is called ....
10. The JavaScript keyword used to create a constant.

JavaScriptcross Solution

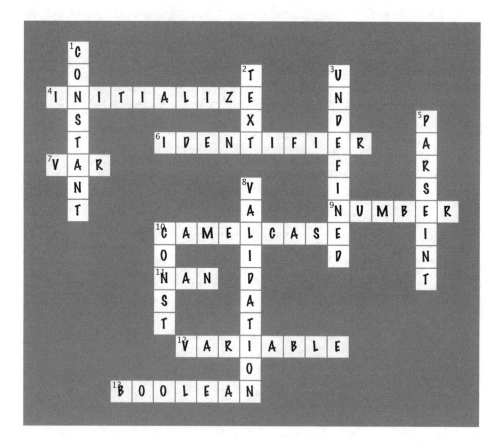

Page Bender

Fold the page vertically
to line up the two brains
and solve the riddle.

What do we all want for our script data?

— It's a meeting of the minds! ←

There are lots of things
I want for my script
data, but one thing in
particular comes to mind.

Yum.

User input is the kind of data that
you shouldn't trust. It's just not safe
to assume that users will enter data and
check to make sure it is OK. A more secure
storage solution involves using JavaScript.

3 exploring the client

Browser Spelunking

Look at this guy, he's the dream client, I tell ya. He's made of money but he can't put it to work without a couple of thinkin' guys like us...

Sometimes JavaScript needs to know what's going on in the world around it. Your scripts may begin as code in web pages, but they ultimately live in a world created by the browser, or client. **Smart scripts** often need to know more about the world they live in, in which case they can **communicate with the browser** to find out more about it. Whether it's finding out the screen size or accessing the browser's snooze button, scripts have an awful lot to gain by cultivating their browser relationships.

Clients, servers, and JavaScript

When you click a hyperlink or type a URL into your web browser, the browser requests the page from a web server, which then delivers the page back to the browser, or web **client**. JavaScript doesn't enter the picture until just before the browser displays the page. The JavaScript code in the page then works in concert with the web browser to **respond to user interactions** and **modify the page** as needed. The part of the web browser that runs JavaScript code is called the JavaScript **interpreter**.

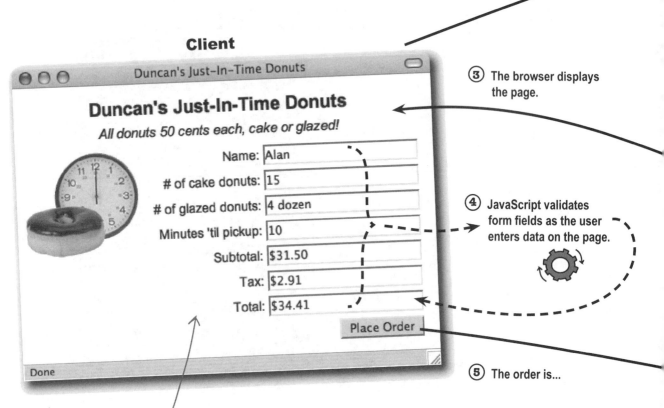

① The browser requests the page from the server.

Client

Duncan's Just-In-Time Donuts

Duncan's Just-In-Time Donuts
All donuts 50 cents each, cake or glazed!

Name: Alan
# of cake donuts: 15
# of glazed donuts: 4 dozen
Minutes 'til pickup: 10
Subtotal: $31.50
Tax: $2.91
Total: $34.41

Place Order

Done

JavaScript code runs entirely on the client, asking nothing of the server.

③ The browser displays the page.

④ JavaScript validates form fields as the user enters data on the page.

⑤ The order is...

Once a page has been delivered to the browser, the server is largely out of the equation. Virtually everything that JavaScript does from there on out is confined to the browser. This makes pages **more responsive** since they don't have to wait for the server to process and return data. This process is why JavaScript is known as a **client language**.

Request page

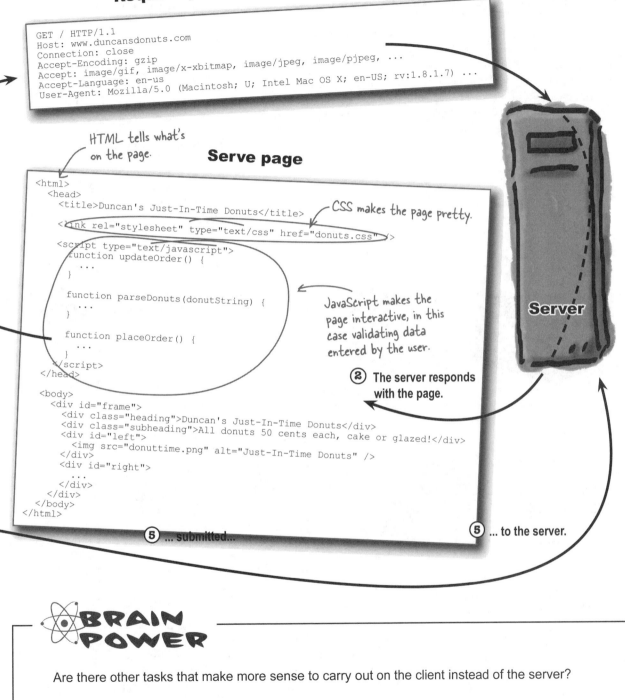

```
GET / HTTP/1.1
Host: www.duncansdonuts.com
Connection: close
Accept-Encoding: gzip
Accept: image/gif, image/x-xbitmap, image/jpeg, image/pjpeg, ...
Accept-Language: en-us
User-Agent: Mozilla/5.0 (Macintosh; U; Intel Mac OS X; en-US; rv:1.8.1.7) ...
```

HTML tells what's on the page.

Serve page

CSS makes the page pretty.

```
<html>
  <head>
    <title>Duncan's Just-In-Time Donuts</title>
    <link rel="stylesheet" type="text/css" href="donuts.css" />

    <script type="text/javascript">
      function updateOrder() {
        ...
      }

      function parseDonuts(donutString) {
        ...
      }

      function placeOrder() {
        ...
      }
    </script>
  </head>

  <body>
    <div id="frame">
      <div class="heading">Duncan's Just-In-Time Donuts</div>
      <div class="subheading">All donuts 50 cents each, cake or glazed!</div>
      <div id="left">
        <img src="donuttime.png" alt="Just-In-Time Donuts" />
      </div>
      <div id="right">
        ...
      </div>
    </div>
  </body>
</html>
```

JavaScript makes the page interactive, in this case validating data entered by the user.

② **The server responds with the page.**

Server

⑤ ... submitted...

⑤ ... to the server.

BRAIN POWER

Are there other tasks that make more sense to carry out on the client instead of the server?

What can a browser do for you?

Your **client** web browser is responsible for **running JavaScript code**, which allows scripts access to the client environment. For example, a script can get the width and height of the browser window, as well as a history of visited web pages. Other interesting browser features that are open to JavaScript include a timing mechanism that works sort of like an alarm clock, and access to cookies, which allow you to store data that hangs around even after you leave a page or close the browser.

Browser metrics

Browser metrics include various measurements associated with the size of the browser window, the viewable web page, and even information about the browser vendor and version number.

Browser history

The browser history is the list of recent pages visited. You can use JavaScript to access this list of pages and direct the browser to one of them, effectively creating your own browser navigation controls.

Cookies

Cookies are like variables that get stored on the user's hard drive by the browser so that they last beyond a single web session. In other words, you can leave a page and come back, and the data's still there.

Timers

Timers allow you to trigger a piece of JavaScript code after a specified amount of time has elapsed.

These features are not all the client has to offer your scripts, but they should give you the idea that there's more to JavaScript than what exists within the page. In fact, there are plenty of situations where it's helpful to **look beyond the page** and get a little help from the browser.

there are no
Dumb Questions

Q: So JavaScript is part of the client?

A: Yes. Web browsers that support JavaScript come with a JavaScript interpreter that's responsible for reading JavaScript code from a page and then running that code.

Q: If JavaScript code runs on the client, how does it relate to the server?

A: JavaScript code doesn't typically have a direct association with a web server since it runs solely on the client. JavaScript is commonly used to intercept web data as it is relayed from server to browser. However, it's possible to write scripts that request information from the server and then process and display that information on the page. That scripting technique is called Ajax, and we talk about how to use it in Chapter 12.

Q: Does JavaScript allow you to control the client?

A: Yes and no. Although web browsers allow JavaScript to access certain parts of the client environment, they don't allow JavaScript unlimited freedom for security reasons. For example, most browsers don't allow scripts to open or close windows without the user's approval.

The iRock is too happy

Remember the iRock? Your JavaScript was such a success that it got bought out by Alan, a young entrepreneur. But he's called you back in, because there are some problems... Users are unnerved by the iRock's **persistent state of happiness**. Sure, we all want our pets to be happy, but the iRock seems to have a severely limited emotional range.

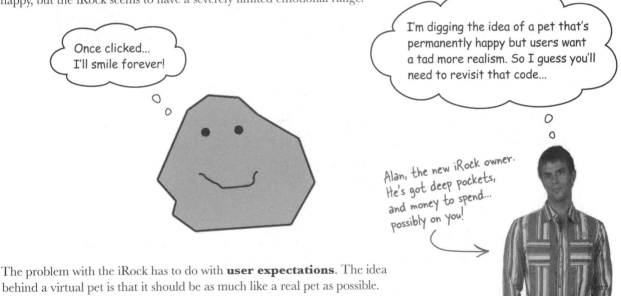

Once clicked...
I'll smile forever!

I'm digging the idea of a pet that's permanently happy but users want a tad more realism. So I guess you'll need to revisit that code...

Alan, the new iRock owner.
He's got deep pockets,
and money to spend...
possibly on you!

The problem with the iRock has to do with **user expectations**. The idea behind a virtual pet is that it should be as much like a real pet as possible. Your challenge is to figure out how to **improve the behavior** of the iRock to make it more realistic. And it seems as if the client web browser may hold some of the solutions to the iRock problem...

The iRock needs to be more responsive

Let's consider some possible behaviors for the iRock, with the goal of trying to make the rock more **realistic** and **engaging** to the user, not to mention more **interactive**. Ideally, the iRock should become more **responsive** to the user as it increases its range of emotional behavior.

Download the latest code for iRock 2.0 at http://www.headfirstlabs.com/books/hfjs.

Rock rage

The iRock randomly gets mad for no reason whatsoever, which makes the owner have to calm the rock down.

Depressed

The iRock cries every time you close the page, requiring the user to leave the browser open to keep the rock from having a breakdown.

Lonely

The iRock reverts back to being lonely when left alone, requiring the user to click it periodically to give it attention.

Which of these behaviors makes sense for the iRock to have? How would you use JavaScript to implement these behaviors in the iRock script?

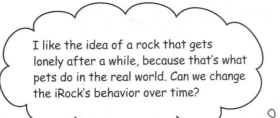

I like the idea of a rock that gets lonely after a while, because that's what pets do in the real world. Can we change the iRock's behavior over time?

JavaScript lets you know when the user is doing something... and when they're not.

The idea of a rock that gets lonely is interesting because it prods the user to interact with the rock without guilt overload, and it **rewards the user** with a **positive response** from the iRock. The challenge is to somehow use JavaScript to change the emotional state of the iRock over time. The idea is to wait for a certain amount of time, and then change the iRock's state if the user hasn't clicked it and the time elapses.

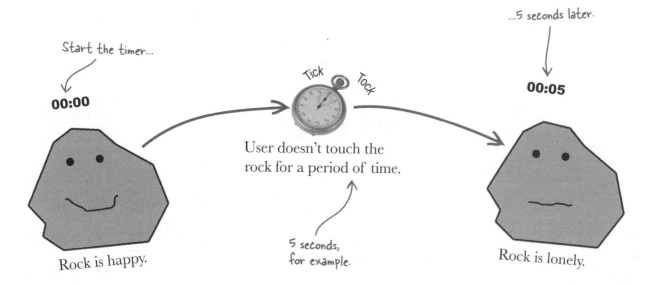

Start the timer...

00:00

Tick Tock

User doesn't touch the rock for a period of time.

5 seconds, for example.

Rock is happy.

...5 seconds later.

00:05

Rock is lonely.

Timers connect action to elapsed time

JavaScript allows you to set **timers**. A JavaScript timer works like an alarm clock: you tell it how long to wait, and when that amount of time expires, a certain piece of code will run. Unlike an alarm clock, however, JavaScript timers are triggered **when a certain amount of time has passed**, as opposed to triggering **at a certain time**. This isn't a problem, it just means you need to think in terms of **time delays** instead of exact times of day.

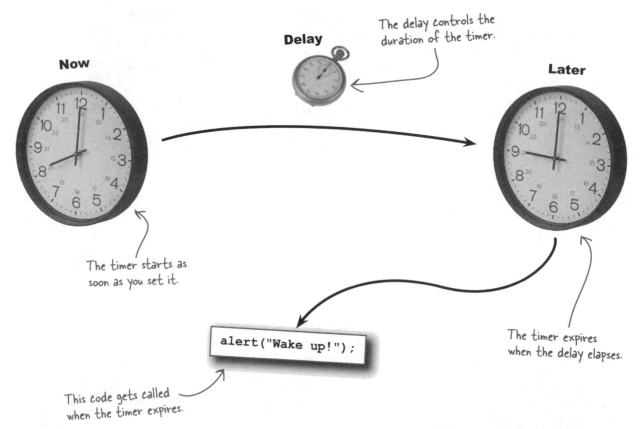

The delay controls the duration of the timer.

Delay

Now

Later

The timer starts as soon as you set it.

```
alert("Wake up!");
```

The timer expires when the delay elapses.

This code gets called when the timer expires.

The cool thing about JavaScript timers is that they allow you to run any code you want when they expire. Some web pages with regularly changing data use timers to refresh themselves after a certain delay, while others use timers to detect when the user hasn't interacted with the page in a while.

Timers let you run JavaScript code <u>after</u> a certain amount of time has elapsed.

Breaking down a timer

The two key pieces to setting a timer in JavaScript are 1) establishing the **time delay** and 2) letting the timer know **what code to run** when the delay elapses. The timer starts ticking down from the moment you set it.

The time delay is expressed in **milliseconds**, which is 1,000th of a second. Multiply the number of seconds you want by 1,000 to figure out the number of milliseconds. For example, 2 seconds is 2,000 milliseconds.

Display a message.

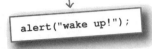

```
alert("wake up!");
```

The code that is run when the timer expires can be any JavaScript code you want, including a single statement, multiple statements (each with a terminating semicolon), or a call to either a built-in or custom function.

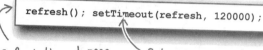

```
refresh(); setTimeout(refresh, 120000);
```

Refresh the web page.   Set another timer.

When normal JavaScript timers expire and the timer code is run, the timer is over, kaput. This type of timer is known as a **one-shot** timer because it triggers a piece of code exactly **one time**. It is also possible to create an **interval** timer, which sets **multiple** intervals instead of a single delay. An interval timer continues to call the timer code **repeatedly** after each interval until you tell it to stop. Although interval timers certainly have their place, the iRock's loneliness timer is <u>definitely</u> a one-shot timer.

> The timer expires, I get lonely, end of story.

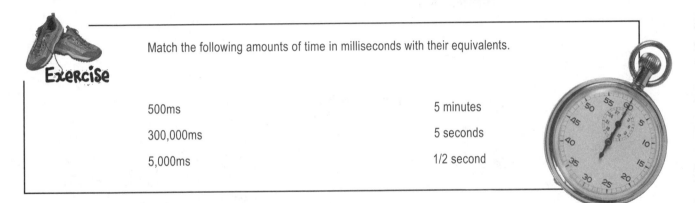

Exercise

Match the following amounts of time in milliseconds with their equivalents.

500ms   5 minutes

300,000ms   5 seconds

5,000ms   1/2 second

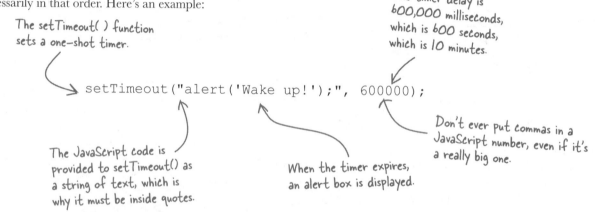

Exercise Solution

Match the following amounts of time in milliseconds with their equivalents in seconds

500ms ———————— 5 minutes

300,000ms ———————— 5 seconds

5,000ms ———————— 1/2 second

Set a timer with setTimeout()

The built-in JavaScript function that makes (one-shot) timers possible is setTimeout(). The two pieces of information you'll need for the function are the **timer delay** and the **code to run** when the timer expires (available at *http://www.headfirstlabs.com/books/hfsd/*), but not necessarily in that order. Here's an example:

The setTimeout( ) function sets a one-shot timer.

The timer delay is 600,000 milliseconds, which is 600 seconds, which is 10 minutes.

```
setTimeout("alert('Wake up!');", 600000);
```

The JavaScript code is provided to setTimeout() as a string of text, which is why it must be inside quotes.

When the timer expires, an alert box is displayed.

Don't ever put commas in a JavaScript number, even if it's a really big one.

This call to the setTimeout() function creates a timer that waits 10 minutes and then displays an alert box.

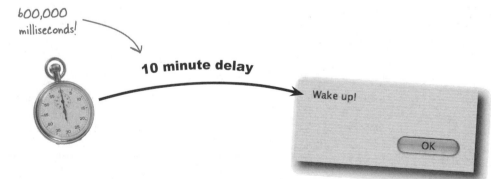

600,000 milliseconds!

10 minute delay

Wake up!

OK

A closer look: the setTimeout() function

Here's the general form that the `setTimeout()` function takes:

Enclose the two function arguments.

`setTimeout` + `(` + `Timer code` + `,` + `Timer delay` + `);`

The code to be run when the timer expires.

Separate the two function arguments.

The delay, in milliseconds.

Terminate the statement.

Setting an interval timer is similar to setting a one-shot timer, except you call the `setInterval()` function instead of `setTimeout()`. The end result of setting an interval timer is code that gets run **over and over** as each interval delay expires:

```
var timerID = setInterval("alert('Wake up!');", 600000);
```

Store away the timer ID.

Set a recurring timer.

The minutes in milliseconds.

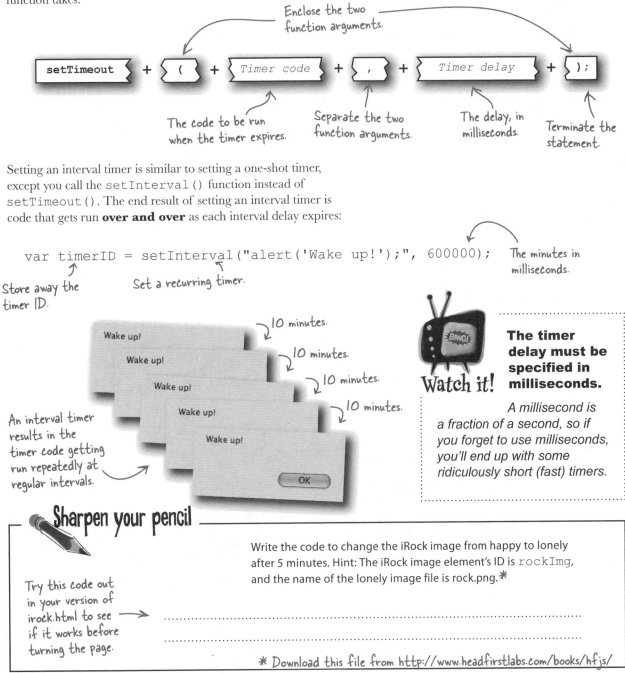

10 minutes.

10 minutes.

10 minutes.

10 minutes.

Wake up!

Wake up!

Wake up!

Wake up!

Wake up!

OK

An interval timer results in the timer code getting run repeatedly at regular intervals.

Watch it!

The timer delay must be specified in milliseconds.

A millisecond is a fraction of a second, so if you forget to use milliseconds, you'll end up with some ridiculously short (fast) timers.

Sharpen your pencil

Try this code out in your version of irock.html to see if it works before turning the page.

Write the code to change the iRock image from happy to lonely after 5 minutes. Hint: The iRock image element's ID is `rockImg`, and the name of the lonely image file is rock.png.✳

....

....

✳ Download this file from http://www.headfirstlabs.com/books/hfjs/

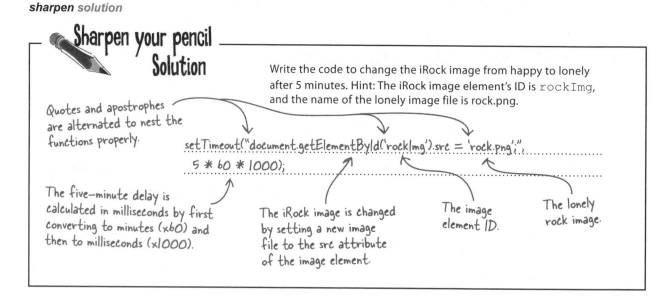

Sharpen your pencil Solution

Write the code to change the iRock image from happy to lonely after 5 minutes. Hint: The iRock image element's ID is `rockImg`, and the name of the lonely image file is rock.png.

Quotes and apostrophes are alternated to nest the functions properly.

```
setTimeout("document.getElementById('rockImg').src = 'rock.png';",
    5 * 60 * 1000);
```

The five-minute delay is calculated in milliseconds by first converting to minutes (x60) and then to milliseconds (x1000).

The iRock image is changed by setting a new image file to the src attribute of the image element.

The image element ID.

The lonely rock image.

Now the iRock gets lonely!

Be sure you made the changes in your `irock.html` that are detailed above, and give the iRock a spin. The iRock now exhibits loneliness when left alone (not clicked by the user) for five minutes. Granted, this time delay may make the rock seem a bit needy but the idea is to keep the user engaged. Besides, a pet in need is a pet indeed! Or something like that...

Tick
Tock

A timer literally counts down the amount of "happy time" remaining for the iRock.

Happiness is now fleeting for the iRock, which is much more realistic.

Geek Bits

You can speed up the iRock's emotional changes by using a smaller timer delay when calling the `setTimeout()` function. This is a great way to test the script without having to wait around.

I guess sometimes the customer really is right - the more emotional iRock is way more engaging.

When the timer expires, happiness switches to loneliness.

there are no Dumb Questions

Q: If the idea is for the iRock to always return to the lonely state after 5 minutes, why isn't an interval timer used?

A: The answer has to do with how the one-shot timer is used. Even though the rock is capable of periodically getting lonely, it only gets lonely *following* a period of happiness. A timer gets set at the initial click, the rock becomes lonely when the timer expires 5 minutes later, and then stays lonely until it is clicked again. That doesn't sound like the role of an interval timer. It's different than how an interval timer works—an interval timer would trigger every five minutes, no matter what the user does.

Q: What happens if the user closes the browser before a timer expires?

A: Nothing. The JavaScript interpreter is shut down when the browser closes, and all JavaScript code is stopped, including any outstanding timers.

Q: How can I create a timer that triggers code at a certain time of day?

A: Since timers are based upon delays, not specific times, you have to convert the time of day into a delay. This can be done by subtracting the current time from the desired trigger time. This calculation requires some help from the JavaScript `Date` object, which you'll learn more about in Chapter 9.

Q: I have a page with data that changes, so I'd like to refresh it every 15 minutes. How do I do it?

A: Use the `setInterval()` function to set an interval timer for 15 minutes, which is 900,000 milliseconds (15 x 60 x 1000). You need the timer code to refresh the page, which is accomplished by calling the `reload()` method of the `location` object, like this:
`location.reload();`
The timer now triggers the page refresh every 15 minutes. Of course, you could also use Ajax (Chapter 12) to dynamically load the data instead of refreshing the page.

Q: I understand that an interval timer continues over and over. How do I make an interval timer stop?

A: A function called `clearInterval()` is used to clear an interval timer that has been set with `setInterval()`. The `clearInterval()` function requires you to pass it the ID of the interval timer to be cleared, which is returned by the `setInterval()` function when you create the timer. Yes, functions are capable of returning information. After storing away the return value of `setInterval()`, in `timerID` for example, just pass it to `clearInterval()` to kill the timer, like this:
`clearInterval(timerID)`.

The Browser Exposed

This week's interview:
Confessions of a web client

Head First: Thanks for taking some time out of your busy day to sit down for a chat.

Browser: Busy is right. As if I didn't have my hands full with HTML and CSS, and all the page rendering headaches involved with those two characters, now I have to contend with JavaScript. That's a whole different animal.

Head First: What do you mean? Is JavaScript wild and untamed?

Browser: Uh, no. I didn't mean "animal" literally. I just meant that JavaScript brings its own unique set of problems that I have to worry about. Now I have this whole new job of reading JavaScript code, hoping for the life of me that it isn't coded poorly, and then running the code while simultaneously keeping a close eye on HTML and CSS.

Head First: I see. How do those three get along?

Browser: Fortunately, that's the least of my problems. Those three guys usually work well together, although occasionally JavaScript will get frisky and mangle some HTML code. Problem is, there usually isn't anything I can do about it because my job is pretty much to do as I'm told.

Head First: So you fashion yourself as somewhat of a "yes man?"

Browser: I suppose that's one way to put it, but it's more accurate to say that I value consistency above all else. I do things by the book. My job is take the code the server gives me and do exactly as it says.

Head First: Even if you know it's wrong?

Browser: I try my best to sort out problems when I see them but that's a tough gig. Besides, that's a topic for another day (Chapter 11). I thought we were going to talk about my role as a web client.

Head First: Oh yeah, I lost track. So what does it mean to be a client?

Browser: Well, it primarily means that I stand on the receiving end of the web page delivery channel, receiving pages after requesting them from the server.

Head First: What does that have to do with JavaScript?

Browser: An awful lot, actually. As I handle all the dirty work of displaying web pages and processing user input, JavaScript is there next to me sticking his nose in and changing things. But that's not all bad. There are lots of neat things JavaScript can do that I wouldn't dare do by myself.

Head First: Such as?

Browser: Well, I would never take it upon myself to do anything special when a user hovers the mouse over an image or resizes my window, for example. JavaScript, on the other hand, is all about doing special things. It's no big deal for a script to change the appearance of the page or otherwise shuffle content in response to client changes. And it's OK by me because JavaScript code runs on a page by page basis, so it only impacts a specific page or web site.

Head First: You talk about JavaScript as if its some other entity. Isn't JavaScript really just you?

Browser: It's both. JavaScript is certainly part of me but you can think of it as its own entity because it can only access the client (me) through a limited interface. In other words, I don't give JavaScript unbridled access to everything about me. That would be a little irresponsible since I can't control who writes scripts and asks me to run them.

Head First: Got it. Well thanks for clearing up some of this client stuff.

Browser: Glad to help.

Multiple size screens, multiple complaints

Alan had barely finished paying you for the iRock's emotional makeover when a new wave of complaints started rolling in from frustrated iRock owners. It seems the **size** of the iRock isn't very consistent, with some users reporting "shrinking rock syndrome," while others are experiencing an acute fear of "giant partial rock formations." You're the guy Alan trusts, so time to ~~earn some more cash~~ fix the iRock again.

Some users are reporting an iRock that is shockingly small.

Other users are seeing only part of a giant iRock.

That's odd, I wonder why?

⚛ **BRAIN POWER**

What's going on with the different rock sizes on different browsers?

Use the document object to get the client window's width

The iRock problem has to do with the fact that the size of the iRock doesn't change when the size of the browser window changes. This might seem like a good thing until you consider the **dramatic variation** in browser sizes across all computers capable of browsing the Web, including **tiny handheld devices** and desktop computers with **gigantic monitors**. You need a way to check the size of the browser window, which can then be used as a measure to **resize the rock image**.

The **client** window is only the part of the browser window that displays a web page.

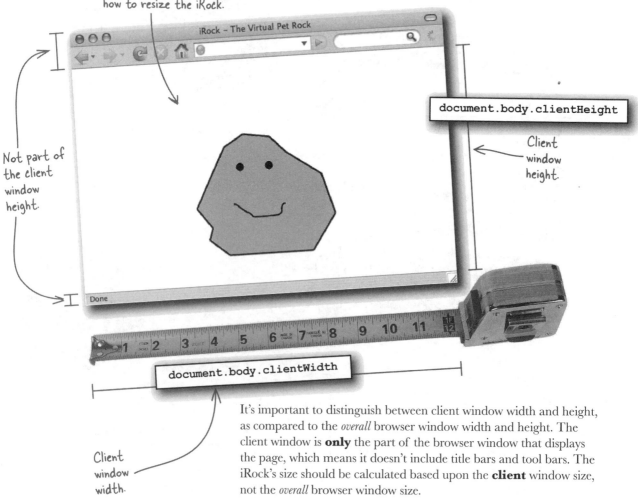

The client window is what holds the rock image, and is therefore what you can use to figure out how to resize the iRock.

document.body.clientHeight

Client window height.

Not part of the client window height.

document.body.clientWidth

Client window width.

It's important to distinguish between client window width and height, as compared to the *overall* browser window width and height. The client window is **only** the part of the browser window that displays the page, which means it doesn't include title bars and tool bars. The iRock's size should be calculated based upon the **client** window size, not the *overall* browser window size.

Use document object properties to set the client window width

The client window size is closely associated with the web page, which you access in JavaScript using the document object. This is the same object you used to access elements on the page with the getElementById() method. The body.clientWidthand body.clientHeight properties of the document hold the width and height of the client window.

```html
<html>
  <head>
    <title>iRock - The Virtual Pet Rock</title>
    <script type="text/javascript">
      var userName;
      function greetUser() {
        alert('Hello, I am your pet rock.');
      }
      function touchRock() {
        if (userName) {
          alert("I like the attention, " + userName + ". Thank you.");
        }
        else {
          userName = prompt("What is your name?", "Enter your name here.");
          if (userName)
            alert("It is good to meet you, " + userName + ".");
        }
        document.getElementById("rockImg").src = "rock_happy.png";
        setTimeout("document.getElementById('rockImg').src = 'rock.png';",
          5 * 60 * 1000);
      }
    </script>
  </head>

  <body onload="greetUser();">
    <div style="margin-top:100px; text-align:center">
      <img id="rockImg" src="rock.png" alt="iRock" style="cursor:pointer"
        onclick="touchRock();" />
    </div>
  </body>
</html>
```

document.body

The body of the document represents the visible part of the page, including client height and client width.

there are no Dumb Questions

Q: So just to be clear, what's the difference between a web client, a browser, a client window, and a browser window?

A: Yeah, it can be a little confusing. In terms of the Web in general, a browser is referred to as the web client because it's on the client side of the serving of web pages. Within a browser, however, "client" takes on a different meaning, because it refers to the specific area of the browser window where the page appears. So the client window is an area within the browser window that doesn't include the other stuff like title bars, tool bars, scroll bars, etc.

Q: Why is the client window the preferred measurement to use when resizing the iRock?

A: The client window provides a better measurement for resizing the rock image because it reflects the actual amount of space in which the image is displayed. This eliminates variations that are difficult to account for, such as add-on toolbars and natural differences in browser windows across different platforms and browser vendors. For example, Safari on the Mac has a different browser window size than Firefox on Windows, even if the displayable part of each—the client window—is the same.

Set the height and width of the iRock image

Knowing the client window size isn't all that useful in the iRock script without being able to **resize the rock image** as well. Fortunately, you can tweak the size of an image using JavaScript with a little help from CSS (even if CSS isn't your style). The `width` and `height` properties of an image element not only allow you to initially determine how big an image is, but also allow you to dynamically resize the image when needed.

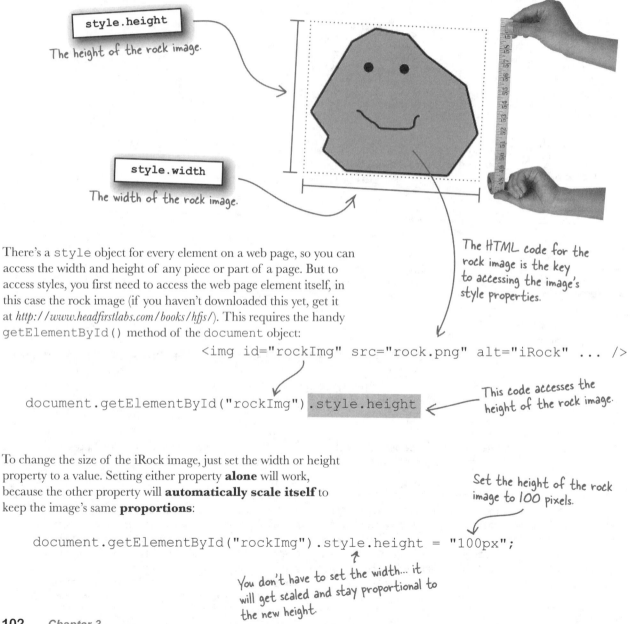

`style.height`

The height of the rock image.

`style.width`

The width of the rock image.

The HTML code for the rock image is the key to accessing the image's style properties.

There's a `style` object for every element on a web page, so you can access the width and height of any piece or part of a page. But to access styles, you first need to access the web page element itself, in this case the rock image (if you haven't downloaded this yet, get it at *http://www.headfirstlabs.com/books/hfjs/*). This requires the handy `getElementById()` method of the `document` object:

```
<img id="rockImg" src="rock.png" alt="iRock" ... />
```

```
document.getElementById("rockImg").style.height
```

This code accesses the height of the rock image.

To change the size of the iRock image, just set the width or height property to a value. Setting either property **alone** will work, because the other property will **automatically scale itself** to keep the image's same **proportions**:

Set the height of the rock image to 100 pixels.

```
document.getElementById("rockImg").style.height = "100px";
```

You don't have to set the width... it will get scaled and stay proportional to the new height.

The iRock should be sized to the page

You still don't have a calculation to use to alter the rock image size based upon the client window size. Since the rock size must change **in proportion** to the client window size, we want to set the rock size as a **percentage** of the client window size.

But should you base the rock size on the width or height of the client window? Since browsers tend to be more tightly constrained **vertically**, it's safer to base the rock image size on the **height** of the client window.

The client window height.

(clientWindowHeight - 100) * 0.9 = rockImageHeight

100 pixels.

90% of what's left vertically.

This calculation accounts for the vertical spacing of the rock on the page (100 pixels), and then sizes the rock image to 90% (0.9) of what's left. Sometimes calculations like this require a little trial and error to test them and find out what works best. You'll have to try out your iRock to see how it works... but first, there's code to write.

Sharpen your pencil

Write the code for the `resizeRock()` function, which should resize the rock image based upon the client window size. Also add code to the onload event handler to call `resizeRock()` in addition to `greetUser()`, which was already being called.

```
function resizeRock() {

   ..................................................................................

   ..................................................................................
   }
...
<body onload=
   ...    ..................................................................... >
</body>
```

Sharpen your pencil
Solution

Your job was to write the code for the `resizeRock()` function, and also to add code to the onload event handler to call `resizeRock()`. Don't forget to make sure `greetUser()` still gets called!

The rock image size is calculated based upon the client window height.

The ID of the rock image is used to get the image element.

```
function resizeRock() {
    document.getElementById("rockImg").style.height =
        (document.body.clientHeight - 100) * 0.9;
}
...
<body onload="resizeRock(); greetUser();"
...
</body>
```

Two different functions are called when the page first loads. It's perfectly fine to tie more than one piece of code to an event.

Subtract 100 pixels to account for the vertical position of the rock.

90% of the remaining window size.

BULLET POINTS

- The `setTimeout()` function allows you to create a **one-shot timer** that triggers JavaScript code after a period of time has elapsed.

- To set a timer that repeats at a certain interval, use `setInterval()`, which will create an **interval timer**.

- Always specify timer durations in milliseconds, which are thousandths of a second.

- Web page elements have a `style` object you use to set style properties, such as `width` and `height`.

- The client window is the part of the browser window that displays the web page and nothing else.

- You can access the width and height of the client window using the `body.clientWidth` and `body.clientHeight` properties of the `document` object.

Your iRock...evolves!

With your code changes, the iRock has evolved to adapt to each unique browser environment. Make sure you update your `iRock.html` (available at *http://www.headfirstlabs.com/books/hfjs/*) to match page 104, and then load it in several browsers and different window sizes. Try it out on your shiny iPhone if you want, too!

The size of the rock image now varies according to the size of the browser window.

Users are no longer reporting problems with their pets, and Alan's just about ready to give you a ton of stock options. Everyone is happy... for now.

there are no Dumb Questions

Q: I still don't get the point of the 100 in the iRock image size calculation. What's the deal?

A: The HTML/CSS code for the iRock page places the rock image 100 pixels down the page so that it isn't jammed against the top of the client window. The calculation accounts for this aesthetic positioning by subtracting the 100-pixel offset before figuring the rock height as a percentage (90%) of the client window height. There's nothing magical about 100 pixels, it just happens to position the rock in a good spot on most browsers.

Q: Can I change the size of anything I want using the `width` and `height` CSS style properties?

A: Pretty much. This hopefully is starting to give you a clue as to how powerful JavaScript can be when it comes to manipulating web page content. In the case of the iRock script, it's the power of being able to query the client window for its size and then using it as the basis for changing the size of an image.

Q: Why not just change the iRock image size in JavaScript code in the head of the page, as opposed to using the `onload` event?

A: This problem has to do with web page content not getting loaded until the `onload` event fires. So if your JavaScript code accesses elements on the page, as the iRock code does, you can't run any code earlier than the `onload` event.

> So what happens to the iRock when the browser is resized? Doesn't the rock image stay the same size?

No, the rock size isn't dynamic.

Some users are bound to resize their browser windows, and the iRock won't change size when this happens. These users won't be happy campers. That's because the rock image size is only altered when the page first loads, in the `onload` event. From then on, nothing that takes place results in an image resize. Unfortunately, we're back to where we started:

The rock image stays the same size when the browser window is resized.

onresize is triggered when the browser's resized

In order for the rock image size to maintain its size in proportion to the client window of the browser, your script needs to know when the user resizes their browser window. Browser resizes are communicated using an event called `onresize`. The `onresize` event is fired whenever the browser window is resized, and it's just what you need to catch in order to resize the rock image when the browser window size changes.

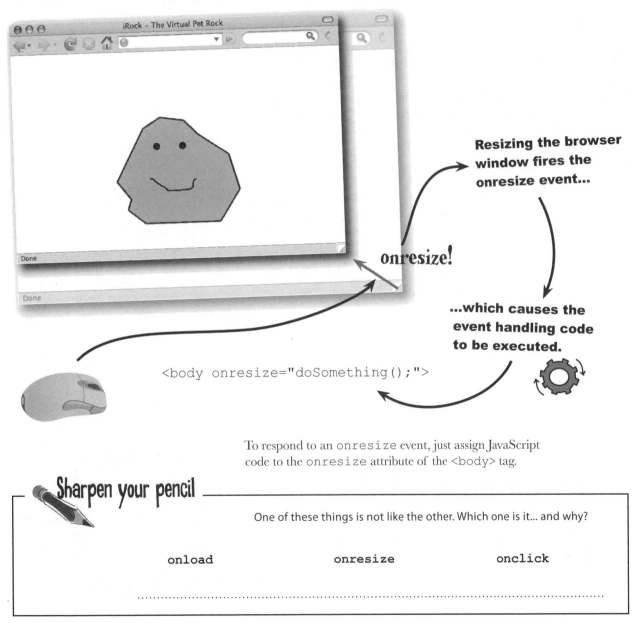

Resizing the browser window fires the onresize event...

onresize!

...which causes the event handling code to be executed.

```
<body onresize="doSomething();">
```

To respond to an `onresize` event, just assign JavaScript code to the `onresize` attribute of the `<body>` tag.

Sharpen your pencil

One of these things is not like the other. Which one is it... and why?

onload   onresize   onclick

....

The onresize event resizes the rock

Now it's time to reap the rewards of creating a function that resizes the rock image. To resize the rock image in response to a browser window resize, you have to call the `resizeRock()` function in response to the `onresize` event:

Triggered when the page first loads.

Triggered when the browser window is resized.

```
<body onload="resizeRock(); greetUser();" onresize="resizeRock();">
```

The resizeRock() function is still called when the page first loads to initially set the rock image size.

You can call more than one piece of code in response to an event.

Now the resizeRock() function is also called any time the browser window is resized.

The iRock's image size now automatically adjusts whenever the user changes the browser window size.

The <u>onresize</u> event makes it possible to detect and respond to changes in the browser window size.

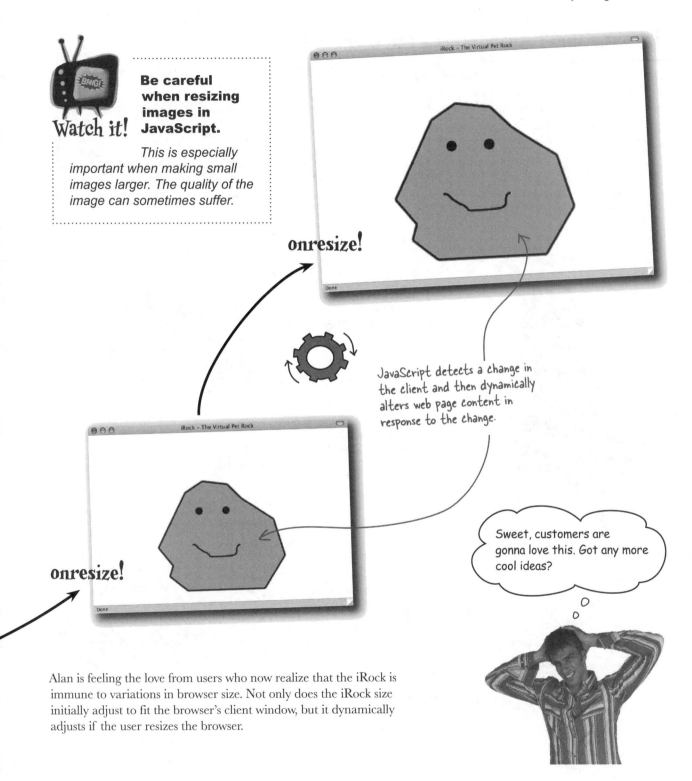

Be careful when resizing images in JavaScript.

This is especially important when making small images larger. The quality of the image can sometimes suffer.

onresize!

JavaScript detects a change in the client and then dynamically alters web page content in response to the change.

onresize!

Sweet, customers are gonna love this. Got any more cool ideas?

Alan is feeling the love from users who now realize that the iRock is immune to variations in browser size. Not only does the iRock size initially adjust to fit the browser's client window, but it dynamically adjusts if the user resizes the browser.

Have we met? Recognizing the user

The iRock size problems are now a thing of the past... but what about when users click the iRock more than once to keep it from feeling lonely? And when they come back to the rock after restarting their computer?

Why don't you remember me? Didn't I make an impression?

The user first meets the iRock and enters his name.

What is your name?

Paul

Cancel   OK

The iRock responds with a personal greeting — a friendship is born!

It is good to meet you, Paul.

OK

Tick   Tock

Time passes and something changes...

Who's Paul? Do I know you?

...the iRock no longer remembers the user.

What is your name?

Cancel   OK

Even though the iRock has definitely met its owner at some point in the past, it is somehow forgetting the user's name...

Every script has a life cycle

The iRock's memory loss is related to the life cycle of a script, which affects the data stored in the script's variables.

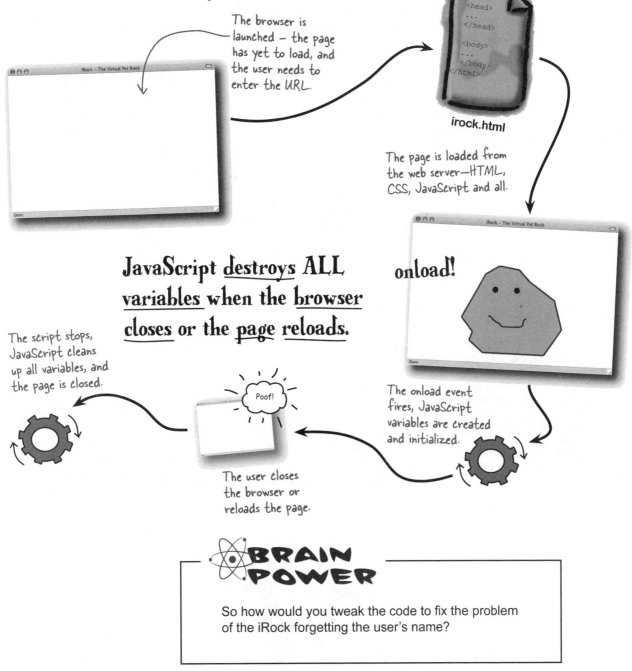

The browser is launched – the page has yet to load, and the user needs to enter the URL.

```
<html>
  <head>
    ...
  </head>

  <body>
    ...
  </body>
</html>
```

irock.html

The page is loaded from the web server—HTML, CSS, JavaScript and all.

onload!

JavaScript <u>destroys</u> ALL variables when the <u>browser</u> closes or the <u>page reloads.</u>

The script stops, JavaScript cleans up all variables, and the page is closed.

Poof!

The user closes the browser or reloads the page.

The onload event fires, JavaScript variables are created and initialized.

BRAIN POWER

So how would you tweak the code to fix the problem of the iRock forgetting the user's name?

Cookies outlive your script's life cycle

The problem that we're having with the iRock has a name, and it's called **persistence**. Or actually it's the lack of persistence. Sometimes you need data that never really goes away. Unfortunately, JavaScript variables are fleeting, and are destroyed the moment the browser closes or the page refreshes. Browser cookies offer a way to store data persistently so that it lasts beyond the life cycle of a script.

A **cookie** is a piece of data stored by the browser on the user's computer. Cookies are a lot like JavaScript variables except that cookies hang around after you close the browser, reload a page, turn off your computer, remodel your house, etc. This makes cookies a handy option for storing the user's name in the iRock script.

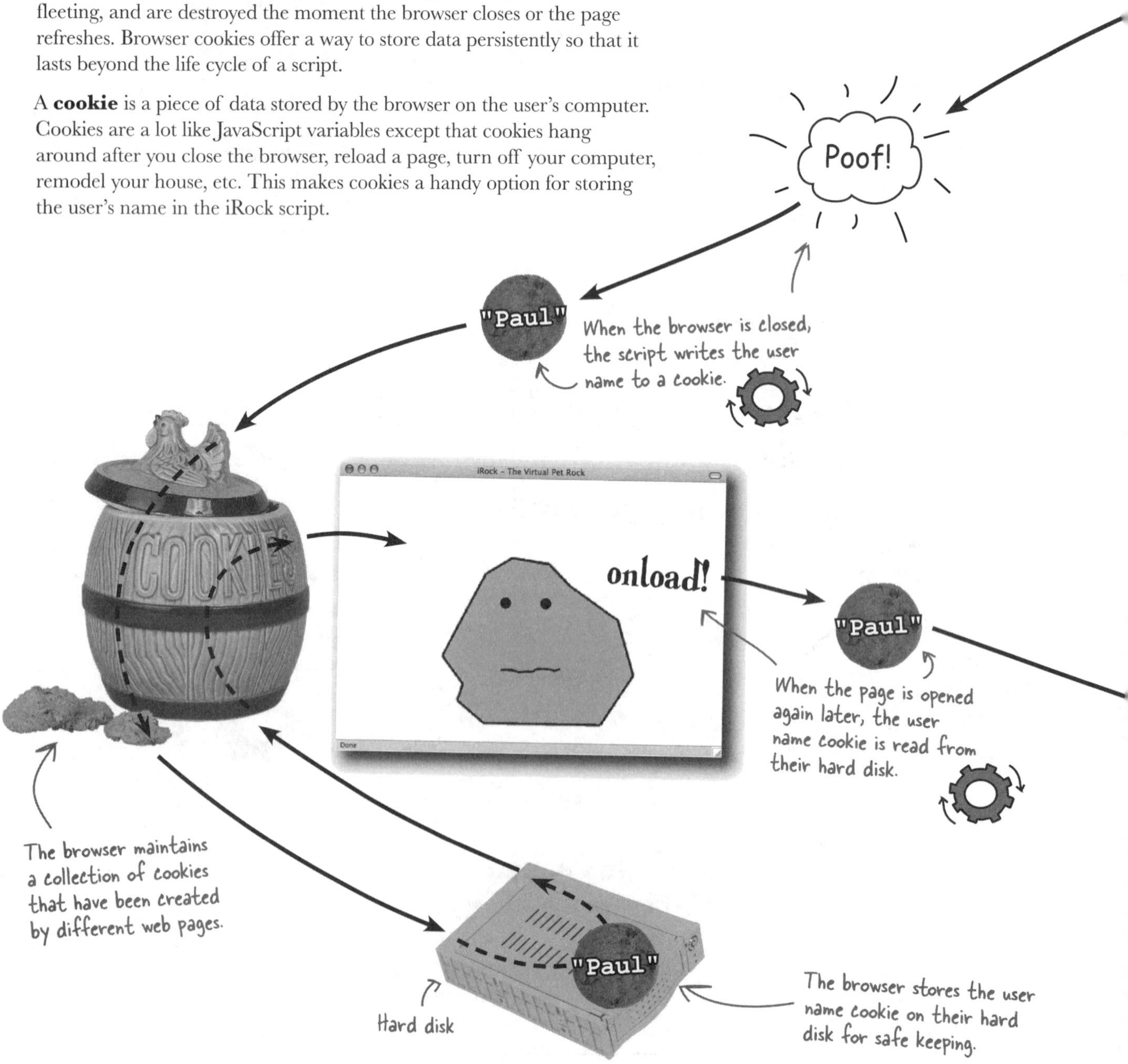

Poof!

"Paul"

When the browser is closed, the script writes the user name to a cookie.

onload!

"Paul"

When the page is opened again later, the user name cookie is read from their hard disk.

The browser maintains a collection of cookies that have been created by different web pages.

"Paul"

Hard disk

The browser stores the user name cookie on their hard disk for safe keeping.

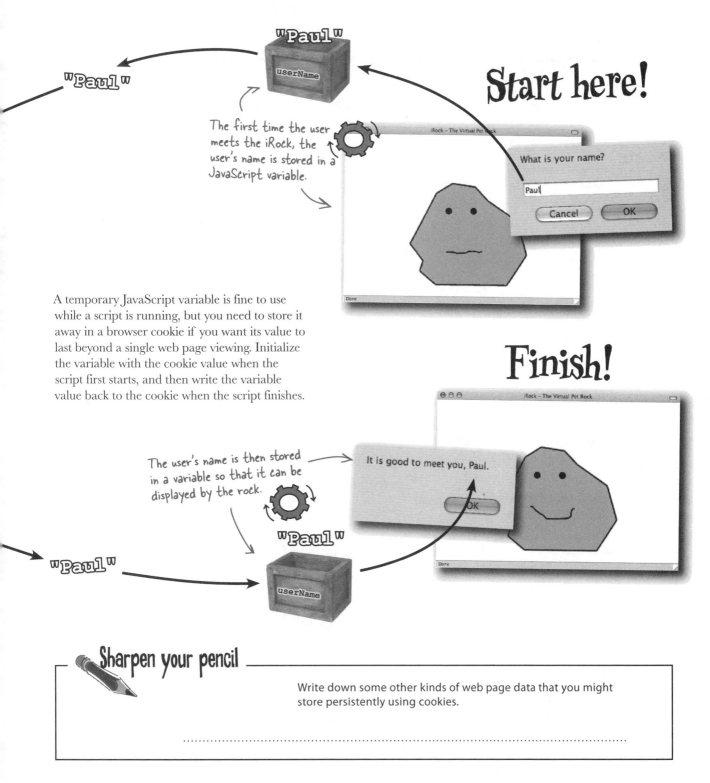

"Paul"

"Paul"

Start here!

The first time the user meets the iRock, the user's name is stored in a JavaScript variable.

A temporary JavaScript variable is fine to use while a script is running, but you need to store it away in a browser cookie if you want its value to last beyond a single web page viewing. Initialize the variable with the cookie value when the script first starts, and then write the variable value back to the cookie when the script finishes.

Finish!

The user's name is then stored in a variable so that it can be displayed by the rock.

"Paul"

"Paul"

It is good to meet you, Paul.

Sharpen your pencil

Write down some other kinds of web page data that you might store persistently using cookies.

....

Fireside Chats

Tonight's talk: **Variable and cookie weigh the importance of persistent data storage**

Variable:

I don't understand why we're talking—you don't really have anything to do with JavaScript.

I see where you're headed. You think that I'm somehow a lesser data storage option because I get clobbered every time the browser is closed or a page is reloaded. Still, I am *very* accessible... unlike some people.

That may be, but don't you live in tight quarters among a bunch of other cookies?

Well, if the rumors are true, it takes a lot of effort to look up a single cookie... you're all just stored in one big list. What a pain! That's what I mean by inaccessible.

Cookie:

Well, you're half right. I definitely do my thing without the help of JavaScript, but I still have an important connection to JavaScript, too. I provide a way to store data persistently. And as you've probably figured out, JavaScript isn't big on persistence.

Inaccessible? I'm always right there in the browser, ready to be called upon at any time.

Yes... and?

Well, yeah, us cookies are stored in a big list, but we have unique names, so it's not all that hard to get to us. You just have to know how to break apart the list to find a particular name.

Sharpen your pencil Solution

Write down some other kinds of web page data that you might store persistently using cookies.

User ID, shopping cart contents, geographical location, language

Variable:

Right, but that's the problem. There are no lists or anything involved in accessing me. Just call my name... and I'll be there!

Permanence is great but it doesn't solve everyday problems. When you really think about it, not all that much data really needs to last forever. In fact, it's usually more efficient to store data temporarily and let it go away when you're finished with it. That's where I come into play. I'm the ultimate temporary storage medium for script data.

Interesting, but how do you think those items got added to the shopping cart to begin with? Most shopping carts rely on me to store temporary data throughout the shopping experience. I'm just as important... maybe even more important. Even if I do tend to forget things a little more quickly.

I think you're right. We solve different problems and really shouldn't ever be competing. Although, I have to admit, I still prefer my ease of accessibility over your ability to store things persistently.

What conversation?

Cookie:

You don't need to sing. I get the point. But here's the real issue. When you store something in me, I always remember it. It doesn't matter if the browser is closed or the page is reloaded. I'm permanent... unless the user chooses to clear out all cookies. But that's another issue.

Whatever... I think you're underestimating how important permanent data storage can be. Haven't you ever been amazed by the magic of returning to a shopping cart days after browsing, only to find everything still there? That's the kind of magic I make possible!

It's starting to sound as if maybe we complement each other. I always saw you as a nemesis.

You couldn't resist a parting jab, eh? I'll take the high road and rest easy knowing that as soon as this page turns you'll forget the entire conversation.

Exactly.

> Why don't you just store persistent web data on the server?

You don't need the server for small pieces of information, like a user's name.

Ah, the server. Yes, the server is a viable option for storing data persistently, but it can be overkill for small pieces of information. Storing data on the server requires programming work on the server, along with a storage medium, like a database. Server programming and database storage are a bit much for storing a piece of data that you want to persist for a simple client script, like the user name in the iRock script.

Cookies allow you to store data persistently on the client without even involving the server. Not only that, but users have the ability to clear out cookie data on the browser if they want to get rid of information web pages have stored persistently. This isn't possible with data stored on the server.

JavaScript + Cookie = Handy persistent data storage on the client!

Cookies have a name and store a value...and can expire

A cookie stores a single piece of data under a unique name, much like a variable. Unlike a variable, though, a cookie can have an expiration date. When this expiration date arrives, the cookie is destroyed. So in reality cookies aren't truly permanent, they just live **longer** than variables. You can create a cookie without an expiration date, but this makes it act just like a JavaScript variable—it gets erased when the browser closes.

Cookies are stored on a user's computer as one big long string of text that is associated with a web site (or domain). Each cookie is separated from the next by a semicolon (;). The semicolons are the key to reading through the cookie list and pulling out a single cookie.

Name
The unique name of the cookie.

Value
The value stored in the cookie.

userName = Paul
Expires 3/9/2009

Expiration date
The date when the cookie expires... and meets its demise.

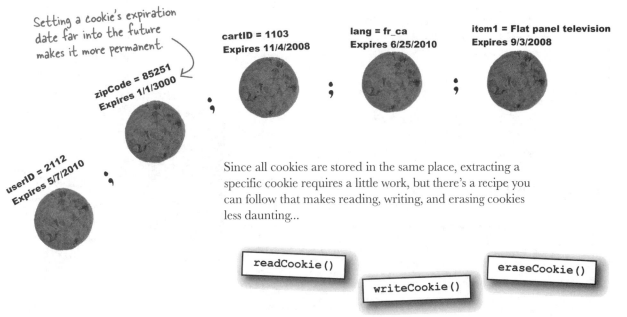

Setting a cookie's expiration date far into the future makes it more permanent.

zipCode = 85251
Expires 1/1/3000

userID = 2112
Expires 5/7/2010

cartID = 1103
Expires 11/4/2008

lang = fr_ca
Expires 6/25/2010

item1 = Flat panel television
Expires 9/3/2008

Since all cookies are stored in the same place, extracting a specific cookie requires a little work, but there's a recipe you can follow that makes reading, writing, and erasing cookies less daunting...

`readCookie()`

`writeCookie()`

`eraseCookie()`

Ready Bake JavaScript

It's okay if you don't get all of this now...you'll understand it by the time you're through the book.

Here's the code for three cookie helper functions, which allow you to write, read, and erase cookies with ease. Sometimes the wisest approach is to coast on the work of others. Take this recipe (available for download at *http://www.headfirstlabs.com/books/hfjs/*) and make the most of your homemade cookie functions.

The expiration date is expressed as the number of days the cookie should exist.

```javascript
function writeCookie(name, value, days) {
  // By default, there is no expiration so the cookie is temporary
  var expires = "";

  // Specifying a number of days makes the cookie persistent
  if (days) {
    var date = new Date();
    date.setTime(date.getTime() + (days * 24 * 60 * 60 * 1000));
    expires = "; expires=" + date.toGMTString();
  }

  // Set the cookie to the name, value, and expiration date
  document.cookie = name + "=" + value + expires + "; path=/";
}

function readCookie(name) {
  // Find the specified cookie and return its value
  var searchName = name + "=";
  var cookies = document.cookie.split(';');
  for(var i=0; i < cookies.length; i++) {
    var c = cookies[i];
    while (c.charAt(0) == ' ')
      c = c.substring(1, c.length);
    if (c.indexOf(searchName) == 0)
      return c.substring(searchName.length, c.length);
  }
  return null;
}

function eraseCookie(name) {
  // Erase the specified cookie
  writeCookie(name, "", -1);
}
```

This expiration date is calculated by converting the number of days to milliseconds, and then adding that number to the current time.

The cookie list is broken into individual cookies by splitting it along semicolons.

You erase a cookie by writing it with no value and an expired expiration date (–1 days).

Create a blank file, name it cookie.js, and add this code to the file.

```
var x;
var y;
function doX()
 ...
function doY()
 ...
```

cookie.js

Files containing only JavaScript code are usually named with a .js file extension.

Your JavaScript can live <u>OUTSIDE</u> your web page

When JavaScript code is stored in its own file, you have to **import** it into any web page that plans on using the code. So in the case of the cookie functions in `cookie.js`, you'll need to import them into your `iRock.html` page. This is done with a variation of the `<script>` tag:

Don't forget to close with the </script> tag.

```
<script type="text/javascript" src="cookie.js"></script>
```

The type of the script code is always text/javascript for JavaScript code.

The name of the file containing the script code, usually ending with .js.

DO THIS! Make this addition to your iRock.html, and make sure cookie.js is in the same directory.

When you import external script code into a page, all of the JavaScript code in the script file is inserted inside of the `<script>` tag in the HTML code, just as if you had placed the code directly in the web page. Any time you have code that could be used in more than one page, it's a good idea to place it in an external file and import the file in the pages.

```
<html>
  <head>
    <title>iRock - The Virtual Pet Rock</title>
    <script type="text/javascript" src="cookie.js"></script>
    <script type="text/javascript">
      var userName;

      function resizeRock() {
        document.getElementById("rockImg").style.height =
          (document.body.clientHeight - 100) * 0.9;
      }

      function greetUser() {
```

The imported script code gets placed into the page when the page is loaded.

Exercise

Write down why it's a good idea to organize reusable code into an external file.

....

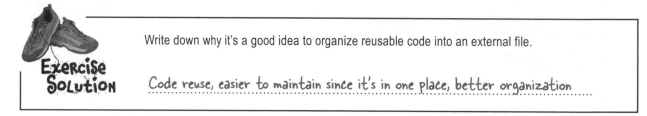

Write down why it's a good idea to organize reusable code into an external file.

Exercise Solution

Code reuse, easier to maintain since it's in one place, better organization

Greet the user with a cookie

We need a cookie-powered version of the iRock script that can greet the user with a personal greeting, assuming their name has already been stored in a cookie. If not, the greeting can just fall back on a generic, impersonal greeting. It's the best of both worlds!

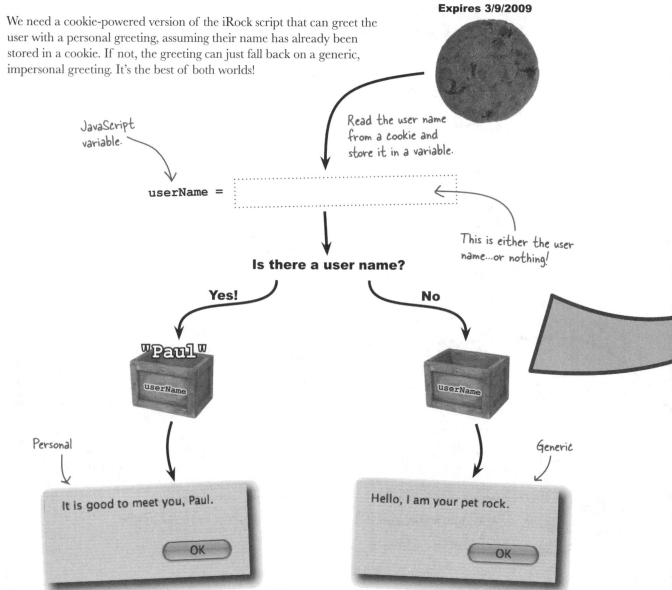

userName = Paul
Expires 3/9/2009

JavaScript variable.

Read the user name from a cookie and store it in a variable.

userName =

This is either the user name...or nothing!

Is there a user name?

Yes!   **No**

Personal

It is good to meet you, Paul.

OK

Generic

Hello, I am your pet rock.

OK

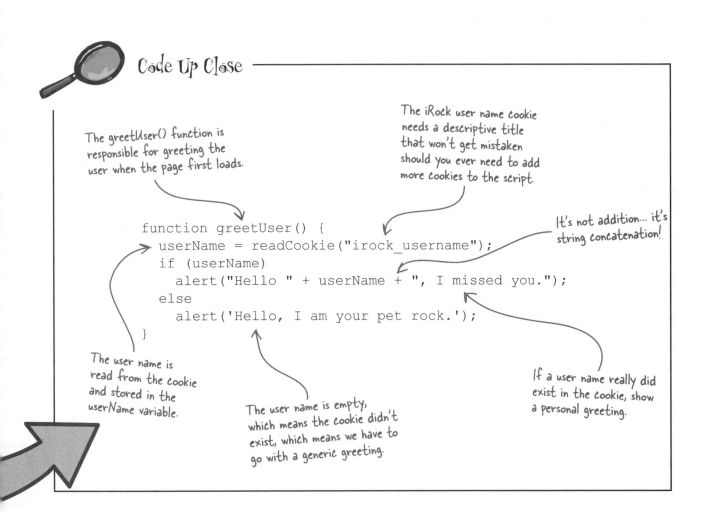

Code Up Close

The greetUser() function is responsible for greeting the user when the page first loads.

The iRock user name cookie needs a descriptive title that won't get mistaken should you ever need to add more cookies to the script.

It's not addition... it's string concatenation!

```javascript
function greetUser() {
  userName = readCookie("irock_username");
  if (userName)
    alert("Hello " + userName + ", I missed you.");
  else
    alert('Hello, I am your pet rock.');
}
```

The user name is read from the cookie and stored in the userName variable.

The user name is empty, which means the cookie didn't exist, which means we have to go with a generic greeting.

If a user name really did exist in the cookie, show a personal greeting.

greetUser() is cookie-powered now

What's really going on in the greetUser() function is a data duet sung by a variable and a cookie. The user's name is read from the cookie and stored in the variable. But you can't count on the cookie holding a name... what if this is the first time the script has run and the user has never entered a name? That's why the code checks to see if the variable really got a name from the cookie—this is the test that determines whether the greeting is personal or generic.

Don't forget to set the cookie, too

Reading the iRock cookie is fine and dandy, but you've still got to set the cookie in the first place. The cookie writing should take place in the `touchRock()` function, which is called when the user clicks the rock image. The `touchRock()` function already prompts the user to enter a name—now it needs to write that name to a cookie after it's entered.

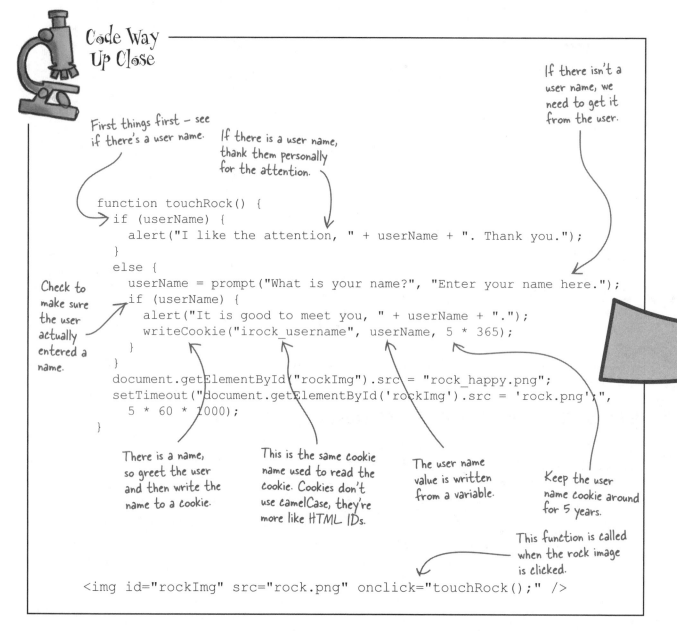

Code Way Up Close

If there isn't a user name, we need to get it from the user.

First things first – see if there's a user name.

If there is a user name, thank them personally for the attention.

```
function touchRock() {
  if (userName) {
    alert("I like the attention, " + userName + ". Thank you.");
  }
  else {
    userName = prompt("What is your name?", "Enter your name here.");
    if (userName) {
      alert("It is good to meet you, " + userName + ".");
      writeCookie("irock_username", userName, 5 * 365);
    }
  }
  document.getElementById("rockImg").src = "rock_happy.png";
  setTimeout("document.getElementById('rockImg').src = 'rock.png';",
    5 * 60 * 1000);
}
```

Check to make sure the user actually entered a name.

There is a name, so greet the user and then write the name to a cookie.

This is the same cookie name used to read the cookie. Cookies don't use camelCase, they're more like HTML IDs.

The user name value is written from a variable.

Keep the user name cookie around for 5 years.

This function is called when the rock image is clicked.

```
<img id="rockImg" src="rock.png" onclick="touchRock();" />
```

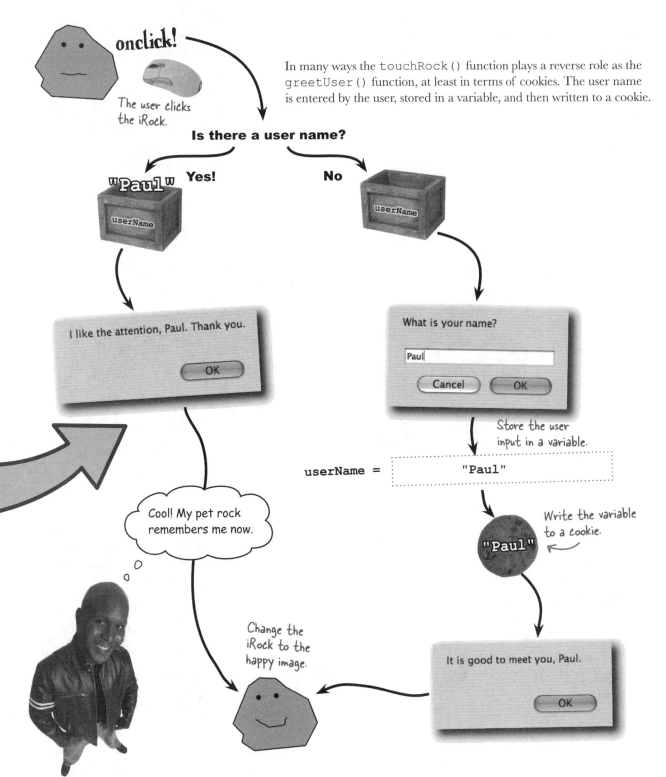

onclick!

The user clicks the iRock.

In many ways the `touchRock()` function plays a reverse role as the `greetUser()` function, at least in terms of cookies. The user name is entered by the user, stored in a variable, and then written to a cookie.

Is there a user name?

"Paul" **Yes!**

userName

No

userName

I like the attention, Paul. Thank you.

OK

What is your name?

Paul

Cancel   OK

Store the user input in a variable.

userName =   "Paul"

Cool! My pet rock remembers me now.

Write the variable to a cookie.

"Paul"

Change the iRock to the happy image.

It is good to meet you, Paul.

OK

Cookies affect browser security

Although most iRock users are thrilled with cookies as a cure for memory loss, a few users have questioned the security risks of cookies. This is a fair question since personal data often gets stored in cookies, but the reality is that cookies **do not** pose a security risk...at least not in terms of accessing sensitive data that is stored on your computer. However cookies themselves aren't considered safe for storage, so it's not a good idea to store **sensitive** data in a cookie

Watch it!

Just because you can, doesn't mean you *should*.

Although you can store anything in a cookie, they aren't terribly secure in terms of how they store data. So it's not a good idea to store sensitive data in a cookie.

A cookie is just a piece of text data stored in a file on your computer

We interrupt this broadcast to bring you a message about JavaScript security...

Although cookies are typically stored on a hard disk, they <u>can't</u> <u>touch</u> <u>anything</u> <u>else</u> on the hard disk.

Since cookies aren't executable programs, they <u>can't</u> <u>spread</u> <u>viruses</u> or <u>worms</u>.

Worms... ick!

Cookies <u>can</u> <u>store</u> personal data, but only when users have knowingly entered data into a web page.

there are no Dumb Questions

Q: Are cookies always stored on the user's hard disk?

A: No. But the hard disk is where the vast majority of browsers store cookies, not all browsers have access to a hard disk. For example, some mobile devices use special memory instead of hard disks for persistent data storage. In this case, the browser uses persistent memory to store cookies. Even so, from the perspective of the browser (and your scripts), cookies remember their values regardless of how they are stored behind the scenes.

Q: How do I know if my cookie name is unique?

A: Cookie names only have to be unique within a given web page. This is because cookies are stored with respect to the page that created them, including the web site of the page. This means the page is effectively part of the cookie name, at least in terms of uniqueness. Bottom line: just make sure your cookies are unique within a given page or site.

Q: Is cookie data shared across different browsers?

A: No. Every browser maintains its own unique database of cookies, so cookies set in Internet Explorer will not be visible to Firefox or Opera.

Q: If cookies are so handy, why would you ever store data on the server?

A: First of all, cookies are only good for storing relatively small (less than 4 Kb) chunks of text. That is one important limitation of cookies. Even more significant is the fact that cookies aren't particularly efficient, meaning that you wouldn't want to be constantly reading and writing lots of data to them. This is where a real database comes into play, and databases typically live on the server. So while cookies are great for storing small pieces of data that don't necessarily warrant storage on the server in a database, they aren't a solution for all of your web data needs. And they also aren't exactly ideal for storing sensitive data since they aren't designed with security in mind.

Q: Is there any way to create a truly permanent cookie?

A: No. Like it or not, every cookie has an expiration date. The idea behind a cookie is not so much true long-term data storage as it is a means to preserve data in the mid-term. In other words, cookies are good for storing data for days, weeks, and months. If you're dealing with data that must linger for longer periods of time, you may want to store it on the server instead. It's not that a cookie can't store data for years, it's just unlikely that the user won't upgrade computers, reinstall their browser, or otherwise clear out cookie data.

Q: Enough about cookies...is there any downside to storing JavaScript code in an external file?

A: Not really. However, keep in mind that the goal with external code is to make it easier to share and maintain the code when it needs to be used in more than one web page. If you're dealing with code that only appears in a single page, you really don't benefit much from moving it to an external file. That is, unless the page is particularly messy and you just want to break up the code for your own sanity.

BULLET POINTS

- A **cookie** is a piece of **text data** stored by the browser on the user's computer.

- Cookies allow scripts to **store data** that survives **beyond a single web session**.

- Every cookie has an **expiration date**, after which the cookie is destroyed by the browser.

- Moving script code to an **external file** is a handy way to make the code more reusable and maintainable.

- Cookies **can't access a user's hard disk** or **spread viruses**, but they are capable of storing personal data that has been entered in web pages.

A world without cookies

Whether it's security concerns or limited browsers, a few iRock users aren't able to benefit from the cookie-powered iRock because cookies aren't available in their browsers. This presents a big problem because the iRock script assumes everyone has cookie support. It's one thing for the iRock to be dependent on cookies for memory, but it's unacceptable to not at least let cookie-less users know they're missing out on the full iRock experience.

> Every user left out is one less customer... that's unacceptable.

JavaScript + Broken cookie = Big problem!

The good news is that the browser has a boolean property you can check to see if cookies are available. The `cookieEnabled` property is part of the `navigator` object, which provides JavaScript with information about the browser itself.

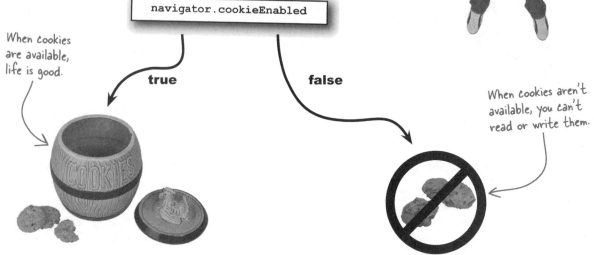

`navigator.cookieEnabled`

When cookies are available, life is good.

true

false

When cookies aren't available, you can't read or write them.

Sharpen your pencil

Write the missing code to check for cookie support in the greetUser() and touchRock() functions. Also add the missing code in touchRock() to let the user know that cookies aren't available.

```
function greetUser() {

    ..............................................................................................
    userName = readCookie("irock_username");
  if (userName)
    alert("Hello " + userName + ", I missed you.");
  else
    alert('Hello, I am your pet rock.');
}

function touchRock() {
  if (userName) {
    alert("I like the attention, " + userName + ". Thank you.");
  }
  else {
    userName = prompt("What is your name?", "Enter your name here.");
    if (userName) {
      alert("It is good to meet you, " + userName + ".");

      ..............................................................................................
        writeCookie("irock_username", userName, 5 * 365);
      else

      ..............................................................................................

    }
  }
  document.getElementById("rockImg").src = "rock_happy.png";
  setTimeout("document.getElementById('rockImg').src = 'rock.png';",
    5 * 60 * 1000);
}
```

Sharpen your pencil
Solution

Write the missing code to check for cookie support in the
`greetUser()` and `touchRock()` functions. Also add the
missing code in `touchRock()` to let the user know that
cookies aren't available.

If cookie support is available, read the user name from the iRock cookie.

```
function greetUser() {

  if (navigator.cookieEnabled)
    userName = readCookie("irock_username");
  if (userName)
    alert("Hello " + userName + ", I missed you.");
  else
    alert('Hello, I am your pet rock.');
}

function touchRock() {
  if (userName) {
    alert("I like the attention, " + userName + ". Thank you.");
  }
  else {
    userName = prompt("What is your name?", "Enter your name here.");
    if (userName) {
      alert("It is good to meet you, " + userName + ".");

      if (navigator.cookieEnabled)
        writeCookie("irock_username", userName, 5 * 365);
      else

        alert("Sorry. Cookies aren't supported/enabled in your browser. I won't remember you later.");

    }
  }
  document.getElementById("rockImg").src = "rock_happy.png";
  setTimeout("document.getElementById('rockImg').src = 'rock.png';",
    5 * 60 * 1000);
}
```

If cookies are supported, write the user name cookie.

Let the user know that their lack of cookie support will limit the iRock.

Make the functions in your iRock.html page look like this... then test things out.

there are no
Dumb Questions

Q: Can you check for client cookie support based upon the type of browser or the version of the browser?

A: Browser detection is a slippery scripting slope that ultimately leads to unreliable results. You can't really trust what browsers say about themselves when it comes to version information, which makes the `navigator.cookieEnabled` property the only truly reliable way to check for cookie support.

Talk to the users... it's better than nothing

Although there's no good way to simulate cookies when they aren't available, gracefully breaking the bad news to the user is worth an awful lot in terms of user satisfaction.

> Sweet! That's a graceful way to deal with cookie-less browsers.

iRock – The Virtual Pet Rock

Cookies aren't supported/enabled in your browser, which means I won't remember you later. I'm sorry.

OK

Done

There are worse things than being up-front about what the user is missing out on.

Alan's happy again... and you collected another nice paycheck.

An iRock fit for a JavaScript king

You've really put some wear and tear on your JavaScript shoes stepping through all the code necessary for making the iRock a success. With a little help from the client, though, the iRock is now more real emotionally, has lost its sizing inconsistencies, and has even improved its memory!

Browser metrics and CSS style properties give the iRock the ability to conform to its environment.

Timers expand the iRock's limited emotional range.

iRock – The Virtual Pet Rock

Thanks to all your hard work, the iRock is now a rock solid pet.

Done

Cookies allow the iRock to remember data beyond the life cycle of the script.

It is good to meet you, Paul.

userName = "Paul"

JavaScriptcross

Take some time to sit back and give your right brain something to do. It's your standard crossword; all of the solution words are from this chapter.

Across

5. One-thousandth of a second.
7. I'm responsible for managing the list of cookies.
8. A JavaScript mechanism that allows you to run code after a certain period of time has elapsed.
10. A cookie has a name, a value, and an ....
11. Use one of these to store a piece of information on the client that you might need later.
12. What you do when you reference external JavaScript code from a Web page.

Down

1. This kind of timer runs a piece of code repeatedly.
2. This function allows you to create a one-shot timer.
3. When data hangs around after a script finishes running, it is considered ....
4. When the browser window is resized, the .... event is fired.
6. Another name for a Web browser.
9. Cookies are incapable of spreading these.

 JavaScriptcross Solution

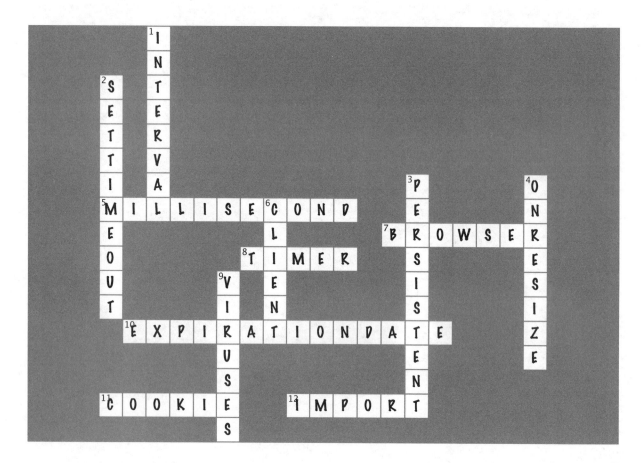

Page Bender

Fold the page vertically to line up the two brains and solve the riddle.

Why should JavaScript care about the client?

— It's a meeting of the minds! ←

The client is where JavaScript code is run,
which means that JavaScript lives
on the browser. This is a positive
thing because it means the server has
less to worry about, such as storing cookies!

4 decision making

If There's a Fork in the Road, Take It

Who can resist a man in uniform...but whom should I choose?

Life is all about making decisions. Stop or go, shake or bake, plea bargain or go to trial... without the ability to make decisions, nothing would ever get done. It works the same in JavaScript—**decisions allow scripts to decide between different possible outcomes**. *Decision-making drives the "story" of your scripts*, and even the most mundane scripts involve a story of some sort. Do I trust what the user entered and book her a trip on a Sasquatch expedition? Or else do I double-check that maybe she really just wanted to ride a bus to Saskatchewan? The choice is yours to make!

Lucky contestant, come on down!

On today's episode of the thrilling new game show, *Wanna Make a Deal*, a lucky contestant is about to be chosen...

Ladies and gentlemen, our lucky contestant is... Eric!

Who, me?

Game show host.

Eric, the lucky contestant.

Although you're no doubt on the edge of your seat in anticipation of Eric's deal-making prowess, the real question is this: how did the game show host know to announce Eric as the lucky contestant?

Choices are all about making a decision

Duh, it's written right there on his card! True, but you're taking for granted the fact that the host can make a **decision** based on what name appears on the card. That's because he's human, and people excel at processing information and making decisions. If the host was a script, things wouldn't be so easy.

The name on the card results in a decision to choose Eric.

The question is **really** this: how does a script use a piece of information as the basis for taking an action? Knowing which name appears on a particular card is only half of the answer. The other half involves being able to **evaluate** the name on the card, and then **choose** the contestant with the matching name, in this case Eric.

"if" this is true... then do something

JavaScript is actually quite adept at processing information and making decisions, and one of the ways this happens is with the `if` statement. The `if` statement allows you to make simple decisions, conditionally running a piece of JavaScript code based upon a true/false test.

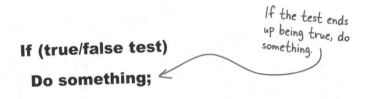

If the test ends up being true, do something.

If (true/false test)

Do something;

If you look at the game show example through the lens of a JavaScript `if` statement, you end up with code like this:

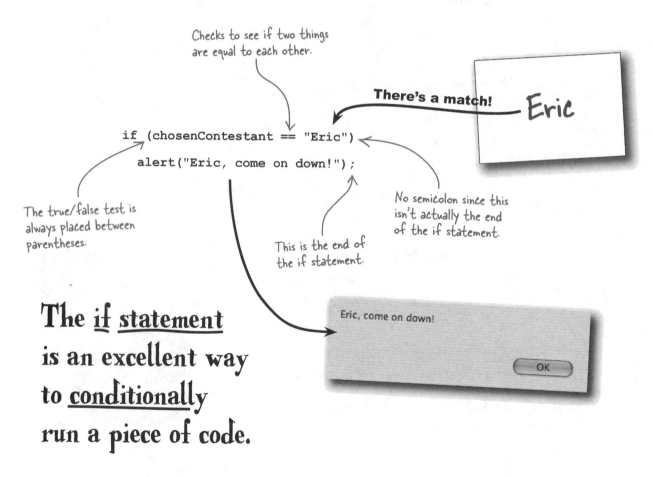

Checks to see if two things are equal to each other.

There's a match!

Eric

```
if (chosenContestant == "Eric")
    alert("Eric, come on down!");
```

The true/false test is always placed between parentheses.

This is the end of the if statement.

No semicolon since this isn't actually the end of the if statement.

The if statement is an excellent way to conditionally run a piece of code.

Eric, come on down!

OK

An if statement evaluates a condition... and then takes action

Every `if` statement sticks to the same format. You used this format already when you added cookies to iRock, but here's the breakdown:

This code MUST somehow evaluate to true or false.

$$\boxed{\texttt{if}} + \boxed{\texttt{(}} + \boxed{\textit{Test condition}} + \boxed{\texttt{)}}$$

$$\boxed{\textit{Statement}} + \boxed{\texttt{;}}$$

Indent to make the code easier to read. The indented statement is part of the "if."

There are a few things to keep in mind about the format of the `if` statement. First off, you can only run one piece of code, and it should appear indented just below `if` and the test condition. Although not strictly required, it's a good idea to indent this code so that you can quickly see that it is part of your `if` statement. Here are the steps required to carry out a decision with an `if` statement:

1 Enclose the true/false test condition in parentheses.

2 Indent the next line of code a couple of spaces.

3 Write the code that gets run if the test condition is true.

Exercise

Match up these `if` statements with the actions that should go with them.

```
if (hungry)                                        numDonuts *= 12;

if (countDown == 0)                                userName = readCookie("irock_username");

if (donutString.indexOf("dozen") != -1)            awardPrize();

if (testScore > 90)                                goEat();

if (!guilty)                                       alert("Houston, we have lift-off.");

if (winner)                                        alert("She's innocent!");

if (navigator.cookieEnabled)                       grade = "A";
```

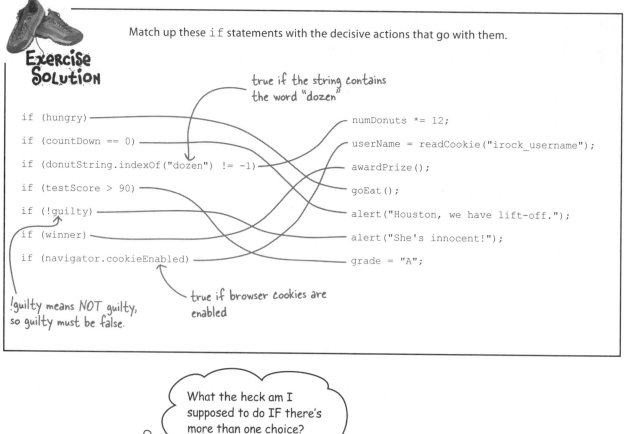

Match up these `if` statements with the decisive actions that go with them.

Exercise Solution

true if the string contains the word "dozen"

```
if (hungry)
if (countDown == 0)
if (donutString.indexOf("dozen") != -1)
if (testScore > 90)
if (!guilty)
if (winner)
if (navigator.cookieEnabled)
```

```
numDonuts *= 12;
userName = readCookie("irock_username");
awardPrize();
goEat();
alert("Houston, we have lift-off.");
alert("She's innocent!");
grade = "A";
```

!guilty means NOT guilty, so guilty must be false.

true if browser cookies are enabled

What the heck am I supposed to do IF there's more than one choice?

Do this...or else.

Just when you thought JavaScript had everything covered, something out of the ordinary appears. Actually, choosing between more than one outcome isn't out of the ordinary at all... chocolate or vanilla, decaf or regular, it seems many choices actually involve one thing ***or*** another. That's why the `if` statement can be tweaked to allow for making a decision and then taking one of two possible actions...or sometimes even more that.

Use if to choose between two things

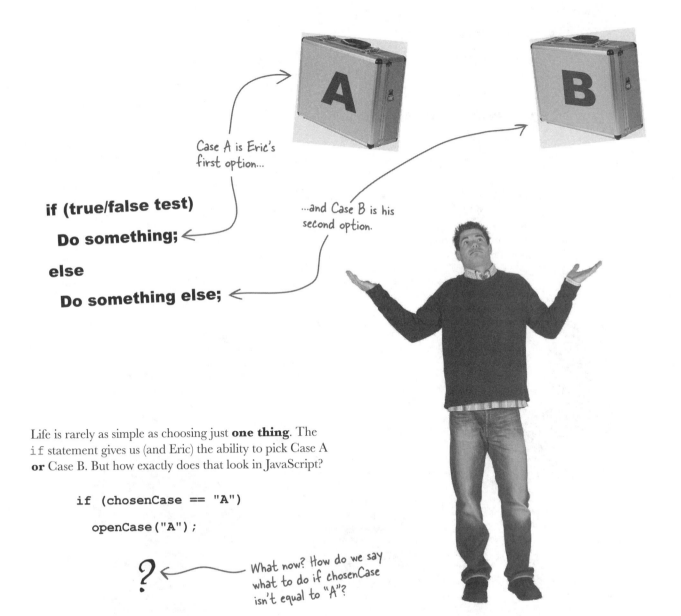

A twist on the if statement allows you to choose between two possible outcomes. Back at *Wanna Make a Deal*, Eric's struggling to make a decision just like that. Presented with two alternatives, he must choose one or the other.

Case A is Eric's first option...

...and Case B is his second option.

if (true/false test)

    Do something;

else

    Do something else;

Life is rarely as simple as choosing just **one thing**. The if statement gives us (and Eric) the ability to pick Case A **or** Case B. But how exactly does that look in JavaScript?

```
if (chosenCase == "A")

    openCase("A");
```

? What now? How do we say what to do if chosenCase isn't equal to "A"?

You can make multiple decisions with if

Using an `if` statement to take more than one action means turning it into an `if/else` statement, which gives you the option of running a different piece of code if the true/false test fails. It's like saying **if** the test is true, run the first piece of code, and if **not** (**else**), run the other piece of code.

```
if (chosenCase == "A")

    openCase("A");          True

else

    openCase("B");          False
```

The if/else statement consists of two possible outcomes, one for each possible value of the test condition.

Eric chooses Case B, which means the `chosenCase` variable will be "B." So since the first test condition is false, that will trigger the `if/else` statement to run the `else` code. Unfortunately for Eric, Case B contains donuts, not the stack of money he was hoping for.

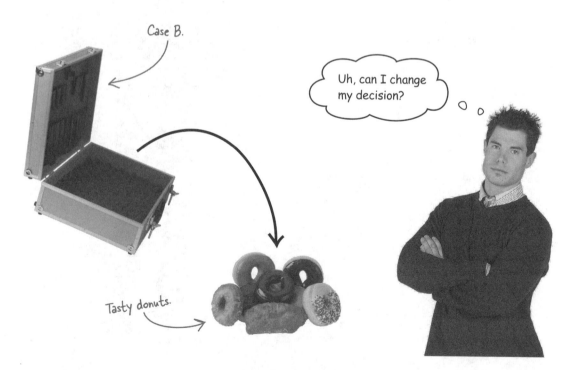

Case B.

Uh, can I change my decision?

Tasty donuts.

Adding an else to your if statement

The formatting of an `if`/`else` statement is very similar to the `if` statement. Just tack on the keyword `else` along with the other piece of code to run if the test condition is false:

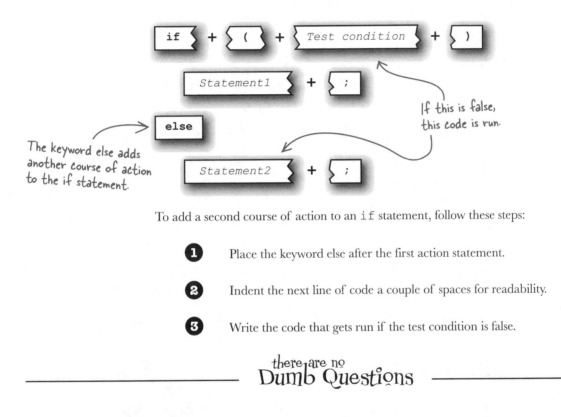

If this is false, this code is run.

The keyword else adds another course of action to the if statement.

To add a second course of action to an `if` statement, follow these steps:

1 Place the keyword else after the first action statement.

2 Indent the next line of code a couple of spaces for readability.

3 Write the code that gets run if the test condition is false.

there are no Dumb Questions

Q: Why isn't there a semicolon after the parentheses in an `if` statement?

A: The rule in JavaScript is that every statement must end with a semicolon, and the `if` statement is no exception. However, the `if` statement isn't just `if (Test Condition)`, it's also the code that gets executed if the condition is true. *That* code does end with a semicolon. So the `if` statement does end in a semicolon, if you understand what exactly constitutes an `if` statement.

Q: What happens when the test condition is false in an `if` statement that has no `else` clause?

A: Nothing at all. In this case the value of the test condition literally results in no action being taken.

Q: Is it possible to use more than one `else` to choose between more than two possible outcomes?

A: Yes. It's certainly possible to structure an `if`/`else` statement to support more than two outcomes, but it isn't as easy as just adding extra `else` clauses. You end up nesting entire `if`/`else` statements within each other, which can quickly get messy if you're making a complex decision with lots of different outcomes. The `if`/`else` approach isn't wrong, but JavaScript offers a better decision-making structure for this situation, the `switch`/`case` statement, which you learn about a bit later in this chapter.

An adventure of epic proportions

Ellie's writing an interactive adventure story called Stick Figure Adventure. Her project involves decision-making at every turn in the story, and she hopes JavaScript decision making may offer the solution to her problem of putting the adventure online for others to enjoy.

Stick Figure Adventure presents the user with a web-based interactive story, experienced by a heroic stick figure.

I'm hoping JavaScript will give Stick Figure Adventure the interactivity it needs.

Ellie dreams about the twists and turns in the plot, but worries a little about how to make them a reality.

Ellie wants the online Stick Figure Adventure to let the user navigate through a story by making one of two choices at each step along the way. You can follow along with the accompanying files available for download at *http://www.headfirstlabs.com/books/hfjs/*.

The adventure setup

The Stick Figure Adventure story is a series of scene screens, where each scene is an image and a description. More importantly, each scene involves making a decision between one of two paths that move the story along to another scene.

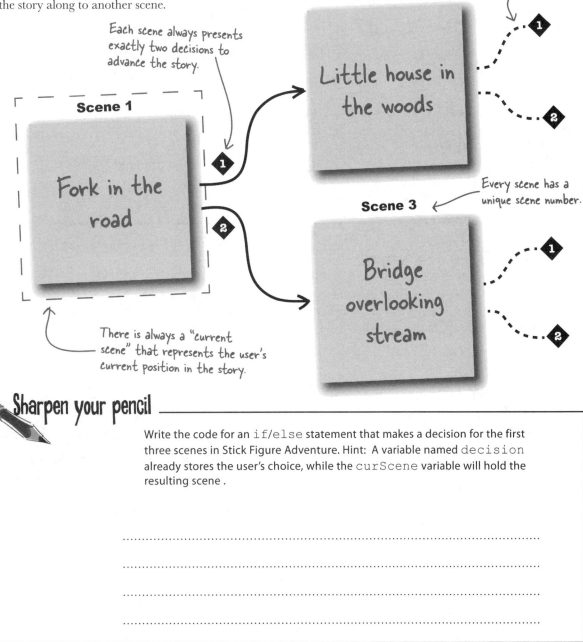

Scenes 2 and 3 have decisions that lead to even more scenes.

Scene 2

Little house in the woods

Each scene always presents exactly two decisions to advance the story.

Scene 1

Fork in the road

Every scene has a unique scene number.

Scene 3

Bridge overlooking stream

There is always a "current scene" that represents the user's current position in the story.

Sharpen your pencil

Write the code for an `if`/`else` statement that makes a decision for the first three scenes in Stick Figure Adventure. Hint: A variable named `decision` already stores the user's choice, while the `curScene` variable will hold the resulting scene .

....

....

....

....

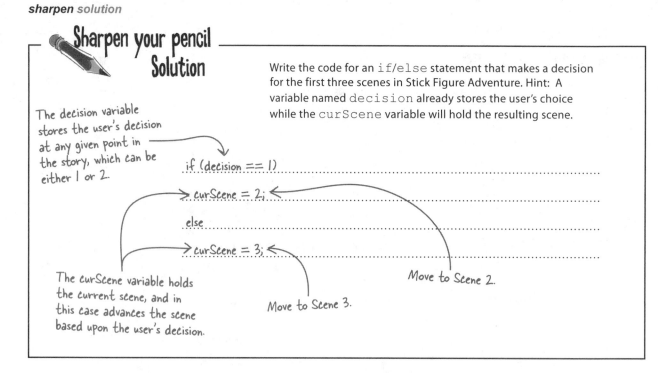

Sharpen your pencil
Solution

Write the code for an `if/else` statement that makes a decision for the first three scenes in Stick Figure Adventure. Hint: A variable named `decision` already stores the user's choice while the `curScene` variable will hold the resulting scene.

The decision variable stores the user's decision at any given point in the story, which can be either 1 or 2.

```
if (decision == 1)
    curScene = 2;
else
    curScene = 3;
```

Move to Scene 2.

Move to Scene 3.

The curScene variable holds the current scene, and in this case advances the scene based upon the user's decision.

Variables drive the story

Let's take a closer look at the two variables used in Stick Figure Adventure, which are critical in responding to user decisions and then moving the story along accordingly.

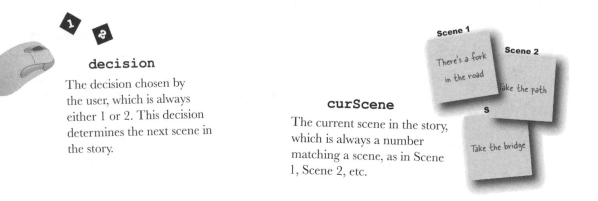

decision

The decision chosen by the user, which is always either 1 or 2. This decision determines the next scene in the story.

curScene

The current scene in the story, which is always a number matching a scene, as in Scene 1, Scene 2, etc.

Scene 1

There's a fork in the road

Scene 2

Take the path

Take the bridge

The `decision` and `curScene` variables work together to store the user's decision, and then use that decision as the basis for moving the story along. This process repeats itself from scene to scene as the story continues to unfold, all thanks to the `if/else` statement.

But part of the story is missing

The if/else statement works great as the engine for the decision making part of Stick Figure Adventure, but the entire story isn't getting told. Each scene involves both an image **and** a text description; both the image and text are displayed for a given scene as the story progresses. Changing the current scene number is sufficient to change the scene image but it doesn't help with the scene description text.

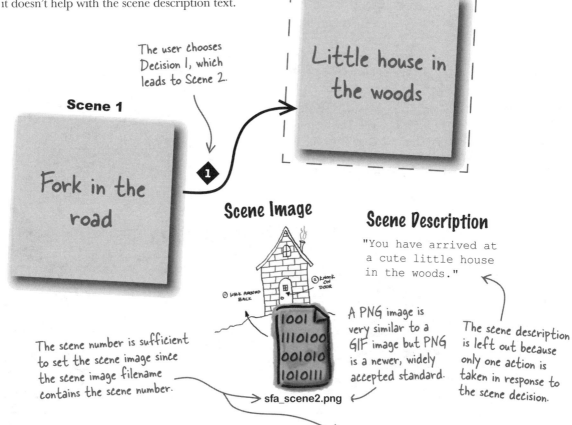

The "new" current scene.

Scene 2

Little house in the woods

The user chooses Decision 1, which leads to Scene 2.

Scene 1

Fork in the road

Scene Image

Scene Description

"You have arrived at a cute little house in the woods."

The scene number is sufficient to set the scene image since the scene image filename contains the scene number.

A PNG image is very similar to a GIF image but PNG is a newer, widely accepted standard.

The scene description is left out because only one action is taken in response to the scene decision.

sfa_scene2.png

```
document.getElementById("sceneimg").src = "scene" + curScene + ".png";
```

With the ability to only run a single piece of code in each part of the if/else statement, you're limited to only one action. In other words, you can't display an image **and** show a text description.

BRAIN POWER

How would you do more than one thing in response to a decision?

Compounding your JavaScript efforts

Ellie needs to be able to do more than one thing in each branch of `if/else` code. She needs to change both the scene number and the scene description text so that the following two lines of code can move the story along:

> Change the scene image to the newly chosen scene.

```
document.getElementById("sceneimg").src = "scene" + curScene + ".png";
alert(message);
```

> Display the scene description message for the new scene to the user.

The challenge is to do more than one thing even though JavaScript only allows you to run a single piece of code. The solution is a **compound statement**, which lets you frame a chunk of code so that it appears in the script as a single piece of code. Creating a compound statement, is done by surrounding the series of statements with curly braces ({ }).

> Ah ha! A compound statement lets me treat a big chunk of code like it's one piece of code.

```
doThis();

doThat();

doSomethingElse();
```
= 3 statements

> Match opening and closing braces to enclose the code.

```
{

  doThis();

  doThat();

  doSomethingElse();

}
```
= 1 statement

With one compound statement, it's possible to build `if/else` statements that do more than one thing in each action branch:

```
if (chosenDoor == "A") {
  prize = "donuts";
  alert("You won a box of donuts!");
}
else {
  prize = "pet rock";
  alert("You won a pet rock!");
}
```

> Do more than one thing in each action branch of an if/else statement.

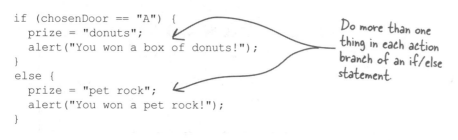

Q: **How exactly does Stick Figure Adventure use variables to drive the story?**

A: At any given moment, the `curScene` variable contains the current scene number. Each scene shows a scene image and a scene description, and also presents the user with a decision allowing them to choose between one of two scenes. The `decision` variable contains the user's scene decision, 1 or 2. When a choice is made, the value of the `decision` variable is used in conjunction with `curScene` to determine the new scene. More specifically, the scene image is changed using the value in `curScene`, and the scene description message is displayed using an alert box.

Q: **Why does it matter that a compound statement crunches multiple statements into one?**

A: It matters because many parts of the JavaScript language are structured around the idea of a single statement. It's kind of like how an airline allows you exactly two carry-on items. Nothing prevents you from stuffing a bunch of stuff into those two carry-ons as long as you stick with just the two. So compound statements are like a piece of carry-on luggage in that they allow you to stuff multiple statements into a single "container" that is **perceived** as a single statement to the rest of the script.

Q: **Why don't compound statements end in a semicolon?**

A: Semicolons are reserved for individual statements, not compound statements. So single statements that appear within a compound statement must have the trailing semicolon but the compound statement itself does not.

Q: **Is a function a compound statement?**

A: Good question! And the answer is yes. You might have noticed that code in a function is surrounded by curly braces. For now you can think of a function as a big compound statement that you can pass data into and out of.

Sharpen your pencil

Rewrite the code for the first `if/else` decision in Stick Figure Adventure. This time, use compound statements to set both the scene number and the scene description message.

....

....

....

....

....

....

....

....

sharpen solution

Sharpen your pencil Solution

Rewrite the code for the first `if/else` decision in Stick Figure Adventure. This time, use compound statements to set both the scene number and the scene description message.

The current scene number is adjusted based upon the decision made by the user.

The scene description message is set to match the new scene.

Start the compound statement with an opening curly brace.

It's a good idea to indent the code within a compound statement.

End the compound statement with a closing curly brace.

A different scene description message is set for Scene 3.

```
if (decision == 1) {
    curScene = 2;
    message = "You have arrived at a cute little house in the woods.";
}
else {
    curScene = 3;
    message = "You are standing on the bridge overlooking a peaceful stream.";
}
```

BULLET POINTS

- Use the `if` statement to conditionally run a single piece of JavaScript code.

- The test condition in an `if` statement must always result in true or false.

- Use the `if/else` statement to conditionally run one of two different pieces of JavaScript code.

- Use a compound statement to run multiple pieces of JavaScript code in place of a single piece of code.

- Create a compound statement by surrounding multiple individual statements with curly braces ({ }).

- Compound statements allow the action parts of `if` and `if/else` statements to do more than one thing.

The adventure begins

A few compound statements combined with an `if/else` decision have turned Stick Figure Adventure into the beginnings of an interactive online story. It's well on its way to becoming a fully-functioning online adventure!

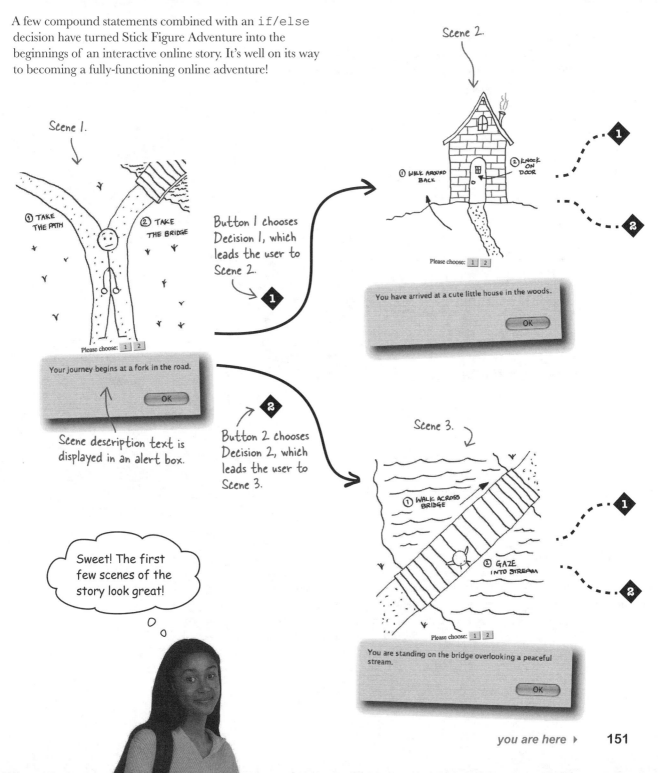

Scene 1.

Button 1 chooses Decision 1, which leads the user to Scene 2.

Scene description text is displayed in an alert box.

Button 2 chooses Decision 2, which leads the user to Scene 3.

Scene 2.

Scene 3.

Sweet! The first few scenes of the story look great!

And now, the rest of the adventure

A single decision hardly makes for an interesting interactive story. But Ellie has plans, including several more scenes that make Stick Figure Adventure considerably more intriguing. Together, these scenes make up a **decision tree** that you can use to chart the different paths through the story.

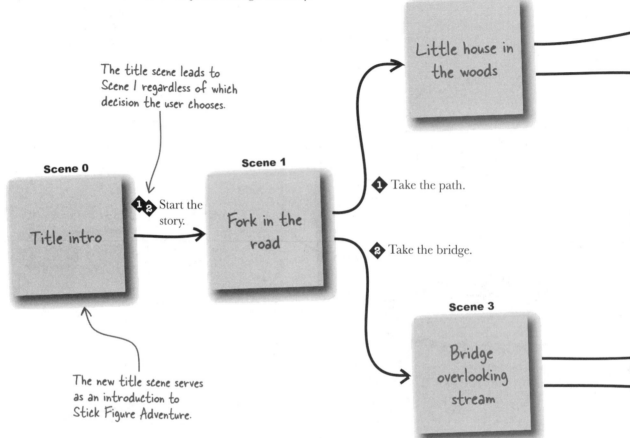

The title scene leads to Scene 1 regardless of which decision the user chooses.

Scene 0

Title intro

1 2 Start the story.

Scene 1

Fork in the road

The new title scene serves as an introduction to Stick Figure Adventure.

Scene 2

Little house in the woods

1 Take the path.

2 Take the bridge.

Scene 3

Bridge overlooking stream

In addition to adding more scenes to the story with new twists and turns, Ellie has also created a new introductory title scene that appears before the first scene in the story (Scene 1). The title scene (Scene 0) is unique in that it leads to Scene 1 regardless of whether you choose Decision 1 or Decision 2. In other words, Scene 0 is not a branch in the story, but instead just the opening credits. The new scenes and openers are ready for you to download at *http://www.headfirstlabs.com/books/hfjs/*.

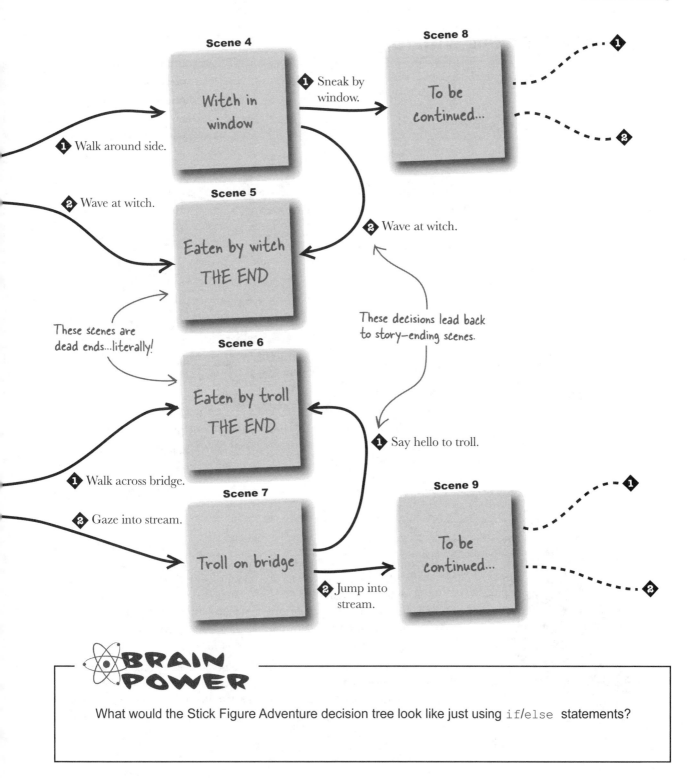

Scene 4 — Witch in window

❶ Walk around side.

❷ Wave at witch.

❶ Sneak by window.

Scene 8 — To be continued...

❶

❷

Scene 5 — Eaten by witch THE END

❷ Wave at witch.

These scenes are dead ends...literally!

These decisions lead back to story-ending scenes.

Scene 6 — Eaten by troll THE END

❶ Say hello to troll.

❶ Walk across bridge.

❷ Gaze into stream.

Scene 7 — Troll on bridge

❷ Jump into stream.

Scene 9 — To be continued...

❶

❷

⚛ BRAIN POWER

What would the Stick Figure Adventure decision tree look like just using `if/else` statements?

Tiered decision making with if/else

Even though each decision within the Stick Figure Adventure decision tree only has two options, Ellie realizes that later decisions are dependent upon earlier ones. For example, to get to Scene 5 from the beginning of the story, the user must follow a specific path:

If (curScene is 2)

   If (decision is 1)

      Jump to Scene 4

Else

   Jump to Scene 5

Scene 1 — Fork in the road

Scene 2 — Little house in the woods

Scene 5 — Eaten by witch — THE END

Scene 1 — Fork in the road

Scene 2 — Little house in the woods

Scene 4 — Witch in window

If (curScene is 4)

   If (decision is 1)

      Jump to Scene 8

Else

   Jump to Scene 5

Is it OK to put one if/else statement inside of another?

Just knowing the option chosen by the user isn't enough information to decide what scene is next. She needs to factor in the current scene. One solution is to use multiple if/else statements in such a way that you first check the current scene, and then take action based upon the user's decision. But this tiered decision-making approach involves an if within an if... a seemingly strange proposition.

That is, until you consider that we make tiered decisions all the time. Have you ever answered the question, "would you like fries with that?" This question rarely follows an order for a salad, the question is based upon an answer you've already provided, such as, "I'll have a cheeseburger." This is a tiered decision because later questions (fries?) are dependent upon the answers to earlier questions (cheeseburger or salad?).

An if can go <u>inside</u> another if

It's perfectly legal to place an `if` within an `if` in JavaScript. Remember, an `if` statement is still just a statement, just being used as the action part of another `if`. In other words, it's OK to follow-up one question with another question. An `if` within another `if` is known as a **nested** `if` statement.

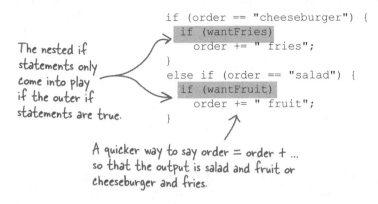

The nested if statements only come into play if the outer if statements are true.

```
if (order == "cheeseburger") {
    if (wantFries)
        order += " fries";
}
else if (order == "salad") {
    if (wantFruit)
        order += " fruit";
}
```

A quicker way to say order = order + ... so that the output is salad and fruit or cheeseburger and fries.

Sharpen your pencil

Write the decision-making code for Scene 0 and Scene 1 of Stick Figure Adventure, making sure to use nested `if` and `if/else` statements when necessary.

....

....

....

....

....

....

....

....

....

....

....

....

....

Sharpen your pencil
Solution

Write the decision-making code for Scene 0 and Scene 1 of Stick Figure Adventure, making sure to use nested `if` and `if/else` statements when necessary.

Scene 0 always leads to Scene 1, so no nested if statement is needed.

Set the Scene 1 description message.

```
if (curScene == 0) {

    curScene = 1;

    message = "Your journey begins at a fork in the road.";

}
```

If the current scene isn't Scene 0, we next check to see if it's Scene 1.

```
else if (curScene == 1) {

    if (decision == 1) {

        curScene = 2;

        message = "You have arrived at a cute little house in the woods.";

    }

    else {

        curScene = 3;

        message = "You are standing on the bridge overlooking a peaceful stream.";

    }

}
```

A nested if/else statement handles the user's decision for Scene 1.

Indentation helps you to see which statements are nested within others.

It is extremely important to carefully match opening and closing braces.

Your functions control your pages

A pair of buttons ("1" and "2") on the Stick Figure Adventure web page is how users move through the story. When they decide to click one of the buttons, the changeScene() function is called to change the scene based upon the decision button that was clicked.

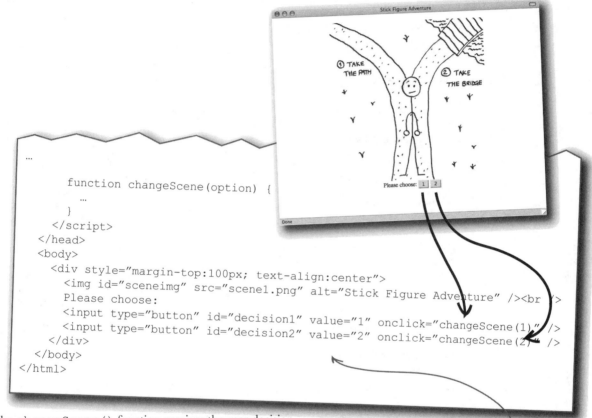

```
...
        function changeScene(option) {
          ...
        }
      </script>
    </head>
    <body>
      <div style="margin-top:100px; text-align:center">
        <img id="sceneimg" src="scene1.png" alt="Stick Figure Adventure" /><br />
        Please choose:
        <input type="button" id="decision1" value="1" onclick="changeScene(1)" />
        <input type="button" id="decision2" value="2" onclick="changeScene(2)" />
      </div>
    </body>
</html>
```

The web page has two buttons that are used to determine the next scene in the story.

The changeScene() function receives the user decision ("1" or "2") as its only argument. This piece of information is all the function needs to change the scene. Specifically the changeScene() function handles three things:

 Set the curScene variable to the new scene number.

 Set the message variable to the new scene description text.

 Change the scene image based upon the value of curScene, and display the scene description text message.

Pseudocode lets you map out your adventure

Ellie has a pretty good general idea of how to build the `changeScene()` function to implement the Stick Figure Adventure decision tree with JavaScript code. But, the sheer number of decisions can make it a confusing proposition once the coding begins. Sometimes, it's helpful to first write the decision tree in pseudocode, which is a casual, more readable, and also very unofficial way of expressing scripting code. Once the pseudocode is knocked out, the real JavaScript code will be much clearer and less error-prone to write.

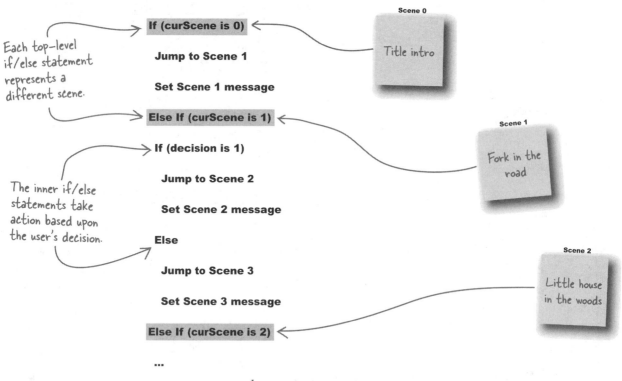

Each top-level if/else statement represents a different scene.

The inner if/else statements take action based upon the user's decision.

If (curScene is 0)

    Jump to Scene 1

    Set Scene 1 message

Else If (curScene is 1)

    If (decision is 1)

        Jump to Scene 2

        Set Scene 2 message

    Else

        Jump to Scene 3

        Set Scene 3 message

Else If (curScene is 2)

    ...

Scene 0 — Title intro

Scene 1 — Fork in the road

Scene 2 — Little house in the woods

there are no
Dumb Questions

Q: Pseudocode looks a lot like JavaScript code. Why bother?

A: You don't have to bother, but the idea is to simplify the process of converting a complex tree of logic into JavaScript code, and at the same time minimize the risk of making errors. Since pseudocode doesn't have the same level of detail of JavaScript code, you can focus your efforts more on the logic of how one scene leads to another, as opposed to making sure every curly brace and semicolon is in the right spot. Once you're comfortable with the pseudocode, translating it into JavaScript code is fairly automatic.

Q: Do you have to use curly braces when nesting `if` statements?

A: No. In fact, if you're only nesting a single `if` statement within another `if` statement with no other code, it can be simpler to leave the curly braces off since you *technically* don't need a compound statement. However, in a complex nesting of `if` statements, it can be advantageous to use curly braces even when not strictly needed just to make the nesting clearer.

JavaScript Magnets

The `changeScene()` function for Stick Figure Adventure is missing a few pieces of code. Use the magnets to finish the missing code from the scene diagram on page 152. Note that not all of the scene decision code is shown—a few scenes have been left out intentionally.

```
function changeScene(option) {
  var message = "";

  ..........(curScene == 0) {
    curScene =........;
    message = "Your journey begins at a fork in the road.";
  }
  ...
  ....................(curScene == 3) {
    ........(option == 1) {
      curScene = ........;
      message = "Sorry, a troll lives on the other side of the bridge and you " +
        "just became his lunch.";
    }
    ........      {
      curScene = ........;
      message = "Your stare is interrupted by the arrival of a huge troll.";
    }
  }
  ....................(curScene == 4) {
    if (option == 1) {
      curScene = ........;
    }
    ............  {
      curScene = ........;
      message = "Sorry, you became part of the witch's stew.";
    }
  }
  ...

  document.getElementById("sceneimg").src = "scene" + curScene + ".png";
  alert(message);
}
```

6   1   5   7   8

if   if   if   if

else   else   else   else

JavaScript Magnets Solution

The changeScene() function for Stick Figure Adventure is missing a few pieces of code. Use the magnets to finish the missing code the scene diagram on page 152. Note that not all of the scene decision code is shown—a few scenes have been left out intentionally.

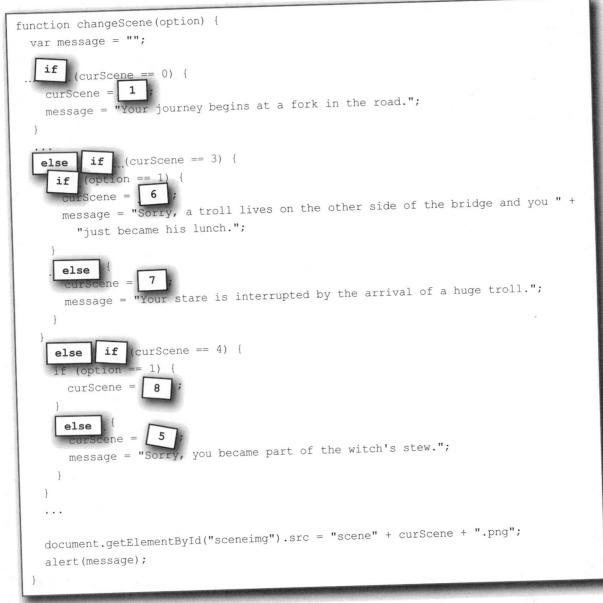

```
function changeScene(option) {
  var message = "";

  if (curScene == 0) {
    curScene = 1;
    message = "Your journey begins at a fork in the road.";
  }

  ...
  else if (curScene == 3) {
    if (option == 1) {
      curScene = 6;
      message = "Sorry, a troll lives on the other side of the bridge and you " +
        "just became his lunch.";
    }
    else {
      curScene = 7;
      message = "Your stare is interrupted by the arrival of a huge troll.";
    }
  }
  else if (curScene == 4) {
    if (option == 1) {
      curScene = 8;
    }
    else {
      curScene = 5;
      message = "Sorry, you became part of the witch's stew.";
    }
  }
  ...

  document.getElementById("sceneimg").src = "scene" + curScene + ".png";
  alert(message);
}
```

Going on a stick figure adventure

The Stick Figure Adventure script now reflects the entire decision tree, allowing you to navigate through the story along several different paths. Here's one of them:

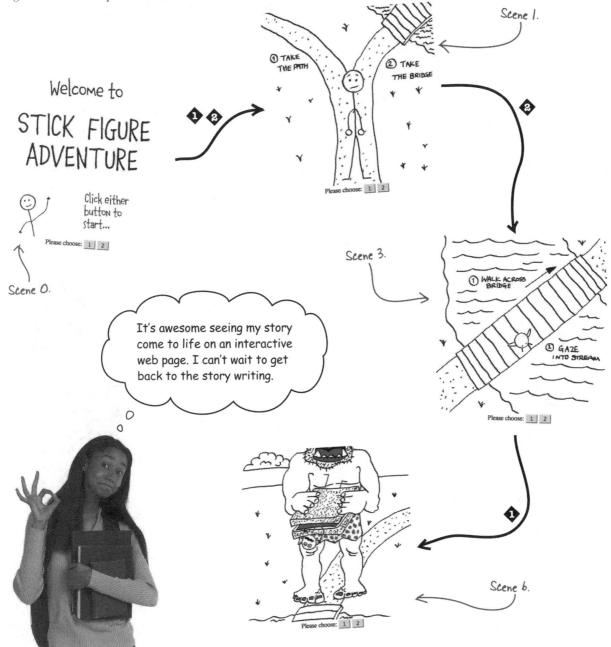

It's awesome seeing my story come to life on an interactive web page. I can't wait to get back to the story writing.

Stick figure inequality

Unfortunately, Ellie is already encountering a problem with Stick Figure Adventure. After releasing the page to a few friends for testing, a few of them have reported a strange window that displays an empty message. The "ghost window" is isolated to when a new adventure is started after ending a previous one. So the problem is somehow associated with moving to Scene 0 from some other scene.

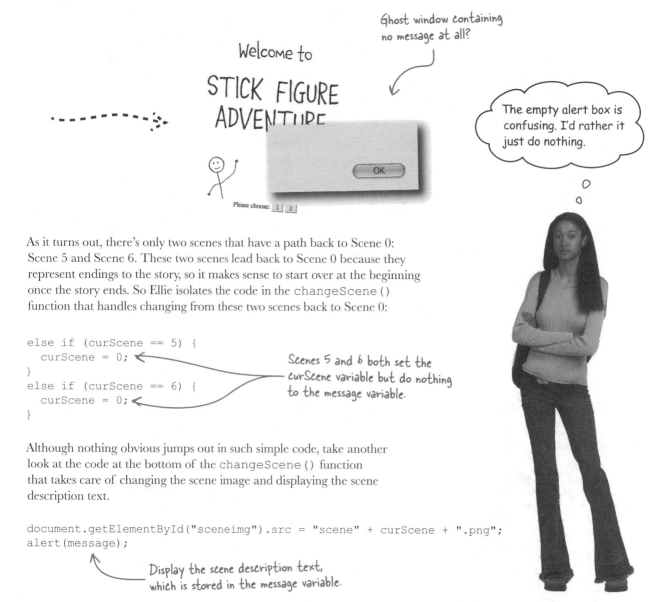

Ghost window containing no message at all?

Welcome to
STICK FIGURE
ADVENTURE

OK

Please choose: 1 | 2

The empty alert box is confusing. I'd rather it just do nothing.

As it turns out, there's only two scenes that have a path back to Scene 0: Scene 5 and Scene 6. These two scenes lead back to Scene 0 because they represent endings to the story, so it makes sense to start over at the beginning once the story ends. So Ellie isolates the code in the changeScene() function that handles changing from these two scenes back to Scene 0:

```
else if (curScene == 5) {
  curScene = 0;
}
else if (curScene == 6) {
  curScene = 0;
}
```

Scenes 5 and 6 both set the curScene variable but do nothing to the message variable.

Although nothing obvious jumps out in such simple code, take another look at the code at the bottom of the changeScene() function that takes care of changing the scene image and displaying the scene description text.

```
document.getElementById("sceneimg").src = "scene" + curScene + ".png";
alert(message);
```

Display the scene description text, which is stored in the message variable.

!= Psst, I've got nothing to tell you...

The problem with the Stick Figure Adventure code is that it always displays an alert box with the scene description message, even when there's no message to display, like with Scene 0 when restarting an adventure. But how can you check to see if the message variable actually contains scene description text?

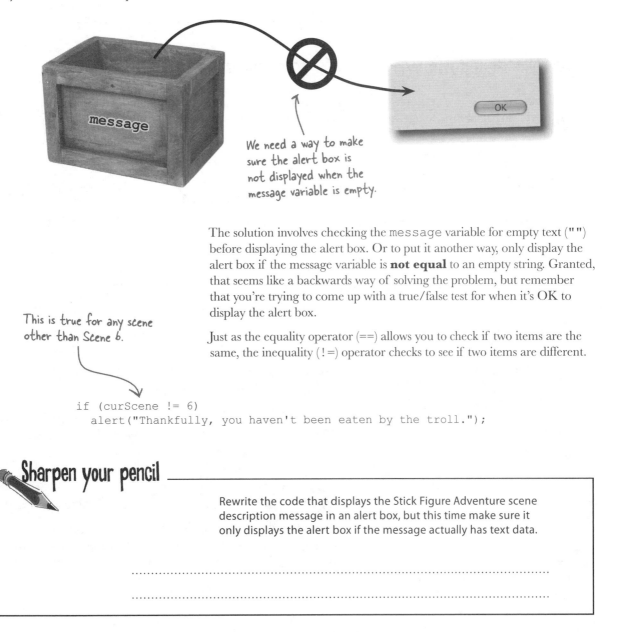

We need a way to make sure the alert box is not displayed when the message variable is empty.

The solution involves checking the message variable for empty text ("") before displaying the alert box. Or to put it another way, only display the alert box if the message variable is **not equal** to an empty string. Granted, that seems like a backwards way of solving the problem, but remember that you're trying to come up with a true/false test for when it's OK to display the alert box.

Just as the equality operator (==) allows you to check if two items are the same, the inequality (!=) operator checks to see if two items are different.

This is true for any scene other than Scene 6.

```
if (curScene != 6)
    alert("Thankfully, you haven't been eaten by the troll.");
```

Sharpen your pencil

Rewrite the code that displays the Stick Figure Adventure scene description message in an alert box, but this time make sure it only displays the alert box if the message actually has text data.

....

....

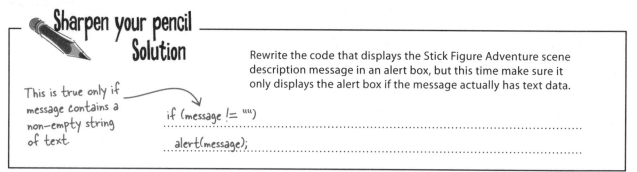

Sharpen your pencil Solution

Rewrite the code that displays the Stick Figure Adventure scene description message in an alert box, but this time make sure it only displays the alert box if the message actually has text data.

This is true only if message contains a non-empty string of text.

```
if (message != "")
    alert(message);
```

Crafting decisions with comparison operators

Equality and inequality aren't the only comparison operators you're likely to find useful as you continue building test conditions and making decisions in your JavaScript code.

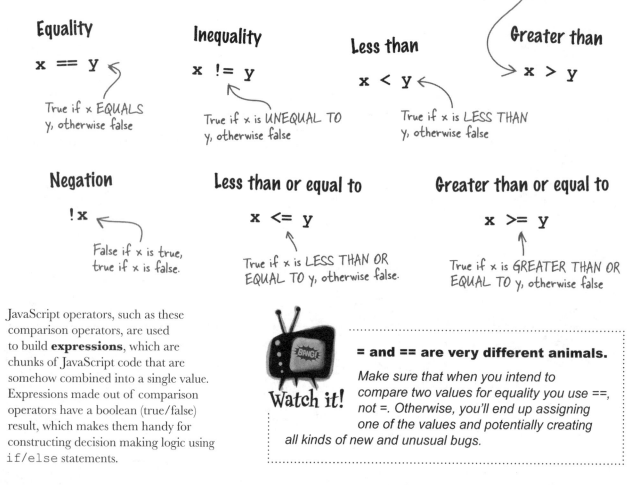

Equality

x == y

True if x EQUALS y, otherwise false

Inequality

x != y

True if x is UNEQUAL TO y, otherwise false

Less than

x < y

True if x is LESS THAN y, otherwise false

Greater than

True if x is GREATER THAN y, otherwise false

x > y

Negation

!x

False if x is true, true if x is false.

Less than or equal to

x <= y

True if x is LESS THAN OR EQUAL TO y, otherwise false.

Greater than or equal to

x >= y

True if x is GREATER THAN OR EQUAL TO y, otherwise false

JavaScript operators, such as these comparison operators, are used to build **expressions**, which are chunks of JavaScript code that are somehow combined into a single value. Expressions made out of comparison operators have a boolean (true/false) result, which makes them handy for constructing decision making logic using `if/else` statements.

Watch it!

= and == are very different animals.

Make sure that when you intend to compare two values for equality you use ==, not =. Otherwise, you'll end up assigning one of the values and potentially creating all kinds of new and unusual bugs.

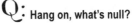

there are no
Dumb Questions

Q: **Why does the negation operator only use a single value?**

A: While most comparison operators require two operands, the negation operator requires only one. And its job is very simple: reverse the value of the operand. So, `true` becomes `false` and `false` become `true`.

Q: **I've seen the negation operator used on a value that isn't a comparison. How does that work?**

A: Code that uses the negation operator on a non-comparison value is taking advantage of a detail regarding how JavaScript determines the "truthiness" of a value. If you use a non-comparison

value in a situation where a comparison is expected, any value other than `null`, `0`, or `" "` will be automatically interpreted as `true`. In other words, the presence of data is considered a `true` value from a comparison perspective. So, when you see the negation operator used on a non-comparison value, `null`, `0`, and `" "` are negated to `true`, while all other values are negated to `false`.

Q: **Hang on, what's null?**

A: `null` is a special JavaScript value that represents the absence of data. It makes more sense in the context of objects, which are covered in Chapters 9 and 10.

Exercise

This code is capable of displaying a **positive** message about Stick Figure Adventure. What values should the four values a, b, c, and d have to successfully complete the message?

```
var quote = "";

if (a != 10)
  quote += "Some guy";
else
  quote += "I";
if (b == (a * 3)) {
  if (c < (b / 6))
    quote += " don't care for";
  else if (c >= (b / 5))
    quote += " can't remember";
  else
    quote += " love";
}
else {
  quote += " really hates";
}
if (!d) {
  quote += " Stick Figure";
}
else {
  quote += " Rock, Paper, Scissors";
}

alert(quote + " Adventure!");
```

a = ...

b = ...

c = ...

d = ...

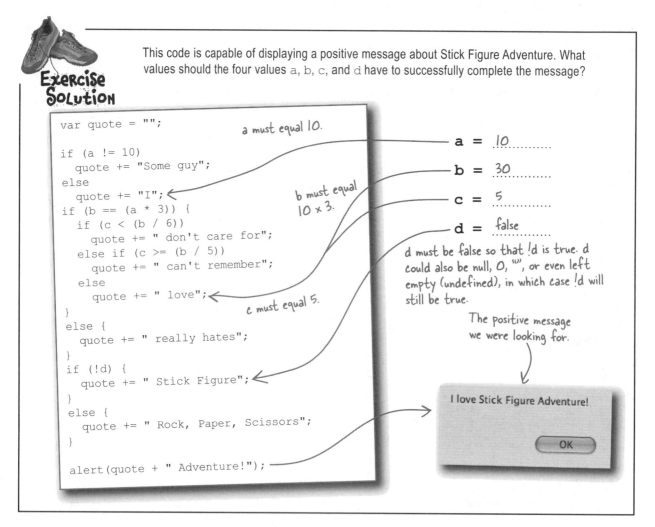

Exercise Solution

This code is capable of displaying a positive message about Stick Figure Adventure. What values should the four values a, b, c, and d have to successfully complete the message?

```
var quote = "";

if (a != 10)
  quote += "Some guy";
else
  quote += "I";
if (b == (a * 3)) {
  if (c < (b / 6))
    quote += " don't care for";
  else if (c >= (b / 5))
    quote += " can't remember";
  else
    quote += " love";
}
else {
  quote += " really hates";
}
if (!d) {
  quote += " Stick Figure";
}
else {
  quote += " Rock, Paper, Scissors";
}

alert(quote + " Adventure!");
```

a must equal 10.

b must equal 10 × 3.

c must equal 5.

a = 10

b = 30

c = 5

d = false

d must be false so that !d is true. d could also be null, 0, "", or even left empty (undefined), in which case !d will still be true.

The positive message we were looking for.

I love Stick Figure Adventure!

OK

Comments, placeholders, and documentation

Stick Figure adventure is a good example of a script that has unfinished chunks of code because the story is still being developed. For example, Scenes 8 and 9 are both "to be continued" scenes still awaiting some creative work from Ellie. It can be helpful to flag unfinished areas of code with placeholder notes so that you don't forget to fill in the details later. JavaScript **comments** make it possible to add notes to code without affecting how the code runs in any way.

A comment starts with a pair of forward slashes.

`//` + `Comment`

The comment text can be anything you want – it all gets ignored by the JavaScript interpreter.

Comments in JavaScript start with //

A comment created with // extends from the slashes to the end of the line.
To create a comment as a placeholder, just follow the slashes with a note
indicating that more code is coming.

These lines
of code are
ignored by the
interpreter.

```
else if (curScene == 8) {
  // TO BE CONTINUED
}
else if (curScene == 9) {
  // TO BE CONTINUED
}
```

Scene 8

To be
continued...

Scene 9

To be
continued...

Comments aren't just for placeholders. They're more commonly used to
document code so that it's better organized and easier to understand. Just
because you know how a piece of code works **now** doesn't mean you'll
have such a great memory about it later. And there's always the chance
someone else will inherit your code, and they'll certainly benefit from
notes about how it works.

This comment
explains the variable
initialization.

```
// Initialize the current scene to Scene 0 (Intro)
var curScene = 0;
```

The initialization of the curScene variable in Stick Figure Adventure
is clearer thanks to a detailed comment. A similar comment could be
used to clarify the initialization of the message variable.

Again, a comment
clarifies what is going on
in the code following it.

```
// Clear the scene message
var message = "";
```

If you need a comment that spans more than one line, you can
create a multiline comment.

Multiline comments
always start with /*.

```
/*  +  Start of comment
```

```
More comment
```

```
End of comment  +  */
```

Multiline comments
always end with */.

Single-line comments start with //, while multiline comments are enclosed between /* and */.

A multiline comment can be as long as you want,
you just have to start it with /* and end it with */.

```
/* All three of these lines of code are one
   big comment. Seriously, I'm not kidding.
   No joke, this is still part of the comment. */
```

Hang on a second. The comments make sense but I don't get why the curScene and message variables are created in different places. What's the deal with that?

curScene is created outside of the changeScene() function.

```
<script type="text/javascript">
// Initialize the current scene to Scene 0 (Intro)
var curScene = 0;

  function changeScene(decision) {
    // Clear the scene message
    var message = "";
    ...
  }
</script>
```

message is created on the inside of the changeScene() function.

Location, location, location of variables

As with real estate, location means everything in JavaScript. In this case, the place where the Stick Figure Adventure variables are created matters a lot. In other words, it's no accident that curScene is created outside of the changeScene() function, while message is created inside the function. The reason is because of **scope**, which controls the life cycle of a variable, as well as what code can access it.

Scope and context: where data lives

In JavaScript, scope refers to the **context of data**, as in where data lives
and how it can be accessed. Depending upon its scope, some data can be
seen everywhere in a script, while other data is limited to a specific block of
code, such as a function. This an example of two variables who live in very
different places:

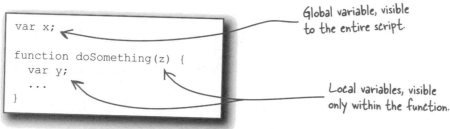

```
var x;

function doSomething(z) {
  var y;
  ...
}
```

Global variable, visible
to the entire script.

Local variables, visible
only within the function.

In this code, x is considered a **global** variable since it's created outside
of any function or other block of code, and therefore can be seen by the
entire script. More importantly, x is "alive" for as long as the script is
running. Unlike x, y is a **local** variable whose visibility is confined to the
code within the doSomething() function. Also, y only exists while the
doSomething() function is running – it gets created when the function
starts, and then destroyed when the function finishes.

So far so good, but where does that leave z, the argument to the
doSomething() function? As it turns out, function arguments act just
like local variables that have already been initialized. So z has the same
scope as y, meaning it can only be accessed from within the function.

Global variables are
kept around for the
entire life of a script.

Local variables are
created and destroyed as
dictated by their scope.

Data visibility is on a "need to know" basis, meaning you should limit
accessibility whenever possible. This helps prevent data from getting
inadvertently changed by code that has no business accessing it. In practical
terms, this means you should use local variables whenever possible.

BRAIN POWER

How could global and local variables fit into the Stick Figure Adventure code?

Check your adventure variable score

Looking back at the Stick Figure Adventure variables with the knowledge of local and global variables, it's now possible to get a better feel for why the variables are created in different places.

The value of the message variable is reset each time through the changeScene() function, so it works fine as a local variable.

The value of the curScene variable must be maintained in between calls to the changeScene() function, so it has to be a global variable.

```html
<script type="text/javascript">
  // Initialize the current scene to Scene 0 (Intro)
  var curScene = 0;

  function changeScene(decision) {
    // Clear the scene message
    var message = "";

    if (curScene == 0) {
      curScene = 1;
      message = "Your journey begins at a fork in the road.";
    }
    else if (curScene == 1) {
      if (decision == 1) {
        curScene = 2;
        message = "You have arrived at a cute little...";
      }
      else {
        curScene = 3;
        message = "You are standing on the bridge...";
      }
    }
    else if (curScene == 2) {
      ...
    }
</script>
```

The issue here is the need to preserve the value of a variable outside the scope of the changeScene() function. The message variable is cleared at the beginning of the function, so its value doesn't have to be preserved outside of the function. The curScene variable, on the other hand, is checked in several if/else test conditions, so this value *has* to persist in between calls to the function. **Bottom line, message can be created locally but curScene has to be global in this example.**

Where does my data live?

If scope still has you a little puzzled, it may help to think of different
parts of a script as self-contained areas where data can live. For
example, the Stick Figure Adventure script has several different
scopes that you could use to store away data.

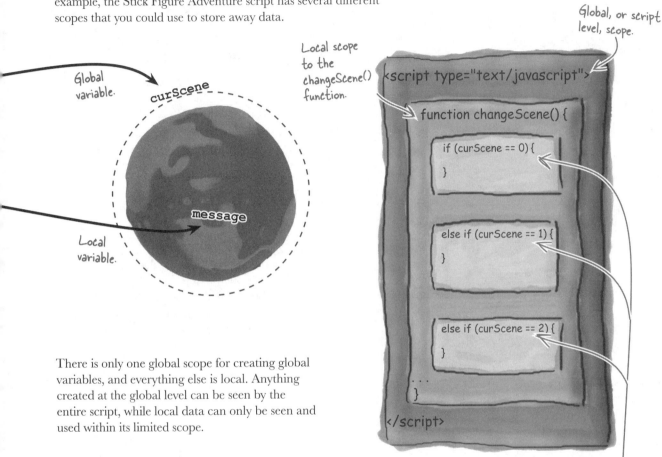

Global, or script level, scope.

Local scope to the changeScene() function.

Global variable.

curScene

message

Local variable.

```
<script type="text/javascript">

    function changeScene() {

        if (curScene == 0) {

        }

        else if (curScene == 1) {

        }

        else if (curScene == 2) {

        }
        ...
    }

</script>
```

Local scope to each different compound statement.

There is only one global scope for creating global
variables, and everything else is local. Anything
created at the global level can be seen by the
entire script, while local data can only be seen and
used within its limited scope.

there are no Dumb Questions

Q: I have some data. Which type of variable should I use to store it: local or global?

A: The way you're using the data will determine whether it needs to be local or global. But
since you asked, the general rule is to try to make all variables local, and only resort to global
if local won't work.

Fireside Chats

Tonight's talk: **Local variable and Global variable discuss the importance of location when finding a home for data**

Local variable:

I find it helpful to focus only on what's going on around me. In fact, I couldn't even tell you what's happening outside of the neighborhood where I live, and I quite like it that way.

Global variable:

Dude, you really need to expand your world view. Get out and travel a little, check out other parts of the script universe.

While that sounds tempting, I like the security of comfortable surroundings. I rest easy knowing that no one from outside of my little area can get to me.

Maybe so, but are you aware of the fact that you're little life is meaningless in the grand script scheme of things. You get created and destroyed over and over every time your little world comes and goes, while I'm here for the long haul. If the script is here, I'm here.

Ouch! I'm not sure I believe in all this reincarnation business, but I can tell you that I'm every bit as handy for storing data as you are. I just don't put myself out there for everyone to see.

That's fair. And I'll admit that I've been abused and misused a time or two, but the upside of me always holding my value through thick and thin has been enough to offset the problems. When a script needs a piece of data that remembers its value and is available everywhere, they come to me.

And when a script needs to keep some information private to a certain section of code, it comes to me because of my knack for discretion.

Sounds great, but I'll take accessibility and persistence over privacy any day.

And that's why people still find us both useful.

there are no
Dumb Questions

Q: What happens if actual JavaScript code is placed within a comment?

A: Nothing! Comments are completely ignored by the JavaScript interpreter, so anything you place within a comment is overlooked when the interpreter starts running script code. Knowing this, comments can be used as a means of temporarily disabling pieces of code when trying to track down a problem or trying different coding approaches.

Q: Can a line of JavaScript code have a single-line comment at the end?

A: Yes. And in this case, the code is still run because it isn't part of the comment. A single-line comment doesn't necessarily take up an entire line—the comment is just from the // to the end of the line. So if the // follows a piece of code, the code will still run just fine.

Q: Why don't comments end with a semicolon?

A: Because they are not JavaScript statements. Comments are labels that do nothing more than describe or provide additional information about code, sort of like footnotes in a book. The main thing to remember is that the JavaScript interpreter ignores all comments—comments are there for the human brain, not JavaScript.

Q: What does "script level" mean in regard to creating global variables?

A: "Script level" is the top level of script code, which is just inside the `<script>` tag. The significance of "script level" is that it is outside of any function or other block of code, and therefore anything created at "script level" is considered global. This means anything created at "script level" lives for the life of the script and can be accessed by any code within the page.

Q: If I create a variable inside of a compound statement, is it a local variable?

A: Yes. A compound statement establishes a new scope level, so anything created inside of a compound statement has a local scope within that statement. Such variables can be thought of as temporary variables since they are created and destroyed every time the flow of script execution goes into and out of the compound statement.

Q: Scope, flow, execution... this local and global variable stuff sounds really complex. Is it as hard as it sounds?

A: Not really. The main thing to remember is that local variables are perfect for storing temporary information that you don't need to remember outside of a function or other chunk of code. If you need the data to stay around for the entire life of the script, then you should make it a global variable. Surprisingly enough, most script data tends to be more temporary than you might initially think, meaning that you will likely use local variables a lot more than global variables.

Local variables store temporary information, global variables are stored for the life of the script.

BULLET POINTS

- **Comments** are a great way to remind yourself of code to add later.

- Don't be afraid to use lots of comments to document your code so that it's easier to understand.

- Use a pair of forward slashes (//) to start a **single-line comment**.

- **Multiline comments** start with /* and end with */.

- Global variables are created at the script level, outside of any function or other body of code, and are kept around for the **life of the script**.

- Local variables are created (and destroyed) inside a body of code, and can only be accessed within that code.

- Local variables are **preferred** over global variables because their access is more tightly controlled.

Choice of five

Remember Eric, our game show contestant from earlier in the chapter? It seems Eric has polished off his donuts and progressed to a later round of *Wanna Make a Deal?* Problem is, he now faces a very challenging decision... he must choose between one of five options.

Geez, I could really use some help making this decision.

BRAIN POWER

How would you code a JavaScript decision involving five different options?

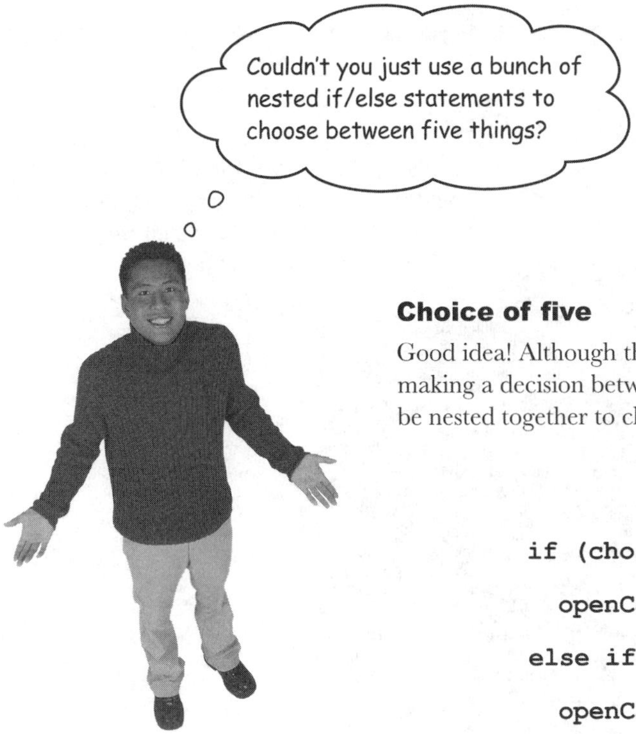

Couldn't you just use a bunch of nested if/else statements to choose between five things?

Choice of five

Good idea! Although the if/else statement is geared toward making a decision between one of two things, several of them can be nested together to choose between as many things as you want.

```
if (chosenCase == "A")

   openCase("A");

else if (chosenCase == "B")

   openCase("B");

else if (chosenCase == "C")

   openCase("C");

else if (chosenCase == "D")

   openCase("D");

else if (chosenCase == "E")

   openCase("E");
```

This code works but the last case requires every test condition to be evaluated, which is inefficient.

Nesting if/else can get complicated

The nested if/else statements work just fine... but they aren't all that efficient, primarily because they aren't really designed for decision-making that involves more than two possibilities. To see why, work through how many boolean tests take place in the process of choosing the last case, Case E. All five test conditions are evaluated, which is a bit inefficient.

Switch statements have multiple cases

JavaScript has a decision-making statement just for making multiple choice decisions. Unlike the `if/else` statement, which is really better suited to choosing between **two things**, the `switch/case` statement allows you to more efficiently choose between any **number of things**. Let's look at Eric's dilemma through the eyes of a `switch/case` statement:

The switch/case statement efficiently chooses between more than two things.

The "case" in switch/case has nothing to do with Eric's metal cases.

```
switch (chosenCase) {

case "A":

    openCase("A");

    break;

case "B":

    openCase("B");

    break;

case "C":

    openCase("C");

    break;

case "D":

    openCase("D");

    break;

case "E":

    openCase("E");

    break;

}
```

The value of Eric's chosen case is the controlling piece of information in the switch/case statement.

Each possible choice is coded using a case statement.

The action code is placed immediately below its matching case statement.

The break statement is necessary to finish each decision branch by immediately exiting from the entire switch/case statement.

The switch/case statement is structured as a big compound statement.

Exercise

Fact or fiction? The `switch/case` statement can do anything the `if/else` statement can do.

☐ **Fact**   ☐ **Fiction**

Fact or fiction? The switch/case statement can do anything the if/else statement can do.

☐ **Fact**   ☑ **Fiction**

Unlike if/else, the test data that controls
a switch/case statement cannot be an
expression—it must simply be a piece of data.

Inside the switch statement

Now that you've seen a switch/case statement in action, let's break it down
and look at the general format for the statement.

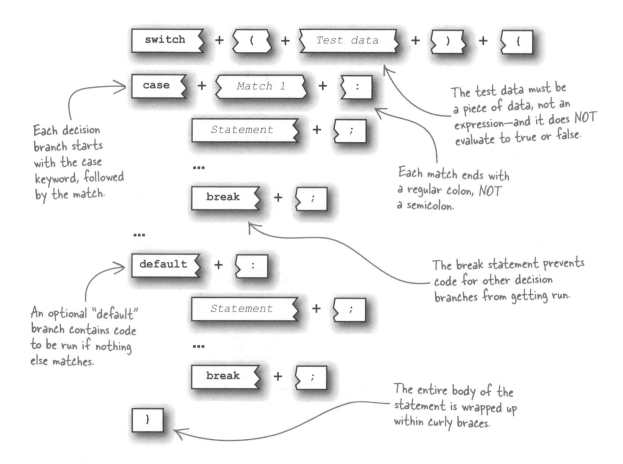

Each decision
branch starts
with the case
keyword, followed
by the match.

The test data must be
a piece of data, not an
expression—and it does NOT
evaluate to true or false.

Each match ends with
a regular colon, NOT
a semicolon.

The break statement prevents
code for other decision
branches from getting run.

An optional "default"
branch contains code
to be run if nothing
else matches.

The entire body of the
statement is wrapped up
within curly braces.

Switch case statements: write your own

Creating a `switch`/`case` statement is admittedly more involved than creating an `if`/`else` statement, but it is much more efficient for dealing with more than two possible outcomes. This is the process:

1 Enclose the test data in parentheses and open the compound statement (`{`).

2 Write the `case` match followed by a colon (`:`).

3 Write the code that gets run if there is a **match**. This can be multiple lines of code—there is no need for a compound statement.

4 Add a `break` statement—don't forget the semicolon (`;`).

5 Optionally include a default branch for when there is no match.

6 Close the compound statement (`}`).

> I wonder if a switch-case statement could be used to make Stick Figure Adventure more efficient...

there are no Dumb Questions

Q: So a `switch`/`case` **statement doesn't make a decision using a true/false expression?**

A: That's correct. Unlike an `if` or `if`/`else` statement, `switch`/`case` uses a piece of test data to make its decisions. That's how it supports more than two outcomes.

Watch it!

Break for safety.

Prevent accidental code from getting run by always finishing off each `switch-case` *match with a break statement.*

Q: So each `case` **match is just a match on the test data?**

A: Yes. The idea is that you use a variable as the test data, and then use literal values to carry out each different match.

Q: **What happens if you leave out all the** `break` **statements in a** `switch`/`case`**?**

A: Unexpected results can occur. The `break` statements serve as dividers between each section of action code in a `switch`/`case` statement. Without them, all of the action code would run as one big chunk, which would defeat the whole purpose of making different decisions. When a match is made in a `switch`/`case` statement, the code below the matching `case` is run until it encounters a `break` statement. Only then does the `switch`/`case` statement exit.

Switch Exposed

This week's interview:
Mover, shaker, decision maker

HeadFirst: Glad you're willing to chat with us. So, in one word tell us how you would describe yourself.

Switch: Choosy.

Head First: Care to elaborate?

Switch: I make it possible to choose between lots of different things. Although some situations involve simple black and white decisions, there are plenty of situations that require, let's say, more nuance. That's where I come in.

Head First: But people say that If can do the same kind of thing, sometimes with less code?

Switch: That may be true. And you can cut a piece of wood with a hammer if you whack at it long enough. Personally, I'd rather just use a saw. The reality is that everyone has their specialty, and mine is efficiently choosing between several different things. I don't have any beef with If, but he's a tool better suited for a different job.

Head First: You mention efficiency. Tell us how efficiency figures into what you do.

Switch: Well, I'm structured to make a decision based upon the value of a piece of data, and all I do is compare that piece of data to possible matches to determine which code to run. That's it. I don't bother trying to evaluate expressions, and I don't require nesting or anything cute like that to choose between multiple outcomes. If you want to make a quick decision based upon a piece of data, I'm your guy!

Head First: Tell us about your buddy Break. We've heard you can't get through the day without him?

Switch: That is a fact. Without Break, I'd be in big trouble because I wouldn't have a way to separate the different pieces of action code. Break lets me know when a section of code has finished running so I can

exit without running some other code by accident.

Head First: I see. What about Case, aren't you guys pretty close as well?

Switch: Absolutely. Case and I have a very close relationship, primarily because Case tells me what all the possible matches are for a given piece of test data. Without Case, I would have no basis for making a decision.

Head First: So I get that Case lays out the different possible matches, and you use those matches to determine what to do. But what happens when the test data has no match?

Switch: It depends. If no special code has been added to deal with a "no match" scenario, then nothing happens. However, my good friend Default makes it possible to run a special chunk of code only in the event that no match was found.

Head First: Wow, I didn't realize that. How does Default get along with Case?

Switch: Just fine, actually. They don't step on each other's toes because they never compete for attention. Case handles all the stuff that matches, while Default takes care of the situations when nothing at all matches. Just between us, I think Case is actually a little relieved that Default is there because he gets nervous when nothing matches.

Head First: I see. Well, we're about out of time. Any parting thoughts before you go?

Switch: Sure. Remember that there's nothing worse than indecision. Nobody likes a waffler. Just because there are lots of possibilities doesn't mean you have to throw your hands up and quit. Give me a call and I'll do my best to help you make a decision that works out best for your script.

Sharpen your pencil

Convert the first two scenes of the Stick Figure Adventure code so that it uses the `switch`/`case` statement instead of `if`/`else`.

```
...
if (curScene == 0) {
  curScene = 1;
  message = "Your journey begins at a fork in the road.";
}
else if (curScene == 1) {
  if (decision == 1) {
    curScene = 2
    message = "You have arrived at a cute little house in the woods.";
  }
  else {
    curScene = 3;
    message = "You are standing on the bridge overlooking a peaceful
stream.";
  }
}
...
```

Here's the original
version of the code
that uses if/else.

Sharpen your pencil
Solution

Convert the first two scenes of the Stick Figure Adventure code so that it uses the `switch`/`case` statement instead of `if`/`else`.

```
...
if (curScene == 0) {
  curScene = 1;
  message = "Your journey begins at a fork in the road.";
}
else if (curScene == 1) {
  if (decision == 1) {
    curScene = 2
    message = "You have arrived at a cute little house in the woods.";
  }
  else {
    curScene = 3;
    message = "You are standing on the bridge overlooking a peaceful
stream.";
  }
}
...
```

Here's the original version of the code that uses if/else.

Set the new scene number and the scene description message text, just like in the if/else version.

```
switch (curScene) {

case 0:

  curScene = 1;

  message = "Your journey begins at a fork in the road.";

  break;

case 1:

  if (decision == 1) {

    curScene = 2

    message = "You have arrived at a cute little house in the woods.";

  }

  else {

    curScene = 3;

    message = "You are standing on the bridge overlooking a peaceful stream.";

  }

  break;

...

}
```

Each case match corresponds to a scene number.

Within each case, it still makes sense to stick with if/else for handling the user's story decision.

The remaining scenes follow a similar structure.

Close the switch/case statement with a }.

A switchy stick figure adventure: test-drive

After completely reworking the decision-making logic for Stick Figure Adventure, Ellie is itching to see the result. The changes are immediately noticeable as you navigate through the story...

Everything looks exactly the same.

Stop right there!

So not all script improvements can be seen on the surface... I can live with that.

Hang on, nothing looks any different! And that's because the `switch/case` changes to Stick Figure Adventure only affect the structure of the code, not its appearance. This is an example of how some coding changes take place purely behind the scenes... literally!

The story goes on...

Stick Figure Adventure is really just the start of the story. It needs some creative storytelling, a little stick figure artwork, and plenty more JavaScript code to be a truly interesting online application. Where will you take it from here?

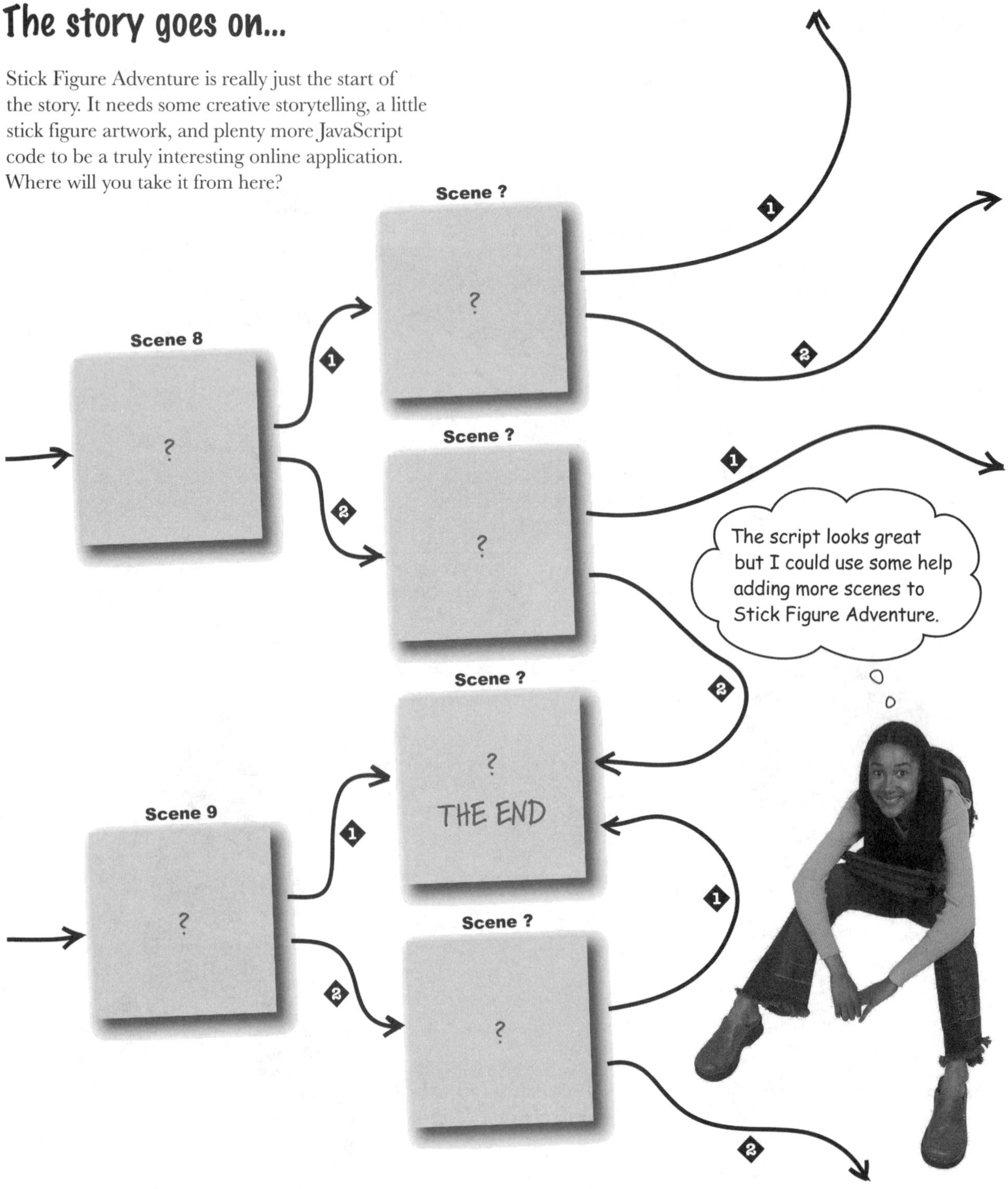

Scene ?

?

Scene 8

?

❶

Scene ?

?

❷

❶

❷

Scene ?

?

❶

❷

> The script looks great but I could use some help adding more scenes to Stick Figure Adventure.

Scene ?

?

THE END

Scene 9

?

❶

❷

Scene ?

?

❶

❷

JavaScriptcross

Here's an easy decision. Is it time to take a break
and knock out a little crossword puzzle? Of course!

Across

1. Writing this first can make it easier to write complex
JavaScript code.
4. Use these to document your code.
5. This kind of statement is actually made up of multiple
statements.
6. When one if statement is placed within another, it is said to
be ....
8. The != operator tests for this.
10. You can use one of these to help visualize a group of
complex decisions.
13. The entire script has access to this kind of variable.

Down

2. Do this, ... do that.
3. These kinds of operators have a true/false result.
4. How code is run when it is part of an if-else statement.
7. A statement that allows you to make a decision based upon
the value of a piece of data.
9. A variable that has limited scope.
11. This statement allows you to conditionally run a piece of
code.
12. Each decision branch inside of a switch statement has one
of these.

 JavaScriptcross Solution

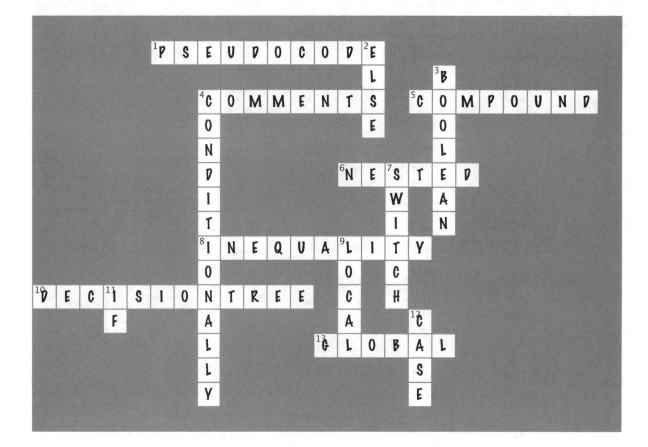

Page Bender

When if/else isn't enough...

Fold the page vertically to line up the two brains and solve the riddle.

It's a meeting of the minds!

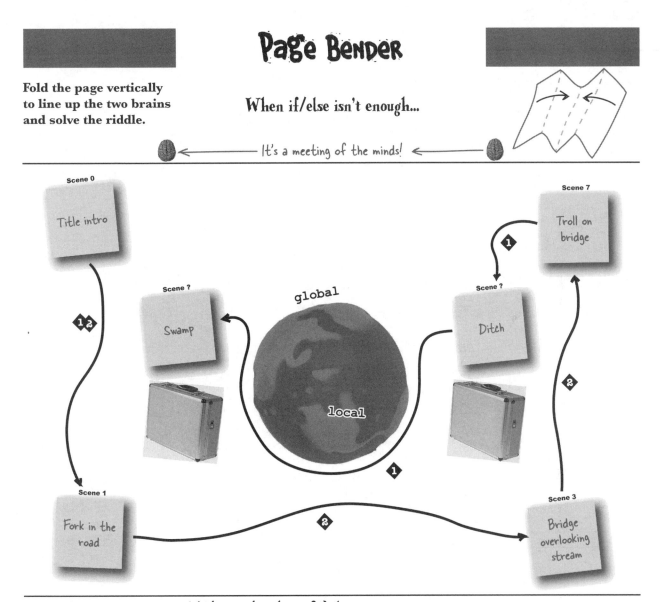

Although the if/else statement is incredibly handy, it does have its limitations. For example, you can't switch between more than two things. In case you don't believe it, try it yourself.

5 looping

At the Risk of Repeating Myself

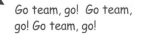

Go team, go! Go team, go! Go team, go!

Some say repetition is the spice of life. Sure, doing something new and interesting is certainly exciting, but it's the little repetitive things that really make it possible to get through the day. Compulsive hand sanitizing, a nervous tick, clicking Reply To All to every freaking message you receive! Okay, maybe repetition isn't always such a great thing in the real world. However, it can be extremely handy in the world of JavaScript. You'd be surprised how often you need a script to run a piece of code several times, and that's where the power of looping really shines. Without loops, you'd be wasting a lot of time cutting and pasting a bunch of wasteful code.

X marks the spot

It's hard to argue the allure of buried treasure.
Here's a treasure map that could use some
JavaScript assistance.

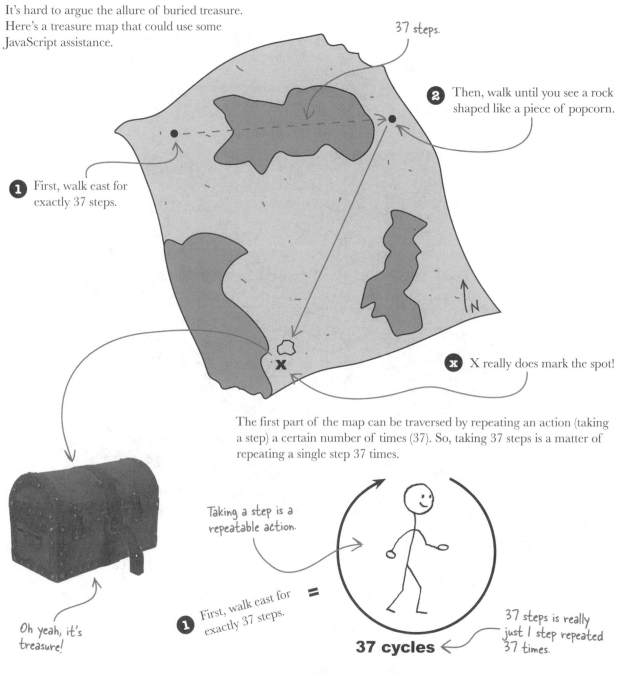

37 steps.

2 Then, walk until you see a rock
shaped like a piece of popcorn.

1 First, walk east for
exactly 37 steps.

x X really does mark the spot!

The first part of the map can be traversed by repeating an action (taking
a step) a certain number of times (37). So, taking 37 steps is a matter of
repeating a single step 37 times.

Taking a step is a
repeatable action.

Oh yeah, it's
treasure!

1 First, walk east for
exactly 37 steps. **=**

37 cycles ←

37 steps is really
just 1 step repeated
37 times.

So the question is... how does JavaScript make repetition possible?

Déjà vu all over again...for loops

Repetition in JavaScript is carried out with **loops**, which allow you to repeat code. The `for` loop in particular is great for repeating something a certain amount of **known** times. For example, `for` loops are great for counting tasks, such as counting down to zero or counting up to some value.

A `for` loop consists of four different parts:

 Initialization
Initialization takes place one time, at the start of a `for` loop.

 Test condition
The test condition checks to see if the loop should continue with another cycle.

 Action
The action part of the loop is the code that is actually repeated in each cycle.

 Update
The update part of the loop updates any loop variables at the end of a cycle.

For loops let you repeat code a certain number of times.

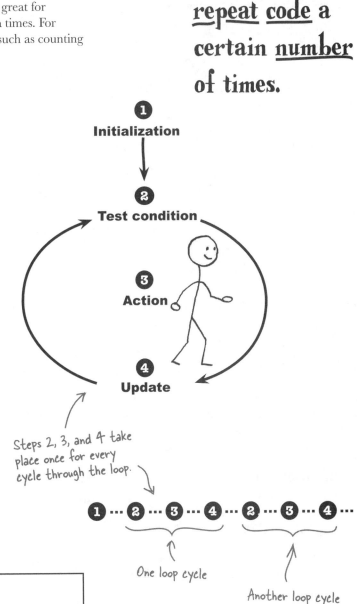

Steps 2, 3, and 4 take place once for every cycle through the loop.

One loop cycle

Another loop cycle

BRAIN POWER

How do the four steps in a `for` loop relate to the treasure map example?

Treasure hunting with a for loop

for loops work for following the treasure map because they involve a known number of steps. Applying a for loop to the first part of the treasure map will look something like this:

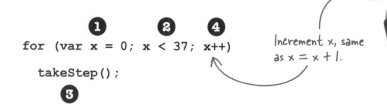

①   **②** **④**

```
for (var x = 0; x < 37; x++)

    takeStep();
```

③

Increment x, same as x = x + 1.

Breaking down the code for the for loop:

It's common to start counting at 0 in JavaScript loops, although the loop could easily be changed to start at 1.

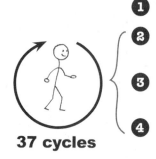

① Initialize the counter variable x to 0.

② Check to see if x is less than 37. If so, move on to Step 3 and continue the cycle through the loop. If not, quit the loop.

③ Run the loop action code, which in this case means running the takeStep() function.

④ Increment x and go back to Step 2 to possibly start another loop cycle.

37 cycles

After 37 cycles through the loop, the loop finishes with x equal to 37. All this thanks to the four pieces of the for loop puzzle that work together to establish JavaScript repetition.

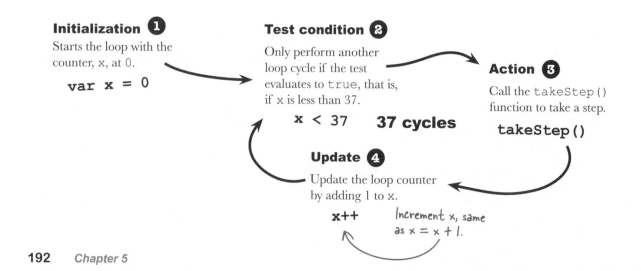

Initialization ①
Starts the loop with the counter, x, at 0.

var x = 0

Test condition ②
Only perform another loop cycle if the test evaluates to true, that is, if x is less than 37.

x < 37   **37 cycles**

Action ③
Call the takeStep() function to take a step.

takeStep()

Update ④
Update the loop counter by adding 1 to x.

x++   *Increment x, same as x = x + 1.*

Dissect the for loop

All `for` loops stick to a consistent format that requires each of the four components to be in specific places. The good news is that there's plenty of flexibility to craft your own custom loops using this format.

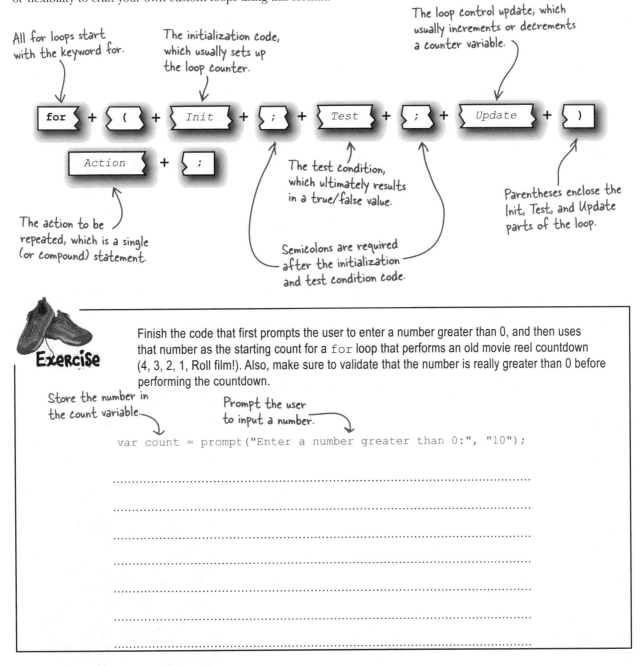

All `for` loops start with the keyword `for`.

The initialization code, which usually sets up the loop counter.

The loop control update, which usually increments or decrements a counter variable.

The action to be repeated, which is a single (or compound) statement.

The test condition, which ultimately results in a true/false value.

Semicolons are required after the initialization and test condition code.

Parentheses enclose the Init, Test, and Update parts of the loop.

Finish the code that first prompts the user to enter a number greater than 0, and then uses that number as the starting count for a `for` loop that performs an old movie reel countdown (4, 3, 2, 1, Roll film!). Also, make sure to validate that the number is really greater than 0 before performing the countdown.

Exercise

Store the number in the count variable.

Prompt the user to input a number.

```
var count = prompt("Enter a number greater than 0:", "10");
```

....

....

....

....

....

....

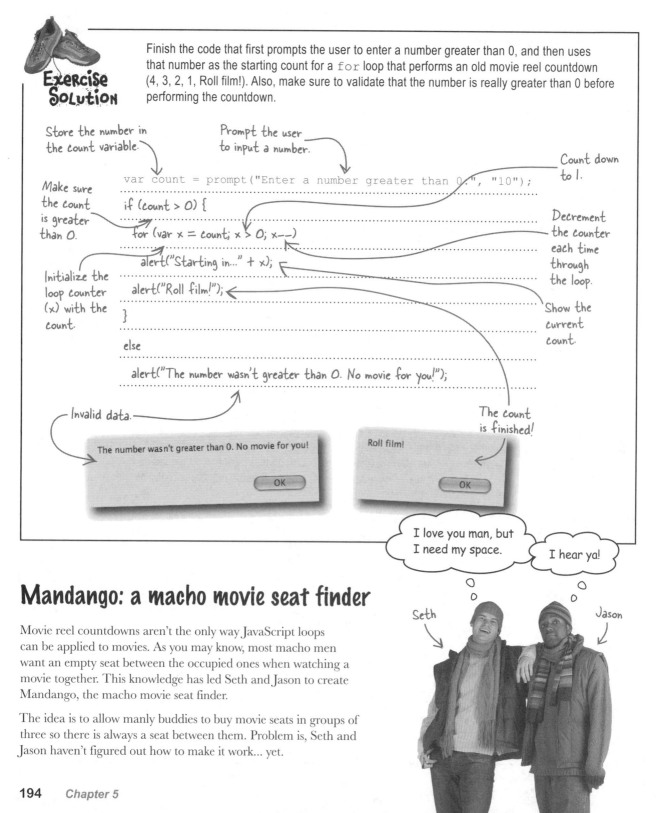

Exercise Solution

Finish the code that first prompts the user to enter a number greater than 0, and then uses that number as the starting count for a `for` loop that performs an old movie reel countdown (4, 3, 2, 1, Roll film!). Also, make sure to validate that the number is really greater than 0 before performing the countdown.

Store the number in the count variable.

Prompt the user to input a number.

Count down to 1.

```
var count = prompt("Enter a number greater than 0.", "10");

if (count > 0) {

    for (var x = count; x > 0; x--)

        alert("Starting in..." + x);

        alert("Roll film!");

}

else

    alert("The number wasn't greater than 0. No movie for you!");
```

Make sure the count is greater than 0.

Initialize the loop counter (x) with the count.

Decrement the counter each time through the loop.

Show the current count.

Invalid data.

The number wasn't greater than 0. No movie for you!

OK

Roll film!

OK

The count is finished!

I love you man, but I need my space.

Seth

I hear ya!

Jason

Mandango: a macho movie seat finder

Movie reel countdowns aren't the only way JavaScript loops can be applied to movies. As you may know, most macho men want an empty seat between the occupied ones when watching a movie together. This knowledge has led Seth and Jason to create Mandango, the macho movie seat finder.

The idea is to allow manly buddies to buy movie seats in groups of three so there is always a seat between them. Problem is, Seth and Jason haven't figured out how to make it work... yet.

First check seat availability

The challenge facing the guys is to be able to search through each
seat in a row, checking for a sequence of three available seats.

All three seats
available!

Only one seat
available.

All three
seats taken.

Not cool.

Anything other than three
available seats together result
in a major lack of "manlitude."

Cool!

Three available seats in a
row means plenty of manly
movie viewing room.

Sharpen your pencil

Using the row of movie seats below, write down how you would
search for three available seats in a row using a `for` loop. Make
sure to draw exactly how the loop works with respect to the seats.

....

....

Sharpen your pencil
Solution

Using the row of movie seats below, write down how you would search for three available seats in a row using a `for` loop. Make sure to draw exactly how the loop works with respect to the seats.

If the availability of each seat is represented by a boolean variable, then you can loop through the seats looking for three in a row that are available (true).

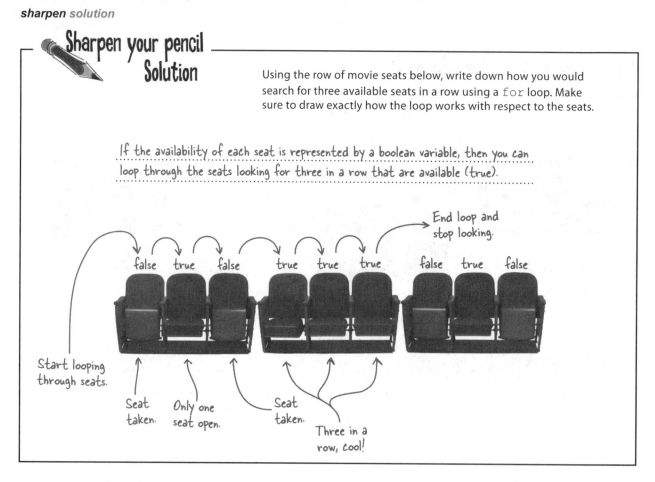

End loop and stop looking.

false   true   false   true   true   true   false   true   false

Start looping through seats.

Seat taken.

Only one seat open.

Seat taken.

Three in a row, cool!

Looping, HTML, and seat availability

The general Mandango design makes some sense but it isn't exactly clear how the availability of each seat translates into HTML code.

Each movie seat is shown visually on the Mandango page as an image.

Full HTML and images for this example are available at http://www.headfirstlabs.com/books/hfjs/.

```
<img id="seat1" src="seat_unavail.png" alt="Unavailable" />
<img id="seat2" src="seat_avail.png" alt="Available" />
<img id="seat3" src="seat_unavail.png" alt="Unavailable" />
<img id="seat4" src="seat_avail.png" alt="Available" />
<img id="seat5" src="seat_avail.png" alt="Available" />
<img id="seat6" src="seat_avail.png" alt="Available" />
<img id="seat7" src="seat_unavail.png" alt="Unavailable" />
<img id="seat8" src="seat_avail.png" alt="Available" />
<img id="seat9" src="seat_unavail.png" alt="Unavailable" />
```

Not only do you need to be able to loop through the HTML image elements, you also need a way to store their availability together as boolean variables in JavaScript code.

Movie seats as variables

Before you can even think about looping through seats looking for availability, you have to represent the availability of each seat in JavaScript code. The availability of a row of nine seats can be represented by nine boolean variables.

```
var seat1 = false;
var seat2 = true;
var seat3 = false;
var seat4 = true;
var seat5 = true;
var seat6 = true;
var seat7 = false;
var seat8 = false;
var seat9 = false;
```

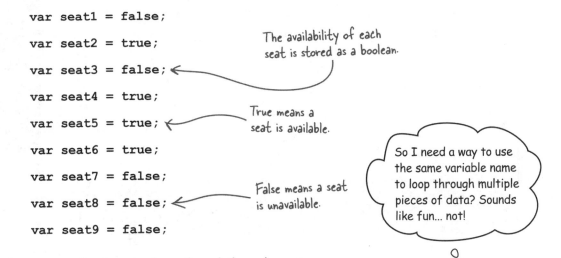

The availability of each seat is stored as a boolean.

True means a seat is available.

False means a seat is unavailable.

So I need a way to use the same variable name to loop through multiple pieces of data? Sounds like fun... not!

Now you're ready to create a `for` loop that loops through these nine seats, checking for three in a row that are available.

```
for (var i = 0; i < 10; i++) {

  if (seat1)

    ...

}
```

You can't change the variable name each time through the loop!

Hang on, there appears to be a problem. The `for` loop needs to be able to check the value of a different seat variable each time through the loop. But there isn't a way to do that since each variable has a different name.

BRAIN POWER

If individual variables don't work so well in loops, how could you store information so that it can be looped through?

Arrays collect multiple pieces of data

JavaScript lets you store multiple pieces of data in a single variable with a special type of data called an **array**. An array variable is like a normal variable since it only has one name, but an array has multiple storage locations. Think of an array as being like a storage cubby in your house— it's one piece of furniture with multiple storage locations.

Each item in an array consists of two pieces of information: a **value** and a unique **key** that is used to access the value. Keys are often just numbers that start at zero and count up with each item. Numeric keys are known as **indexes**, making this an **indexed array**:

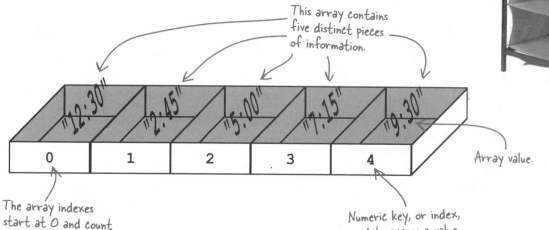

This array contains five distinct pieces of information.

Array value.

The array indexes start at 0 and count up with each item.

Numeric key, or index, used to access a value.

Creating an array is similar to creating a normal variable except you have to let JavaScript know you want an array, as opposed to a single unit of storage. In fact, you're really telling JavaScript to create an **object**.

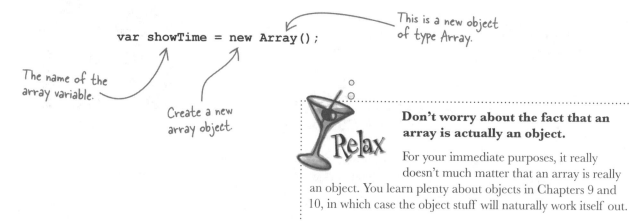

```
var showTime = new Array();
```

This is a new object of type Array.

The name of the array variable.

Create a new array object.

Don't worry about the fact that an array is actually an object.

For your immediate purposes, it really doesn't much matter that an array is really an object. You learn plenty about objects in Chapters 9 and 10, in which case the object stuff will naturally work itself out.

Array values are stored with keys

Object or not, once you've created an array you can start adding and accessing data in it. The key to getting to the data stored in an array is, well, the **key**! The unique key associated with a piece of data is what you use to access that data. In the case of an indexed array, you just use the index of the array element you want to access.

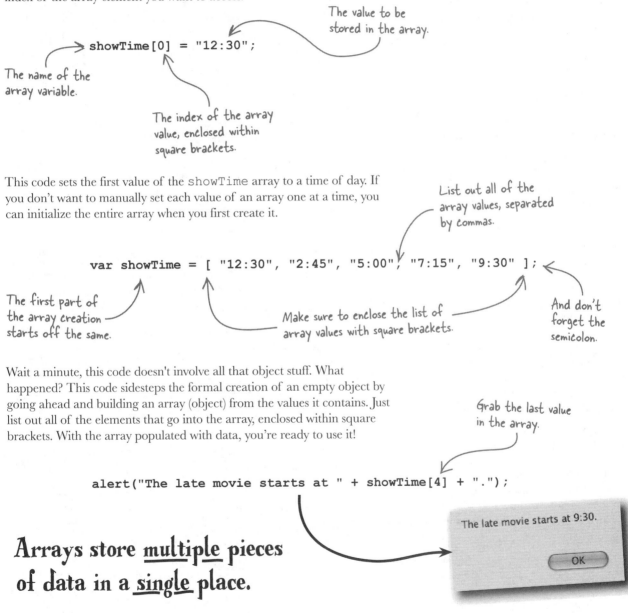

The name of the array variable.

```
showTime[0] = "12:30";
```

The value to be stored in the array.

The index of the array value, enclosed within square brackets.

This code sets the first value of the showTime array to a time of day. If you don't want to manually set each value of an array one at a time, you can initialize the entire array when you first create it.

List out all of the array values, separated by commas.

```
var showTime = [ "12:30", "2:45", "5:00", "7:15", "9:30" ];
```

The first part of the array creation starts off the same.

Make sure to enclose the list of array values with square brackets.

And don't forget the semicolon.

Wait a minute, this code doesn't involve all that object stuff. What happened? This code sidesteps the formal creation of an empty object by going ahead and building an array (object) from the values it contains. Just list out all of the elements that go into the array, enclosed within square brackets. With the array populated with data, you're ready to use it!

Grab the last value in the array.

```
alert("The late movie starts at " + showTime[4] + ".");
```

The late movie starts at 9:30.

OK

Arrays store <u>multiple</u> pieces of data in a <u>single</u> place.

Arrays Exposed

This week's interview:
Inside the mind of a serial data storer

Head First: Good to meet you, Array. So I hear you're good at storing multiple pieces of data.

Array: That's true. I'm all about volume. You need a place to store 50 strings of text or 300 numbers, I'm your guy.

Head First: Sounds intriguing. But can't people already store quantities of data in normal variables?

Array: Sure, and people can also walk to work barefoot if they want. Look, there's always more than one way to do things. In this case, I provide a better way to store multiple pieces of information than regular variables.

Head First: Well, I do prefer wearing shoes to work. But how exactly are you better?

Array: Think about it this way. If you're keeping a diary and you write down something every day, how do you keep up with all of those pages after a few years?

Head First: The pages are all right there in the diary. What's the big deal?

Array: You're making a big assumption about the pages being organized together with some sense of connectedness. What if they were just a bunch of random sticky notes thrown in a shoebox? That diary would suddenly get a lot tougher to manage.

Head First: Right, but how is storing data in an array like keeping diary pages in a book?

Array: Because I organize the data in such a way that it is very easy to access. For example, if I ask what you wrote in the diary on last June 6th, you would probably tell me to turn to page 124. Same thing with array data, except the page numbers for an array are called keys.

Head First: I've heard of array indexes, but not keys. What's a key?

Array: Oh, sorry. A key is a general term used to describe a piece of information used to look up a piece of data. An index is just a certain kind of key, a numeric key. So the diary page numbers are not only keys, they are also indexes. If you're talking about looking up data with unique numbers, keys and indexes are really the same thing.

Head First: Got it. I guess the thing I still don't understand is what any of this has to do with looping.

Array: Well, not necessarily anything. I'm plenty handy for storing data without loops ever entering the picture. However, I do make it incredibly handy for loops to cycle through a bunch of data.

Head First: How so?

Array: Remember that loops often use numeric counters to control the looping, right? Just use the counter as the index into an array, and voila, you now have a way to cycle through all of the data I have stored away.

Head First: Hang on, you're saying people can use a loop counter as an array index to look up data?

Array: That's exactly what I'm saying.

Head First: That's pretty powerful!

Array: I know. That's why scripts that need to loop through data find me indispensable. In just a few lines of code, you can loop through an entire array of data. It's really quite cool.

Head First: I can imagine. I want to thank you for shining a light on yourself and your connection to loops.

Array: Glad to do it. Look me up any time!

Sharpen your pencil

Write code to create a `seats` array for Mandango, and then loop through the seats in the array, alerting the user to the availability of each seat.

....

....

....

....

....

....

....

there are no
Dumb Questions

Q: Is it possible for a `for` loop to never stop looping?

A: Ah, yes, the dreaded infinite loop. Sure, it's very possible to create a loop that never exits, destined to cycle on and on to the limits of space and time... or at least until you reload the web page. Infinite loops are considered bad things because they prevent your script from doing anything else—it's the JavaScript equivalent of a locked-up application. Think Windows blue screen, only not quite as ominous.

Infinite loops occur when a loop counter either doesn't get updated properly, or when it otherwise never changes to cause the loop's test condition to result in a `false` value. Knowing this, you should always double and triple check the test condition and update logic in your `for` loops very carefully. Oh, and you'll know you have an infinite loop on your hands when your script just sits there apparently doing nothing.

Q: Is it possible to use a compound statement as the action part of a `for` loop?

A: Absolutely! In fact, in all but the most simple of looping scenarios, you will need to use a compound statement. This is because most practical loops end up needing to loop through more than one statement.

Q: When the loop condition tests `false`, does the action part of the loop run one last time?

A: No. The action part of a `for` loop only gets executed if the test condition evaluates to `true`. Once the test condition evaluates to `false`, the loop immediately exits with no other code getting run.

Q: Do indexed arrays always start their indexing with 0?

A: Yes and no. By default, all indexed arrays start at 0. However, you can override this behavior and set numeric keys to any number values you want, although inconventional. Unless there is a very good design decision for not using zero-based indexes, don't do it...it's unconventional behavior and could cause confusion.

Q: Does the data stored in an array always have to be the same type?

A: No, not at all. For the purposes of looping, it is important for array data to be of the same type because the whole idea is to loop through a set of similar data. For example, if you want to loop through an array of scores to calculate an average, it wouldn't make much sense for some of the array entries to be booleans—they should all be numbers in this case. So although arrays can contain values of different types, it's generally a good idea to store data of the same type in arrays, especially when you're storing a collection of like data.

Sharpen your pencil
Solution

Write code to create a `seats` array for Mandango, and then loop through the seats in the array, alerting the user to the availability of each seat.

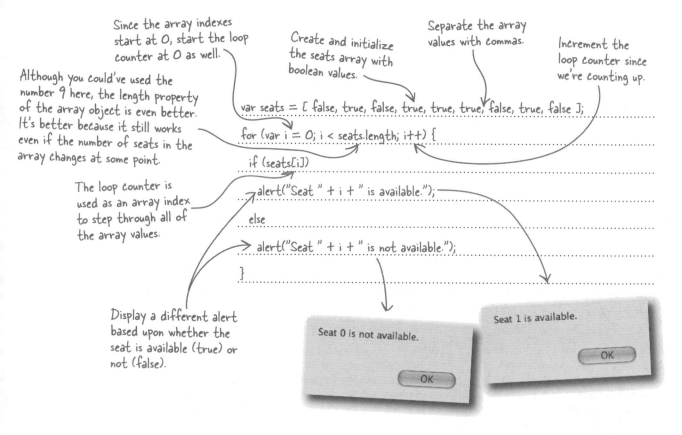

Since the array indexes start at 0, start the loop counter at 0 as well.

Create and initialize the seats array with boolean values.

Separate the array values with commas.

Increment the loop counter since we're counting up.

Although you could've used the number 9 here, the length property of the array object is even better. It's better because it still works even if the number of seats in the array changes at some point.

```
var seats = [ false, true, false, true, true, true, false, true, false ];
for (var i = 0; i < seats.length; i++) {
    if (seats[i])
        alert("Seat " + i + " is available.");
    else
        alert("Seat " + i + " is not available.");
}
```

The loop counter is used as an array index to step through all of the array values.

Display a different alert based upon whether the seat is available (true) or not (false).

Seat 0 is not available.

OK

Seat 1 is available.

OK

BULLET POINTS

- `for` loops repeat a piece of JavaScript code a **specific number of times**.

- The increment (++) and decrement (--) operators provide a handy way to update loop counters.

- An array allows you to store multiple pieces of data in a **single place**.

- Although an array holds multiple pieces of information, it has a single variable name.

- Indexed arrays are accessed using numeric keys called **indexes**.

- Indexed arrays work great with loops because they allow you to use a loop counter to loop through array data.

From JavaScript to HTML

Mandango seat availability is represented by an array of booleans. So the next step is translating this array into HTML images (which are available at *http://www.headfirstlabs.com/books/hfjs/*) that reflect the seat availability on the Mandango web page.

```
var seats = [ false, true, false, true, true, true, false, true, false ];
```

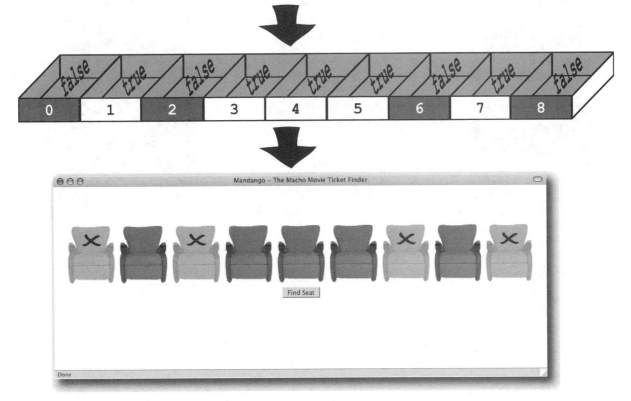

Although this looks nice, there isn't actually any code to map the array of booleans to visual seat images on the web page. Now this is a problem.

> How could you make the connection between the JavaScript seat availability array and the seat images on the Mandango page?

Visualizing Mandango seats

To tie the JavaScript array to the HTML images, first make sure the images are laid out in an accessible way, then determine what images are going to be used to represent the different seat states. Let's tackle the last task first.

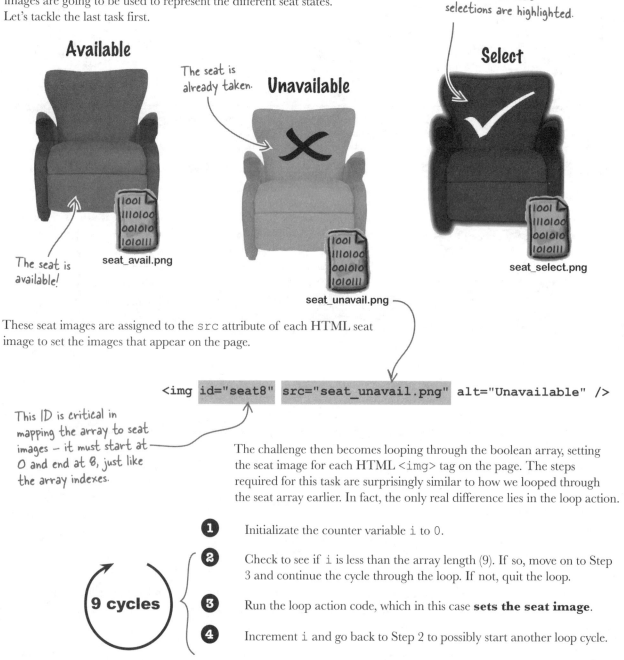

This seat image applies to the Mandango seat search, when seat selections are highlighted.

Available

The seat is available!

seat_avail.png

The seat is already taken.

Unavailable

seat_unavail.png

Select

seat_select.png

These seat images are assigned to the src attribute of each HTML seat image to set the images that appear on the page.

```
<img id="seat8" src="seat_unavail.png" alt="Unavailable" />
```

This ID is critical in mapping the array to seat images — it must start at 0 and end at 8, just like the array indexes.

The challenge then becomes looping through the boolean array, setting the seat image for each HTML <img> tag on the page. The steps required for this task are surprisingly similar to how we looped through the seat array earlier. In fact, the only real difference lies in the loop action.

1 Initialize the counter variable i to 0.

2 Check to see if i is less than the array length (9). If so, move on to Step 3 and continue the cycle through the loop. If not, quit the loop.

9 cycles

3 Run the loop action code, which in this case **sets the seat image**.

4 Increment i and go back to Step 2 to possibly start another loop cycle.

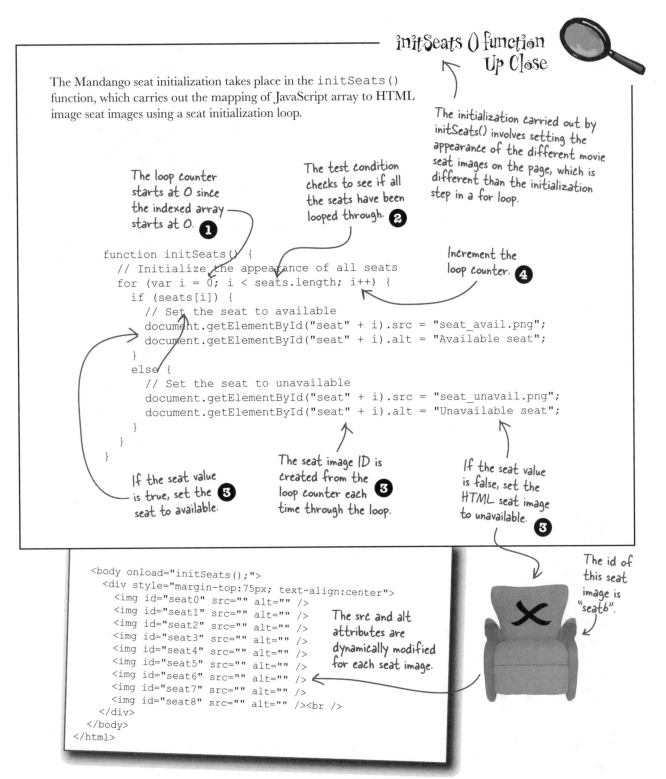

initSeats () function
Up Close

The Mandango seat initialization takes place in the initSeats() function, which carries out the mapping of JavaScript array to HTML image seat images using a seat initialization loop.

The initialization carried out by initSeats() involves setting the appearance of the different movie seat images on the page, which is different than the initialization step in a for loop.

The loop counter starts at 0 since the indexed array starts at 0. **1**

The test condition checks to see if all the seats have been looped through. **2**

Increment the loop counter. **4**

```
function initSeats() {
  // Initialize the appearance of all seats
  for (var i = 0; i < seats.length; i++) {
    if (seats[i]) {
      // Set the seat to available
      document.getElementById("seat" + i).src = "seat_avail.png";
      document.getElementById("seat" + i).alt = "Available seat";
    }
    else {
      // Set the seat to unavailable
      document.getElementById("seat" + i).src = "seat_unavail.png";
      document.getElementById("seat" + i).alt = "Unavailable seat";
    }
  }
}
```

If the seat value is true, set the seat to available. **3**

The seat image ID is created from the loop counter each time through the loop. **3**

If the seat value is false, set the HTML seat image to unavailable. **3**

The id of this seat image is "seat6".

```
<body onload="initSeats();">
  <div style="margin-top:75px; text-align:center">
    <img id="seat0" src="" alt="" />
    <img id="seat1" src="" alt="" />
    <img id="seat2" src="" alt="" />
    <img id="seat3" src="" alt="" />
    <img id="seat4" src="" alt="" />
    <img id="seat5" src="" alt="" />
    <img id="seat6" src="" alt="" />
    <img id="seat7" src="" alt="" />
    <img id="seat8" src="" alt="" /><br />
  </div>
</body>
</html>
```

The src and alt attributes are dynamically modified for each seat image.

Not so macho seat searching

With the seats initialized, it's now possible to move on to the seat searching, which is really the point of Mandango. Seth and Jason have determined that it might be better to first get the script finding individual seats before embarking on the eventual three-seat search. This simplifies the immediate task, allowing them to build the application incrementally.

Since they want to search for a single available seat, the first thing the script is going to need is a variable to keep track of the seat selection.

Global variable, which means it is accessible throughout the script.

selSeat

This variable stores the seat selection, and needs to hang around for the life of the script, which means it must be a global variable. So, the `findSeat()` function, which handles the job of finding a seat for the user, will rely on the `selSeat` variable for storing the index of the selected seat.

> The selSeat variable makes sense, but what value indicates an unselected seat?

Seth brings up a good question. The `selSeat` variable stores the seat selection, which is in the range 0 to 8 when a seat has been selected. But you also need to know when a user **hasn't** chosen any seats yet. A special value can indicate this state of **unselection**, which can be noted as -1 (no seats selected yet). So `selSeat` really needs to start out initialized to -1.

The selSeat variable is now initialized to –1 so that the script starts off with no seat selection.

```
var selSeat = -1;
```

With the seat selection variable in place, we're ready to assemble the `findSeat()` function. `findSeat()` will search through each seat in the seats array, find available seats, and then prompt the user to accept or reject each available seat. While it's true that macho guys won't be happy with this initial version of Mandango, it's a step in the right direction!

JavaScript Magnets

The Mandango `findSeat()` function is where the user searches for
an available seat, and then confirms or denies any seats that are found.
Help out Seth and Jason by finishing the missing code with the magnets.

```
function findSeat() {
  // If seat is already selected, reinitialize all seats to clear them

  if (................>= 0) {

    ................ = -1;

    ...................... ();
  }

  // Search through all the seats for availability
  for (var i = 0; i < seats.length; i++) {
    // See if the current seat is available

    if (.....................) {
      // Set the seat selection and update the appearance of the seat

      ................ = i;

      document.getElementById("seat" + i)............. = "seat_select.png";

      document.getElementById("seat" + i)............. = "Your seat";

      // Prompt the user to accept the seat

      var ............... = confirm("Seat " + (i + 1) + " is available. Accept?");

      if (................ ) {
        // The user rejected the seat, so clear the seat selection and keep looking

        .................. = -1;

        document.getElementById("seat" + i)............= "seat_avail.png";

        document.getElementById("seat" + i)............= "Available seat";
      }
    }
  }
}
```

```
initSeats   alt   accept   selSeat   src   seats[i]   !accept
```

JavaScript Magnets Solution

The Mandango `findSeat()` function is where the user searches for an available seat, and then confirms or denies any seats that are found. Help out Seth and Jason by finishing the missing code with the magnets.

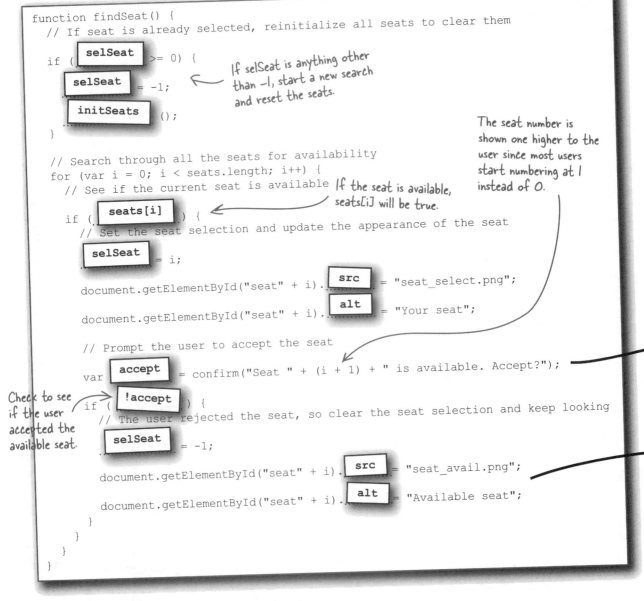

```
function findSeat() {
  // If seat is already selected, reinitialize all seats to clear them
  if (  selSeat  >= 0) {
       selSeat  = -1;
       initSeats ();
  }

  // Search through all the seats for availability
  for (var i = 0; i < seats.length; i++) {
    // See if the current seat is available
    if (  seats[i]  ) {
      // Set the seat selection and update the appearance of the seat
         selSeat  = i;
      document.getElementById("seat" + i). src  = "seat_select.png";
      document.getElementById("seat" + i). alt  = "Your seat";

      // Prompt the user to accept the seat
      var  accept  = confirm("Seat " + (i + 1) + " is available. Accept?");
      if (  !accept  ) {
        // The user rejected the seat, so clear the seat selection and keep looking
           selSeat  = -1;
        document.getElementById("seat" + i). src  = "seat_avail.png";
        document.getElementById("seat" + i). alt  = "Available seat";
      }
    }
  }
}
```

If selSeat is anything other than –1, start a new search and reset the seats.

If the seat is available, seats[i] will be true.

The seat number is shown one higher to the user since most users start numbering at 1 instead of 0.

Check to see if the user accepted the available seat.

Test drive: the solo seat finder

The solo seat searching version of Mandango uses a `for` loop and
an array to allow the user to search for individual available seats.
Not very macho, but functional nonetheless...

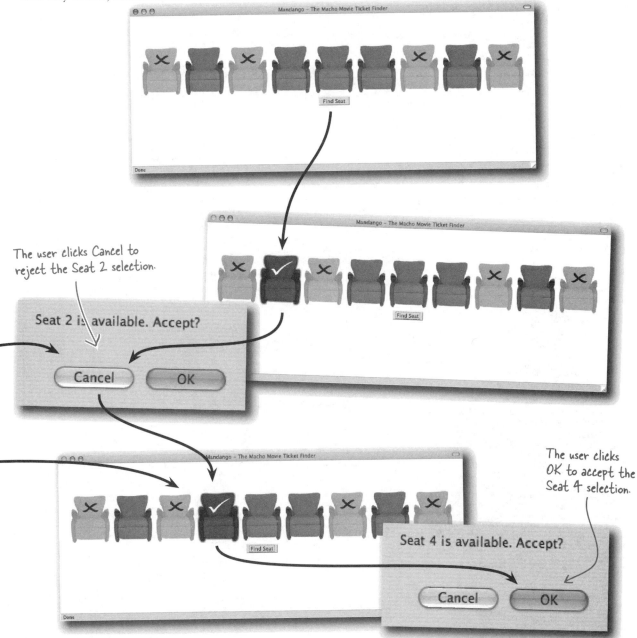

The user clicks Cancel to
reject the Seat 2 selection.

Seat 2 is available. Accept?

The user clicks
OK to accept the
Seat 4 selection.

Seat 4 is available. Accept?

Too much of a good thing: endless loops

Although the Mandango single-seat search technically works at finding an individual seat that is available, there's a problem in that the loop doesn't know when to stop. Even after the user accepts a seat by clicking OK, the script keeps on looping through the remaining available seats.

Seat 4 has already been accepted but Mandango keeps on looking for more seats anyway.

Ohhh, that's not good. Kinda defeats the whole point if you have to search through every seat anyway.

... a few clicks later...

Loops always need an exit condition (or two!)

Since the overzealous seat searching seems to be caused by the loop never ending, Jason thinks a closer look at the `for` loop in the `findSeat()` function is in order.

> The confirm() function prompts the user to answer a yes/no question, returning true (yes) or false (no).

```
for (var i = 0; i < seats.length; i++) {
    // See if the current seat is available
    if (seats[i]) {
        // Set the seat selection and update the appearance of the seat
        selSeat = i;
        document.getElementById("seat" + i).src = "seat_select.png";
        document.getElementById("seat" + i).alt = "Your seat";

        // Prompt the user to accept the seat
        var accept = confirm("Seat " + (i + 1) + " is available. Accept?");
        if (!accept) {
            // The user rejected the seat, so clear the seat selection and keep looking
            selSeat = -1;
            document.getElementById("seat" + i).src = "seat_avail.png";
            document.getElementById("seat" + i).alt = "Available seat";
        }
    }
}
```

?

If the user accepts an available seat, nothing happens and the loop just keeps on trucking.

This is the code that runs when the user does NOT accept an available seat.

So when the user clicks Cancel to reject a seat, the `selSeat` variable is set to -1 (no selection), and the loop continues. However, there's no code at all for when the user accepts a seat. This is good since it allows the `selSeat` variable to remember the current seat, but there's nothing stopping the loop from continuing looking for seats.

BRAIN POWER

What needs to happen when the user clicks the OK button to accept the current seat?

A "break" in the action

The problem with the Mandango code is that you need to bail out of the loop once the user accepts a seat. One possible fix is to trick the `for` loop by setting the counter to a value larger than the length of the array.

```
i = seats.length + 1;
```

This ends the loop by forcing the test condition to fail... but there's a better way to force loops to end.

Although this code is a clever little hack that gets this done, there's a better way that doesn't involve monkeying around with the loop counter to trick the loop condition. The `break` statement is designed specifically for breaking out of a section of code, including loop code.

```
break;
```

Immediately exit a loop, do not pass Go, do not collect $200.

When a loop encounters the `break` statement, the loop immediately ends, ignoring the test condition completely. So the `break` statement provides you with a handy way to immediately exit a loop, no questions asked.

Closely related to `break` is the `continue` statement, which bails out of the current loop cycle but doesn't exit the loop itself. In other words, you can use `continue` to force the loop to jump to the next cycle.

Jump out of the current loop cycle, continuing with the next one.

```
continue;
```

Both `break` and `continue` are extremely useful in fine-tuning the control of loops, but `break` offers a solution to Seth and Jason's immediate Mandango looping problem.

I'm digging the break statement. It'll get rid of all that unnecessary looping.

there are no
there are no
Dumb Questions

Q: **Does the remaining action code in a** `for` **loop finish the current cycle when the** `break` **statement is used?**

A: No. The `break` statement forces an immediate end to the loop, completely short-circuiting the normal flow of the loop.

Q: **Why is tinkering with the loop counter to force a loop exit a bad thing?**

A: Because you're not really using the loop counter for what it was intended, and therefore run the risk of introducing unusual bugs. Instead of counting through the array elements as expected, you're forcing the counter to an artificial value beyond the range of the array just to end the loop. In general, you want to be able to trust that the update part of the loop is the only place where the loop counter gets changed. There are always special cases that arise where tricks are allowed, but this isn't one of them—the `break` statement handles breaking out of the loop admirably and without any confusion as to what's going on.

Sharpen your pencil

The `for` loop in the `findSeat()` function of Mandango needs some help breaking out when the user accepts a seat. Write the missing lines of code that handle breaking out of the loop, making sure to include a comment to explain how the code works.

```
// Search through all the seats for availability
for (var i = 0; i < seats.length; i++) {
  // See if the current seat is available
  if (seats[i]) {
    // Set the seat selection and update the appearance of the seat
    selSeat = i;
    document.getElementById("seat" + i).src = "seat_select.png";
    document.getElementById("seat" + i).alt = "Your seat";

    // Prompt the user to accept the seat
    var accept = confirm("Seat " + (i + 1) + " is available. Accept?");

    ...................................................................................................

    ...................................................................................................

    ...................................................................................................

    ...................................................................................................

    else {
      // The user rejected the seat, so clear the seat selection and keep looking
      selSeat = -1;
      document.getElementById("seat" + i).src = "seat_avail.png";
      document.getElementById("seat" + i).alt = "Available seat";
    }
  }
}
```

Sharpen your pencil
Solution

The `for` loop in the `findSeat()` function of Mandango needs some help breaking out when the user accepts a seat. Write the missing lines of code that handle breaking out of the loop, making sure to include a comment to explain how the code works.

```
// Search through all the seats for availability
for (var i = 0; i < seats.length; i++) {
  // See if the current seat is available
  if (seats[i]) {
    // Set the seat selection and update the appearance of the seat
    selSeat = i;
    document.getElementById("seat" + i).src = "seat_select.png";
    document.getElementById("seat" + i).alt = "Your seat";

    // Prompt the user to accept the seat
    var accept = confirm("Seat " + (i + 1) + " is available. Accept?");
    if (accept) {
      // The user accepted the seat, so we're done
      break;
    }
    else {
      // The user rejected the seat, so clear the seat selection and keep looking
      selSeat = -1;
      document.getElementById("seat" + i).src = "seat_avail.png";
      document.getElementById("seat" + i).alt = "Available seat";
    }
  }
}
```

Putting the 'man' in Mandango

The original intent of Mandango is to allow users to search for available movie seats in groups of three. With the single-seat search now working, Seth and Jason are ready to turn their attention to a truly macho movie seat search. They need a way to check for a series of three available seats.

Three available seats in a row... plenty of space!

All this movie talk just gets me thinking about popcorn... Oh, sorry. I think a few nested if statements could knock out the three-seat search with no problem. That's how I'd do it!

Code Up Close

A sequence of three seats is checked using nested if statements.

If three seats in a row are found, set the selection to the first one.

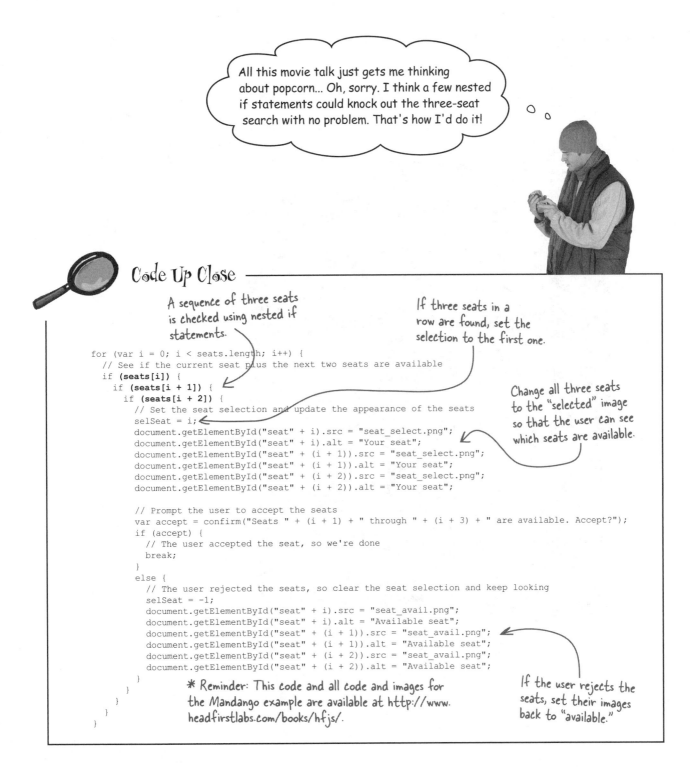

Change all three seats to the "selected" image so that the user can see which seats are available.

```
for (var i = 0; i < seats.length; i++) {
  // See if the current seat plus the next two seats are available
  if (seats[i]) {
    if (seats[i + 1]) {
      if (seats[i + 2]) {
        // Set the seat selection and update the appearance of the seats
        selSeat = i;
        document.getElementById("seat" + i).src = "seat_select.png";
        document.getElementById("seat" + i).alt = "Your seat";
        document.getElementById("seat" + (i + 1)).src = "seat_select.png";
        document.getElementById("seat" + (i + 1)).alt = "Your seat";
        document.getElementById("seat" + (i + 2)).src = "seat_select.png";
        document.getElementById("seat" + (i + 2)).alt = "Your seat";

        // Prompt the user to accept the seats
        var accept = confirm("Seats " + (i + 1) + " through " + (i + 3) + " are available. Accept?");
        if (accept) {
          // The user accepted the seat, so we're done
          break;
        }
        else {
          // The user rejected the seats, so clear the seat selection and keep looking
          selSeat = -1;
          document.getElementById("seat" + i).src = "seat_avail.png";
          document.getElementById("seat" + i).alt = "Available seat";
          document.getElementById("seat" + (i + 1)).src = "seat_avail.png";
          document.getElementById("seat" + (i + 1)).alt = "Available seat";
          document.getElementById("seat" + (i + 2)).src = "seat_avail.png";
          document.getElementById("seat" + (i + 2)).alt = "Available seat";
        }
      }
    }
  }
}
```

✱ Reminder: This code and all code and images for the Mandango example are available at http://www.headfirstlabs.com/books/hfjs/.

If the user rejects the seats, set their images back to "available."

A logical, elegant, well-designed solution with &&

There is a better way to handle the three-seat check in Mandango. The nested `if` version works but there's room for improvement, and the change primarily involves making the code more elegant.

> Elegant!? Are you kidding me? Oh man, that's a good one!

Despite Seth's objections, there are times when it's worth making changes to your code so that is more "elegant," which is another way of saying the code is clean, efficient, and easy to understand and maintain. In the case of the nested `if` statements, it would be more elegant to combine them all into a single `if` statement... but how?

The boolean AND operator compares two boolean values to see if they are both true.

```
if (seats[i] && seats[i + 1] && seats[i + 2]) {
    ...
}
```

true   true   true

The boolean AND operator (`&&`) compares two boolean values to see if they are both `true`. In this Mandango code, two AND operators are used together to see if the three seat values are all `true`. If so, you know you have a series of three available seats. Problem solved... and with a little touch of elegance!

Boolean operator logic uncovered

You've already seen several comparison operators, such as == and
<. Most of the comparison operators you've seen compare two
values and yield a boolean result. Boolean **logic** operators also yield
a boolean result, but they operate only on boolean values—they
perform boolean logical comparisons.

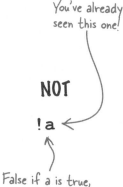

You've already seen this one!

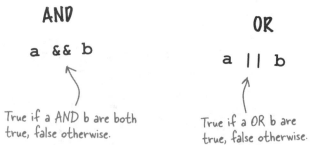

AND

`a && b`

True if a AND b are both true, false otherwise.

OR

`a || b`

True if a OR b are true, false otherwise.

NOT

`!a`

False if a is true, true if a is false.

Boolean logic operators can be combined with one another to
create more interesting logical comparisons, typically for the sake
of making complex decisions.

Parentheses allow you to group together boolean logic expressions.

```
if ((largeDrink && largePopcorn) || coupon)
    freeCandy();
```

You can get free candy by buying a combo OR by having a coupon.

In this example, an AND operator is used to check for a large
drink and large popcorn...combo! You get free candy with a
combo. Or, there is another path to the free candy thanks to the
OR operator—a coupon. So, you can get free candy by ordering
a large drink AND large popcorn, OR by presenting a coupon.
This kind of decision would be extremely difficult to carry out
without the help of boolean logic operators.

**Boolean logic operators
can be combined to carry
out complex decisions.**

there are no
Dumb Questions

Q: I still don't understand the difference between a normal boolean operator and a boolean logic operator. What is it?

A: Well, first off, they're all boolean operators, which means they always result in a boolean value when they're finished doing their thing. The only difference is the kind of data they operate on. Normal boolean operators work on all kinds of data since they carry out general comparisons such as "equal to," "not equal to," "greater than,"

etc. Boolean logic operators work only on boolean data, and therefore carry out logical comparisons such as AND, OR, and NOT. So boolean logic operators work solely on true/false information, while normal boolean operators work on all kinds of data.

Q: So, is the NOT operator a boolean logic operator?

A: Yes. It operates only on a boolean value, so it qualifies as a boolean logic operator. It's also a *unary* operator since it operates on only one piece of data.

Q: How do parentheses work with respect to boolean operators?

A: Parentheses allow you to alter the default order of evaluation of all operators, not just boolean operators. Grouping an operation inside parentheses forces that operation to take place before others around it. So, `largeDrink && largePopcorn` is forced to take place before the `||` operation in the free candy code because it appears within `()`.

Sharpen your pencil

It's the sixth pass through the Mandango `for` loop (`i = 5`), and your help is needed to determine if three consecutive seats are available by checking the seat availability and carrying out some boolean logic.

```
for (var i = 0; i < seats.length; i++) {

  // See if the current seat plus the next two seats are available

  if (seats[i] && seats[i + 1] && seats[i + 2]) {

    ...

  }

  ...

}
```

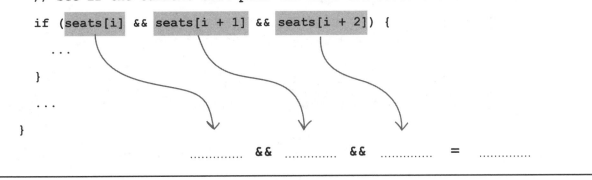

.... && .... && .... = ...

Sharpen your pencil Solution

It's the sixth pass through the Mandango `for` loop (i = 5), and your help is needed to determine if three consecutive seats are available by checking the seat availability and carrying out some boolean logic.

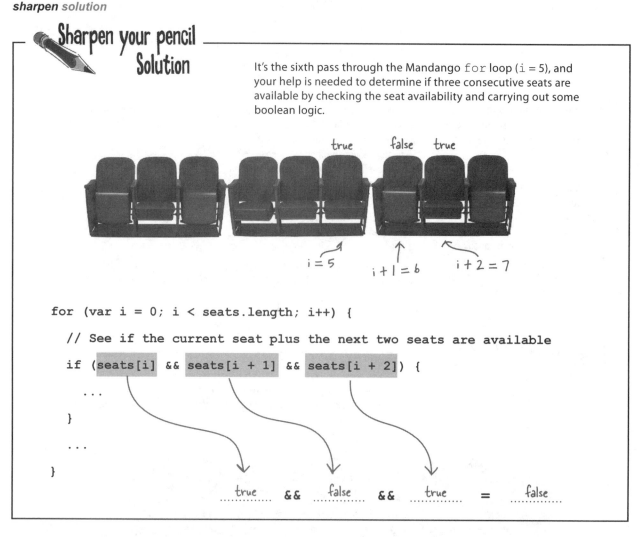

```
for (var i = 0; i < seats.length; i++) {

    // See if the current seat plus the next two seats are available

    if (seats[i] && seats[i + 1] && seats[i + 2]) {

        ...

    }

    ...

}
```

___true___ && ___false___ && ___true___ = ___false___

Finally, a manly seat finder

Now Mandango correctly searches for a sequence of three available seats, resulting in a movie ticket service that even the toughest of tough guys will appreciate.

The user is now prompted to accept a range of three seats.

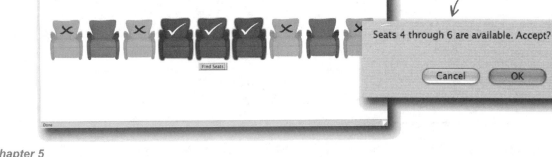

Back to the treasure map

With Mandango in good shape for the time being, we can return to the search for hidden treasure. Remember the treasure map?

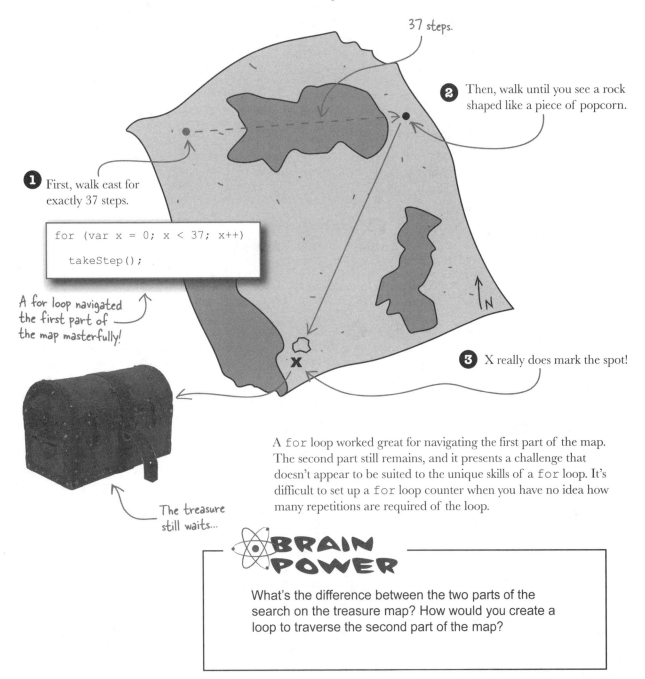

37 steps.

2 Then, walk until you see a rock shaped like a piece of popcorn.

1 First, walk east for exactly 37 steps.

```
for (var x = 0; x < 37; x++)
    takeStep();
```

A for loop navigated the first part of the map masterfully!

3 X really does mark the spot!

The treasure still waits...

A `for` loop worked great for navigating the first part of the map. The second part still remains, and it presents a challenge that doesn't appear to be suited to the unique skills of a `for` loop. It's difficult to set up a `for` loop counter when you have no idea how many repetitions are required of the loop.

BRAIN POWER

What's the difference between the two parts of the search on the treasure map? How would you create a loop to traverse the second part of the map?

Looping for just a "while"...until a condition is met

Although it's possible to create a `for` loop that walks the second part of the treasure map, there is a better option. Unlike the `for` loop, which is structured around the notion of a loop counter, the `while` loop is geared toward looping **while** a certain condition is met. And that condition doesn't necessarily have anything to do with a loop counter.

while loops let you <u>repeat</u> code while a certain condition is <u>true</u>.

A `while` loop consists of two different parts:

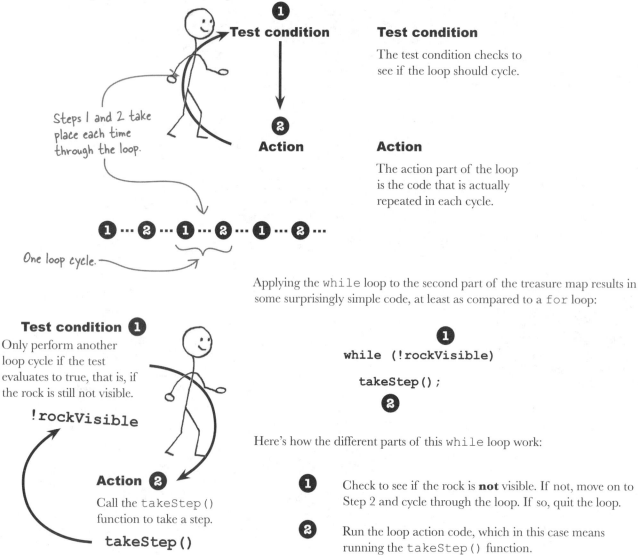

Test condition

The test condition checks to see if the loop should cycle.

Action

The action part of the loop is the code that is actually repeated in each cycle.

Steps 1 and 2 take place each time through the loop.

One loop cycle.

Applying the `while` loop to the second part of the treasure map results in some surprisingly simple code, at least as compared to a `for` loop:

Test condition ❶

Only perform another loop cycle if the test evaluates to true, that is, if the rock is still not visible.

`!rockVisible`

Action ❷

Call the `takeStep()` function to take a step.

`takeStep()`

```
❶
while (!rockVisible)
    takeStep();
❷
```

Here's how the different parts of this `while` loop work:

❶ Check to see if the rock is **not** visible. If not, move on to Step 2 and cycle through the loop. If so, quit the loop.

❷ Run the loop action code, which in this case means running the `takeStep()` function.

Breaking down the while loop

Much simpler in structure than `for` loops, `while` loops must still adhere to a predictable formula:

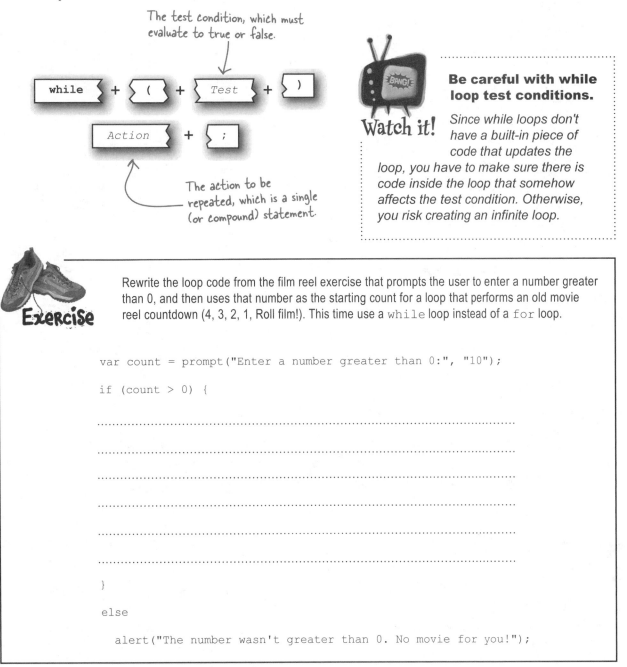

The test condition, which must evaluate to true or false.

```
while + ( + Test + )
```

```
Action + ;
```

The action to be repeated, which is a single (or compound) statement.

Watch it!

Be careful with while loop test conditions.

Since while loops don't have a built-in piece of code that updates the loop, you have to make sure there is code inside the loop that somehow affects the test condition. Otherwise, you risk creating an infinite loop.

Exercise

Rewrite the loop code from the film reel exercise that prompts the user to enter a number greater than 0, and then uses that number as the starting count for a loop that performs an old movie reel countdown (4, 3, 2, 1, Roll film!). This time use a `while` loop instead of a `for` loop.

```
var count = prompt("Enter a number greater than 0:", "10");

if (count > 0) {




    ...................................................................................

    ...................................................................................

    ...................................................................................

    ...................................................................................

    ...................................................................................

    ...................................................................................

}

else

    alert("The number wasn't greater than 0. No movie for you!");
```

Exercise Solution

Rewrite the loop code from an earlier exercise that prompts the user to enter a number greater than 0, and then uses that number as the starting count for a loop that performs an old movie reel countdown (4, 3, 2, 1, Roll film!). This time use a `while` loop instead of a `for` loop.

Store the number in the count variable.

Prompt the user to input a number.

Make sure the count is greater than 0.

```
var count = prompt("Enter a number greater than 0:", "10");

if (count > 0) {

    var x = count;

    while (x > 0) {

        alert("Starting in..." + x);

        x--;
    }

    alert("Roll film!");

}

else

    alert("The number wasn't greater than 0. No movie for you!");
```

Count down to 0.

There is still a counter, but it is created outside of the while loop.

Decrement the counter as part of the loop action, same as x=x–1.

The loop action is a compound statement.

Invalid data.

The count is finished!

The number wasn't greater than 0. No movie for you!

OK

Roll film!

OK

BULLET POINTS

- The `break` statement **immediately** breaks out of a loop, skipping any remaining loop code.

- Boolean logic operators allow you to create powerful true/false logic for making decisions.

- The `while` loop runs a piece of code **as long as** a certain test condition remains true.

- Avoid an infinite loop by making sure the test condition is somehow affected by code within the `while` loop.

Use the right loop for the job

The movie reel countdown exercise revealed that `for` loops and `while` loops are often capable of solving the same problems. In fact, any `for` loop can be reconstructed as a `while` loop using the following form:

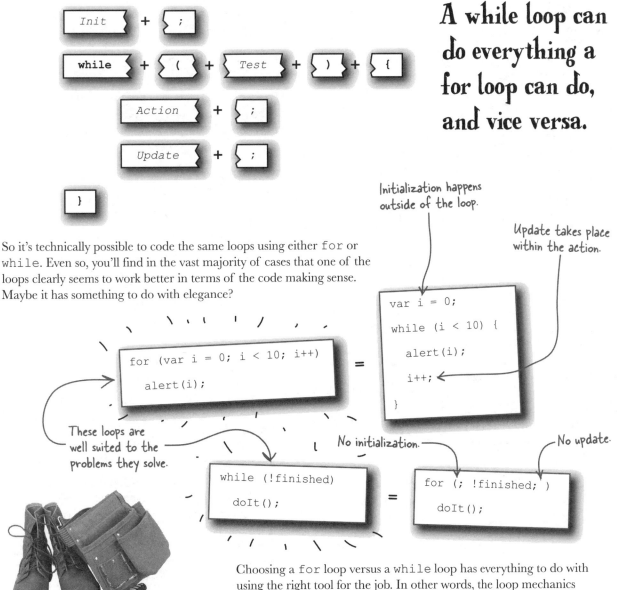

A while loop can do everything a for loop can do, and vice versa.

So it's technically possible to code the same loops using either `for` or `while`. Even so, you'll find in the vast majority of cases that one of the loops clearly seems to work better in terms of the code making sense. Maybe it has something to do with elegance?

Initialization happens outside of the loop.

Update takes place within the action.

```
var i = 0;
while (i < 10) {
    alert(i);
    i++;
}
```

```
for (var i = 0; i < 10; i++)
    alert(i);
```

These loops are well suited to the problems they solve.

No initialization.

No update.

```
while (!finished)
    doIt();
```

```
for ( ; !finished; )
    doIt();
```

Choosing a `for` loop versus a `while` loop has everything to do with using the right tool for the job. In other words, the loop mechanics should fit the problem at hand.

Fireside Chats

Tonight's talk: **For loop and While loop try really hard to repeat themselves**

For loop:	**While loop:**
Ah, here we are, just a couple of repetitive fellas hanging out together.	
	Yep. Although I have to say, I'm not that crazy about all the different steps involved in making you work. Seems kinda complicated to me.
I'm not complicated at all, I just add a little more structure for creating certain kinds of loops. When people want to loop using some kind of numeric counter, they find comfort in how easy I make it to initialize and update the counter that controls me.	
	That's true, but looping isn't all about counting, you know. There are all kinds of cool loops that don't even involve numbers. Sometimes you just need the simplicity of saying, "Hey, just keep doing this for a while." That's my kind of loop.
Sounds kinda vague to me, although I suppose it could work. I like to be more exacting, you know, keep close tabs on what makes me tick. That's why I make a special effort to initialize myself before I even start looping. I also keep myself updated at the end of each loop, just to make sure I keep running as expected. Guess I'm a little compulsive about making sure I repeat like clockwork.	
	While I applaud your work ethic, you do realize that it's every bit as possible to loop reliably and predictably without all that formal initializating and updating stuff? Besides, I often repeat code in situations where there isn't a need to initialize anything, and the updating takes place right there in the action code. So I'm content to do without the formality and just focus on the looping.
I am aware that there are lot of different ways to structure loops. I just like to run a tight ship.	

For loop:

That's true. The good news is that we both get the job done in our own way. And I can even see where my style is a bit much for a loop with simple logic controls.

You can say that again!

No problem at all, I understand. Thanks for the chat.

While loop:

I suppose it really just comes down to style, and each loop has its own. You like to keep all the loop controls in their place, while I'm a little more casual about how I'm controlled.

Now you're talking! I think there's room in this town for both of us after all.

I think there's room in this town... oh, I suppose instincts kicked in there for a moment. Sorry.

---

there are no Dumb Questions

Q: The `while` loop looks pretty simple. Am I missing something?

A: Not at all. Just keep in mind that simple doesn't necessarily mean weak or limited. In other words, you may be surprised by how powerful `while` loops can be. Sure, the `while` loop consists solely of a test condition and a piece of action code, but that's often all you need to do some really slick looping. Especially when you consider that the test condition can be made more interesting thanks to boolean logic operators. Not only that, but the action part of the `while` loop can contain as much code as you want if you use a compound statement.

Q: What happens if I created a while loop that started off `while (true)`..., will it work?

A: Yes, it will...perhaps too well. The problem is that you've just created an infinite loop because the test condition is permanently `true`. A `while` loop continues looping until the test condition evaluates to `false`, and in this case that time never comes. It's scary to think about how many infinite loops are running right this moment as you read this, destined to repeat themselves for ever and ever... and ever... and ever... hey, break out of it!

Q: Is it possible for the loop action code (the code in the parentheses) to never get called?

A: Yes. Both `for` loops and `while` loops require their test conditions to be `true` before initially running the action code. So, if for some reason the test condition fails at the get-go, the action code won't run and the loop exits before ever starting.

Q: Can loops be nested inside each other?

A: Oh yeah! Nested loops allow more than one level of repetition. This sounds strange right now, but it's quite cool. We explore nested loops later when Mandango grows to search an entire theater!

Treasure at the end of the loop

By using a `for` loop followed up by a `while` loop, the treasure map can be fully traversed, leading to the treasure at the spot marked X.

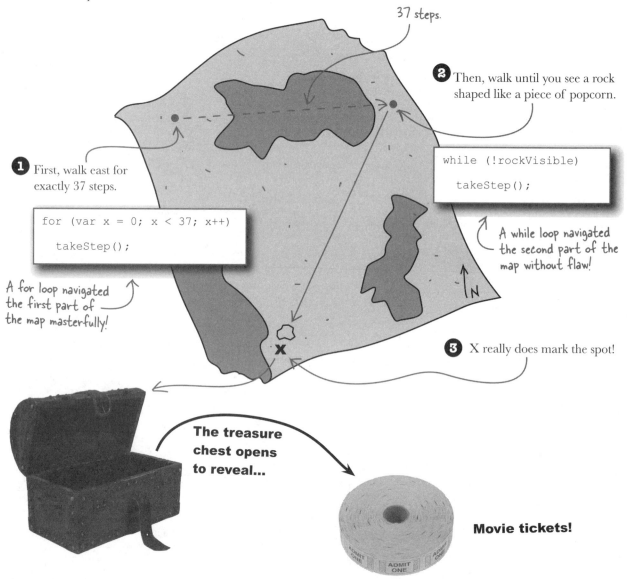

37 steps.

❷ Then, walk until you see a rock shaped like a piece of popcorn.

```
while (!rockVisible)
    takeStep();
```

A while loop navigated the second part of the map without flaw!

❶ First, walk east for exactly 37 steps.

```
for (var x = 0; x < 37; x++)
    takeStep();
```

A for loop navigated the first part of the map masterfully!

N

❸ X really does mark the spot!

The treasure chest opens to reveal...

Movie tickets!

Could this be a sign? Your newfound `while` looping knowledge and movie tickets can only lead back to one thing... Mandango!

Sharpen your pencil

Rewrite the loop in the Mandango `findSeats()` function so that it uses a `while` loop instead of a `for` loop. Add a new loop control variable, `finished`, that is used as a means of exiting the loop through the test condition, as opposed to using `break`.

```
...............................................................................

...............................................................................

...............................................................................

// See if the current seat plus the next two seats are available
if (seats[i] && seats[i + 1] && seats[i + 2]) {
  // Set the seat selection and update the appearance of the seats
  ...

  // Prompt the user to accept the seats
  var accept = confirm("Seats " + (i + 1) + " through " + (i + 3) +
    " are available. Accept?");

  .............................................................................

  .............................................................................

  .............................................................................

  .............................................................................

  else {
    // The user rejected the seats, so clear the seat selection and keep looking
    ...
  }
}

// Increment the loop counter

.............................................................................

}
```

Sharpen your pencil
Solution

Rewrite the loop in the Mandango `findSeats()` function so that it uses a `while` loop instead of a `for` loop. Add a new loop control variable, `finished`, that is used as a means of exiting the loop through the test condition, as opposed to using `break`.

Initialize the loop counter and the "finished" variable.

Loop as long as the loop counter is less than the number of seats AND "finished" isn't true.

This loop is somewhat of a hybrid of what we've seen so far in that it is dependent on both a count and a boolean logic expression. It's usually simpler to code hybrid loops using while.

```
var i = 0, finished = false;
while ((i < seats.length) && !finished) {
  // See if the current seat plus the next two seats are available
  if (seats[i] && seats[i + 1] && seats[i + 2]) {
    // Set the seat selection and update the appearance of the seats

    ...

    // Prompt the user to accept the seats
    var accept = confirm("Seats " + (i + 1) + " through " + (i + 3) +
      " are available. Accept?");

    if (accept) {
      // The user accepted the seats, so we're done
      finished = true;
    }
    else {
      // The user rejected the seats, so clear the seat selection and keep looking
      ...
    }
  }

  // Increment the loop counter
  i++;
}
```

Increment the loop counter.

Set "finished" to true to bail out of the loop. Since this affects the test condition, there's no need to break here.

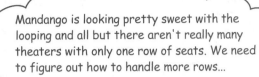

Mandango is looking pretty sweet with the looping and all but there aren't really many theaters with only one row of seats. We need to figure out how to handle more rows...

Movie seat data modeling

Jason's right. Mandango really needs to be able to handle more rows of seats in order to truly be functional. Thus far the single row of seats has made sense because it cleanly maps to an array of booleans representing the seat availability. To expand the idea to multiple rows of seats requires expanding the array, and that requires another dimension. That's right, we're talking about a two-dimensional array!

This movie theater has four rows of seats with nine seats in each row. Yeah, it's cozy!

We need an array that is 9 x 4 in size to match up with the actual seats, which are four rows with nine seats in each.

Each item in the 2-D array is still a boolean.

Now there is another dimension of array indexes.

	false	true	false	true	true	true	false	true	false
0	0	1	2	3	4	5	6	7	8
1	0	1	2	3	4	5	6	7	8
2	0	1	2	3	4	5	6	7	8
3	0	1	2	3	4	5	6	7	8

An array of an array: two-dimensional arrays

You don't need any special glasses or anything to create a two-dimensional array. In fact, creating a two-dimensional array is similar to creating a normal (one-dimensional) array except that you create multiple sub-arrays as elements of the array. These sub-arrays are what add the second dimension, resulting in a **table** of data that has rows and columns.

Then create sub-arrays to serve as elements in the outer array. That's two dimensions!

First create an array to house the sub-arrays. That's one dimension!

```
var seats = new Array(new Array(9), new Array(9), new Array(9), new Array(9));
```

Four sub-arrays result in four rows of array data.

In the case of Mandango, we already know the initial values of the array elements, so it makes sense to use a **different** approach to create the 2-D array, one that involves an array literal. This **creates** the array and **initializes** it at the same time—a win-win situation!

Double brackets indicate a 2-D array.

```
var seats = [[ false, true, false, true, true, true, false, true, false ],
   [ false, true, false, false, true, false, true, true, true ],
   [ true, true, true, true, true, true, false, true, false ],
   [ true, true, true, false, true, false, false, true, false ]];
```

The first list of boolean values is the first row of the 2-D array.

Each sub-array has its own array index, in this case between 0 and 3.

False – the seat is already taken.

True – the seat is available.

Two keys to access 2-D array data

Accessing data in a 2-D array is no different than accessing a 1-D array except you have to provide an additional piece of information: the index of the extra array. More specifically, you specify the indexes of the **row** and the **column** where the data sits in the array. For example, to grab the value of the fourth seat in the second row of seats, use this code:

The index of the second row in the array is 1 (starts at 0).

```
alert(seats[1][3]);
```

The index of the fourth element in a row is 3 (starts at 0).

Two-dimensional arrays allow you to store <u>tabular</u> <u>data</u>.

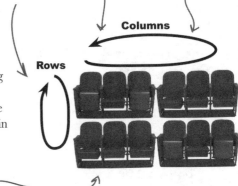

Two dimensions.

One dimension.

Columns

Rows

Looping through an array with more than one dimension involves nesting a loop for each dimension. So, looping through a 2-D array involves a total of two loops, one inside the other. The outer loop cycles through the rows of array data, while the inner loop cycles through the columns within a row.

Nested loops allow you to iterate through two dimensions of data.

Sharpen your pencil

Write code to loop through the seats in the 2-D seats array, alerting the user to the availability of each seat.

....

....

....

....

....

....

....

....

Sharpen your pencil
Solution

Write code to loop through the seats in the 2-D `seats` array, alerting the user to the availability of each seat.

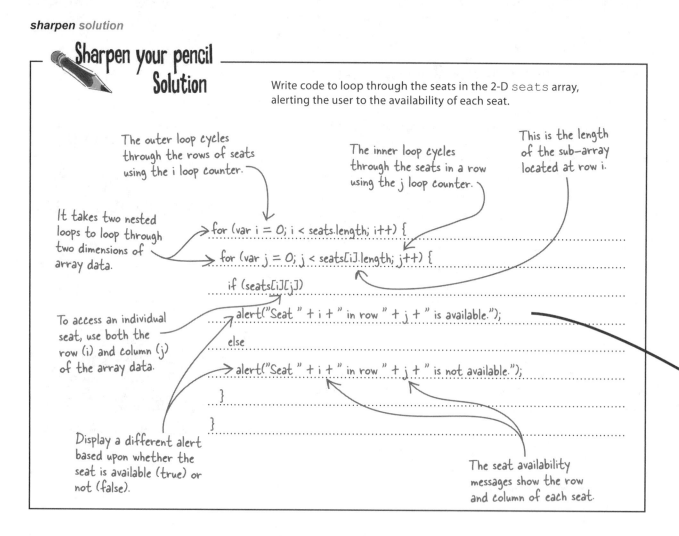

The outer loop cycles through the rows of seats using the i loop counter.

The inner loop cycles through the seats in a row using the j loop counter.

This is the length of the sub-array located at row i.

It takes two nested loops to loop through two dimensions of array data.

```
for (var i = 0; i < seats.length; i++) {
    for (var j = 0; j < seats[i].length; j++) {
        if (seats[i][j])
            alert("Seat " + i + " in row " + j + " is available.");
        else
            alert("Seat " + i + " in row " + j + " is not available.");
    }
}
```

To access an individual seat, use both the row (i) and column (j) of the array data.

Display a different alert based upon whether the seat is available (true) or not (false).

The seat availability messages show the row and column of each seat.

---

there are no Dumb Questions

Q: Can arrays be more than 2-D?

A: Yes, although at some point it can get tricky to visualize the data. Three dimensions can be handy for modeling real-world data such as the x-y-z coordinate of a point in space. Beyond that, additional dimensions are probably relegated to very isolated situations. When adding another dimension, just think in terms of replacing individual array elements with sub-arrays.

Q: Can I add additional data to an array later if I initialize it with data upon creation?

A: Absolutely. You're always free to add more data to an array by assigning new data to an unused array element. In the Mandango example, you could add another row of seats by adding a new sub-array as a fifth row (at index 4 in the array). Just assign the sub-array to `seats[4]`. You can also call the `push()` method of the `Array` object to add a new item to the end of an array.

Q: Do 2-D arrays have to contain the same number of rows?

A: No, not exactly. Just keep in mind that if the rows don't contain the same number of elements, you're setting up a recipe for looping disaster because nested loops are typically designed to cycle through a consistent sub-array length. So, yes, it's possible to vary the length of 2-D array rows, but it's a risky proposition that's safer to avoid.

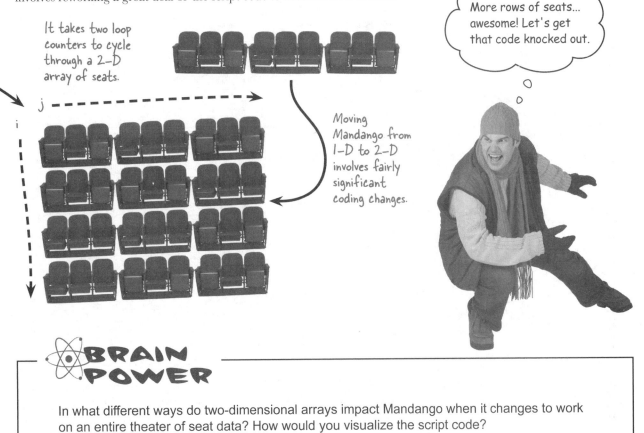

BULLET POINTS

- Two-dimensional arrays allow you to store rows and columns of data in **tabular** structures.

- When accessing an individual piece of data in a 2-D array, you must specify both the **row and column** of the index.

- **Nested loops** can be used to iterate through the data in a 2-D array.

- Just like normal arrays, 2-D arrays can be created and initialized from array object literals

Mandango in 2-D

Although you've already worked through pieces and parts of the code, moving Mandango from a single row of seats to a full theater of seats involves reworking a great deal of the script code to account for 2-D data.

It takes two loop counters to cycle through a 2-D array of seats.

More rows of seats... awesome! Let's get that code knocked out.

Moving Mandango from 1-D to 2-D involves fairly significant coding changes.

BRAIN POWER

In what different ways do two-dimensional arrays impact Mandango when it changes to work on an entire theater of seat data? How would you visualize the script code?

2-D Mandango Up Close

No need to visualize... here's the complete code for 2-D Mandango! →

```html
<html>
  <head>
    <title>Mandango - The Macho Movie Ticket Finder</title>

    <script type="text/javascript">
      var seats = [[ false, true, false, true, true, true, false, true, false ],
                   [ false, true, false, false, true, false, true, true, true ],
                   [ true, true, true, true, true, true, false, true, false ],
                   [ true, true, true, false, true, false, false, true, false ]];
      var selSeat = -1;

      function initSeats() {
        // Initialize the appearance of all seats
        for (var i = 0; i < seats.length; i++) {
          for (var j = 0; j < seats[i].length; j++) {
            if (seats[i][j]) {
              // Set the seat to available
              document.getElementById("seat" + (i * seats[i].length + j)).src = "seat_avail.png";
              document.getElementById("seat" + (i * seats[i].length + j)).alt = "Available seat";
            }
            else {
              // Set the seat to unavailable
              document.getElementById("seat" + (i * seats[i].length + j)).src = "seat_unavail.png";
              document.getElementById("seat" + (i * seats[i].length + j)).alt = "Unavailable seat";
            }
          }
        }
      }

      function findSeats() {
        // If seats are already selected, reinitialize all seats to clear them
        if (selSeat >= 0) {
          selSeat = -1;
          initSeats();
        }

        // Search through all the seats for availability
        var i = 0, finished = false;
        while (i < seats.length && !finished) {
          for (var j = 0; j < seats[i].length; j++) {
            // See if the current seat plus the next two seats are available
            if (seats[i][j] && seats[i][j + 1] && seats[i][j + 2]) {
              // Set the seat selection and update the appearance of the seats
              selSeat = i * seats[i].length + j;
              document.getElementById("seat" + (i * seats[i].length + j)).src = "seat_select.png";
              document.getElementById("seat" + (i * seats[i].length + j)).alt = "Your seat";
              document.getElementById("seat" + (i * seats[i].length + j + 1)).src = "seat_select.png";
              document.getElementById("seat" + (i * seats[i].length + j + 1)).alt = "Your seat";
              document.getElementById("seat" + (i * seats[i].length + j + 2)).src = "seat_select.png";
              document.getElementById("seat" + (i * seats[i].length + j + 2)).alt = "Your seat";

              // Prompt the user to accept the seats
              var accept = confirm("Seats " + (j + 1) + " through " + (j + 3) +
                " in Row " + (i + 1) + " are available. Accept?");
              if (accept) {
                // The user accepted the seats, so we're done (break out of the inner loop)
                finished = true;
                break;
              }
              else {
```

mandango.html

The 2-D array of boolean seat availability variables is created.

Reinitialize the seats if the user is starting a new search for seats by clicking the Find Seats button again.

Taking advantage of the best of both worlds, a while loop is used to cycle through the rows, while a for loop cycles through individual seats in a row.

```
            // The user rejected the seats, so clear the seat selection and keep looking
            selSeat = -1;
            document.getElementById("seat" + (i * seats[i].length + j)).src = "seat_avail.png";
            document.getElementById("seat" + (i * seats[i].length + j)).alt = "Available seat";
            document.getElementById("seat" + (i * seats[i].length + j + 1)).src = "seat_avail.png";
            document.getElementById("seat" + (i * seats[i].length + j + 1)).alt = "Available seat";
            document.getElementById("seat" + (i * seats[i].length + j + 2)).src = "seat_avail.png";
            document.getElementById("seat" + (i * seats[i].length + j + 2)).alt = "Available seat";
          }
        }
      }

      // Increment the outer loop counter
      i++;
    }
  }
  </script>
</head>
```

The row and column loop counters are required to change the seat images and alternate text.

The initSeats() function is called when the page first loads.

```
<body onload="initSeats();">
  <<div style="margin-top:25px; text-align:center">
    <img id="seat0" src="" alt="" />
    <img id="seat1" src="" alt="" />
    <img id="seat2" src="" alt="" />
    <img id="seat3" src="" alt="" />
    <img id="seat4" src="" alt="" />
    <img id="seat5" src="" alt="" />
    <img id="seat6" src="" alt="" />
    <img id="seat7" src="" alt="" />
    <img id="seat8" src="" alt="" /><br />
    <img id="seat9" src="" alt="" />
    <img id="seat10" src="" alt="" />
    <img id="seat11" src="" alt="" />
    <img id="seat12" src="" alt="" />
    <img id="seat13" src="" alt="" />
    <img id="seat14" src=" alt="" />
    <img id="seat15" src="" alt="" />
    <img id="seat16" src="" alt="" />
    <img id="seat17" src="" alt="" /><br />
    <img id="seat18" src="" alt="" />
    <img id="seat19" src="" alt="" />
    <img id="seat20" src="" alt="" />
    <img id="seat21" src="" alt="" />
    <img id="seat22" src="" alt="" />
    <img id="seat23" src="" alt="" />
    <img id="seat24" src="" alt="" />
    <img id="seat25" src="" alt="" />
    <img id="seat26" src="" alt="" /><br />
    <img id="seat27" src="" alt="" />
    <img id="seat28" src="" alt="" />
    <img id="seat29" src="" alt="" />
    <img id="seat30" src="" alt="" />
    <img id="seat31" src="" alt="" />
    <img id="seat32" src="" alt="" />
    <img id="seat33" src="" alt="" />
    <img id="seat34" src="" alt="" />
    <img id="seat35" src="" alt="" /><br />
    <input type="button" id="findseats" value="Find Seats" onclick="findSeats();" />
  </div>
  </body>
</html>
```

Four rows with nine seats each require 36 HTML images... yikes!

Don't be intimidated by the sheer size of this code.

It's using the same 2-D array techniques but now it's folded into the context of Mandango, with all of the HTML code and images (which is all available for download at *http://www.headfirstlabs.com/books/hfjs/*).

The findSeats() function is called when the user clicks the Find Seats button.

An entire theater of manly seats

With two dimensions to work with, Seth and Jason are able to take Mandango to the next level and support theater-wide seat searching... with a macho twist! The guys are stoked.

We never have to sit together again!

Wicked!

Mandango now offers manly moviegoers a choice of three seats in a row within a theater of options.

 # JavaScriptcross

All this talk about seats probably has you itching to go see a movie. Before you leave, do a little mental stretch and take a stab at this crossword puzzle.

Across

2. This kind of loop keeps on running code as long as a test condition is true.

4. Use this statement to jump out of the current loop cycle but continue looping.

8. If a is true or b is true, then a .. b is true; otherwise a .. b is false.

9. A type of data that lets you store multiple pieces of data in a single variable.

10. The part of a loop that contains the code to run repetitively.

11. The part of a loop that gets the loop ready to start.

13. A type of loop that is ideally suited for counting.

Down

1. The part of a loop that must have a boolean result.

3. A ... is used to access a value in an array.

5. Boolean ..... operators operate on boolean values and return a boolean result.

6. The part of a loop that is responsible for changing the state of any loop controls.

7. If you want to end a loop immediately, use this statement.

10. If a is true and b is true, then a ... b is true; otherwise a ... b is false.

12. Accessing an array value using a number requires an ......

 # JavaScriptcross Solution

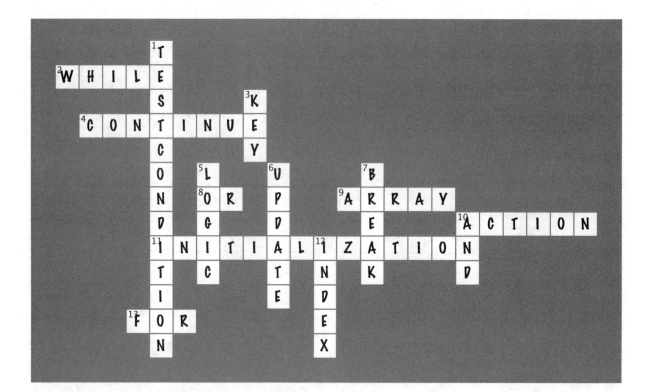

Page Bender

Fold the page vertically to line up the two brains and solve the riddle.

What do loops and movies have in common?

🧠 ← — It's a meeting of the minds! ← 🧠

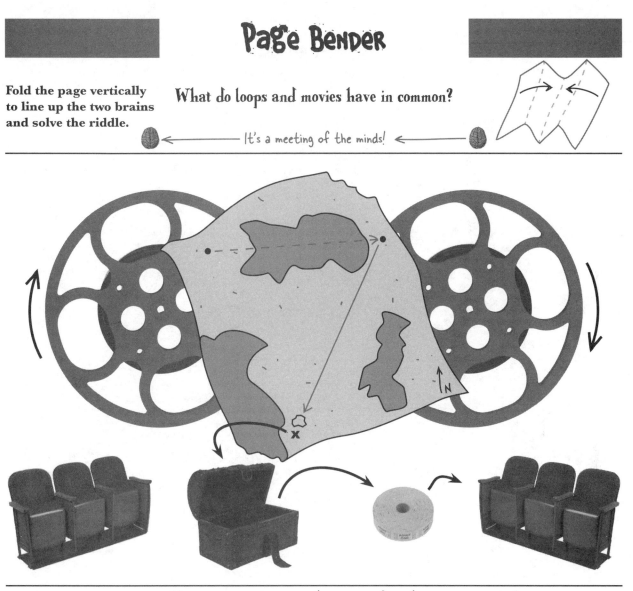

Some movies are known for having circular plots that are difficult to follow.

There are other movies that use motion and lots of action to attract people.

In the end, a movie is just a movie.

6 functions

Reduce, Reuse, Recycle

That's the thing about meatloaf, you cook it once and then eat it for weeks and weeks... somebody help me!

If there was an environmental movement within JavaScript, it would be led by functions. Functions allow you to make JavaScript code more efficient, and yes, more reusable. Functions are task-oriented, good at code organization, and excellent problem solvers. Sounds like the makings of a good resume! In reality, all but the simplest of scripts stand to benefit from a functional reorganization. While it's hard to put a number on the carbon footprint of the average function, let's just say they do their part in making scripts as eco-friendly as possible.

The mother of all problems

When it comes down to it, web scripting is about solving problems. No matter how large the problem, with enough thought and planning, there's always a solution. But what about the **really huge problems**?

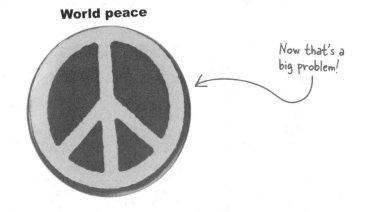

World peace

Now that's a big problem!

The trick to solving big problems is to break them down into smaller, more manageable problems. And if those problems are still too big, then break them down again.

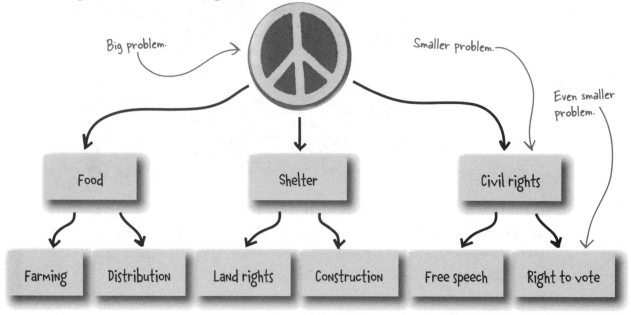

Big problem.

Smaller problem.

Even smaller problem.

Food

Shelter

Civil rights

Farming

Distribution

Land rights

Construction

Free speech

Right to vote

Continue this process again…and again…and again…

Solve big problems by solving small problems

Continuing to break down the world peace problem into smaller problems, you eventually arrive at a problem that is small enough for JavaScript to handle.

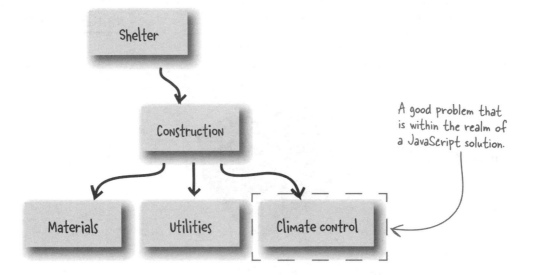

A good problem that is within the realm of a JavaScript solution.

Think of a JavaScript equivalent to the climate control problem, which would involve the scripting equivalent of a thermostat, which is used to control the temperature of an environment. The most basic thermostat would simply have a "heat" button.

The easiest thermostat ever — push the button and it goes.

You don't care how the heating is done, you only need to know how to turn it on.

Note how the thermostat reveals nothing about how the heating is carried out. You press the Heat button and you get heat. Climate control problem solved!

Functions as problem solvers

The Heat button on the thermostat is the equvalent of a **function** in JavaScript. The idea is similar to a real-world thermostat—someone requests heat, the function provides it. The details of the heating are handled inside the function, and aren't important to the code calling the function. In this way, you can think of a function as a "black box"—information can flow into it and out of it but what goes on inside is the box's responsibility, and therefore not important to code outside of the box.

Functions turn <u>big problems</u> into <u>small</u> problems.

Request heat ──────▶   It gets warmer

Translating the Heat button into JavaScript code involves calling a function called heat()...

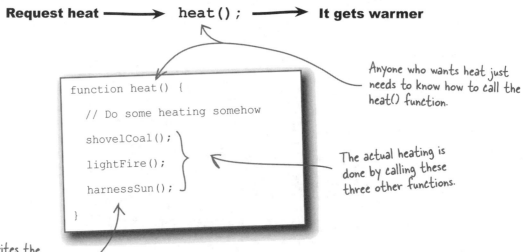

Request heat ──────▶ heat(); ──────▶ It gets warmer

```
function heat() {

    // Do some heating somehow

    shovelCoal();

    lightFire();

    harnessSun();

}
```

Anyone who wants heat just needs to know how to call the heat() function.

The actual heating is done by calling these three other functions.

The person who writes the heat() function is the only person who has to worry about how the function heats.

It's not terribly important **how** the heat() function does the heating. What matters is that it serves as a self-contained solution to a problem. If you need some heat, just call the heat() function. The details of solving the problem are left to the inner workings of the function.

The nuts and bolts of a function

When you elect to create a function, you become the problem solver. Creating a function requires you to use a consistent syntax that ties the name of the function with the code that it runs. Following is the syntax for the most basic JavaScript function:

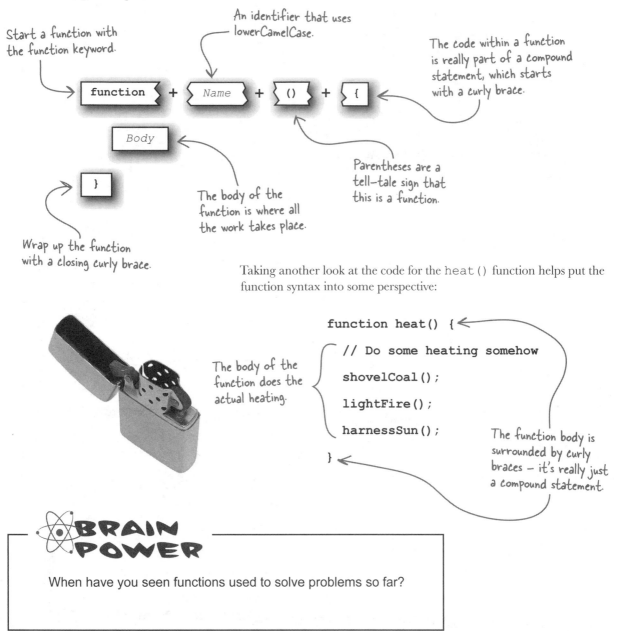

Start a function with the function keyword.

An identifier that uses lowerCamelCase.

The code within a function is really part of a compound statement, which starts with a curly brace.

```
function  +  Name  +  ()  +  {
```

```
Body
```

```
}
```

Parentheses are a tell-tale sign that this is a function.

The body of the function is where all the work takes place.

Wrap up the function with a closing curly brace.

Taking another look at the code for the heat() function helps put the function syntax into some perspective:

```
function heat() {
    // Do some heating somehow
    shovelCoal();
    lightFire();
    harnessSun();
}
```

The body of the function does the actual heating.

The function body is surrounded by curly braces — it's really just a compound statement.

BRAIN POWER

When have you seen functions used to solve problems so far?

A function you've already met

You don't have to look any further than the Mandango macho seat finder (full files available at *http://www.headfirstlabs.com/books/hfjs/.*) script to find a good example of a function solving a problem—in this case, the problem of initializing movie seat data. Here's how the Mandango problem was broken down:

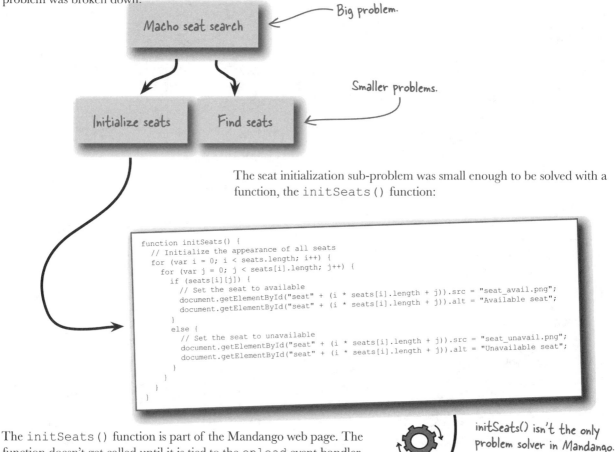

Big problem.

Macho seat search

Smaller problems.

Initialize seats   Find seats

The seat initialization sub-problem was small enough to be solved with a function, the `initSeats()` function:

```
function initSeats() {
  // Initialize the appearance of all seats
  for (var i = 0; i < seats.length; i++) {
    for (var j = 0; j < seats[i].length; j++) {
      if (seats[i][j]) {
        // Set the seat to available
        document.getElementById("seat" + (i * seats[i].length + j)).src = "seat_avail.png";
        document.getElementById("seat" + (i * seats[i].length + j)).alt = "Available seat";
      }
      else {
        // Set the seat to unavailable
        document.getElementById("seat" + (i * seats[i].length + j)).src = "seat_unavail.png";
        document.getElementById("seat" + (i * seats[i].length + j)).alt = "Unavailable seat";
      }
    }
  }
}
```

The `initSeats()` function is part of the Mandango web page. The function doesn't get called until it is tied to the `onload` event handler. This causes the function to run when the page loads.

initSeats() isn't the only problem solver in Mandango.

```
<body
onload="initSeats();">
    <div style="height:25px"></div>
    <div style="text-align:center">
      <img id="seat0" src="" alt="" />

      ...
      <img id="seat35" src="" alt="" /><br />
      <input type="button" id="findseats" value="Find Seats" onclick="findSeats();" />
    </div>
  </body>
</html>
```

there are no Dumb Questions

Q: **How does the naming convention for functions work again?**

A: lowerCamelCase is a convention for naming JavaScript identifiers where the first word in an identifier is all lowercase but additional words are mixed case. So, a function that rates a movie might be called `rateMovie()`, while a function that kicks out a guy who insists on talking on his mobile phone during a movie might be called `removeInappropriateGuy()`.

Q: **Are functions always about turning big problems into smaller problems?**

A: Not necessarily. There are situations where functions are helpful purely as a division of coding labor. In other words, it may be one problem being solved by

several functions working together. In this case, the rationale for dividing up the code into functions is to help divide the work and give each function its own singular purpose. Kind of like how people are given different job titles so that they can each focus on one specific type of task. Such functions may or may not be solving unique problems, but they definitely improve the structure of scripts by dividing up the work.

Q: **How do you know when a chunk of code should be placed into a function?**

A: Unfortunately, there is no magical way to know when it makes the most sense to place a piece of code into a function. But there are some signs you can look for as clues. One sign is if you find yourself duplicating a piece of code. Duplicate code

is almost never a good thing because you have to maintain it in more than one place. So duplicate code is a great target for placing in a function. Another sign is a situation where a piece of code grows to become unwieldy, and you're able to make out several logical parts to it. This is a good time to apply the "division of labor" idea to the code, and consider breaking it out into multiple functions.

Q: **I thought I remember seeing functions that accepted arguments and then passed data back. Am I missing something?**

A: No, not at all. There certainly are functions that both accept and return data. In fact, you're about to see the `heat()` function turn into one if you hang in there.

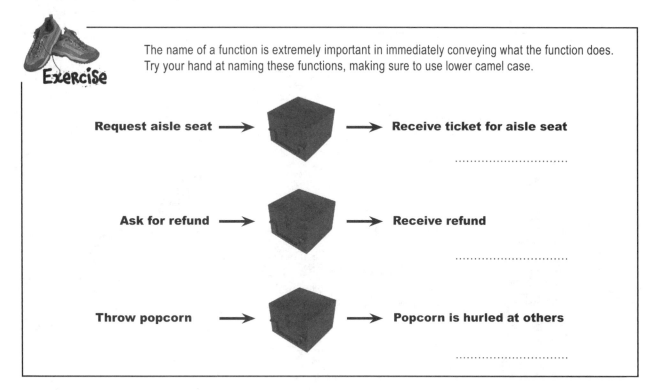

Exercise

The name of a function is extremely important in immediately conveying what the function does. Try your hand at naming these functions, making sure to use lower camel case.

Request aisle seat ⟶ ⟶ Receive ticket for aisle seat

....

Ask for refund ⟶ ⟶ Receive refund

....

Throw popcorn ⟶ ⟶ Popcorn is hurled at others

....

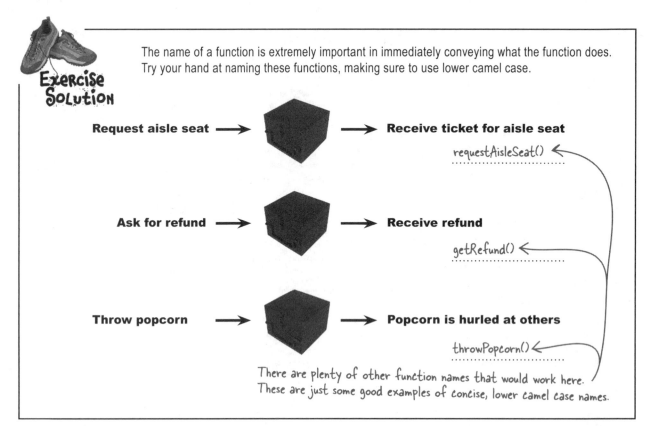

Exercise Solution

The name of a function is extremely important in immediately conveying what the function does. Try your hand at naming these functions, making sure to use lower camel case.

Request aisle seat ⟶ ⟶ Receive ticket for aisle seat

requestAisleSeat() ⟵

Ask for refund ⟶ ⟶ Receive refund

getRefund() ⟵

Throw popcorn ⟶ ⟶ Popcorn is hurled at others

throwPopcorn() ⟵

There are plenty of other function names that would work here. These are just some good examples of concise, lower camel case names.

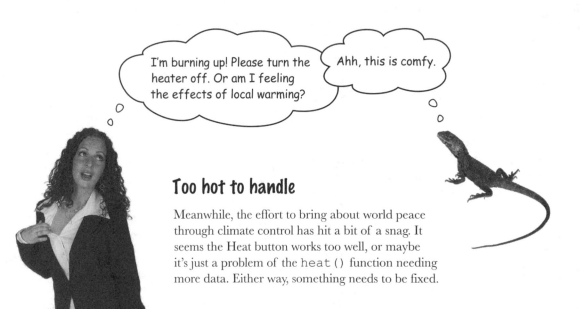

I'm burning up! Please turn the heater off. Or am I feeling the effects of local warming?

Ahh, this is comfy.

Too hot to handle

Meanwhile, the effort to bring about world peace through climate control has hit a bit of a snag. It seems the Heat button works too well, or maybe it's just a problem of the heat() function needing more data. Either way, something needs to be fixed.

Build a better thermostat with more data

So back to the thermostat…It doesn't know when to stop heating because we never set a target temperature. There simply isn't enough information to solve the problem effectively, which means someone presses the Heat button and they get heat... forever!

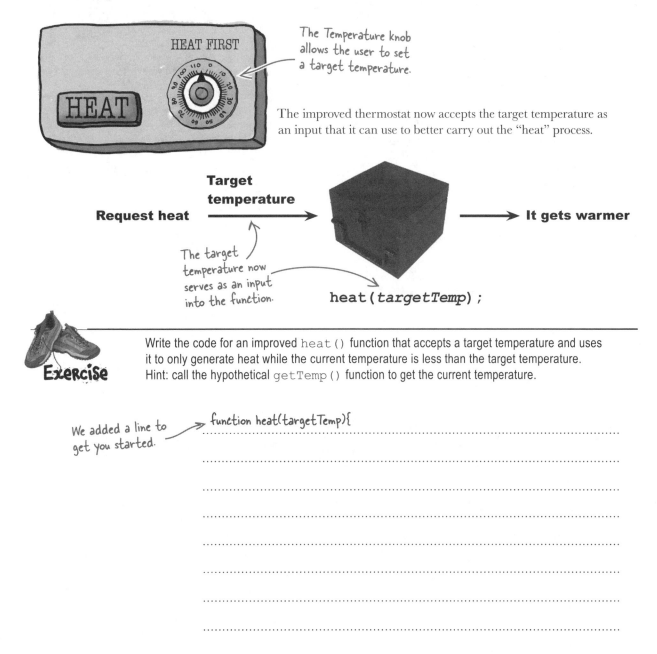

The Temperature knob allows the user to set a target temperature.

The improved thermostat now accepts the target temperature as an input that it can use to better carry out the "heat" process.

Request heat **Target temperature** ⟶ **It gets warmer**

The target temperature now serves as an input into the function.

heat(*targetTemp*);

ExeRCiSe

Write the code for an improved `heat()` function that accepts a target temperature and uses it to only generate heat while the current temperature is less than the target temperature.
Hint: call the hypothetical `getTemp()` function to get the current temperature.

We added a line to get you started. ⟶ function heat(targetTemp){

Exercise Solution

Write the code for an improved `heat()` function that accepts a target temperature and uses it to only generate heat while the current temperature is less than the target temperature. Hint: call the hypothetical `getTemp()` function to get the current temperature.

```
function heat(targetTemp){

    while (getTemp() < targetTemp) {

        // Do some heating somehow

        shovelCoal();

        lightFire();

        harnessSun();

    }

}
```

The target temperature is passed into the function as a function argument.

The target temperature is used as part of the test condition for a while loop.

The function now only heats if the current temperature is less than the target temperature.

Passing information to functions

Data is passed into JavaScript functions using function **arguments**, which are like inputs. Look again at the syntax for functions; see how arguments are placed inside the parentheses when you create a function.

One or more arguments can appear inside the parentheses.

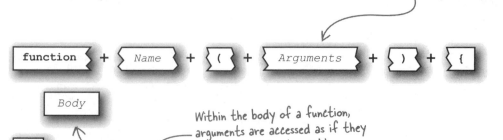

function + *Name* + (+ *Arguments* +) + {

Body

}

Within the body of a function, arguments are accessed as if they are initialized local variables.

There isn't really a limit on the number of arguments you can pass into a function, although it makes practical sense to try and keep them to within no more than two or three. You can pass just about any piece of data to a function as an argument: a constant (`Math. PI`), a variable (`temp`), or a literal (`72`).

Function arguments as data

When data is passed into a function as an argument, it acts as an initialized local variable inside the function. As an example, here the `heat()` function is getting supplied with a target temperature that is passed to the function as an argument:

```
heat(72);
```

The target temperature is passed into the function as a <u>literal</u> number.

Inside the `heat()` function, the `targetTemp` argument is accessible as if it was a local variable initialized to 72. Replacing the normal `heat()` function code with an alert reveals the argument value.

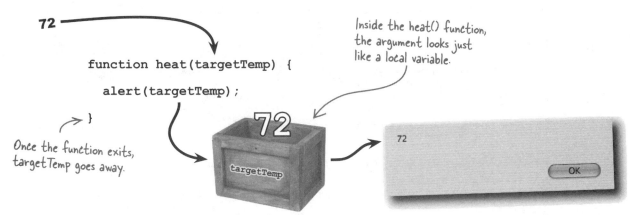

72

```
function heat(targetTemp) {

    alert(targetTemp);

}
```

Inside the heat() function, the argument looks just like a local variable.

Once the function exits, targetTemp goes away.

Although function arguments act much like local variables from within a function, changing an argument value **inside** a function does **not** affect anything **outside** of the function. This rule does not apply to objects that are passed as arguments—we'll dig into objects in Chapters 9 and 10.

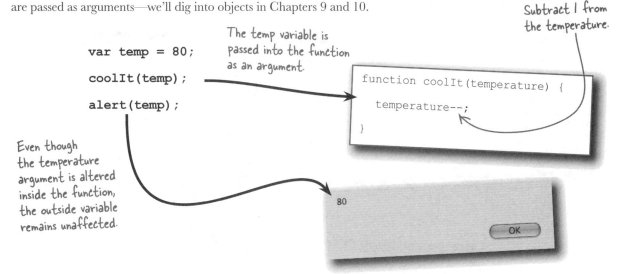

```
var temp = 80;

coolIt(temp);

alert(temp);
```

The temp variable is passed into the function as an argument.

Subtract 1 from the temperature.

```
function coolIt(temperature) {

    temperature--;

}
```

Even though the temperature argument is altered inside the function, the outside variable remains unaffected.

80

Functions eliminate duplicate code

In addition to breaking down problems so that they can be solved more easily, functions serve as a great way to eliminate duplicate code by generalizing tasks. A **generalized task** can be used to eliminate similar code that appears in more than one place. Even though the code may not be identical, in many cases you can generalize it into identical code that can be placed in a function. Then you call the function instead of duplicating similar code.

Following are three different pieces of code that all involve similar tasks that could be generalized into a single, **reusable** task:

The discount percentage calculation is unnecessarily duplicated.

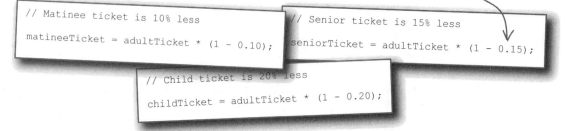

```
// Matinee ticket is 10% less

matineeTicket = adultTicket * (1 - 0.10);
```

```
// Senior ticket is 15% less

seniorTicket = adultTicket * (1 - 0.15);
```

```
// Child ticket is 20% less

childTicket = adultTicket * (1 - 0.20);
```

The specific tasks involve calculating the prices of three different kinds of discounted movie tickets. But these tasks can be generalized into a task that involves calculating the price of a ticket based upon any discount percentage.

Functions can return data as well.

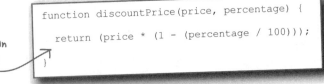

```
function discountPrice(price, percentage) {
    return (price * (1 - (percentage / 100)));
}
```

With a generalized ticket discount function in hand, the other three pieces of code can be rewritten much more efficiently:

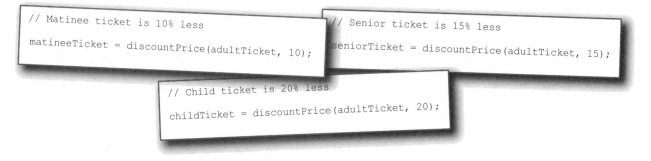

```
// Matinee ticket is 10% less
matineeTicket = discountPrice(adultTicket, 10);
```

```
// Senior ticket is 15% less
seniorTicket = discountPrice(adultTicket, 15);
```

```
// Child ticket is 20% less
childTicket = discountPrice(adultTicket, 20);
```

BE the Efficiency Expert

Below is the findSeats() function from the Mandango macho seat finder in all its prior glory. Using your newfound efficiency knowledge, circle similar code that could be rewritten as a generalized, reusable function.

```
function findSeats() {
  // If seats are already selected, reinitialize all seats to clear them
  if (selSeat >= 0) {
    selSeat = -1;
    initSeats();
  }

  // Search through all the seats for availability
  var i = 0, finished = false;
  while (i < seats.length && !finished) {
    for (var j = 0; j < seats[i].length; j++) {
      // See if the current seat plus the next two seats are available
      if (seats[i][j] && seats[i][j + 1] && seats[i][j + 2]) {
        // Set the seat selection and update the appearance of the seats
        selSeat = i * seats[i].length + j;
        document.getElementById("seat" + (i * seats[i].length + j)).src = "seat_select.png";
        document.getElementById("seat" + (i * seats[i].length + j)).alt = "Your seat";
        document.getElementById("seat" + (i * seats[i].length + j + 1)).src = "seat_select.png";
        document.getElementById("seat" + (i * seats[i].length + j + 1)).alt = "Your seat";
        document.getElementById("seat" + (i * seats[i].length + j + 2)).src = "seat_select.png";
        document.getElementById("seat" + (i * seats[i].length + j + 2)).alt = "Your seat";

        // Prompt the user to accept the seats
        var accept = confirm("Seats " + (j + 1) + " through " + (j + 3) +
          " in Row " + (i + 1) + " are available. Accept?");
        if (accept) {
          // The user accepted the seats, so we're done (break out of the inner loop)
          finished = true;
          break;
        }
        else {
          // The user rejected the seats, so clear the seat selection and keep looking
          selSeat = -1;
          document.getElementById("seat" + (i * seats[i].length + j)).src = "seat_avail.png";
          document.getElementById("seat" + (i * seats[i].length + j)).alt = "Available seat";
          document.getElementById("seat" + (i * seats[i].length + j + 1)).src = "seat_avail.png";
          document.getElementById("seat" + (i * seats[i].length + j + 1)).alt = "Available seat";
          document.getElementById("seat" + (i * seats[i].length + j + 2)).src = "seat_avail.png";
          document.getElementById("seat" + (i * seats[i].length + j + 2)).alt = "Available seat";
        }
      }
    }

    // Increment the outer loop counter
    i++;
  }
}
```

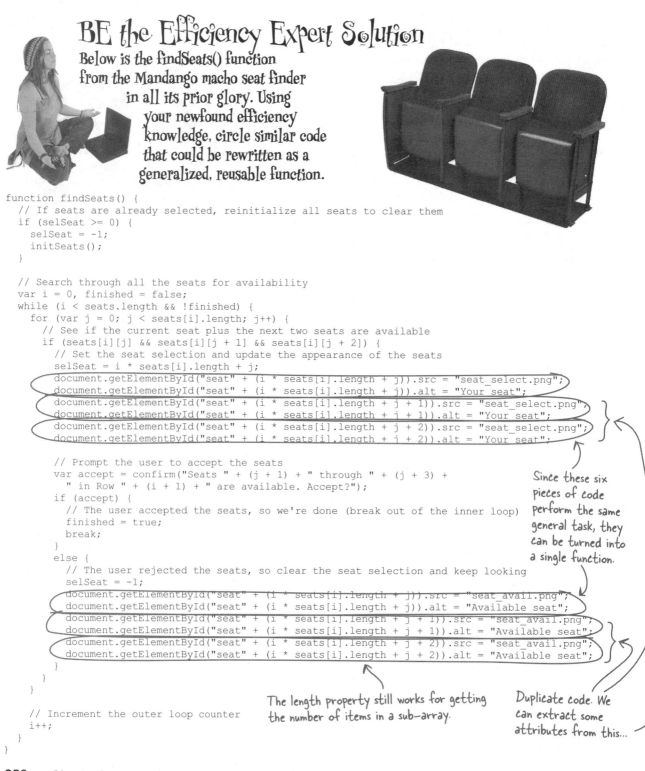

BE the Efficiency Expert Solution

Below is the findSeats() function from the Mandango macho seat finder in all its prior glory. Using your newfound efficiency knowledge, circle similar code that could be rewritten as a generalized, reusable function.

```
function findSeats() {
  // If seats are already selected, reinitialize all seats to clear them
  if (selSeat >= 0) {
    selSeat = -1;
    initSeats();
  }

  // Search through all the seats for availability
  var i = 0, finished = false;
  while (i < seats.length && !finished) {
    for (var j = 0; j < seats[i].length; j++) {
      // See if the current seat plus the next two seats are available
      if (seats[i][j] && seats[i][j + 1] && seats[i][j + 2]) {
        // Set the seat selection and update the appearance of the seats
        selSeat = i * seats[i].length + j;
        document.getElementById("seat" + (i * seats[i].length + j)).src = "seat_select.png";
        document.getElementById("seat" + (i * seats[i].length + j)).alt = "Your seat";
        document.getElementById("seat" + (i * seats[i].length + j + 1)).src = "seat_select.png";
        document.getElementById("seat" + (i * seats[i].length + j + 1)).alt = "Your seat";
        document.getElementById("seat" + (i * seats[i].length + j + 2)).src = "seat_select.png";
        document.getElementById("seat" + (i * seats[i].length + j + 2)).alt = "Your seat";

        // Prompt the user to accept the seats
        var accept = confirm("Seats " + (j + 1) + " through " + (j + 3) +
          " in Row " + (i + 1) + " are available. Accept?");
        if (accept) {
          // The user accepted the seats, so we're done (break out of the inner loop)
          finished = true;
          break;
        }
        else {
          // The user rejected the seats, so clear the seat selection and keep looking
          selSeat = -1;
          document.getElementById("seat" + (i * seats[i].length + j)).src = "seat_avail.png";
          document.getElementById("seat" + (i * seats[i].length + j)).alt = "Available seat";
          document.getElementById("seat" + (i * seats[i].length + j + 1)).src = "seat_avail.png";
          document.getElementById("seat" + (i * seats[i].length + j + 1)).alt = "Available seat";
          document.getElementById("seat" + (i * seats[i].length + j + 2)).src = "seat_avail.png";
          document.getElementById("seat" + (i * seats[i].length + j + 2)).alt = "Available seat";
        }
      }
    }

    // Increment the outer loop counter
    i++;
  }
}
```

Since these six pieces of code perform the same general task, they can be turned into a single function.

The length property still works for getting the number of items in a sub-array.

Duplicate code. We can extract some attributes from this...

Creating a seat setter function

Now that the Mandango guys have gotten wind of this efficiency stuff, they're fired up about adding a function to Mandango that makes the seat setting code more efficient (code available at *http://www.headfirstlabs.com/books/hfjs/*). In order to write the `setSeat()` function, however, they really need to figure out what arguments are required. You can isolate the necessary arguments by examining what pieces of information are different in the duplicate code. A closer look at the duplicate parts of the `findSeats()` function reveals these arguments:

Seat Number

The number of the seat to be set. This is not an array index; it's just the number of the seat if you were to start counting from left to right and top to bottom, starting at 0.

The findSeats() attributes are extracted from the duplicated code that will be placed in the function.

Status

The status of the seat, as in available, unavailable, and selected. This is used to determine what seat image to display.

Dude, functions rule! We need more of these things.

I know, but let me call you back... I have someone on the other line.

Description

The description of the seat status, as in "Available seat", "Unavailable seat", and "Your seat". This is used to set the `alt` text for the seat images.

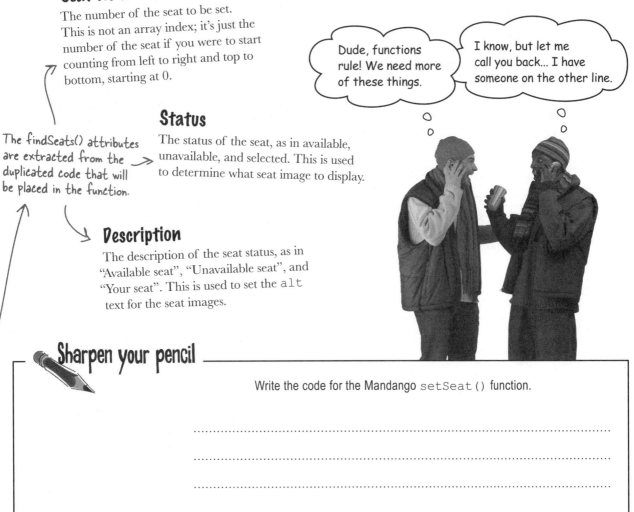

Sharpen your pencil

Write the code for the Mandango `setSeat()` function.

....

....

....

....

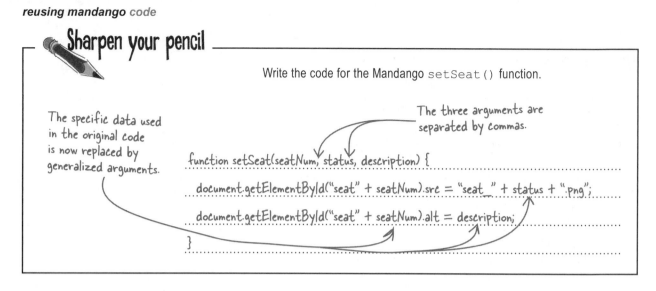

Sharpen your pencil

Write the code for the Mandango `setSeat()` function.

The specific data used in the original code is now replaced by generalized arguments.

The three arguments are separated by commas.

```
function setSeat(seatNum, status, description) {
    document.getElementById("seat" + seatNum).src = "seat_" + status + ".png";
    document.getElementById("seat" + seatNum).alt = description;
}
```

A leaner, cleaner Mandango with functions

Breaking out similar, duplicate code into the `setSeat()` function simplifies the code for the `findSeats()` function considerably. There are now six calls to the `setSeat()` function, which is a significant improvement in terms of code reuse.

The seat number, status, and description are passed to setSeat() in each function call.

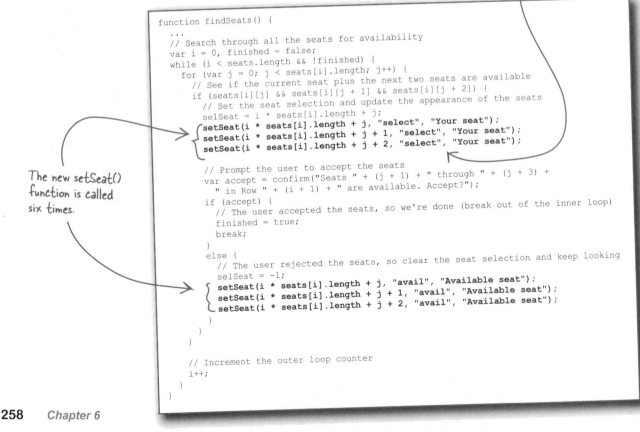

```
function findSeats() {
  ...
  // Search through all the seats for availability
  var i = 0, finished = false;
  while (i < seats.length && !finished) {
    for (var j = 0; j < seats[i].length; j++) {
      // See if the current seat plus the next two seats are available
      if (seats[i][j] && seats[i][j + 1] && seats[i][j + 2]) {
        // Set the seat selection and update the appearance of the seats
        selSeat = i * seats[i].length + j;
        setSeat(i * seats[i].length + j, "select", "Your seat");
        setSeat(i * seats[i].length + j + 1, "select", "Your seat");
        setSeat(i * seats[i].length + j + 2, "select", "Your seat");

        // Prompt the user to accept the seats
        var accept = confirm("Seats " + (j + 1) + " through " + (j + 3) +
          " in Row " + (i + 1) + " are available. Accept?");
        if (accept) {
          // The user accepted the seats, so we're done (break out of the inner loop)
          finished = true;
          break;
        }
        else {
          // The user rejected the seats, so clear the seat selection and keep looking
          selSeat = -1;
          setSeat(i * seats[i].length + j, "avail", "Available seat");
          setSeat(i * seats[i].length + j + 1, "avail", "Available seat");
          setSeat(i * seats[i].length + j + 2, "avail", "Available seat");
        }
      }
    }

    // Increment the outer loop counter
    i++;
  }
}
```

The new setSeat() function is called six times.

The setSeat() function makes Mandango even better

But the `setSeat()` function doesn't just benefit `findSeats()`. It also helps make the `initSeats()` function more **efficient** because that function has similar seat setting code as well.

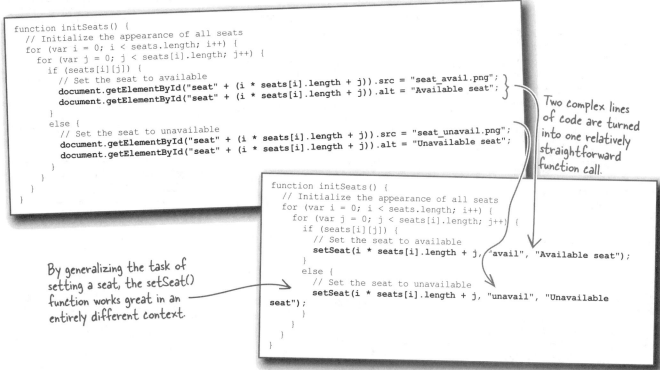

```
function initSeats() {
  // Initialize the appearance of all seats
  for (var i = 0; i < seats.length; i++) {
    for (var j = 0; j < seats[i].length; j++) {
      if (seats[i][j]) {
        // Set the seat to available
        document.getElementById("seat" + (i * seats[i].length + j)).src = "seat_avail.png";
        document.getElementById("seat" + (i * seats[i].length + j)).alt = "Available seat";
      }
      else {
        // Set the seat to unavailable
        document.getElementById("seat" + (i * seats[i].length + j)).src = "seat_unavail.png";
        document.getElementById("seat" + (i * seats[i].length + j)).alt = "Unavailable seat";
      }
    }
  }
}
```

Two complex lines of code are turned into one relatively straightforward function call.

```
function initSeats() {
  // Initialize the appearance of all seats
  for (var i = 0; i < seats.length; i++) {
    for (var j = 0; j < seats[i].length; j++) {
      if (seats[i][j]) {
        // Set the seat to available
        setSeat(i * seats[i].length + j, "avail", "Available seat");
      }
      else {
        // Set the seat to unavailable
        setSeat(i * seats[i].length + j, "unavail", "Unavailable seat");
      }
    }
  }
}
```

By generalizing the task of setting a seat, the setSeat() function works great in an entirely different context.

So, a fairly simple function consisting of two lines of code is now used eight times throughout the Mandango script. Not only does this **simplify** the script code, but it makes the script more maintainable because if you ever need to change how a seat is set, you only have to change the one `setSeat()` piece of code, as opposed to eight separate pieces. No JavaScript coder in their right mind wants to change multiple pieces of code, when they don't have to. Maintainabilty... it's a good thing.

BULLET POINTS

- Functions allow you to turn **big problems into small problems**, which become much easier to solve.

- Functions provide a mechanism to separate script tasks and then complete them with **reusable** chunks of code.

- Functions serve as a great way to **eliminate duplicate code** since the code in a function can be reused as many times as you want.

- **Arguments** allow you to pass data into functions as **input** for a given task.

Q: Is there a limit to the number of arguments that can be passed into a function?

A: No and yes. No, there isn't a real limit on the number of arguments that can be passed into a function, unless you factor in the limits on computer memory. If you're passing so many arguments that memory becomes an issue, you might want to take a break and rethink what you're doing because it takes an awful lot of arguments to cause a memory problem. The more practical limitation has to do with good design, and that means keeping the number of arguments to a manageable amount just so function calls don't get too ridiculously complicated. It's generally a good idea to not use more than a handful of arguments.

Q: I've learned that functions turn big problems into small problems, divide scripting labor, and eliminate duplicate code. Which is it?

A: All of the above. Functions are good at more than one thing, and in many cases the best functions accomplish several goals at once. It's not out of the question to create a function that solves a sub-problem, performs a division-of-labor task, and eliminates duplicate code, all at the same time. In fact, those are three pretty good goals to have when creating any function. But if you must focus on one thing, you will typically want to err on the side of dividing labor, which really means giving every function a singular purpose. If every function excels at one unique thing, your scripts will benefit greatly.

Q: One more time, where do functions go in the header or the body of a web page?

A: Functions should appear inside the `<script>` tag within the head of the page, or in an external JavaScript file that is imported into the head of the page.

Q: If I truly want a function to change the value of an argument, how do I do it?

A: Function arguments can't be directly altered, or at least the changes won't carry on outside of the function. So if you want to change a piece of data that has been passed as an argument, you need to return the changed value from the function. Read on to find out how return values work!

Something isn't right with this thermostat— I'm freezing!

I feel great!

Winter in July: feedback with functions

Although Mandango has made some big strides thanks to functions, they aren't faring so well on the climate change front. It seems the JavaScript thermostat still isn't quite working properly, resulting in some frigid users who now long for the old Heat button that never stopped heating.

The significance of feedback

Our current thermostat allows you to set the temperature thanks to function arguments but it doesn't report the current temperature. The current temperature is important because it gives you a basis for determining a target temperature. Besides, different thermostats often report different temperatures, even within the same space. What this boils down to is the need for feedback... you need to know the current temperature in order to set a meaningful target temperature.

The "current temperature" display lets users know the current temperature so that they can make adjust the heat with more accuracy.

The thermostat now periodically displays the current temperature as feedback to help assist in determining an optimal temperature.

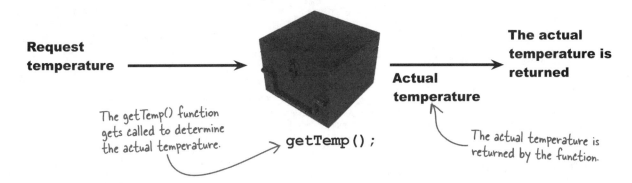

Request temperature

The actual temperature is returned

The getTemp() function gets called to determine the actual temperature.

Actual temperature

`getTemp();`

The actual temperature is returned by the function.

So we really need a way for JavaScript functions to return information back to the code that called them.

BRAIN POWER

How do you think a function could be coaxed into returning data?

Returning data from functions

Returning information from a function involves using the `return` keyword, followed by the data to be returned. This data is then returned to the code that called the function.

A return value allows you to <u>return</u> <u>a</u> <u>piece</u> <u>of</u> <u>data</u> from a function.

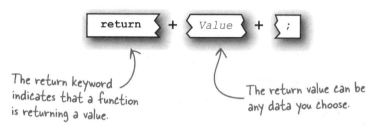

The return keyword indicates that a function is returning a value.

The return value can be any data you choose.

A `return` statement can be placed anywhere within a function; just know that the function will exit immediately upon encountering a `return`. So the `return` statement not only returns data but also ends a function. As an example, the `getTemp()` function ends by returning the actual temperature, as read from a sensor.

```
function getTemp() {

  // Read and convert the actual temperature

  var rawTemp = readSensor();

  var actualTemp = convertTemp(rawTemp);

  return actualTemp;

}
```

The sensor data is in a weird format and needs to be converted to degrees.

The actual temperature is returned from the function using the return statement.

If you think back carefully, the `getTemp()` function has already been used in the thermostat code:

```
function heat(targetTemp) {

  while (getTemp() < targetTemp) {

    // Do some heating somehow

    ...

  }

}
```

The getTemp() function provides the value that is used in the test condition for the heat() while loop.

The return value of the `getTemp()` function **replaces** the `getTemp()` function call and becomes part of the test condition in the `while` loop.

The return value of a function <u>replaces</u> the call to the function.

Many happy return values

Since the `return` statement immediately ends a function, you can use it to control the flow of a function, in addition to returning data. Not only that, but it's very common for functions to indicate their success using return values. The `heat()` function presents an opportunity to do both:

```
function heat(targetTemp) {

  if (getTemp() >= targetTemp)

    return false;

  while (getTemp() < targetTemp) {

    // Do some heating somehow

    ...

  }

    return true;

}
```

Remember the actualTemp variable? It provides the return value of getTemp().

No need to do any heating, so return false and end the function.

This code does the actual heating, which affects the temperature, and therefore the return value of getTemp().

Finished heating, so return true to indicate success.

The `heat()` function demonstrates how a boolean return value can control the flow of a function and also indicate success or failure. For pure flow control, you can use the `return` statement with no return value at all as a means of bailing out of a function. For example, here's another version of the `heat()` function that doesn't rely on the return value to indicate success or failure.

```
function heat(targetTemp) {

  if (getTemp() >= targetTemp)

    return;

  while (getTemp() < targetTemp) {

    // Do some heating somehow

    ...

  }

}
```

The return statement cuts the function short since no heating is required.

The function still ends when it ends, without the help of a return statement.

The return statement can be used by itself to end a function.

Return Exposed

This week's interview:
Secrets of a function escape artist

Head First: So I hear that you're pretty slippery, able to get out of just about anything.

Return: That's true. Put me in any function and I'll get out of it in no time. I'll even take a piece of data with me.

Head First: Where do you go when you leave a function?

Return: Well, don't forget that functions are always called by other code, so returning from a function just means returning to the code that called it. And in the case, of returning data, it means the data is returned to the code that called the function.

Head First: How does that work?

Return: It helps if you think of a function call as an expression that has a result. If the function doesn't return any data, the result of the expression is nothing. But if the function does return data, and many of them do, then the result of the expression is that piece of data.

Head First: So if a function is just an expression, does that mean you can assign the return value of a function to a variable?

Return: No and yes. No, the function itself is not an expression—it's the call to the function that is the expression. And yes, you can and often should place a function call so that the result gets assigned to a variable. That's where the expression comes into play—when a function call is evaluated, it is treated as an expression where the result is the return value of the function.

Head First: I see. But what happens to the expression when you don't return anything?

Return: If you use me with no return data, then the function returns nothing and the expression is empty.

Head First: Isn't that a problem?

Return: No, not really. You have to remember that people only worry about doing something with function return values when they know the function is capable of returning data. If a function isn't intended to return anything, you shouldn't worry about trying to do anything with a return value.

Head First: Gotcha. So getting back to your escape skills, isn't it a bad idea to keep a function from finishing its natural course of execution?

Return: No, and here's why. Just because a function has a first line and a last line does not mean it is designed to always run every line of code from start to finish. In fact, it's dangerous to even think of a function as having a start and a finish. The "natural" finish of a function could very well be in the middle of the code thanks to some crafty developer putting me in the right place.

Head First: I don't get it. Are you saying that it's normal for some function code to never get called?

Return: I never say never, but I will say that there is usually more than one path through a function, and I often help establish those paths. If something takes place that indicates the function shouldn't continue running, I'm there to give it an early exit. In other scenarios, a function may run all the way to its last line of code and exit without ever encountering me, or it may end with me just so I can return some data.

Head First: Oh, I see. You provide options, both in terms of returning data and controlling the flow of execution through a function.

Return: Hey, you're catching on!

Head First: Yeah, I'm quick like that. Thanks for your time.

Return: No worries. I gotta get out of here!

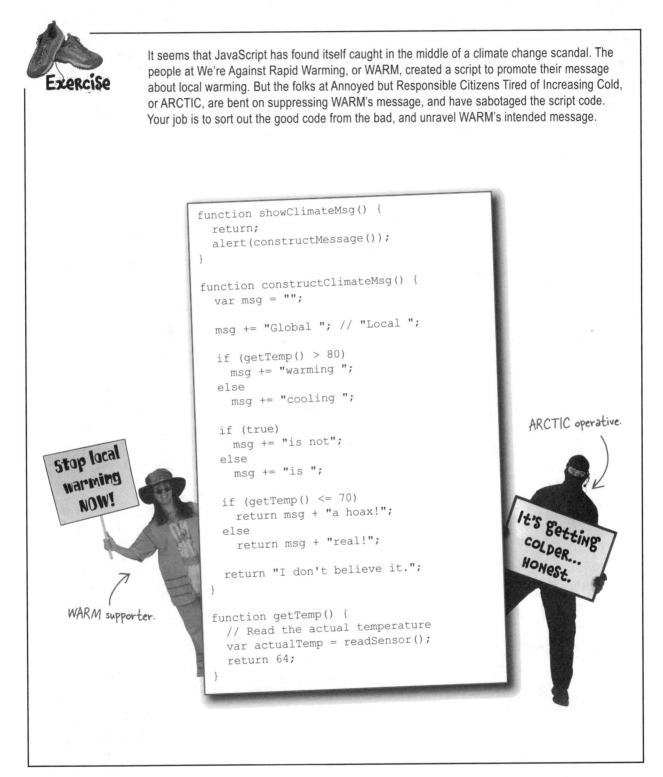

Exercise

It seems that JavaScript has found itself caught in the middle of a climate change scandal. The people at We're Against Rapid Warming, or WARM, created a script to promote their message about local warming. But the folks at Annoyed but Responsible Citizens Tired of Increasing Cold, or ARCTIC, are bent on suppressing WARM's message, and have sabotaged the script code. Your job is to sort out the good code from the bad, and unravel WARM's intended message.

```javascript
function showClimateMsg() {
  return;
  alert(constructMessage());
}

function constructClimateMsg() {
  var msg = "";

  msg += "Global "; // "Local ";

  if (getTemp() > 80)
    msg += "warming ";
  else
    msg += "cooling ";

  if (true)
    msg += "is not";
  else
    msg += "is ";

  if (getTemp() <= 70)
    return msg + "a hoax!";
  else
    return msg + "real!";

  return "I don't believe it.";
}

function getTemp() {
  // Read the actual temperature
  var actualTemp = readSensor();
  return 64;
}
```

Stop local warming NOW!

WARM supporter.

ARCTIC operative.

It's getting COLDER... HONEST.

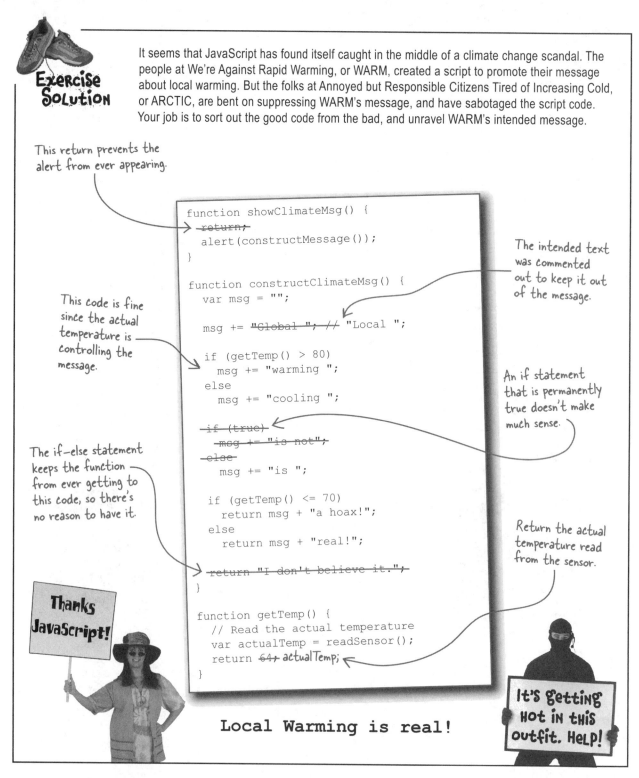

Exercise Solution

It seems that JavaScript has found itself caught in the middle of a climate change scandal. The people at We're Against Rapid Warming, or WARM, created a script to promote their message about local warming. But the folks at Annoyed but Responsible Citizens Tired of Increasing Cold, or ARCTIC, are bent on suppressing WARM's message, and have sabotaged the script code. Your job is to sort out the good code from the bad, and unravel WARM's intended message.

This return prevents the alert from ever appearing.

```
function showClimateMsg() {
  return;
  alert(constructMessage());
}

function constructClimateMsg() {
  var msg = "";

  msg += "Global "; // "Local ";

  if (getTemp() > 80)
    msg += "warming ";
  else
    msg += "cooling ";

  if (true)
    msg += "is not";
  else
    msg += "is ";

  if (getTemp() <= 70)
    return msg + "a hoax!";
  else
    return msg + "real!";

  return "I don't believe it.";
}

function getTemp() {
  // Read the actual temperature
  var actualTemp = readSensor();
  return 64; actualTemp;
}
```

The intended text was commented out to keep it out of the message.

This code is fine since the actual temperature is controlling the message.

An if statement that is permanently true doesn't make much sense.

The if-else statement keeps the function from ever getting to this code, so there's no reason to have it.

Return the actual temperature read from the sensor.

Thanks JavaScript!

It's getting hot in this outfit. Help!

Local Warming is real!

Getting the status of a seat

Back at Mandango, Seth and Jason are sick of hearing about climate
change, and are ready to make some more improvements to their script
code. Some users have reported difficulty in making out the different
colors of seats, and would like to be able to click and query any seat for its
availability. Sounds as if Mandango needs a new function.

> All this temperature
> talk is killing me. I've got
> Mandango stuff to fix!

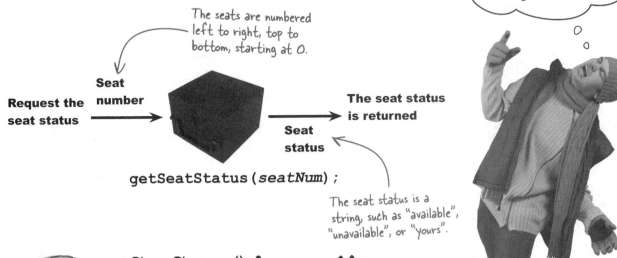

The seats are numbered
left to right, top to
bottom, starting at 0.

Request the seat status → **Seat number** → **The seat status is returned**

Seat status

`getSeatStatus(`*seatNum*`);`

The seat status is a
string, such as "available",
"unavailable", or "yours".

getSeatStatus() function Magnets

The `getSeatStatus()` function in Mandango is missing some important code that helps it figure out
the status of a given seat. The function first checks to see if the seat is part of the series of three selected
seats. If not, it looks up the seat in the seat array to see if it is available or unavailable. Use the magnets
below to finish the missing pieces of code.

```
function getSeatStatus(seatNum) {
  if (............ != -1 &&
    (............ == ............ || ............ == (............ + 1) || ............ == (............ + 2)))
    return "yours";
  else if (........[Math.floor(............ / ........ [0].length)][............ % ........ [0].length])
    return "available";
  else
    return "unavailable";
}
```

`seats`   `selSeat`   `seatNum`

getSeatStatus() function Magnets Solution

The `getSeatStatus()` function in Mandango is missing some important code that helps it figure out the status of a given seat. The function first checks to see if the seat is part of the series of three selected seats. If not, it looks up the seat in the seat array to see if it is available or unavailable. Use the magnets below to finish the missing pieces of code.

The selSeat global variable is −1 when no seat is selected, so check it first.

We're dealing with three seats in a row, so you must check this seat and the next two.

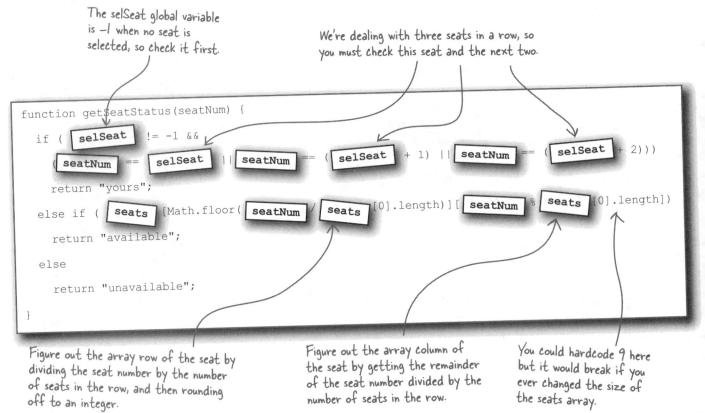

```
function getSeatStatus(seatNum) {
  if ( selSeat != -1 &&
  ( seatNum == selSeat || seatNum == ( selSeat + 1) || seatNum == ( selSeat + 2)))
    return "yours";
  else if ( seats [Math.floor( seatNum / seats [0].length)][ seatNum % seats [0].length])
    return "available";
  else
    return "unavailable";

}
```

Figure out the array row of the seat by dividing the seat number by the number of seats in the row, and then rounding off to an integer.

Figure out the array column of the seat by getting the remainder of the seat number divided by the number of seats in the row.

You could hardcode 9 here but it would break if you ever changed the size of the seats array.

Showing the seat status

Getting the seat status is handy but allowing the user to query any seat for its status requires a means of showing the seat status when the user clicks a seat. The `showSeatStatus()` function provides a simple solution to this problem, delegating the dirty work to the `getSeatStatus()` function that we just wrote.

Pass along the seat number to getSeatStatus() to get the seat status.

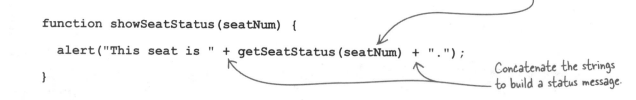

```
function showSeatStatus(seatNum) {

  alert("This seat is " + getSeatStatus(seatNum) + ".");

}
```

Concatenate the strings to build a status message.

You can link the function to an image

Wiring this function to a seat image on the Mandango page allows the user to query the seat for its status by clicking the image. Each image must have its `onclick` event tied to `showSeatStatus()`, like this:

The showSeatStatus() function is called when the user clicks the "seat23" image.

```
<img id="seat23" src="" alt="" onclick="showSeatStatus(23);" />
```

onclick!

Mandango – The Macho Movie Ticket Finder

This seat is yours.

OK

Find Seats

Seat number 23.

Done

A click is all it takes to view the status of any seat in an alert box, which is useful for anyone who has trouble making out the seat images, and just wants to click an individual seat for its status.

BULLET POINTS

- The `return` statement allows functions to return data back to the code that called them.

- When a piece of data is returned from a function, it stands in for the code that called the function.

- A function can only return a single piece of data.

- The `return` statement can be used without any data to simply end a function early.

Repetitive code is never a good thing

The Mandango script is working pretty well but the guys are starting to worry about maintaining the script over the long haul. In particular, Jason has been doing some research, and has learned that modern web applications often benefit from separating HTML, JavaScript, and CSS code.

I see a lot of different code mixed up in there.

```
<html>
  <head>
    <title>Mandango - The Macho Movie Ticket Finder</title>

    <script type="text/javascript">
      ...

      function initSeats() {
        ...      }

      function getSeatStatus(seatNum) {
        ...
      }

      function showSeatStatus(seatNum) {
        alert("This seat is " + getSeatStatus(seatNum) + ".");
      }

      function setSeat(seatNum, status, description) {
        document.getElementById("seat" + seatNum).src = "seat_" + status + ".png";
        document.getElementById("seat" + seatNum).alt = description;
      }

      function findSeats() {
        ...
      }
    </script>
  </head>
  <body onload="initSeats();">
    <div style="margin-top:25px; text-align:center">
      <img id="seat0" src="" alt="" onclick="showSeatStatus(0);" />
      <img id="seat1" src="" alt="" onclick="showSeatStatus(1);" />
      <img id="seat2" src="" alt="" onclick="showSeatStatus(2);" />
      <img id="seat3" src="" alt="" onclick="showSeatStatus(3);" />
      <img id="seat4" src="" alt="" onclick="showSeatStatus(4);" />
      <img id="seat5" src="" alt="" onclick="showSeatStatus(5);" />
      <img id="seat6" src="" alt="" onclick="showSeatStatus(6);" />
      <img id="seat7" src="" alt="" onclick="showSeatStatus(7);" /><br />
      <img id="seat8" src="" alt="" onclick="showSeatStatus(8);" />
      <img id="seat9" src="" alt="" onclick="showSeatStatus(9);" />
      <img id="seat10" src="" alt="" onclick="showSeatStatus(10);" />
      <img id="seat11" src="" alt="" onclick="showSeatStatus(11);" />
      <img id="seat12" src="" alt="" onclick="showSeatStatus(12);" />
      <img id="seat13" src="" alt="" onclick="showSeatStatus(13);" />
      <img id="seat14" src="" alt="" onclick="showSeatStatus(14);" />
      <img id="seat15" src="" alt="" onclick="showSeatStatus(15);" />
      <img id="seat16" src="" alt="" onclick="showSeatStatus(16);" /><br />
      <img id="seat17" src="" alt="" onclick="showSeatStatus(17);" />
      <img id="seat18" src="" alt="" onclick="showSeatStatus(18);" />
      <img id="seat19" src="" alt="" onclick="showSeatStatus(19);" />
      <img id="seat20" src="" alt="" onclick="showSeatStatus(20);" />
      <img id="seat21" src="" alt="" onclick="showSeatStatus(21);" />
      <img id="seat22" src="" alt="" onclick="showSeatStatus(22);" />
      <img id="seat23" src="" alt="" onclick="showSeatStatus(23);" />
      <img id="seat24" src="" alt="" onclick="showSeatStatus(24);" />
      <img id="seat25" src="" alt="" onclick="showSeatStatus(25);" />
      <img id="seat26" src="" alt="" onclick="showSeatStatus(26);" /><br />
      <img id="seat27" src="" alt="" onclick="showSeatStatus(27);" />
      <img id="seat28" src="" alt="" onclick="showSeatStatus(28);" />
      <img id="seat29" src="" alt="" onclick="showSeatStatus(29);" />
      <img id="seat30" src="" alt="" onclick="showSeatStatus(30);" />
      <img id="seat31" src="" alt="" onclick="showSeatStatus(31);" />
      <img id="seat32" src="" alt="" onclick="showSeatStatus(32);" />
      <img id="seat33" src="" alt="" onclick="showSeatStatus(33);" />
      <img id="seat34" src="" alt="" onclick="showSeatStatus(34);" />
      <img id="seat35" src="" alt="" onclick="showSeatStatus(35);" /><br />
      <input type="button" id="findseats" value="Find Seats" onclick="findSeats();" />
    </div>
  </body>
</html>
```

The mixed JavaScript and HTML code can be isolated to event handler HTML attributes.

JavaScript and HTML code are mixed together throughout the Mandango web page.

Separate your functionality from your content

So what's the big deal with mixing code? It obviously works, right? The problem has a lot to do with viewing your JavaScript-powered web pages not as pages, but as **applications**. And like any good application, JavaScript applications require careful planning and design for long-term success. More to the point, good applications are less buggy and easier to maintain when there is a separation of content, presentation, and functionality. As it stands, Mandango very much represents a murky merger of all three.

Content

This is the HTML code in the page, which provides the structure for how the page physically goes together, as well as housing the data in the page.

Separating content, presentation, and functionality turns a big problem into small problems.

Functionality

This is the JavaScript code that drives the page and makes it interactive. You can think of this part of the page as the part that **does things**.

Presentation

This is the CSS part of the page, which dresses up the content and determines its appearance, such as fonts, colors, and even layout.

Think about the code separation issue this way. Let's say Seth and Jason find a really slick movie seat management script that they'd like to use instead of their own code. They would need to overhaul Mandango so that it uses the new script code, but they would have to risk screwing up the structure of the page because the JavaScript code is intimately tied to the HTML code. It would be much better if the HTML code was isolated, and the JavaScript-to-HTML connection occurred purely in JavaScript.

Separating functionality from content makes web applications easier to build and maintain.

How would you go about using functions to separate functionality from content in Mandango?

Functions are just data

In order to effectively separate code you'll need to understand how functions are wired to events; so far, we've done this using HTML attributes. There's another way, which a lot of people consider to be superior to mixing JavaScript and HTML code. This other way of wiring event handlers requires a different view of functions.

Surprisingly enough, functions are really just variables. It's true. The twist is that the function body is the value, while the function name is the variable name. Here's the way you're accustomed to viewing functions:

The function is created just like always.

```
function showSeatStatus(seatNum) {

  alert("This seat is " + getSeatStatus(seatNum) + ".");

}
```

That code works fine, but here's the same function created in a different way.

The function name is the variable name.

```
var showSeatStatus = function(seatNum) {

  alert("This seat is " + getSeatStatus(seatNum) + ".");

};
```

The function body is the value of the variable, also known as a function literal when expressed like this.

This code shows how a function can be created using the same syntax as a variable, and even consists of the same pieces and parts: a unique identifier (function name) plus a value (function body). When a function body appears by itself without a name, it is known as a **function literal**.

What makes this revelation about functions so interesting is that it shows that functions can be manipulated like variables. For example, what do you think the following code does?

```
var myShowSeatStatus = showSeatStatus;
```

Assign the showSeatStatus() function to the myShowSeatStatus variable.

Calling or referencing your functions

When you assign the name of a function to another variable, you're giving that variable access to the body of the function. In other words, you can write code like this to call the same function:

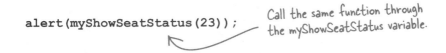

```
alert(myShowSeatStatus(23));
```

Call the same function through the myShowSeatStatus variable.

The end result of calling myShowSeatStatus() is the same as calling showSeatStatus() because both functions ultimately **reference** the same code. For this reason, a function name is also known as a **function reference**.

```
showSeatStatus              function() {
                                ...
myShowSeatStatus            };
```

A function is really just a variable whose value is a reference to the function body.

The distinction between **referencing** a function and **calling** a function has to do with whether you follow the function name with parentheses (). Function references appear by themselves, while function calls are always followed by parentheses, and in many cases function arguments.

Run the myShowSeatStatus() function, which is the same as showSeatStatus().

```
var myShowSeatStatus = showSeatStatus;
myShowSeatStatus(23);
```

Assign a function reference to myShowSeatStatus.

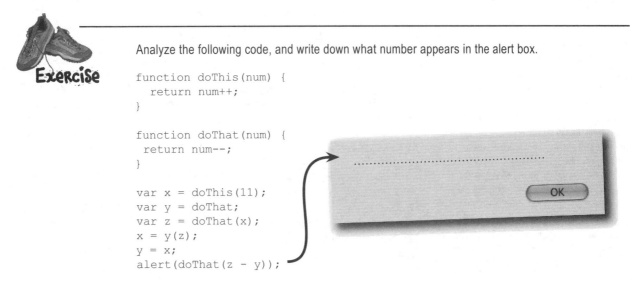

Exercise

Analyze the following code, and write down what number appears in the alert box.

```
function doThis(num) {
   return num++;
}

function doThat(num) {
 return num--;
}

var x = doThis(11);
var y = doThat;
var z = doThat(x);
x = y(z);
y = x;
alert(doThat(z - y));
```

Exercise Solution

Analyze the following code, and write down what number appears in the alert box.

```
function doThis(num) {
   return num++;
}

function doThat(num) {
  return num--;
}

var x = doThis(11);
var y = doThat;
var z = doThat(x);
x = y(z);
y = x;
alert(doThat(z - y));
```

0

OK

x = 12
y = doThat
z = doThat(12) = 11
x = doThat(11) = 10
y = 10
alert(doThat(11 – 10))

---

there are no Dumb Questions

Q: Is separating content really that big of a deal?

A: Yes and no. For simple applications, it's not necessarily wrong to blend HTML, CSS, and JavaScript code. The benefits of code separation become significant in more complex applications that involve lots of code. It's much harder to get a handle on the big picture in larger applications, which means it's easy to get in trouble when making changes, especially when different kinds of code are all mixed together. By cleanly separating the code, you can feel safer making functional changes without breaking something in the structure or appearance of the page. This also allows people with different areas of expertise to work on the same project.

For example, web designers can work on the structure and presentation of an application without fear of creating errors in functional JavaScript code that they may not understand.

Q: If a function is just data, how can I distinguish a function from a normal variable?

A: The difference between a function and a "normal" variable comes down to what you do with the data. The data (code) associated with functions is capable of being executed. You indicate that you want to run a function by following the function name with parentheses, including arguments if the function requires them.

Q: What's the point of function references?

A: Unlike a normal variable, which stores its data as a value in an area of memory, functions store a reference to their code. So the value of a function variable isn't the code itself but a reference to the location in memory where the code is stored. It's kind of like how your mailing address is a reference to your house, not the house itself.

Functions use references instead of actual values because it is more efficient than storing multiple copies of function code. So when you assign a function to an event handler, as you do in a moment, you're really just assigning a reference to the function code, not the code itself.

OK, so function references sound pretty neat, but what do they have to do with separating content from functionality?

*69 (callback features) for functions

Function references are closely linked to a special way of calling functions that has a lot to do with separating content from functionality. You're familiar with calling a function from your own Mandango code.

```
setSeat(i * seats[i].length + j, "select", "Your seat");
```

```
function setSeat(seatNum, status, description) {
   ...
}
```

But this isn't the only way functions can get called in scripts. Another kind of function known as a **callback function** can get called without you having anything directly to do with it.

BRAIN POWER

How do you think Mandango could take advantage of callback functions?

Fireside Chats

Tonight's talk: **Normal function and Callback function confront each other**

Normal function:

So you're the guy I keep hearing about, who won't accept local calls. What's with the attitude?

You mean like the browser? Real exotic. I think you're just a little stuck up about those of us who talk with script code on a regular basis.

Boy, that sure would be a loss. Not! Who cares what goes on outside of the script?

You may have a point there. I do like knowing when the page loads or when the user clicks or types something. So you're saying I wouldn't know about those things without you?

Well, I'm glad to hear that we really aren't so different after all.

Don't call me, I'll call you.

Callback function:

No attitude, I just serve a different purpose. I prefer to only be called from exotic, faraway places.

Look, it's not about who is better or worse. We're all script code, it's just that I give outsiders a means of accessing script code. Without me, you would never know when anything takes place outside of the script.

Actually, everyone. Don't forget that the whole point of scripting is to provide web users with a better experience. If a script had no means of detecting events outside of itself, the user experience would be awful tough to improve.

That's right. The browser calls me, and in many cases I call you since responding to outside happenings often requires several functions.

Yep. So I guess I'll see you around.

Good luck with that.

Events, callbacks, and HTML attributes

We've been using callback functions all along, which are called by the browser, instead of your own code. The most common use of callback functions is in handling events. Mandango already heavily relies upon callback functions. In fact, event handling functions are the basis of the problem involving the mixing of HTML and JavaScript code.

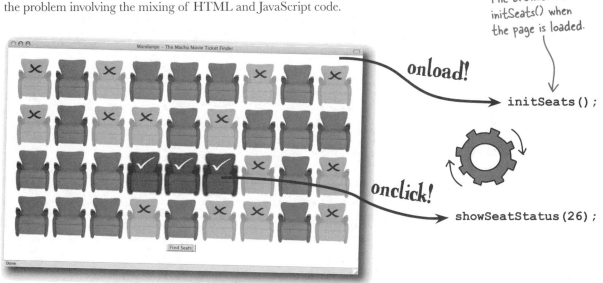

The browser calls initSeats() when the page is loaded.

onload!

`initSeats();`

onclick!

`showSeatStatus(26);`

These callback functions are wired to events in the HTML code for the Mandango page.

The onload HTML attribute is used to wire the initSeats() function to the onload event.

```
<body onload="initSeats();">
```

```
<img id="seat26" src="" alt="" onclick="showSeatStatus(26);" />
```

The onclick HTML attribute is used to wire the showSeatStatus() function to the onclick event.

Can I call you back?

This technique of tying event handling functions to events via HTML attributes works just fine, but it has the downside of requiring JavaScript code to be mixed with HTML code. Function references make it possible to separate this mixture and break apart HTML and JavaScript...

Wiring events using function references

Instead of using an HTML attribute to wire a callback function to an event as an event handler, you can assign a function reference directly in JavaScript code. In other words, you don't have to venture into HTML code at all—just set the callback function using a function reference, all from within JavaScript code.

```
window.onload = initSeats;
```

There are no parentheses following the function name because you don't want to run the function, you just want to reference it.

The onload event is a property of the window object.

A reference to the initSeats() function is assigned to the onload event property.

So setting an event handler purely in JavaScript code involves assigning a function reference to an event property of an object. In the case of this `onload` event handling code, the assignment of the function reference causes the `initSeats()` function to get called when the event is triggered. Even though this call happens automatically when the event is fired, the effect is this:

onload! ⟶ `window.onload();` ⟶ `initSeats();`

The onload event triggers an event handler through the window.onload property...

...and since the property is set to a function reference, the initSeats() function gets called to handle the event.

The upside to using a function reference to assign an event handler function to an event is that it allows us to cleanly separate JavaScript code from HTML code—there's no need to assign JavaScript code to HTML event attributes.

~~`<body onload="initSeats();">`~~ ⟶ `<body>`

Now the `<body>` tag can just be the `<body>` tag since the function handler is wired purely in JavaScript code. We just have to make sure that the event assignment code gets run as early as possible, so usually it takes place in the head of the page.

But there's a problem. What happens if we need to pass an argument into an event handler to help it do its job? This isn't a problem with `onload` in Mandango, but the `onclick` event needs to pass along the number of the seat that was clicked. Function references offer no means of passing through arguments, so we need another option...

Function references provide a convenient way to wire event handler functions to events.

Function literals to the rescue

The `onlick` event for seat images in Mandango must call the `showSeatStatus()` function with an argument (the seat number) indicating the seat that was clicked. Simply assigning a reference to the function won't pass along the argument, which presents a big problem, but there is another way. The solution is to use a function literal as the function reference, and then call the `showSeatStatus()` function from inside the function literal.

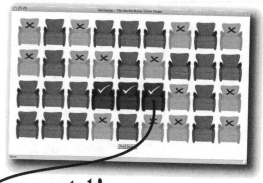

The seat image object is retrieved so that its onclick property can be accessed.

onclick!

```
document.getElementById("seat26").onclick = function(evt) {

    showSeatStatus(26);

};
```

The function literal "wraps" the call to showSeatStatus(), allowing an argument to be passed into it.

The function literal is assigned to the onclick event property as a function reference.

An event object is automatically passed to an event handler as its first argument.

The function literal is used purely as a wrapper around the call to the `showSeatStatus()` function, but it plays a critical role in allowing us to pass along the appropriate seat number to the function. You can think of the function literal as a nameless function that handles the event. For this reason, function literals are sometimes called **anonymous functions**.

This code reveals how JavaScript offers an event object that is passed into event handlers, in this case through the `evt` argument. The event object contains information specific to each different event. In this case we don't need to know any detailed information about the event, so it's OK to just not use the `evt` argument.

Function literals let you create anonymous event handler functions.

Exercise

Wire the `initSeats()` function to the `onload` event handler, but this time use a function literal instead of a function reference.

....

....

....

Exercise Solution

Wire the `initSeats()` function to the `onload` event handler, but this time use a function literal instead of a function reference.

```
window.onload = function(evt) {

    initSeats();

};
```

The initSeats() function is called inside of the onload event handler function literal.

The evt argument is ignored since the onload event handler has no need for the event object.

Where's the wiring?

There's still an unresolved issue related to event wiring through function literals. We know that the `onload` event handler can just be assigned in the head of the page inside the `<script>` tag, just like normal script code. And that works great because the code tied to `onload` doesn't run until after the page is loaded (when the `onload` event fires), just as if we had used the old approach of assigning `initSeats()` to the HTML `onload` attribute of the `<body>` tag. But where do other function literal event handlers get wired?

The answer goes back to the `onload` event handler callback function, which serves as a great place to wire all events for a page.

The onload event handler is an excellent place to initialize all events.

```
window.onload = function() {

  // Wire other events here

  ...

  // Initialize the seat appearances

  initSeats();

};
```

All other events on the page can be wired inside of the onload event handler.

The code specific to the onload event is still run inside the event handler.

What this code boils down to is that the `onload` event handler becomes an event initialization function where all other events in a page are set. So the `onload` event handler not only performs normal start-up duties for the page, such as initializing the seats, but also wires all other event handler callback functions for the application.

Q: Why do callback functions matter?

A: Callback functions are significant because they allow you to react to things that take place outside of your code. Instead of you calling a function from your own code, you create a callback function that is essentially on standby waiting for something to take place so that it can leap into action. When that something takes place, it is the browser's responsibility to let the callback function know it can run. All you do is set the stage by wiring the callback function to a trigger, usually an event.

Q: Are there callback functions other than event handlers?

A: Yes. We explore another common usage of callback functions in Chapter 12 when they are called to process data sent by the server in a request for data using Ajax.

Q: I'm still confused about function literals. What are they, and why are they such a big deal?

A: A function literal is just a function body without a name, kind of like a literal piece of data such as a number or string. Function literals are important because they are ideal in situations where you need a quick one-off callback function. In other words, the function is only called once, and not by your code. So you create a function literal and assign it directly to an event property, as opposed to creating a named function and assigning its reference. It's really more of a coding efficiency issue, taking advantage of the fact that you don't need a formally named function in some situations. And don't forget that function literals are really only necessary when you need to do more than simply reference a function, such as pass an argument to a function.

Sharpen your pencil

Finish the missing code in Mandango's new `onload` event handler function.

```
window.onload = function() {

  // Wire the Find Seat button event
  document.getElementById("findseats"). .......... = .............. ;


  // Wire the seat image events
  document.getElementById("seat0"). .......... = function(evt) { ........................... };
  document.getElementById("seat1"). .......... = function(evt) { ........................... };
  document.getElementById("seat2"). .......... = function(evt) { ........................... };

  ...


  // Initialize the seat appearances

  ................

};
```

Sharpen your pencil
Solution

Finish the missing code in Mandango's new `onload` event handler function.

The entire onload event handler is a function literal.

The `findSeats()` function is tied to the onclick event using a function reference.

```
window.onload = function() {
  // Wire the Find Seat button event
  document.getElementById("findseats").  onclick  =  findSeats ;


  // Wire the seat image events
  document.getElementById("seat0").  onclick  = function(evt) {  showSeatStatus(0);   };
  document.getElementById("seat1").  onclick  = function(evt) {  showSeatStatus(1);   };
  document.getElementById("seat2").  onclick  = function(evt) {  showSeatStatus(2);   };

  ...


  // Initialize the seat appearances
  initSeats();

};
```

The initSeats() function is called to finish up the onload tasks.

The onclick property for each seat image is accessed to set onclick event handlers.

showSeatStatus() is called from within a function literal so that an argument can be passed into it.

BULLET POINTS

- Callback functions are called by the browser in response to things that take place **outside of the script**.

- Function references can be used to **assign functions** as if they were **variables**.

- Function references let you wire event handler functions in JavaScript code **without altering HTML code**.

- Function literals are **nameless functions** that are handy in situations when a named function isn't necessary.

there are no
Dumb Questions

Q: Why is the `onload` event handler in Mandango created as a function literal?

A: Because there isn't really any reason to create a named function for it. The function only gets called once, and that's in response to the `onload` event. We could've just as easily created a named function and assigned its reference to `window.onload`, but the connection between callback function and event is clearer when the function is directly tied to the event using a function literal.

Q: Do the other callback functions have to be wired in the `onload` event handler?

A: Yes. You might think you could wire them directly within the `<script>` tag in the head of the page. But remember that the content for the page hasn't finished loading at that point. So, all of the `getElementById()` calls would fall flat on their faces and the event handlers wouldn't get wired. The `onload` handler guarantees you that the page has loaded.

A shell of an HTML page

Separating the JavaScript code from the HTML code in Mandango reveals how truly minimal the structural part of the page becomes. This makes the HTML code much easier to maintain without fear of trampling JavaScript code that might break the application.

Dude, I need a picture of that!

Look at that code! It's so maintainable.

```html
<body>
  <div style="margin-top:75px; text-align:center">
    <img id="seat0" src="" alt="" />
    <img id="seat1" src="" alt="" />
    <img id="seat2" src="" alt="" />
    <img id="seat3" src="" alt="" />
    <img id="seat4" src="" alt="" />
    <img id="seat5" src="" alt="" />
    <img id="seat6" src="" alt="" />
    <img id="seat7" src="" alt="" />
    <img id="seat8" src="" alt="" />
    <img id="seat9" src="" alt="" /><br />
    <img id="seat10" src="" alt="" />
    <img id="seat11" src="" alt="" />
    <img id="seat12" src="" alt="" />
    <img id="seat13" src="" alt="" />
    <img id="seat14" src="" alt="" />
    <img id="seat15" src="" alt="" />
    <img id="seat16" src="" alt="" />
    <img id="seat17" src="" alt="" />
    <img id="seat18" src="" alt="" />
    <img id="seat19" src="" alt="" /><br />
    <img id="seat20" src="" alt="" />
    <img id="seat21" src="" alt="" />
    <img id="seat22" src="" alt="" />
    <img id="seat23" src="" alt="" />
    <img id="seat24" src="" alt="" />
    <img id="seat25" src="" alt="" />
    <img id="seat26" src="" alt="" />
    <img id="seat27" src="" alt="" />
    <img id="seat28" src="" alt="" />
    <img id="seat29" src="" alt="" /><br />
    <img id="seat30" src="" alt="" />
    <img id="seat31" src="" alt="" />
    <img id="seat32" src="" alt="" />
    <img id="seat33" src="" alt="" />
    <img id="seat34" src="" alt="" />
    <img id="seat35" src="" alt="" />
    <img id="seat36" src="" alt="" />
    <img id="seat37" src="" alt="" />
    <img id="seat38" src="" alt="" />
    <img id="seat39" src="" alt="" /><br />
    <input type="button" id="findseats" value="Find Seats" />
  </div>
</body>
```

One small step for JavaScript...

Although we didn't manage to solve world peace, we did take a step in
the right direction by using JavaScript to get a handle on climate control.
Turning big problems into small problems, focusing on a singularity
of purpose, and striving for code reuse are all ways that functions can
improve scripts.

And of course, Seth and Jason put the same problem-solving techniques
to work by creating a better organized and more maintainable version of
Mandango. If nothing else, the world of macho movie-going is at peace...

JavaScriptcross

Well, it's that time again. Take a load off and twist
your cerebellum around this crossword puzzle.

Across

3. When you assign a function to a variable, you use a
function ....
5. Functions help eliminate this kind of code.
6. You never call this kind of function yourself.
10. A nameless function body.
12. When code is relatively easy to modify, it is considered to
have good ....
13. HTML code represents this part of a Web page.

Down

1. .... is at peace with Mandango now.
2. Functions improve the .... of code so that you don't
unnecessarily duplicate it.
4. JavaScript represents this part a Web page.
7. To pass data back from a function, just ...... it.
8. A piece of reusable JavaScript code.
9. Functions are good at breaking these down.
11. This is how you pass data into a function.

 # JavaScriptcross Solution

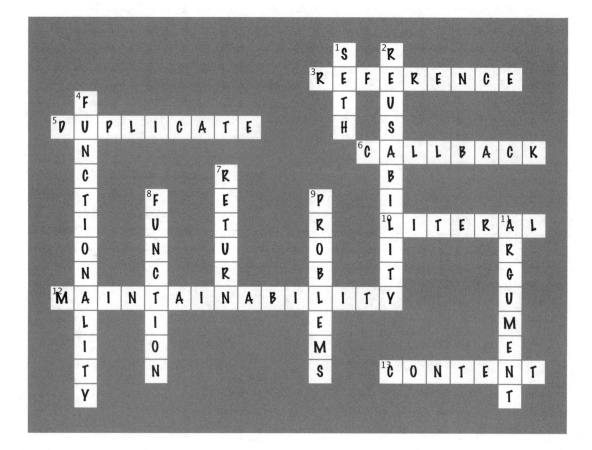

Page Bender

Fold the page vertically
to line up the two brains
and solve the riddle.

What do functions add to your JavaScript life?

It's a meeting of the minds!

Food

I'm so cold.

It's hot. I'm not comfortable.

Shelter

Civil rights

Peace is always a tricky proposition. Even
with JavaScript code, only the most
organized code leads to tranquility and
calm. It's not easy to lead a life of
comfort, at least in terms of JavaScript.

7 forms and validation

Getting the User to Tell All

I wonder if my suave, debonair personality will be enough to get this Betty's phone number...looking for some validation here, you know?

You don't have to be suave or sneaky to successfully get information from users with JavaScript. But you do have to be careful. Humans have this strange tendency to make mistakes, which means *you can't* always count on the data provided in online forms being *accurate* or valid. Enter JavaScript. By **passing form data through the right JavaScript code** as it is being entered, you can **make web applications much more reliable**, and also **take some load off of the server**. We need to *save that precious bandwidth for important things* like stunt videos and cute pet pictures.

Bannerocity: messaging the friendly skies

Stunt-loving aviator Howard has turned his love of flying into an aerial banner business, Bannerocity. Howard wants to put a whole new meaning to the term "banner ad" by taking online orders for aerial banners. In addition to kick starting his new business, Howard hopes the online order system will free up his time so he can spend more of it enjoying the friendly skies.

Howard got an awesome deal on this vintage WWII era plane.

Bannerocity...banner ads in the sky!

Currently, Howard's paper order form captures all of the information necessary for an aerial banner order.

> message: Duncan's Donuts... only the best!
>
> ZIP code: 74129
>
> Fly date: December 14th, 2008
>
> Name: Duncan Glutenberg
>
> Phone #: 408-555-5309

It's very important for the Bannerocity online order form to capture all of the order information that is associated with an aerial banner order. Howard figures the online order form should include all of the fields on the paper form, plus an email field since customers will be filling out the form online.

Message
The message to be displayed in the aerial banner ad.

ZIP code
The geographical area where the message is to be displayed. Howard flies over a specified ZIP code when showing an ad.

Fly date
The date on which the banner ad is flown.

Name
The customer's name.

Phone number
The customer's phone number.

Email
The customer's email address.

The Bannerocity HTML form

With a little help from HTML, Howard's first stab at an online order form for Bannerocity looks great.

Bannerocity – Personalized Online Sky Banners
BANNEROCITY
Enter the banner message:
Enter ZIP code of the location:
Enter the date for the message to be shown:
Enter your name:
Enter your phone number:
Enter your email address:
Order Banner
Done

Wow, the online order form looks really good.

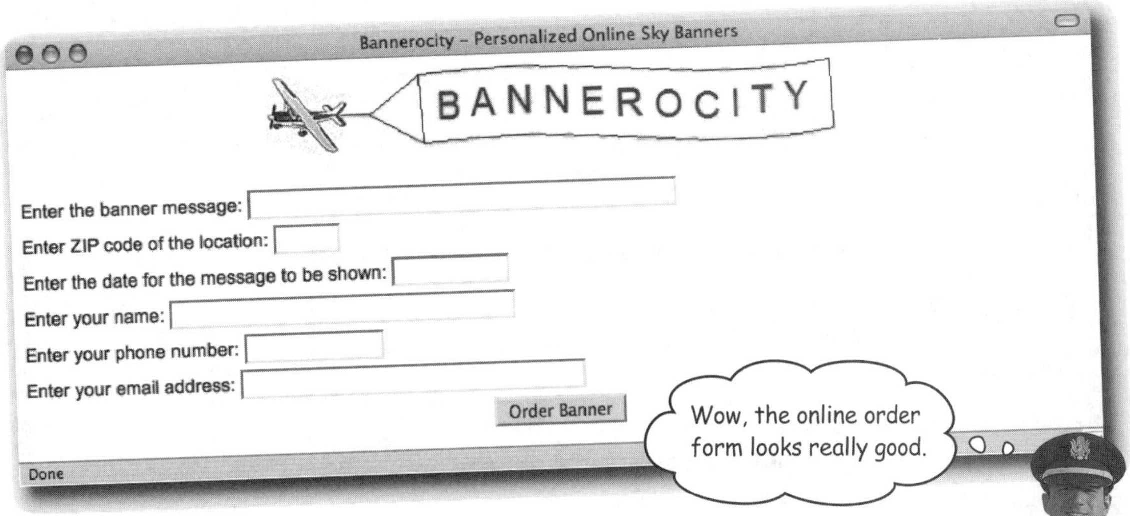

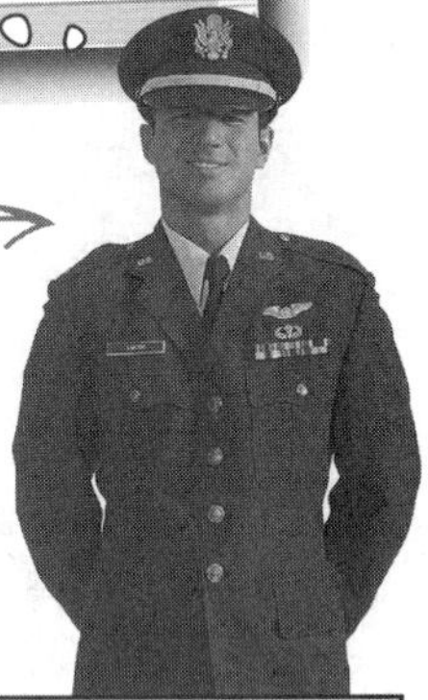

Howard has been in the private sector for a while now, but he can't seem to let go of that handsome uniform.

The shiny new Bannerocity order form has all of the necessary form fields, and is ready for taking orders without using any JavaScript code. What's the catch?

Download it from http://www.headfirstlabs.com/books/hfjs/ and get to work!

Sharpen your pencil

Try your hand at writing an order using Howard's HTML order form. Don't worry, you won't be charged for the banner ad!

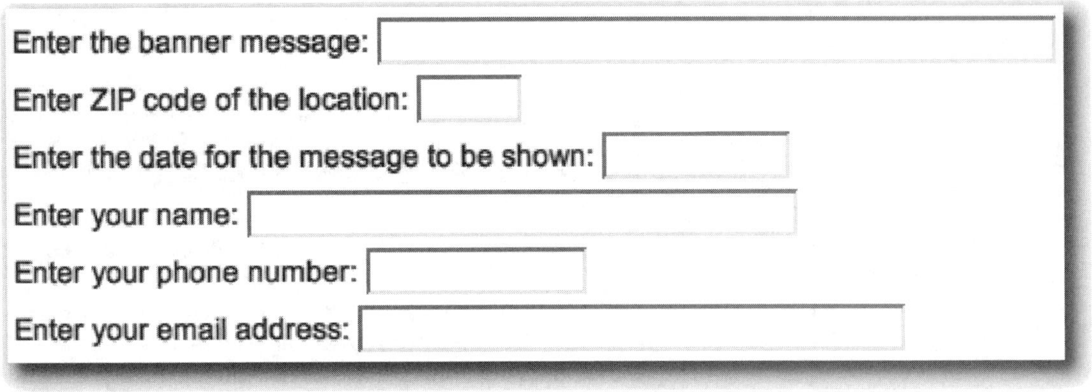

Enter the banner message:
Enter ZIP code of the location:
Enter the date for the message to be shown:
Enter your name:
Enter your phone number:
Enter your email address:

Sharpen your pencil Solution

Try your hand at writing an order using Howard's HTML order form. Don't worry, you won't be charged for the banner ad!

You didn't know but Howard can only display 32 characters on his aerial banner, so this one is too long.

Too many numbers in the ZIP code – should just be five.

Enter the banner message: Mandango... the movie seat picker for tough guys!

Enter ZIP code of the location: 100012

Enter the date for the message to be shown: March 11, 2009

Enter your name: Seth Tinselman

Enter your phone number: (212) 555-5339

Enter your email address: setht@mandango

OK, the name is fine.

This is an invalid email address – it's missing the domain extension, such as .biz

The phone number is supposed to be in the form ###-###-####, with no parentheses.

The date is not in the MM/DD/YYYY format that the form expects.

When HTML is not enough

Online forms are only as good as the data entered into them, Howard realizes he's going to need the help of JavaScript to make sure his form data is reliable. And he needs to help clarify to the user what exactly constitutes "good data." For example, without some kind of cue from the Bannerocity page, the user has no clue that there is a 32-character limit on the banner ad message, or that the date must be entered as MM/DD/YYYY.

I'm sorry, there's a 32-character limit on banner ad text.

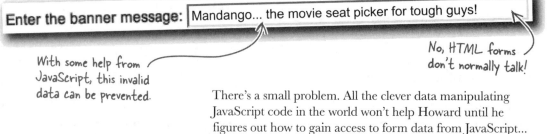

Enter the banner message: Mandango... the movie seat picker for tough guys!

With some help from JavaScript, this invalid data can be prevented.

No, HTML forms don't normally talk!

There's a small problem. All the clever data manipulating JavaScript code in the world won't help Howard until he figures out how to gain access to form data from JavaScript...

Accessing form data

In order to access the data that has been entered into a form, it's first necessary to uniquely identify each field in a form. This is handled in HTML code, using one of two (or both!) attributes.

The id attribute uniquely identifies any element in a page.

The name attribute uniquely identifies a field within a form.

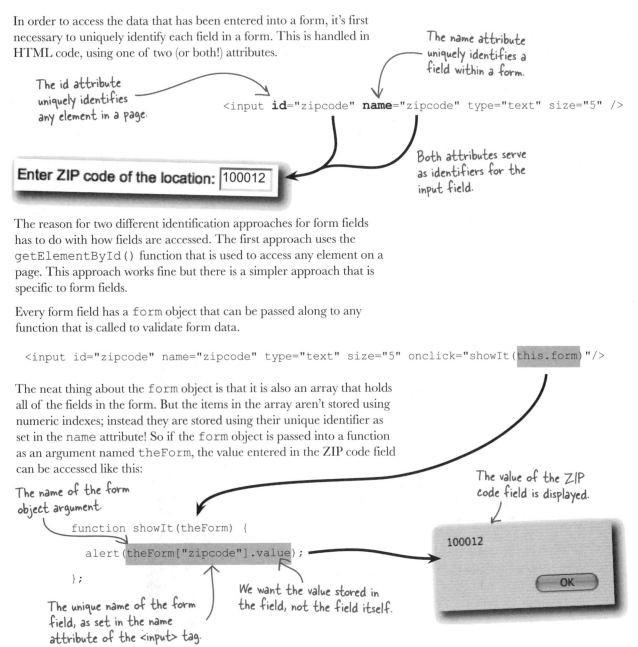

```
<input id="zipcode" name="zipcode" type="text" size="5" />
```

Enter ZIP code of the location: 100012

Both attributes serve as identifiers for the input field.

The reason for two different identification approaches for form fields has to do with how fields are accessed. The first approach uses the getElementById() function that is used to access any element on a page. This approach works fine but there is a simpler approach that is specific to form fields.

Every form field has a form object that can be passed along to any function that is called to validate form data.

```
<input id="zipcode" name="zipcode" type="text" size="5" onclick="showIt(this.form)"/>
```

The neat thing about the form object is that it is also an array that holds all of the fields in the form. But the items in the array aren't stored using numeric indexes; instead they are stored using their unique identifier as set in the name attribute! So if the form object is passed into a function as an argument named theForm, the value entered in the ZIP code field can be accessed like this:

The name of the form object argument.

The value of the ZIP code field is displayed.

```
function showIt(theForm) {
    alert(theForm["zipcode"].value);
};
```

100012

OK

The unique name of the form field, as set in the name attribute of the <input> tag.

We want the value stored in the field, not the field itself.

This approach to accessing form data is no better or worse than using getElementById(), other than making code easier to read since it involves less of it. The form object provides a shortcut, so you might as well use it.

---

there are no
Dumb Questions

Q: Why does an individual form field even have access to the `form` object?

A: Sometimes it doesn't, but keep in mind that a form field is capable of calling a validation function that needs access to the data in other form fields. In this case, the `form` object made available within each field becomes the key to conveniently accessing other form fields. This object is typically passed into the validation function so that the function can quickly grab any field it needs. The Bannerocity example continues to lean heavily on the form object to access fields in its order form.

Q: So is value a property of a form field? Does that mean each form field is really an object?

A: Yes and yes. Each form field is represented by an object to JavaScript code, and the `form` object provides a quick and easy way to access such an object for any field in a form. Once you have a form field object in hand by way of `form["objectname"]`, you can then access its value by tacking on the `value` property. You'll learn all about objects in Chapters 9 and 10.

> I get that knowing **how** to access form data in JavaScript is important for making sure data is OK. But how do you know **when** to check it?

Knowing when to check form data is dependent upon choosing the correct user input event to handle.

The answer to the "when" of data validation involves events, and understanding which event lets you know when the user has entered data into a particular field. In other words, the challenge is to respond to the event that is triggered immediately after data has been entered. But the question still remains... which event is it?

Form field follow a chain of events

When data is entered into a form, a flurry of events are generated. You can use these events as an entry point for validating data on a field by field basis. But doing so involves taking a look at a typical input sequence and understanding exactly which events are fired... and when.

1 Select the input field (`onfocus`).

2 Enter data into the field.

3 Leave the input field to move to the next one (`onblur/onchange`).

4 Select the next input field (`onfocus`).

5 Enter data into the field...

Entering data into a form sets off a chain of interesting JavaScript events.

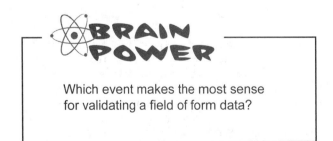

1 onfocus!

2 Enter the banner message: `Mandango... the movie seat picker for tough guys!`

Enter ZIP code of the location: `100012` **4** onfocus! **3** onblur! onchange!

5 Enter the date for the message to be shown: `[          ]`

Enter your name: `[          ]`

Enter your phone number: `[          ]`

Enter your email address: `[          ]`

The `onfocus` event is fired when a field first gets selected for input, while `onblur` is fired when a field loses input selection. The `onchange` event is similar to `onblur` except that it only gets triggered if the field loses input selection **and** its contents have been changed.

BRAIN POWER

Which event makes the most sense for validating a field of form data?

Losing focus with onblur

While there is an argument to be made for using the `onchange` event for data validation, there is a particular problem in that you can't use it to validate an empty field. The reason is that nothing is present when a form is first loaded, but since the form data hasn't changed either, `onchange` won't trigger even if a user navigates through empty form fields. The `onblur` event solves this problem by always being triggered any time the input selection, or **focus**, leaves a field.

The onblur event is a perfect trigger for data validation.

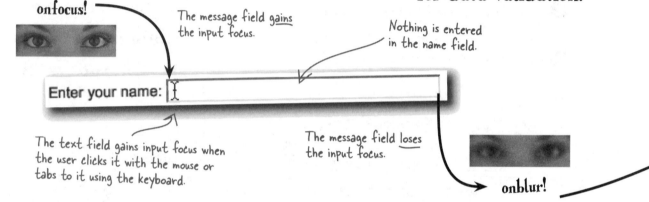

onfocus!

The message field gains the input focus.

Nothing is entered in the name field.

Enter your name:

The text field gains input focus when the user clicks it with the mouse or tabs to it using the keyboard.

The message field loses the input focus.

onblur!

Unlike `onchange`, `onblur` gets fired every time a field loses focus, even if the data hasn't been touched. This means `onblur` is very powerful, but also means you have to be careful about how and when you go about notifying the user of data validation issues. Case in point... the alert box, which can be an easy but risky proposition for validation notification.

---

there are no Dumb Questions

Q: Aren't some events generated when the user actually enters form data?

A: Yes. Several events are generated in response to keypresses, such as `onkeypress`, `onkeyup`, `onkeydown`, etc. While there are certainly situations where it makes sense to respond to these events, they aren't usually a good idea for validating data because the user is typically still in the midst of entering information when these events get triggered. Validating data using these events would be somewhat overbearing, notifying the user of every typo and unfinished piece of data as it is being entered. It's probably better to wait until users leave a field, which is an indication that they are finished entering data into it. And this is done by responding to the onblur event.

Q: `onblur` seems like a weird name for an event. What does it mean?

A: The idea is that `onblur` is supposed to be the counterpart to `onfocus`. So if `onfocus` is fired when an element or form field **gains** input focus, then `onblur` is fired when a field **loses** focus. Even though the word "focus" in this context isn't exactly referring to vision, the word "blur" is used to indicate a lack of focus. It's a JavaScript play on words that ends up being a little confusing. Just remember that `onblur` is fired when a field loses focus.

You can use an alert box for validation messages

Alert boxes are certainly handy for quickly displaying information to the user, and they happen to represent the most simple form of notification for letting the user know something is wrong with form data. Just call the `alert()` function while handling the `onblur` event if a problem is detected with the form data.

Check to see if the form field is empty.

A validation function is called to validate the name data.

```
function validateNonEmpty(inputField) {
  // See if the input value contains any text
  if (inputField.value.length == 0) {
    // The data is invalid, so notify the user
    alert("Please enter a value.");
    return false;
  }

  return true;
}
```

Instructs the user on how to remedy the problem.

> Please enter a value.
>
> OK

Since the name field is empty, an alert is displayed.

Sharpen your pencil

How many `onblur` events are generated by the following input sequence? How many `onchange` events? Don't worry about `onfocus`.

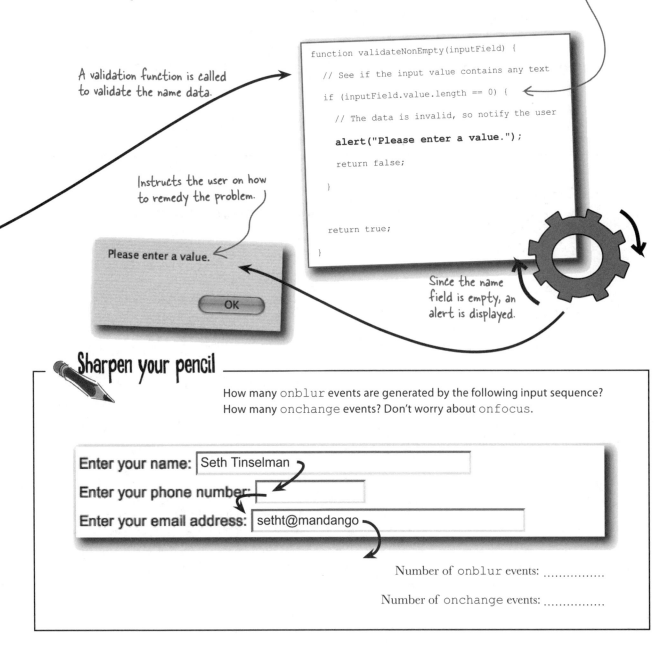

Enter your name: Seth Tinselman

Enter your phone number:

Enter your email address: setht@mandango

Number of `onblur` events: ....

Number of `onchange` events: ....

Sharpen your pencil
Solution

How many `onblur` events are generated by the following input sequence? How many `onchange` events? Don't worry about `onfocus`.

Enter your name: | Seth Tinselman — **onblur!** **onchange!**

Enter your phone number: — **onblur!**

Enter your email address: | setht@mandango — **onblur!** **onchange!**

Number of `onblur` events: __3__

Number of `onchange` events: __2__

Fireside Chats

Tonight's talk: **onblur and onchange discuss when to react to bad form data**

onblur:

These days it seems as if scripts are always worried about what the user is up to. I guess that's where you and I come in.

onchange:

That's right. We're quite a pair, always there to let somebody know when an element or form field loses focus or some data has changed... or both!

That's something I've been meaning to talk to you about. Rumor is there has been some empty data floating around and a lot of fingers have been pointing your way.

I'm frankly a little shocked by the accusation. You know I never miss a beat when it comes to notifying a script of data that has changed.

That's true. Nobody is questioning your reliability when data has changed. Problem is, what happens if a form starts off with empty data that never changes?

onblur:

That's true, it doesn't make any sense, and neither do some users, but they try to do it just the same.

Calm down, it's OK. It's not your fault. Look, it's not your responsibility to worry about data that never changes. Remember, you're name is on**change**.

Let's not get carried away. Like I was saying, it's not your responsibility. So if a script is worried about validating a form to make sure fields aren't empty, it really shouldn't be using you to trigger the validation code.

Hang on, try not to react so much. Even though you may not be ideal for triggering validation code, that doesn't mean scripts aren't sometimes interested in whether data has changed or not. What about a form that lets people edit data that gets stored away? You would make perfect sense for only allowing a save if the data has truly changed.

Absolutely! So there's no need to keep beating yourself up.

You're welcome. All right, I'd love to chat some more but I have some data to validate... see ya!

onchange:

Are you saying a user is capable of trying to submit a form with blank fields? That doesn't make any sense.

OK, so a form starts off blank with empty fields. The user skips entering some of the data and submits the form with the fields still empty... oh man, I think I'm starting to have a panic attack!

But what about the scenario we just talked about where I fail the script miserably on the empty data and the world starts coming apart at the seams?

Well that's a relief, even if it does mean I might not be of use to anyone anymore. Wait, I think I feel the panic coming on again...

Hey, that's true. So you're saying I still have a purpose?

Thanks. That's very reassuring,

Checking for... something

Back at Bannerocity, Howard knows that at the very least he needs to be validating the Bannerocity form to make sure all fields have data. But from a JavaScript point of view, this involves looking at things from an odd perspective. More specifically, instead of checking to see if a field **has something**, you have to check and see if the field **doesn't have nothing**. In other words, "something" equals "not nothing."

Something = Not nothing

The reason for this counterintuitive thinking is because it's easier to check a form field for emptiness than "fullness." So a first line of defense for data validation involves checking to see if a field is non-empty.

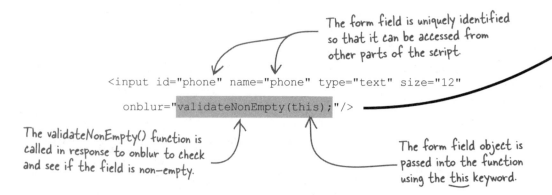

Non-empty.

Enter your name: Seth Tinselman

Enter your phone number:

Empty.

Howard's validation function must respond to the `onblur` event for each form field in order to perform the non-empty validation. For example:

The form field is uniquely identified so that it can be accessed from other parts of the script.

```
<input id="phone" name="phone" type="text" size="12"
    onblur="validateNonEmpty(this);"/>
```

The validateNonEmpty() function is called in response to onblur to check and see if the field is non-empty.

The form field object is passed into the function using the *this* keyword.

The `this` keyword is used in this code to reference the form field itself. By passing the form field as an object to the validation function, it gives the function an opportunity to access both the value of the form field as well as the `form` object that holds all form fields, which is sometimes helpful.

Validate fields to make sure you have "not nothing"

Each form field has similar code that wires the `onblur` event to the `validateNonEmpty()` function. By tying the `onblur` event of each field to the function, all of the data on the form gets validated.

```
<input id="name" name="name" type="text" size="32"
    onblur="validateNonEmpty(this);"/>
```

The name form field calls the validation function to see if there is a name.

The phone number form field calls the validation function to see if there is a phone number.

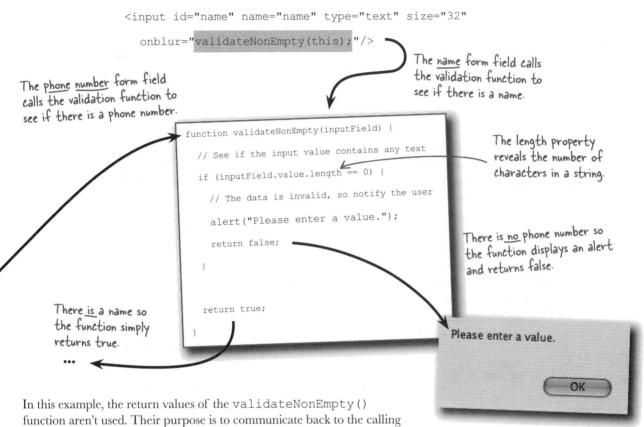

```
function validateNonEmpty(inputField) {
  // See if the input value contains any text
  if (inputField.value.length == 0) {
    // The data is invalid, so notify the user
    alert("Please enter a value.");
    return false;
  }

  return true;
}
```

The length property reveals the number of characters in a string.

There is <u>no</u> phone number so the function displays an alert and returns false.

There <u>is</u> a name so the function simply returns true.

Please enter a value.

OK

In this example, the return values of the `validateNonEmpty()` function aren't used. Their purpose is to communicate back to the calling code the result of the validation: `true` if the data is OK, or `false` if it's not. A little later we'll see how these return values are used to make sure form data is OK before submitting a form to the server for processing.

A non-empty validation function checks to make sure form fields aren't left empty.

⚛ BRAIN POWER

Can you think of any drawbacks to using an alert box to notify the user of bad form data?

Validation without aggravating alert boxes

It didn't take long for Howard to realize that alert boxes aren't ideal for notifying the user of invalid data. He's getting lots of complaints about all of the alert boxes that pop up when users are trying to enter Bannerocity orders. We've all become somewhat conditioned to be annoyed when a pop-up window interrupts the online experience, and data validation is no different, even though the alert boxes in this case are trying to be helpful.

Howard's solution is a "passive help system," which doesn't involve alert boxes, and therefore doesn't interrupt the flow of data entry. This passive approach to notifying the user does require adding a few new HTML elements to the form, however.

A new HTML element provides a place for displaying validation help messages.

> Enter your phone number: [   ] *Please enter a value.*

The new HTML help element represents a significant improvement over alert boxes because it doesn't get in the way, yet it still conveys the same information to the user. And all it requires structurally is the addition of an HTML `<span>` tag that is named to match the form field that it sits next to. This new `<span>` tag appears in the code for the web page form just below the input field.

A second argument to validateNonEmpty() now passes along the help text element.

```
<input id="phone" name="phone" type="text" size="12"
    onblur="validateNonEmpty(this, document.getElementById('phone_help'))" />
<span id="phone_help" class="help"></span>
```

The <span> tag is initially empty but it does have an ID that associates it with the phone number form field.

These two IDs must match in order for help text to be displayed for the input field.

The style class is used to format the help text in a red italic font, although it's hard to see red on this printed page!

With the `span` element in place that houses the help text, all that's missing is the code that actually displays the help message. And based upon the new second argument to the `validateNonEmpty()` function, there's a good chance that function will be responsible for making sure the help text gets seen by the user.

A more subtle non-empty validator

Howard's ingenious passive help message solution reveals itself in a new and improved `validateNonEmpty()` function that now also handles the task of setting and clearing help messages for a form field.

> The help text object is passed into the function as the second argument.

```
function validateNonEmpty(inputField, helpText) {

  // See if the input value contains any text

  if (inputField.value.length == 0) {

    // The data is invalid, so set the help message

    if (helpText != null)

      helpText.innerHTML = "Please enter a value.";

    return false;

  }

  else {

    // The data is OK, so clear the help message

    if (helpText != null)

      helpText.innerHTML = "";

    return true;

  }

}
```

> First make sure the help text element exists (helpText != null), then set its innerHTML property to the help message.

> It's important to also clear the help text once data has been entered into a form field.

Data validation in Bannerocity is now greatly improved thanks to the new passive help approach, which still uses a healthy dose of JavaScript but in a much cleaner way, at least in terms of streamlining the user experience.

> That's much better...no alert boxes...less intrusive.

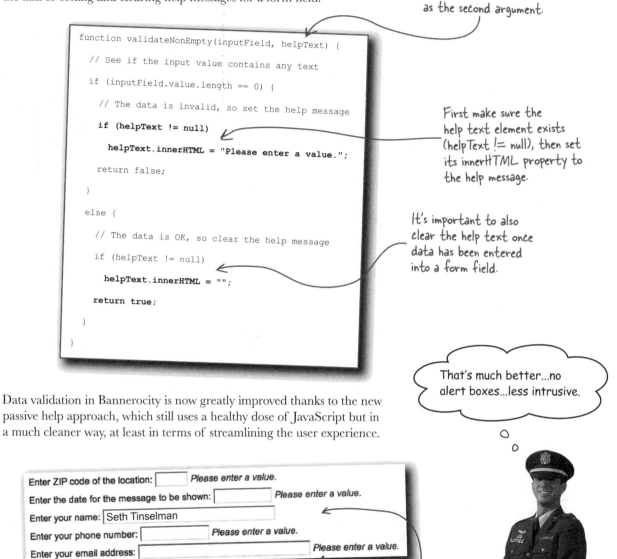

Enter ZIP code of the location: [ ] *Please enter a value.*
Enter the date for the message to be shown: [ ] *Please enter a value.*
Enter your name: [Seth Tinselman]
Enter your phone number: [ ] *Please enter a value.*
Enter your email address: [ ] *Please enter a value.*

> When data is missing, Bannerocity now just displays a passive help message.

> Name data is present so the help message isn't shown.

Too much of a good thing

As it turns out, non-empty validation works great but too much data can be as problematic as not enough. Check out Howard's latest banner, which reveals a new problem with the Bannerocity order form.

Only part of the banner ad text is displayed on the aerial banner... Seth and Jason are not happy!

Mandango... the movie seat picker fo

Hey, what's wrong, guys?

Dude, where's the rest of our banner?

I don't know, but flyboy Howard is about to get a strongly worded text message!

⚛️ BRAIN POWER

What's wrong with this banner, and what can be done to solve the problem?

Size matters...

The trouble with Bannerocity is that Howard's aerial banner can only hold 32 characters but the message field on the order form has no limit. Sure, it's great that the user gets warned if they don't enter a message at all, but a message that is too long still gets through with no problem. And this is in fact a big problem for Howard!

The user has entered too much text but Bannerocity doesn't tell them it's a problem.

Enter the banner message: Mandango... the movie seat picker for tough guys!

Mandango...the movie seat picker fo

Since there is more text than the banner can hold, the ad text gets chopped... not good!

Attempting to show unlimited text in a limited space doesn't work, and ultimately results in unhappy customers... like Seth and Jason. The solution is to validate the message field so that it has a maximum length. A more customized help message for the new validation is also a good idea to make sure that users understand the message size limitation.

This banner text is within the 32-character limit.

Enter the banner message: Mandango... macho movie tickets!

The text fits on the banner just fine when it is constrained within the maximum size limit.

Mandango... macho movie tickets!

Sharpen your pencil

Write pseudocode that shows how a new Bannerocity length validation function will work, making sure to validate both the minimum and maximum lengths.

....

....

....

....

Write pseudocode that shows how a new Bannerocity length validation function will work, making sure to validate both the minimum and maximum lengths.

If (fieldValue is shorter than minLength OR fieldValue is longer than maxLength)

Show the help text

Else

Clear the help text

Validating the length of data

The role of the new `validateLength()` function is to check and see if the value in a form field adheres to certain minimum and maximum lengths. In the case of Bannerocity, the function is primarily used to limit the length of the banner text field, although it does enforce a minimum length of one character as well. It's unlikely that Howard will find a client who wants to fly a letter L by itself, for example, but the main idea is to make sure there are no more than 32 characters and no less than one.

In addition to the minimum and maximum lengths to be enforced by `validateLength()`, the function also requires two more arguments for the input field to be validated and the help text element used to display a help message. That makes for a total of four arguments to the function.

`validateLength(minLength, maxLength, inputField, helpText);`

maxLength

The maximum amount of text allowed in the input field.

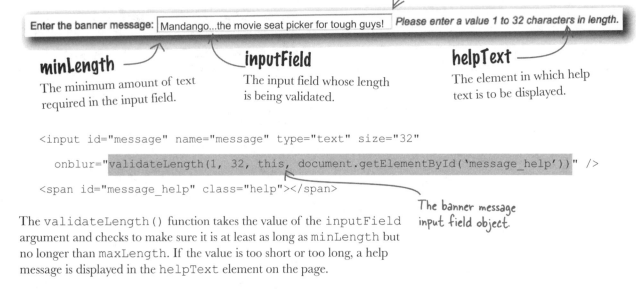

Enter the banner message: `Mandango...the movie seat picker for tough guys!` *Please enter a value 1 to 32 characters in length.*

minLength
The minimum amount of text required in the input field.

inputField
The input field whose length is being validated.

helpText
The element in which help text is to be displayed.

```
<input id="message" name="message" type="text" size="32"
    onblur="validateLength(1, 32, this, document.getElementById('message_help'))" />
<span id="message_help" class="help"></span>
```

The banner message input field object.

The `validateLength()` function takes the value of the `inputField` argument and checks to make sure it is at least as long as `minLength` but no longer than `maxLength`. If the value is too short or too long, a help message is displayed in the `helpText` element on the page.

BULLET POINTS

- Every form field is accessible as a JavaScript object.

- Within a form field object there is a property called `form` that represents the **entire form** as an array of fields.

- The `onblur` event is fired when the input focus leaves a form field, and is a great way to trigger a data validation function.

- Alert boxes are a very clunky and often annoying way of notifying users of data validation problems.

- A passive approach to validation help is much more intuitive and less of a hassle for users.

- The `length` property of a string reveals the number of characters in the string.

Sharpen your pencil

Finish the code for the `validateLength()` function, making sure to pay close attention to the arguments being passed to it.

```
function validateLength(minLength, maxLength, inputField, helpText) {
```

// See if the input value contains at least minLength but no more than maxLength characters

....

// The data is invalid, so set the help message

....

....

....

....

....

// The data is OK, so clear the help message

....

....

....

....

```
}
```

Sharpen your pencil Solution

Finish the code for the `validateLength()` function, making sure to pay close attention to the arguments being passed to it.

```
function validateLength(minLength, maxLength, inputField, helpText) {
    // See if the input value contains at least minLength but no more than maxLength characters
    if (inputField.value.length < minLength || inputField.value.length > maxLength) {
        // The data is invalid, so set the help message
        if (helpText != null)
            helpText.innerHTML = "Please enter a value " + minLength + " to " + maxLength +
            " characters in length.";
        return false;
    }
    else {
        // The data is OK, so clear the help message
        if (helpText != null)
            helpText.innerHTML = "";
        return true;
    }
}
```

Check both the minimum and maximum lengths of the form field value.

Set the help message to reflect the field length problem.

Clear the help text if the field length is OK.

Message problem solved

Howard is relieved that the banner length problem is solved. Short of buying a longer banner, he didn't have any other good options, so attacking the problem at the JavaScript level turned out being a good idea. At least users now know the limitations of Bannerocity banners up front before they order.

The help text now calls out a banner message that exceeds the limit.

Enter the banner message: Get your adventure on with Stick Figure Adventure! *Please enter a value 1 to 32 characters in length.*

there are no
Dumb Questions

Q: What's really so wrong with alert box validation? Don't most people realize that an alert box isn't a pop-up ad?

A: While it's probably true that most people realize a JavaScript alert box isn't a pop-up ad, it still doesn't eliminate the fact that alert boxes are regarded to be highly intrusive. Anything that requires the user to stop what they're doing and click something in another window is disruptive. So while alert boxes have a place in JavaScript programming, data validation isn't it.

Q: The usage of `this` in the `onblur` code for form fields is still confusing. Is the form field an object or is the form itself an object?

A: The answer is both. Within the context of an HTML element, the `this` keyword refers to the element as an object. So in the case of a form field, `this` is a reference to the form field object. Within a given form field object, there is a property called `form` that provides access to the entire form as an object. So when you see `this.form` in the `onblur` code for a form field, what you're really seeing is a reference to the form itself, as an object.

The purpose of `this.form` in the Bannerocity code is to gain access to the help text element that is associated with a particular input field. Remember that `this.form` is a reference to the `form` object, which is also an associative array containing all of the form fields. So you can quickly access a field named `my_field` using array notation with the code `this.form["my_field"]`. You could also use `getElementById()`, but the form approach is a little more concise.

Q: When a help text element is associated within an input field, what is the significance of the name and id attributes of each?

A: The `id` of a help text element is based upon the `id`/`name` of its associated input field but it's not exactly the same. More specifically, the help text ID uses the input field ID with the text `_help` tacked on to the end. The point of this naming convention is to create a clear and consistent connection between an input field and the element that displays help text for the field. In reality, you can name the help text element IDs anything you want as long as they are unique and get properly passed into the validation functions.

Q: Why is it necessary to clear the help message when data validates as being OK in a validation function?

A: Keep in mind that the point of help text is to give the user help when there is a problem. If the data entered into a form field checks out OK, there is no problem and therefore no reason to display a help message. And since a help message may already be visible from an earlier validation on the same field, the safe play is to clear the help message any time a field validates with good data.

Q: What happens if a help text element isn't provided as an argument to a validation function?

A: The script searches and searches for the missing element, overheats the page, and leaves a charred mess in the browser. OK, not really. By design, the passive help system in Bannerocity quietly disappears if the text help argument isn't used in a validation function. So the help text for the input field just isn't shown. This means the help text system is designed to be entirely optional. What's nice about this approach is that it allows help text to be used as much or as little as desired; even with individual fields, you aren't forced to add a help text element for every field on a form.

The validation code that checks to see if the `htmlText` argument is non-null is what allows the help text element to be optional. If the help text element is not `null`, it means the element exists and help text can be displayed. Otherwise, it just does nothing because the element is missing.

Q: Doesn't the `size` attribute of an HTML form field already limit the length of the field?

A: The HTML `size` attribute only limits the physical size of the form field on the page—it has nothing to do with limiting how much data is entered. As an example, the ZIP code field in Bannerocity has its `size` attribute set to 5, which means the field is sized on the page to fit about five characters of text. It is possible to limit the actual length of text in HTML using the `maxlength` attribute, but there is no `minlength` equivalent. A validation function provides the utmost flexibility in controlling the length of characters that may be entered into a field, although in the case of a ZIP code it would really be better to not only look for five characters of text, but to also make sure that they are five numbers. Maybe this is something Howard should consider adding to Bannerocity...

Right banner, wrong location

Howard's online form continues to cause problems despite his best validation efforts. This time a ZIP code has been entered incorrectly, resulting in Howard flying around for several hours over the wrong location. Perhaps worse than Howard's wasted time is his unhappy customer, Duncan, who missed out on some donut sales.

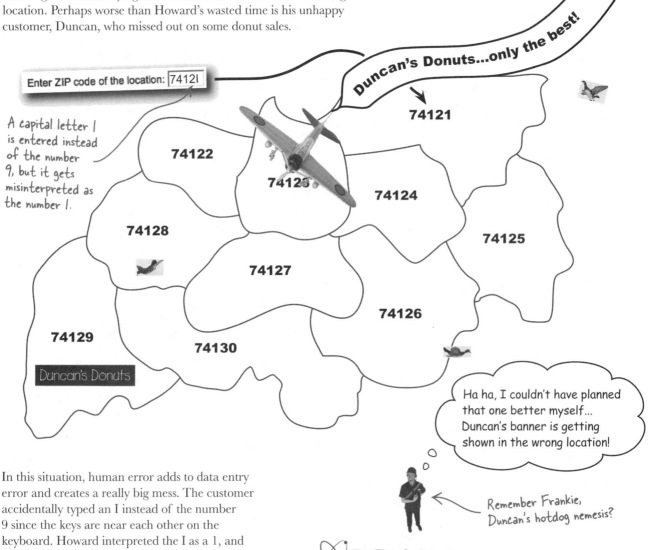

Enter ZIP code of the location: 7412I

A capital letter I is entered instead of the number 9, but it gets misinterpreted as the number 1.

Duncan's Donuts...only the best!

74121

74122

74123

74124

74128

74125

74127

74126

74129

74130

Duncan's Donuts

Ha ha, I couldn't have planned that one better myself... Duncan's banner is getting shown in the wrong location!

Remember Frankie, Duncan's hotdog nemesis?

In this situation, human error adds to data entry error and creates a really big mess. The customer accidentally typed an I instead of the number 9 since the keys are near each other on the keyboard. Howard interpreted the I as a 1, and ends up flying a banner over the wrong location.

⚛ BRAIN POWER

How would you validate a ZIP code?

Validating a ZIP code

Howard's problem has to do with a ZIP code not getting entered properly. At its simplest, a U.S. ZIP code consists of exactly five numbers. So validating a ZIP code can be as simple as making sure the user enters exactly five numbers... nothing more and nothing less.

 # # # # # ——— Exactly five numbers.

No letters allowed.

A3492 ⊘ ← → 007JB ⊘

37205

Too long. → 741265 ⊘

OK! ↗

5280 ⊘ ← Too short.

✏️ Sharpen your pencil

Finish the code for the `validateZIPCode()` function that validates ZIP codes to make sure they are exactly five characters long, as well as numeric.

```
function validateZIPCode(inputField, helpText) {
  // First see if the input value length is anything other than 5

  if ( ................................. ) {

    // The data is invalid, so set the help message
    if (helpText != null)
      helpText.innerHTML = "Please enter exactly five digits.";


    ........................
  }
  // Then see if the input value is a number

  else if ( ................................. ) {

    // The data is invalid, so set the help message
    if (helpText != null)
      helpText.innerHTML = "Please enter a number.";


    ........................
  }
  else {
    // The data is OK, so clear the help message
    if (helpText != null)
      helpText.innerHTML = "";


    ........................
  }
}
```

Sharpen your pencil
Solution

Finish the code for the `validateZIPCode()` function that validates ZIP codes to make sure they are exactly five characters long, as well as numeric.

See if the length of the ZIP code string is anything other than 5.

```
function validateZIPCode(inputField, helpText) {
  // First see if the input value length is anything other than 5

  if (   inputField.value.length != 5   ) {

    // The data is invalid, so set the help message
    if (helpText != null)
      helpText.innerHTML = "Please enter exactly five digits.";

    return false;
  }
```

Return false since the length of the ZIP code isn't exactly 5.

```
  // Then see if the input value is a number

  else if (   isNaN(inputField.value)   ) {
```

The isNaN() function checks to see if a value is Not a Number.

```
    // The data is invalid, so set the help message
    if (helpText != null)
      helpText.innerHTML = "Please enter a number.";

    return false;
  }
```

Return false since the ZIP code is not a number.

```
  else {
    // The data is OK, so clear the help message
    if (helpText != null)
      helpText.innerHTML = "";

    return true;
  }
}
```

Return true to indicate that the ZIP code validated OK.

It isn't always safe to assume postal codes are purely numeric.

If a web form is capable of receiving postal codes for addresses outside of the U.S., then validating for a purely numeric ZIP code won't be such a good idea. This is because plenty of other countries rely on postal codes that contain a mixture of letters and numbers. Additionally, full U.S. ZIP codes actually consist of 9 digits in the form #####-####, in which case the hyphen would make the ZIP code data non-numeric.

The Bannerocity validation functions are neat and all, but what happens if the user ignores the help messages and clicks the Order Banner button with bad data? Does the form still get submitted to the server?

Bad data should never make it to the server.

Yikes! All the data validation code in the world won't matter if the user can sidestep all of it by clicking a button and submitting the form despite a bunch of good intentions. Bannerocity's fatal flaw is that it doesn't subject the form fields to validation before submitting the form, which is why bad form data is currently capable of getting sent along to the server.

None of the data validation matters if the user has the option of ignoring it and submitting the form with bad data anyway.

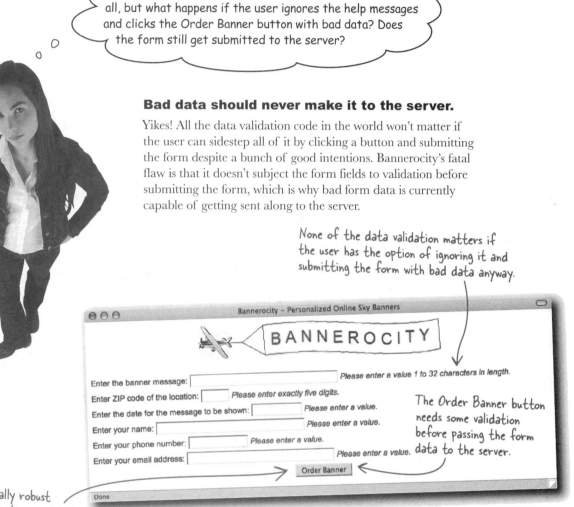

A really robust application would also validate the data on the server just to be safe.

The Order Banner button needs some validation before passing the form data to the server.

Bannerocity needs another function, and its job is to validate all of the form fields before submitting the form to the server for processing. The custom `placeOrder()` function is tied to the Order Banner button, and gets called to make a final round of validation before completing the order.

```
<input type="button" value="Order Banner" onclick="placeOrder(this.form);" />
```

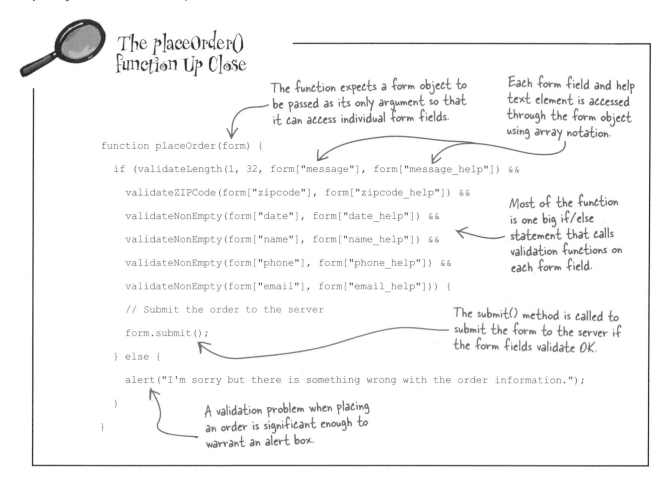

The placeOrder()
function Up Close

The function expects a form object to be passed as its only argument so that it can access individual form fields.

Each form field and help text element is accessed through the form object using array notation.

```
function placeOrder(form) {

  if (validateLength(1, 32, form["message"], form["message_help"]) &&

    validateZIPCode(form["zipcode"], form["zipcode_help"]) &&

    validateNonEmpty(form["date"], form["date_help"]) &&

    validateNonEmpty(form["name"], form["name_help"]) &&

    validateNonEmpty(form["phone"], form["phone_help"]) &&

    validateNonEmpty(form["email"], form["email_help"])) {

    // Submit the order to the server

    form.submit();

  } else {

    alert("I'm sorry but there is something wrong with the order information.");

  }

}
```

Most of the function is one big if/else statement that calls validation functions on each form field.

The submit() method is called to submit the form to the server if the form fields validate OK.

A validation problem when placing an order is significant enough to warrant an alert box.

there are no Dumb Questions

Q: How does the placeOrder() function control whether or not the form gets submitted to the server?

A: First off, the if/else statement in the function is structured so that the conditional involves a validation of every field in the form, which means if any of the form data is invalid, the else clause will run. The else clause only contains a call to the alert() function, so nothing else happens if the function makes it into this clause. On the other hand, if the data validates OK, the submit() method is called on the form object, which submits the form to the server. So the submission of the form to the server is controlled by calling or not calling the form's submit() method. This method is the JavaScript equivalent of an HTML submit button.

Q: I thought alert boxes were bad for data validation. What's the deal?

A: In many cases they are, but the real issue here is when it's OK to interrupt the flow of a page to display a pop-up message (alert) and require the user to read a message and click OK. Since the Order Banner button is only clicked when the user intends to submit an order, it's worth making sure they know there is a problem with the data. So in this case the problem is severe enough that an alert is appropriate. And don't forget that passive help messages are still displayed to help guide the user to a fix.

Timing is everything...date validation

Unfortunately, Howard's ZIP code and form submission validation fixes provide only a fleeting sense of relief because there is now an entirely new problem. He no longer flies over the wrong location thanks to validated ZIP codes, but now he finds himself sometimes flying banners on the wrong date, which is perhaps even worse. Something is amiss with the fly dates that are being entered...

Enter the date for the message to be shown: 05/1o/2008

A typo resulted in a date containing the letter o instead of a 9...it seems no one can type a 9 correctly.

Howard interpreted the letter o as a zero, and flew on the 10th instead of the intended date, the 19th.

Go on a Stick Figure Adventure!

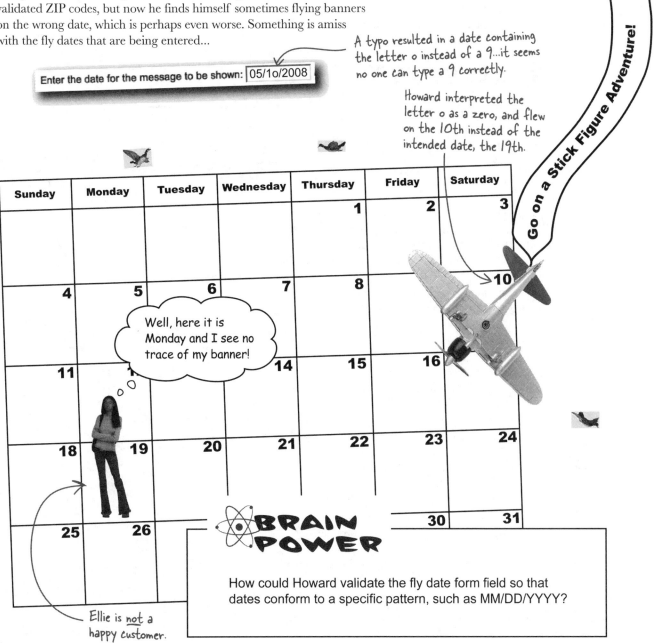

Sunday	Monday	Tuesday	Wednesday	Thursday	Friday	Saturday
				1	2	3
4	5	6	7	8		10
11	1	14	15	16		
18	19	20	21	22	23	24
25	26				30	31

Well, here it is Monday and I see no trace of my banner!

Ellie is <u>not</u> a happy customer.

⚛ BRAIN POWER

How could Howard validate the fly date form field so that dates conform to a specific pattern, such as MM/DD/YYYY?

Validating a date

Howard apparently isn't going to get by with just checking to see if the user entered data into the date field—he's going to have to actually check to see if a valid date has been entered. The key to validating a date is deciding on a specific date format, and then enforcing it. A common date format involves specifying the two-digit month, then the two-digit day, then the four-digit year, separated by slashes.

MM/DD/YYYY

The year consists of four characters... we'd hate to create a Y3K problem!

The month and day consist of two characters each.

Each portion of the date is separated by a forward slash.

Enter the date for the message to be shown: 05/1o/2008

Nailing down a format for a date is the easy part... coming up with code to validate a piece of data against that format is where things get messy. There are some powerful string functions that make it possible to tear a string apart based upon a certain character, such as a forward slash. But it's a fairly complex endeavor breaking apart a string into pieces and then analyzing each piece to make sure it is numeric and that it adheres to a certain length. It's kind of like the ZIP code validation challenge taken to the extreme.

Let's work through the steps of how a date validation function might work:

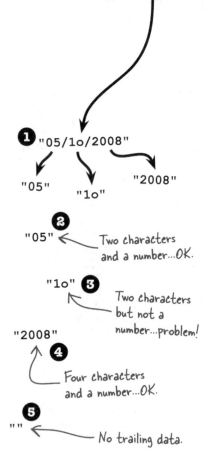

1 "05/1o/2008"

"05"   "1o"   "2008"

2 "05" Two characters and a number...OK.

"1o" **3** Two characters but not a number...problem!

"2008" **4** Four characters and a number...OK.

5 "" No trailing data.

1 Break apart the form field value into a collection of substrings, using a forward slash as the basis for separating the string.

2 Analyze the month substring to make sure it is exactly two characters in length and that it is a number.

3 Analyze the day substring to make sure it is exactly two characters in length and that it is a number.

4 Analyze the year substring to make sure it is exactly four characters in length and that it is a number.

5 Ignore any other data following the second forward slash.

While this series of steps isn't necessarily nightmarish from a coding perspective, it seems like an awful lot of work to validate a relatively simple pattern.

Wouldn't it be dreamy if there was a better way to validate data than hacking apart strings...A girl can dream, can't she?

Regular expressions aren't "regular"

JavaScript happens to have an extremely powerful built-in tool called a **regular expression** that is designed specifically for matching patterns in text. A regular expression allows you to create a pattern and then apply it to a string of text, searching for a match much like a suspect in a police lineup... but with more cooperative characters!

Sounds like a case of height, hair style, and vision profiling to me...

I don't see the point in any of this. When can I leave?

There must be some kind of mix up.

No worries... I'm always ready for trouble. I have my alibi right here!

A match!

Pattern = Tall, no glasses, short hair

The pattern involves physical attributes of a person.

A regular expression is used to match patterns in text.

The pattern describes physical properties of a person that are then matched against actual people. Regular expressions allow you to do the same kind of pattern matching with strings.

Regular expressions define patterns to match

Just as a pattern for a police lineup might involve the height, hair style, and other physical attributes of a person, a text pattern involves a certain sequence of characters, such as five numbers in a row. Wait a minute, that sounds like a familiar pattern... a ZIP code maybe?

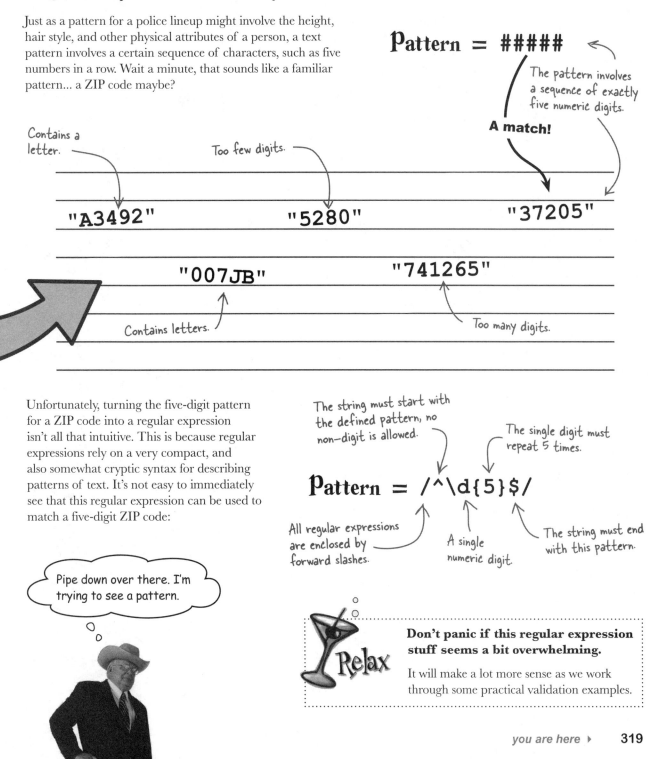

Pattern = #####

The pattern involves a sequence of exactly five numeric digits.

A match!

Contains a letter.

Too few digits.

"A3492"   "5280"   "37205"

"007JB"   "741265"

Contains letters.

Too many digits.

Unfortunately, turning the five-digit pattern for a ZIP code into a regular expression isn't all that intuitive. This is because regular expressions rely on a very compact, and also somewhat cryptic syntax for describing patterns of text. It's not easy to immediately see that this regular expression can be used to match a five-digit ZIP code:

The string must start with the defined pattern, no non-digit is allowed.

The single digit must repeat 5 times.

Pattern = /^\d{5}$/

All regular expressions are enclosed by forward slashes.

A single numeric digit.

The string must end with this pattern.

Pipe down over there. I'm trying to see a pattern.

Don't panic if this regular expression stuff seems a bit overwhelming.

It will make a lot more sense as we work through some practical validation examples.

Regular expressions exposed

Creating a regular expression is sort of like creating a string
literal except that the regular expression appears inside of
forward slashes (/ /) instead of inside quotes or apostrophes.

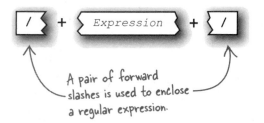

/ + Expression + /

A pair of forward
slashes is used to enclose
a regular expression.

**Regular expressions
always start and end
with a forward slash.**

Within the expression itself, a collection of special symbols known as
metacharacters are used in conjunction with letters and numbers
to create highly descriptive text patterns. The good news is that it isn't
necessary to know every nuance of the regular expression "language" in
order to create practical regular expressions. Following are some of the
more commonly used regular expression metacharacters:

Yes, it's just a period.

.

Match any character
other than a newline.

Whitespace includes
spaces, tabs, newlines,
and returns.

\s

Match a whitespace
character.

\d

Match any numeric digit.

Many metacharacters
start with a backslash...
very different than
the forward slashes
used to enclose a
regular expression.

\w

Match any alphanumeric
(letter or number) character.

The string being
matched can't have
any text preceding
the pattern.

^

The string must begin
with the pattern.

The pattern must be the
very last characters in
the string.

$

The string must end
with the pattern.

Although these descriptions of the regular expression metacharacters
are accurate, the metacharacters are much easier to understand when
examined in the context of a real pattern...

Metacharacters represent more than one literal character

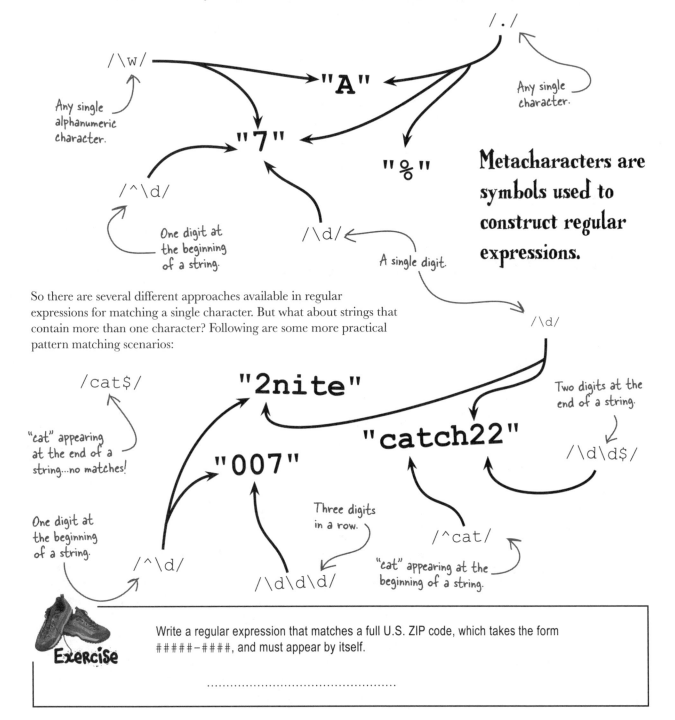

/./

/\w/ → "A"

Any single character.

Any single alphanumeric character.

"7"

Metacharacters are symbols used to construct regular expressions.

/^\d/

One digit at the beginning of a string.

"%"

/\d/

A single digit.

So there are several different approaches available in regular expressions for matching a single character. But what about strings that contain more than one character? Following are some more practical pattern matching scenarios:

/\d/

/cat$/

"2nite"

"catch22"

Two digits at the end of a string.

"cat" appearing at the end of a string...no matches!

/\d\d$/

"007"

Three digits in a row.

One digit at the beginning of a string.

/^\d/

/\d\d\d/

/^cat/

"cat" appearing at the beginning of a string.

Write a regular expression that matches a full U.S. ZIP code, which takes the form #####-####, and must appear by itself.

Exercise

....

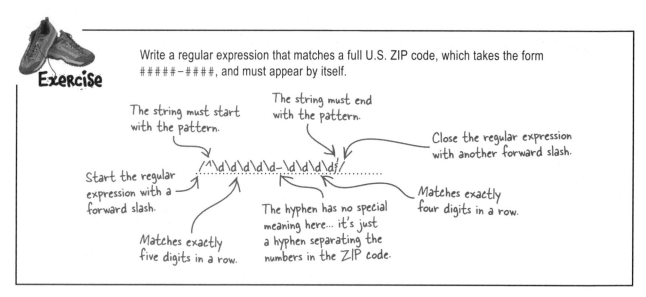

Write a regular expression that matches a full U.S. ZIP code, which takes the form #####-####, and must appear by itself.

The string must start with the pattern.

The string must end with the pattern.

Close the regular expression with another forward slash.

/^\d\d\d\d\d-\d\d\d\d$/

Start the regular expression with a forward slash.

Matches exactly four digits in a row.

Matches exactly five digits in a row.

The hyphen has no special meaning here... it's just a hyphen separating the numbers in the ZIP code.

Drilling into regular expressions: quantifiers

Any text that isn't a metacharacter is matched as-is in a regular expression, meaning that /howard/ matches the text "howard" in any part of a string. Additionally, there are some other regular expression constructs called **quantifiers** that further refine patterns. Quantifiers are applied to sub-patterns that precede them within a regular expression, and provide control over how many times a sub-pattern appears in a pattern.

*

Preceding sub-pattern must appear **0 or more times.**

The sub-pattern is optional, and can appear any number of times.

{*n*}

Preceding sub-pattern must appear exactly ***n*** times in a row.

Control exactly how many times a sub-pattern can appear.

+

Preceding sub-pattern must appear **1 or more times.**

The sub-pattern is required, and can appear any number of times.

Although not technically a quantifier, parentheses are used to group together sub-patterns much as you group together mathematical expressions.

?

Preceding sub-pattern must appear 0 or 1 time.

The sub-pattern is optional, but can only appear once if it does appear.

()

Group characters and/or metacharacters together in a sub-pattern.

Pattern quantification

Quantifiers allow regular expressions to be written much more concisely than with metacharacters alone. Instead of repeating sub-patterns explicitly, a quantifier can specify exactly how many times a sub-pattern should appear. As an example, the following pattern matches a ZIP code using quantifiers:

Quantifiers control the number of times a sub-pattern appears in a regular expression.

`/^\d{5}-\d{4}$/`

With the help of the {} quantifier, it's no longer necessary to list out each digit.

It's possible to get very creative with metacharacters and quantifiers to create quite powerful regular expressions that match just about anything that can appear in a string.

`/\w*/`

Matches any number of alphanumeric characters, including an empty string!

`/.+/`

Any character must appear one or more times...matches a non-empty string.

`/(Hot)? ?Donuts/`

Matches either "Donuts" or "Hot Donuts".

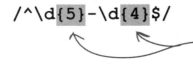

------ **WHAT'S MY PURPOSE?** ------

Match each regular expression metacharacter or quantifier to what it does within a pattern.

.   The pattern finishes at the end of the string.

\w   The sub-pattern is **required**, and can appear any number of times.

$ Match any alphanumeric (letter or number) character.

\d   Match any character other than a newline.

+   Match any numeric digit.

*   The sub-pattern is **optional**, and can appear any number of times.

WHAT'S MY PURPOSE?

Match each regular expression metacharacter or quantifier to what it does within a pattern.

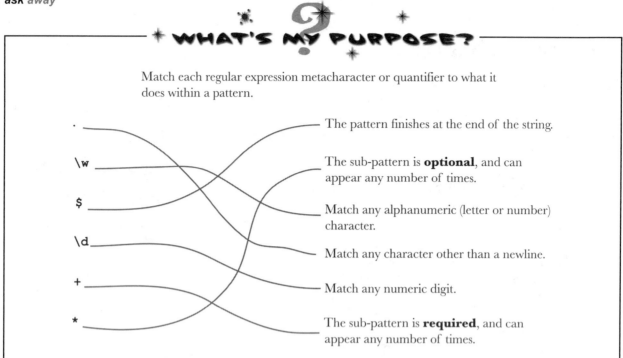

- `.`
- `\w`
- `$`
- `\d`
- `+`
- `*`

- The pattern finishes at the end of the string.
- The sub-pattern is **optional**, and can appear any number of times.
- Match any alphanumeric (letter or number) character.
- Match any character other than a newline.
- Match any numeric digit.
- The sub-pattern is **required**, and can appear any number of times.

there are no Dumb Questions

Q: Is a regular expression a string?

A: No. You can think of a regular expression more as a **description** of a string, or at least a description of part of a string. Regular expressions are closely tied to strings, and are used to match patterns of text that appear in strings, but they are not strings themselves.

Q: Can regular expressions be applied to other kinds of data?

A: No, regular expressions are designed solely for matching patterns of characters within a string of text, so they only apply to strings. But that doesn't limit them from being extremely useful in carrying out complex text-matching tasks that would be extremely difficult using strings alone.

Q: What happens if you want to match a metacharacter, such as a dollar sign?

A: Similar to JavaScript strings, characters with special meaning in regular expressions can be escaped with a backslash. So to match a dollar sign within a regular expression, you would specify the $ character as \$. This same rule applies to any other character that has a special meaning within a regular expression, such as ^, *, and +, to name a few. Any character that doesn't have a special meaning can be placed directly in a regular expression with no special formatting.

Q: Do regular expressions have anything to do with data validation? Weren't we originally trying to validate a date form field in Bannerocity?

A: Ah, patience, young Jedi. Soon use regular expressions you will. Yes, the reason for this little detour into regular expressions is to work out a way to validate data with a complex format, such as a date or an email address. Bannerocity still needs plenty of help on the data formatting front, so there will be plenty of opportunities to apply regular expressions. Just hang in there a little while longer.

Q: How are regular expressions used in JavaScript?

A: We're getting there...really! Regular expressions are represented in JavaScript by an object, which supports several methods for using regular expressions to match patterns within strings.

Master of Patterns

This week's interview:
The cryptic but powerful
regular expression

Head First: So you're the one I keep hearing about who is capable of looking into strings and recognizing patterns. Is that true?

Regular Expression: Yes, I'm a code breaker of sorts, able to look at a string of text and immediately pick apart patterns. The CIA could really use a guy like me... but they haven't returned my calls.

Head First: So you have an interest in spying?

Regular Expression: No, I just love looking for patterns in text. In fact, I **am** a pattern, any pattern. Just give me some parameters about what you're looking for and I'll find it, or at least let you know whether it exists in a string or not.

Head First: Sounds great, but can't the `indexOf()` method of the `String` object already handle string searching?

Regular Expression: Please tell me you didn't just go there... that amateur doesn't know the first thing about patterns. Look, if you need a painfully simple search feature that just looks for the word "lame" in a string, then `indexOf()` is your answer. Otherwise, you're going to quickly realize that `indexOf()` falls way short of doing anything serious when it comes to analyzing strings.

Head First: But isn't a string search a form of pattern matching?

Regular Expression: Yes, and walking to the mailbox is a form of exercise but you don't see it in the Olympics... yet. My point is that a simple string search is really the most simplistic form of pattern matching possible—the pattern is a static word or phrase. Now consider something like a date or a web site URL. Those are true patterns because although they adhere to strict formats, the specifics of what is being searched for is not static.

Head First: I think I see what you mean. A pattern is a **description** of text that can appear in a string but not necessarily the text itself?

Regular Expression: Exactly. It's like if I ask you to let me know when a person walks by who is tall, has short hair, and no glasses. That is a description of a person but not an actual person. If a guy named Alan walks by matching that description, we can say that the pattern has been matched. But there could be plenty of other people who also match that description. Without patterns, we wouldn't be able to look for a person based upon a description—we'd have to look for an actual person. So the difference between searching for a specific piece of text using `indexOf()` and matching a pattern using me is the difference between looking for Alan or looking for a person who is tall, has short hair, and no glasses.

Head First: That makes sense now. But how does pattern matching apply to data validation?

Regular Expression: Well, validating data is primarily about making sure data fits a certain preconceived format, or pattern. So my job is to take a pattern and see if a string of text conforms to it. If so, then the data is considered valid. Otherwise, the data is bad.

Head First: So is there a different regular expression for matching different kinds of data?

Regular Expression: Oh yes. And that's really where most of the work takes place in using me to validate data—coming up with a regular expression that successfully models a data format.

Head First: That is very interesting. I appreciate you explaining the role you play in data validation.

Regular Expression: No problem. I often have to explain myself...I suppose that's a behavioral pattern.

Validating data with regular expressions

As thrilling as it may be to create regular expressions purely for the sake of seeing patterns in text, we have a pressing need for regular expressions to help validate the date field in Bannerocity and get Howard back in the air. A regular expression in JavaScript is represented by the `RegExp` object, which includes a method called `test()` that is the key to using regular expressions for data validation. The `test()` method checks for the existence of a pattern within a string.

The test() method of the RegExp object is used to test a string for a regular expression pattern.

The regular expression matches a 5-digit ZIP code.

This object literal automatically creates a RegEx object.

The value of an input field, a string, is passed into the method.

```
var regex = /^\d{5}$/;

if (!regex.test(inputField.value))
    // The ZIP code is invalid!
```

If the test() method returns false, the pattern failed and the data is invalid.

The test() method is called on the regular expression object.

The return value of test() is true if the pattern matches with the string, or false otherwise.

Although we could make a call to the `test()` method inside of each different validation function, there is an opportunity to create a general regular expression-based validation function that more specific functions can call to do the generic validation work. The following steps must be carried out by the general `validateRegEx()` function:

 Perform a test on the regular expression that is passed as an argument, using the input string that is also passed in.

 If the pattern matches, set the help message to the help text that is passed as an argument, and then return `false`.

3 If the pattern doesn't match, clear the help message and return `true`.

```
validateRegEx(regex,
    inputStr, helpText,
    helpMessage);
```

Now all that's missing is the code for the function, which as it turns out, isn't so bad. In fact, the vast majority of this code already appeared in the other validation functions, so `validateRegEx()` is as much about code reuse as it is about creating an all-purpose regular expression validator.

The regular expression, input string, help message text, and help message element are all passed in as arguments.

```
function validateRegEx(regex, inputStr, helpText, helpMessage) {
  // See if the inputStr data validates OK
  if (!regex.test(inputStr)) {
    // The data is invalid, so set the help message and return false
    if (helpText != null)
      helpText.innerHTML = helpMessage;
    return false;
  }
  else {
    // The data is OK, so clear the help message and return true
    if (helpText != null)
      helpText.innerHTML = "";
    return true;
  }
}
```

The regular expression is tested against the input string.

If the test fails, the data is invalid, so the help message text is displayed.

If the data checks out OK, the help message is cleared.

Sharpen your pencil

Write the code for the validateDate() function, which calls both validateNonEmpty() and validateRegEx() to validate the date form field in Bannerocity. Hint: The function accepts two arguments, the date input field and its related help text element.

....

....

....

....

....

....

....

....

....

Sharpen your pencil
Solution

The validateNonEmpty()
function is called first to make
sure the field isn't empty.

Write the code for the validateDate() function, which calls
both validateNonEmpty() and validateRegEx() to
validate the date form field in Bannerocity. Hint: The function
accepts two arguments, the date input field and its related help
text element.

```
function validateDate(inputField, helpText) {

    // First see if the input value contains data

    if (!validateNonEmpty(inputField, helpText))

        return false;


    // Then see if the input value is a date

    return validateRegEx(/^\d{2}\/\d{2}\/\d{4}$/, inputField.value, helpText,

        "Please enter a date (for example, 01/14/1975).");

}
```

The date regular
expression is
passed into the
validateRegEx()
function.

Since forward slashes have a special
meaning in regular expressions, they
have to be escaped with a backslash.

The date regular expression uses
metacharacters and quantifiers to enforce
the MM/DD/YYYY format.

It might be a good
idea to also allow
people to enter the
year as only two digits.

It's debatable whether
your scripts will still be
used in the year 2100.

Y2100 is a long way away...

Knowing that we won't change centuries again for quite some time, it's
probably OK to allow users to enter the year as two digits instead of
four. Realistically, it's unlikely that any JavaScript code written today will
survive the 90 or so years it will take to present a problem. Howard briefly
considered a strict approach to future-proofing Bannerocity by sticking
with four-digit years, and then decided that he can live with a tweak later
if the code is still in use at the turn of the next century.

there are no
Dumb Questions

Q: **Why is it necessary to call the** `validateNonEmpty()` **function in** `validateDate()`**? Doesn't the regular expression already factor in empty data?**

A: Yes, the regular expression does inherently validate the date to make sure it isn't empty, and the non-empty validation could be removed and the date would still get validated just fine. However, by first checking to see if data has been entered, the page becomes more intuitive to the user, offering up specific help messages based upon the particular validation problem. If no data has been entered, a different message is displayed then if an invalid date has been entered. The end result is a passive help system that feels as if it guides the user through filling out the form. This subtle usability enhancement seems to be a worthy tradeoff for how little extra code is required.

Q: **What if I really want to future-proof my script code? Is that a problem?**

A: No, not at all. It's rarely a problem attempting to anticipate future needs and writing code that can adapt to those needs. In the case of Bannerocity, a four-year date field is certainly more future-proof than the two-year version. And keep in mind that if you really wanted to be crafty, you could allow the user to enter only two digits, and then prepend the number of the century to those digits behind the scenes. So the effect on the form is a two-digit year but the date is actually being stored as a four-digit year.

Matching mins and maxes

The {} quantifier accepts a number that determines how many times a sub-pattern can appear in a string. There is another version of this quantifier that takes two numbers, which specify the minimum and maximum number of times a sub-pattern can appear. This provides a handy way to fine-tune the presence of a sub-pattern.

Watch it!

Not all dates are in the format MM/DD/YYYY.

It's not necessarily safe to assume that all users are comfortable entering dates as MM/DD/YYYY. Many parts of the world reverse the months and days so that the format is DD/MM/YYYY.

`{min,max}` ← Control how many times a sub-pattern can appear as a minimum and maximum range.

Preceding sub-pattern must appear at least **min** times in a row but no more than **max** times.

`/^\w{5,8}$/` Some passwords allow between five and eight alphanumeric characters, which is perfect for the min/max {} quantifier.

Sharpen your pencil

Rewrite the regular expression used in the `validateDate()` function so that it allows both 2-digit years and 4-digit years.

Sharpen your pencil
Solution

Rewrite the regular expression used in the `validateDate()` function so that it allows both 2-digit years and 4-digit years.

The min/max version of the {} quantifier sets the minimum and maximum number of year digits allowed in the date.

/^\d{2}\/\d{2}\/\d{2,4}$/

Hang on a second. It looks as if the new date validation code also allows 3-digit years? That doesn't make much sense...

The date regular expression matches 3–digit years as OK...not good!

Enter the date for the message to be shown: | 03/01/200 |

No amount of revisionist history can add JavaScript support to the first through tenth centuries.

And since it wasn't supported back then, there's no reason to allow users to enter the year part of a date in the hundreds. In fact, there's no need to let users order aerial banners at any point in the past if we can possibly help it. So eliminating 3-digit years from the validation code is an important fix, and will help prevent Howard from facing an onslaught of new Bannerocity data entry problems.

BULLET POINTS

- A regular expression matches a **pattern** of text in a string, and is enclosed within forward slashes.

- In addition to normal text, regular expressions are built out of metacharacters and quantifiers, which provide careful control over how a text pattern is matched.

- In JavaScript, regular expressions are supported by the built-in `RegExp` object, but it is rarely seen because regular expressions are typically created as literals.

- The `test()` method in the `RegExp` object is used to a test a regular expression pattern on a string of text.

Eliminating three-digit years with this...or that

Another very useful metacharacter in the regular expression toolbox is the alternation metacharacter, which looks and works a lot like the logical OR operator in JavaScript. Unlike the JavaScript OR operator, the alternation metacharacter involves only one vertical bar, |, but it does allow a pattern to specify a list of alternate sub-patterns. In other words, the pattern will successfully match if any of the alternate sub-patterns match. This is a lot like the logical OR operator because it's basically saying "this, or this, or this..."

`this|that`

The pattern matches if the **this** sub-pattern **or** the **that** sub-pattern match.

The alternation metacharacter provides a handy way to specify alternate matches.

`/small|medium|large/`

Multiple possibilities can be specified using more than one alternation metacharacter.

`/(red|blue) pill/`

A simple choice of two, this pattern matches both "red pill" and "blue pill".

Sharpen your pencil

Rewrite the regular expression used in the `validateDate()` function one more time, and this time make sure the year can only be 2 digits or 4 digits, and nothing else.

....

is this your real number?

**Sharpen your pencil
Solution**

Rewrite the regular expression used in the `validateDate()` function one more time, and this time make sure the year can only be 2 digits or 4 digits, and nothing else.

The alternation metacharacter (|) lets the pattern accept both 2-digit and 4-digit years.

`/^\d{2}\/\d{2}\/(\d{2}|\d{4})$/`

Leave nothing to chance

Howard really likes the new, robust date validator that relies on regular expressions for precise pattern matching. In fact, he likes the validator so much that he wants to move forward and use regular expressions to validate the remaining two fields on the Bannerocity form: the phone number and email address.

Looking good...but I want more!

Bannerocity – Personalized Online Sky Banners

BANNEROCITY

Enter the banner message: Mandango...macho movie tickets!

Enter ZIP code of the location: 10012

Enter the date for the message to be shown: 03/11/200 *Please enter a date (for example, 01/14/1975).*

Enter your name:

Enter your phone number:

Enter your email address:

Order Banner

Done

The date form field is now validated using a regular expression, which is very accurate about enforcing the date format.

Howard's idea about validating the phone number and email address on the Bannerocity order form is a very good one, but it does mean we'll need to cook up some new regular expressions to successfully reign in those data formats.

Can you hear me now? Phone number validation

From a validation perspective, phone numbers aren't too terribly difficult to grasp because they follow such a rigid format. Of course, without regular expressions, they would still involve a fair amount of string hacking, but regular expressions make phone numbers a breeze to validate. Phone numbers in the U.S. conform to the following pattern:

$$\text{Pattern} = \text{###-###-####}$$

Since Howard doesn't plan on flying outside of his local area, it's safe to assume a U.S. phone number format.

By changing the dashes in the phone number pattern to slashes and tweaking the number of digits, it becomes apparent that the phone number pattern is very similar to the date pattern.

The date pattern conforms a date to MM/DD/YYYY or MM/DD/YY using the \d metacharacter and {} quantifier.

`/^\d{2}\/\d{2}\/\d{2,4}$/`

The phone number pattern is similar to the date pattern except it uses hyphens to separate a different number of digits.

`/^\d{3}-\d{3}-\d{4}$/`

The `validatePhone()` function becomes fairly predictable thanks to the phone number regular expression and the `validateRegEx()` function.

```
function validatePhone(inputField, helpText) {
  // First see if the input value contains data
  if (!validateNonEmpty(inputField, helpText))
    return false;

  // Then see if the input value is a phone number
  return validateRegEx(/^\d{3}-\d{3}-\d{4}$/,
    inputField.value, helpText,
    "Please enter a phone number (for example, 123-456-7890).");
}
```

You've got mail: validating email

With the phone number validation task nailed down, Howard's final challenge is to validate the email address field on the Bannerocity form. Like any other data, the key to validating an email address is to break the format down to a consistent pattern that can be modeled using a regular expression.

2 or 3 character alphanumeric.

Pattern = `LocalName@DomainPrefix.DomainSuffix`

Alphanumeric.

That doesn't look too bad—an email address is just three pieces of alphanumeric text with an at symbol (@) and a period thrown in.

All of these email addresses conform to the email pattern. Our work is done here...or is it?

`howard@bannerocity.com`

`sales@duncansdonuts.com`

`puzzler@youcube.ca`

Creating a regular expression to match this email pattern is fairly straightforward considering that everything is so predictable.

The period must be escaped since it is a special character in regular expressions.

The email address must start with one or more alphanumeric characters.

`/^\w+@\w+\.\w{2,3}$/`

The email address must end with a 2- or 3-character alphanumeric.

Following the @ symbol, one or more alphanumeric characters appear.

Although this pattern does the job, something seems amiss. Do all email addresses truly adhere to such a predictable format?

BRAIN POWER

What other variations of the email pattern are possible? Think about all the different email addresses you've ever seen.

The exception is the rule

Email addresses are actually more complex than they appear to be at first glance. There are quite a few variations on the basic email format that have to be considered when formulating a reliable email pattern for data validation. Here are some examples of perfectly valid email addresses:

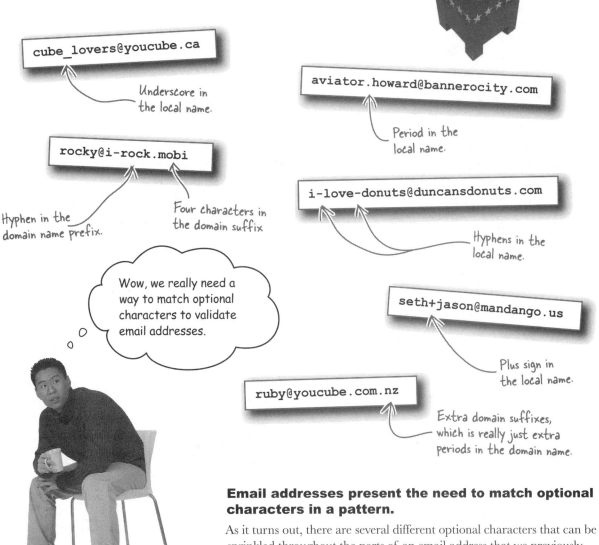

`cube_lovers@youcube.ca`

Underscore in the local name.

`aviator.howard@bannerocity.com`

Period in the local name.

`rocky@i-rock.mobi`

Hyphen in the domain name prefix.

Four characters in the domain suffix

`i-love-donuts@duncansdonuts.com`

Hyphens in the local name.

Wow, we really need a way to match optional characters to validate email addresses.

`seth+jason@mandango.us`

Plus sign in the local name.

`ruby@youcube.com.nz`

Extra domain suffixes, which is really just extra periods in the domain name.

Email addresses present the need to match optional characters in a pattern.

As it turns out, there are several different optional characters that can be sprinkled throughout the parts of an email address that we previously handled as purely alphanumeric. We need a way to incorporate such optional characters into a pattern...

Matching optional characters from a set

Another very handy regular feature that directly affects the email address pattern is **character classes**, which allow you to create tightly controlled sub-patterns within a pattern. More specifically, character classes excel at establishing rules where optional characters play heavily into a sub-pattern. You can think of a character class as a set of rules for matching a single character.

`[CharacterClass]`

CharacterClass is a set of regular expression rules for matching a single character.

Character classes are always enclosed within square brackets.

Within a character class, every character listed is considered legal for the character match, kind of like how the alternation between metacharacters lets you build a list of alternate sub-patterns. However, the result of a character class is always a match for a single character unless the character class is followed by a quantifier. A few examples will help put character classes into perspective."

Character classes offer an efficient way to control optional characters in a regular expression pattern.

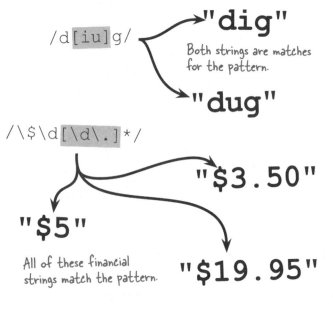

`/d[iu]g/`

"dig"

Both strings are matches for the pattern.

"dug"

`/\$\d[\d\.]*/`

"$3.50"

"$5"

All of these financial strings match the pattern.

"$19.95"

Character classes are exactly what we need to whip the email address pattern into shape and add email validation to Bannerocity...

Watch it!

Don't forget to escape special characters in regular expressions.

Characters that have special meaning in regular expressions must be escaped to include the actual character in a regular expression. Escape one of the following characters by preceding it with a backslash (\): `[\^$.|?*+()`.

Constructing an email validator

It's now possible to create a much more robust pattern for email addresses by factoring in all of the possible optional characters that can appear in the local name and domain name.

> This part of the email address can appear one or more times.

$$\text{Pattern} = LocalName@DomainPrefix.DomainSuffix$$

Any alphanumeric, as well as ., -, _, and +.

Any alphanumeric, as well as -.

The period is considered part of the domain suffix.

Any 2-, 3-, or 4-character alphanumeric, preceded by a period.

Keep in mind that there are many different ways to approach the creation of patterns, including the email address pattern. It can be surprisingly tough to create a pattern that successfully addresses every little nuance of a particular data format. We've already experienced how once the general pattern design is worked out, translating it to an actual regular expression is fairly straightforward.

Sharpen your pencil

Finish the missing code for the `validateEmail()` function, which is used to validate an email address in Bannerocity.

```
function validateEmail(inputField, helpText) {

  // First see if the input value contains data

  if (!......................... (inputField, helpText))

    return false;


  // Then see if the input value is an email address

  return validateRegEx(.............................................,

    inputField.value, helpText,

    ...........................................................);

}
```

Sharpen your pencil Solution

Finish the missing code for the `validateEmail()` function, which is used to validate an email address in Bannerocity.

```
function validateEmail(inputField, helpText) {
    // First see if the input value contains data
    if (!  validateNonEmpty  (inputField, helpText))
        return false;

    // Then see if the input value is an email address
    return validateRegEx( /^[\w\.-_\+]+@[\w-]+(\.\w{2,4})+$/ ,
        inputField.value, helpText,
        "Please enter an email address (for example, johndoe@acme.com)." );
}
```

The validateNonEmpty() function is still called initially to check for a lack of data.

The email regular expression uses most of the regular expression tricks we've learned to validate an email address.

The domain name suffix can be 2 to 4 alphanumeric characters at the end of the string.

The local name can be an alphanumeric, as well as ., -, _, and +, and must be at the start of the string.

If the email validation fails, a help message is displayed that clarifies the input format with an example.

A bulletproof Bannerocity form

The aerial banner order data collection in Bannerocity is now sheer perfection thanks to some intense validation efforts. Howard is so excited that he has decided to fly a banner ad of his very own.

Data validation is a good thing!

Howard is thrilled that he can get back to what he loves...flying!

The phone number and email address fields now validate according to very strict data formats.

```
Enter the banner message: Mandango...macho movi    ets!
Enter ZIP code of the location: 10012
Enter the date for the message to be shown: 03/11/2009
Enter your name: Seth Tinselman
Enter your phone number: (212) 555-5339  Please enter a phone number (for example, 123-456-7890).
Enter your email address: setht@mandango     Please enter an email address (for example, johndoe@acme.com).
                    Order Banner
```

JavaScriptcross

Here's a pattern you might recognize... a crossword
puzzle! No validation required—just a few answers.

Across

1. The JavaScript object that supports regular expressions.
2. Triggered when the data in a form field changes.
4. A handy way to specify optional characters in a regular expression.
7. This object contains all of the individual fields in a form.
9. A special character in a regular expression.
10. A description of a data format.
12. This kind of validation checks to make sure a form field has data.
13. Controls how many times a sub-pattern appears in a regular expression.

Down

1. Used to match patterns of text.
3. Do this to form data to make sure it is legit.
5. The method used to match a string with a regular expression.
6. Triggered when the user leaves a form field.
8. HTML attribute that uniquely identifies a field within a form.
11. Handy in many cases but usually not the best way to notify the user about invalid data.

 # JavaScriptcross Solution

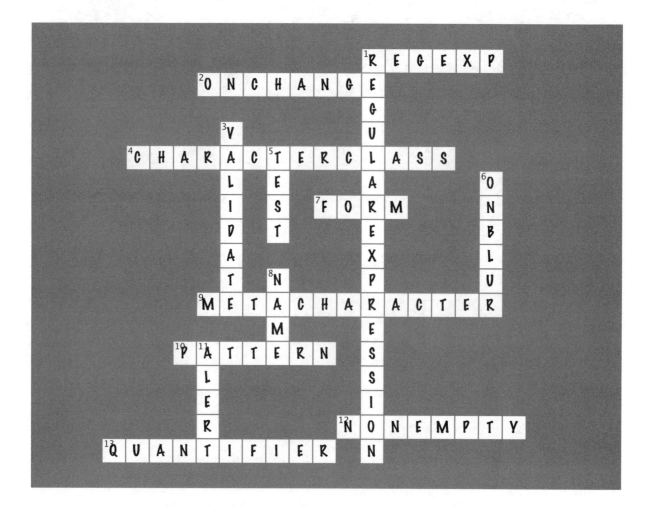

Page Bender

Fold the page vertically to line up the two brains and solve the riddle.

What does JavaScript bring to Web forms?

← ———— It's a meeting of the minds! ←

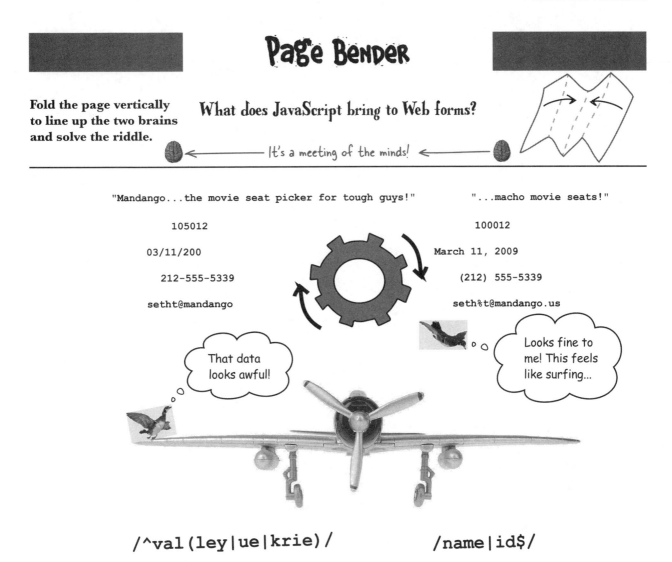

"Mandango...the movie seat picker for tough guys!"   "...macho movie seats!"

105012   100012

03/11/200   March 11, 2009

212-555-5339   (212) 555-5339

setht@mandango   seth%t@mandango.us

Looks fine to me! This feels like surfing...

That data looks awful!

`/^val(ley|ue|krie)/`   `/name|id$/`

JavaScript has a lot to offer web forms, so it's difficult to make a valid argument for any one thing. The answer almost certainly involves data on some level, but how, specifically?

8 wrangling the page

Slicing and Dicing HTML with the DOM

> With the right ingredients and a few flicks of the wrist, I can whip up just about anything. I just have to get close to what I'm making... you know, be the pie.

Taking control of web page content with JavaScript is a lot like baking. Well, without the mess... and unfortunately, also without the edible reward afterward. However; you get **full access to the HTML** ingredients that go into a web page, and more importantly, you have the ability to **alter** the recipe of the page. So **JavaScript makes it possible to manipulate the HTML code within a web page** to your heart's desire, which opens up all kinds of interesting opportunities all made possible by a **collection of standard objects** called **the DOM** (Document Object Model).

Functional but clumsy...interface matters

The Stick Figure adventure script from Chapter 4 is a good example of interactive decision making with JavaScript, but the user interface is a bit clumsy, especially by modern web standards. The alert boxes tend to feel tedious to navigate through, and the cryptic option buttons aren't very intuitive, seeing as how they are simply labeled 1 and 2.

Alerts can get annoying, and they break up the flow of the application.

Your journey begins at a fork in the road.

OK

Stick Figure Adventure works fine... but it could work a lot better.

Welcome to

STICK FIGURE ADVENTURE

Click either button to start...

Please choose: 1 2

The decision options are very cryptic, providing little context for making decisions.

Ellie realizes that it's time to right the wrongs in the Stick Figure Adventure user interface...

Describing scenes without alert boxes

The problem with the alert box approach to displaying the scene descriptions is that the text disappears once the user clicks OK. It could be better if the description was displayed directly on the page to get rid of annoying alerts and bring the story into the body of the web page. This is what Ellie wants the Stick Figure Adventure to look like:

The newest set of files for the Stick Figure Adventure are ready for you at http://www.headfirstlabs.com/books/hfjs/.

The scene description area now appears on the page as a replacement for alert boxes.

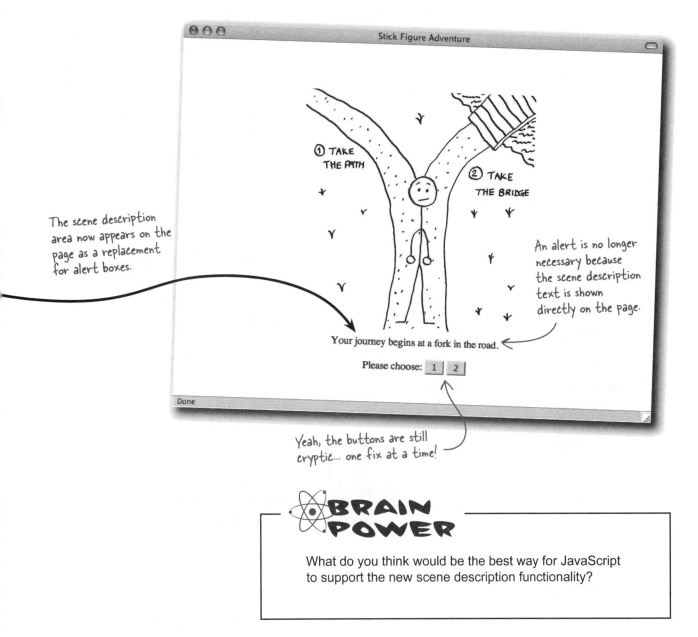

An alert is no longer necessary because the scene description text is shown directly on the page.

Yeah, the buttons are still cryptic... one fix at a time!

BRAIN POWER

What do you think would be the best way for JavaScript to support the new scene description functionality?

Creating space on the page with div

In order to display scene description on the page, we first need to define a physical area on the page as an HTML element before we can get serious about using JavaScript code. Since the scene description text appears as its own paragraph, a `<div>` tag should work fine for holding the scene text.

The `<div>` tag has an ID that uniquely identifies the element for holding scene description text.

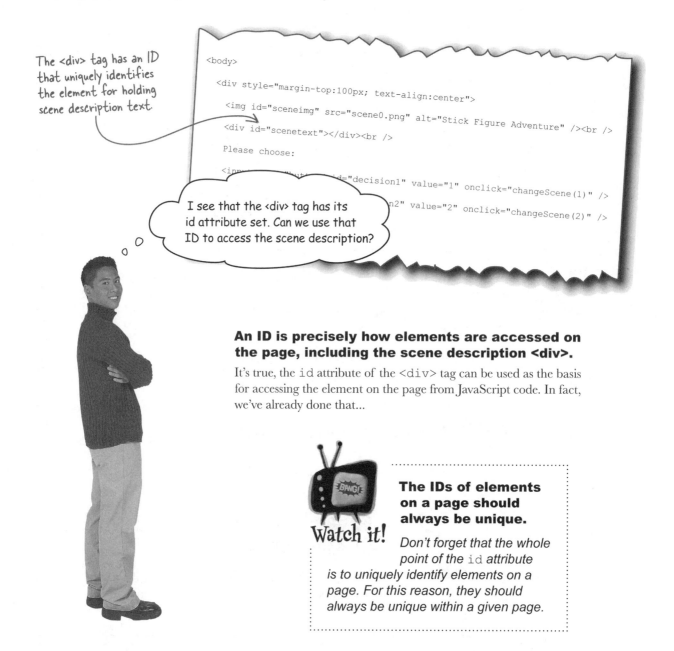

```
<body>

  <div style="margin-top:100px; text-align:center">

    <img id="sceneimg" src="scene0.png" alt="Stick Figure Adventure" /><br />
    <div id="scenetext"></div><br />

    Please choose:

    <inp           id="decision1" value="1" onclick="changeScene(1)" />
               n2" value="2" onclick="changeScene(2)" />
```

I see that the `<div>` tag has its id attribute set. Can we use that ID to access the scene description?

An ID is precisely how elements are accessed on the page, including the scene description <div>.

It's true, the `id` attribute of the `<div>` tag can be used as the basis for accessing the element on the page from JavaScript code. In fact, we've already done that...

Watch it!

The IDs of elements on a page should always be unique.

Don't forget that the whole point of the `id` *attribute is to uniquely identify elements on a page. For this reason, they should always be unique within a given page.*

Accessing HTML elements

The `getElementById()` method of the standard `document` object that we've used quite a lot. It allows you to reach within a page and access an HTML element...as long as that element has a unique ID.

> This must match the id attribute of the HTML element, in this case a div.

```
var sceneDesc = document.getElementById("scenetext");
```

> The div element is accessed using its id attribute.

```
<img id="sceneimg" src="scene0.png" ...
<div id="scenetext"></div><br />
Please choose:
```

With the scene description element in hand, we're one step closer to manipulating the content stored in it. But there's one other method worth investigating first. It's the `getElementsByTagName()` method, which grabs all of the elements on a page of a certain kind, like `div` or `img`. This method returns an array containing all of the elements on the page, in the order that they appear in the HTML.

> The name of the tag itself, without the <>.

```
var divs = document.getElementsByTagName("div");
```

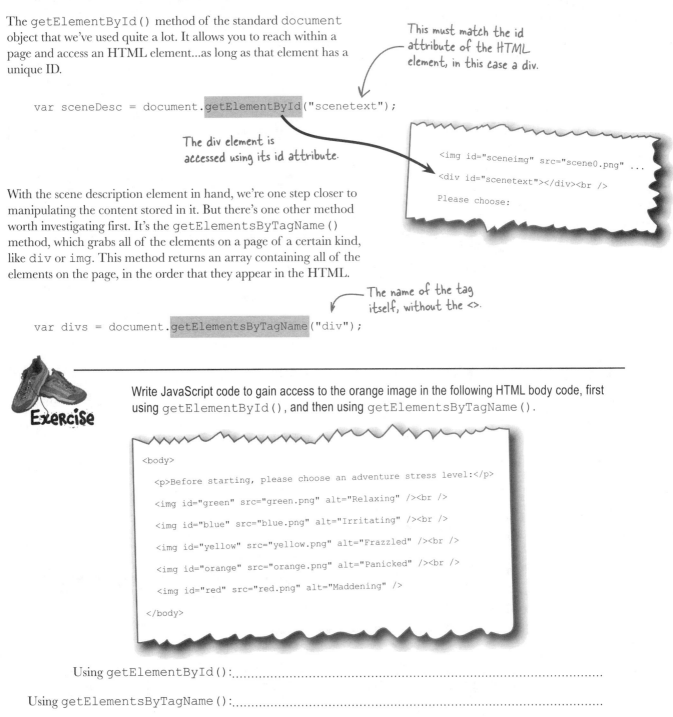

Exercise

Write JavaScript code to gain access to the orange image in the following HTML body code, first using `getElementById()`, and then using `getElementsByTagName()`.

```
<body>
  <p>Before starting, please choose an adventure stress level:</p>
  <img id="green" src="green.png" alt="Relaxing" /><br />
  <img id="blue" src="blue.png" alt="Irritating" /><br />
  <img id="yellow" src="yellow.png" alt="Frazzled" /><br />
  <img id="orange" src="orange.png" alt="Panicked" /><br />
  <img id="red" src="red.png" alt="Maddening" />
</body>
```

Using `getElementById()`:..

Using `getElementsByTagName()`:..

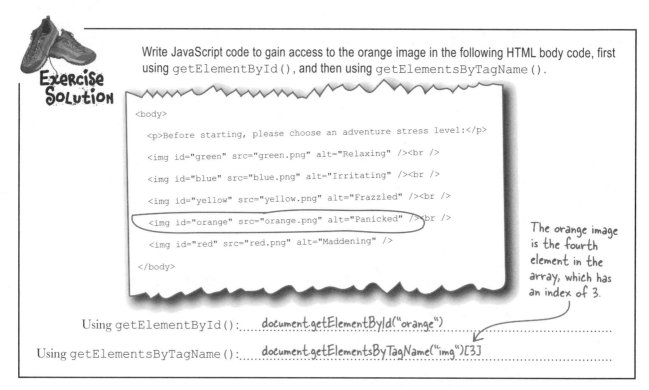

Write JavaScript code to gain access to the orange image in the following HTML body code, first using `getElementById()`, and then using `getElementsByTagName()`.

```
<body>
  <p>Before starting, please choose an adventure stress level:</p>
  <img id="green" src="green.png" alt="Relaxing" /><br />
  <img id="blue" src="blue.png" alt="Irritating" /><br />
  <img id="yellow" src="yellow.png" alt="Frazzled" /><br />
  <img id="orange" src="orange.png" alt="Panicked" /><br />
  <img id="red" src="red.png" alt="Maddening" />
</body>
```

The orange image is the fourth element in the array, which has an index of 3.

Using `getElementById()`: _document.getElementById("orange")_

Using `getElementsByTagName()`: _document.getElementsByTagName("img")[3]_

Getting in touch with your inner HTML

OK, the real point of all this HTML element access business is getting to the content stored in an element. You can access HTML elements that are capable of holding text content, such as `div` and `p`, by using a property called `innerHTML`.

The innerHTML property provides access to all of the content stored in an element.

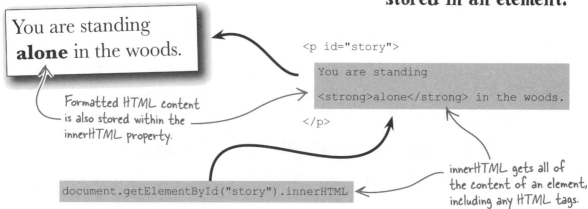

You are standing **alone** in the woods.

Formatted HTML content is also stored within the innerHTML property.

```
<p id="story">
  You are standing
  <strong>alone</strong> in the woods.
</p>
```

```
document.getElementById("story").innerHTML
```

innerHTML gets all of the content of an element, including any HTML tags.

It seems as if you should be able to set the content of an HTML element as easily as you can get it. Is that possible?

innerHTML can also be used to set content on the page.

The innerHTML property is actually used for **setting** HTML content just as much as it is for **getting** it. The content of an element can be set to a string of HTML text just by assigning the string of text to the element's innerHTML property. The new content replaces any content that previously belonged to the element.

```
document.getElementById("story").innerHTML =
    "You are <strong>not</strong> alone!";
```

Element content is set, or in this case replaced, by assigning a string to the innerHTML property.

You are **not** alone!

Sharpen your pencil

Assuming the scene description message is already being correctly set based upon decisions made by the user, write the line of code that sets the message text to the scene description element on the Stick Figure Adventure page using innerHTML.

....

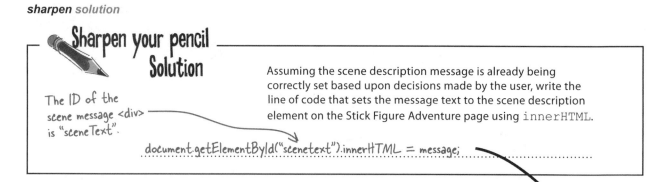

Sharpen your pencil Solution

The ID of the scene message <div> is "sceneText".

Assuming the scene description message is already being correctly set based upon decisions made by the user, write the line of code that sets the message text to the scene description element on the Stick Figure Adventure page using innerHTML.

```
document.getElementById("scenetext").innerHTML = message;
```

An adventure with less interruptions

The dynamically changing scene description area gives Stick Figure Adventure a smoother and more enjoyable user experience with no pesky alerts.

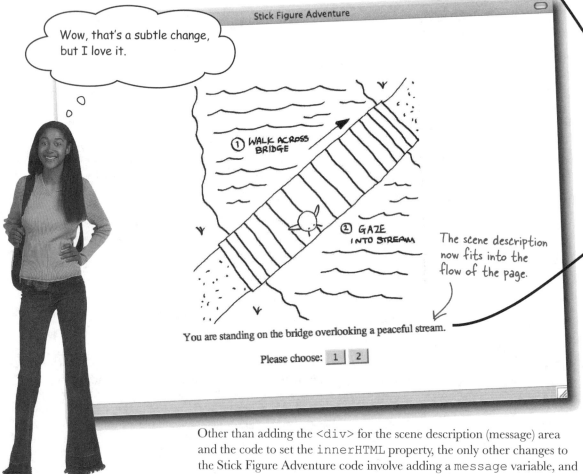

Wow, that's a subtle change, but I love it.

The scene description now fits into the flow of the page.

Other than adding the <div> for the scene description (message) area and the code to set the innerHTML property, the only other changes to the Stick Figure Adventure code involve adding a message variable, and then setting it in each different scene...

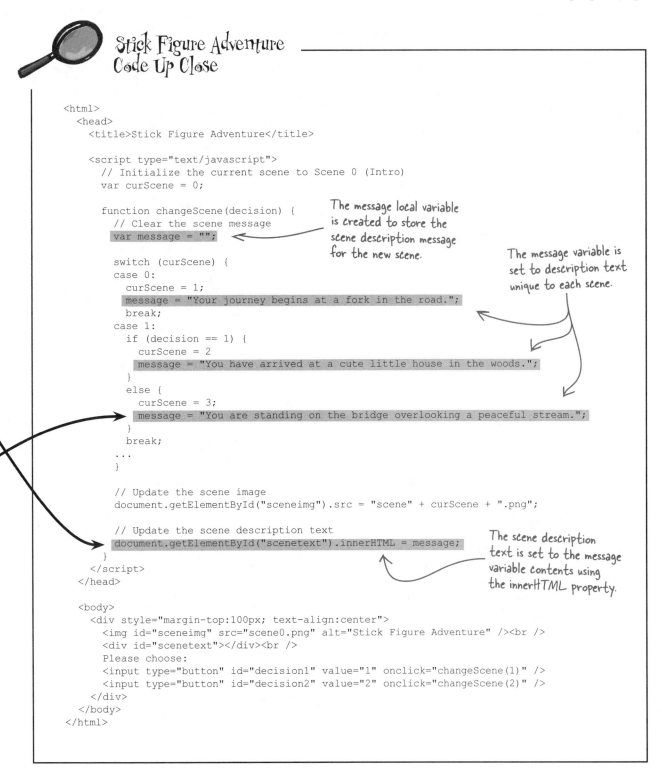

**Stick Figure Adventure
Code Up Close**

```
<html>
  <head>
    <title>Stick Figure Adventure</title>

    <script type="text/javascript">
      // Initialize the current scene to Scene 0 (Intro)
      var curScene = 0;

      function changeScene(decision) {
        // Clear the scene message
        var message = "";

        switch (curScene) {
        case 0:
          curScene = 1;
          message = "Your journey begins at a fork in the road.";
          break;
        case 1:
          if (decision == 1) {
            curScene = 2
            message = "You have arrived at a cute little house in the woods.";
          }
          else {
            curScene = 3;
            message = "You are standing on the bridge overlooking a peaceful stream.";
          }
          break;
        ...
        }

        // Update the scene image
        document.getElementById("sceneimg").src = "scene" + curScene + ".png";

        // Update the scene description text
        document.getElementById("scenetext").innerHTML = message;
      }
    </script>
  </head>

  <body>
    <div style="margin-top:100px; text-align:center">
      <img id="sceneimg" src="scene0.png" alt="Stick Figure Adventure" /><br />
      <div id="scenetext"></div><br />
      Please choose:
      <input type="button" id="decision1" value="1" onclick="changeScene(1)" />
      <input type="button" id="decision2" value="2" onclick="changeScene(2)" />
    </div>
  </body>
</html>
```

The message local variable is created to store the scene description message for the new scene.

The message variable is set to description text unique to each scene.

The scene description text is set to the message variable contents using the innerHTML property.

there are no

Dumb Questions

Q: Can I use `getElementById()` to access any element on a page?

A: Yes, but only if the element has its `id` attribute set to a unique value. The `id` attribute is absolutely essential to using the `getElementById()` method.

Q: Can `innerHTML` be used to set the content of any HTML element?

A: No. In order to set the "inner HTML" content of an element, the element must be capable of containing HTML content. So in reality, `innerHTML`.is for setting the content of elements like `div`, `span`, `p`, and other elements that act as content containers.

Q: When you set the content of an element with `innerHTML` **what happens to the content?**

A: The `innerHTML` property always completely overwrites any prior content when you set it. So there is no concept of **appending** content to `innerHTML`, although you can get the effect of appending content by concatenating the new content onto the old content, and then assigning the result to `innerHTML`, like this:
```
elem.innerHTML += " This
sentence gets appended.
```

Not so fast. I heard innerHTML isn't even a Web standard. Is that true?

Well, yes, but are web standards really anything to worry about?

It's true, `innerHTML` was originally created by Microsoft as a proprietary feature for the Internet Explorer browser. Since then, other browsers have adopted `innerHTML`, and it has become an **unofficial** standard for quickly and easily changing the content of web page elements.

But the fact remains that `innerHTML` isn't standard. That may not seem like a big deal but the idea behind standards is to make web pages and applications work on as many browsers and platforms as possible. Besides, there is a standards-compliant way of accomplishing the same task that is ultimately more flexible and more powerful, even if it isn't quite as simple. This approach involves the DOM, or Document Object Model, a collection of objects that provide JavaScript with complete and total control over the structure and content of web pages.

Seeing the forest <u>and</u> the trees: the Document Object Model (DOM)

The DOM offers a script-friendly view into the structure and content of a web page, which is important if you'd like to use JavaScript to dynamically alter a page. Through the lens of the DOM, a page looks like a hierarchy of elements in the shape of a tree. Each leaf on the tree is a **node**, which directly relates to each element on a page. When a node appears beneath another node on the tree, it is considered a **child** of that node.

Yeah, it's a strange-looking tree, but the nodes for a page do resemble a tree.

```html
<html>

  <head></head>


  <body>

    <p id="story">

      You are standing <strong>alone</strong> in the woods.

    </p>

  </body>

</html>
```

At the top of every DOM tree sits the Document node, which is just above the HTML element.

The DOM "sees" a web page as a hierarchical tree of nodes.

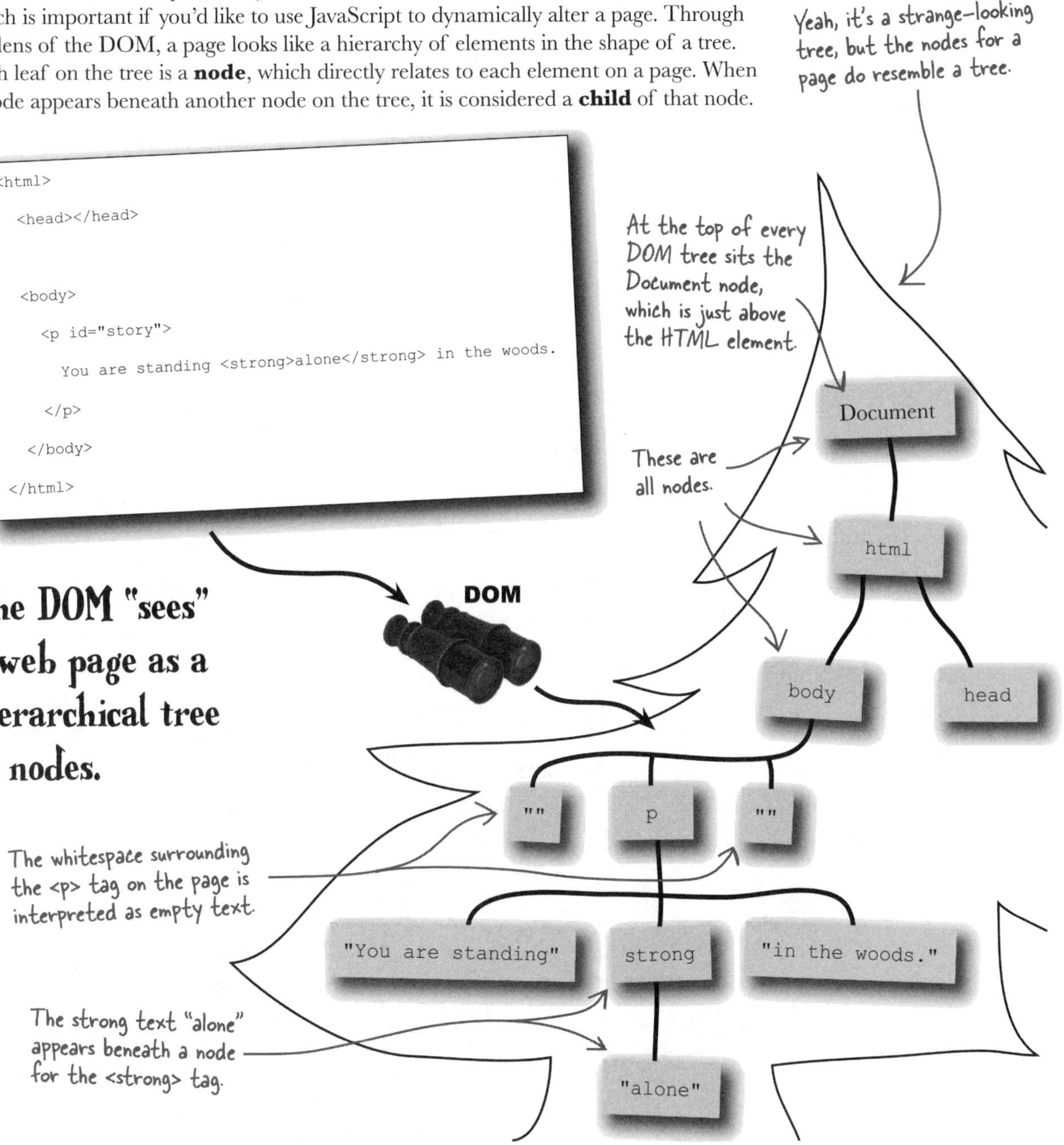

DOM

These are all nodes.

Document

html

body   head

The whitespace surrounding the `<p>` tag on the page is interpreted as empty text.

`""`   `p`   `""`

`"You are standing"`   `strong`   `"in the woods."`

The strong text "alone" appears beneath a node for the `<strong>` tag.

`"alone"`

Your page is a collection of DOM nodes

Every node in a DOM tree is classified according to its **type**. The main node types correspond to structural parts of a page, primarily consisting of element nodes and text nodes.

DOM nodes are classified according to their node types.

DOCUMENT

The top node in a DOM tree, representing the document itself, and appearing just above the `html` element.

ELEMENT

Any HTML element that corresponds to a tag in HTML code.

TEXT

The text content for an element, always stored as a child node beneath an element.

ATTRIBUTE

An attribute of an element, accessible through an element node, but not present directly in the DOM tree.

Applying node types to the DOM tree for a web page helps to clarify exactly how each piece of a page is perceived by the DOM. Of particular interest is how the TEXT nodes always appear immediately beneath an ELEMENT node as part (or all) of the node's content.

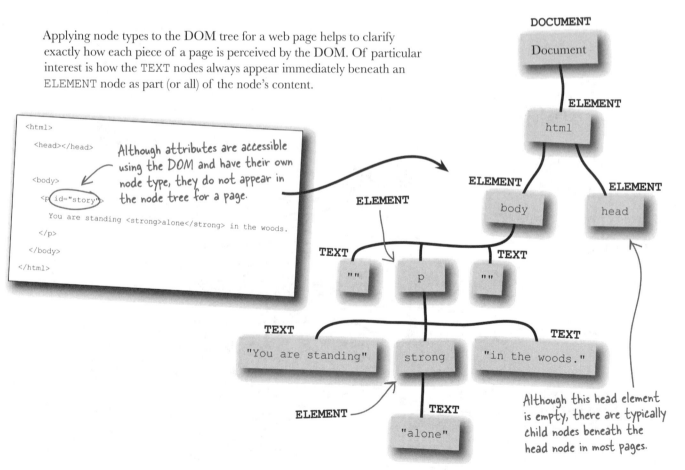

```
<html>
 <head></head>

 <body>
  <p id="story">
   You are standing <strong>alone</strong> in the woods.
  </p>
 </body>
</html>
```

Although attributes are accessible using the DOM and have their own node type, they do not appear in the node tree for a page.

Although this head element is empty, there are typically child nodes beneath the head node in most pages.

Sharpen your pencil

Complete the DOM tree representation of the Stick Figure Adventure HTML code by writing in the name of each node. Also annotate the type of each node.

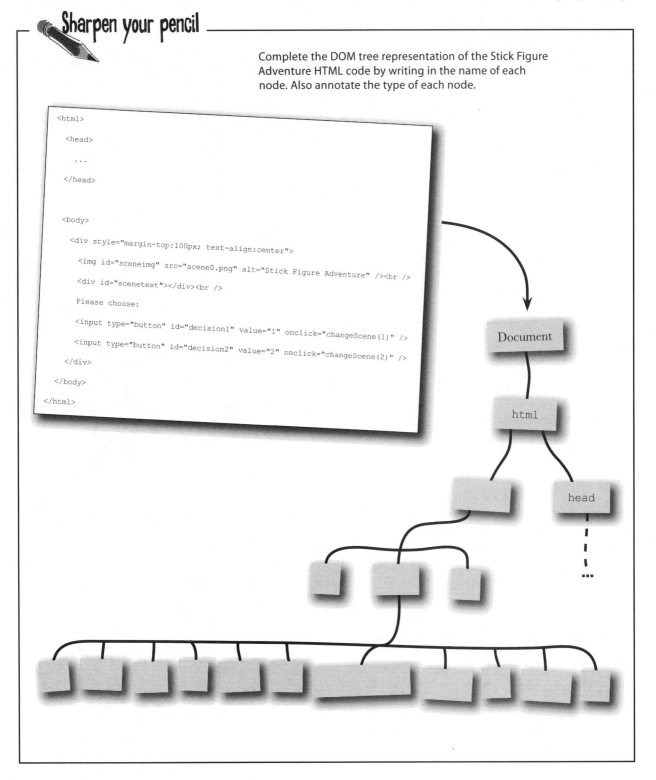

```
<html>

  <head>

    ...

  </head>


  <body>

    <div style="margin-top:100px; text-align:center">

      <img id="sceneimg" src="scene0.png" alt="Stick Figure Adventure" /><br />

      <div id="scenetext"></div><br />

      Please choose:

      <input type="button" id="decision1" value="1" onclick="changeScene(1)" />

      <input type="button" id="decision2" value="2" onclick="changeScene(2)" />

    </div>

  </body>

</html>
```

Sharpen your pencil Solution

Complete the DOM tree representation of the Stick Figure Adventure HTML code by writing in the name of each node. Also annotate the type of each node.

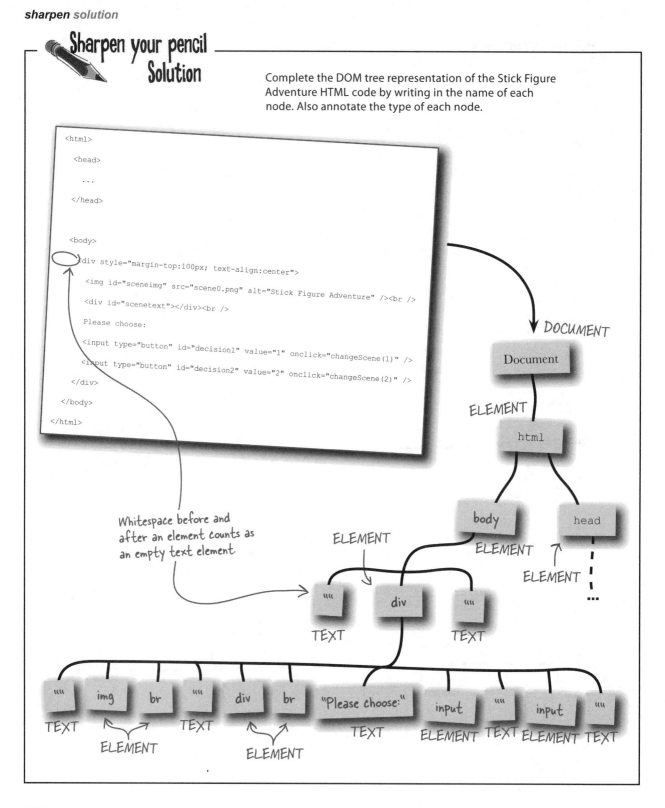

```
<html>
  <head>
    ...
  </head>

  <body>
    <div style="margin-top:100px; text-align:center">
      <img id="sceneimg" src="scene0.png" alt="Stick Figure Adventure" /><br />
      <div id="scenetext"></div><br />
      Please choose:
      <input type="button" id="decision1" value="1" onclick="changeScene(1)" />
      <input type="button" id="decision2" value="2" onclick="changeScene(2)" />
    </div>
  </body>
</html>
```

Whitespace before and after an element counts as an empty text element.

DOCUMENT

Document

ELEMENT

html

ELEMENT   body   head   ELEMENT

ELEMENT

ELEMENT   """ TEXT   div   """ TEXT

""" TEXT   img   br   """ TEXT   div   br   "Please choose:" TEXT   input   """ TEXT   input   """ TEXT

ELEMENT   ELEMENT   ELEMENT   ELEMENT TEXT   ELEMENT TEXT

Climbing the DOM tree with properties

Most interactions with the DOM begin with the `document` object, which is the topmost node in a document's node tree. The document object offers useful methods like `getElementById()` and `getElementsByTagName()`, and quite a few properties too. Many of the properties of the `document` object are available from **every** node in a tree. Some of these objects even allow you to navigate to other nodes. This means node properties can be used to navigate through the node tree.

> **Node properties are handy for traversing through nodes in the DOM tree.**

nodeValue

The value stored in a node, only for text and attribute nodes (not elements).

nodeType

The type of a node, such as DOCUMENT or TEXT, but expressed as a number.

childNodes

Arrays containing all of the child nodes beneath a node, in the order that the nodes appear in the HTML code.

firstChild

The first child node beneath a node.

lastChild

The last child node beneath a node.

These properties are key to being able to manuver through the document tree to access specific node data. For example, you can use node properties with the `getElementById()` node access method to quickly isolate a specific node.

```
alert(document.getElementById("scenetext").nodeValue);
```

The nodeValue property accesses the text content stored in a node.

The nodeValue property always contains pure text with no additional formatting.

The scene description text in Stick Figure Adventure initially starts out empty.

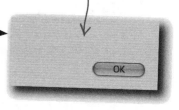

OK, so maybe that's not the best example, seeing as how the scene description text `div` starts out empty in Stick Figure Adventure. But it should eventually get set to some very compelling text as the story progresses, in which case this code would look much smarter.

Exercise

The following code is referencing a node in the tree on page 356. Carefully study the code and then circle which node it references.

```
document.getElementsByTagName("body")[0].childNodes[1].lastChild
```

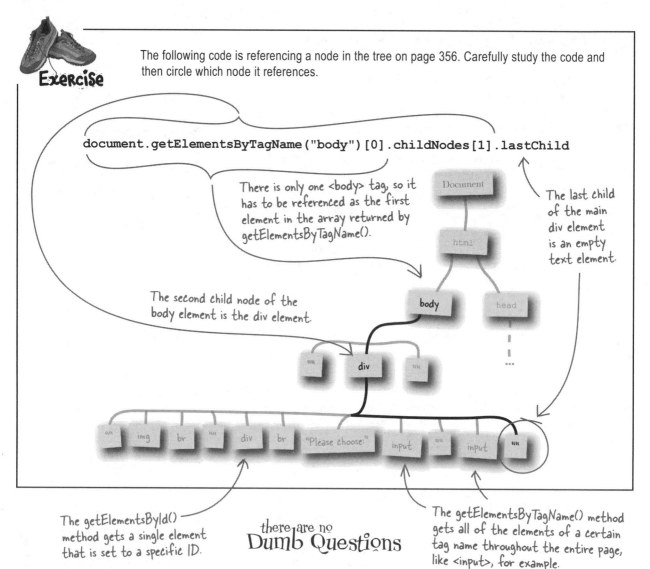

Exercise

The following code is referencing a node in the tree on page 356. Carefully study the code and then circle which node it references.

```
document.getElementsByTagName("body")[0].childNodes[1].lastChild
```

There is only one <body> tag, so it has to be referenced as the first element in the array returned by getElementsByTagName().

The last child of the main div element is an empty text element.

The second child node of the body element is the div element.

The getElementsById() method gets a single element that is set to a specific ID.

there are no
Dumb Questions

The getElementsByTagName() method gets all of the elements of a certain tag name throughout the entire page, like <input>, for example.

Q: **What's the difference between** `getElementById()` **and** `getElementsByTagName()` **in the DOM tree? Why would I choose one over the other?**

A: The two methods offer different approaches that basically have to do with whether or not your goal is to isolate a **single** element or a **group** of similar elements. To isolate a single element, you can't beat `getElementById()`—just hang an ID on the element and you're good to go.

But if you want to target a group of nodes, `getElementByTagName()` is a much better option. For

example, if you wanted to hide all of the images on a page using JavaScript, you would first call `getElementsByTagName()` and pass it `"img"` to get all of the image nodes on the page. Then you would change the `visibility` CSS style property on each of the image elements to hide them. Oops, we're getting way ahead of ourselves... we get back to the DOM and CSS later in the chapter. For now, just understand that while `getElementsByTagName()` isn't as popular as `getElementById()`, it still has its place in special situations.

So node properties make it possible to drill into HTML code and access web page content...but can they be used to **change** that content?

DOM properties allow you to change web page content <u>and</u> maintain web standards compliance.

Since the DOM views everything in a web page document as a node, changing a page involves changing its nodes. In the case of text content, the text for an element like div, span, or p always appears as a child node or nodes, immediately beneath the element (node) in the tree. If the text is contained in a single text node with no additional HTML elements, then the node is located in the first child. Like this:

```
document.getElementById("story").firstChild.nodeValue
```

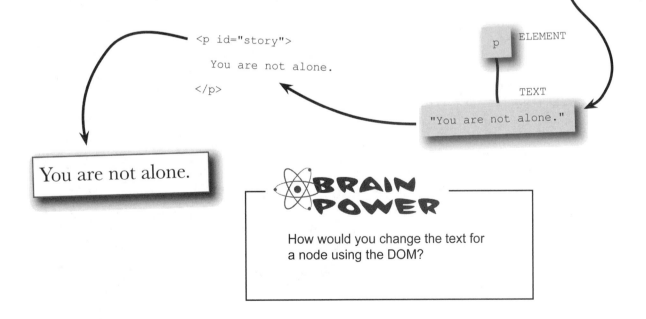

```
<p id="story">
    You are not alone.
</p>
```

You are not alone.

⚛ BRAIN POWER

How would you change the text for a node using the DOM?

Changing node text with the DOM

If you could safely assume that a node only has one child that holds its text content, then it's possible to simply assign new text content to the child using its `nodeValue` property. This approach works just fine, again, but only if there's a single child node.

```
document.getElementById("story").firstChild.nodeValue = "OK, maybe you are alone.";
```

The new text content replaces the existing content in the child.

p ELEMENT

TEXT

"OK, maybe you are alone."

But things aren't always so simple. What happens if a node has more than one child? Like this code:

```
<p id="story">

    You are <strong>not</strong> alone.

</p>
```

This paragraph breaks down into multiple child nodes.

p ELEMENT

TEXT

"You are"

ELEMENT

strong

TEXT

"alone."

TEXT

"not"

Changing the content in the first child isn't enough to change the entire content of the paragraph.

Since there is a tag in the paragraph content, there are multiple child nodes.

If we replace only the first child, the remaining child nodes are still there, and we'll get some strange results like these:

```
document.getElementById("story").firstChild.nodeValue = "OK, maybe you are alone.";
```

Only the first child is replaced, which still leaves the remaining content...and some confusing results.

OK, maybe you are alone **not** alone.

Three (safe) steps for changing node text

The problem with changing the content of a node by only changing the first child is that it doesn't factor in the prospects of other child nodes. So to change the content of a node, we really should clear all of its children, and then add a new child that contains the new content.

 Remove all child nodes.

 Create a new text node based upon the new content.

 Append the newly created text node as a child node.

We can do this with three DOM methods:

① removeChild()

Remove a child node from a node; pass in the child node to be removed.

② createTextNode()

Create a text node from a string of text.

③ appendChild()

Add a node as the last child of the node; pass in the child node to be added.

To change the text content in the "you are not alone" example, we have to work through these three steps, first making sure to remove all of the child nodes, then creating a new text node, and finally appending the text node to the paragraph.

First grab the element (node) using its ID.

```
var node = document.getElementById("story");

while (node.firstChild) ①

    node.removeChild(node.firstChild);

node.appendChild(document.createTextNode("OK, maybe you are alone."));
③                            ②
```

Remove the first child node until there are no more child nodes.

Create a new text node.

After removing all the child nodes, append the new text node to the parent node.

OK, maybe you are alone.

DOM Building Blocks

This week's interview:
Node discusses the wisdom of
DOM trees

Head First: I'm told you're the smallest unit of storage in a DOM tree, kind of like an atom for HTML content. Is that true?

Node: I'm not sure how atomic I am but yes, I do represent a discrete piece of information in a DOM tree. Think of the DOM as breaking down every web page into tiny bite-sized pieces of information... and I'm that bite-sized portion!

Head First: Why does that matter? I mean, is it really that important to be able to break down a web page into little chunks of data?

Node: It's only important if you care about accessing or altering the information in a web page. Many scripts care about this very thing, in which case the DOM matters quite a lot. But the real reason it matters is because it is quite empowering to be able to disassemble a web page into all of its little pieces and parts.

Head First: Don't you run the risk of losing a part when taking apart a page? Far too many people take something apart only to have pieces left over, and next thing you know they've broken the thing.

Node: No, that's not a problem with the DOM because you don't have to literally take anything apart to access a web page as a tree of nodes. The DOM provides the tree view regardless of whether you actually plan on doing any shaping or pruning to the web data.

Head First: That's a relief. But if I really do want to do some web page pruning, is that where you enter the picture?

Node: Yes. Except that you aren't limited to pruning—you're free to add to the tree of web data as well.

Head First: Wow, that's pretty amazing. How does that work?

Node: Well, remember that every piece of information

on a page is modeled in the tree as a node. So you can go through me to access anything within a page. Or you can create entirely new pieces of web data using me, and then add them to the tree. The DOM is really quite flexible.

Head First: That's neat. One thing that still confuses me, however, is how you relate to elements. Are you guys really the same person?

Node: Yes, actually we are. But I do take things a step further. Remember that an element is just another way of looking at a tag, such as `<div>` or `<span>`. Every element on a page is represented by a node in the document tree, so in that sense element and I are the same. However, I also represent content stored within an element. So the text stored in a `<div>` is also its own node, stored just beneath the `div` node in the tree.

Head First: That sounds kinda confusing. How can you tell the difference between elements and their content?

Node: Well, first of all, the content stored within an element, or node, always appears as a child of the node in the DOM tree. And second, all nodes are distinguishable by type: an element node has the ELEMENT node type, while its text content has the TEXT node type.

Head First: So if I want to access the text content of an element, do I just look for the TEXT node type?

Node: You could; just keep in mind that the `nodeType` property actually returns a number for each node type. For example, the TEXT node type is 3, while ELEMENT is 1. But even that's not really necessary because all you have to do is look to the children of an element node in order to access its content.

Head First: I see. Well thanks for your time, and for illuminating the wonders of the DOM tree.

Node: You're very welcome. And if you're ever in the mood for some tree surgery, don't forget to look me up!

there are no Dumb Questions

Q: I'm still a little confused about child nodes and how they are organized. For example, how does the `childNodes` property work?

A: When a node contains data within it, the node is considered a parent node and the data within it is perceived by the DOM as child nodes. If the data consists of anything more than raw text data, then it is broken apart into multiple child nodes. The child nodes beneath a parent node appear in the parent's `childNodes` property as an array, and their order in the array matches the order that they appear in the HTML code itself. So the first child node in the `childNodes` array can be accessed using `childNodes[0]`. The array can

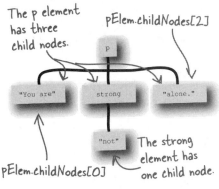

The p element has three child nodes.

pElem.childNodes[2]

pElem.childNodes[0]

The strong element has one child node.

also be looped through to access each of the child nodes.

Q: In the code that removes all of the child nodes from a node, how does the `while` loop test condition work?

A: The while loop test looks like this:

`while(node.firstChild)`

What this test is doing is checking to see if the node still contains a first child node. If there is still a first child node, its presence results in a value of `true` in the context of the `while` loop, and the loop continues for another iteration. If there is no first child node, that means there are no children at all. And if that's the case, the code `node.firstChild` results in `null`, which automatically gets converted to `false` in the context of the `while` loop. So what's really going in is that the `while` loop is looking to see if the first child node is `null`, which is conclusive evidence that there aren't any other child nodes lurking around.

JavaScript Magnets

The DOM-compliant version of Stick Figure Adventure is missing several pieces of important code. Use the magnets below to finish up the code that changes the node text for the scene text element. Magnets can be used more than once.

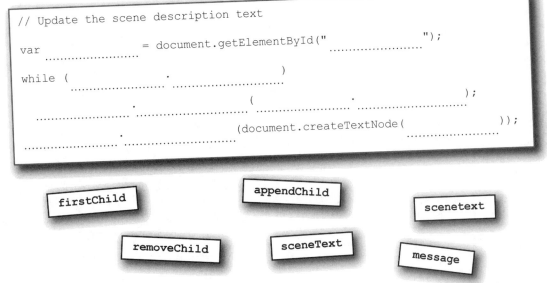

```
// Update the scene description text

var ............... = document.getElementById("...............");

while ( ...............  .  ............... )
    ...............  .  ...............  ( ...............  .  ............... );
    ...............  .  ............... (document.createTextNode( ...............  ));
```

firstChild

appendChild

scenetext

removeChild

sceneText

message

JavaScript Magnets Solution

The DOM-compliant version of Stick Figure Adventure is missing several pieces of important code. Use the magnets below to finish up the code that changes the node text for the scene text element. Magnets can be used more than once.

As long as the scene text node has child nodes, keep looping.

The loop will continue looping as long as a first child exists.

First grab the scene text element using its ID.

The message must be pure text with no formatting or HTML tags.

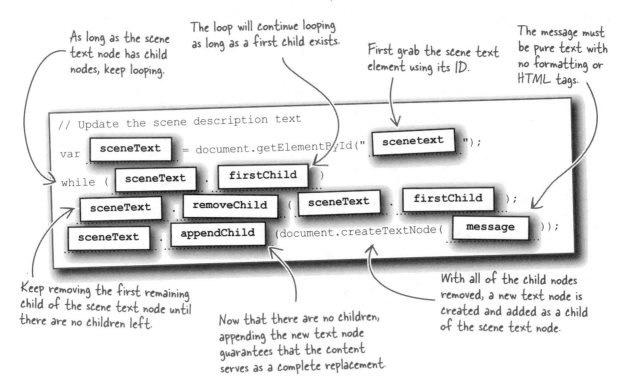

```
// Update the scene description text
var  sceneText  = document.getElementById(" scenetext ");
while ( sceneText . firstChild )
  sceneText . removeChild ( sceneText . firstChild );
  sceneText . appendChild (document.createTextNode( message ));
```

Keep removing the first remaining child of the scene text node until there are no children left.

Now that there are no children, appending the new text node guarantees that the content serves as a complete replacement.

With all of the child nodes removed, a new text node is created and added as a child of the scene text node.

BULLET POINTS

- Although not a web standard, the `innerHTML` property provides access to all of the content stored in an element.

- The Document Object Model, or DOM, provides a **standardized** mechanism of accessing and modifying web page data.

- The DOM looks at a web page like a hierarchical **tree** of related nodes.

- The DOM alternative to changing web page content with `innerHTML` involves removing all of the child nodes of an element, and then creating and appending a new child node that contains the new content.

Standards compliant adventuring

Boy, that sounds fun! The mark of any good adventure is standards compliance... or not. But it can be a good thing in the context of modern web apps. And more importantly, take a look at the dramatic changes the DOM approach to altering the scene description text have brought to Stick Figure Adventure...

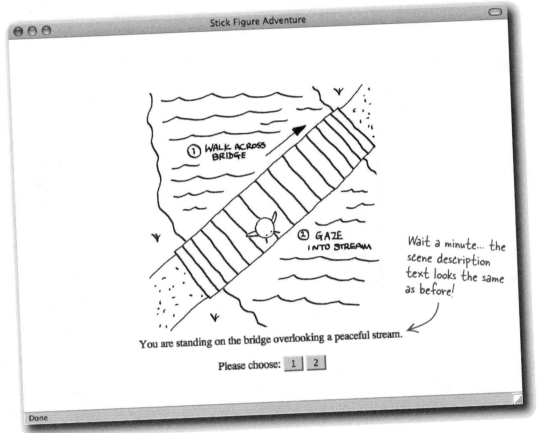

Hmm. OK, so maybe the page doesn't look any different, but behind the scenes it adheres to the latest web standards thanks to its usage of the DOM. Not everything in JavaScript code can be appreciated visually, and in this case our satisfaction with the DOM-powered version of Stick Figure Adventure will have to come from within.

The DOM is a web standard way of manipulating HTML that allows more control than using the innerHTML property.

In search of better options

So now the dynamic scene description text has now been overhauled twice, but those cryptic option buttons still remain in Stick Figure Adventure. Surely something could be done to make the story navigation a little more engaging and intuitive than choosing between the numbers 1 and 2!

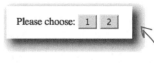

The numeric option buttons just aren't cutting it — they say nothing about the decision facing the user.

I know they get the job done but the option buttons really are underwhelming. They should be much more descriptive.

A decent improvement to the option buttons would be to change them so that they actually reflect the available decisions. They could include text on the buttons that spell out exactly what the two options are at each point like this:

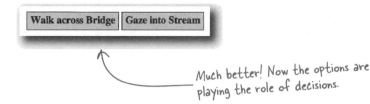

Much better! Now the options are playing the role of decisions.

Come to think of it, there really isn't any reason we have to use form buttons for this—any HTML element that can contain text could feasibly work. CSS styles could be used to dress them up and make them look more like input controls.

BRAIN POWER

How would you implement data-driven options in Stick Figure Adventure so that they display option text specific to each different scene?

Designing better, cleaner options

Since the new and improved decision-making options in Stick Figure Adventure are HTML elements that contain text, the DOM can be used to dynamically alter the decision text in each scene. This means each scene will set its decision text along with its description. And it also means the changeScene() function needs two new variables to store this decision text, decision1 and decision2.

Here's how we could go about setting Scene 1 decision text as it transitions to Scene 3 in the changeScene() function:

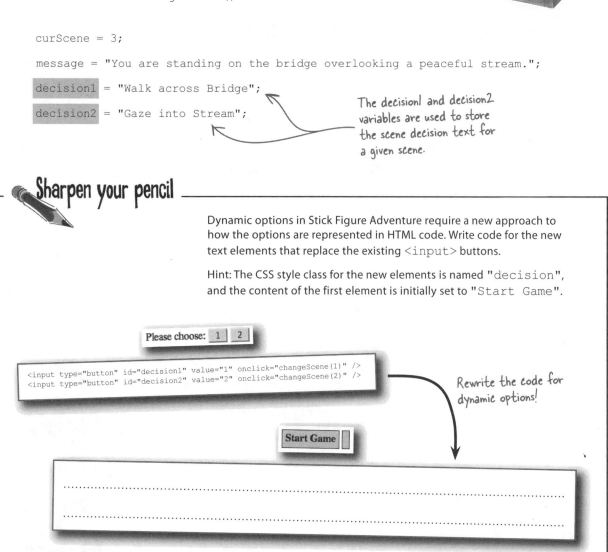

```
curScene = 3;

message = "You are standing on the bridge overlooking a peaceful stream.";

decision1 = "Walk across Bridge";

decision2 = "Gaze into Stream";
```

The decision1 and decision2 variables are used to store the scene decision text for a given scene.

Sharpen your pencil

Dynamic options in Stick Figure Adventure require a new approach to how the options are represented in HTML code. Write code for the new text elements that replace the existing <input> buttons.

Hint: The CSS style class for the new elements is named "decision", and the content of the first element is initially set to "Start Game".

Please choose: 1 2

```
<input type="button" id="decision1" value="1" onclick="changeScene(1)" />
<input type="button" id="decision2" value="2" onclick="changeScene(2)" />
```

Rewrite the code for dynamic options!

Start Game

....
....

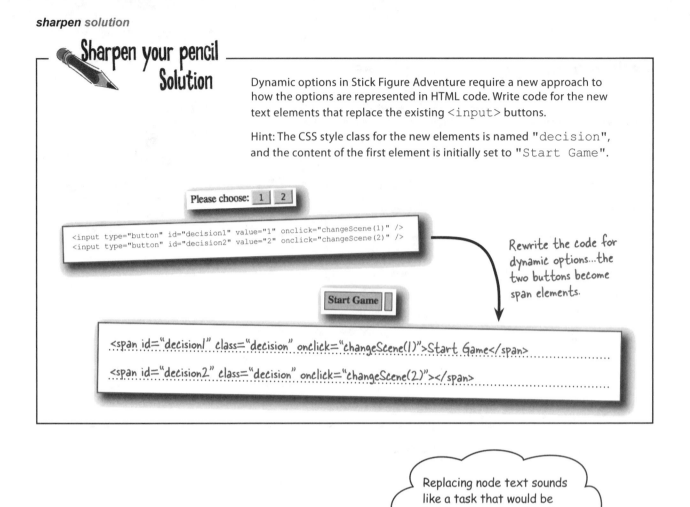

Sharpen your pencil Solution

Dynamic options in Stick Figure Adventure require a new approach to how the options are represented in HTML code. Write code for the new text elements that replace the existing `<input>` buttons.

Hint: The CSS style class for the new elements is named `"decision"`, and the content of the first element is initially set to `"Start Game"`.

Please choose: 1 2

```
<input type="button" id="decision1" value="1" onclick="changeScene(1)" />
<input type="button" id="decision2" value="2" onclick="changeScene(2)" />
```

Rewrite the code for dynamic options...the two buttons become span elements.

Start Game

```
<span id="decision1" class="decision" onclick="changeScene(1)">Start Game</span>

<span id="decision2" class="decision" onclick="changeScene(2)"></span>
```

> Replacing node text sounds like a task that would be handy to have in a function.

Rethinking node text replacement

All that's missing now in Stick Figure Adventure for the new dynamic decision text is the code that actually sets the text for the new span elements. This code is ultimately doing the exact same thing as the DOM code we wrote earlier in the chapter that dynamically changes the scene description text. In fact, this presents a problem because we now need to carry out the exact same task on three different elements: the scene description and the two scene decisions...

Replacing node text with a function

An all-purpose node text replacement function is a handy thing, and not just in Stick Figure Adventure. This type of function operates much like the scene description text replacement code we worked through earlier, except this time the code goes to work on function arguments.

The ID of the node whose content is to be replaced.

```
function replaceNodeText(id, newText) {

    ...

}
```

The new text content to place in the node.

The custom `replaceNodeText()` function accepts two arguments: the ID of the node whose content is to be replaced and the new text to place in the node. Use this function to change the text content of any element on a page that can hold text. In Stick Figure Adventure, the function allows you to now dynamically change the scene description text and the text for the two decisions at one time..but of course you need to write it first.

Instead of duplicating the same code three times, the function is called three times.

```
replaceNodeText("scenetext", message);
replaceNodeText("decision1", decision1);
replaceNodeText("decision2", decision2);
```

Replace the scene description text with a new message.

Change the decision text for each of the two decisions.

Sharpen your pencil

Write the code for the `replaceNodeText()` function, the all-purpose function for replacing the text within a node that is referenced by ID.

Don't forget that the function accepts two arguments, `id` and `newText`.

....

....

....

....

....

....

Sharpen your pencil Solution

Write the code for the `replaceNodeText()` function, the all-purpose function for replacing the text within a node that is referenced by ID.

Don't forget that the function accepts two arguments, `id` and `newText`.

Get the element using its unique ID.

```
function replaceNodeText(id, newText) {

    var node = document.getElementById(id);

    while (node.firstChild)

        node.removeChild(node.firstChild);

    node.appendChild(document.createTextNode(newText));

}
```

Remove all children from the node.

Create a new child text element using the text passed into the function.

The createTextNode() function is only available in the document object, and has no direct tie to a particular node.

Dynamic options are a good thing

The new dynamic text decisions in Stick Figure Adventure are much more intuitive than their cryptic button counterparts.

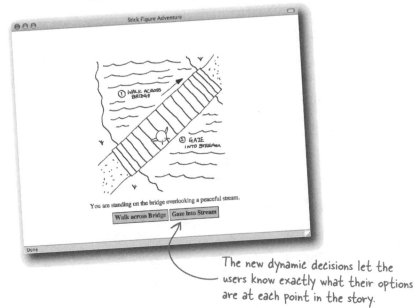

Dynamic, descriptive, delightful!

The new dynamic decisions let the users know exactly what their options are at each point in the story.

there are no
Dumb Questions

Q: Why are `span` elements used for the Stick Figure Adventure decisions, as opposed to `div` elements?

A: Because the decision elements need to appear side by side, which means they can't be block elements that start on a new line. A `div` is a block element, whereas a `span` is inline. Inline is what we want for the decisions, so `span` is the ticket.

Q: When I create a new node with `createTextNode()`, where does the node go?

A: Nowhere. When a new text node is first created, it's in limbo, at least with respect to the DOM tree for a given page. It's not until you append the node as a child of another node that it actually gets added to the tree, which then adds it to the page.

Q: Does the content of a text node created with `createTextNode()` have to be just text?

A: Yes. The DOM doesn't work like `innerHTML`, where you can assign text that has tags mixed in with it. When the DOM talks about a "text node," it really means pure text with no other tags or formatting tacked on.

Interactive options are even better

So the dynamic text decisions in Stick Figure Adventure are an improvement over their cryptic predecessors, but they could still be better. For example, they could highlight when the mouse pointer hovers over them to make it clear that they are clickable.

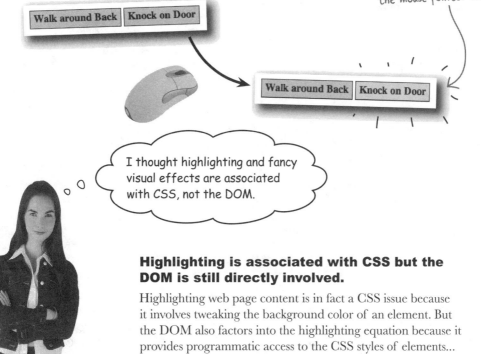

The decision text element highlights when the user drags the mouse pointer over it.

I thought highlighting and fancy visual effects are associated with CSS, not the DOM.

Highlighting is associated with CSS but the DOM is still directly involved.

Highlighting web page content is in fact a CSS issue because it involves tweaking the background color of an element. But the DOM also factors into the highlighting equation because it provides programmatic access to the CSS styles of elements...

A matter of style: CSS and DOM

CSS styles are tied to HTML elements, and the DOM provides access to
styles through elements (nodes). By using the DOM to tweak CSS styles,
it's possible to dynamically manipulate the content presentation. One way
that CSS styles are exposed through the DOM is in an element's `style`
class, which is where a group (class) of styles is applied to an element.

```
<span id="decision1" class="decision" onclick="changeScene(1)">Start Game</span>

<span id="decision2" class="decision" onclick="changeScene(2)"></span>
```

```
<style type="text/css">

  span.decision {

    font-weight:bold;

    border:thin solid #000000;

    padding:5px;

    background-color:#DDDDDD;

  }

</style>
```

*The decision style class is
what gives the decisions
their visual appeal.*

Start Game

The DOM provides access to an element's style class through the
`className` property of the node object.

```
alert(document.getElementById("decision1").className);
```

*The className property
provides access to an
element's style class.*

decision

OK

The className property of a node
provides access to the style class.

**Try not to
get CSS
style
classes
confused
with JavaScript
classes.**

*CSS style classes and
JavaScript classes are very
different animals. A CSS
style class is a collection of
styles that can be applied
to an element on the page,
while a JavaScript class
is a template for creating
JavaScript objects. We
uncover the details of
JavaScript classes and
objects in Chapter 10.*

Watch it!

Swapping style classes

To change the appearance of an element using a completely different style class, just change its style class name to a different CSS style class.

> The decisioninverse style class reverses the color scheme of the decision text.

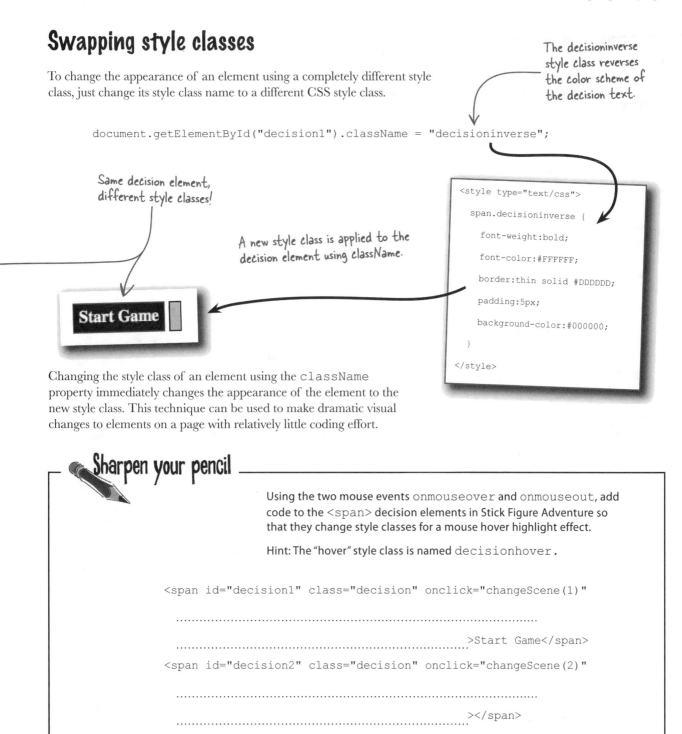

```
document.getElementById("decision1").className = "decisioninverse";
```

> Same decision element, different style classes!

> A new style class is applied to the decision element using className.

Start Game

```
<style type="text/css">
  span.decisioninverse {
    font-weight:bold;
    font-color:#FFFFFF;
    border:thin solid #DDDDDD;
    padding:5px;
    background-color:#000000;
  }
</style>
```

Changing the style class of an element using the `className` property immediately changes the appearance of the element to the new style class. This technique can be used to make dramatic visual changes to elements on a page with relatively little coding effort.

Sharpen your pencil

Using the two mouse events `onmouseover` and `onmouseout`, add code to the `<span>` decision elements in Stick Figure Adventure so that they change style classes for a mouse hover highlight effect.

Hint: The "hover" style class is named `decisionhover`.

```
<span id="decision1" class="decision" onclick="changeScene(1)"

    .........................................................................

    ...............................................................>Start Game</span>
<span id="decision2" class="decision" onclick="changeScene(2)"

    .........................................................................

    ...............................................................></span>
```

![Sharpen your pencil pencil icon] **Sharpen your pencil**
Solution

Using the two mouse events onmouseover and onmouseout, add code to the <span> decision elements in Stick Figure Adventure so that they change style classes for a mouse hover highlight effect.

Hint: The "hover" style class is named decisionhover.

The decisionhover style class is set in response to the onmouseover event.

```
<span id="decision1" class="decision" onclick="changeScene(1)"
  onmouseover="this.className = 'decisionhover'"
  onmouseout="this.className = 'decision'"                    >Start Game</span>
<span id="decision2" class="decision" onclick="changeScene(2)"
  onmouseover="this.className = 'decisionhover'"
  onmouseout="this.className = 'decision'"                    ></span>
```

This event is triggered when the mouse pointer moves over the span element.

The unhighlighted decision style is restored in response to the onmouseout event.

This event is triggered when the mouse pointer moves off of the span element.

---

there are no Dumb Questions

Q: Can't I just use CSS to create buttons that highlight when the mouse moves over them?

A: Yes. And in many cases that is a better way to create "hover" buttons because CSS is more widely supported than JavaScript in browsers, such as on some mobile devices. However, Stick Figure Adventure is a JavaScript application, and does all kinds of things that are impossible to do in CSS alone. So in this case it's not a liability in any way to use JavaScript for the scene decision buttons.

Classy options

Applying style classes to the Stick Figure Adventure code yields two different appearances for the decision elements: normal and highlighted.

```
<style type="text/css">
  span.decision {
    font-weight:bold;
    border:thin solid #000000;
    padding:5px;
    background-color:#DDDDDD;
  }
</style>
```

The only difference between the two style classes is the background color.

```
<style type="text/css">
  span.decisionhover {
    font-weight:bold;
    border:thin solid #000000;
    padding:5px;
    background-color:#EEEEEE;
  }
</style>
```

Normal

Walk around Back   Knock on Door

Highlighted

Walk around Back   Knock on Door

Test drive the stylized adventure options

The user interface for Stick Figure Adventure is now improved thanks to the DOM's ability to change an element's style class on demand. Ellie is feeling pretty good about her script.

Wow, the new mouse hover highlighting effect rocks!

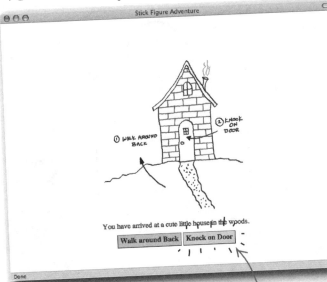

The decision elements now highlight when the mouse pointer hovers over them.

there are no Dumb Questions

Q: I don't remember the onmouseover **and** onmouseout **events. Are those standard events?**

A: Yes. In fact, there are lots of standard JavaScript events that we haven't explored. But the thing about events is how you can react to them even when you don't necessarily know everything about them. In the case of the two mouse events, their names are really all you needed to know to understand that one of them is fired when the mouse pointer hovers **over** an element, and the other one fires when the mouse pointer moves **out** of an element.

Q: Why wasn't it necessary to use getElementById() **in the code that sets the style class of the decision elements?**

A: Every element in JavaScript is an object, and in the HTML code for an element we have access to that object through the this keyword. So in the Stick Figure Adventure code, the this keyword references the node object for the span element. And that's the same object with the className property that accesses its style class. So changing the style class only involves setting this.className.

Q: Style classes are cool but I'd really like to just change one style property. Is that possible?

A: Wow, what intuition! There's a nagging problem with Stick Figure Adventure that Ellie has been eager to resolve. And it just so happens to involve using JavaScript and the DOM to manipulate style properties individually...

Options gone wrong: the empty button

It's been there all along, and up until this point Ellie coped with it. But it's time to go ahead and address the weirdness associated with the empty decisions in Stick Figure Adventure. In some scenes there is only one viable decision yet both decision elements are still displayed, like the screenshot here. It's a little unsettling for the user to see an interactive decision element with no information in it.

It's been bugging me that some of the scenes have empty options. An empty option doesn't make much sense and can only cause confusion.

Welcome to

STICK FIGURE ADVENTURE

Click either button to start...

The empty decision element is both strange and confusing.

Start Game

> **⚛BRAIN POWER**
>
> Which other scenes have the empty option problem? What options exist to fix this?

A la carte style tweaking

Sometimes changing the entire style class of an element is just too much. For times when a little more granularity is required, there is the `style` object. The `style` object is accessible as a property of a node object, and provides access to individual styles as properties. The `visibility` style property can be used to show and hide elements. In the HTML for Stick Figure Adventure, the second decision element can be initially hidden using the following code:

The style property of a node provides access to individual style properties.

```
<span id="decision2" class="decision" onclick="changeScene(2)"
  onmouseover="this.className = 'decisionhover'"
  onmouseout="this.className = 'decision'"
  style="visibility:hidden"></span>
```

From then on, showing and hiding the element is just a matter of setting the `visibility` style property to `visible` or `hidden`.

```
document.getElementById("decision2").style.visibility = "visible";

document.getElementById("decision2").style.visibility = "hidden";
```

Sharpen your pencil

Some scenes in Stick Figure Adventure must alter the visibility of the second option element when changing to a new scene. Circle these scenes, and then annotate the decision where each scene should show or hide the option.

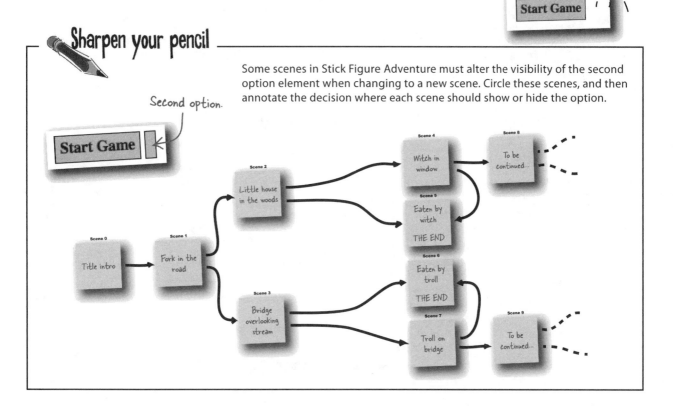

Second option.

Sharpen your pencil Solution

Some scenes in Stick Figure Adventure must alter the visibility of the second option element when changing to a new scene. Circle these scenes, and then annotate the decision where each scene should show or hide the option.

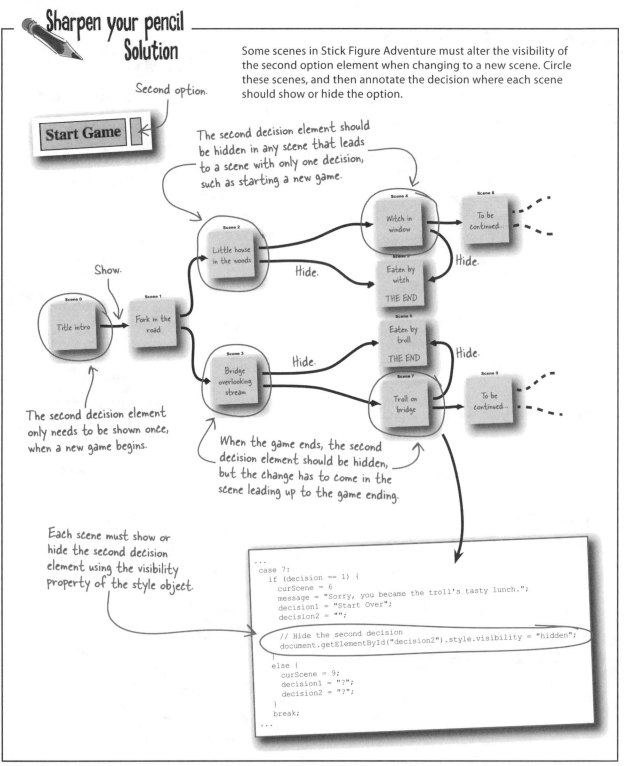

Second option.

Start Game

The second decision element should be hidden in any scene that leads to a scene with only one decision, such as starting a new game.

Scene 4 — Witch in window

Scene 8 — To be continued...

Scene 2 — Little house in the woods

Hide.

Scene 6 — Eaten by witch — THE END

Hide.

Show.

Scene 0 — Title intro

Scene 1 — Fork in the road

Scene 5 — Eaten by troll — THE END

Scene 3 — Bridge overlooking stream

Hide.

Hide.

Scene 7 — Troll on bridge

Scene 9 — To be continued...

The second decision element only needs to be shown once, when a new game begins.

When the game ends, the second decision element should be hidden, but the change has to come in the scene leading up to the game ending.

Each scene must show or hide the second decision element using the visibility property of the style object.

```
...
case 7:
  if (decision == 1) {
    curScene = 6
    message = "Sorry, you became the troll's tasty lunch.";
    decision1 = "Start Over";
    decision2 = "";

    // Hide the second decision
    document.getElementById("decision2").style.visibility = "hidden";
  }
  else {
    curScene = 9;
    decision1 = "?";
    decision2 = "?";
  }
  break;
...
```

BULLET POINTS

- The `className` node property makes big style changes by changing the **entire style class** of a node.

- The `style` node property makes small style changes by providing access to **individual style properties** of a node.

- A CSS style class has nothing to do with a JavaScript class—they are completely different things.

- Elements on a page can be dynamically shown or hidden using the `visibility` style property of the element object.

  The display style property can accomplish a similar show/hide effect by setting it to display:none (hide) or display: block (show).

No more bogus options

Manipulating individual styles using the DOM allows the second decision element to be selectively shown and hidden. The end result is a user interface that makes a lot more sense now that the empty decision elements are gone.

Ah, much better... those empty decisions were really annoying!

The second decision element is now hidden when it isn't needed, such as on the title scene.

More options, more complexity

Ellie envisions the Stick Figure Adventure storyline growing by leaps and bounds to reveal all kinds of interesting new scenes and decisions. There are ways the DOM can factor into helping manage the complexity of a much deeper Stick Figure Adventure narrative.

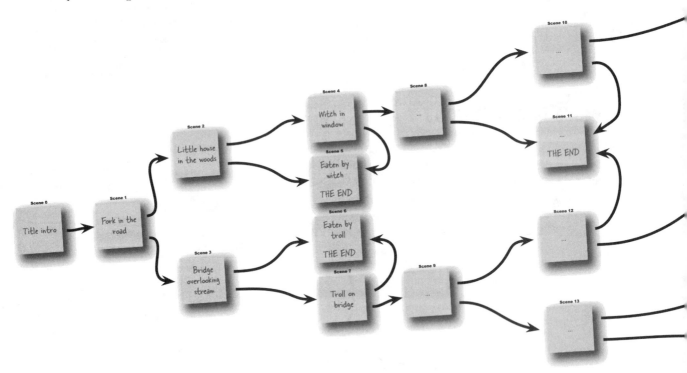

Deeper adventure = Bigger decision tree!

* The latest version of the Stick Figure Adventure is online and waiting for your coding assistance. Download this at http://www.headfirstlabs.com/books/hfjs/ if you haven't already.

Scene 14

Scene 18

Scene 24

Scene 28

Scene 19

THE END

Scene 29

Scene 25

Scene 20

Scene 30

THE END

Scene 26

Scene 15

Scene 21

Scene 31

Scene 27

Scene 22

THE END

THE END

Scene 16

Scene 23

> Wow! That's a lot of decisions... but it seems like it would be a nightmare to test.

Scene 17

THE END

Big stories can certainly turn into big problems without a way to test the decision tree.

As the story continues to unfold with more scenes and decisions, it becomes increasingly difficult to test the logic of the story and make sure every decision path leads to the right place. Stick Figure Adventure is in desperate need of a way to analyze paths through the story.

BRAIN POWER

What do you think might be the best way to create testing paths through such a monstrous decision tree?

Tracking the decision tree

Similar to the history feature in a web browser, which keeps track of the sequence of pages you've visited, a decision history feature in Stick Figure Adventure can be used to test and debug the storyline. The idea is to reveal the series of decisions that leads to a particular outcome. By doing this Ellie can make sure the decision path works as expected.

The decision history is built as a list of the options and scenes that occur in any given path through the story. The history then serves as a story debugger that lets Ellie trace back through options and scenes.

Start Scene 0 - Title intro.

Decision 1
is chosen...

1 Scene 1 - Fork in the road.

1 Scene 2 - Little house in the woods.

1 Scene 4 - Witch in window. ... which leads to scene 4.

1 Scene 8 - ...

2 Scene 11 - ...

End

Each scene traversed is added to the decision history, along with the decision made to arrive there.

☢ BRAIN POWER

What kind of changes are required to the Stick Figure Adventure Web page to support a decision history feature?

Turn your decision history into HTML

From an HTML perspective, the code for the decision history isn't too terribly complex: a `div` element and a paragraph of text for each decision is all that is needed.

Each p element contains a decision in the decision history.

```
<div id="history">

  <p>Decision 1 -> Scene 1 : Fork in the road.</p>

  <p>Decision 1 -> Scene 2 : Little house in the woods.</p>

  <p>Decision 1 -> Scene 4 : Witch in window.</p>

  ...

</div>
```

All that remains is writing some JavaScript to use the DOM to generate the decision history as a collection of nodes.

A decision history feature in Stick Figure Adventure can be a very useful story debugging tool.

> That's crazy. You can't just create new paragraphs at will... can you?

The DOM can create any HTML element at will, including paragraphs of text.

Actually, you can. And it involves another method of the document object, `createElement()`, which can be used to create any HTML element. The idea is that you create a new container element using `createElement()`, and then you add text content to it by creating a child text node with `createTextNode()`. The end result is an entirely new branch of nodes grafted onto the node tree of a page.

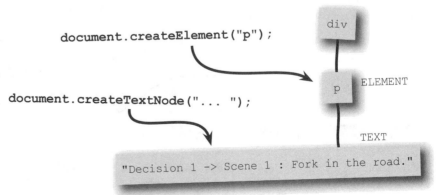

```
document.createElement("p");
```

```
document.createTextNode("... ");
```

div

p   ELEMENT

TEXT

"Decision 1 -> Scene 1 : Fork in the road."

Manufacturing HTML code

Creating a new element with the `createElement()` method only
requires the name of the tag. So creating a paragraph (p) element simply
means having to call the method with an argument of `"p"`, making sure
to hang on to the resulting element that is created.

*We start off with a new p
element floating in space.*

```
var decisionElem = document.createElement("p");
```

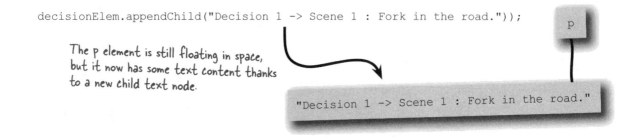

At this point there's a new paragraph element with no content, and it's
not yet part of any page either. So to add the text content to the element,
create a text node and then add it as a child of the new p node.

```
decisionElem.appendChild("Decision 1 -> Scene 1 : Fork in the road."));
```

*The p element is still floating in space,
but it now has some text content thanks
to a new child text node.*

"Decision 1 -> Scene 1 : Fork in the road."

The last step is to add the new paragraph element to the page as a child of
the history `div` element.

```
document.getElementById("history").appendChild(decisionElem);
```

*The p element is added as
a child of an existing div
element, which merges the
paragraph into the web page.*

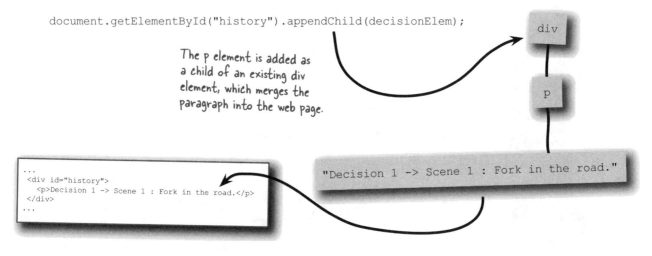

```
...
  <div id="history">
    <p>Decision 1 -> Scene 1 : Fork in the road.</p>
  </div>
...
```

"Decision 1 -> Scene 1 : Fork in the road."

By repeating these steps whenever each scene is traversed in Stick Figure
Adventure, a decision history can be created dynamically.

BULLET POINTS

- Any HTML element can be created using the `document` object's `createElement()` method.

- To add text content to an element, a child text node must be created and appended to the element.

- By carefully adding and removing nodes in the DOM tree, a web page can be disassembled and reassembled at will.

Sharpen your pencil

Add code to the `changeScene()` function to support the decision history feature in Stick Figure Adventure. Hint: You need to add a new paragraph element with a child text node to the decision history element when the current scene isn't Scene 0, and clear the decision history if the Scene is 0.

```
function changeScene(decision) {

  ...

  // Update the decision history
```

....

....

....

....

....

....

....

....

....

....

....

....

....

```
}
```

Sharpen your pencil
Solution

Add code to the changeScene() function to support the decision history feature in Stick Figure Adventure. Hint: You need to add a new paragraph element with a child text node to the decision history element when the current scene isn't Scene 0, and clear the decision history if the Scene is 0.

Append the new text node to the new paragraph element.

The changeScene() function already has a local variable named decision, so this variable must be named something else.

```
function changeScene(decision) {

    ...

    // Update the decision history

    var history = document.getElementById("history");

    if (curScene != 0) {

        // Add the latest decision to the history

        var decisionElem = document.createElement("p");

        decisionElem.appendChild(document.createTextNode("decision " + decision +

        " -> Scene " + curScene + " : " + message));

        history.appendChild(decisionElem);

    }

    else {

        // Clear the decision history

        while (history.firstChild)

            history.removeChild(history.firstChild);

    }

}
```

Grab the history div using its ID.

Append the paragraph element to the div to add it to the page.

Clear the history div by removing all of its children.

Create a new text node with the decision history information.

Tracing the adventure story

The decision history feature in Stick Figure Adventure now makes it possible to carefully track the story logic as it unfolds.

The story hasn't started so there is no history.

The decision history is awesome! I can finally cut loose creatively and still keep the decision tree under control.

The history grows as the story unfolds.

The story path completes in the decision history when an ending is reached.

A long strange trip...

It's time to flex your creative muscle by expanding the Stick Figure
Adventure story into something worthy of some serious decision history
debugging. Your stick figure friend is waiting for adventure...

Exercise

Dream up your very own continuation of the Stick Figure Adventure story, and add code to
incorporate it into the Stick Figure Adventure application so that you can share it online as an
interactive adventure.

There is no solution to this exercise... just have fun dreaming up adventures!

JavaScriptcross

Before you dig too deeply into stick figure story writing, take
a moment to experience a little crossword adventure!

Across

1. A node appearing below another node in the DOM tree is
called a ......
4. The property of a node object used to get its value.
5. Used to set the style class of an element.
7. Call this method to get all of the elements of a certain type,
such as div.
10. This type of node holds text content.
11. A DOM node type that equates to an HTML tag.
12. Use this method to add a node to another node as a child.

Down

1. Call this method to create an HTML element.
2. The topmost node in a DOM tree.
3. A non-standard way to change the content of an HTML
element.
6. A clumsy way to tell an online story.
8. A leaf in a DOM tree of Web page content.
9. Use this property to access individual style properties of an
element.
13. Set this attribute on an HTML tag to make it accessible from
JavaScript.

JavaScriptcross Solution

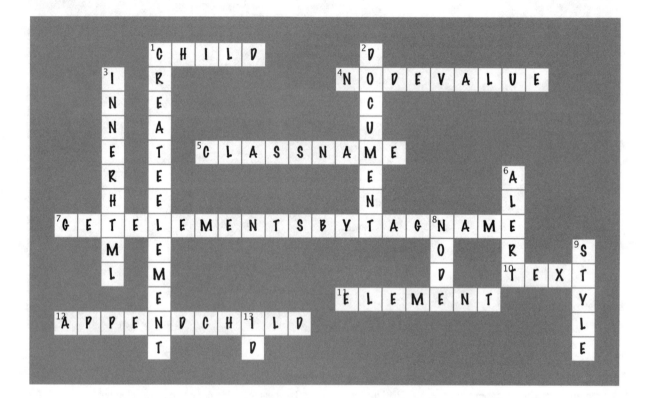

Page Bender

Fold the page vertically
to line up the two brains
and solve the riddle.

What is the DOM, really?

← ——— It's a meeting of the minds! ←

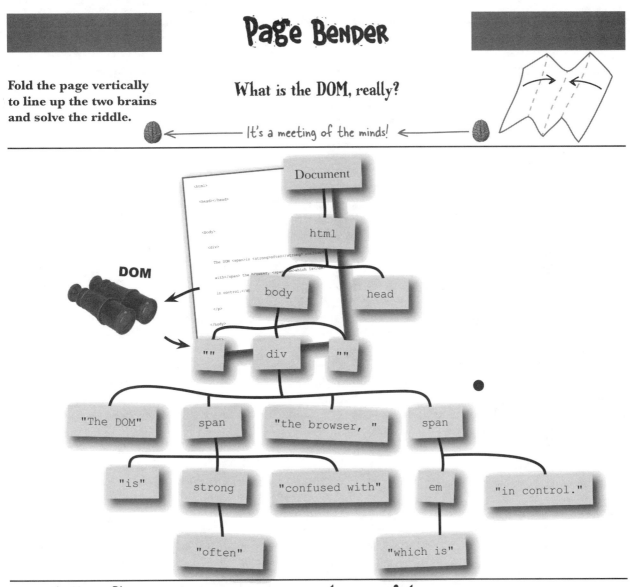

A JavaScript programmer must be careful not to
get carried away with the DOM. It
is certainly handy for accessing HTML
tags. But try not to become a total
manipulator, or you may wear out your nodes.

9 bringing data to life

Objects as Frankendata

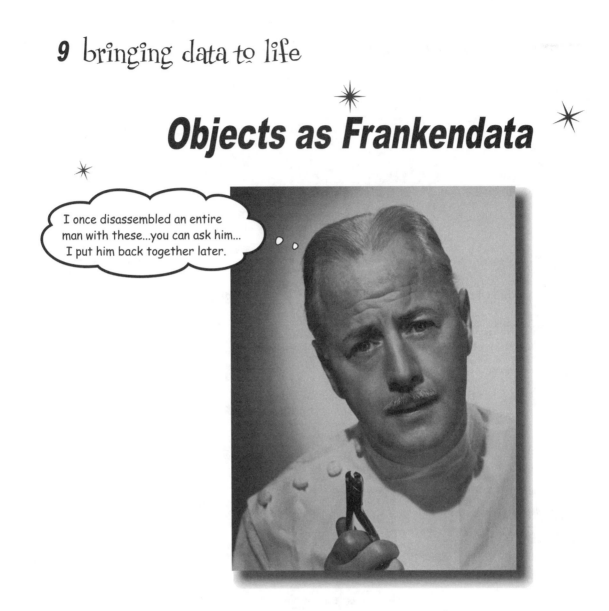

I once disassembled an entire man with these...you can ask him... I put him back together later.

JavaScript objects aren't nearly as gruesome as the good doctor might have you think. But they are interesting in that they combine pieces and parts of the JavaScript language together so that they're more powerful together. **Objects combine data with actions** to create a new **data type** that is much more "alive" than data you've seen thus far. You end up with *arrays that can sort themselves*, *strings that can search themselves*, and scripts that can grow fur and howl at the moon! OK, maybe not that last one but you get the idea...

A JavaScript-powered party

There's a party, and you're responsible for the invitations. So the first
question is what information goes into the perfect party invitation?

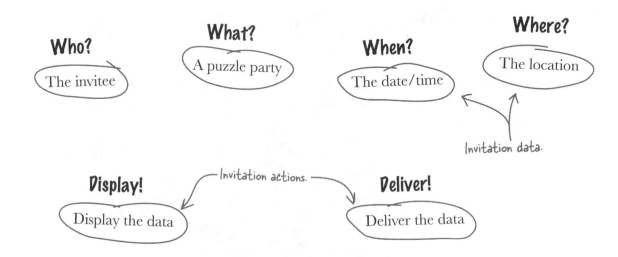

A party invitation for JavaScript would model the data as variables
and the actions as functions. Problem is, in the real world the
ability to separate data and actions doesn't really exist.

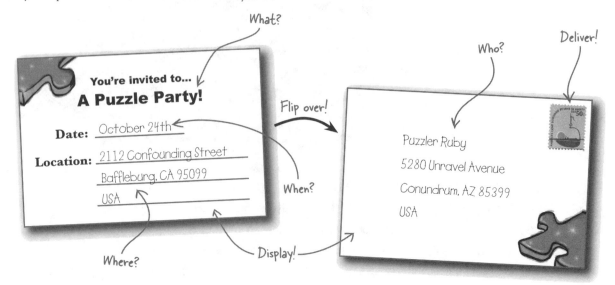

In the real world, the invitation card combines data and actions
into a single entity, an object.

Data + actions = object

You don't always have to work with data and actions as separate things in JavaScript. In fact, JavaScript **objects** combine the two into an entirely unique data structure that both **stores** data and **acts on** that data. This functionality allows JavaScript to apply real-world thinking to scripts. So you can think in terms of "things" as opposed to separate data and actions.

When you look at the party invitation in terms of a JavaScript object, you get this:

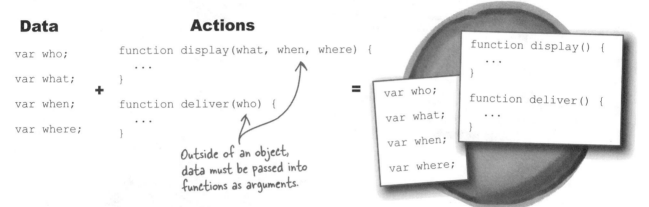

Data

```
var who;

var what;

var when;

var where;
```

+

Actions

```
function display(what, when, where) {
    ...
}

function deliver(who) {
    ...
}
```

Outside of an object, data must be passed into functions as arguments.

=

Object

```
var who;

var what;

var when;

var where;
```

```
function display() {
    ...
}

function deliver() {
    ...
}
```

Inside the invitation object, data and functions now co-exist and have closer ties than they had outside of the object. More specifically, functions placed within an object can access variables in the object without having to pass the variables into the functions as arguments.

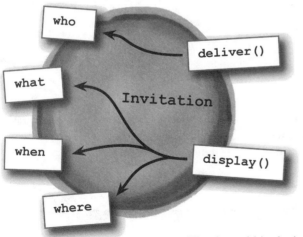

who

deliver()

what

Invitation

when

display()

where

Objects link variables and functions together inside a storage container.

The data within the invitation object is accessible to the functions but hidden from the outside world. So the object serves as a container that stores data **and** links it to code that can take action on it.

An object <u>owns</u> its data

When variables and functions are placed within an object, they are referred to as **object members**. More specifically, variables are called object **properties** and functions are called object **methods**. They still store data and take actions on data, they just do so within the context of a specific object.

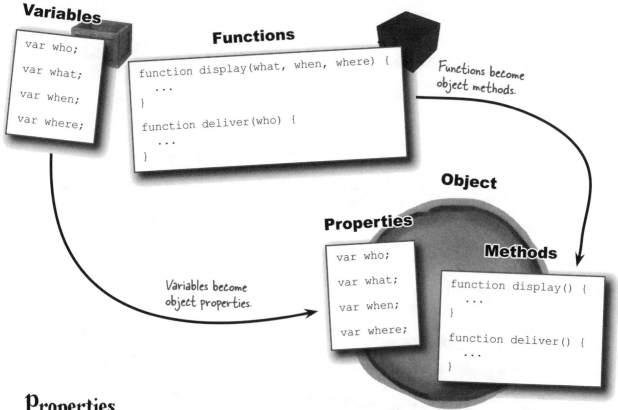

Variables

```
var who;
var what;
var when;
var where;
```

Functions

```
function display(what, when, where) {
    ...
}

function deliver(who) {
    ...
}
```

Functions become object methods.

Object

Properties

```
var who;
var what;
var when;
var where;
```

Variables become object properties.

Methods

```
function display() {
    ...
}

function deliver() {
    ...
}
```

> **Properties and methods are the object equivalents of variables and functions.**

Properties and methods are "owned" by an object, which means they are stored within the object much like data is stored in an array. Unlike arrays, however, you typically access object properties and methods using a special operator called the **dot operator**.

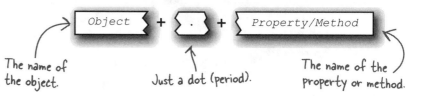

Object **+** . **+** Property/Method

The name of the object.

Just a dot (period).

The name of the property or method.

Object member references with a dot

The dot operator establishes a reference between a property or method and the object to which it belongs. It's kind of like how people's first names tell you who **they** are, but their last names tell you what **family** they belong to. Same thing for objects—a property name tells you what the property is, while the **object name** tells you what object the property belongs to. And the dot operator connects the two together.

Now it's possible to actually put together the data for a JavaScript invitation object using properties and the dot operator:

The dot operator references a property or method from an object.

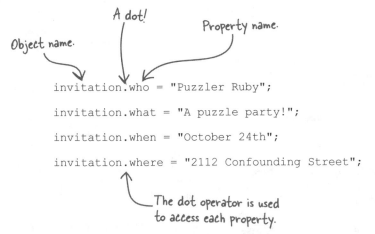

A dot!

Object name.

Property name.

```
invitation.who = "Puzzler Ruby";

invitation.what = "A puzzle party!";

invitation.when = "October 24th";

invitation.where = "2112 Confounding Street";
```

The dot operator is used to access each property.

Keep in mind that since the data and the actions are all part of the same object, you don't have to pass along anything to a method in order for it to be able to use the data. This makes taking an action on the invitation object quite simple:

```
invitation.deliver();
```

Object name.

Method name.

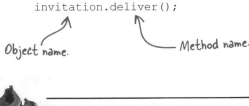

Exercise

The party invitation is missing an RSVP property that allows invitees to respond with whether they will be coming to the party or not. Write code to add an `rsvp` property to the Puzzler Ruby invitation (she plans to attend), and then call the `sendRSVP()` method to send the response.

....

....

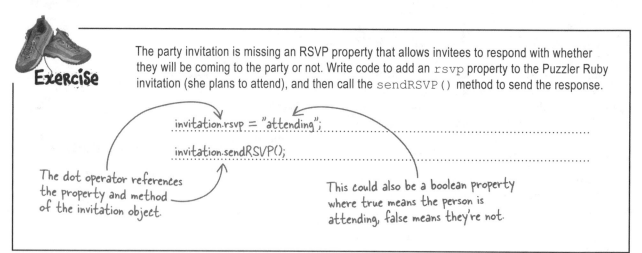

Exercise

The party invitation is missing an RSVP property that allows invitees to respond with whether they will be coming to the party or not. Write code to add an `rsvp` property to the Puzzler Ruby invitation (she plans to attend), and then call the `sendRSVP()` method to send the response.

invitation.rsvp = "attending";

invitation.sendRSVP();

The dot operator references the property and method of the invitation object.

This could also be a boolean property where true means the person is attending, false means they're not.

there are no Dumb Questions

Q: What exactly is an object? Does it have a data type?

A: Yes, objects have a data type. An object is a named collection of properties and methods. Or put more exactly, objects **are** a data type. Other data types you've learned about include number, text, and boolean. These are known as *primitive* data types because they represent a single piece of information. Objects are considered *complex* data types because they encompass multiple pieces of data. You can add "object" as a fourth data type to the list of primitive types you already know (number, string, and boolean). So, any object you create or any built-in JavaScript object you use has a data type of object.

Q: Couldn't I just use global variables and functions instead of object properties and methods? Functions can access global variables just fine, right?

A: Yes they can. Problem is, there is nothing stopping any other code from accessing the global variables as well. This is problematic because you always want to try and limit data exposure only to code that

truly needs access to the data. This helps prevent the data from getting accidentally changed by other code.

Unfortunately, JavaScript doesn't currently allow you to truly prevent an object property from being accessed by outside code. And there are situations where you specifically want an object property to be accessed directly. However, the idea is that you place data in an object to logically associate it with the object. A piece of data tied to an object has much more context and meaning than a piece of data floating freely in a script (a global variable).

Q: I've seen object notation with the dot operator used several times already. Was I really using objects all this time?

A: Yes. You'll find that it's actually quite difficult to use JavaScript without using objects, and that's because JavaScript itself is really one big collection of objects. For example, the `alert()` function is technically a method of the `window` object, which means it can be called with `window.alert()`. The `window` object represents the browser window, and doesn't have to be explicitly referenced as

an object, which is why you can get away with `alert()` by itself.

Q: OK, this is really confusing. So you're telling me that functions are really methods?

A: Yes, although it can get confusing thinking of functions in this manner. You already know that a function is a chunk of code that can be called by other code by name. A method is just a function that has been placed within an object. The confusion arises when you realize that every function actually belongs to an object.

So `alert()` is both a function and a method, which explains why it can be called as a function or as a method—most methods have to be called as a method using object notation. In reality, every JavaScript function belongs to an object, thereby making it a method. And in many cases this object is the browser's `window` object. Since this object is assumed to be the default object if no object is specified for a method call, such as `alert()`, it's OK to think of these methods as functions. Their ownership by the `window` object is incidental since they have no logical connection to the object.

BULLET POINTS

- Objects are a special kind of **data structure** that combine data with **code that acts on the data**.

- In practical terms, an object is really just variables and functions combined into a **single structure**.

- When placed into an object, variables become known as **properties**, while functions become known as **methods**.

- Properties and methods are referenced by supplying the name of the **object** followed by a **dot** followed by the **name** of the property or method.

A blog for cube puzzlers

On the other end of the party invitation is Ruby, a cube puzzle enthusiast who can't wait to get together with her other puzzler friends. But Ruby has more on her mind than just going to parties—she wants to create a blog where she can share her love of cube puzzles with the world. She's ready to start sharing her cubist wisdom on YouCube!

> I've heard that objects will make my code easier to maintain when I need to make changes. That will give me more time for my cube puzzles!

Ruby has heard that JavaScript supports custom objects as a means of creating more robust, and ultimately more manageable code. She has also heard that lots of blogs eventually get stale because bloggers get tired of maintaining them. So Ruby wants to start her blog out on the right foot by building YouCube as an **object-oriented** script using custom objects that will carry her far into the puzzling future.

Object-oriented YouCube = **More cube time!**

Deconstructing YouCube

Ruby currently has a handwritten diary, and she's read enough blogs to know hers will need to consist of dates and text, but she can't figure out how to store them using JavaScript. She just knows she's sick of writing her cube diary (soon to be blog) entries by hand!

The handwritten YouCube.

08/14/2008
Got the new cube I ordered. It's a real pearl.

08/19/2008
Solved the new cube but of course, now I'm bored and shopping for a new one.

Date of the entry.

08/16/2008
Managed to get a headache toiling over the new cube.
Gotta nap.

Body text of the entry.

08/21/2008
Found a 7x7x7 cube for sale online. Yikes! That one could be a beast.

Each entry consists of a date combined with a string of text.

Ruby's favorite cube puzzle.

Ruby desperately needs a straightforward way to store and access multiple pairs of information (date + text). This sure sounds an awful lot like what JavaScript objects have to offer...combining multiple pieces of information into a single entity.

Blog date + Blog body = Blog object

A custom object allows the two pieces of blog data to be combined into a single entity.

Custom objects extend JavaScript

The JavaScript language includes lots of handy standard objects, several of which we explore later in this chapter. As useful as these objects are, there are times when they simply aren't enough. The YouCube blog is a good example of this limitation since it involves a data storage problem that can't be solved with built-in JavaScript data types...a custom object is in order.

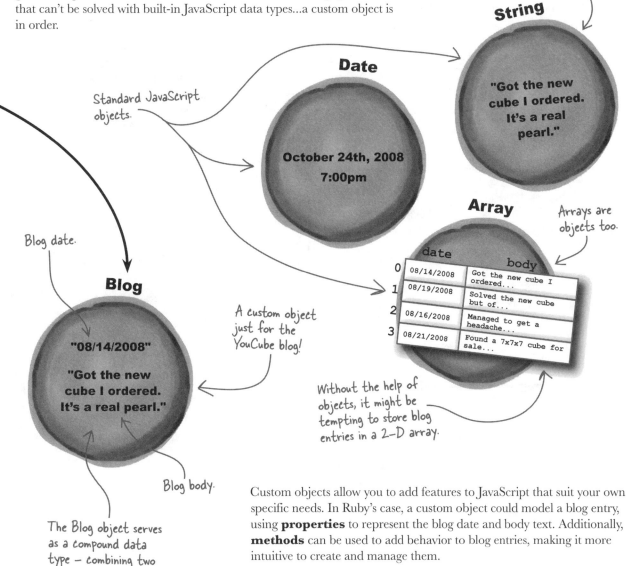

It's true, strings are really objects!

String

"Got the new cube I ordered. It's a real pearl."

Standard JavaScript objects.

Date

October 24th, 2008
7:00pm

Arrays are objects too.

Array

	date	body
0	08/14/2008	Got the new cube I ordered...
1	08/19/2008	Solved the new cube but of...
2	08/16/2008	Managed to get a headache...
3	08/21/2008	Found a 7x7x7 cube for sale...

Blog date.

Blog

"08/14/2008"

"Got the new cube I ordered. It's a real pearl."

A custom object just for the YouCube blog!

Without the help of objects, it might be tempting to store blog entries in a 2-D array.

Blog body.

The Blog object serves as a compound data type — combining two pieces of data into one.

Custom objects allow you to add features to JavaScript that suit your own specific needs. In Ruby's case, a custom object could model a blog entry, using **properties** to represent the blog date and body text. Additionally, **methods** can be used to add behavior to blog entries, making it more intuitive to create and manage them.

In order to bring such a custom object to life, however, we must first find out how custom objects are created...

Construct your custom objects

Since objects have data associated with them that must be initialized when an object is created, a special method called a **constructor** is required to get an object up and running. Every custom object requires its own constructor, which is named the same as the object. The constructor is called to initialize an object upon creation. When creating a custom object, it's your job to write a suitable constructor that brings the object to life.

A constructor is responsible for <u>creating an object</u>.

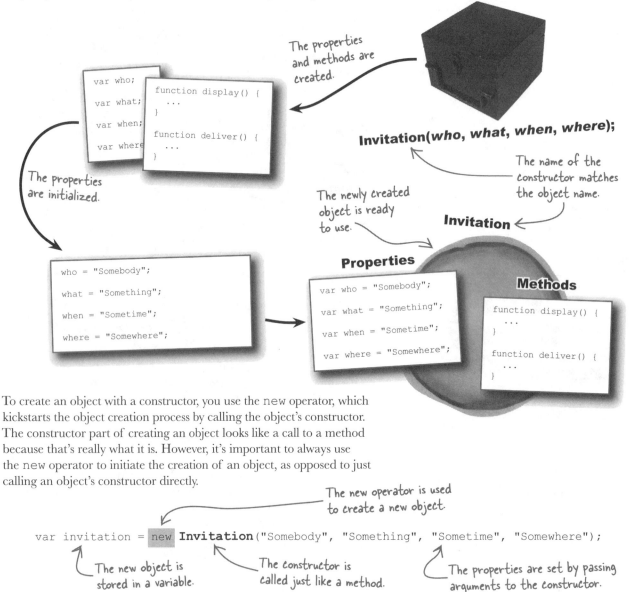

The properties and methods are created.

```
var who;
var what;
var when;
var where
```

```
function display() {
    ...
}

function deliver() {
    ...
}
```

The properties are initialized.

```
who = "Somebody";
what = "Something";
when = "Sometime";
where = "Somewhere";
```

Invitation(*who, what, when, where*);

The name of the constructor matches the object name.

The newly created object is ready to use.

Invitation

Properties

```
var who = "Somebody";
var what = "Something";
var when = "Sometime";
var where = "Somewhere";
```

Methods

```
function display() {
    ...
}

function deliver() {
    ...
}
```

To create an object with a constructor, you use the new operator, which kickstarts the object creation process by calling the object's constructor. The constructor part of creating an object looks like a call to a method because that's really what it is. However, it's important to always use the new operator to initiate the creation of an object, as opposed to just calling an object's constructor directly.

The new operator is used to create a new object.

```
var invitation = new Invitation("Somebody", "Something", "Sometime", "Somewhere");
```

The new object is stored in a variable.

The constructor is called just like a method.

The properties are set by passing arguments to the constructor.

What's in a constructor?

A big part of the constructor's job is establishing the properties of an object, along with their initial values. To create a property within a constructor, you set the property using a JavaScript keyword called `this`. The `this` keyword assigns ownership of the property to the object, and also sets its initial value at the same time. The word literally does what it means—you're creating a property that belongs to "this" object, as opposed to just being a local variable within the constructor.

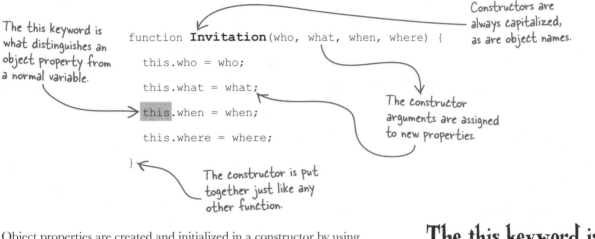

The this keyword is what distinguishes an object property from a normal variable.

Constructors are always capitalized, as are object names.

```
function Invitation(who, what, when, where) {
    this.who = who;
    this.what = what;
    this.when = when;
    this.where = where;
}
```

The constructor arguments are assigned to new properties.

The constructor is put together just like any other function.

Object properties are created and initialized in a constructor by using object notation (the dot operator) and the `this` keyword. Without the `this` keyword, the constructor would not know that you're creating object properties. The result of this constructor is the creation of four properties, which are assigned the four values passed as arguments into the constructor.

The _this_ keyword is the key to creating object properties inside a constructor.

Sharpen your pencil

Write a constructor for a `Blog` object that creates and initializes properties for the date and body text of a blog entry.

....

....

....

....

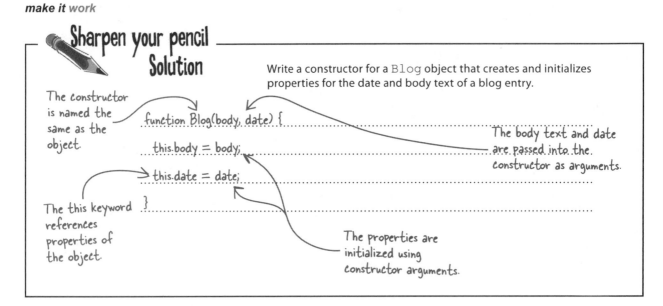

Sharpen your pencil
Solution

Write a constructor for a `Blog` object that creates and initializes properties for the date and body text of a blog entry.

The constructor is named the same as the object.

```
function Blog(body, date) {
    this.body = body;
    this.date = date;
}
```

The body text and date are passed into the constructor as arguments.

The properties are initialized using constructor arguments.

The this keyword references properties of the object.

Bringing blog objects to life

The `Blog` object is certainly shaping up but it hasn't actually been created yet. As good as it may seem in theory, it's still just a hypothesis yet to be proven. Remember that the constructor establishes the design of an object but none are physically created until you use the `new` operator, which then builds the object by calling the constructor. So let's go ahead and create a real live `Blog` object.

Follow along with the examples, available for download at http://www.headfirstlabs.com/books/hfjs/.

JavaScript Blog object.

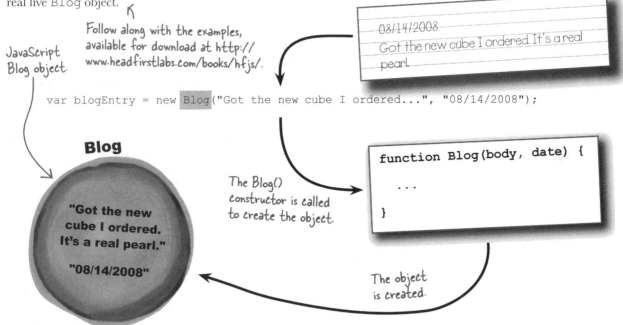

Handwritten blog entry.

```
08/14/2008
Got the new cube I ordered. It's a real pearl.
```

```
var blogEntry = new Blog("Got the new cube I ordered...", "08/14/2008");
```

Blog

"Got the new cube I ordered. It's a real pearl."

"08/14/2008"

The Blog() constructor is called to create the object.

```
function Blog(body, date) {
    ...
}
```

The object is created.

<h1 style="text-align:center">there are no
Dumb Questions</h1>

Q: **I'm confused about object creation. Does the** `new` **operator create an object or does the constructor?**

A: Both! The `new` operator is responsible for setting the object creation in motion, and a big part of its job is to make sure the constructor gets called. Just calling a constructor like a function without using the `new` operator would not create an object, and using the `new` operator with no constructor would be meaningless.

Q: **Does every custom object require a constructor?**

A: Yes. The reason is because the constructor is responsible for creating the object's properties, so without a constructor you wouldn't have any properties. And without any properties, you wouldn't have a very meaningful object.

There is an exception to this rule about constructors, and it applies when creating a purely organizational object consisting of a collection of methods that don't act on object properties. In this case, it's technically possible to do without a constructor. But keep in mind that such an object isn't exactly a shining example of good object-oriented programming practices because it's really just a collection of related functions. Even so, JavaScript itself employs an organizational object for grouping together math related tasks, as you learn later in the chapter.

Q: **What exactly is** `this`?

A: `this` is a JavaScript keyword used to refer to an object. More specifically, `this` references an object from within that **same** object. Yeah, that sounds pretty weird, and slightly schizophrenic. But it makes sense once you wrap your brain around it. To look at it in real world terms, think about what would happen if you lost your watch and someone found it in a room full of people. When they hold the watch up, you would probably yell, "It's my watch!" You used the word "my" to refer to yourself. More importantly, the word "my" is used to clarify that you are the owner of the watch. `this` works exactly the same way—it implies object **ownership**. So `this.date` means that the `date` property belongs to the object in which the code appears.

Sharpen your pencil

08/14/2008
Got the new cube I ordered. It's a real pearl.

08/19/2008
Solved the new cube but of course, now I'm bored and shopping for a new one.

08/16/2008
Managed to get a headache toiling over the new cube.
Gotta nap.

08/21/2008
Found a 7x7x7 cube for sale online. Yikes! That one could be a beast.

Create an array of `Blog` objects in a variable named `blog` that is initialized to the blog entries in the YouCube blog. Feel free to just write the first few words of body text in each entry.

```
var blog =
  [ ..................................................................
  ....................................................................
  ....................................................................
  ....................................................... ];
```

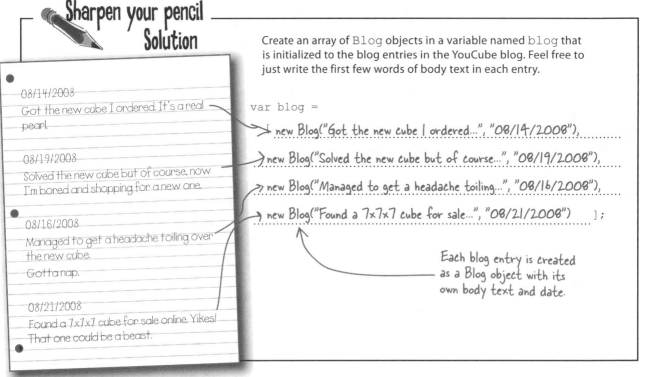

Sharpen your pencil Solution

Create an array of `Blog` objects in a variable named `blog` that is initialized to the blog entries in the YouCube blog. Feel free to just write the first few words of body text in each entry.

08/14/2008
Got the new cube I ordered. It's a real pearl.

08/19/2008
Solved the new cube but of course, now I'm bored and shopping for a new one.

08/16/2008
Managed to get a headache toiling over the new cube.
Gotta nap.

08/21/2008
Found a 7x7x7 cube for sale online. Yikes! That one could be a beast.

```
var blog =
    new Blog("Got the new cube I ordered...", "08/14/2008"),
    new Blog("Solved the new cube but of course...", "08/19/2008"),
    new Blog("Managed to get a headache toiling...", "08/16/2008"),
    new Blog("Found a 7x7x7 cube for sale...", "08/21/2008")   ];
```

Each blog entry is created as a Blog object with its own body text and date.

YouCube 1.0

The data stored in each Blog object is neatly displayed on the YouCube page.

Combining the array of `Blog` objects with some JavaScript code for displaying the blog data yields an initial version of YouCube. Ruby knows her work is not done, but the blog is up and running, and she's happy with the early results.

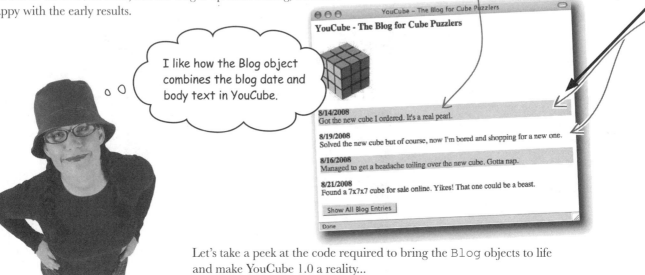

I like how the Blog object combines the blog date and body text in YouCube.

Let's take a peek at the code required to bring the `Blog` objects to life and make YouCube 1.0 a reality...

YouCube Up Close

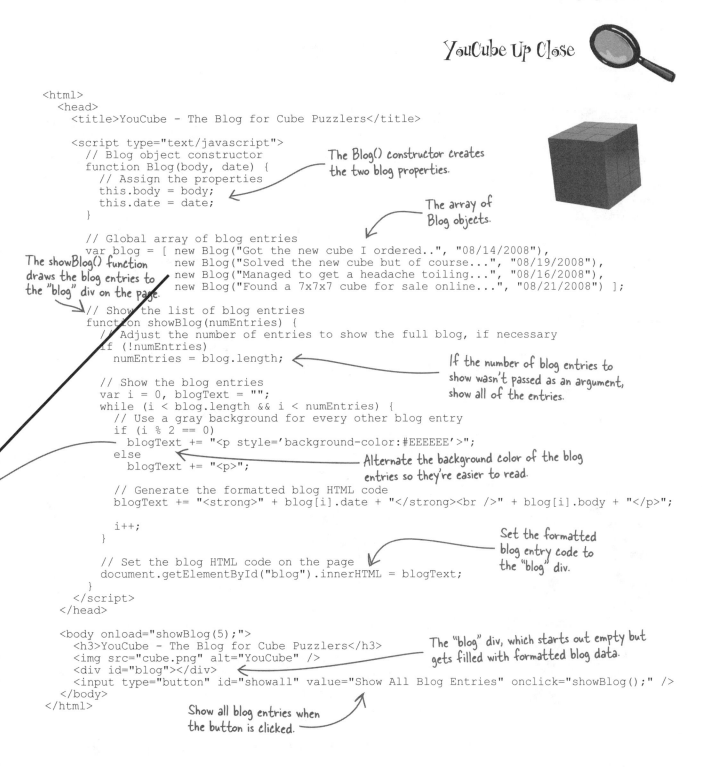

```html
<html>
  <head>
    <title>YouCube - The Blog for Cube Puzzlers</title>

    <script type="text/javascript">
      // Blog object constructor
      function Blog(body, date) {
        // Assign the properties
        this.body = body;
        this.date = date;
      }

      // Global array of blog entries
      var blog = [ new Blog("Got the new cube I ordered..", "08/14/2008"),
        new Blog("Solved the new cube but of course...", "08/19/2008"),
        new Blog("Managed to get a headache toiling...", "08/16/2008"),
        new Blog("Found a 7x7x7 cube for sale online...", "08/21/2008") ];

      // Show the list of blog entries
      function showBlog(numEntries) {
        // Adjust the number of entries to show the full blog, if necessary
        if (!numEntries)
          numEntries = blog.length;

        // Show the blog entries
        var i = 0, blogText = "";
        while (i < blog.length && i < numEntries) {
          // Use a gray background for every other blog entry
          if (i % 2 == 0)
            blogText += "<p style='background-color:#EEEEEE'>";
          else
            blogText += "<p>";
          // Generate the formatted blog HTML code
          blogText += "<strong>" + blog[i].date + "</strong><br />" + blog[i].body + "</p>";

          i++;
        }

        // Set the blog HTML code on the page
        document.getElementById("blog").innerHTML = blogText;
      }
    </script>
  </head>

  <body onload="showBlog(5);">
    <h3>YouCube - The Blog for Cube Puzzlers</h3>
    <img src="cube.png" alt="YouCube" />
    <div id="blog"></div>
    <input type="button" id="showall" value="Show All Blog Entries" onclick="showBlog();" />
  </body>
</html>
```

The Blog() constructor creates the two blog properties.

The array of Blog objects.

The showBlog() function draws the blog entries to the "blog" div on the page.

If the number of blog entries to show wasn't passed as an argument, show all of the entries.

Alternate the background color of the blog entries so they're easier to read.

Set the formatted blog entry code to the "blog" div.

The "blog" div, which starts out empty but gets filled with formatted blog data.

Show all blog entries when the button is clicked.

there are no Dumb Questions

Q: Why is the Show All Blog Entries button necessary in YouCube?

A: In the current state of the blog, the button is not necessary at all since there are only four blog entries total. But as the blog grows, it becomes increasingly important to limit the number of entries shown initially on the main YouCube page to keep from overwhelming visitors. So the blog code defaults to only showing the first five entries. The Show All Blog Entries button overrides this default by displaying all blog entries.

Q: Why is `innerHTML` used to show the blog entries instead of DOM methods?

A: Although DOM methods are certainly preferred in terms of web standards compliance, they are fairly unwieldy when it comes to dynamically generating highly formatted HTML code. The reason is because every container tag such as `<p>` and `<strong>` has to be created as a parent with child nodes for their content. `innerHTML` is a tremendous convenience in this case, and simplifies the YouCube code considerably.

Q: Why doesn't the `Blog` object have any methods?

A: Ambition, that's good! The truth is that there are plenty of other aspects of YouCube to work on before `Blog` methods become a true priority. But don't worry, methods are definitely part of the long-range plan for YouCube. Methods are an important part of any well-designed object, and the `Blog` object is no different.

A disorderly blog

YouCube 1.0 looks good but it isn't without its flaws. Ruby has noticed that the blog entries are in the wrong order—they really should appear with the most recent post first. Right now they are displayed in whatever order they are stored, which we can't count on being chronological.

The order of blog entries should be most recent first.

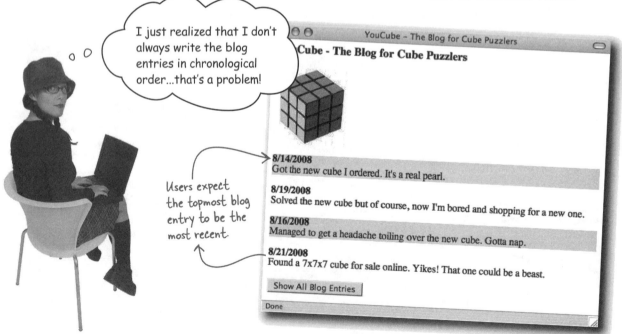

I just realized that I don't always write the blog entries in chronological order...that's a problem!

Users expect the topmost blog entry to be the most recent.

YouCube – The Blog for Cube Puzzlers

Cube - The Blog for Cube Puzzlers

8/14/2008
Got the new cube I ordered. It's a real pearl.

8/19/2008
Solved the new cube but of course, now I'm bored and shopping for a new one.

8/16/2008
Managed to get a headache toiling over the new cube. Gotta nap.

8/21/2008
Found a 7x7x7 cube for sale online. Yikes! That one could be a beast.

Show All Blog Entries

Done

The need for sorting

Ruby's solution to the blog ordering problem is to sort the blog array by
date. Since JavaScript supports looping and comparisons, it should be
possible to loop through the blog entries, compare dates to each other, and
sort them into reverse chronological order (most recent posts first).

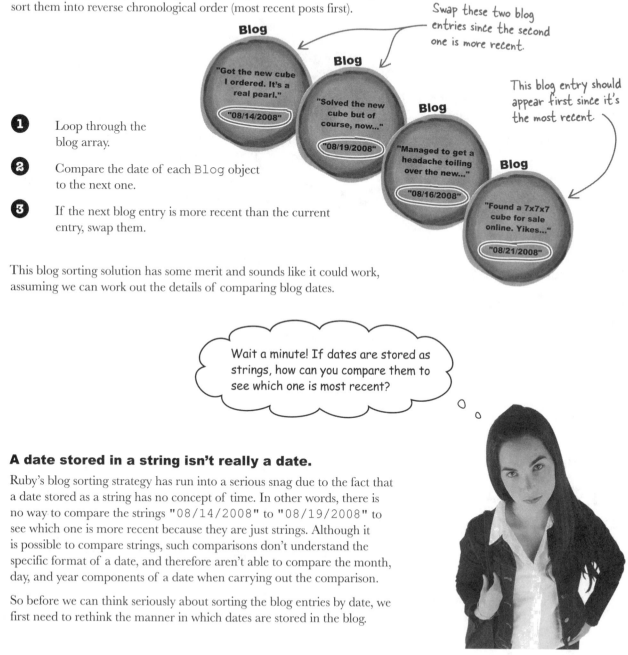

Swap these two blog
entries since the second
one is more recent.

Blog

"Got the new cube
I ordered. It's a
real pearl."

"08/14/2008"

Blog

"Solved the new
cube but of
course, now..."

"08/19/2008"

This blog entry should
appear first since it's
the most recent.

Blog

"Managed to get a
headache toiling
over the new..."

"08/16/2008"

Blog

"Found a 7x7x7
cube for sale
online. Yikes..."

"08/21/2008"

1 Loop through the
blog array.

2 Compare the date of each `Blog` object
to the next one.

3 If the next blog entry is more recent than the current
entry, swap them.

This blog sorting solution has some merit and sounds like it could work,
assuming we can work out the details of comparing blog dates.

> Wait a minute! If dates are stored as
> strings, how can you compare them to
> see which one is most recent?

A date stored in a string isn't really a date.

Ruby's blog sorting strategy has run into a serious snag due to the fact that
a date stored as a string has no concept of time. In other words, there is
no way to compare the strings `"08/14/2008"` to `"08/19/2008"` to
see which one is more recent because they are just strings. Although it
is possible to compare strings, such comparisons don't understand the
specific format of a date, and therefore aren't able to compare the month,
day, and year components of a date when carrying out the comparison.

So before we can think seriously about sorting the blog entries by date, we
first need to rethink the manner in which dates are stored in the blog.

A JavaScript object for dating

What Ruby needs is the ability to store a date in such a way that it can be compared to other dates. In other words, the date needs to **understand** that it is a date, and **behave** accordingly. Wait a minute, that sounds a lot like an object! And as it turns out, JavaScript offers a built-in Date object that could very well be what Ruby needs.

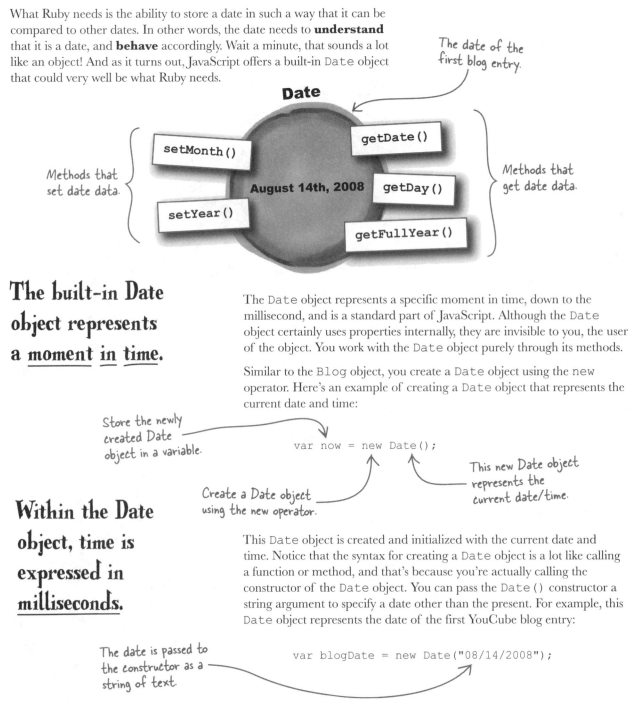

The date of the first blog entry.

Date

setMonth()

getDate()

August 14th, 2008

getDay()

setYear()

getFullYear()

Methods that set date data.

Methods that get date data.

The built-in Date object represents a moment in time.

The Date object represents a specific moment in time, down to the millisecond, and is a standard part of JavaScript. Although the Date object certainly uses properties internally, they are invisible to you, the user of the object. You work with the Date object purely through its methods.

Similar to the Blog object, you create a Date object using the new operator. Here's an example of creating a Date object that represents the current date and time:

Store the newly created Date object in a variable.

```
var now = new Date();
```

Create a Date object using the new operator.

This new Date object represents the current date/time.

Within the Date object, time is expressed in milliseconds.

This Date object is created and initialized with the current date and time. Notice that the syntax for creating a Date object is a lot like calling a function or method, and that's because you're actually calling the constructor of the Date object. You can pass the Date() constructor a string argument to specify date other than the present. For example, this Date object represents the date of the first YouCube blog entry:

The date is passed to the constructor as a string of text.

```
var blogDate = new Date("08/14/2008");
```

Calculating time

One of the most powerful features of objects is how they inherently know how to manipulate themselves. For example, think about how tricky it would be to calculate the number of days between two dates on your own. You'd have to somehow convert a date into a number of days from some known reference, making sure to factor in leap years. Or you could just let the `Date` object do the work for you...check out this function that does the heavy lifting with a couple of `Date` objects:

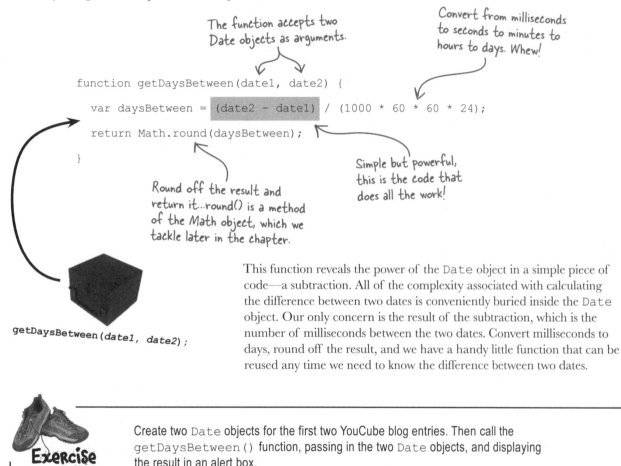

The function accepts two Date objects as arguments.

Convert from milliseconds to seconds to minutes to hours to days. Whew!

```
function getDaysBetween(date1, date2) {
    var daysBetween = (date2 - date1) / (1000 * 60 * 60 * 24);
    return Math.round(daysBetween);
}
```

Round off the result and return it...round() is a method of the Math object, which we tackle later in the chapter.

Simple but powerful, this is the code that does all the work!

getDaysBetween(*date1*, *date2*);

This function reveals the power of the `Date` object in a simple piece of code—a subtraction. All of the complexity associated with calculating the difference between two dates is conveniently buried inside the `Date` object. Our only concern is the result of the subtraction, which is the number of milliseconds between the two dates. Convert milliseconds to days, round off the result, and we have a handy little function that can be reused any time we need to know the difference between two dates.

Exercise

Create two `Date` objects for the first two YouCube blog entries. Then call the `getDaysBetween()` function, passing in the two `Date` objects, and displaying the result in an alert box.

....

....

....

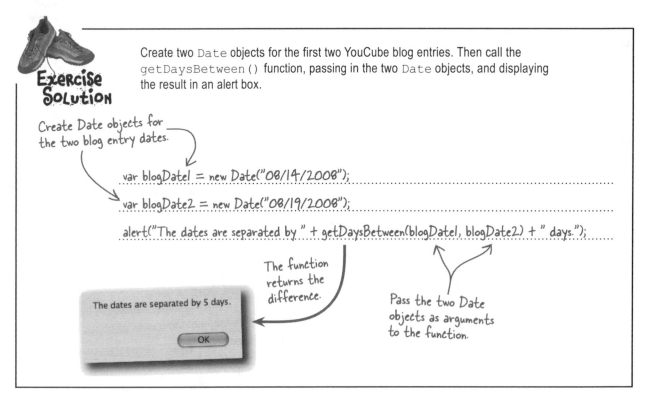

Create two `Date` objects for the first two YouCube blog entries. Then call the `getDaysBetween()` function, passing in the two `Date` objects, and displaying the result in an alert box.

Exercise Solution

Create Date objects for the two blog entry dates.

```
var blogDate1 = new Date("08/14/2008");
var blogDate2 = new Date("08/19/2008");
alert("The dates are separated by " + getDaysBetween(blogDate1, blogDate2) + " days.");
```

The dates are separated by 5 days.

OK

The function returns the difference.

Pass the two Date objects as arguments to the function.

Rethinking blog dates

While it's great that JavaScript offers a `Date` object that makes it possible to manipulate dates intelligently, the YouCube `Blog` object currently still stores dates as strings, not `Date` objects. In order to take advantage of the features made available by the `Date` object, we need to change the blog so that the blog dates are `Date` objects.

Blog

"Got the new cube I ordered. It's a real pearl."

"08/14/2008"

The date property of the Blog object needs to be converted from a string to a Date object.

Date

August 14th, 2008

The question is, can the `date` property of the `Blog` object store a `Date` object instead of a string?

An object within an object

The Blog object is a good example of how objects must often **contain** other objects. The two properties of the Blog object are actually already objects themselves—both properties are String objects. The String objects don't really look like objects because they are created as **object literals** by simply quoting a string of text. Date objects aren't as flexible, and must be created using the new operator.

To create a blog date property as a Date object, we must use the new operator to create a new Date while creating the Blog object. If this sounds nightmarish, maybe some code will ease the fear.

The string literal automatically creates a String object.

The Blog object is created using the new operator.

```
var blogEntry = new Blog("Nothing going on but the weather.",
    new Date("10/31/2008"));
```

A Date object is created and passed into the Blog() constructor, also using the new operator.

This code reveals how a YouCube blog entry is now created as an object that contains two other objects (a String object and a Date object). Of course, we still need to build an array of Blog objects in order to successfully represent all of the YouCube blog entries.

String

"Got the new cube I ordered. It's a real pearl."

body property.

Date

August 14th, 2008

Blog

"Got the new cube I ordered. It's a real pearl."

August 14th, 2008

date property.

The <u>new</u> operator creates objects with the help of constructors.

Sharpen your pencil

Rewrite the code to create an array of YouCube Blog objects where each date is now a Date object. Feel free to shorten the body text.

....

....

....

....

Sharpen your pencil Solution

Rewrite the code to create an array of YouCube `Blog` objects where each date is now a `Date` object. Feel free to shorten the body text.

Each blog entry is still created as a Blog object.

```
var blog = [ new Blog("Got the new cube I ordered...", new Date("08/14/2008")),

new Blog("Solved the new cube but of course...", new Date("08/19/2008")),

new Blog("Managed to get a headache toiling...", new Date("08/16/2008")),

new Blog("Found a 7x7x7 cube for sale...", new Date("08/21/2008")) ];
```

String literals work fine for the body text of each blog entry.

The date for each Blog object is created as a Date object.

---

there are no Dumb Questions

Q: Why is the date in a `Date` object stored in milliseconds?

A: First off, understand that the `Date` object represents an instant in time. If you could click the Pause button on the universe, you'd have a frozen moment in time. But you wouldn't have any way to tell people when the moment occurred without some kind of reference. So you decide on January 1, 1970 as the arbitrary reference point for your moment in time. Now you need a measurement from this offset. Maybe it's 38 years, 8 months, 14 days, 3 hours, 29 minutes, and 11 seconds. But that's a cumbersome way to keep track of a time offset. It's much easier to stick with a single unit of measurement, one that is capable of representing the

tiniest fractions of time. How about a millisecond? So instead of all those different units of time, you now have 1,218,702,551,000 milliseconds. Yeah, that's a whole bunch of milliseconds but big numbers aren't a problem for JavaScript.

Q: Do I have to worry about converting milliseconds when using the `Date` object?

A: It depends. The `Date` object includes several methods for extracting meaningful parts of a date that avoid dealing directly with milliseconds. However, if you need to deal with a **difference** between two dates, then milliseconds will almost certainly enter the picture.

BULLET POINTS

- The standard JavaScript `Date` objects represents an **instant in time**, expressed in milliseconds.

- The `Date` object includes several methods for accessing the different pieces and parts of a date and time.

- The `Date` object is smart enough to know how to manipulate dates mathematically, as well as compare dates to each other.

- Like most objects other than `String`, you create a `Date` object using the `new` operator.

Dates aren't useful...for humans

With the date property of the Blog object converted into a Date object, Ruby is ready to turn her attention back to sorting the blog entries by date. Well, almost ready. It seems she has introduced a new problem in that the dates of the blog entries are now extremely cryptic. Ruby suspects that users won't really care about the time zone of each post, and it will only distract from the YouCube experience. Clearly, the injection of `Date` objects into YouCube needs to be examined more closely!

The blog dates are quite messy...information overload!

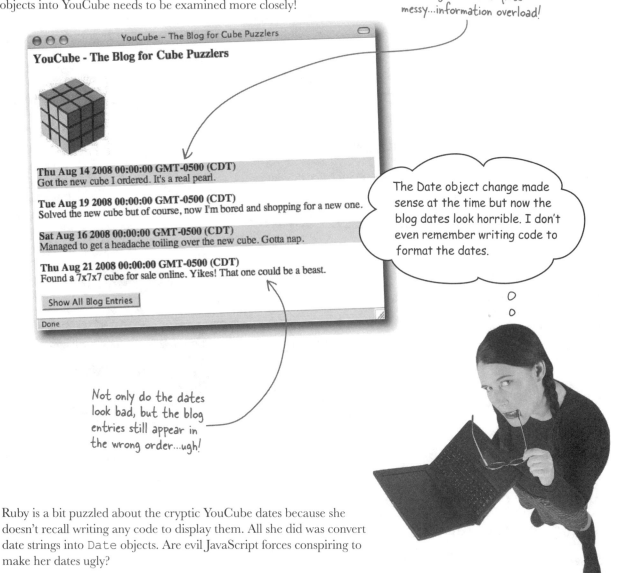

The Date object change made sense at the time but now the blog dates look horrible. I don't even remember writing code to format the dates.

Not only do the dates look bad, but the blog entries still appear in the wrong order...ugh!

Ruby is a bit puzzled about the cryptic YouCube dates because she doesn't recall writing any code to display them. All she did was convert date strings into `Date` objects. Are evil JavaScript forces conspiring to make her dates ugly?

Converting objects to text

Fortunately, there are no evil forces to blame for the ugly YouCube dates. In fact, it's the very natural forces of JavaScript objects that are responsible for the date formatting—the dates formatted themselves! It works like this: every JavaScript object has a method called `toString()` that attempts to provide a text representation of the object. The cryptic date is the output of the `Date` object's **default** `toString()` method.

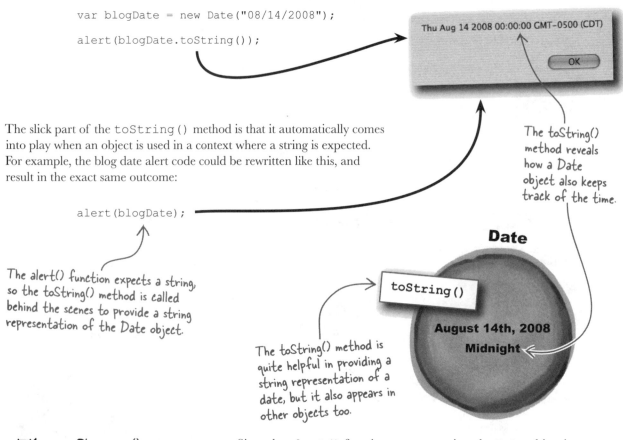

```
var blogDate = new Date("08/14/2008");

alert(blogDate.toString());
```

Thu Aug 14 2008 00:00:00 GMT-0500 (CDT)

OK

The slick part of the `toString()` method is that it automatically comes into play when an object is used in a context where a string is expected. For example, the blog date alert code could be rewritten like this, and result in the exact same outcome:

```
alert(blogDate);
```

The toString() method reveals how a Date object also keeps track of the time.

The alert() function expects a string, so the toString() method is called behind the scenes to provide a string representation of the Date object.

Date

`toString()`

August 14th, 2008
Midnight

The toString() method is quite helpful in providing a string representation of a date, but it also appears in other objects too.

The toString() method provides a string representation of an object.

Since the `alert()` function expects a string, the `Date` object is smart enough to know that it must provide a string representation of itself. So it calls upon the `toString()` method to handle the task.

This `toString()` business wouldn't be a problem except for the fact that YouCube really needs dates to be displayed in an easy-to-read format, such as *MM/DD/YYYY*. Bottom line, it doesn't look as if YouCube will be able to take advantage of the default string representation of the `Date` object made possible by its `toString()` method.

Accessing pieces and parts of a date

Ruby needs a way to customize the format of a date. The key to custom formatting a `Date` object is accessing the individual pieces of the date, such as the month, day, and year. Then we can reassemble a date in any format we want. Fortunately, the `Date` object provides methods for accessing these pieces of information.

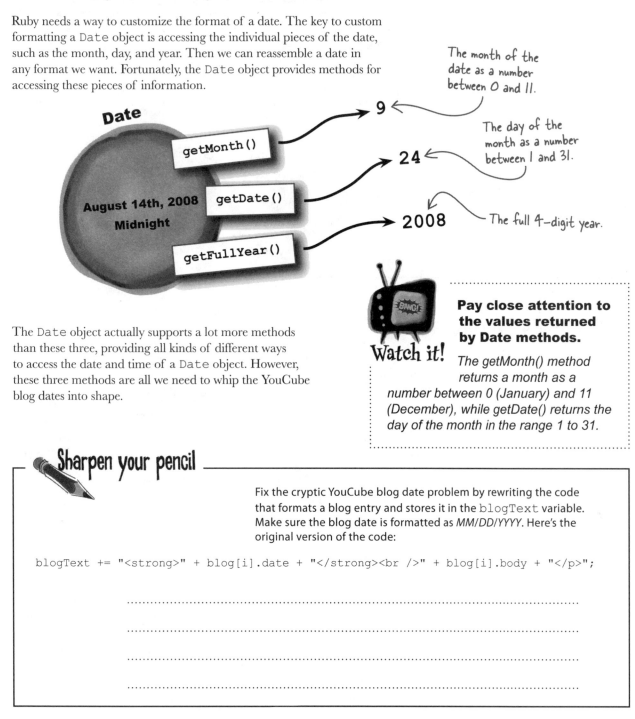

The month of the date as a number between 0 and 11.

The day of the month as a number between 1 and 31.

The full 4-digit year.

The `Date` object actually supports a lot more methods than these three, providing all kinds of different ways to access the date and time of a `Date` object. However, these three methods are all we need to whip the YouCube blog dates into shape.

Watch it!

Pay close attention to the values returned by Date methods.

The getMonth() method returns a month as a number between 0 (January) and 11 (December), while getDate() returns the day of the month in the range 1 to 31.

Sharpen your pencil

Fix the cryptic YouCube blog date problem by rewriting the code that formats a blog entry and stores it in the `blogText` variable. Make sure the blog date is formatted as *MM/DD/YYYY*. Here's the original version of the code:

```
blogText += "<strong>" + blog[i].date + "</strong><br />" + blog[i].body + "</p>";
```

....

....

....

....

Sharpen your pencil Solution

Fix the cryptic YouCube blog date problem by rewriting the code that formats a blog entry and stores it in the `blogText` variable. Make sure the blog date is formatted as *MM/DD/YYYY*. Here's the original version of the code:

```
blogText += "<strong>" + blog[i].date + "</strong><br />" + blog[i].body + "</p>";
```

blogText += "" + (blog[i].date.getMonth() + 1) + "/" +
blog[i].date.getDate() + "/" +
blog[i].date.getFullYear() + "<br />" +
blog[i].body + "</p>";

We get more control by not relying on the Date object to format itself.

Each piece of the date is extracted from the Date object by calling methods.

The blog date displayed is now custom built in the MM/DD/YYYY format.

Dates make sorting easy

Now that the blog dates have been successfully converted to Date objects, which are much more suited to sorting than strings, it's time to revisit the blog order. The problem is that the blog entries are currently displayed in the same order that they are stored in the blog array, which isn't necessarily chronological. Most blogs are displayed in reverse chronological order, where the most recent posts appear first in the list of blog entries. Knowing this, it's possible to revisit the original blog sorting strategy:

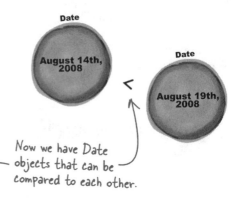

Now we have Date objects that can be compared to each other.

① Loop through the blog array.

② Compare the Date object within each Blog object to the next one.

③ If the date of the next blog entry is more recent than the current entry, swap the entries.

Although the date comparison part of this strategy certainly looks much less daunting with the help of the Date object, the rest of the plan still involves a fair amount of custom coding. Sorting a sequence of data sure does seem like a common programming problem that has been solved many times before. You hate to reinvent the wheel...

Wouldn't it be dreamy if JavaScript had some kind of built-in sort feature that took the drudgery out of sorting a sequence of data?

Arrays as objects

Could it be that an array is capable of sorting itself? If a date knows how to turn itself into a string, it's not so far-fetched to think that an array might be able to sort itself. For that to be possible, however, an array would have to be an object so that the sorting could take place in a method. And indeed it is. Remember this code from the Mandango script?

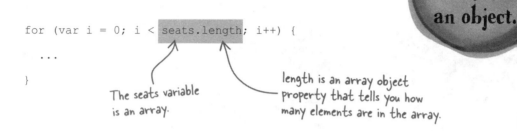

An array is really just an object.

```
for (var i = 0; i < seats.length; i++) {
    ...
}
```

The seats variable is an array.

length is an array object property that tells you how many elements are in the array.

So the cat's out of the bag, arrays are objects, but does that mean they can sort themselves? Not only do arrays have properties such as `length`, but they also have methods that act on the array data, bringing it to life. And yes, there's a method named `sort()` that sorts the data in an array. Let's see how it works:

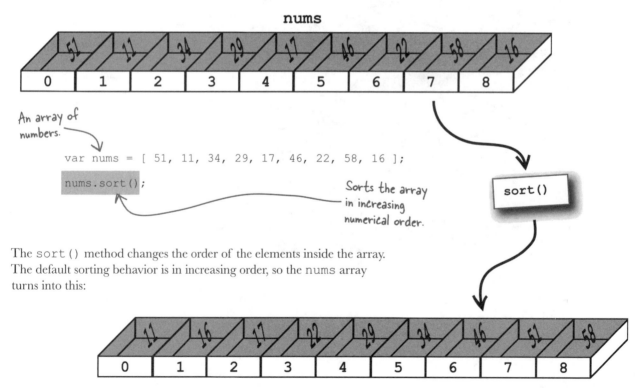

nums

0	1	2	3	4	5	6	7	8
51	11	34	29	17	46	22	58	16

An array of numbers.

```
var nums = [ 51, 11, 34, 29, 17, 46, 22, 58, 16 ];
nums.sort();
```

Sorts the array in increasing numerical order.

sort()

The `sort()` method changes the order of the elements inside the array. The default sorting behavior is in increasing order, so the `nums` array turns into this:

0	1	2	3	4	5	6	7	8
11	16	17	22	29	34	46	51	58

Custom sorting an array

The default behavior of the `Array` object's `sort()` method is often not enough. The good news is that the sorting behavior is determined by a **comparison function** that `sort()` calls to handle the comparison of each sorted item in an array. You can fine-tune the sort order by providing your own version of this comparison function. Here's an example of what the function typically looks like:

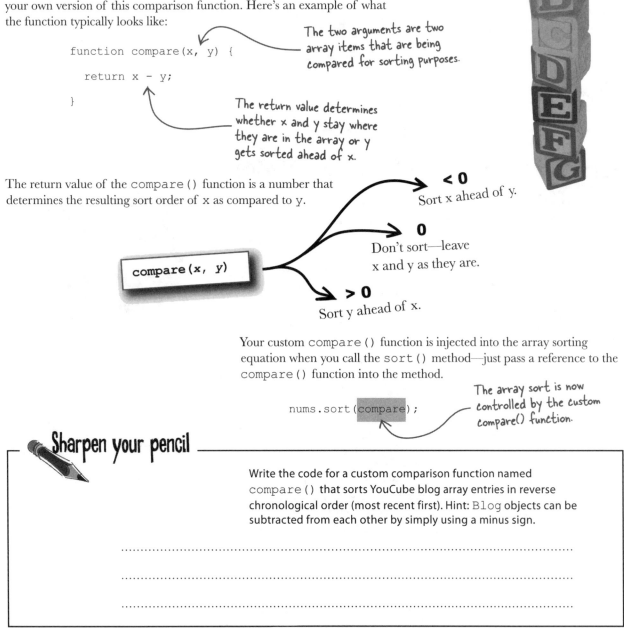

```
function compare(x, y) {

    return x - y;

}
```

The two arguments are two array items that are being compared for sorting purposes.

The return value determines whether x and y stay where they are in the array or y gets sorted ahead of x.

The return value of the `compare()` function is a number that determines the resulting sort order of x as compared to y.

< 0
Sort x ahead of y.

0
Don't sort—leave x and y as they are.

compare(x, y)

> 0
Sort y ahead of x.

Your custom `compare()` function is injected into the array sorting equation when you call the `sort()` method—just pass a reference to the `compare()` function into the method.

```
nums.sort(compare);
```

The array sort is now controlled by the custom compare() function.

Sharpen your pencil

Write the code for a custom comparison function named `compare()` that sorts YouCube blog array entries in reverse chronological order (most recent first). Hint: `Blog` objects can be subtracted from each other by simply using a minus sign.

....

....

....

Sharpen your pencil
Solution

Write the code for a custom comparison function named `compare()` that sorts YouCube blog array entries in reverse chronological order (most recent first). Hint: `Blog` objects can be subtracted from each other by simply using a minus sign.

These two arguments are Blog objects since the array contains Blog objects.

```
function compare(blog1, blog2) {

    return blog2.date - blog1.date;

}
```

Subtracting the first date from the second results in a reverse chronological sort.

We're subtracting the two dates as numbers (milliseconds).

Sorting made simple with function literals

When you think about the role of the array sort comparison function, it's really only used by the `sort()` method and nothing else. Since it is never called by any of the YouCube script code, there's really no reason for it to be a named function.

Remember function literals from the thermostat in Chapter 6? The `compare()` function is an excellent candidate for a function literal because of how it is used. In fact, YouCube blog sorting can be simplified by converting the `compare()` function into a function literal that's passed directly into the `sort()` method.

```
blog.sort(function(blog1, blog2) {

    return blog2.date - blog1.date;

});
```

The function literal is passed directly into the array sort() method.

As a devout puzzler, Ruby is all about efficiency. And in this case that equates to eliminating an unnecessary named function that is really just a sidekick of the `sort()` method. Ruby is so bent on efficiency, in fact, that she doesn't see why the comparison function needs to take up three lines of code. Although the organization of JavaScript code doesn't make the code run any differently, in this case the function literal is simple enough that it makes some sense shrinking it to a single line of code.

The function literal is crunched into a single line of code.

```
blog.sort(function(blog1, blog2) { return blog2.date - blog1.date; });
```

there are no Dumb Questions

Q: Does every object have a `toString()` method?

A: Yes. Even if you create a custom object and don't give it a `toString()` method, JavaScript will at least report that it is an object if you use it in a context where a string is expected. Granted, the string won't be very meaningful but it's up to you to provide a `toString()` method for custom objects if you want it to convey meaning about the object.

Q: How does the sort comparison work between `Date` objects?

A: The goal of a sort comparison function is to return a number whose value controls the sorting of the two arguments. In the case of comparing dates, you want the more recent date to be sorted first. The more recent date is the larger date, so subtracting the second date from the first date achieves the result of sorting recent dates ahead of later dates. This means the second date is sorted above the first date only if the second date is larger (the result is greater than 0).

Q: How does the `Array.sort()` method know to use a custom comparison function or a default comparison?

A: This decision is made based upon whether or not an argument is passed into the `sort()` function. If there is no argument, a default sort comparison is assumed. If an argument is provided, it is interpreted as a function reference and used as the basis for comparing items in the sort. So the comparison function reference is an **optional** argument.

Ruby and her cubes are happy

The YouCube blog is now approaching Ruby's vision of a cube puzzle blog that shares her every cubist thought with the universe.

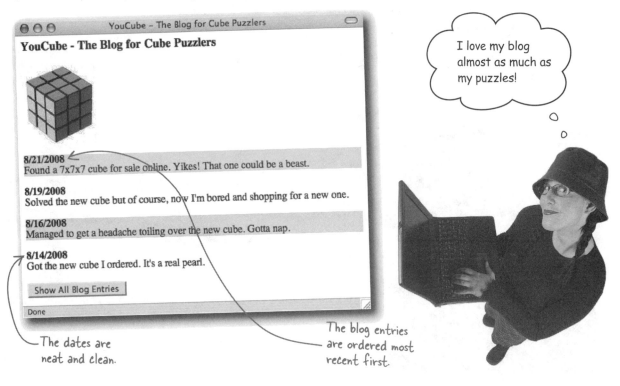

I love my blog almost as much as my puzzles!

The dates are neat and clean.

The blog entries are ordered most recent first.

Searching would be nice

YouCube is running pretty smoothly but several users have requested a search feature that allows them to search all of the blog posts. Since Ruby plans on eventually having lots of blog posts, she agrees that this could be a very handy feature, especially over the long haul.

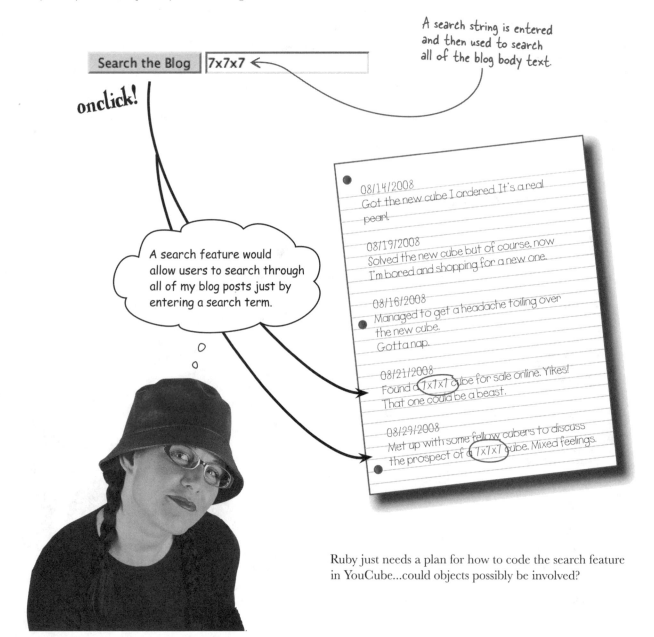

Search the Blog | 7x7x7 ←

onclick!

A search string is entered and then used to search all of the blog body text.

A search feature would allow users to search through all of my blog posts just by entering a search term.

08/14/2008
Got the new cube I ordered. It's a real pearl.

08/19/2008
Solved the new cube but of course, now I'm bored and shopping for a new one.

08/16/2008
Managed to get a headache toiling over the new cube.
Gotta nap.

08/21/2008
Found a 7x7x7 cube for sale online. Yikes! That one could be a beast.

08/29/2008
Met up with some fellow cubers to discuss the prospect of a 7x7x7 cube. Mixed feelings.

Ruby just needs a plan for how to code the search feature in YouCube...could objects possibly be involved?

Searching the blog array

A search feature for YouCube involves looping through each entry in the
blog array looking for matching text in each blog post.

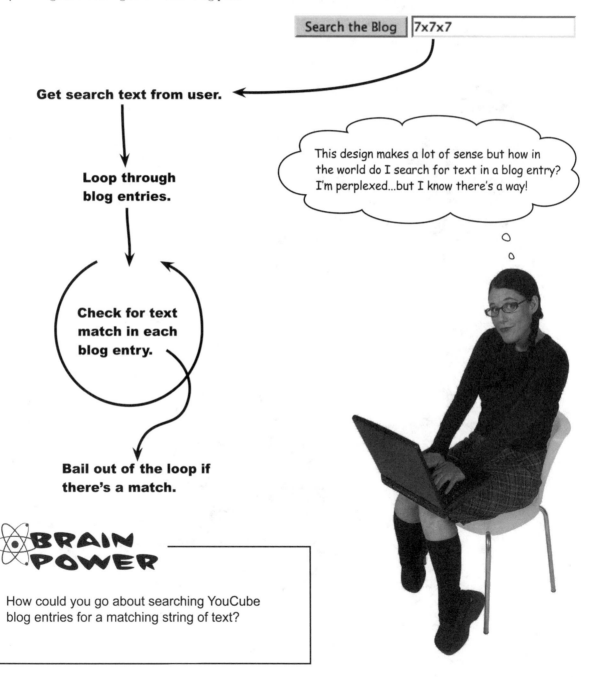

Search the Blog | 7x7x7

Get search text from user.

**Loop through
blog entries.**

This design makes a lot of sense but how in
the world do I search for text in a blog entry?
I'm perplexed...but I know there's a way!

**Check for text
match in each
blog entry.**

**Bail out of the loop if
there's a match.**

BRAIN POWER

How could you go about searching YouCube
blog entries for a matching string of text?

> We already know that a string is really an object. So is it possible that string could just search itself?

A string is a searchable object.

You're maybe starting to figure out that objects are everywhere in JavaScript. Strings are objects, and include lots of handy methods for interacting with string data (text). And yes, one of these methods allows you to search for a piece of text within a string. A string within a string is sometimes referred to as a **substring**.

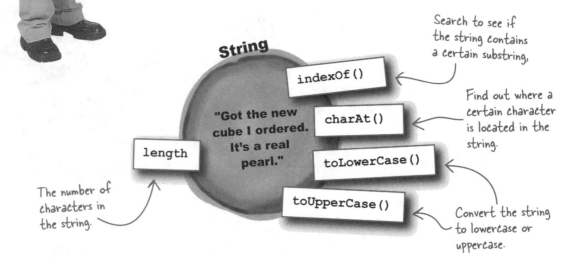

String

"Got the new cube I ordered. It's a real pearl."

length

The number of characters in the string.

indexOf()

Search to see if the string contains a certain substring,

charAt()

Find out where a certain character is located in the string.

toLowerCase()

toUpperCase()

Convert the string to lowercase or uppercase.

Searching within strings: indexOf()

The `indexOf()` method allows you to search for a string of text, a substring, within a `String` object. The substring is passed as an argument to the `indexOf()` method—since you call the method on a `String` object, there's no need to pass anything else. The `indexOf()` method returns the index where the substring is located, or -1 if there is no match.

```
var str = "Got the new cube I ordered. It's a real pearl.";

alert(str.indexOf("new"));
```

> 8
>
> OK

To understand where the number 8 comes from in this example, you have to look at a string very much like it's an array of individual characters.

```
 0         10        20        30        40
 |||||||||||||||||||||||||||||||||||||||||||||
"Got the new cube I ordered. It's a real pearl."
```

The search string "new" appears at index 8 in the string.

Each character in the string is located at a unique index that counts up from 0 at the beginning of the string.

When `indexOf()` is used to search for a string that doesn't exist, the result of the method is -1.

```
var searchIndex = str.indexOf("used");
```

The result is -1 since the search string doesn't appear in the String object.

Exercise

Below is one of Ruby's favorite riddles. Identify the index of each occurrence of the substring `"cube"` in the riddle string.

```
"A cubist cubed two cubes and ended up with eight. Was she Cuban?"
```

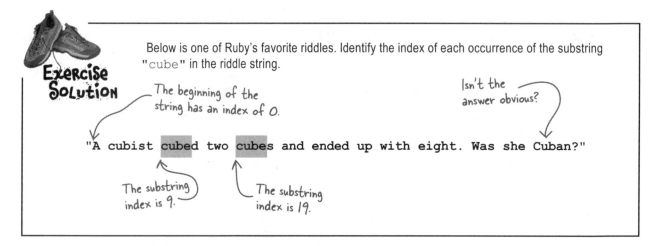

Exercise Solution

Below is one of Ruby's favorite riddles. Identify the index of each occurrence of the substring "cube" in the riddle string.

The beginning of the string has an index of 0.

Isn't the answer obvious?

"A cubist cubed two cubes and ended up with eight. Was she Cuban?"

The substring index is 9.

The substring index is 19.

Searching the blog array

String searching isn't too difficult thanks to the indexOf() method of the String object, but Ruby still has an entire blog to search. Her plan is to loop through the array of blog entries, and use the indexOf() method to search for a substring within the body text of each blog entry. If there is a match, she wants to display the blog entry in an alert box.

Before writing a function to handle the actual blog search, the YouCube blog needs a text field for the search text, as well as a button for initiating a search.

```
<input type="button" id="search" value="Search the Blog" onclick="searchBlog();" />
<input type="text" id="searchtext" name="searchtext" value="" />
```

Blog search text is accessible through the searchtext ID.

Search text!

The Search button calls the searchBlog() function to search the blog.

Search the Blog | 7x7x7

With the HTML search elements in place, all that's left is to put together the code for the searchBlog() function. Since the function uses an alert to display the search results, there's no need to return any information from it. There also isn't any need for an argument since the function directly reads the search text from the HTML text field.

JavaScript Magnets

The YouCube `searchBlog()` function is responsible for looping through the array of blog entries and searching for matching text in a blog body. Help Ruby finish the function by filling in missing code with the magnets. Hint: The matching search result should be displayed with its date in the form *MM/DD/YYYY* inside of square brackets, followed by the blog body text.

```javascript
function searchBlog() {

  var ................ = document.getElementById(" ................ ").value;

  for (var i = 0; i < ........................ ; i++) {

    // See if the blog entry contains the search text

    if (blog[i]. ................ .toLowerCase().indexOf(searchText.toLowerCase()) != -1) {

      alert("[" + (blog[i]. ................ . ........................ + ........ ) + "/" +

        blog[i].date.getDate() + "/" + blog[i]. ................ .getFullYear() + "] " +

        blog[i]. ................ );

      break;
    }
  }

  // If the search text wasn't found, display a message

  if (i == ........................ )

    alert("Sorry, there are no blog entries containing the search text.");
}
```

Magnets:

`date`

`searchText`

`blog.length`

`1`

`searchtext`

`body`

`getMonth()`

JavaScript Magnets Solution

The YouCube `searchBlog()` function is responsible for looping through the array of blog entries and searching for matching text in a blog body. Help Ruby finish the function by filling in missing code with the magnets. Hint: The matching search result should be displayed with its date in the form *MM/DD/YYYY* inside of square brackets, followed by the blog body text.

First grab the search text from the HTML text field.

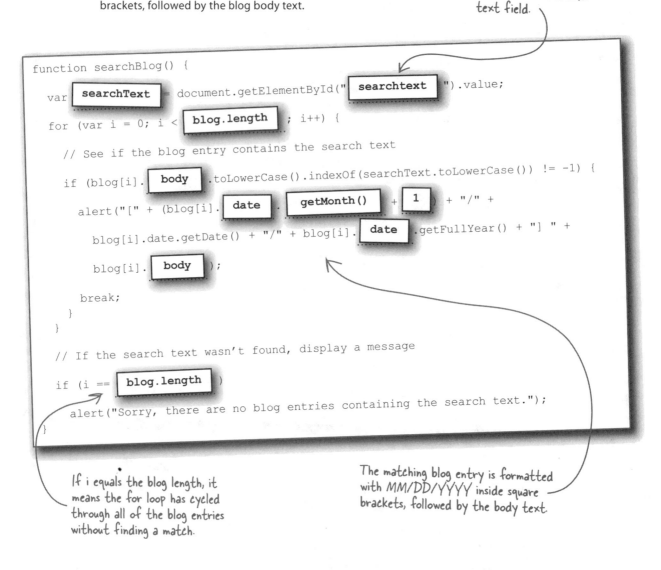

```javascript
function searchBlog() {

  var  searchText  = document.getElementById("  searchtext  ").value;

  for (var i = 0; i <  blog.length  ; i++) {

    // See if the blog entry contains the search text

    if (blog[i].  body  .toLowerCase().indexOf(searchText.toLowerCase()) != -1) {

      alert("[" + (blog[i].  date  .  getMonth()  +  1  ) + "/" +

        blog[i].date.getDate() + "/" + blog[i].  date  .getFullYear() + "] " +

        blog[i].  body  );

      break;
    }
  }

  // If the search text wasn't found, display a message

  if (i ==  blog.length  )

    alert("Sorry, there are no blog entries containing the search text.");
}
```

If i equals the blog length, it means the for loop has cycled through all of the blog entries without finding a match.

The matching blog entry is formatted with MM/DD/YYYY inside square brackets, followed by the body text.

Searching works now, too!

YouCube 2.0 is now complete with a search feature that relies heavily on the search capabilities built into the `String` object. It's a great example of how objects make data active, in this case turning a string of text (pure data) into an entity that has a behavior (it can search itself). And perhaps more importantly, it kept Ruby from having to invent her own search routine, allowing her to focus on writing her blog.

Ruby is thrilled with the new blog feature, but she's not one to rest on her laurels. She already has YouCube 3.0 in mind...

there are no
Dumb Questions

Q: I still don't quite understand how every string is really an object. Is that really true?

A: Yes. Every single string in JavaScript is an object. If you put your name in quotes in JavaScript code, as in `"Ruby"`, you just created an object. Although it may seem like overkill, the upside to JavaScript treating every string as an object is that every string has the ability to do useful things such as know its own length, search for substrings within itself, and so forth.

Q: So I get that a string is an object, but it also seems to be a lot like an array with the character indexes and all. Is a string also an array?

A: No. A string is most definitely not an array. However, it is true that many of the `String` methods operate on string data as if it was an array of individual characters. For example, the characters within a string start at index 0 and count up a character at a time as you move through the string. But you can't access a character within a string using square brackets (`[ ]`), as you can with an array. So while it does help to think of the characters within a string as being similar to elements in an array, you don't literally work with a `String` object the same way you work with an `Array` object.

Q: Could the `searchBlog()` function have used `charAt()` instead of `indexOf()` for the blog search?

A: No. The `charAt()` method only searches for a single character, which wouldn't be very helpful in searching the blog for a phrase of text. The `indexOf()` method searches for a string, not just a single character, and is the best tool for the job in this case.

Q: Is it possible to search a string for more than one occurrence of a search substring?

A: Yes. The `indexOf()` method defaults to searching for the first occurrence of the search substring. But you can pass in a second, optional argument that tells `indexOf()` where to start the search. So let's say you're searching for the string "cube" and you've found a match at index 11. You can call `indexOf()` again with a second argument of 11, which forces it to start searching at index 12. So the general solution is to pass the previous search index into the `indexOf()` method to continue searching throughout a string.

Q: What's the purpose of the two calls to `toLowerCase()` in the `searchBlog()` function?

A: Great question! The answer has to do with the problem of case when searching for text in the blog. If someone searches the blog for the word "cube", they probably want all matches for the word, including "cube", "Cube", "CUBE", and any other variations in the case of the word. A simple way to get around this problem is to convert both the search substring and the blog body text to a common case before carrying out the search. Although the `searchBlog()` function uses `toLowerCase()`, the `toUpperCase()` method would work just as well. The point is to remove case from the search entirely.

BULLET POINTS

- The `toString()` method is used to convert any object to a text representation.

- Arrays and strings are both really just objects, relying on the standard `Array` and `String` objects in JavaScript for their methods and data storage.

- The `sort()` method of the `Array` object can be used to sort an array in any order you want.

- The `indexOf()` method in the `String` object searches for a string of text within another string, returning the index of the search string location.

A random YouCube

In the neverending quest to keep users interested in her blog, Ruby has come up with one more addition to YouCube that she thinks her fellow puzzlers will enjoy. She wants to add a Random button that allows visitors to view a blog entry at random.

08/14/2008
Got the new cube I ordered. It's a real p...

08/16/2008
Managed to get a headache toiling over the new cube. Gotta nap.

08/29/2008
Met up with some fellow cubers to discuss the prospect of a 1x1x1 cube. Mixed feelings.

08/21/2008
Found a 1x1x1 cube for sale online. Yikes! That one could be a beast.

...e new cube but of course, now I'm bored and shopping for a new one.

A random blog feature adds a touch of fun and mystery to YouCube. I'm all about fun and mystery!

Ruby, cube puzzle blogger and woman of mystery.

⚛ BRAIN POWER

How could you go about choosing a YouCube blog entry at random?

The Math object is an <u>organizational object</u>

To help Ruby add a random feature to YouCube, we desperately need a
way to generate random numbers. This involves using a built-in JavaScript
object that isn't quite as "alive" as some of the other objects we've used.
The standard `Math` object is where random numbers can be generated,
and it is a unique object in that it doesn't have any data that changes, and
no methods that act on internal data.

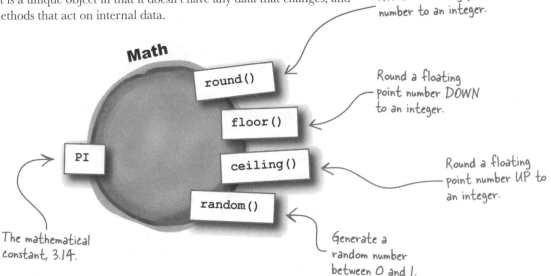

Math

round()

floor()

PI

ceiling()

random()

Round a floating point number to an integer.

Round a floating point number DOWN to an integer.

Round a floating point number UP to an integer.

The mathematical constant, 3.14.

Generate a random number between 0 and 1.

The `Math` object is an **organizational object**, which means it is just
a collection of math-related utility methods and constants. There are no
variables, which means the `Math` object maintains no state—you can't use
it to store anything. The only data it contains are a few constants such as
`PI` (3.14). The methods in the `Math` object, however, are quite handy. For
one, the `random()` method generates a random floating point number
between 0 and 1.

> **The Math object is an <u>organizational object</u> that houses math methods and constants.**

Exercise

Write the results of the following calls to `Math` methods.

        Math.round(Math.PI)   ....

        Math.ceiling(Math.PI)   ....

        Math.random()   ....

⟶ Answers on page 436.

The Math Object Exposed

This week's interview:
When math functions collide

Head First: OK, I'm really confused. You're an object, but I'm hearing that you don't really do anything other than hold a bunch of mathematical methods and a few constants. I thought the whole point of objects was to make data active. You know, wrap up some data and then have methods that do cool things with it.

Math: That's what conventional JavaScript wisdom leads people to think, but not all objects are about bringing data to life. It's perfectly acceptable for an object to play the role of organizer, like me.

Head First: But couldn't all those math methods have just been created as standard functions?

Math: Yes, they could've, but you're forgetting that the JavaScript language is built out of objects. So in reality, there's no such thing as a "standard" function.

Head First: But I can create a function outside of an object and it seems to work just fine.

Math: Right, but in reality all functions really are methods because they belong to an object somewhere, even if it's hidden. This helps explain why there are no "standard functions."

Head First: Ah, I see. It's starting to make more sense why you contain those math methods.

Math: And don't forget that just because I don't have internal data that gets manipulated by my methods, it doesn't mean I don't play an important role in being an object.

Head First: What do you mean?

Math: Well, imagine a group of people who all share a common interest, such as cube puzzles. In many cases, such people organize together so that they can interact with each other about their interest. While math methods aren't exactly as social as people, they do benefit from the organization I provide.

Head First: You mean because they're all related to a common interest.

Math: Yes! And that interest is carrying out mathematical tasks, such as rounding numbers, carrying out trigonometric operations, and generating random numbers.

Head First: You mention generating random numbers. I've heard your numbers aren't truly random. Any truth to the rumor?

Math: I have to confess that no, they are not truly random. And neither are most computer-generated random numbers. My random numbers are "pseudorandom," which is good enough for most situations.

Head First: Pseudorandom, is that like pseudo-science...or pseudocode?

Math: Uh, no and yes. No, nothing at all like pseudo-science. And yes, a little like pseudocode since pseudocode is intended to represent the idea behind code without actually being code. In the case of pseudorandom numbers, they approximate randomness without truly being random.

Head First: So, can I trust that pseudorandom numbers are sufficiently random for most JavaScript applications?

Math: Yes, and that's a good way to put it: "sufficiently random." You probably wouldn't want to trust pseudorandom numbers for issues involving national security, but they work great for injecting randomness into everyday scripts.

Head First: Got it. Well, thanks for your time...and your honesty regarding random numbers.

Math: Glad to do it...you know I can't lie.

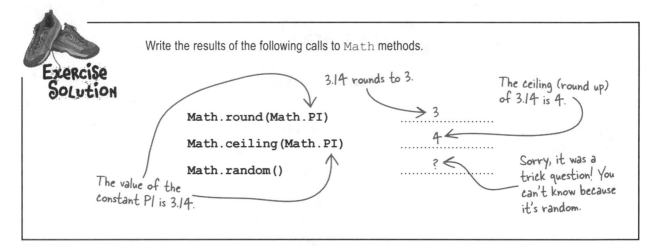

Exercise Solution

Write the results of the following calls to `Math` methods.

3.14 rounds to 3.

The ceiling (round up) of 3.14 is 4.

```
Math.round(Math.PI)
```
............3............

```
Math.ceiling(Math.PI)
```
............4............

```
Math.random()
```
............?............

The value of the constant PI is 3.14.

Sorry, it was a trick question! You can't know because it's random.

Generate random numbers with Math.random

Pseudorandom or not, random numbers generated by the `random()` method of the `Math` object are extremely useful in applications such as YouCube that need to make a random selection from a collection of data. The problem is, `random()` returns a random number in the range 0 and 1, while Ruby needs a random number that is in the range 0 to the end of blog array. In other words, she needs to generate a random blog index.

Each of the random numbers is in the range 0 to 1.

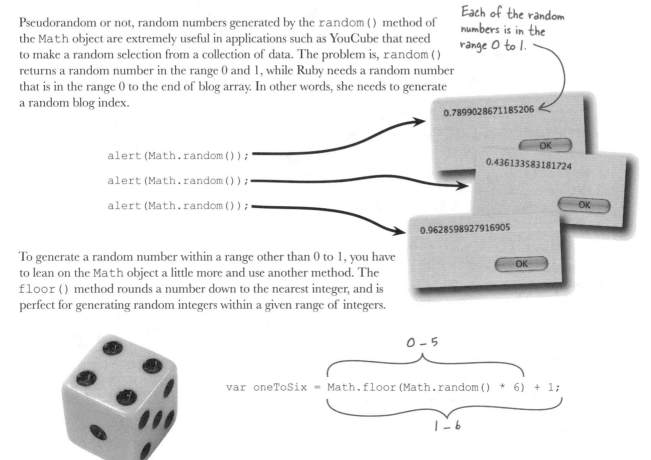

```
alert(Math.random());
```
0.7899028671185206

OK

```
alert(Math.random());
```
0.436133583181724

OK

```
alert(Math.random());
```
0.9628598927916905

OK

To generate a random number within a range other than 0 to 1, you have to lean on the `Math` object a little more and use another method. The `floor()` method rounds a number down to the nearest integer, and is perfect for generating random integers within a given range of integers.

0 - 5

```
var oneToSix = Math.floor(Math.random() * 6) + 1;
```

1 - 6

Q: Why isn't it necessary to create a Math **object before using it?**

A: Ah, that's a perceptive question, and it touches on a very important concept related to objects. Since the Math object doesn't actually contain data that can change, also known as instance data, there is no need to create an object. Remember that the Math object is just a collection of static methods and constants, so everything that goes into the Math object already exists—there's nothing **to** create. This will make much more sense in Chapter 10 when you learn the details of object instances and classes.

Q: What's the difference between the round() **and** floor() **methods of the** Math **object?**

A: The round() method rounds the number up or down depending upon its decimal part. For example, Math. round(11.375) results in 11, while Math.round(11.625) results in 12. The floor() method, on other hand, always rounds down, no matter what the decimal part is. You can just think of the floor() method as always chopping off the decimal part.

Q: What else can the Math **object do?**

A: Lots of things. Two handy methods that we haven't had the need for yet are min() and max(), which analyze two numbers and return the lesser or greater of the two. abs() is another very useful Math method—its job is to return a positive number no matter what number you give it.

Geek Bits

If you find yourself working on a JavaScript application that desperately needs true random numbers, stop by http://random.org to learn more about how to go beyond the realm of pseudorandom numbers.

Sharpen your pencil

Write the code for a randomBlog() function that selects a blog entry at random and then displays it in an alert box. Hint: The blog entry in the alert box can be formatted the same as the search result in searchBlog().

....

....

....

....

....

....

Sharpen your pencil Solution

Write the code for a `randomBlog()` function that selects a blog entry at random and then displays it in an alert box. Hint: The blog entry in the alert box can be formatted the same as the search result in `searchBlog()`.

Use a random number to select a blog entry.

Generate a random number between 0 and one less than the blog length.

```
function randomBlog() {
  // Pick a random number between 0 and blog.length - 1
  var i = Math.floor(Math.random() * blog.length);
  alert("[" + (blog[i].date.getMonth() + 1) + "/" + blog[i].date.getDate() + "/" +
    blog[i].date.getFullYear() + "] " + blog[i].body);
}
```

Format the blog entry with a MM/DD/YYYY date followed by the body text.

Random but still lacking

Ruby's blog now supports a random blog search feature, which she is very happy about. Users can now view the YouCube blog with a healthy sense of intrigue since they don't know what entry they'll get.

Randomly chosen blog entry.

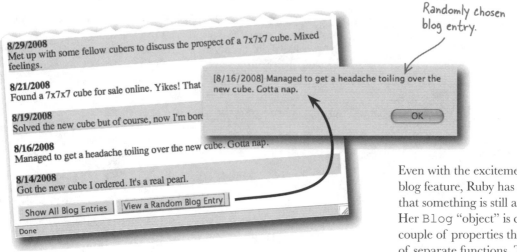

Even with the excitement over the new blog feature, Ruby has a nagging feeling that something is still amiss with YouCube. Her `Blog` "object" is currently just a couple of properties that rely on a bunch of separate functions. That doesn't seem like a very good object design...

An object in search of actions

Ruby's instincts about the YouCube object are dead-on. The behavioral part of the object is extremely lacking, and could use some serious restructuring so that it uses methods to handle blog-specific tasks. Ruby needs methods that add some **actions** to the Blog object!

> I really could use some blog methods.

Sharpen your pencil

Study the YouCube code and circle any code you think could be placed within Blog methods; make sure to name each method.

```javascript
function showBlog(numEntries) {
  // First sort the blog in reverse chronological order (most recent first)
  blog.sort(function(blog1, blog2) { return blog2.date - blog1.date; });

  // Adjust the number of entries to show the full blog, if necessary
  if (!numEntries)
    numEntries = blog.length;

  // Show the blog entries
  var i = 0, blogText = "";
  while (i < blog.length && i < numEntries) {
    // Use a gray background for every other blog entry
    if (i % 2 == 0)
      blogText += "<p style='background-color:#EEEEEE'>";
    else
      blogText += "<p>";

    // Generate the formatted blog HTML code
    blogText += "<strong>" + (blog[i].date.getMonth() + 1) + "/" +
      blog[i].date.getDate() + "/" +
      blog[i].date.getFullYear() + "</strong><br />" +
      blog[i].body + "</p>";

    i++;
  }

  // Set the blog HTML code on the page
  document.getElementById("blog").innerHTML = blogText;
}

function searchBlog() {
  var searchText = document.getElementById("searchtext").value;
  for (var i = 0; i < blog.length; i++) {
    // See if the blog entry contains the search text
    if (blog[i].body.toLowerCase().indexOf(searchText.toLowerCase()) != -1) {
      alert("[" + (blog[i].date.getMonth() + 1) + "/" + blog[i].date.getDate() + "/" +
        blog[i].date.getFullYear() + "] " + blog[i].body);
      break;
    }
  }

  // If the search text wasn't found, display a message
  if (i == blog.length)
    alert("Sorry, there are no blog entries containing the search text.");
}

function randomBlog() {
  // Pick a random number between 0 and blog.length - 1
  var i = Math.floor(Math.random() * blog.length);
  alert("[" + (blog[i].date.getMonth() + 1) + "/" + blog[i].date.getDate() + "/" +
    blog[i].date.getFullYear() + "] " + blog[i].body);
}
```

Sharpen your pencil Solution

Study the YouCube code and circle any code you think could be placed within `Blog` methods; make sure to name each method.

```javascript
function showBlog(numEntries) {
  // First sort the blog in reverse chronological order (most recent first)
  blog.sort(function(blog1, blog2) { return blog2.date - blog1.date; });

  // Adjust the number of entries to show the full blog, if necessary
  if (!numEntries)
    numEntries = blog.length;

  // Show the blog entries
  var i = 0, blogText = "";
  while (i < blog.length && i < numEntries) {
    // Use a gray background for every other blog entry
    if (i % 2 == 0)
      blogText += "<p style='background-color:#EEEEEE'>";
    else
      blogText += "<p>";

    // Generate the formatted blog HTML code
    blogText += "<strong>" + (blog[i].date.getMonth() + 1) + "/" +
      blog[i].date.getDate() + "/" +
      blog[i].date.getFullYear() + "</strong><br />" +
      blog[i].body + "</p>";

    i++;
  }

  // Set the blog HTML code on the page
  document.getElementById("blog").innerHTML = blogText;
}

function searchBlog() {
  var searchText = document.getElementById("searchtext").value;
  for (var i = 0; i < blog.length; i++) {
    // See if the blog entry contains the search text
    if (blog[i].body.toLowerCase().indexOf(searchText.toLowerCase()) != -1) {
      alert("[" + (blog[i].date.getMonth() + 1) + "/" + blog[i].date.getDate() + "/" +
        blog[i].date.getFullYear() + "] " + blog[i].body);
      break;
    }
  }

  // If the search text wasn't found, display a message
  if (i == blog.length)
    alert("Sorry, there are no blog entries containing the search text.");
}

function randomBlog() {
  // Pick a random number between 0 and blog.length - 1
  var i = Math.floor(Math.random() * blog.length);
  alert("[" + (blog[i].date.getMonth() + 1) + "/" + blog[i].date.getDate() + "/" +
    blog[i].date.getFullYear() + "] " + blog[i].body);
}
```

Convert the blog entry to formatted HTML – Blog.toHTML().

Blog.toHTML()
Convert a blog entry to formatted HTML code, which takes a huge burden off of other code that wants to display a cleanly formatted blog.

Blog.containsText()
Not much code but still worthy of a method since a blog entry should be capable of searching its own body for text.

Blog.toString()
Convert a blog entry to a string, which makes sense to use in any situation where the date is shown in square brackets with the body text beside it.

Q: **How do you know what script code should go into a method?**

A: Well, you have to first remind yourself what a method is ideally intended to do, and that is to take some kind of action based upon the state (data) of an object. To some extent, figuring out methods for an object involves figuring out what it is the object is exactly doing, or needs to do. Then focus on empowering objects to do things for themselves.

As an example, it makes sense for the Blog object to turn itself into a string or formatted HTML code since those two actions require access to internal blog data. Similarly, searching for text within a blog entry is an action that should be internal to the Blog object, and therefore makes perfect sense as a method.

Q: **So is there an example of an action that the Blog object shouldn't take?**

A: Actions that are very much outside of the scope of the Blog object could be things like showing or searching the list of blog entries. This is because the Blog object represents a single blog entry. That's why the blog array consists of multiple **individual** Blog objects. So each individual Blog object doesn't need to concern itself with a collection of Blog objects. Instead, an individual Blog object should take care of its own business, which involves taking action based solely upon its own date and body text.

Turn a function into a method

Now that some pieces of YouCube code have been isolated that would make a good fit as methods of the Blog object, let's take a closer look at converting one of them into a Blog method. The method is containsText(), which takes on the responsibility of searching the body of a blog entry for a substring. Moving the search code to a method primarily involves operating directly on the body property of a Blog object, as opposed to a local variable in the searchBlog() function. These steps help clarify the process:

1 Declare the method, complete with an argument list, if required, such as the search text argument to containsText().

2 Move the existing code to the new method.

3 Change relevant code to use object properties, such as this.body in the containsText() method.

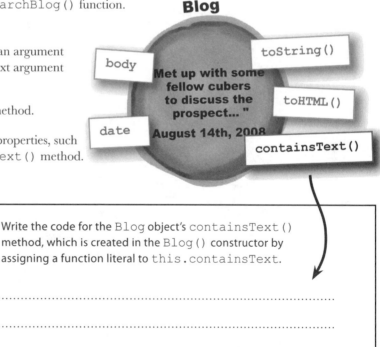

Blog

body

Met up with some fellow cubers to discuss the prospect... "

date   August 14th, 2008

toString()

toHTML()

containsText()

 Sharpen your pencil

Write the code for the Blog object's containsText() method, which is created in the Blog() constructor by assigning a function literal to this.containsText.

....

....

....

Sharpen your pencil
Solution

Write the code for the Blog object's containsText() method, which is created in the Blog() constructor by assigning a function literal to this.containsText.

The method is created by assigning a function literal to a method reference.

```
this.containsText = function(text) {

    return (this.body.toLowerCase().indexOf(text.toLowerCase()) != -1);

};
```

The this keyword is used to create a method similarly to how it is used to create properties.

The code within the method accesses an object property directly using the this keyword.

Unveiling the shiny new blog object

The other two new blog methods join the containsText() method in a new version of the Blog object that has both properties **and** behaviors.

Hey, I've shaped up quite nicely!

Create and initialize the properties.

```
function Blog(body, date) {
    // Assign the properties
    this.body = body;
    this.date = date;

    // Return a string representation of the blog entry
    this.toString = function() {
        return "[" + (this.date.getMonth() + 1) + "/" + this.date.getDate() + "/" +
            this.date.getFullYear() + "] " + this.body;
    };

    // Return a formatted HTML representation of the blog entry
    this.toHTML = function(highlight) {
        // Use a gray background as a highlight, if specified
        var blogHTML = "";
        blogHTML += highlight ? "<p style='background-color:#EEEEEE'>" : "<p>";

        // Generate the formatted blog HTML code
        blogHTML += "<strong>" + (this.date.getMonth() + 1) + "/" +
            this.date.getDate() + "/" + this.date.getFullYear() + "</strong><br />" +
            this.body + "</p>";
        return blogHTML;
    };

    // See if the blog body contains a string of text
    this.containsText = function(text) {
        return ((this.body.toLowerCase().indexOf(text.toLowerCase()) != -1);
    };
}
```

The toString() method returns the blog entry formatted as a string of text

The toHTML() method returns the blog entry as fancy formatted HTML code.

The containsText() method returns true if the body text contains the search string, or false otherwise.

What do objects really offer YouCube?

It's not until the new version of the `Blog` object (available at *http://www. headfirstlabs.com/books/hfjs/*) is plugged into the YouCube script that the real benefits of object-oriented programming are revealed. Now that several important blog-specific tasks are delegated to `Blog` methods, the script code gets considerably simpler.

The new Blog object simplifies the YouCube script.

```
// Show the list of blog entries
function showBlog(numEntries) {
  // First sort the blog in reverse chronological order (most recent first)
  blog.sort(function(blog1, blog2) { return blog2.date - blog1.date; });

  // Adjust the number of entries to show the full blog, if necessary
  if (!numEntries)
    numEntries = blog.length;

  // Show the blog entries
  var i = 0, blogListHTML = "";
  while (i < blog.length && i < numEntries) {
    blogListHTML += blog[i].toHTML(i % 2 == 0);
    i++;
  }

  // Set the blog HTML code on the page
  document.getElementById("blog").innerHTML = blogListHTML;
}

// Search the list of blog entries for a piece of text
function searchBlog() {
  var searchText = document.getElementById("searchtext").value;
  for (var i = 0; i < blog.length; i++) {
    // See if the blog entry contains the search text
    if (blog[i].containsText(searchText)) {
      alert(blog[i]);
      break;
    }
  }

  // If the search text wasn't found, display a message
  if (i == blog.length)
    alert("Sorry, there are no blog entries containing the search text.");
}

// Display a randomly chosen blog entry
function randomBlog() {
  // Pick a random number between 0 and blog.length - 1
  var i = Math.floor(Math.random() * blog.length);
  alert(blog[i]);
}
```

The toHTML() method is entirely responsible for formatting a blog entry as HTML code.

The containsText() method takes care of searching a blog entry for a substring.

The toString() method is a little more subtle, getting called automatically when a blog entry is used in a context where a string is expected.

YouCube 3.0!

It's been quite a project but Ruby has officially deemed YouCube 3.0 good enough for her to take a break and get back to puzzling. She's also excited about spending some time preparing for that party she was invited to...

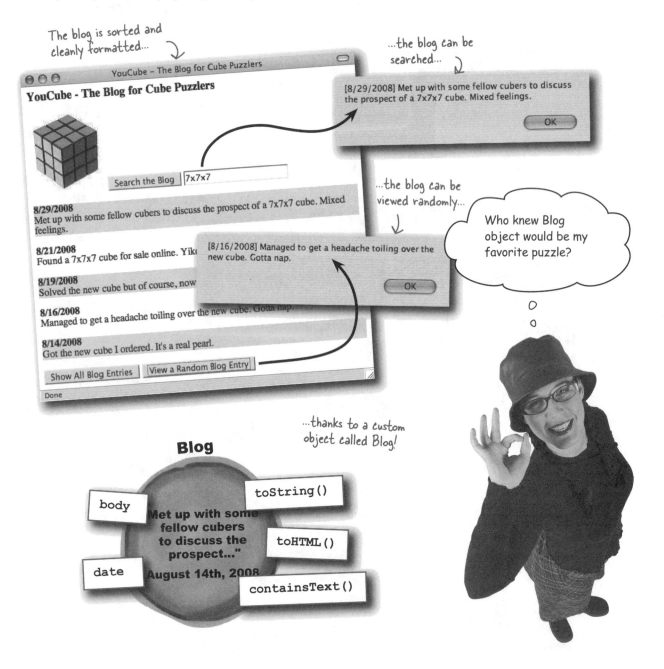

The blog is sorted and cleanly formatted...

...the blog can be searched...

YouCube – The Blog for Cube Puzzlers

[8/29/2008] Met up with some fellow cubers to discuss the prospect of a 7x7x7 cube. Mixed feelings.

OK

Search the Blog 7x7x7

8/29/2008
Met up with some fellow cubers to discuss the prospect of a 7x7x7 cube. Mixed feelings.

8/21/2008
Found a 7x7x7 cube for sale online. Yik

8/19/2008
Solved the new cube but of course, now

8/16/2008
Managed to get a headache toiling over the new cube. Gotta nap.

8/14/2008
Got the new cube I ordered. It's a real pearl.

[8/16/2008] Managed to get a headache toiling over the new cube. Gotta nap.

OK

...the blog can be viewed randomly...

Who knew Blog object would be my favorite puzzle?

Show All Blog Entries   View a Random Blog Entry

Done

...thanks to a custom object called Blog!

Blog

body

"Met up with some fellow cubers to discuss the prospect..."

date   August 14th, 2008

toString()

toHTML()

containsText()

JavaScriptcross

Ruby has been waiting all chapter for this...a puzzle!
But it's not a cube puzzle, it's a crossword puzzle. Oh
well, you can't have it all.

Across

1. Use this String method to search for a string of text.
4. When you place a function in an object, it becomes a ....
6. JavaScript arrays and strings are really ....
8. Use this to access a member of an object.
11. Nearly random.
13. This method converts any object into a string of text.
14. Ruby's hometown.

Down

2. Use this object to work with time.
3. A Math method that rounds down a number.
5. In an object, properties store this.
7. Object properties are created here.
9. A piece of data in an object.
10. Methods allow objects to take these.
12. Call this method to change the order of the items in an array.

JavaScriptcross Solution

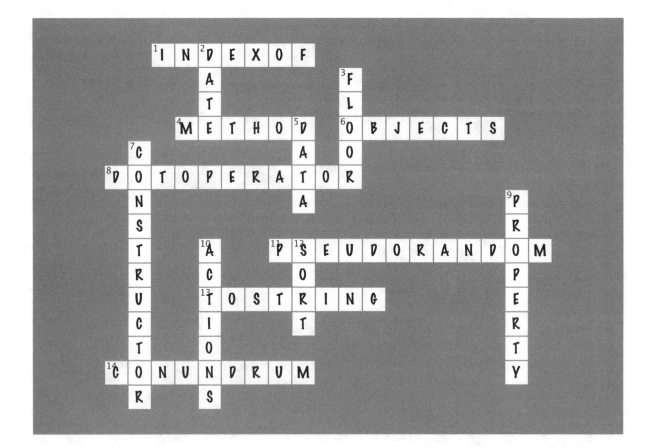

Page Bender

Fold the page vertically to line up the two brains and solve the riddle.

What can JavaScript objects do to their data?

← —— It's a meeting of the minds! ←

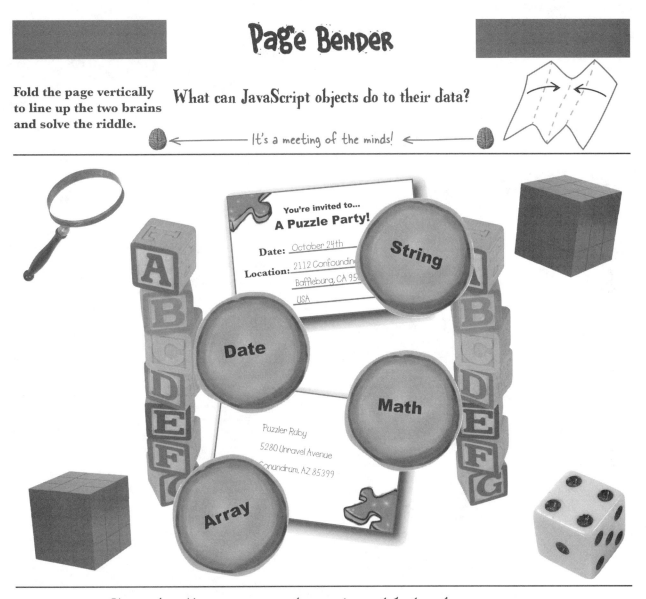

Search all you want, but it's unlikely that
you'll find anything better than a
JavaScript object to do things like sort
and analyze data. They're even able to
randomize numbers without any trouble at all.

10 creating custom objects

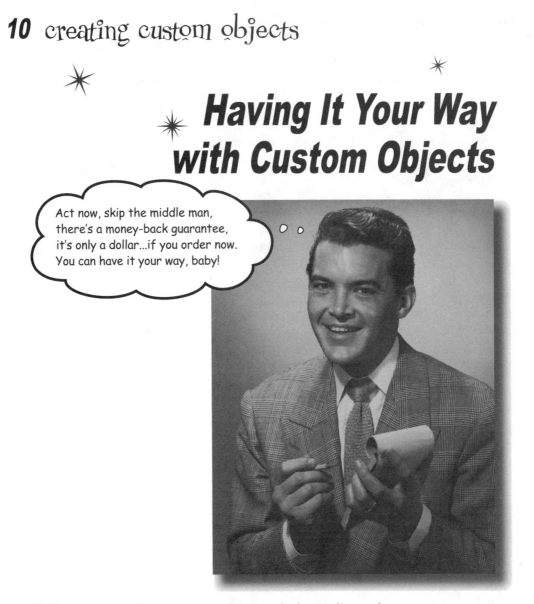

Having It Your Way
with Custom Objects

Act now, skip the middle man, there's a money-back guarantee, it's only a dollar...if you order now. You can have it your way, baby!

If it was only that easy, we'd surely have it made. JavaScript doesn't have a money-back guarantee, but you can definitely have it your way. Custom objects are the JavaScript equivalent of a decaf triple shot grande extra hot no whip extra drizzle no foam marble mocha macchiato. That is one custom cup of coffee! And with custom JavaScript objects, you can brew up some code that does exactly what you want, while taking advantage of the benefits of properties and methods. The end result is reusable object-oriented code that effectively extends the JavaScript language...just for you!

Revisiting the YouCube Blog methods

When we last left Ruby, she was quite excited about having created an object-powered blog for writing about her interest in cube puzzles. Although Ruby did a decent job of creating the `Blog` object that drives the YouCube blog, she unknowingly missed some key opportunities to apply object-oriented principles to YouCube. More importantly, she didn't fully explore the different ways the `Blog` object can be made more efficient, more organized, and therefore more maintainable into the future.

The last tweak Ruby made to the `Blog` object involved the creation of three methods to handle several blog-specific tasks.

The YouCube blog works but it still isn't a shining beacon of object-oriented programming design.

The latest version of the files can be downloaded at http://www.headfirstlabs.com/books/hfjs/.

The three Blog methods take care of several tasks that make sense being handled from within a blog entry.

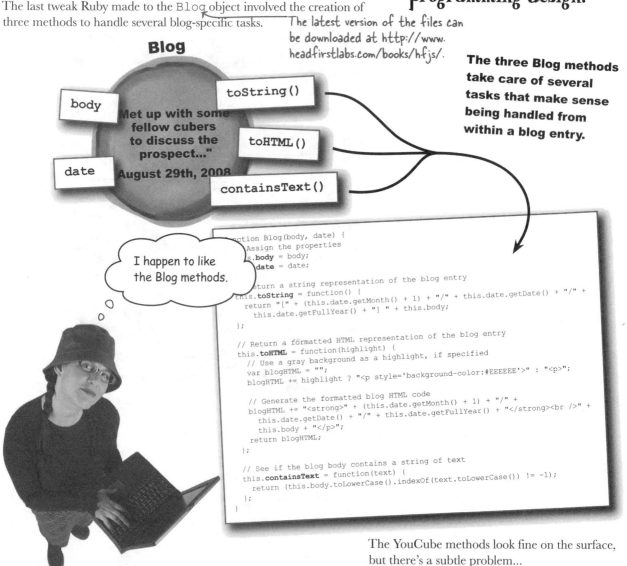

Blog

body

date

toString()

toHTML()

containsText()

"Met up with some fellow cubers to discuss the prospect..."

August 29th, 2008

I happen to like the Blog methods.

```
function Blog(body, date) {
  // Assign the properties
  this.body = body;
  this.date = date;

  // Return a string representation of the blog entry
  this.toString = function() {
    return "[" + (this.date.getMonth() + 1) + "/" + this.date.getDate() + "/" +
      this.date.getFullYear() + "] " + this.body;
  };

  // Return a formatted HTML representation of the blog entry
  this.toHTML = function(highlight) {
    // Use a gray background as a highlight, if specified
    var blogHTML = "";
    blogHTML += highlight ? "<p style='background-color:#EEEEEE'>" : "<p>";

    // Generate the formatted blog HTML code
    blogHTML += "<strong>" + (this.date.getMonth() + 1) + "/" +
      this.date.getDate() + "/" + this.date.getFullYear() + "</strong><br />" +
      this.body + "</p>";
    return blogHTML;
  };

  // See if the blog body contains a string of text
  this.containsText = function(text) {
    return (this.body.toLowerCase().indexOf(text.toLowerCase()) != -1);
  };
}
```

The YouCube methods look fine on the surface, but there's a subtle problem...

Method overload

Similar to the blog properties, the methods in the `Blog` object are created inside the constructor using the `this` keyword. This approach works but it ends up creating a new copy of the methods for every `Blog` object that is created. So if the blog contains six entries, there are six copies of the three `Blog` methods.

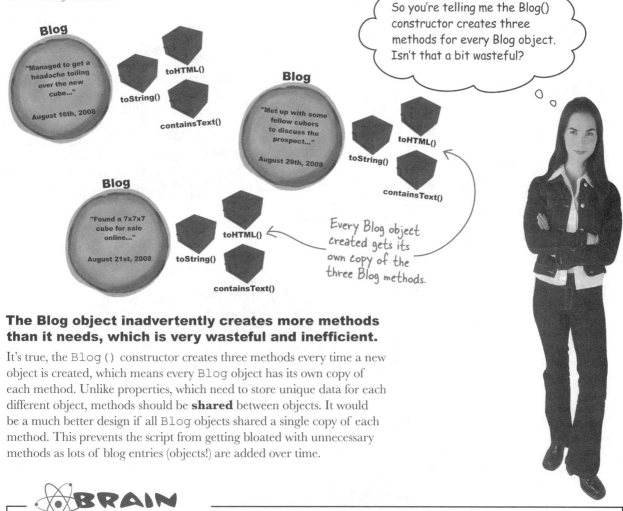

> So you're telling me the Blog() constructor creates three methods for every Blog object. Isn't that a bit wasteful?

Every Blog object created gets its own copy of the three Blog methods.

The Blog object inadvertently creates more methods than it needs, which is very wasteful and inefficient.

It's true, the `Blog()` constructor creates three methods every time a new object is created, which means every `Blog` object has its own copy of each method. Unlike properties, which need to store unique data for each different object, methods should be **shared** between objects. It would be a much better design if all `Blog` objects shared a single copy of each method. This prevents the script from getting bloated with unnecessary methods as lots of blog entries (objects!) are added over time.

⚛️ BRAIN POWER

How could you redesign the `Blog` object so that the method code doesn't get duplicated in each new object?

Classes vs. instances

The duplicate method problem touches on an extremely important concept related to JavaScript objects: the difference between an object **class** and an object **instance**. A class is an object description, a template that outlines what an object is made of. An instance is an actual object that has been created from a class. In real world terms, a class is the blueprint for a house, while an object is the house itself. And similar to JavaScript objects, you can build many house instances from a single class (blueprint).

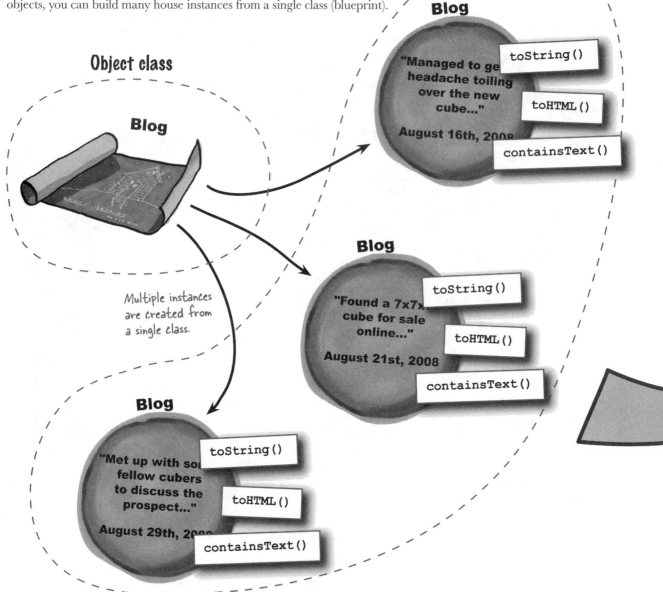

Object class

Object instances

Blog

Blog

"Managed to ge
headache toiling
over the new
cube..."

August 16th, 2008

toString()

toHTML()

containsText()

Multiple instances
are created from
a single class.

Blog

"Found a 7x7x
cube for sale
online..."

August 21st, 2008

toString()

toHTML()

containsText()

Blog

"Met up with so
fellow cubers
to discuss the
prospect..."

August 29th, 20

toString()

toHTML()

containsText()

Instances are created from classes

A class describes the properties and methods of an object, while an
instance puts real data in the properties and brings them to life. Each
instance gets its own copies of properties, which is what allows instances to
be uniquely different from one another.

An object class is a template, while an object instance is the thing created from the template.

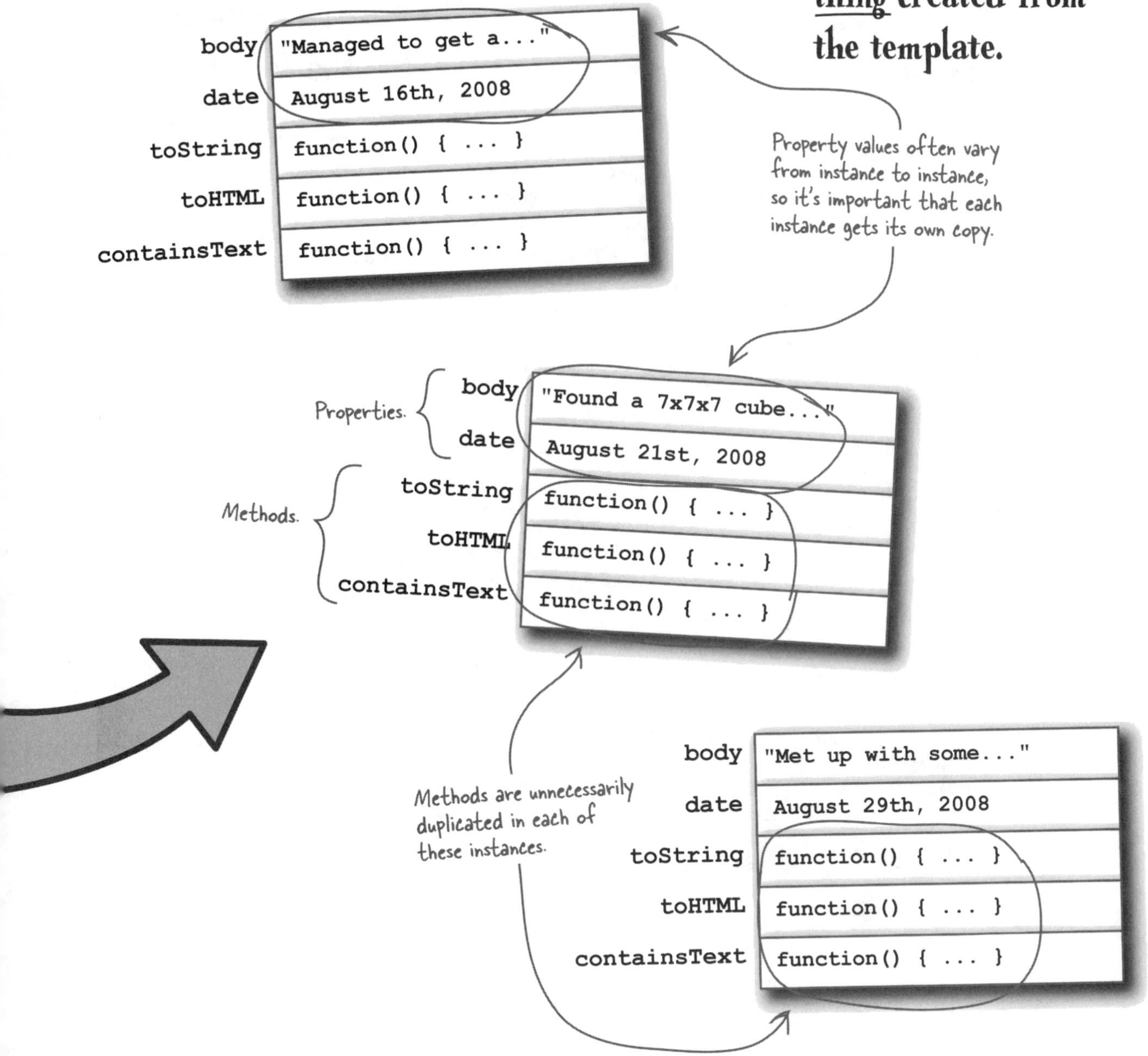

body	"Managed to get a..."
date	August 16th, 2008
toString	function() { ... }
toHTML	function() { ... }
containsText	function() { ... }

Property values often vary from instance to instance, so it's important that each instance gets its own copy.

Properties. {

body	"Found a 7x7x7 cube..."
date	August 21st, 2008
toString	function() { ... }
toHTML	function() { ... }
containsText	function() { ... }

Methods. {

Methods are unnecessarily duplicated in each of these instances.

body	"Met up with some..."
date	August 29th, 2008
toString	function() { ... }
toHTML	function() { ... }
containsText	function() { ... }

Access an instance's properties with "this"

All the properties we've dealt with thus far have been **instance properties**, meaning that they are owned by an instance, and more importantly, each instance gets its own copy. You can easily identify an instance property because it is set in the constructor using the `this` keyword.

```
function Blog(body, date) {

    this.body = body;

    this.date = date ;

    ...

}
```

These are instance properties because they are referenced using the this keyword.

> The <u>this</u> keyword is used to set properties and methods that are <u>owned</u> <u>by</u> <u>an instance</u>.

There are also instance methods, but they are a little trickier since they can be owned by an instance **or** by the class. So far we've only created instance methods that are set using the `this` keyword, which means they are **owned by each instance**. This explains why the method code is duplicated in each instance.

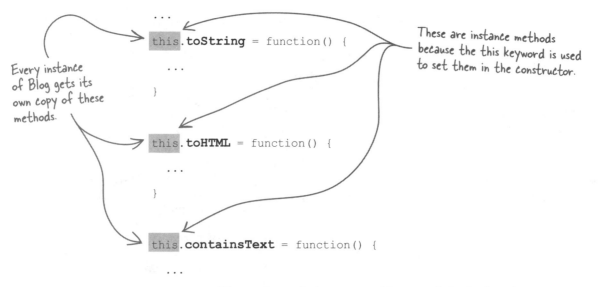

```
function Blog(body, date) {

    ...

    this.toString = function() {

        ...

    }

    this.toHTML = function() {

        ...

    }

    this.containsText = function() {

        ...

    }

}
```

Every instance of Blog gets its own copy of these methods.

These are instance methods because the this keyword is used to set them in the constructor.

The good news is that custom objects aren't destined to always waste method code by duplicating it in every new instance. The solution is to create methods in such a way that the instances all share a common copy of the method code.

Own once, run many: class-owned methods

There is another kind of instance method that is owned by the class itself, which means that there is only one copy shared for **all** instances. This **class-owned** instance method is much more efficient than storing a copy of a method in each and every instance.

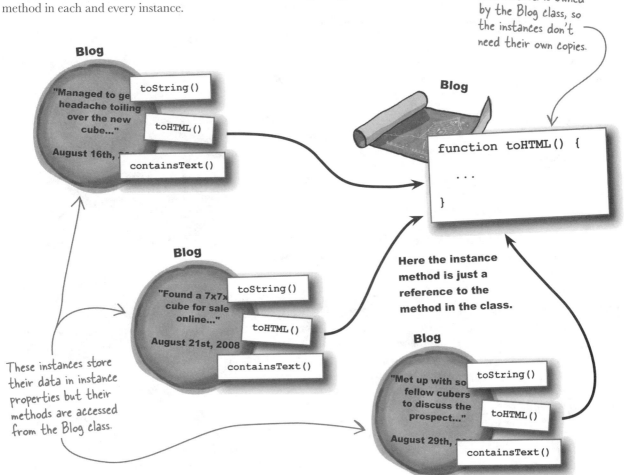

The method is owned by the Blog class, so the instances don't need their own copies.

These instances store their data in instance properties but their methods are accessed from the Blog class.

Here the instance method is just a reference to the method in the class.

When a method is owned by the class, all instances of the class have access to it, and therefore don't have their own copies. This is much more efficient, especially when you consider how many method copies could end up taking up space in an application that creates lots of object instances. In the case of YouCube, three methods (`toString()`, `toHTML()`, and `containsText()`) would be unnecessarily duplicated for every blog entry that is created.

Of course, we still need a mechanism for assigning the ownership of a method to the class, as opposed to individual instances...

Storing a method in a _class_ allows all instances to _share_ one copy.

Use prototype to work at a class-level

Classes in JavaScript are made possible in JavaScript thanks to a hidden object called `prototype` that exists in every object as a property. The `prototype` object allows you to set properties and methods that are owned at the **class level**, as opposed to within an instance. In the case of methods, the `prototype` object is how you establish that a **class** owns a method.

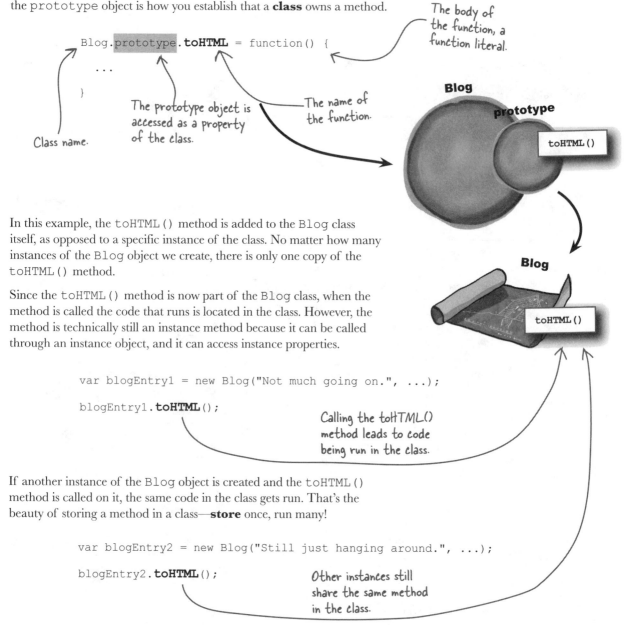

```
Blog.prototype.toHTML = function() {

    ...

}
```

The body of the function, a function literal.

Class name.

The prototype object is accessed as a property of the class.

The name of the function.

Blog

prototype

toHTML()

Blog

toHTML()

In this example, the `toHTML()` method is added to the `Blog` class itself, as opposed to a specific instance of the class. No matter how many instances of the `Blog` object we create, there is only one copy of the `toHTML()` method.

Since the `toHTML()` method is now part of the `Blog` class, when the method is called the code that runs is located in the class. However, the method is technically still an instance method because it can be called through an instance object, and it can access instance properties.

```
var blogEntry1 = new Blog("Not much going on.", ...);

blogEntry1.toHTML();
```

Calling the toHTML() method leads to code being run in the class.

If another instance of the `Blog` object is created and the `toHTML()` method is called on it, the same code in the class gets run. That's the beauty of storing a method in a class—**store** once, run many!

```
var blogEntry2 = new Blog("Still just hanging around.", ...);

blogEntry2.toHTML();
```

Other instances still share the same method in the class.

Classes, prototypes, and YouCube

Ruby is a little overwhelmed with all the talk about classes and prototypes, but she has a pretty good sense that YouCube could benefit from rethinking the `Blog` method storage with the aid of the `prototype` object.

> Wow, using the prototype object to store blog methods could make the YouCube code much more efficient.

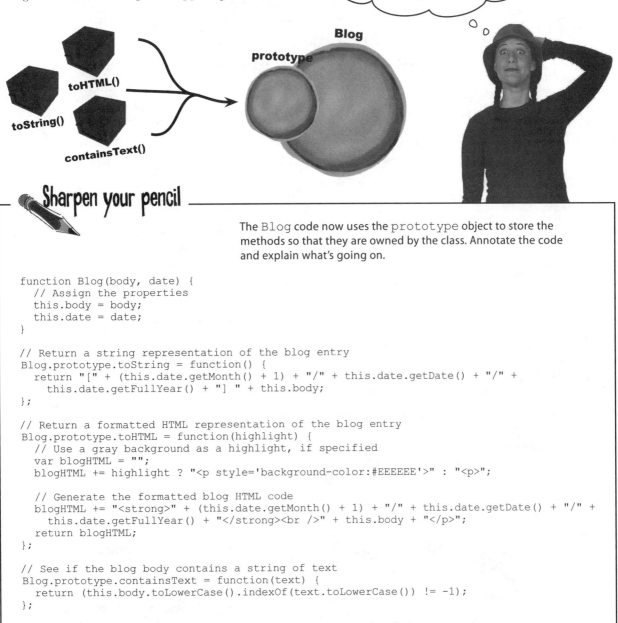

Sharpen your pencil

The `Blog` code now uses the `prototype` object to store the methods so that they are owned by the class. Annotate the code and explain what's going on.

```javascript
function Blog(body, date) {
  // Assign the properties
  this.body = body;
  this.date = date;
}

// Return a string representation of the blog entry
Blog.prototype.toString = function() {
  return "[" + (this.date.getMonth() + 1) + "/" + this.date.getDate() + "/" +
    this.date.getFullYear() + "] " + this.body;
};

// Return a formatted HTML representation of the blog entry
Blog.prototype.toHTML = function(highlight) {
  // Use a gray background as a highlight, if specified
  var blogHTML = "";
  blogHTML += highlight ? "<p style='background-color:#EEEEEE'>" : "<p>";

  // Generate the formatted blog HTML code
  blogHTML += "<strong>" + (this.date.getMonth() + 1) + "/" + this.date.getDate() + "/" +
    this.date.getFullYear() + "</strong><br />" + this.body + "</p>";
  return blogHTML;
};

// See if the blog body contains a string of text
Blog.prototype.containsText = function(text) {
  return (this.body.toLowerCase().indexOf(text.toLowerCase()) != -1);
};
```

Sharpen your pencil
Solution

The `Blog` code now uses the `prototype` object to store the methods so that they are owned by the class. Annotate the code and explain what's going on.

```
function Blog(body, date) {
  // Assign the properties
  this.body = body;
  this.date = date;
}

// Return a string representation of the blog entry
Blog.prototype.toString = function() {
  return "[" + (this.date.getMonth() + 1) + "/" + this.date.getDate() + "/" +
    this.date.getFullYear() + "] " + this.body;
};

// Return a formatted HTML representation of the blog entry
Blog.prototype.toHTML = function(highlight) {
  // Use a gray background as a highlight, if specified
  var blogHTML = "";
  blogHTML += highlight ? "<p style='background-color:#EEEEEE'>" : "<p>";

  // Generate the formatted blog HTML code
  blogHTML += "<strong>" + (this.date.getMonth() + 1) + "/" + this.date.getDate() + "/" +
    this.date.getFullYear() + "</strong><br />" + this.body + "</p>";
  return blogHTML;
};

// See if the blog body contains a string of text
Blog.prototype.containsText = function(text) {
  return (this.body.toLowerCase().indexOf(text.toLowerCase()) != -1);
};
```

Now the constructor focuses solely on creating and initalizing the properties.

Since the methods aren't being assigned to a particular Blog instance, the assignment takes place outside of the constructor.

Each method is set in the prototype object instead of using the this keyword in the Blog() constructor.

A more efficient YouCube

The YouCube blog now uses **class-owned methods** to eliminate wasteful code, thanks to object prototyping. No matter how many `Blog` instances are created, only one copy of the methods are created since they now reside in the class. The cool thing is that from the YouCube script's perspective of using the `Blog` object, nothing has changed.

Blog instances calling methods in the class.

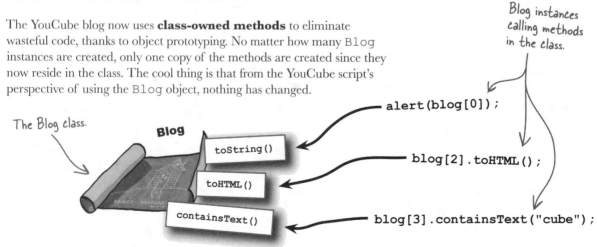

The Blog class.

Blog

`toString()`

`toHTML()`

`containsText()`

`alert(blog[0]);`

`blog[2].toHTML();`

`blog[3].containsText("cube");`

BULLET POINTS

- A class is a **description** of an object, while an instance is an **actual** object that has been created based upon that description.

- A class lays out the properties and methods of an object, while an instance places real data in the properties, giving the methods something to work with.

- The `this` keyword is used to access an instance from within its **own code**.

- The `prototype` object allows methods to be stored in a **class**, preventing instances from unnecessarily duplicating code.

there are no Dumb Questions

Q: I'm still not quite understanding the big picture of classes vs. instances. What's the deal?

A: The idea behind a class is to make it easier to create and reuse objects. You could create one-off objects as object literals all day long and never have a problem other than wasting a lot of energy unnecessarily. It's wasteful because you'd be duplicating your efforts. Kind of like an architect who insists on redrawing the plans for the same house every time he wants to build it again.

Why not create a template that can be used to create as many instances as you want, resulting in a lot less effort? That's where classes enter the picture—create one class, and then use it to create as many instances as needed.

Q: OK, so classes are about making it easier to create objects that are similar to each other. But what do `this` and `prototype` have to do with that?

A: The `this` keyword lets you access an instance from within one of its own methods. Its primary usage is in accessing instance properties. So if you want to access a property named `x` from within a method, you say `this.x`. If you were to just say

`x`, the code wouldn't know you were trying to access a property of the instance; it would just think `x` was a variable. That's why constructors require you to use `this` when creating and initializing properties.

`prototype` is a different animal altogether. It provides the mechanism for creating classes. Unlike some other programming languages such as C++ and Java, JavaScript doesn't truly support classes as a concrete part of the language. Instead, JavaScript uses prototypes to simulate classes. The end result is similar but JavaScript requires you to create "classes" by manipulating the `prototype` object, which appears as a "hidden" property of every JavaScript object. By storing a property or method in the `prototype` object, you effectively make it accessible as part of a class, as opposed to just part of an instance.

Q: How do constructors fit into the class equation?

A: Constructors are a very important part of establishing JavaScript classes because they are responsible for creating object instances. You can think of a constructor and a prototype as representing the two major pieces of the JavaScript class puzzle. Constructors take care of setting up

everything for instances, while prototypes handle everything at the class level. Both entities working in concert give you the ability to do some pretty cool things because there are compelling reasons for positioning some members at the instance level and some at the class level. We continue exploring this issue throughout the chapter.

Q: I'm a little confused by the naming convention used with objects. Sometimes an object is capitalized, sometimes it's in lower camel case. Is there some rule I'm missing?

A: The only rule is that class names are capitalized, while instance names are in lower camel case. This is because an instance is really just a variable, and variable identifiers use lower camel case. The inconsistency mainly has to do with the fact that we've been using the term "object" fairly loosely. To be accurate, however, classes such as `Blog` should be capitalized, while instances such as `blogEntry` or `blog[0]` should be in lowerCamelCase.

This naming convention makes sense if you think back to other standard objects that we've used. You might store the current date/time in a variable (instance) called `now`, which is created from the `Date` object (class).

Signing the blog

Ruby is digging the efficiency and organizational improvements that object-oriented programming, or OOP, has brought to YouCube but she's interested in doing more than just improve the code behind the scenes... she wants to add a new feature.

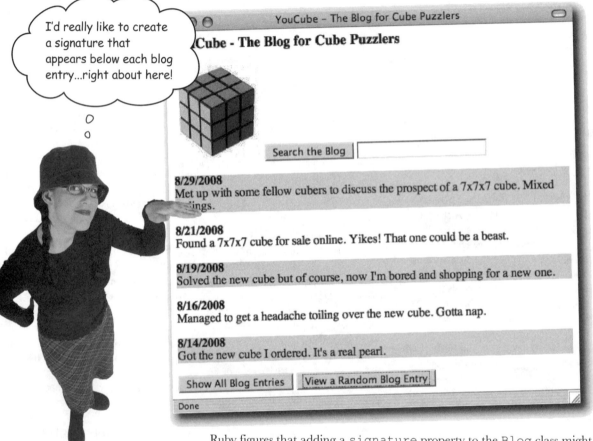

Ruby figures that adding a `signature` property to the `Blog` class might do the trick. Then she can just set the property in the constructor and display it with each blog entry...problem solved!

Should Ruby create the signature as an instance property? Can you think of any reason why this might not be such a good idea?

Q: I keep seeing the term object-oriented. What does it mean?

A: The term **object-oriented** gets used (and abused) an awful lot in programming circles, and it can mean different things to different people. In general, object-oriented programming (OOP) involves building software out of objects, such as how the `Date` object is used in the `date` property of YouCube blog entries.

Most programmers associate OOP with using objects extensively throughout a program. At least in theory, a truly object-oriented program can be broken down into a collection of objects that interact with each other. There are object-oriented purists out there who will argue that JavaScript doesn't qualify as an OOP language. Save yourself the energy and try to avoid that debate. There are valid arguments on both sides, but at the end of the day nobody wins.

The signature is the same for all blog entries.

08/14/2008
Got the new cube I or~
by Puzzler Ruby

08/19/2008
Solved the ne~
and shopping
by Puzzler Ruby

08/16/2008
Managed to get a headache toiling over the new cube.
Gotta nap.
by Puzzler Ruby

08/21/2008
Found a 7x7x7 cube for sale online. Yikes! That one could be a beast.
by Puzzler Ruby

08/29/2008
Met up with some fellow cubers to discuss the prospect of a 7x7x7 cube. Mixed feelings.
by Puzzler Ruby

> Wait a minute. Doesn't Ruby have just one signature? If so, why does each instance need its own signature property?

Maybe one signature is enough.

Knowing that the blog signature is the same for all instances, there's no need for each instance to have its own signature property. What Ruby needs is a **class property**, a property where there is only one copy that is stored in the class instead of a different copy in each individual instance.

The signature property should be stored in the Blog class, not in each blog instance.

Blog

signature

Class properties are shared, too

Class properties are very similar to class-owned instance methods in that they are owned by the class with a **single copy** available to all instances. In some ways this is more significant when it comes to data because it means that the property has only **one value** that is shared by all instances. This is exactly what Ruby is looking for when it comes to the new `signature` property because there is only one signature for the entire YouCube blog.

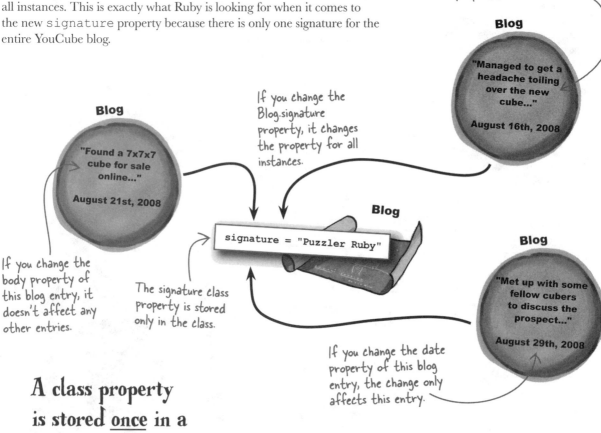

Each instance stores its own instance properties.

Blog

"Managed to get a headache toiling over the new cube..."

August 16th, 2008

If you change the Blog.signature property, it changes the property for all instances.

Blog

"Found a 7x7x7 cube for sale online..."

August 21st, 2008

```
signature = "Puzzler Ruby"
```

Blog

If you change the body property of this blog entry, it doesn't affect any other entries.

The signature class property is stored only in the class.

Blog

"Met up with some fellow cubers to discuss the prospect..."

August 29th, 2008

If you change the date property of this blog entry, the change only affects this entry.

A class property is stored <u>once</u> in a class but accessible to all instances.

Even though the `signature` property is stored in the `Blog` class, it is readily accessible to any instance that wants to access the blog author's signature.

BRAIN POWER

How do you think you could go about creating a class property?

Creating class properties with prototype

For all the talk about where a class property is stored and the sweeping impact that has on life as we know it, creating a class property is surprisingly mundane. In fact, a single line of code is all it takes:

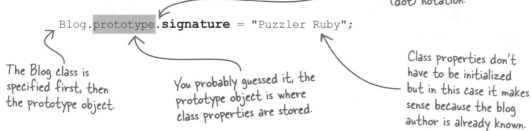

The class property is accessed using object (dot) notation.

```
Blog.prototype.signature = "Puzzler Ruby";
```

The Blog class is specified first, then the prototype object.

You probably guessed it, the prototype object is where class properties are stored.

Class properties don't have to be initialized but in this case it makes sense because the blog author is already known.

One of the most interesting things about this code is what you can't fully appreciate by looking at it by itself—the code doesn't appear inside of a constructor like the code that creates instance properties. The reason is because constructors are used to bring instances to life, and therefore aren't capable of creating class properties. Instead, class properties must be created outside of the constructor.

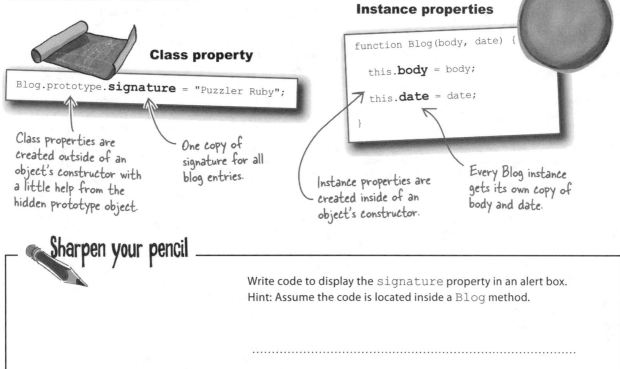

Instance properties

Class property

```
Blog.prototype.signature = "Puzzler Ruby";
```

Class properties are created outside of an object's constructor with a little help from the hidden prototype object.

One copy of signature for all blog entries.

```
function Blog(body, date) {
    this.body = body;
    this.date = date;
}
```

Instance properties are created inside of an object's constructor.

Every Blog instance gets its own copy of body and date.

Sharpen your pencil

Write code to display the signature property in an alert box.
Hint: Assume the code is located inside a Blog method.

....

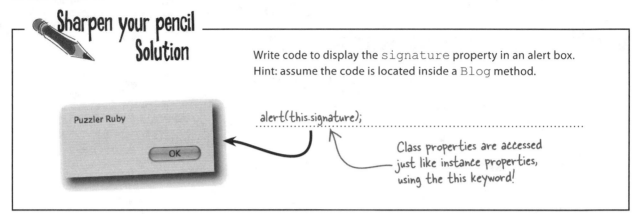

Sharpen your pencil Solution

Write code to display the `signature` property in an alert box. Hint: assume the code is located inside a `Blog` method.

> Puzzler Ruby
>
> OK

`alert(this.signature);`

Class properties are accessed just like instance properties, using the this keyword!

there are no Dumb Questions

Q: Why do you even need to store the YouCube signature in a property? Couldn't it just be entered as part of the body text for each entry?

A: It's certainly possible to include a signature in every blog entry as part of the body text, but that requires unnecessary time and effort, assuming there is only one person posting to the blog. It would get tiresome for Ruby to sign every blog entry when there is such a cleaner way to handle the signature using JavaScript. And who's to say she might accidentally enter a typo and become "Puzzled Ruby"? Not a good thing!

Another option that is more viable is to just use a string literal for the signature when formatting a blog entry as HTML. This approach works fine but it buries an important piece of data, the signature, down in the blog formatting code where it's difficult to find and maintain. By placing the signature in a class property, you make it easily accessible, and therefore much easier for the blogger to identify and change.

Q: How would creating a blog entry change if the signature was an instance property?

A: Remember that each instance of an object gets its own set of instance properties that are initialized in the constructor. If the signature property was an instance property, the `Blog()` constructor would need to set it in each and every instance. This wouldn't necessarily be all that big of a coding hassle since the constructor could set the property to the signature string. However, behind the scenes, there would be as many copies of the signature as there are instances, and that would be extremely wasteful. Not only that, but it would be possible to change the signature for different instances independently of others.

Q: So if I wanted to modify YouCube to support multiple bloggers, would I change the signature to an instance property?

A: Yes, and that would be a good idea because in a multi-blogger scenario the `signature` property has the prospect of **needing** to hold different values for each instance. The best way to handle this would probably be to add an argument to the `Blog()` constructor that allows the signature string to be passed in. Then use that string to initialize the `signature` instance property. In other words, handle the

`signature` property exactly the same as the other `Blog` instance properties.

Q: Class properties seem to work kind of like global variables. How are they different?

A: Class properties are in fact a lot like global variables since they can be accessed from just about anywhere. Class properties are also created similarly to global variables, at least in terms of where they're created—from the main script level outside of other code. Where class properties differ from global variables is in their association with a class, and therefore with instance objects. This means you always have to access a class property with respect to an instance.

Q: Hang on. Class properties *have* to be accessed through an instance?

Q: Even though class properties are created using the `prototype` object, which stores them in a class, they must be accessed through instances. So a class property is accessed just like an instance property, using the `this` keyword and object (dot) notation. The difference is really just where the property is stored—in the class (class property) or in a specific instance (instance property).

Signed and delivered

With the `signature` class property created, initialized, and ready to use, Ruby is ready to see it put in action. Looking back at the code that formats a blog entry for display in a browser, the `toHTML()` method is where the signature enters into the presentation of each blog entry.

The `toHTML()` method now formats the signature as part of a blog entry.

```
Blog.prototype.toHTML = function(highlight) {

  // Use a gray background as a highlight, if specified

  var blogHTML = "";

  blogHTML += highlight ? "<p style='background-color:#EEEEEE'>" : "<p>";


  // Generate the formatted blog HTML code

  blogHTML += "<strong>" + (this.date.getMonth() + 1) + "/" + this.date.getDate() + "/" +

    this.date.getFullYear() + "</strong><br />" + this.body + "<br /><em>" + this.signature +

    "</em></p>";

  return blogHTML;

};
```

The signature class property is referenced just like a normal instance property.

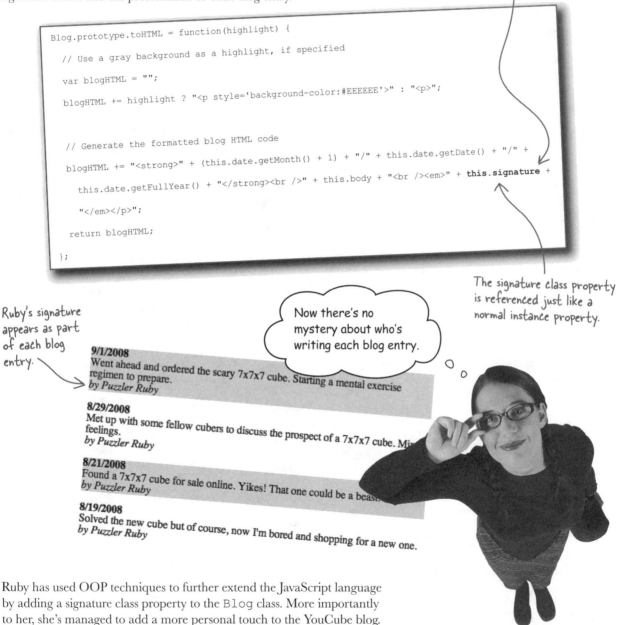

Ruby's signature appears as part of each blog entry.

Now there's no mystery about who's writing each blog entry.

9/1/2008
Went ahead and ordered the scary 7x7x7 cube. Starting a mental exercise regimen to prepare.
by Puzzler Ruby

8/29/2008
Met up with some fellow cubers to discuss the prospect of a 7x7x7 cube. Mi feelings.
by Puzzler Ruby

8/21/2008
Found a 7x7x7 cube for sale online. Yikes! That one could be a beas
by Puzzler Ruby

8/19/2008
Solved the new cube but of course, now I'm bored and shopping for a new one.
by Puzzler Ruby

Ruby has used OOP techniques to further extend the JavaScript language by adding a signature class property to the `Blog` class. More importantly to her, she's managed to add a more personal touch to the YouCube blog.

Fireside Chats

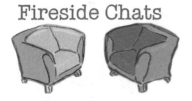

Tonight's talk: **Instance and class properties talk data ownership and secret societies**

Instance property:

So you're the other guy I've been hearing about. I have to say I don't see why you're here. I do an excellent job of allowing object instances to be unique and keep track of their own property values.

Now that's hard believe. Go on...

So you're saying I wouldn't be the best way to store a secret handshake?

I see. But what about a secret password? Can I store that?

Awesome! So let's get started. I'm starting a secret club and we're both getting our own passwords.

Good one! So what is it? Really. I'm serious...

Class property:

I'm sure you do, and that's an admirable thing. But did you know that sometimes instances don't want the hassle of keeping up with their own data?

Well, there are situations where a piece of data is common to all instances, kinda like how a secret club has a secret handshake. Each person in the club knows the secret handshake but it's a club-wide handshake. If some gal in the club invents her own secret handshake, it screws everything up. Then some other girl has to top that with her handshake, and before you know it nobody knows the secret handshake anymore because there are lots of them.

That's right. No offense, but in this case the club members just need one handshake, even though all of the people need to know about it.

Maybe. If each person has their own secret password that is personal to them, then yes, you would be excellent for storing secret passwords.

But you don't know the secret handshake...gotcha!

Duplicate code is a no-no

Ruby is at it again. Never one to rest on her laurels, she's decided to look even further at improving the efficiency of the YouCube code. She has spotted some duplicate date formatting code that she's convinced can be eliminated somehow with a crafty application of OOP principles.

> This code seems to be duplicated unnecessarily. How can I cut it?

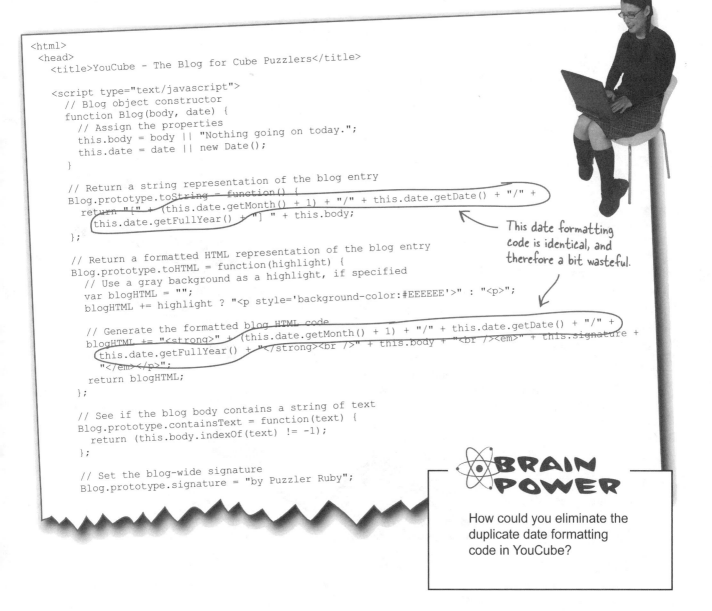

```
<html>
 <head>
   <title>YouCube - The Blog for Cube Puzzlers</title>

   <script type="text/javascript">
     // Blog object constructor
     function Blog(body, date) {
       // Assign the properties
       this.body = body || "Nothing going on today.";
       this.date = date || new Date();
     }

     // Return a string representation of the blog entry
     Blog.prototype.toString = function() {
       return "[" + (this.date.getMonth() + 1) + "/" + this.date.getDate() + "/" +
         this.date.getFullYear() + "] " + this.body;
     };

     // Return a formatted HTML representation of the blog entry
     Blog.prototype.toHTML = function(highlight) {
       // Use a gray background as a highlight, if specified
       var blogHTML = "";
       blogHTML += highlight ? "<p style='background-color:#EEEEEE'>" : "<p>";

       // Generate the formatted blog HTML code
       blogHTML += "<strong>" + (this.date.getMonth() + 1) + "/" + this.date.getDate() + "/" +
         this.date.getFullYear() + "</strong><br />" + this.body + "<br /><em>" + this.signature +
         "</em></p>";
       return blogHTML;
     };

     // See if the blog body contains a string of text
     Blog.prototype.containsText = function(text) {
       return (this.body.indexOf(text) != -1);
     };

     // Set the blog-wide signature
     Blog.prototype.signature = "by Puzzler Ruby";
```

This date formatting code is identical, and therefore a bit wasteful.

☀️ BRAIN POWER

How could you eliminate the duplicate date formatting code in YouCube?

A date formatting method

Ruby thinks a decent solution to the duplicate date formatting code is to add a date formatting method to the Blog object. In order to reuse the code, it must be placed in a function or method, and she might as well go with a method since the Blog object is responsible for formatting dates as part of formatting a blog entry. Or should she?

> If formatting a date is really a behavior of the Date object, would it make more sense for the method to be a Date method? Is there any way to add a method to a standard JavaScript object?

Back to the prototype object

What could be more powerful than taking a pre-existing object and making it even better? As it turns out, there is a way to modify a standard object, and it turns out providing the ultimate option in terms of extending the JavaScript language. The key to extending standard objects, or any JavaScript object for that matter, is the prototype object. We've already used the prototype object to extend the Blog class with class properties and class-owned methods. There's nothing stopping us from doing the same kind of extending to built-in JavaScript classes.

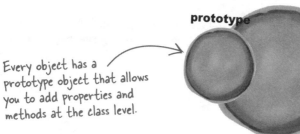

prototype

Every object has a prototype object that allows you to add properties and methods at the class level.

Any old object, even a standard JavaScript object.

Extending standard objects

The key to extending an object lies in the `prototype` object, and every object in JavaScript has one. So you can extend any object by adding properties and methods to its `prototype` object, which establishes class properties and class-owned methods. In the case of a built-in JavaScript object, adding a property or method to its `prototype` object means any new instances of the built-in object will have access to the property or method.

> The prototype object allows you to extend built-in JavaScript objects.

String

prototype

`scramble()`

Adding a method to the prototype of a built-in object places the method in the object class.

String

`scramble()`

New objects created from the class can then use the method.

```
String.prototype.scramble = function() {
  // Return scrambled string
  ...
};
```

Create the method as a member of String's prototype object.

Using the new `String` method is just a matter of calling it on an instance of the `String` object.

```
alert(this.signature.scramble());
```

String
"Puzzler Ruby"

String
"Met up with some fellow cubers to discuss the prospect..."

String
"Went ahead and ordered the scary 7x7x7 cube..."

luzPrb uzyRe

OK

Sharpen your pencil

Write the code for a method called `shortFormat()` that is an extension to the standard `Date` object, and whose job it is to format a date as *MM/DD/YYYY*.

....

....

....

Sharpen your pencil Solution

Write the code for a method called `shortFormat()` that is an extension to the standard `Date` object, and whose job it is to format a date as *MM/DD/YYYY*.

The method is added to the prototype of the Date object.

```
Date.prototype.shortFormat = function() {
  return (this.getMonth() + 1) + "/" + this.getDate() + "/" + this.getFullYear();
};
```

Custom date object = better YouCube

The customized `Date` object makes YouCube more efficient and extends the features of the built-in object. YouCube also becomes easier to maintain since the date format can now be altered in one location, yet affect the appearance of dates throughout the blog. Granted, OOP improvements to script code don't always present immediate sizzle in the form of visual changes, but they do often result in code that just seems to work better over the long haul.

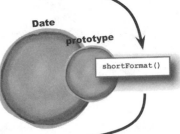

Date
prototype
`shortFormat()`

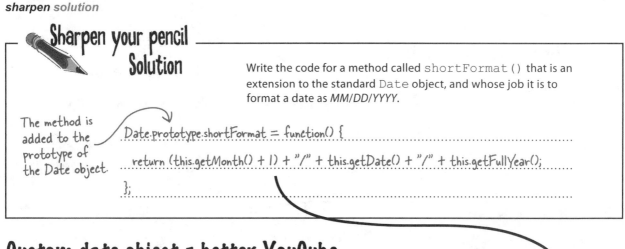

9/3/2008
Attended a rally outside of a local toy store that stopped carrying cube puzzles. Power to the puzzlers!
by Puzzler Ruby

9/1/2008
Went ahead and ordered the scary 7x7x7 cube. Starting a mental exercise regimen to prepare.
by Puzzler Ruby

8/29/2008
Met up with some fellow cubers to discuss the prospect of a 7x7x7 cube. Mixed feelings.
by Puzzler Ruby

8/21/2008
Found a 7x7x7 cube for sale online. Yikes! That one could be a beast.
by Puzzler Ruby

8/19/2008
Solved the new cube but of course, now I'm bored and shopping for a new one.
by Puzzler Ruby

Blog dates are now formatted using a custom method of the Date object.

A class can have its own method

The custom `shortFormat()` method of the `Date` object is a **class-owned instance method**, meaning that it has access to instance properties even though it is owned by the class. This is what allows the method to format the date stored within a given instance. It is also possible to create a **class method**, which is a method owned by a class that **cannot** access instance properties. Class methods can access class properties, however, such as the `signature` property in the `Blog` class.

Class methods are owned by a class, and can only access class properties.

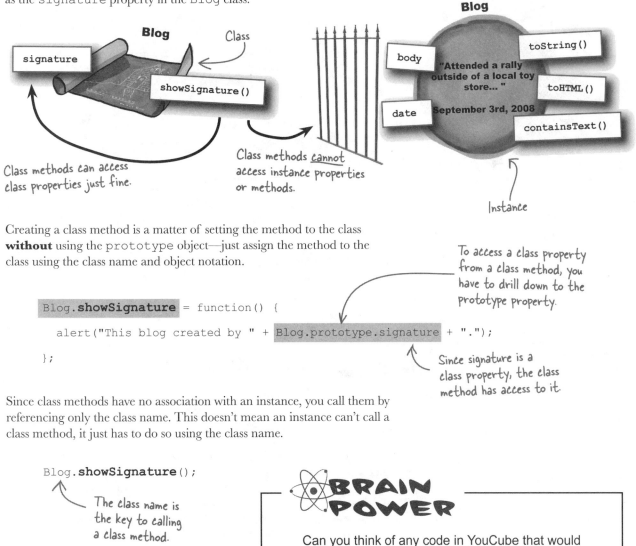

Blog

signature

Class

showSignature()

Class methods can access class properties just fine.

Class methods *cannot* access instance properties or methods.

Blog

body

"Attended a rally outside of a local toy store... "

toString()

toHTML()

date   September 3rd, 2008

containsText()

Instance

Creating a class method is a matter of setting the method to the class **without** using the `prototype` object—just assign the method to the class using the class name and object notation.

To access a class property from a class method, you have to drill down to the prototype property.

```
Blog.showSignature = function() {
    alert("This blog created by " + Blog.prototype.signature + ".");
};
```

Since *signature* is a class property, the class method has access to it.

Since class methods have no association with an instance, you call them by referencing only the class name. This doesn't mean an instance can't call a class method, it just has to do so using the class name.

```
Blog.showSignature();
```

The class name is the key to calling a class method.

⚛ BRAIN POWER

Can you think of any code in YouCube that would make sense as a class method of `Blog`?

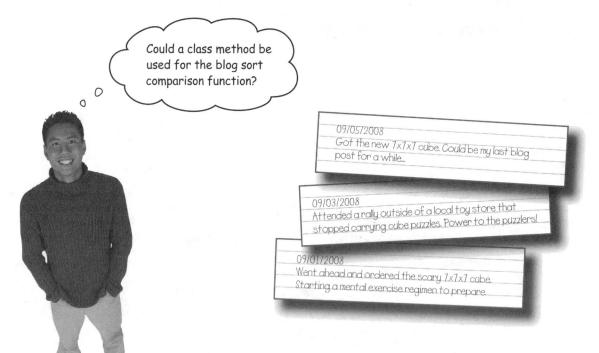

Could a class method be used for the blog sort comparison function?

09/05/2008
Got the new 7x7x7 cube. Could be my last blog post for a while...

09/03/2008
Attended a rally outside of a local toy store that stopped carrying cube puzzles. Power to the puzzlers!

09/01/2008
Went ahead and ordered the scary 7x7x7 cube. Starting a mental exercise regimen to prepare.

Rethinking the blog sorter

This is an intriguing idea because the sort comparison function is definitely playing a role that is specific to the `Blog` object. Currently, this function is created as a function literal inside the `showBlog()` function, which is where it is needed.

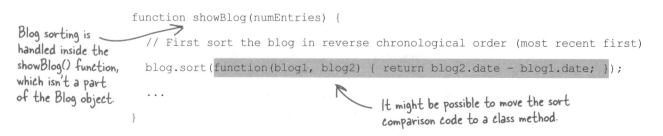

Blog sorting is handled inside the showBlog() function, which isn't a part of the Blog object.

```
function showBlog(numEntries) {
    // First sort the blog in reverse chronological order (most recent first)
    blog.sort(function(blog1, blog2) { return blog2.date - blog1.date; });
    ...
}
```

It might be possible to move the sort comparison code to a class method.

One of the fundamental concepts of OOP is to **encapsulate** the functionality of an object within the object itself, meaning that outside code shouldn't be doing work that an object can do for itself. In this case, the comparison of blog entries for sorting purposes could be done inside the object instead of in the `showBlog()` function. But, can the sort comparison code be placed into a class method of the `Blog` class? In order to answer this question, we have to figure out if the method requires access to instance data or methods. That would be a big problem since class methods can't access anything in an instance.

Examine the sort comparison function

The only way to know if this will work is to break down the function and
see what's going on. Here's the sort comparison function literal with the
code formatted more like a normal function:

*Two blog instances are passed
into the function as arguments.*

```
function(blog1, blog2) {

    return blog2.date - blog1.date;

}
```

*The sort comparison
involves a subtraction
of the two arguments.*

Although the function deals directly with blog instances, they are passed
in as arguments. This is different than attempting to access a property
or method **inside** an instance through the `this` keyword, which isn't
possible in a class method. So the sort comparison function doesn't need
access to anything within an instance, which makes it a perfect candidate
for a class method.

In fact, the sort comparison function doesn't even require class properties,
although it could do so if necessary because class methods do have access
to class properties.

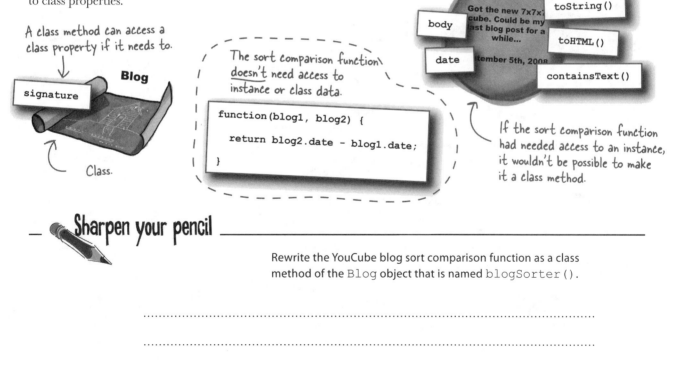

*A class method can access a
class property if it needs to.*

Blog

signature

Class.

*The sort comparison function
doesn't need access to
instance or class data.*

```
function(blog1, blog2) {

    return blog2.date - blog1.date;

}
```

Instance.

Blog

body

Got the new 7x7x7 cube. Could be my last blog post for a while...

date

tember 5th, 2008

toString()

toHTML()

containsText()

*If the sort comparison function
had needed access to an instance,
it wouldn't be possible to make
it a class method.*

Sharpen your pencil

Rewrite the YouCube blog sort comparison function as a class
method of the `Blog` object that is named `blogSorter()`.

....

....

....

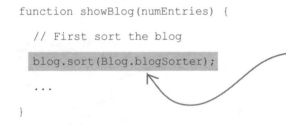

Sharpen your pencil
Solution

Rewrite the YouCube blog sort comparison function as a class method of the `Blog` object that is named `blogSorter()`.

```
Blog.blogSorter = function(blog1, blog2) {
    return blog2.date - blog1.date;
};
```

The sort comparison method is now a class method of the Blog object named blogSorter().

Calling a class method

The benefit of moving the blog sort comparison function to a `Blog` method becomes a little easier to appreciate when you see the code that calls the method.

```
function showBlog(numEntries) {

    // First sort the blog
    blog.sort(Blog.blogSorter);

    ...

}
```

The details of sorting the blog are now delegated to the blogSorter() class method of the Blog class.

The beauty of this code is subtle but important. The `showBlog()` function no longer has to concern itself with how blog entries are sorted. Instead, the details of how blog entries are sorted is handled within the `Blog` class where it logically belongs.

What's neat is how the sorting is still initiated outside of the `Blog` class in the `showBlog()` function, which makes sense because sorting affects an entire collection of blog instances. But the specifics of how the sorting is carried out with respect to individual blog entries is within the realm of something the `Blog` class can handle. Good OOP design often involves a careful orchestration of objects and their surrounding code.

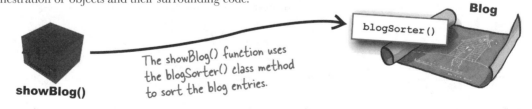

showBlog()

The showBlog() function uses the blogSorter() class method to sort the blog entries.

Blog

`blogSorter()`

A picture is worth a thousand ⌄blog⌄ words

Ruby continues to be thrilled by the OOP improvements to YouCube but she also knows that users won't necessarily share her enthusiasm because the OOP enhancements have yet to dramatically impact the user experience. She has therefore decided that it's time to add some noticeable sizzle to the blog!

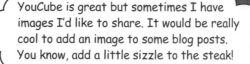

YouCube is great but sometimes I have images I'd like to share. It would be really cool to add an image to some blog posts. You know, add a little sizzle to the steak!

Ruby's idea is to allow each individual blog entry to support an optional image that is displayed along with the date and body text. Since not all blog entries require images, it's important for the image to be optional. This also prevents existing blog entries that she has already written from breaking.

⚛ BRAIN POWER

How could you alter the `Blog` object in YouCube to support images?

Incorporating images into YouCube

Adding image support to the YouCube blog involves figuring out how to incorporate an image into the `Blog` object in such a way that it doesn't interfere with the way the object already works. This brings up two important questions that will drive the design:

 1   **What is the best way to store a blog image within the Blog object?**

2   **How can the blog image be added to YouCube but remain entirely optional?**

Regardless of how a blog image is stored, we know that it will ultimately get fed into an HTML `<img>` tag so that it can be displayed on the YouCube web page.

```
<img src="cube777.png" />
```

A blog image is sufficiently described using a string filename.

This code tells us that as far as the blog is concerned, an image is really just a string. Sure, the string ultimately references an image file stored somewhere on a web server, but from the perspective of the `Blog` object, it's just a string.

As far as the Blog object is concerned, an image is just a string.

So an image could be added to the `Blog` object simply as a property that stores a string, similar to the `body` property.

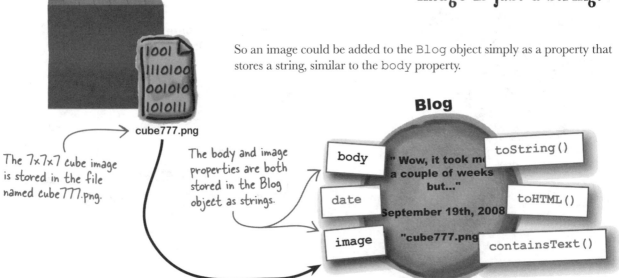

The 7×7×7 cube image is stored in the file named cube777.png.

cube777.png

The body and image properties are both stored in the Blog object as strings.

Blog

body	" Wow, it took me a couple of weeks but..."	toString()
date	September 19th, 2008	toHTML()
image	"cube777.png"	containsText()

An optional blog image

So the blog image gets stored in the Blog object as a string property named image, but the question still remains as to how this property can be added to the blog as a purely optional feature. This question ultimately has to lead back to the constructor, which is where the object is both created and initialized. Surely some special code has to be placed in the constructor to deal with the fact that the property is optional.

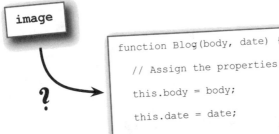

```
function Blog(body, date) {
  // Assign the properties
  this.body = body;
  this.date = date;
}
```

> I'm not so sure about that. What happens if you don't pass an argument to a constructor? Doesn't the property just get set to null?

Missing function arguments become null.

When an argument isn't passed into a function, method, or constructor, it takes on the value of null in any code that attempts to use it. And in the case of a constructor specifically, this means the property associated with a missing argument gets set to null, which isn't necessarily a bad thing. The real trick is then to make sure that the optional constructor argument is specified at the end of the argument list so that it can be left off without disrupting the other arguments. This technique actually works for any function or method, but it's particularly handy for the image argument of the Blog() constructor.

Sharpen your pencil

Rewrite the YouCube Blog() constructor to support a new image property for storing a blog entry image.

....

....

....

....

....

....

Sharpen your pencil Solution

Rewrite the YouCube `Blog()` constructor to support a new image property for storing a blog entry image.

```
function Blog(body, date, image) {

    // Assign the properties

    this.body = body;

    this.date = date;

    this.image = image;

}
```

An image argument is added as the last argument to the constructor.

The image property is created and initialized to the image argument.

there are no Dumb Questions

Q: Is it important that the `image` argument appears last in the `Blog()` constructor's argument list?

A: Yes, and the reason is because the image is considered an optional part of a blog entry. The real issue here is how you go about passing arguments to functions, especially as it pertains to optional arguments. If a function has two arguments, you have the option of passing both arguments, passing only the first argument, or passing none of the arguments. There is no way to pass **only** the second argument.

So when it comes to optional arguments, think about them in terms of being able to leave them off the end of the argument list. Also try to think about arguments in terms of importance, with more important arguments appearing first. Less important arguments that are more likely to be considered optional should appear near the end of the argument list. Since the `image` argument to `Blog()` is optional, it must appear last in the argument list where it can be easily left off.

Adding imagery to YouCube

The shiny new `Blog()` constructor with support for images wouldn't be very useful without some blog entries that use it. In order to create a blog entry that supports images, two things have to happen:

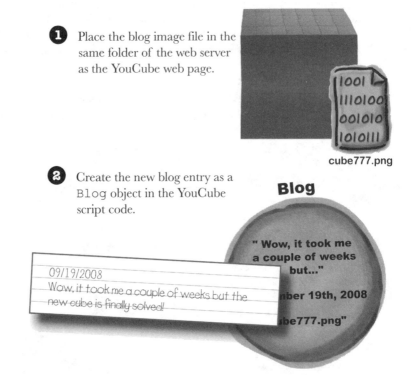

1 Place the blog image file in the same folder of the web server as the YouCube web page.

cube777.png

2 Create the new blog entry as a `Blog` object in the YouCube script code.

Blog

" Wow, it took me a couple of weeks but..."

09/19/2008
Wow, it took me a couple of weeks but the new cube is finally solved!

nber 19th, 2008

be777.png"

Completing these steps results in the following code, which successfully creates a new blog entry that passes an image string into the last argument of the Blog() constructor:

```
new Blog("Wow, it took me a couple of weeks but the new cube is finally solved!",

   new Date("09/19/2008"), "cube777.png")
```

The blog image is passed into the last argument of the Blog() constructor.

Showing the blog image

Now that a blog entry has been created with an image, there is one last piece of business left for the image enhancement to YouCube. All this talk of constructors and optional arguments wouldn't mean much if the code that displays a blog entry didn't actually factor in the new image property.

This code is located in the toHTML() method. We already know that this method is responsible for formatting the blog as HTML code, except now it has to take into account whether or not the image property has a meaningful value. What's really going on is that there are two different ways of displaying a blog entry, one with an image and one without, and the existence of an image is what determines which way the blog gets displayed.

A blog entry should now be displayed according to the logic in this pseudocode.

If (image exists)

   Display blog entry with image

Else

   Display blog entry without image

___

Sharpen your pencil

The Blog object's toHTML() method is missing a piece of code that will allow optional images to be displayed. Write the piece of missing code, and annotate what it does.

```
if (.............................) {
   blogHTML += "<strong>" + this.date.shortFormat() +

      "</strong><br /><table><tr><td><img src='" + this.image +

      "'/></td><td style='vertical-align:top'>" + this.body + "</td></tr></table><em>" +

      this.signature + "</em></p>";
}
else {
   blogHTML += "<strong>" + this.date.shortFormat() + "</strong><br />" + this.body +

      "<br /><em>" + this.signature + "</em></p>";
}
```

Sharpen your pencil Solution

The Blog object's toHTML() method is missing a piece of code that will allow optional images to be displayed. Write the piece of missing code, and annotate what it does.

```
if (    this.image    ) {
```
If the image property is set to an actual image, the if test condition evaluates to true and the image is shown.

```
  blogHTML += "<strong>" + this.date.shortFormat() +
    "</strong><br /><table><tr><td><img src='" + this.image +
```
this.image

```
    "'/></td><td style='vertical-align:top'>" + this.body + "</td></tr></table><em>" +
    this.signature + "</em></p>";
}
else {
```
Otherwise, the blog entry is shown like normal with no image.

```
  blogHTML += "<strong>" + this.date.shortFormat() + "</strong><br />" + this.body +
    "<br /><em>" + this.signature + "</em></p>";
}
```

I know...it's beautiful.

An object-powered YouCube

Ruby is ecstatic. Her blog has grown by leaps and bounds thanks to objects, and it now sports a slick new image feature that she just knows her visitors will love.

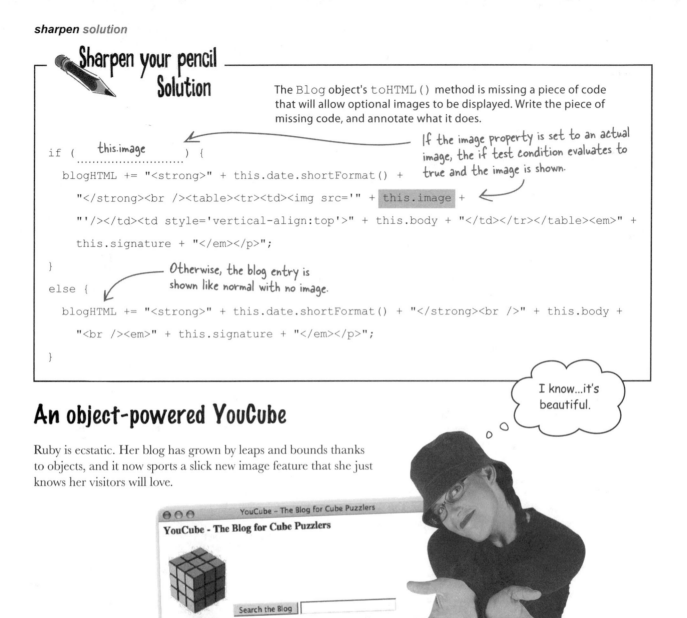

A blog entry with an image.

JavaScriptcross

You know the drill...boxes and words. Fill 'em in!

Across

2. A real live object with its own data.
4. The operator used to create object instances.
6. The signature in YouCube is one of these.
9. Software that is designed using objects.
11. A keyword that references an object from within its own code.
12. An object that inherits properties and methods from another object.

Down

1. The object equivalent of a function.
3. The blog sort comparison code in YouCube is one of these.
5. When a piece of data is placed in an object, it is called a ....
7. Every object has one of these objects hidden within it.
8. A template used to create instances of an object.
10. Object notation uses these to access properties and methods.

JavaScriptcross Solution

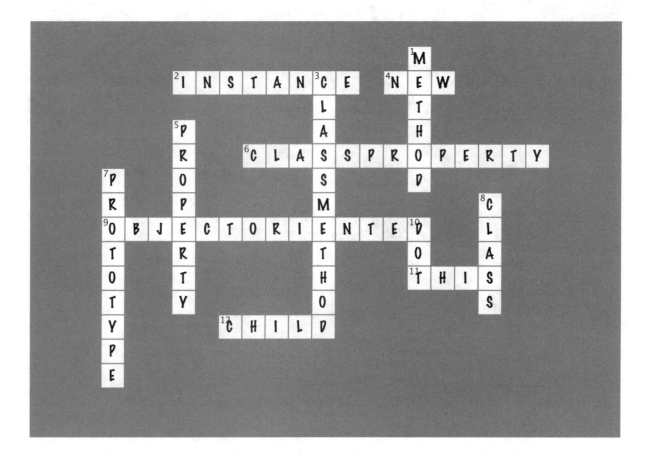

Page Bender

Fold the page vertically to line up the two brains and solve the riddle.

What do objects add to most scripts?

It's a meeting of the minds!

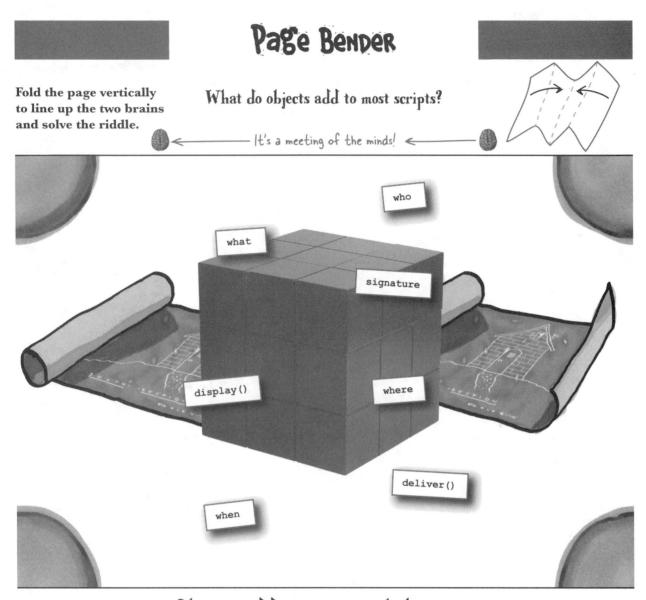

who

what

signature

display()

where

deliver()

when

Objects add so many cool things to
scripts that it can be hard to pick
one thing. It's true, some objects outclass
others and make it even tougher,
but in the end the answer is clear.

11 kill bugs dead

Good Scripts Gone Wrong

> You never know with these things. One day everything works great, everybody's happy... and the next day, bam! Stuff flying everywhere. Bottom line—it's good to have a guy like me around to fix things.

Even the best laid JavaScript plans sometimes fail. When this happens, and it will, your job is not to panic. The best JavaScript developers are not the ones who never create bugs—those people are called liars. No, the best JavaScript developers are those who are able to **successfully hunt down and eradicate** the **bugs** they create. More importantly, top notch JavaScript bug exterminators **develop good coding habits** that minimize the sneakiest and nastiest of bugs. *A little prevention can go a long way.* But bugs happen, and you'll need an arsenal of weapons to combat them...

Real-world debugging

It's a shocking fact of snack food life... a chocolate bar can contain up to 60 bug pieces. As scary as that little tidbit of information may be, there's no reason to fear bugs in JavaScript code. JavaScript code can be more tightly controlled than chocolate processing equipment. There's even a taskforce devoted solely to the removal of JavaScript bugs.

BUG SCENE INVESTIGATORS

It's Bug Scene Investigators, or BSI, as those in the business refer to them. Owen has recently joined BSI as a JavaScript investigator, and is eager to prove himself and help rid the Web of JavaScript bugs.

Owen, BSI JavaScript investigator and former chocolate lover.

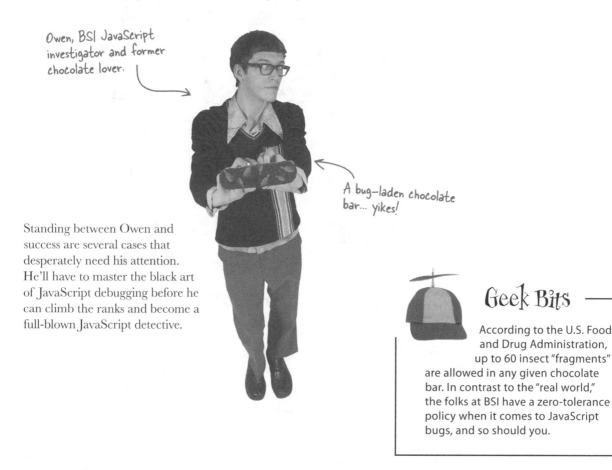

A bug-laden chocolate bar... yikes!

Standing between Owen and success are several cases that desperately need his attention. He'll have to master the black art of JavaScript debugging before he can climb the ranks and become a full-blown JavaScript detective.

Geek Bits

According to the U.S. Food and Drug Administration, up to 60 insect "fragments" are allowed in any given chocolate bar. In contrast to the "real world," the folks at BSI have a zero-tolerance policy when it comes to JavaScript bugs, and so should you.

The case of the buggy IQ calculator

The first case across Owen's desk is an IQ calculator script that's part of a page that calculates an average IQ from an array of IQs, and then groups users together whose results are similar. So the script is given an array of numbers, and then calculates an average and indicates the intelligence of that average.

The files for Owen are available at http://www.headfirstlabs.com/ books/hfjs/.

Owen has been informed that this script is quite buggy. Unfortunately, no other information has been provided beyond, "it doesn't work."

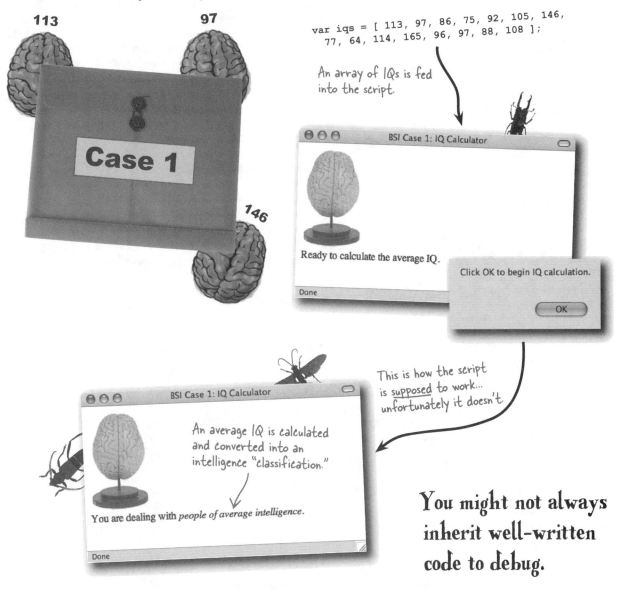

113   **97**

146

Case 1

```
var iqs = [ 113, 97, 86, 75, 92, 105, 146,
    77, 64, 114, 165, 96, 97, 88, 108 ];
```

An array of IQs is fed into the script.

BSI Case 1: IQ Calculator

Ready to calculate the average IQ.

Done

Click OK to begin IQ calculation.

OK

This is how the script is supposed to work... unfortunately it doesn't.

BSI Case 1: IQ Calculator

An average IQ is calculated and converted into an intelligence "classification."

You are dealing with *people of average intelligence*.

Done

You might not always inherit well-written code to debug.

Try different browsers

Owen figures that running the problematic
script through a few different browsers might
help shine some light on the problem. He starts
out with Internet Explorer...

**Internet
Explorer**

Double-clicking the yellow sign
in the bottom left corner of
IE opens an error window.

Internet Explorer reports an error when the page first loads but Owen
isn't sure he can trust it. A quick look at the code for the script shows
that the variable `iqs` exists, but the IE browser shows it doesn't.
Knowing that browsers aren't always accurate when reporting errors,
he decides to press on with the Safari browser...

The iqs variable is defined in
the code, so IE's error doesn't
appear to make any sense.

Safari

If you count down the
lines of code starting at 1,
Safari points to an error
on a line of code that
initially appears to be OK.

Safari points out that the error is on entirely different line of code,
which doesn't immediately appear to Owen to have anything wrong
with it. So he decides to take a stab at locating the error with Opera...

The line number is different but
the code in the Opera error
matches the Safari error.

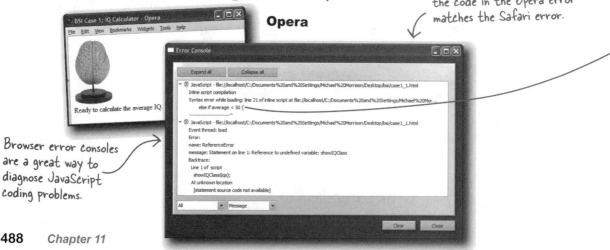

Opera

Browser error consoles
are a great way to
diagnose JavaScript
coding problems.

Something is strange here. Opera mentions a different line number but it's clearly referring to the same line of code as Safari, which is actually good news for Owen. But he still doesn't see anything wrong with the code. So he decides to try one more option, Firefox...

Firefox is pretty helpful in pinpointing the nature of the bug.

Firefox has yet another take on the line number of the problematic code.

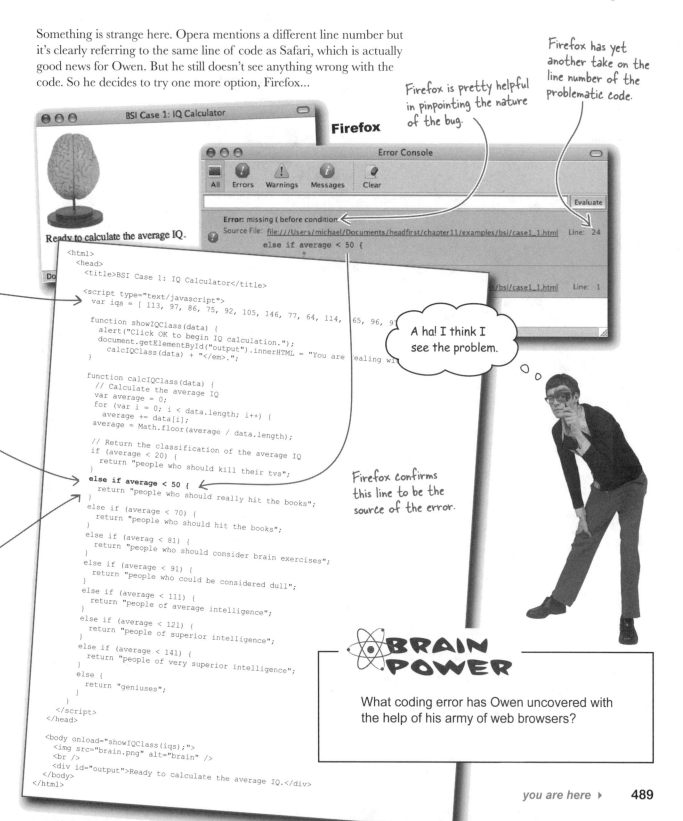

Firefox

BSI Case 1: IQ Calculator

Ready to calculate the average IQ.

Error Console

All | Errors | Warnings | Messages | Clear

Evaluate

Error: missing (before condition
Source File: file:///Users/michael/Documents/headfirst/chapter11/examples/bsi/case1_1.html   Line: 24

```
           else if average < 50 {
```

...bsi/case1_1.html   Line: 1

A ha! I think I see the problem.

```html
<html>
  <head>
    <title>BSI Case 1: IQ Calculator</title>

    <script type="text/javascript">
      var iqs = [ 113, 97, 86, 75, 92, 105, 146, 77, 64, 114,     65, 96, 9

      function showIQClass(data) {
        alert("Click OK to begin IQ calculation.");
        document.getElementById("output").innerHTML = "You are  ealing wi
          calcIQClass(data) + "</em>.";
      }

      function calcIQClass(data) {
        // Calculate the average IQ
        var average = 0;
        for (var i = 0; i < data.length; i++) {
          average += data[i];
        average = Math.floor(average / data.length);

        // Return the classification of the average IQ
        if (average < 20) {
          return "people who should kill their tvs";
        }
        else if average < 50 {
          return "people who should really hit the books";
        }
        else if (average < 70) {
          return "people who should hit the books";
        }
        else if (averag < 81) {
          return "people who should consider brain exercises";
        }
        else if (average < 91) {
          return "people who could be considered dull";
        }
        else if (average < 111) {
          return "people of average intelligence";
        }
        else if (average < 121) {
          return "people of superior intelligence";
        }
        else if (average < 141) {
          return "people of very superior intelligence";
        }
        else {
          return "geniuses";
        }
      }
    </script>
  </head>

  <body onload="showIQClass(iqs);">
    <img src="brain.png" alt="brain" />
    <br />
    <div id="output">Ready to calculate the average IQ.</div>
  </body>
</html>
```

Firefox confirms this line to be the source of the error.

⚛**BRAIN POWER**

What coding error has Owen uncovered with the help of his army of web browsers?

Firefox to the rescue

Given how specific Firefox is in describing the bug, Owen decides to dig a little further using Firefox. So he clicks the link in the Firefox error console window, and it takes him to the line just before the suspicious line of code.

Firefox is widely considered the best debugging browser around, at least for the time being.

Geek Bits

Not only does Firefox have excellent built-in bug detection capabilities, but it also has a debugger plug-in called **Firebug** that takes debugging to an entirely different level. The Firebug debugger for Firefox can be downloaded for free at *http://www.getfirebug.com/*.

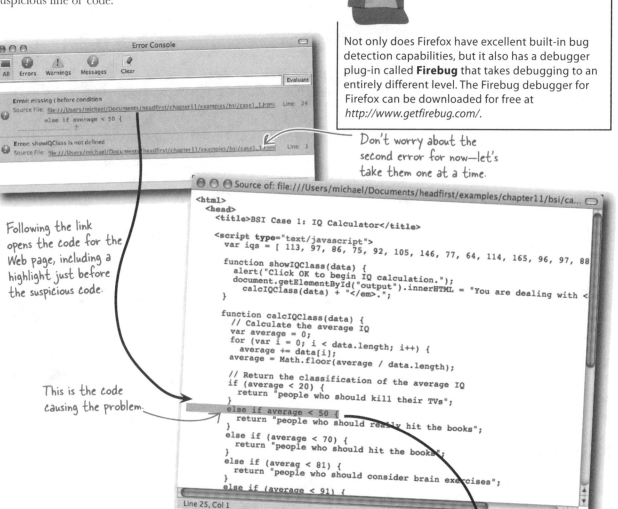

Don't worry about the second error for now—let's take them one at a time.

Following the link opens the code for the Web page, including a highlight just before the suspicious code.

This is the code causing the problem.

```
<html>
  <head>
    <title>BSI Case 1: IQ Calculator</title>

    <script type="text/javascript">
      var iqs = [ 113, 97, 86, 75, 92, 105, 146, 77, 64, 114, 165, 96, 97, 88

      function showIQClass(data) {
        alert("Click OK to begin IQ calculation.");
        document.getElementById("output").innerHTML = "You are dealing with <
          calcIQClass(data) + "</em>.";
      }

      function calcIQClass(data) {
        // Calculate the average IQ
        var average = 0;
        for (var i = 0; i < data.length; i++) {
          average += data[i];
        average = Math.floor(average / data.length);

        // Return the classification of the average IQ
        if (average < 20) {
          return "people who should kill their TVs";
        }
        else if average < 50 {
          return "people who should really hit the books";
        }
        else if (average < 70) {
          return "people who should hit the books";
        }
        else if (averag < 81) {
          return "people who should consider brain exercises";
        }
        else if (average < 91) {
```

Line 25, Col 1

By analyzing the Firefox error message, Owen's figured out that Safari is actually right about the line number (25). Firefox highlights and mentions line 24 but correctly shows the code on line 25. More importantly, Firefox explains exactly what is wrong with the code, which is a simple problem yet deceptively easy to overlook.

```
else if average < 50 {
```

The if statement is missing parentheses around the test condition.

there are no Dumb Questions

Q: I can't figure out how to view the error console in my browser. How do I open it?

A: Unfortunately, every browser is different, and some make it a challenge to find the JavaScript error console. For example, Safari on the Mac only allows access to the error console from the Debug menu, which is disabled by default. You have to issue the following command (write it on one line, with no carriage return) in the Terminal application to change the settings and enable the Debug menu:

```
defaults write com.apple.Safari
IncludeDebugMenu 1
```

Check the documentation for your specific browser to find out how to open the error console and view script errors. The error console in Firefox is opened by selecting Error Console from the Tools menu.

Q: What makes Firefox so special?

A: The developers of Firefox did a great job on its error reporting capabilities. It simply outperforms other browsers when it comes to assessing script errors and pointing you in the right direction for finding them. This isn't to say some other browser may come along and do a better job at some point in the future, but Firefox has proven itself a very capable browser for debugging pages containing JavaScript code.

Q: What error was Internet Explorer talking about?

A: There's not really any way to know for sure. The reason is because the error reported by Internet Explorer has to do with the script code not loading property, which is the result of an error encountered by the JavaScript interpreter. You know the code is not loading properly because the `iqs` variable is being reported as "undefined," even though the code clearly shows the `iqs` variable getting created. So the only way it can be a problem is if some other error is somehow preventing the script from fully loading.

And that begs the question... is there some other error in the script, and what does "undefined" really mean?

Debugging on easy street

Owen is pretty excited about isolating the bug in the IQ calculator script so quickly. And with such a simple coding fix to make, he figures he'll be able to cruise along in this job and make BSI detective in no time.

> This debugging stuff is easy. With a little help from Firefox, my job is a piece of cake... with coffee.

```
else if (average < 50) {
```

Placing the test condition inside parentheses solves the bug in the IQ calculator.

Adding the missing parentheses squashes the bug.

Is there a chance Owen has gotten an early dose of overconfidence? He really needs to test the newly repaired script before taking the rest of the day off...

The bug report isn't always the bug source

Unfortunately, Owen isn't finished with the IQ calculator case because Firefox is still complaining, except now it's a completely different problem. While he's tempted to stick with the same tactic of trusting Firefox's assessment implicitly, this time Owen has his doubts about the validity of the reported bug.

> This function brace matches up with the brace mentioned by Firefox, so nothing is missing with the function braces.

> Again, one bug at a time, so let's continue to ignore this one for now.

```html
<html>
  <head>
    <title>BSI Case 1: IQ Calculator</title>

    <script type="text/javascript">
      var iqs = [ 113, 97, 86, 75, 92, 105, 146, 77, 64, 114, 165, 96, 97, 88, 108 ];

      function showIQClass(data) {
        alert("Click OK to begin IQ calculation.");
        document.getElementById("output").innerHTML = "You are dealing with <em>" +
          calcIQClass(data) + "</em>.";
      }

      function calcIQClass(data) {
        // Calculate the average IQ
        var average = 0;
        for (var i = 0; i <
          average += data[i]
        average = Math.floor

        // Return the classi
        if (average < 20) {
          return "people who
        }
        else if (average < 50
          return "people who
        }
        else if (average < 70
          return "people who
        }
        else if (averag < 81)
          return "people who
        }
        else if (average < 91)
          return "people who
        }
        else if (average < 111
          return "people of av
        }
        else if (average < 121)
          return "people of superior int
        }
        else if (average < 141) {
          return "people of very superior intelligence
        }
        else {
          return "geniuses";
        }
      }
    </script>
  </head>

  <body onload="showIQClass(iqs);">
    <img src="brain.png" alt="brain" />
    <br />
    <div id="output">Ready to calculate the average IQ.</div>
  </body>
</html>
```

> This is the brace Firefox is complaining about.

Error Console

All · Errors · Warnings · Messages · Clear

Evaluate

Error: missing } after function body
Source File: file:///Users/michael/Documents/headfirst/chapter11/examples/bsi/case1_2.html   Line: 53

Error: showIQClass is not defined
Source File: file:///Users/michael/Documents/headfirst/chapter11/examples/bsi/case1_2.html   Line: 1

> I think your magical debugger just screwed up. Clearly, the braces around the function in this code are just fine.

You can't always trust the browser.

It's true, the function braces are OK. As good as it may be in some cases, it appears that Firefox is barking up the wrong tree on this bug. However, it's worth taking the mention of a missing curly brace as a clue to study all of the braces in the code a bit closer.

BE the JavaScript Interpreter

Your job is to play JavaScript interpreter and follow the trail of curly braces in the code to find out what has gone wrong.

```html
<html>
  <head>
    <title>BSI Case 1: IQ Calculator</title>

    <script type="text/javascript">
      var iqs = [ 113, 97, 86, 75, 92, 105, 146, 77, 64, 114, 165, 96, 97, 88, 108 ];

      function showIQClass(data) {
        alert("Click OK to begin IQ calculation.");
        document.getElementById("output").innerHTML = "You are dealing with <em>" +
          calcIQClass(data) + "</em>.";
      }

      function calcIQClass(data) {
        // Calculate the average IQ
        var average = 0;
        for (var i = 0; i < data.length; i++) {
          average += data[i];
        average = Math.floor(average / data.length);

        // Return the classification of the average IQ
        if (average < 20) {
          return "people who should kill their tvs";
        }
        else if (average < 50) {
          return "people who should really hit the books";
        }
        else if (average < 70) {
          return "people who should hit the books";
        }
        else if (averag < 81) {
          return "people who should consider brain exercises";
        }
        else if (average < 91) {
          return "people who could be considered dull";
        }
        else if (average < 111) {
          return "people of average intelligence";
        }
        else if (average < 121) {
          return "people of superior intelligence";
        }
        else if (average < 141) {
          return "people of very superior intelligence";
        }
        else {
          return "geniuses";
        }
      }
    </script>
  </head>

  <body onload="showIQClass(iqs);">
    <img src="brain.png" alt="brain" />
    <br />
    <div id="output">Ready to calculate the average IQ.</div>
  </body>
</html>
```

BE the JavaScript Interpreter Solution

Your job is to play JavaScript interpreter
and follow the trail of curly braces in
the code to find out what has gone wrong.

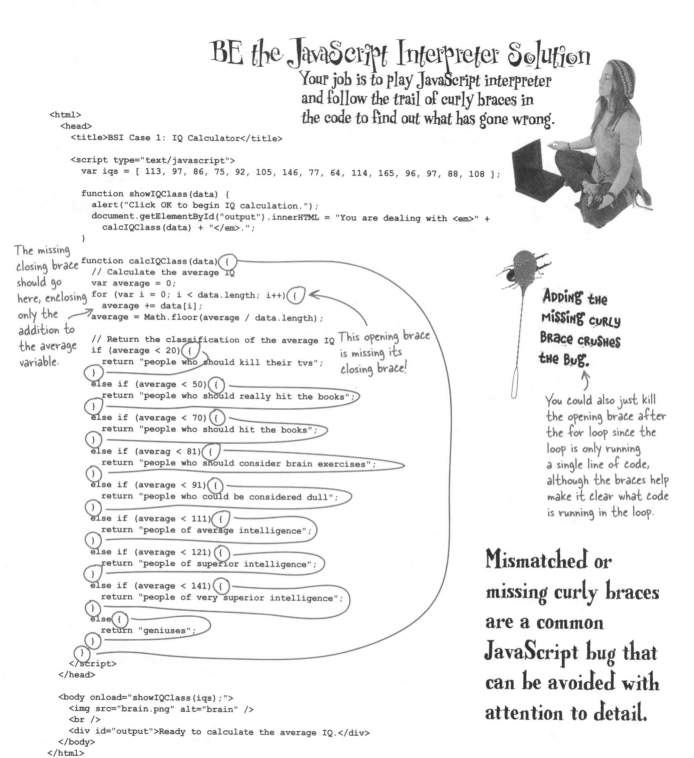

```html
<html>
  <head>
    <title>BSI Case 1: IQ Calculator</title>

    <script type="text/javascript">
      var iqs = [ 113, 97, 86, 75, 92, 105, 146, 77, 64, 114, 165, 96, 97, 88, 108 ];

      function showIQClass(data) {
        alert("Click OK to begin IQ calculation.");
        document.getElementById("output").innerHTML = "You are dealing with <em>" +
          calcIQClass(data) + "</em>.";
      }

      function calcIQClass(data) {
        // Calculate the average IQ
        var average = 0;
        for (var i = 0; i < data.length; i++) {
          average += data[i];
        average = Math.floor(average / data.length);

        // Return the classification of the average IQ
        if (average < 20) {
          return "people who should kill their tvs";
        }
        else if (average < 50) {
          return "people who should really hit the books";
        }
        else if (average < 70) {
          return "people who should hit the books";
        }
        else if (averag < 81) {
          return "people who should consider brain exercises";
        }
        else if (average < 91) {
          return "people who could be considered dull";
        }
        else if (average < 111) {
          return "people of average intelligence";
        }
        else if (average < 121) {
          return "people of superior intelligence";
        }
        else if (average < 141) {
          return "people of very superior intelligence";
        }
        else {
          return "geniuses";
        }
      }
    </script>
  </head>

  <body onload="showIQClass(iqs);">
    <img src="brain.png" alt="brain" />
    <br />
    <div id="output">Ready to calculate the average IQ.</div>
  </body>
</html>
```

The missing closing brace should go here, enclosing only the addition to the average variable.

This opening brace is missing its closing brace!

Adding the missing curly brace crushes the bug.

You could also just kill the opening brace after the for loop since the loop is only running a single line of code, although the braces help make it clear what code is running in the loop.

Mismatched or missing curly braces are a common JavaScript bug that can be avoided with attention to detail.

Variables gone ~~wild~~ undefined

Owen can't seem to catch a break as the stream of IQ calculator bugs just keeps on flowing. Now Firefox is reporting that a variable is "not defined," which sounds sort of like the bogus error Internet Explorer reported early on. Except this time the undefined variable is named `averag`, not `iqs`.

> Notice that the second error has now gone away. Sometimes fixing one bug will naturally resolve more than one error.

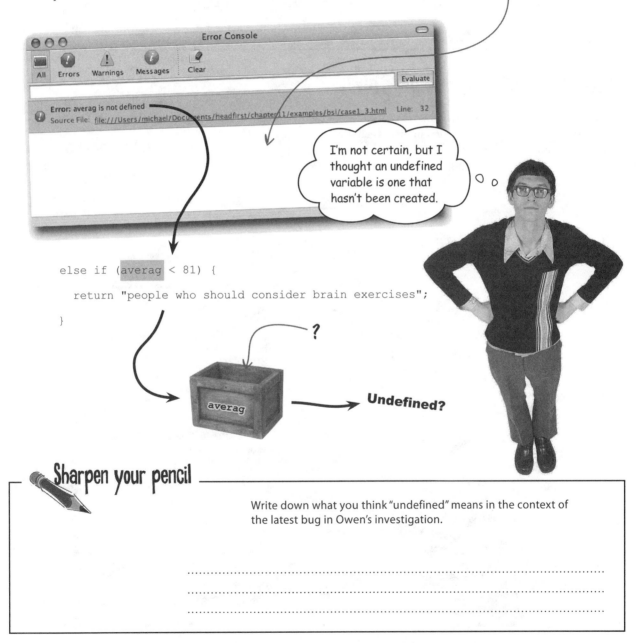

> I'm not certain, but I thought an undefined variable is one that hasn't been created.

```
else if (averag < 81) {

    return "people who should consider brain exercises";

}
```

averag → **Undefined?**

Sharpen your pencil

Write down what you think "undefined" means in the context of the latest bug in Owen's investigation.

....

....

....

Sharpen your pencil
Solution

Write down what you think "undefined" means in the context of the latest bug in Owen's investigation.

"Undefined" refers to a variable that has either not been created (using var) or that has been created but not yet assigned a value. Either way, the problem is that the variable is being referenced even though it has no value.

Sometimes it's the simple things

In this case "undefined" definitely refers to a variable that has been used without having been created, although in this case it's by accident. The only reason the variable is undefined is because of a typo that results in the JavaScript interpreter thinking it is an entirely new variable.

Something as simple as a typo can often wreak havoc on a script.

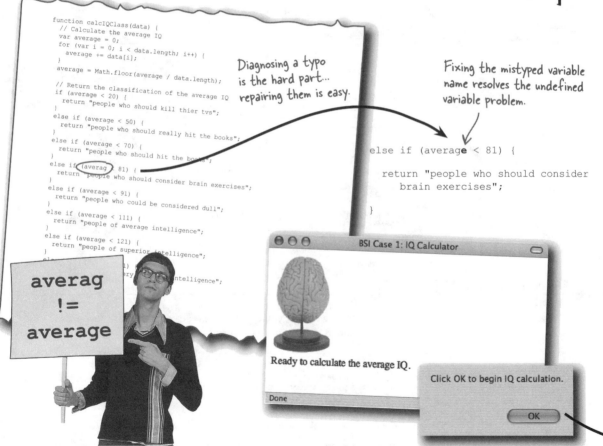

```
function calcIQClass(data) {
  // Calculate the average IQ
  var average = 0;
  for (var i = 0; i < data.length; i++) {
    average += data[i];
  }
  average = Math.floor(average / data.length);

  // Return the classification of the average IQ
  if (average < 20) {
    return "people who should kill thier tvs";
  }
  else if (average < 50) {
    return "people who should really hit the books";
  }
  else if (average < 70) {
    return "people who should hit the books";
  }
  else if (averag < 81) {
    return "people who should consider brain exercises";
  }
  else if (average < 91) {
    return "people who could be considered dull";
  }
  else if (average < 111) {
    return "people of average intelligence";
  }
  else if (average < 121) {
    return "people of superior intelligence";
  }
```

Diagnosing a typo is the hard part... repairing them is easy.

Fixing the mistyped variable name resolves the undefined variable problem.

```
else if (average < 81) {

    return "people who should consider
          brain exercises";

}
```

averag != average

BSI Case 1: IQ Calculator

Ready to calculate the average IQ.

Done

Click OK to begin IQ calculation.

OK

there are no Dumb Questions

Q: Is there a difference between "undefined" and "not defined"?

A: No. They mean exactly the same thing, it's just that some browsers use one term and some use the other. Consider the two terms to be entirely interchangeable.

Q: OK then, so is there a difference between "undefined" and null?

A: That one's a little trickier. Yes, on a very technical level there is a difference between "undefined' and null, but not really enough to worry about. Unlike null, "undefined" is not a value that you should ever think about assigning to a variable. There is an undefined data type that variables automatically assume when they have yet to be assigned a value. On the other hand, variables are never automatically set to null. However, it's sometimes a good idea to set object variables to null as an initialization step to make sure it is clear an object has not yet been created.

Nitty gritty technical details aside, the main thing to know about "undefined" and null is that they both convert to false when placed in a boolean context, such as the test condition of an if statement. That's why code such as if (someObject) is often used to check if an object has been created before attempting to access its members.

Q: I still don't quite understand how a typo somehow turned the average variable into undefined. How did that happen?

A: Even though a variable named average had already been created and initialized, JavaScript has no ability to make the connection between averag and average just because they have **nearly** the same name. The variable averag could just as easily be named shazbot or lederhosen for all JavaScript cares. Which is to say that JavaScript interprets it as an entirely new variable. And since this new variable has yet to be assigned a value, it's a big problem trying to compare something to it in an if statement. It's like trying to write a movie review before you've decided what movie to watch.

Q: Are you kidding me? I make typo mistakes all the time in my word processor and it doesn't break everything. Why is JavaScript so sensitive?

A: Take a deep breath and commit these four very important and insightful words to memory: GET USED TO IT. We're not writing scripts for people, we're writing them for machines, and machines are anything but forgiving regardless of what language you're scripting in. Even one character in the wrong place can send a script over the edge. There is some flexibility in the whitespace surrounding JavaScript code, such as spaces and newlines, but the code itself must be very exact.

Crunching the intelligence numbers

With the typo bug under control, the IQ calculator script now works properly, calculating an average IQ from an array and then displaying the result as a text classification. Owen can close this case and bask in the glory of a job well done... but for how long?

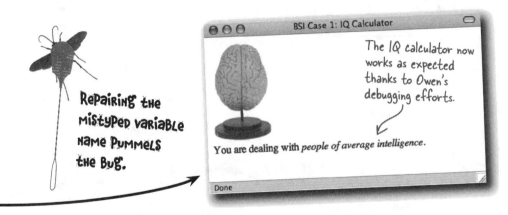

Repairing the mistyped variable name pummels the bug.

The IQ calculator now works as expected thanks to Owen's debugging efforts.

You are dealing with *people of average intelligence.*

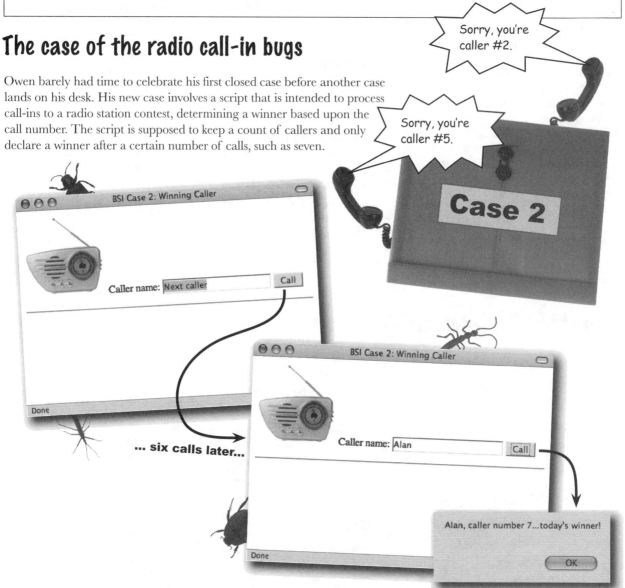

BULLET POINTS

- Although most browsers provide an error console that provides information about JavaScript errors, they can't always be trusted as completely accurate.

- Even though browsers often yield sketchy error information, they do usually provide valuable **clues** about where to start looking for trouble.

- Curly braces around blocks of code are a common source of bugs—be careful to always **match** opening and closing braces.

- Simple typographical errors are easy to make but not necessarily easy to find—always check the naming of identifiers.

The case of the radio call-in bugs

Owen barely had time to celebrate his first closed case before another case lands on his desk. His new case involves a script that is intended to process call-ins to a radio station contest, determining a winner based upon the call number. The script is supposed to keep a count of callers and only declare a winner after a certain number of calls, such as seven.

Sorry, you're caller #2.

Sorry, you're caller #5.

Case 2

BSI Case 2: Winning Caller

Caller name: Next caller   Call

Done

... six calls later...

BSI Case 2: Winning Caller

Caller name: Alan   Call

Alan, caller number 7...today's winner!

OK

Done

Opening up the investigation

Before firing up the radio call-in page in a browser, Owen thinks it's worth taking a quick look at the code (available at *http://www.headfirstlabs.com/books/hfjs/*) and getting a feel for how it is put together. Maybe something will jump out that is obviously wrong, or maybe he'll at least gain some understanding of how the code is **supposed** to work.

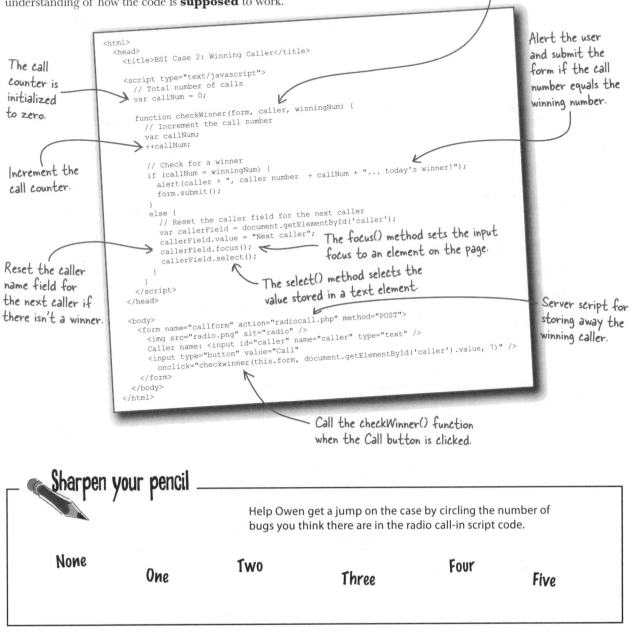

The name of the caller and the winning call number are passed into the checkWinner() function, along with the form object.

Alert the user and submit the form if the call number equals the winning number.

The call counter is initialized to zero.

Increment the call counter.

Reset the caller name field for the next caller if there isn't a winner.

The focus() method sets the input focus to an element on the page.

The select() method selects the value stored in a text element.

Server script for storing away the winning caller.

Call the checkWinner() function when the Call button is clicked.

```html
<html>
  <head>
    <title>BSI Case 2: Winning Caller</title>

    <script type="text/javascript">
    // Total number of calls
    var callNum = 0;

    function checkWinner(form, caller, winningNum) {
      // Increment the call number
      var callNum;
      ++callNum;

      // Check for a winner
      if (callNum = winningNum) {
        alert(caller + ", caller number  " + callNum + "... today's winner!");
        form.submit();
      }
      else {
        // Reset the caller field for the next caller
        var callerField = document.getElementById('caller');
        callerField.value = "Next caller";
        callerField.focus();
        callerField.select();
      }
    }
    </script>
  </head>

  <body>
    <form name="callform" action="radiocall.php" method="POST">
      <img src="radio.png" alt="radio" />
      Caller name: <input id="caller" name="caller" type="text" />
      <input type="button" value="Call"
        onclick="checkwinner(this.form, document.getElementById('caller').value, 7)" />
    </form>
  </body>
</html>
```

Sharpen your pencil

Help Owen get a jump on the case by circling the number of bugs you think there are in the radio call-in script code.

None   One   Two   Three   Four   Five

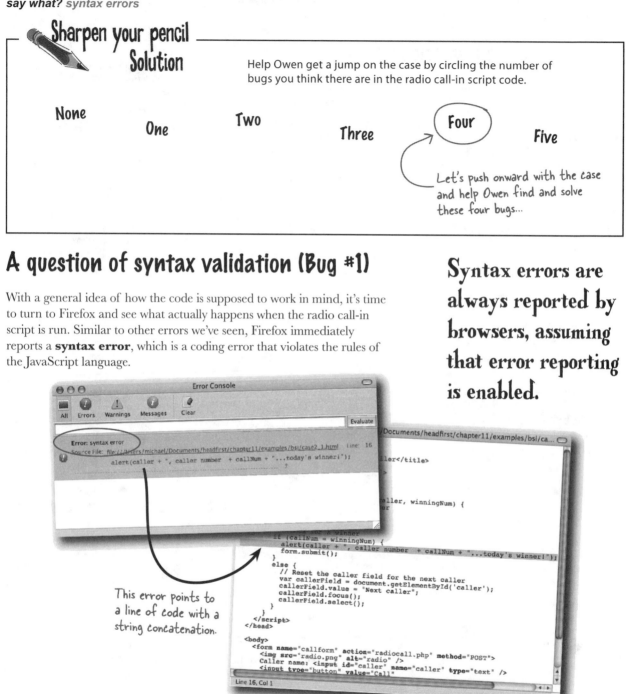

Sharpen your pencil Solution

Help Owen get a jump on the case by circling the number of bugs you think there are in the radio call-in script code.

None

One

Two

Three

(Four)

Five

Let's push onward with the case and help Owen find and solve these four bugs...

A question of syntax validation (Bug #1)

With a general idea of how the code is supposed to work in mind, it's time to turn to Firefox and see what actually happens when the radio call-in script is run. Similar to other errors we've seen, Firefox immediately reports a **syntax error**, which is a coding error that violates the rules of the JavaScript language.

Syntax errors are always reported by browsers, assuming that error reporting is enabled.

This error points to a line of code with a string concatenation.

Syntax errors always result in a browser notification of some sort, assuming the browser is set to report errors. This gives us a very important jumpstart in tracking down errors.

Careful with those strings

Firefox pinpointed a line of code with a string concatenation, which is a clue to analyze the line of code very carefully. The code calls the `alert()` function with several string literals concatenated with the `caller` and `callNum` variables.

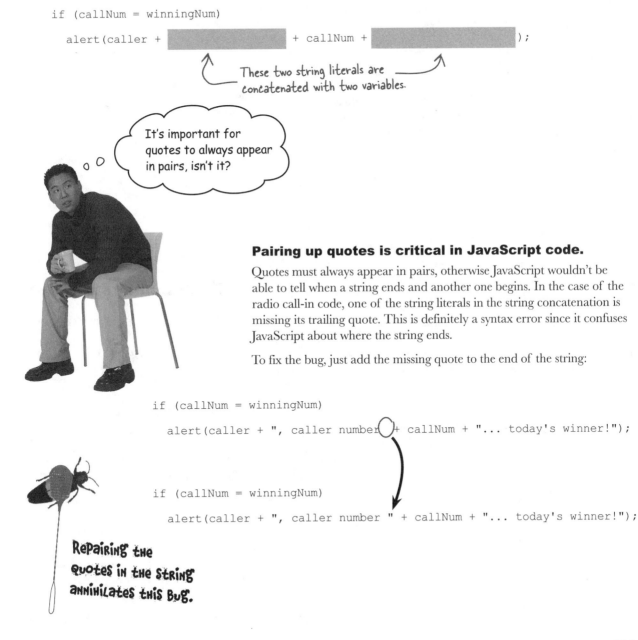

```
if (callNum = winningNum)
    alert(caller +                    + callNum +                    );
```

These two string literals are concatenated with two variables.

It's important for quotes to always appear in pairs, isn't it?

Pairing up quotes is critical in JavaScript code.

Quotes must always appear in pairs, otherwise JavaScript wouldn't be able to tell when a string ends and another one begins. In the case of the radio call-in code, one of the string literals in the string concatenation is missing its trailing quote. This is definitely a syntax error since it confuses JavaScript about where the string ends.

To fix the bug, just add the missing quote to the end of the string:

```
if (callNum = winningNum)
    alert(caller + ", caller number  + callNum + "... today's winner!");
```

```
if (callNum = winningNum)
    alert(caller + ", caller number " + callNum + "... today's winner!");
```

Repairing the quotes in the string annihilates this bug.

Quotes, apostrophes, and consistency

Missing quotes are only half the story when it comes to tracking down quote-related errors in strings. Since JavaScript and HTML equally support both quotes and apostrophes for enclosing strings (JavaScript) and attributes (HTML), it's critical to be consistent when mixing the two.

```
<input type="button" value="Call"

   onclick="checkwinner(this.form, document.getElementById('caller').value, 7)" />
```

Quotes are used to enclose all of the HTML attributes.

Apostrophes are used to enclose JavaScript strings within an attribute.

This approach to using quotes for HTML attributes and apostrophes for JavaScript strings within attributes works perfectly fine, and is a good idea. However, it is also possible in HTML to reverse the two, as this code reveals::

The modern XHTML web page standard doesn't allow apostrophes to be used to enclose attributes.

```
<input type='button' value='Call'

   onclick='checkwinner(this.form, document.getElementById("caller").value, 7)' />
```

Now apostrophes are used for the HTML attributes and quotes are used for the JavaScript strings.

The idea here is to stick with quotes for one type of code, and apostrophes for the other type. And since the modern version of HTML, XHTML, requires quotes around attributes, it makes sense to stick with quotes around attributes and apostrophes around the JavaScript strings inside attributes.

Quotes and apostrophes should be alternated when using JavaScript strings in HTML attributes.

But a problem arises when you specifically need a quote or an apostrophe but you've already committed to one of them as the string-enclosing character, or string **boundary**. Consider the following code:

```
alert('It's so exciting!');
```

Does this code work?

BRAIN POWER

What happens when you specifically need a quote or an apostrophe character in a string that is enclosed using the same kind of character?

When a quote isn't a quote, use escape characters

A common bug involves using a quote or apostrophe as a character within a string but having it interpreted as a string boundary. So the alert code we just saw is a syntax error because the JavaScript interpreter can't figure out which apostrophes are boundaries and which are real apostrophes. Fortunately, there is an easy way to declare that a character is a "real" character. It's called an **escape character**, and it involves placing a backslash (****) in front of the character to be used literally.

```
alert('It\'s so exciting!');
```

Now the apostrophe has been escaped, and JavaScript knows without a doubt that we really want an apostrophe character in the string, as opposed to declaring the end of the string. Of course, we could've dodged the escape by changing the string boundary to quotes.

Escape characters are used to specify literal characters in strings.

```
alert("It's so exciting!");
```
Escape no longer needed.

That works fine, but what about this code:

```
alert("They said, "you've won!"");
```

The string contains literal quotes and a literal apostrophe, so escape is the only option available. In such a scenario, it's usually safer to escape all of the literal characters, even though the apostrophe could get by without it.

```
alert("They said, \"you\'ve won!\"");
```
Escape not needed but still a good idea.

Exercise

Fix the quotes and apostrophes in the following code snippets, using escape characters whenever possible.

```
var message = 'Hey, she's the winner!';
```
....

```
var response = "She said, "I can't believe I won.""
```
....

```
<input type="button" value="Winner" onclick="givePrize("Ruby");" />
```
....

Exercise Solution

Fix the quotes and apostrophes in the following code snippets, using escape characters whenever possible.

```
var message = 'Hey, she's the winner!';
```

var message = 'Hey, she\'s the winner!';

The apostrophe doesn't have to be escaped since it appears within a string surrounding by quotes.

```
var response = "She said, "I can't believe I won.""
```

var response = "She said, \"I can\'t believe I won.\""

```
<input type="button" value="Winner" onclick="givePrize("Ruby");" />
```

<input type="button" value="Winner" onclick="givePrize('Ruby');" />

Escape characters won't work in this case since this is a JavaScript string inside an HTML attribute. Mixing quotes and apostrophes solves the problem.

Undefined isn't just for variables (Bug #2)

One bug is taken care of but Owen knows his work is not finished. The radio call-in script now starts up fine with no errors, but a click of the Call button to enter a caller is all it takes to reveal another problem. And this one seems to have something to do with the checkWinner() function.

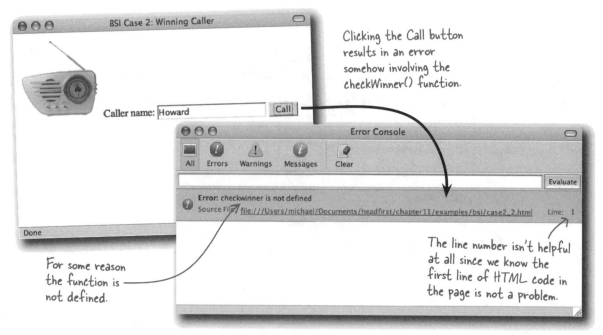

Clicking the Call button results in an error somehow involving the checkWinner() function.

For some reason the function is not defined.

The line number isn't helpful at all since we know the first line of HTML code in the page is not a problem.

The usual suspects: the checklist

With some debugging experience under his belt, Owen decides to run through his newly constructed checklist of common JavaScript errors. Maybe this bug will match up with one of the bugs he has already encountered.

* Unmatched or missing parentheses.

* Unmatched or missing curly braces.

* Misnamed identifier from typo.

* Quote or apostrophe misuse.

Owen's bug detection cheat sheet.

```
function checkWinner(form, caller, winningNum) {
    // Increment the call number
    var callNum;
    ++callNum;

    // Check for a winner
    if (callNum = winningNum) {
        alert(caller + ", caller number " + callNum + "... today\'s winner!");
        form.submit();
    }
    else {
        // Reset the caller field for the next caller
        var callerField = document.getElementById('caller');
        callerField.value = "Next caller";
        callerField.focus();
        callerField.select();
    }
}
</script>
</head>

<body>
    <form name="callform" action="radiocall.php" method="POST">
        <img src="radio.png" alt="radio" />
        Caller name: <input id="caller" name="caller" type="text" />
        <input type="button" value="Call"
            onclick="checkwinner(this.form, document.getElementById('caller').value,
    </form>
</body>
</html>
```

Hmmm... .

The checkWinner() function is only referenced twice in the code.

Sharpen your pencil

Help Owen by checking the type of problem you think is plaguing the radio call-in script.

☐ Unmatched or missing curly braces.

☐ Unmatched or missing parentheses.

☐ Misnamed identifier from typo.

☐ Quote or apostrophe misuse.

☐ Some entirely new kind of problem.

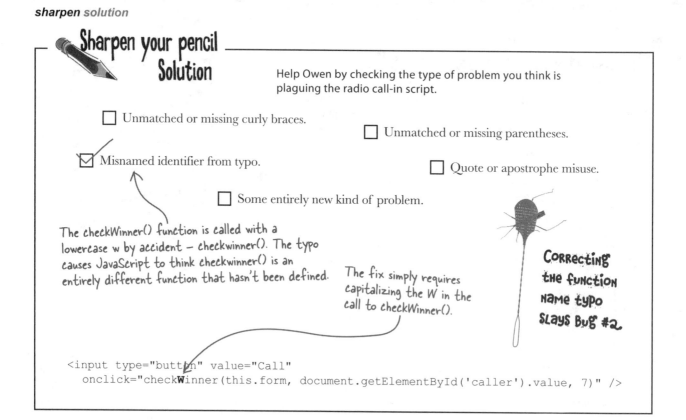

Sharpen your pencil Solution

Help Owen by checking the type of problem you think is plaguing the radio call-in script.

☐ Unmatched or missing curly braces.

☐ Unmatched or missing parentheses.

☑ Misnamed identifier from typo.

☐ Quote or apostrophe misuse.

☐ Some entirely new kind of problem.

The checkWinner() function is called with a lowercase w by accident – checkwinner(). The typo causes JavaScript to think checkwinner() is an entirely different function that hasn't been defined.

The fix simply requires capitalizing the W in the call to checkWinner().

CORRECTING the function name typo SLAYS Bug #2

```
<input type="button" value="Call"
   onclick="checkWinner(this.form, document.getElementById('caller').value, 7)" />
```

Everyone's a winner (Bug #3)

With the pesky "undefined" typo bug taken care of, the radio call-in script is still triggering errors. The good news is that the browser is no longer reporting any problems. But the bad news is that **every** caller is now a winner—the script is even declaring them the correct caller number even when they aren't. That's a lot of prizes to give away if Owen doesn't come up with a fix!

The really strange thing is that the call number is being shown as the winning number even though the caller isn't the winning caller.

Ellie, caller number 7...today's winner!

OK

Jason, caller number 7...today's winner!

OK

Ruby, caller number 7...today's winner!

OK

Every call is being declared a winner.

Alert box debugging

We know that the test for the winning number takes place by comparing the `callNum` variable to the `winningNum` argument to `checkWinner()` function. But this code appears to be OK... we really need a way to look a little closer at what's going on with the `callNum` variable.

> Nothing obvious jumps out as being wrong with this code.

```
...

if (callNum = winningNum) {

...
```

> It's worth trying to track the value of callNum to see how it is changing leading up to this code.

> Is there a way to look at the value of a variable at different points in a script?

Alert boxes can be very handy for getting a quick look at the value of a variable.

Alert boxes can serve as a debug watch window.

As it turns out, alert boxes aren't just for displaying pop-up information to end users. They can also be useful purely on the development side of JavaScript code as temporary watch windows for looking at variables. Not only that, but alerts can be used to make sure a certain section of code is getting called as expected. In this case, we need to use an alert simply for keeping an eye on the `callNum` variable.

> The alert box provides a watch on the variable's value, in this case the value of the callNum variable.

Watching variables with alert

A **watch** is a debugging term that refers to constantly watching
a variable as a program runs. An alert provides a primitive
watch that isn't exactly a constant view of a variable but can still
be very helpful. An alert can be used as a watch anywhere in
JavaScript code where a variable is in question.

```
alert(callNum);
if (callNum = winningNum) {
  alert(caller + ", caller number " + callNum + "... today\'s
winner!");
  form.submit();
}
```

*Something isn't right...
callNum should be set to the
number of the current call.*

NaN

OK

Owen realizes that the radio call-in script is somehow seeing `callNum`
and `winningNum` as equal, even though `callNum` is showing up as NaN
just before the `if` statement. While it's already confusing that `callNum`
is coming up as NaN, he decides to move the alert just inside the `if`
statement to see if anything changes.

*Bingo! I think I
figured it out.*

```
if (callNum = winningNum) {
  alert(callNum);
  alert(caller + ", caller number " + callNum + "... today\'s
winner!");
  form.submit();
}
```

*The callNum variable is now
showing up set to 7 just
after the if test conditional.*

7

OK

BRAIN POWER

With the alert watch confirming that `callNum` is
somehow miraculously getting set to 7 within a
single line of code, what do you think is the cause
of the bug? What has Owen figured out?

Debugging with Alert

This week's interview:
Alert shares his disdain of bugs

Head First: I have to admit, I've heard mixed things about you. People say you can be really annoying. Yet I hear you could very well be a debugger's best friend. Can you enlighten us on who the real alert is?

Alert: Those first people are crazy. I'm a wonderful guy. I'm also pretty simple—you give me some information to display, and boom, I pop up and display it. That's it. Where's the harm in that?

Head First: I guess it's the "pop-up" part. Pop-ups have gotten a bad rep as of late with all the ridiculous ads that sometimes pop up everywhere.

Alert: Oh, I gotcha. Yeah, I can see where that could get really annoying. But you can't go around blaming a hammer for a dimwitted carpenter who doesn't know how to use it. See what I mean?

Head First: So you're saying that any bad things I've heard about you have to do with you being misused?

Alert: There you go. Like I said, I just do as I'm told. You tell me to pop up a whole bunch of times with silly ads, I'll do it. I'm not saying I'll like it, but I don't really have a choice in the matter. Hey, I thought you were going to ask me about my contribution to the world of debugging.

Head First: Oh, I'm sorry. Yes, I have heard some really good things about how you help JavaScript developers track down bugs in their code. How do you do it?

Alert: It's pretty simple, really. Let's say there's a variable that has gone haywire, getting set to some value that makes no sense. The programmer is freaking out, overcaffeinated, you know what I mean, and desperately needs a way to take a peek at the variable at different places in the script to see how it's getting changed. So she asks me to pop up and show the variable.

Head First: But how are you able to show the variable change value at different points in a script? That sounds difficult.

Alert: Not at all. All you do is call me multiple times, with each call at a different point in the script.

Head First: I see. Have you ever run into any problems when helping out as a debugging tool.

Alert: Well, I have to admit that I'm not so good at popping up debugging information when there is a piece of code getting run a bunch of times, like in a loop.

Head First: Why is that?

Alert: Well, remember that I am a pop-up window, so I have to be clicked to go away. If I'm popping up a bunch of times, that's a whole lot of clicks.

Head First: That makes sense. I also hear that you can be handy even when there isn't data to be looked at.

Alert: Oh yes. There are plenty of situations where it isn't quite clear if or when a piece of code is getting called. A quick call to me within the code will let you know if the code is really getting called. I become somewhat of an alarm just to let you know if code is called.

Head First: In all of these debugging scenarios, are you telling me you are just temporary?

Alert: Oh, absolutely. And I don't mind. It's not like I don't have my permanent role as well—I just do the debugging thing on the side as a little public service.

Head First: Well, I appreciate you taking the time to explain your role in bug detection. I look forward to seeing you around.

Bad logic is legal but buggy

Owen has honed in on a **logic error**, an error that is perfectly legal according to the rules of JavaScript but entirely wrong in terms of what it is intended to do. In this case, = is used instead of ==, which means winningNum is getting **assigned** to callNum instead of being **compared** to it. Subtle? Yes. But still highly problematic.

The code that "looked" OK earlier turned out to have a subtle bug that was difficult to spot.

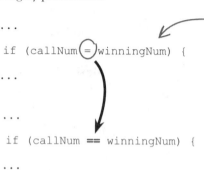

```
...
if (callNum = winningNum) {
...

...
if (callNum == winningNum) {
...
```

CHANGING
= to ==
PULVERIZES
BUG #3.

The real problem with this error is that it doesn't trip up the browser and generate an error like the syntax errors. The JavaScript interpreter didn't complain because an assignment "returns" the value being assigned, in this case winningNum, which is then automatically converted to true (non-zero) in the if test condition. In other words, the code is perfectly legal even though it didn't do what we wanted it to.

So logic errors don't ever show up in a browser's error console?

Logic errors like to fly below the radar.

What makes logic errors such a pain to deal with is that they often don't reveal themselves the way that syntax errors do. Although a script error in a browser may seem a bit deflating, it's really a blessing in disguise because it's a bug that has been detected for you. Logic errors don't violate any JavaScript syntax rules, so they are often tougher to detect.

On the other hand, logic errors do sometimes result in a script error **while** a script is running. For example, if a logic error results in a variable not getting initialized, an "undefined" error will show up when the script tries to reference the variable. So sometimes a logic error will spare you the suffering of an exhausting bug hunt.

BULLET POINTS

- Syntax errors involve code that violates JavaScript language rules, and are usually caught by the JavaScript interpreter.

- Strings must be carefully enclosed within matching quotes or apostrophes.

- Quotes and apostrophes should be mixed (but still in matching pairs) in HTML event handler attributes that contain JavaScript code.

- Alert boxes offer a primitive but useful option for watching variables throughout a script.

- It's a common error to accidentally code a test condition with = when you really mean ==.

there are no Dumb Questions

Q: **Are escape characters only used for escaping quotes and apostrophes?**

A: No, there are several escape characters supported by JavaScript. For example, you can use \t to insert a tab into a string. Similarly, a newline is represented by the \n escape character. And a literal backslash must also be escaped with \\.

One place where escape characters can be used effectively is in formatting the text displayed in an alert box. You can use \t and \n to align text using tabs and control how it flows onto new lines.

Q: **What's the deal with the limitation on escape characters in HTML attributes?**

A: The limitation has to do with the fact that HTML attributes aren't subject to the rules of JavaScript, at least not when it comes to the characters used to bound an attribute value. So while it's fine to escape a character within a JavaScript string that is enclosed in an HTML attribute, it can't be the same character used to enclose the attribute.

If this is still confusing, think about it like this. HTML sees an attribute simply as a value that must appear between quotes or apostrophes. Nothing more. So whichever boundary character you use to start the

attribute, HTML assumes the next one it encounters is its matching partner that closes the attribute value. This happens because HTML doesn't process the attribute value for JavaScript escape characters.

Escape characters do still work within an HTML attribute, provided they don't conflict with the character used to enclose the attribute. This is because the attribute value does eventually get interpreted as JavaScript code, assuming we're talking about an event handler attribute.

Q: **Aren't there fancier debuggers for JavaScript that provide detailed control over the debugging process?**

A: Yes, there are a few out there. And it's not a bad idea at all to investigate them further and consider trying one out. However, understand that good coding habits coupled with the debugging techniques explored in this chapter will go a long way toward helping you create error-free scripts.

Q: **What exactly is happening when JavaScript code tries to reference an undefined variable or function?**

A: Remember that an undefined variable is a variable that has either not been created or that has been created but not set to anything. In both cases the value stored in the variable is unknown, or more specifically, it is undefined. So attempting to read that value and do something meaningful with it makes no sense, which is why JavaScript generates an error.

A similar situation occurs with functions when a function is called but the JavaScript interpreter can't find a function by that name. The function is undefined, which means that calling it makes no sense—there's nothing to call. Again, JavaScript considers it an error because there is no way to meaningfully execute the code.

Q: **What's the deal with the callNum variable turning up as NaN before the if test condition in the radio call-in script?**

A: We still don't know. Although it does tell us that something is still amiss in the script code. So it's important to keep sleuthing for more bugs...

Fireside Chats

Tonight's talk: **Syntax error and Logic error share their love of poor scripting**

Syntax error:

Hey, I've heard of you. I hear you're pretty sneaky. But what I'm wondering is if you enjoy a really badly written script as much as I do?

Logic error:

Oh yeah. There's nothing better than a script that looks fine on the surface, but just barely out of sight are all kinds of strange problems.

I disagree. I like scripts that are a trainwreck right there in plain view. That's where I excel. You sprinkle a few of me throughout a script, and it's guaranteed to make a browser squeal in pain.

But what fun is that? Everybody knows a sneak attack is much more effective. You know, lull them into thinking everything is OK, and then slowly start revealing little problems here and there. If you do a good enough job, they'll be questioning whether or not their browser is even working right.

I can appreciate your twisted way of seeing things, but the problem is that you still allow a script to run. That's no good to me. I like to stop it dead in its tracks.

You've got a point there. It's a shame I haven't figured out a good way to reveal myself by stopping a script like you do. Or even better, crash the whole browser in a big puff of smoke. That would be cool!

It would, but we're unfortunately pretty limited in terms of how much damage we can do. Sure, it's fun to screw up a page and keep it from working right, but I hate that we can't get access to anything else. Boy, what fun I could have with a hard drive full of important data!

Oh man, that would be incredible. You sure there isn't an angle for us to get in there?

Syntax error:

Nah, the JavaScript interpreter has us locked down pretty tight.

No, how does it work?

How do you get away with that?

I have a good one sorta like that where people forget to end each JavaScript statement with a semicolon. It's great because the interpreter will let it slide if the statements are on lines by themselves. But eventually some cocky programmer will try to "optimize" the code and combine the statements onto a single line, and that's when I show up. That one never gets old—I always get a good laugh!

I love it because if the interpreter does notice, then I get to spring into action and shock them with an error. Hey, I'm starting to realize we should think about teaming up—I think we could do more damage that way.

I'm right behind you!

Logic error:

Well, there's still plenty of fun to be had. Did I tell you about my little trick with = and ==?

It's great. The programmer means to type == to compare two values, but they accidentally type = and it does an assignment instead. It's hilarious because they'll go hours without seeing the problem. And the JavaScript interpreter is none the wiser because the code is still technically legit.

Oh, I have loads of them. It's a fine line I walk being just inside the law but still able to stir up trouble.

Hey, that reminds me of one more I have to share. I love it when people decide to change the arguments to a function after they've written the function. It never fails—they'll forget to change all of the calls to the function, which all are supposed to be updated to match the new arguments. If all goes well, the interpreter won't notice and they'll get unexpected results from the bad arguments.

I agree. Let's get started.

Everyone's a loser! (Bug #4)

Owen is starting to realize that this debugging stuff is not as easy as he once thought. With the `if` statement logic error fixed, now the script never declares a winner. So we went from everyone being a winner to everyone now being a loser. Some people's self-esteem will definitely be affected by this bug if Owen doesn't get it fixed quickly.

Caller 1.

Caller 3.

Caller 7.

It seems that everyone has gone from winners to losers since now no one can win.

This is really confusing. I guess I'll use some alert boxes to try and figure out what's still wrong with the call number variable.

This caller should be a winner.

Overwhelmed by annoying alerts

Owen attempts to use alerts to put a watch on the `callNum` variable and try to figure out what's going on. However, he runs into a problem in that it gets tedious having to wade through so many alert boxes en route to the seventh caller. He's tried using several alerts in different parts of the code, but he's just getting overwhelmed with so many less than helpful pop-up windows, and doesn't know where to start...

The drawback to alerts as watch windows is that they can get tedious when used in repetitive code.

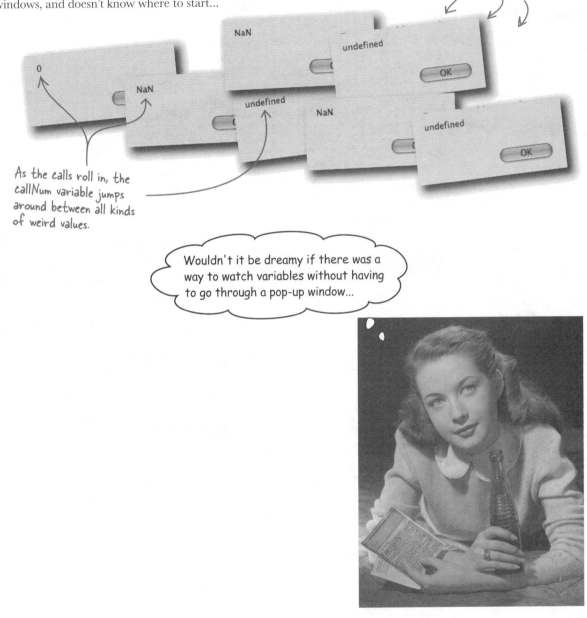

As the calls roll in, the `callNum` variable jumps around between all kinds of weird values.

Wouldn't it be dreamy if there was a way to watch variables without having to go through a pop-up window...

Browser debugging consoles can help

Most browsers have a debugging console, really an **error** console, that is responsible for displaying errors that occur in a script. Error consoles are very useful for finding out when something goes wrong in a script, and in many cases helping to diagnose exactly what went wrong. Firefox in particular has proven to have an excellent error console.

Browser error consoles are great for finding out about script errors, especially syntax errors.

We've already leaned heavily on the Firefox error console to track bugs.

Error consoles are great and all, but how do they help me watch variables?

Error consoles don't really help at all when it comes to watching variables.

As handy as error consoles may be, they don't offer any means of watching variables. But there's good news—it's not outside the realm of possibility to create your own debug console from scratch that can serve as a watch window.

Build a custom console for debugging

The idea of a custom debug console might sound intimidating at first, but all it really has to do is display text when asked. The key is that the console must display the debug information directly on the page, not in an alert box. A separate pop-up window could be used as long as it doesn't require the user to click OK, but it's simpler and just as effective to show the debug messages directly on the page.

Debug messages are displayed just below the main page in a special debug area.

Each line is a different debug message.

BSI Case 2: Winning Caller

Caller name: Next caller | Call

```
callNum: 1
callNum: 2
callNum: 3
callNum: 4
callNum: 5
```

Done

Sharpen your pencil

Imagine a design of a JavaScript debugging console that allows Owen to display debugging messages in a list within a dynamically created area on the page. Draw what you think the necessary components of this design are, and how they fit together, including a custom JavaScript object for the debugging console.

Sharpen your pencil
Solution

The debugging console is designed as an object named DebugConsole that has one property and one method.

Imagine a design of a JavaScript debugging console that allows Owen to display debugging messages in a list within a dynamically created area on the page. Draw what you think the necessary components of this design are, and how they fit together, including a custom JavaScript object for the debugging console.

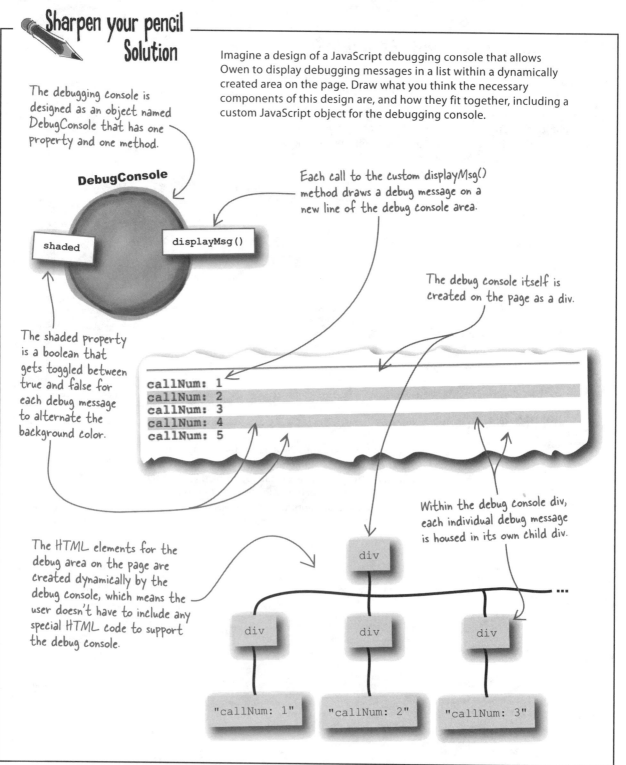

DebugConsole

shaded

displayMsg()

Each call to the custom displayMsg() method draws a debug message on a new line of the debug console area.

The debug console itself is created on the page as a div.

The shaded property is a boolean that gets toggled between true and false for each debug message to alternate the background color.

```
callNum: 1
callNum: 2
callNum: 3
callNum: 4
callNum: 5
```

Within the debug console div, each individual debug message is housed in its own child div.

The HTML elements for the debug area on the page are created dynamically by the debug console, which means the user doesn't have to include any special HTML code to support the debug console.

div

div   div   div   ...

"callNum: 1"   "callNum: 2"   "callNum: 3"

JavaScript Magnets

The code for the debugging console is missing a few pieces.
Fill in the blanks with the code magnets to finish building the
DebugConsole object.

```
function DebugConsole() {
  // Create the debug console area

  var consoleElem = document. ........................... ( ......... );

  consoleElem.id = "debug";
  consoleElem.style.fontFamily = "monospace";
  consoleElem.style.color = "#333333";

  document.body. ..................... (consoleElem);
  consoleElem. ..................... (document. ..................... ("hr"));

  // Create the alternating background color property

  this. ........... = false;

}

DebugConsole.prototype.displayMsg = function(msg) {
  // Create the message
  var msgElement = document.createElement("div");

  msgElement.appendChild(document. ..................... (msg));

  msgElement.style.backgroundColor = this.shaded ? "#EEEEEE" : "#FFFFFF";

  var consoleElem = document.getElementById( ............... );

  consoleElem.appendChild( ............... );

  // Toggle the alternating background color property

  this.shaded = ........ this.shaded;

}
```

```
"div"          msgElement          "debug"          !

shaded     appendChild      createElement     createTextNode
```

JavaScript Magnets Solution

The code for the debugging console is missing a few pieces.
Fill in the blanks with the code magnets to finish building the
DebugConsole object.

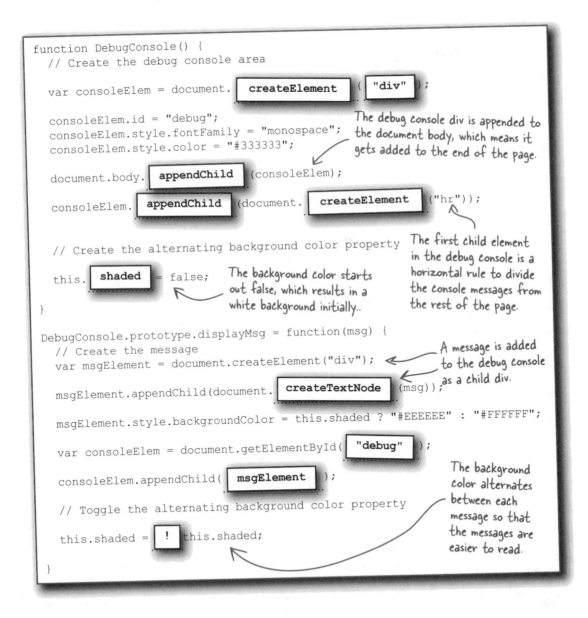

```
function DebugConsole() {
  // Create the debug console area

  var consoleElem = document. createElement ( "div" );

  consoleElem.id = "debug";
  consoleElem.style.fontFamily = "monospace";
  consoleElem.style.color = "#333333";

  document.body. appendChild (consoleElem);

  consoleElem. appendChild (document. createElement ("hr"));


  // Create the alternating background color property

  this. shaded = false;
}

DebugConsole.prototype.displayMsg = function(msg) {
  // Create the message
  var msgElement = document.createElement("div");

  msgElement.appendChild(document. createTextNode (msg));

  msgElement.style.backgroundColor = this.shaded ? "#EEEEEE" : "#FFFFFF";

  var consoleElem = document.getElementById( "debug" );

  consoleElem.appendChild( msgElement );

  // Toggle the alternating background color property

  this.shaded = ! this.shaded;

}
```

The debug console div is appended to the document body, which means it gets added to the end of the page.

The first child element in the debug console is a horizontal rule to divide the console messages from the rest of the page.

The background color starts out false, which results in a white background initially..

A message is added to the debug console as a child div.

The background color alternates between each message so that the messages are easier to read.

Debug your debugger

Owen can't wait to put the new debug console through its paces to find out what's still wrong with the radio call-in script. So he imports the **debug.js** file into the page and creates the DebugConsole object in the head of the page.

```
<script type="text/javascript">

    // Debug console global variable

    var console = new DebugConsole();

    ...
```

This code creates the DebugConsole object as a global variable in the head of the page.

Unfortunately, things don't go as planned. When he first attempts to use the debug console, Owen learns that he has compounded his problems by introducing an entirely new bug of his own into the new debug console.

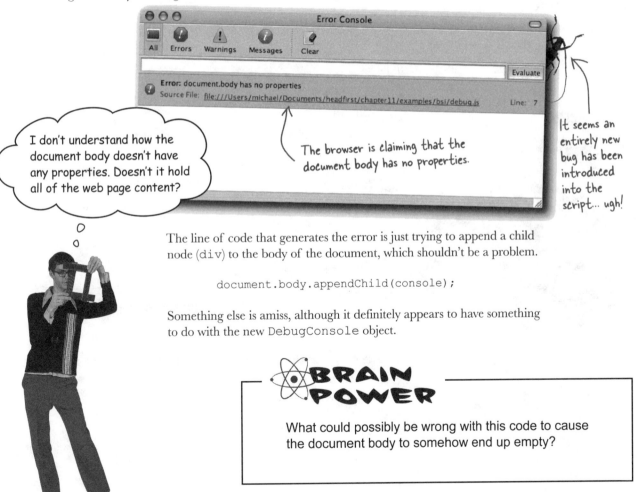

Error Console

All | Errors | Warnings | Messages | Clear

Evaluate

Error: document.body has no properties
Source File: file:///Users/michael/Documents/headfirst/chapter11/examples/bsi/debug.js   Line: 7

The browser is claiming that the document body has no properties.

It seems an entirely new bug has been introduced into the script... ugh!

> I don't understand how the document body doesn't have any properties. Doesn't it hold all of the web page content?

The line of code that generates the error is just trying to append a child node (div) to the body of the document, which shouldn't be a problem.

```
document.body.appendChild(console);
```

Something else is amiss, although it definitely appears to have something to do with the new DebugConsole object.

⚛ BRAIN POWER

What could possibly be wrong with this code to cause the document body to somehow end up empty?

Waiting on the page

The problem with the debug console has to do with the timing of how a
page loads and when script code has access to the body of the page.

The head of the page is
loaded before the body, so
none of the body content
is available at this point.

The HTML elements that
actually reside on the page
aren't loaded until the body
loads... after the head.

Ah, so script code that
runs in the head of the
page can't access HTML
elements on the page.

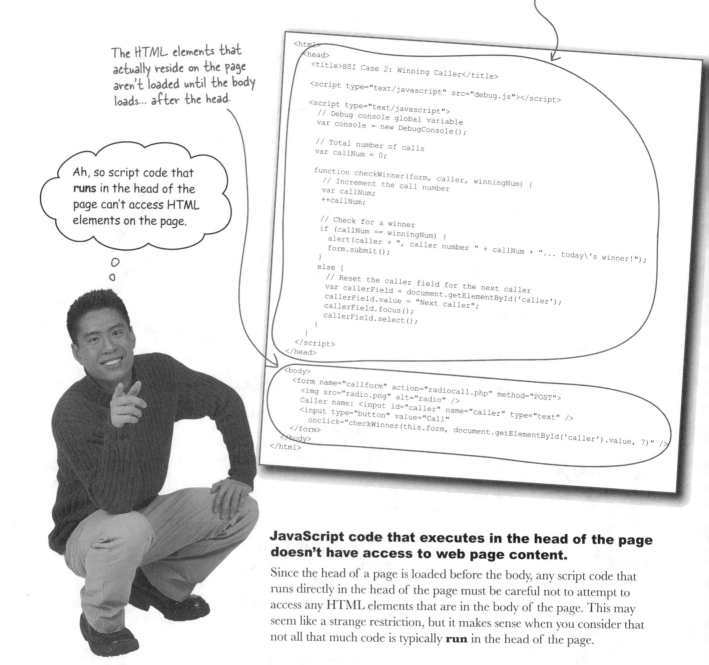

```html
<html>
  <head>
    <title>BSI Case 2: Winning Caller</title>

    <script type="text/javascript" src="debug.js"></script>

    <script type="text/javascript">
      // Debug console global variable
      var console = new DebugConsole();

      // Total number of calls
      var callNum = 0;

      function checkWinner(form, caller, winningNum) {
        // Increment the call number
        var callNum;
        ++callNum;

        // Check for a winner
        if (callNum == winningNum) {
          alert(caller + ", caller number " + callNum + "... today\'s winner!");
          form.submit();
        }
        else {
          // Reset the caller field for the next caller
          var callerField = document.getElementById('caller');
          callerField.value = "Next caller";
          callerField.focus();
          callerField.select();
        }
      }
    </script>
  </head>

  <body>
    <form name="callform" action="radiocall.php" method="POST">
      <img src="radio.png" alt="radio" />
      Caller name: <input id="caller" name="caller" type="text" />
      <input type="button" value="Call"
        onclick="checkWinner(this.form, document.getElementById('caller').value, 7)" />
    </form>
  </body>
</html>
```

JavaScript code that executes in the head of the page doesn't have access to web page content.

Since the head of a page is loaded before the body, any script code that
runs directly in the head of the page must be careful not to attempt to
access any HTML elements that are in the body of the page. This may
seem like a strange restriction, but it makes sense when you consider that
not all that much code is typically **run** in the head of the page.

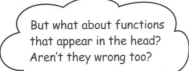

But what about functions that appear in the head? Aren't they wrong too?

Not all code in the head of a page is <u>executed</u> in the head of the page.

Placing code in a function that appears in the head of a page is not the same as **running** the code in the head of the page—function code doesn't run until the function is called. But code that is placed outside of a function is executed immediately when the header is loaded. This is the code that can cause problems.

In the case of the `DebugConsole` object, it can't be created directly in the head of the page because its constructor is very much dependent on content in the body of the page.

Sharpen your pencil

Write down when and where you think the `DebugConsole` object should be created to make sure that it can safely access elements on the page.

....

....

....

....

....

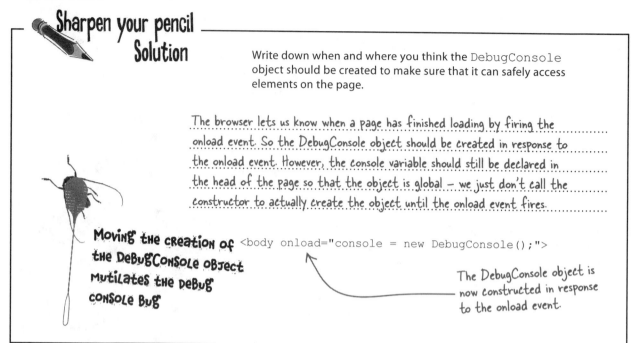

Sharpen your pencil Solution

Write down when and where you think the DebugConsole object should be created to make sure that it can safely access elements on the page.

The browser lets us know when a page has finished loading by firing the onload event. So the DebugConsole object should be created in response to the onload event. However, the console variable should still be declared in the head of the page so that the object is global — we just don't call the constructor to actually create the object until the onload event fires.

MoviNg the cReatioN of the DeBugConsole oBject MutiLates the DeBug console Bug

```
<body onload="console = new DebugConsole();">
```

The DebugConsole object is now constructed in response to the onload event.

The peskiest errors of all: runtime

The unloaded document body problem is an example of a **runtime error**—an error that only shows its face in certain conditions while a script is actually running. Sometimes runtime errors only surface under very specific circumstances, such as a certain type of user input or a certain number of loop iterations taking place. Runtime errors are often the toughest errors of all to find because they are so difficult to predict. Sometimes it's a challenge just reproducing a runtime error when someone else encounters it.

Runtime errors occur only because of specific conditions that take place while a script is running.

Error Console

All	Errors	Warnings	Messages	Clear

Evaluate

Error: document.body has no properties
Source File: file:///Users/michael/Documents/headfirst/chapter11/examples/bsi/debug.js   Line: 7

The debug console bug was a runtime error caused by attempting to access data before it had been loaded, which is an issue that is only revealed when a script is run.

The JavaScript bug trifecta

Along with runtime errors, two other errors we saw earlier round out the JavaScript bug trifecta: syntax errors, logic errors, and runtime errors. Any of these kinds of errors are capable of manifesting themselves in any script, often at the same time! Understanding their differences is an important part of being able to successfully find and eradicate them.

Syntax error

An error resulting from a violation of the rules of the JavaScript language, meaning that the code is unfit to run in the JavaScript intepreter.

Runtime error

An error revealed only by runtime conditions, such as the user entering a certain kind of data into a form that the script can't handle or attempting to access an object before it has been created or initialized.

Logic error

An error caused by bad logic, often involving code that is intended to do one thing but is accidentally coded to do something else. Some code with logic errors performs exactly as intended, in which case the programmer misunderstood the task to begin with.

```html
<html>
  <head>
    <title>BSI Case 2: Winning Caller</title>

    <script type="text/javascript" src="debug.js"></script>

    <script type="text/javascript">
      // Debug console global variable
      var console = new DebugConsole();

      // Total number of calls
      var callNum = 0;

      function checkWinner(form, caller, winningNum) {
        // Increment the call number
        var callNum;
        ++callNum;

        console.displayMsg("callNum: " + callNum);

        // Check for a winner
        if (callNum = winningNum) {
          alert(caller + ", caller number " + callNum + "... today's winner!");
          form.submit();
        }
        else {
```

Exercise

Write down the type of error for each of the following error descriptions.

Missing parentheses around the test condition of an if statement.   ....

Forgetting to initialize a counter variable to 0.   ....

Creating a loop that loops beyond the last element in an array.   ....

Forgetting to close a function with a closing curly brace.   ....

Write down the type of error for each of the following error descriptions.

Exercise

Missing parentheses around the test condition of an if statement.　　Syntax

Forgetting to initialize a counter variable to 0.　　Logic

Creating a loop that loops beyond the last element in an array.　　Runtime

Forgetting to close a function with a closing curly brace.　　Syntax

> The call number is showing up as "not a number." That's pretty strange...

It's not a num-bah

With the debug console finally up and running, it's now possible to take a look at the callNum variable as the calls come in without having to sift through all those alerts. And as it turns out, an old problem Owen ignored has finally come home to roost. The callNum variable is showing up as NaN, which means it isn't a number. But why isn't it?

```
console.displayMsg("callNum: " + callNum);
```

A single line of code sets up a watch on the callNum variable.

At least the debug console is working!

```
BSI Case 2: Winning Caller

Caller name: [Next caller]    [Call]

callNum:  NaN
callNum:  NaN
callNum:  NaN
callNum:  NaN
callNum:  NaN

Done
```

When watching isn't enough

Sometimes watching a variable creates more questions than answers. Why is `callNum` not a number? Why is it not getting incremented? What's the point of this debug console if it only confirms what you already know...that there's a problem. So how do we go about finding out specifically what it is?

What now?

> It might help to try eliminating code until the call number changes in value.

Removing code is a great way to simplify a script while hunting down bugs.

Sometimes less is more when it comes to JavaScript debugging. In this case, removing code and watching to see what changes is an excellent idea. But just deleting code doesn't sound all that appetizing since the vast majority of it will remain as is when you're finished debugging. We really need a way to **disable** code, as opposed to truly removing it.

Comments as temporary code disablers

Hiding executable code inside comments is an extremely handy way to disable the code while debugging. This allows code to be selectively pulled out of the execution of a script without actually deleting the code. Think of commenting out code as a means of subtracting lines or chunks of code as needed to help isolate a bug.

Comments are extremely useful for temporarily disabling code.

```
function checkWinner(form, caller, winningNum) {
  console.displayMsg("callNum: " + callNum);

/*
  // Increment the call number
  var callNum;
  ++callNum;

  // Check for a winner
  if (callNum == winningNum) {
    alert(caller + ", caller number " + callNum + "... today\'s
winner!");
    form.submit();
  }
  else {
    // Reset the caller field for the next caller
    var callerField = document.getElementById('caller');
    callerField.value = "Next caller";
    callerField.focus();
    callerField.select();
  }
*/
}
```

> Hey, the call number is now showing up as 0. So something in the disabled code is turning it into "not a number."

This multiline comment disables everything in the function but the code that displays the debug message.

The callNum variable is now 0, which means something in the disabled code is trashing it.

BSI Case 2: Winning Caller

Caller name: [   ] Call

callNum: 0
callNum: 0
callNum: 0
callNum: 0
callNum: 0

Done

BRAIN POWER

What do you think will happen if only the line of code that increments the call number is added back?

Problem solved...sort of

By switching to single-line comments, it becomes possible to be more selective about the code that is disabled. If the line of code that increments the `callNum` variable is added back, the `callNum` variable starts working as it should. So one of the remaining lines of disabled code is causing the problem.

Single-line comments are used so that individual lines can be enabled and disabled.

```
function checkWinner(form, caller, winningNum) {
  console.displayMsg("callNum: " + callNum);

  // Increment the call number
//  var callNum;
  ++callNum;

  // Check for a winner
//  if (callNum == winningNum) {
//    alert(caller + ", caller number " + callNum + "... today\'s
winner!");
```

Uncommenting the increment line of code finally gets the callNum variable working.

BSI Case 2: Winning Caller

Caller name: [   ]   Call

```
callNum: 1
callNum: 2
callNum: 3
callNum: 4
callNum: 5
```

Done

```
ld for the next caller
ument.getElementById('caller');
Next caller";
```

The callNum variable finally works like it's supposed to, incrementing with each call.

Sharpen your pencil

Write down what's wrong with the callNum bug in the debug console, along with how to fix it.

....
....
....
....
....
....

Sharpen your pencil Solution

Write down what's wrong with the callNum bug in the debug console, along with how to fix it.

Another variable named callNum is accidentally created as a local variable using var inside the checkWinner() function. So the callNum local variable "hides" the callNum global variable, creating a subtle problem to detect. Since the local variable isn't initialized, incrementing it and then comparing it to the winning number results in "not a number." The fix is to just remove the line inside the function that creates the local callNum variable with var.

KiLLiNG the LiNE of code that creates the LOCaL VaRiaBLE OBLiteRates BuG #4.

```
// Increment the call number
var callNum;
++callNum;
```

By removing the line of code that accidentally creates a local variable named callNum, the function uses the global callNum variable, as originally intended.

The dangers of shadowy variables

The `callNum` bug in the radio call-in script is an example of a **shadow variable**, which is a variable that accidentally hides another variable with the same name. The problem arises when a local variable is created with the same name as a global variable. JavaScript creates the local variable and gives it precedence in the local block of code. So any changes made to the local variable do not carry over to the global variable—the local variable effectively casts a shadow over the global variable, temporarily hiding it from the script.

A shadow variable occurs when local and global variables are created with the same name...not good!

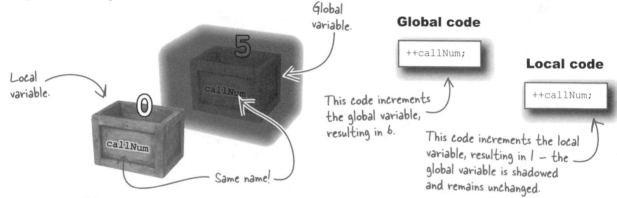

Global variable.

Local variable.

Same name!

Global code

```
++callNum;
```

This code increments the global variable, resulting in 6.

Local code

```
++callNum;
```

This code increments the local variable, resulting in 1 — the global variable is shadowed and remains unchanged.

there are no
Dumb Questions

Q: **When commenting out code to track down bugs, how do I know how much code to disable?**

A: This is a judgment call that you'll get better at as you get more experienced with JavaScript debugging. However, it's never wrong to err on the side of disabling most, if not all of the code near a problematic area of a script. And if a really nasty problem arises, don't hesitate to disable all of the script code on a page. And also don't forget to temporarily remove any import tags that pull external code into the page.

There is another approach that can work if you've already isolated a bug to a particular section of script code. This approach involves disabling a line of code at a time until the bug goes away. So instead of disabling everything and slowly enabling code until the bug

appears, you slowly disable the code a line at a time until the bug **disappears**. The former approach works better if you're clueless about where a bug is located, while the latter approach works better if you've isolated the bug's location to some degree.

Q: **What if I intend to create a shadow variable? Is it OK then?**

A: That's like asking if you **intend** to break your leg, is it OK? And the answer is no. Just because you deliberately bring pain and suffering onto yourself doesn't somehow make it acceptable. Besides, there's plenty of hurt to go around in debugging code that is intended to work perfectly, so you shouldn't be gunning to up the risk factor deliberately. So the real answer to the question is that shadow variables introduce such confusion and sneakiness in JavaScript code that they should be avoided in all situations.

Case closed!

With a healthy dose of patience and some help from his new debugging skills., Owen closes the case and bags a promotion to JavaScript Detective at Bug Scene Investigators.

Case closed!

Detective Owen, grizzled JavaScript debugging sleuth

```
BSI Case 2: Winning Caller

        Caller name: Alan              [ Call ]

callNum: 1
callNum: 2
callNum: 3
callNum: 4
callNum: 5                 Alan, caller number 7...today's winner!
callNum: 6
callNum: 7
                                                  ( OK )

Done
```

The bug free radio call-in script is complete with a working debug console.

Owen's bug-squashing checklist

Make sure parentheses are always matched in pairs.

Make sure curly braces around blocks of code are always matched in pairs - careful indentation of code helps in matching pairs of curly braces.

Try hard to avoid typos in identifier names—both variables and functions can cause big problems if their names aren't used consistently.

Be consistent with the use of quotes and apostrophes, and carefully mix the two in HTML attributes if necessary.

Use escape characters to code characters that have a special meaning in strings, such as a quote (\") or an apostrophe (\').

Never, ever, ever use = when you mean ==. JavaScript probably won't see it as an error but your code will not work as intended.

Make sure an object has been created before attempting to access it—this primarily applies to web page elements, which aren't created until just before the onload event is triggered.

Don't ever name local variables and global variables the same thing because the local variable will shadow the global one, resulting in some very unpredictable behavior.

JavaScriptcross

Before you turn your newfound respect of bugs into
an ant farm purchase, try your hand at this puzzle.

Across

2. Use this to quickly take a peek at a variable.
4. Use apostrophes mixed with these when placing JavaScript strings in HTML attributes.
7. The special window browsers use to display errors.
10. An error that violates JavaScript language rules.
12. An error that gives the wrong result despite being perfectly legal in JavaScript.
13. A variable that hasn't been assigned a value is ....
14. The custom object Owen created to battle bugs.

Down

1. Use these to temporarily disable code.
3. Make one of these on a variable name and there will be problems.
5. The current Web browser of choice for JavaScript debugging.
6. Miss one of these surrounding a block of code and you'll have trouble.
8. The number of bug fragments allowed in a chocolate bar.
9. An error that only reveals itself when a script is running.
11. Use this to code special characters in strings.

 JavaScriptcross Solution

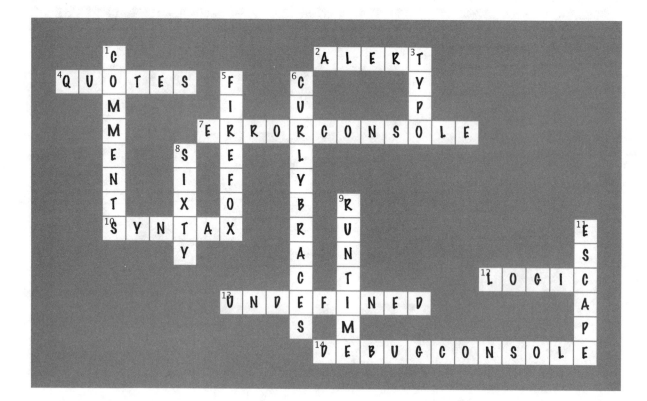

Page Bender

Fold the page vertically to line up the two brains and solve the riddle.

What do all JavaScript bugs deserve?

It's a meeting of the minds!

Cases closed!

Case 1
CLOSED

Case 2
CLOSED

Hey, it's cool... I'm not a bug. Honest.

Turning the other cheek is an erroneous approach that might overload your tolerance for bugs. The overall ickiness of bugs will cause the debilitation of your code, which is a problem.

12 dynamic data

Touchy-Feely Web Applications

Don't let my eyes fool you. Behind this pretty face is raw emotion just waiting to get out. In fact, my dynamic personality is my biggest asset.

The modern Web is a very responsive place where pages are expected to react to the user's every whim. Or at least that's the dream of many web users and developers. JavaScript plays a vital role in this dream through a programming technique known as **Ajax** that provides a mechanism for dramatically changing the "feel" of web pages. With Ajax, web pages act much more like full-blown applications since they are able to **quickly load and save data dynamically** while **responding to the user in real time** without any page refreshes or browser trickery.

Yearning for dynamic data

Remember Ruby, cube puzzle afficionado and blogger? Ruby loves her JavaScript-powered YouCube blog but she is frustrated with having to edit the HTML file for the entire page just to add new entries. She'd like to be able to somehow separate the blog entries from the HTML code that describes the blog page, freeing her up to focus on the blog content itself.

Adding new blog entries to YouCube shouldn't require editing the web page.

I'd *really* like to be able to add new blog entries without having to edit HTML code.

Frustrated blogger and cube dreamer, Ruby.

Adding a new blog entry requires Ruby to edit the HTML file for the YouCube web page.

A data-driven YouCube

Ruby's files for the data-driven pages are available at http://www.headfirstlabs.com/books/hfjs/.

Ruby is onto something. A version of her blog that separates blog content from web page structure involves dynamic data, data that is fed into a page dynamically as the page is processed by the browser. Web pages built out of dynamic data are known as **data-driven** pages because the page really just defines a structure that gets filled out by the data. In other words, the data is in charge of the page's content.

The blog data is stored in a physically separate file that can be edited without touching the web page.

Blog data

Web page

The web page contains HTML code for web page structure plus JavaScript code for incorporating dynamic blog data into the page.

JavaScript is responsible for processing the blog data and blending it into a final HTML Web page.

The blog entries are fed to the blog page from a separate file.

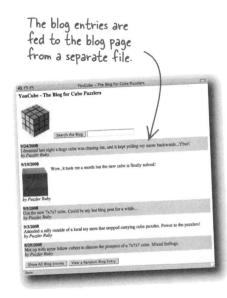

With the help of JavaScript, raw blog data is dynamically merged with HTML code to generate a final YouCube page that looks identical to the original. But this data-driven page is assembled from separate parts: the structural page and the blog data. With the blog data broken out into its own file, Ruby is free to manipulate the blog content separate from the HTML, CSS, and JavaScript code for the web page.

Ruby only has to edit this file to update her new data-driven blog.

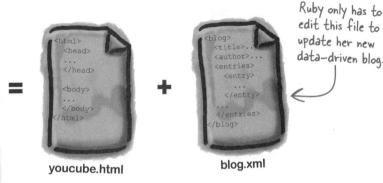

youcube.html   blog.xml

Dynamic data sounds pretty complicated. I bet it requires a bunch of messy JavaScript code, right?

Dynamic data requires a little more coding effort up front but it pays huge returns on the back end.

Although a page driven by dynamic data certainly requires some additional planning and effort up front, it more than pays for itself in the long run with quick and easy page updates. Besides, JavaScript has built-in support for dynamic data thanks to a nifty programming technique dubbed Ajax.

Ajax is all about communication

Ajax makes dynamic data possible by allowing for tiny "conversations" between the client web browser and web server. More specifically, a script is able to ask the server for some data, like a collection of blog entries, and the server delivers it using Ajax. The script then takes the blog data and dynamically incorporates it into the page.

Ajax allows a web page to dynamically receive data from a web server.

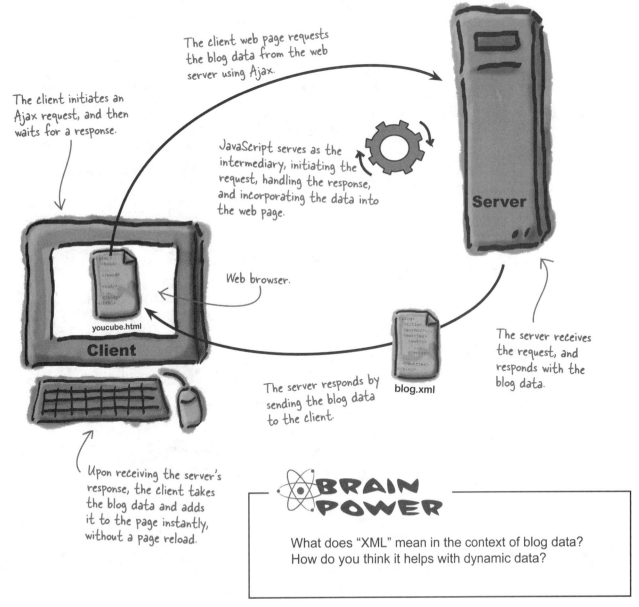

The client web page requests the blog data from the web server using Ajax.

The client initiates an Ajax request, and then waits for a response.

JavaScript serves as the intermediary, initiating the request, handling the response, and incorporating the data into the web page.

Server

Web browser.

youcube.html

Client

The server receives the request, and responds with the blog data.

The server responds by sending the blog data to the client.

blog.xml

Upon receiving the server's response, the client takes the blog data and adds it to the page instantly, without a page reload.

⚛ **BRAIN POWER**

What does "XML" mean in the context of blog data? How do you think it helps with dynamic data?

An HTML for everything: XML

The "ML" in HTML stands for **markup language**, and it refers to the fact that HTML uses tags and attributes to create hypertext (the "HT"). Just as HTML is used to create hypertext web pages, XML is another markup language that is used to create, well, anything you want. That's what the "X" means—anything! The idea is that there are all kinds of data that could benefit from being stored as tags and attributes. So why not extend the reach of markup languages to solve other data problems?

XML is a markup language used to format _any_ kind of data.

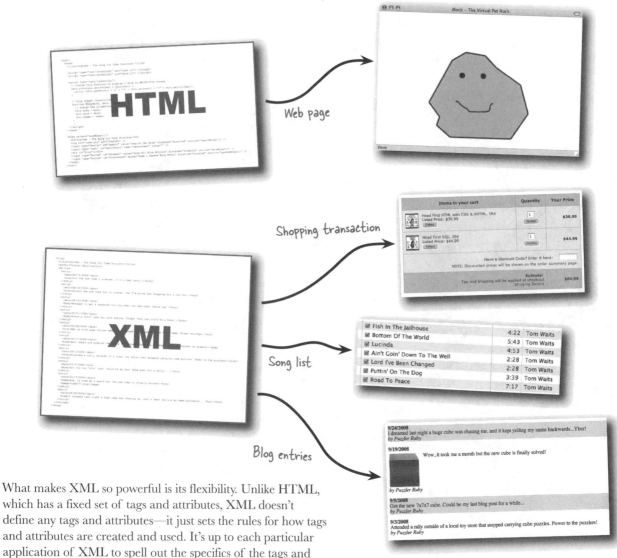

What makes XML so powerful is its flexibility. Unlike HTML, which has a fixed set of tags and attributes, XML doesn't define any tags and attributes—it just sets the rules for how tags and attributes are created and used. It's up to each particular application of XML to spell out the specifics of the tags and attributes that represent the specific data.

XML lets you tag YOUR data YOUR way

The real beauty of XML is that it can turn anyone into a custom tagmaker by using a little tag and attribute alchemy to cook up an entirely custom markup language for any purpose. There are certainly lots of existing XML languages that have already been created to solve lots of different problems, and it's not a bad idea to use one of those if it happens to fit your needs. But creating a custom markup language of your very own is a tough temptation to resist.

Similar to HTML code, this XML code consists of a hierarchy of elements.

```
<movie>
    <title>Gleaming the Cube</title>
    <releaseDate>01/13/1989</releaseDate>
    <director>Graeme Clifford</director>
    <summary>A skateboarder investigates the death of his adopted brother.</summary>
</movie>
```

Each aspect of the movie is stored within its own unique tag.

The movie details are contained within the <movie> tag.

Even though you've never seen this example XML markup language, which is entirely custom, the descriptive tags make it possible to decipher the data. Even more importantly, the tags are very specific to the data being stored—it just makes sense to use a tag named `<director>` when storing the director of a movie!

Exercise

Match the following tags with their descriptions, and then write down next to each description if the tag is an HTML or XML tag.

....	`<itunes:author>`	Bold text in a web page.
....	`<span>`	The title of an online news feed.
....	`<title>`	An input control in a web page.
....	`<strong>`	Text that is converted to speech for a telephone caller.
....	`<input>`	The artist of an iTunes podcast.
....	`<prompt>`	Inline content in a web page.

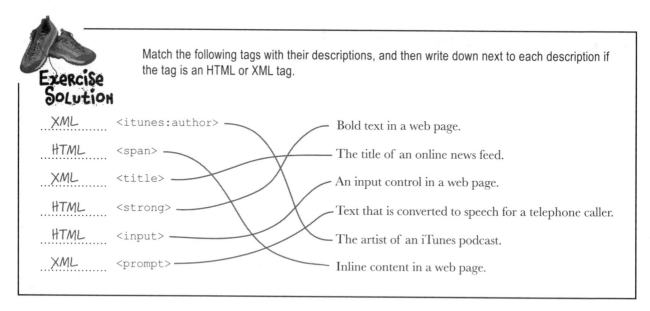

Match the following tags with their descriptions, and then write down next to each description if the tag is an HTML or XML tag.

Exercise Solution

XML	`<itunes:author>`	Bold text in a web page.
HTML	`<span>`	The title of an online news feed.
XML	`<title>`	An input control in a web page.
HTML	`<strong>`	Text that is converted to speech for a telephone caller.
HTML	`<input>`	The artist of an iTunes podcast.
XML	`<prompt>`	Inline content in a web page.

XML is just text

Similar to HTML, XML data is **just text**, which means it is stored in a normal plain text file. However, XML files are named with a **.xml** file extension, as opposed to the .html or .htm extensions used in HTML files.

XML data is typically stored in files with a .xml file extension.

So the data-driven version of YouCube can be updated by editing an XML document... cool!

```
<blog>
   <title>..
   <author>...
   <entries>
      <entry>
         ...
      </entry>
   ...
   </entries>
</blog>
```

blog.xml

XML + HTML = XHTML

They may have different file extensions but XML and HTML have a very important connection, and it's called XHTML. XHTML is a modern version of HTML that follows the stricter rules of XML. For example, every starting tag in an XHTML web page must have a closing tag. HTML plays fast and loose with its syntax, meaning that you can get away without pairing up tags such as <p> and </p>. XHTML isn't so forgiving, and requires such tags to always appear as matched pairs.

XHTML is a version of HTML that adheres to the more rigid syntax rules of XML.

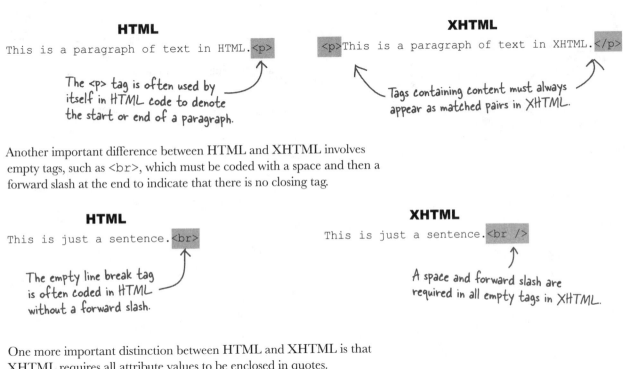

HTML

This is a paragraph of text in HTML.`<p>`

The <p> tag is often used by itself in HTML code to denote the start or end of a paragraph.

XHTML

`<p>`This is a paragraph of text in XHTML.`</p>`

Tags containing content must always appear as matched pairs in XHTML.

Another important difference between HTML and XHTML involves empty tags, such as <br>, which must be coded with a space and then a forward slash at the end to indicate that there is no closing tag.

HTML

This is just a sentence.`<br>`

The empty line break tag is often coded in HTML without a forward slash.

XHTML

This is just a sentence.`<br />`

A space and forward slash are required in all empty tags in XHTML.

One more important distinction between HTML and XHTML is that XHTML requires all attribute values to be enclosed in quotes.

HTML

<a href=`home.html`>Go home</a>

The attribute value isn't in quotes, which violates the rules of XHTML.

XHTML

<a href="`home.html`">Go home</a>

All XHTML attribute values must appear within quotes.

Although XHTML doesn't directly factor into Ruby's immediate needs in terms of modeling blog data in XML, it does illuminate some of the most important syntax rules of XML, which apply to all XML-based languages, including Ruby's custom blog data language.

Fireside Chats

Tonight's talk: **HTML and XML drop the dime on web data**

The latest version of HTML has been reformulated using XML, and is called XHTML.

XHTML:

You know, you've really made things confusing for me. Here I am the backbone of the Web, and now many people are confused about me thanks to you.

But you're still no good without me because browsers only display HTML code. They don't even know what to make of you.

How is that possible? Who cares about data with no appearance?

All that stuff can be seen thanks to me—it's all right there on the Web.

I see. So are you suggesting that we actually work together?

That's a huge relief!

XML:

It's not my fault that you have tunnel vision, always thinking about web pages. I broadened my mind, and in doing so I can represent any kind of data.

Hey, I'm a mysterious fella. The truth is I'm a man without a face—all substance and no appearance. I need you when it comes time to reveal myself.

Wow, you really don't get out much, do you? The rest of the world operates on data that can't be seen the majority of the time. Bank transactions, political polls, weather conditions, you name it.

That's true, but how do you think it gets stored before it makes it to a web browser? Not as paragraphs and tables, I can tell you that. It often gets stored using me because I provide lots of structure and context—I make data easy to process.

Absolutely! I have no concept of what data looks like. Instead, I focus on what it **means**. As long as people keep using web browsers, I'll continue to need your help displaying the data I represent.

XML and the YouCube blog data

XHTML is a great application of XML that is rapidly improving the structure and reliability of web pages. With respect to the YouCube blog, however, Ruby needs a custom XML language that models her specific blog data. This requires assessing the different data required of the blog, and considering how it might fit into the context of hierarchical XML tags.

```
<blog>
  <title> ——          YouCube - The Blog for Cube Puzzlers
  <author> ——          Blog.prototype.signature = "by Puzzler Ruby";
  <entries>
    <entry>
      <date> ——        blog[0] = new Blog("Got the new cube I ordered. It's a real pearl.",
      <body> ——          new Date("08/14/2008"));
```

Sharpen your pencil

Invent your own XML language for storing a blog, and use the language to code a blog entry. Items such as title, date, author, and the entry itself should be considered.

```
<blog>
.................................................................
.................................................................
.................................................................
.................................................................
.................................................................
.................................................................
.................................................................
.................................................................
</blog>
```

Sharpen your pencil Solution

Invent your own XML language for storing a blog, and use the language to code a blog entry. Items such as title, date, author, and the entry itself should be considered.

The entire blog is contained inside the `<blog>` tag.

```
<blog>
    <title>YouCube — The Blog for Cube Puzzlers</title>
    <author>Puzzler Ruby</author>
    <entries>
        <entry>
            <date>11/14/2007</date>
            <body>Got the new cube I ordered. It's a real pearl.</body>
        </entry>
    </entries>
</blog>
```

The `<title>` tag houses the blog title.

Guess what tag holds the blog author?

The collection of blog entries is stored within the `<entries>` tag.

Each blog entry is represented by the `<entry>` tag.

The date and body of each blog entry have their own respective tags.

there are no Dumb Questions

Q: Why not just store blog data as regular unformatted text?

A: You could but then it would put a huge burden on the script code to sift through the data and try to break it apart into separate blog entries with their own dates and bodies. XML adds a predictable structure to data so that you can easily distinguish between separate fields of data, such as unique blog entries with their own dates and bodies, not to mention the title and author of the blog itself.

Q: Is the `<entries>` tag really necessary in the XML blog data?

A: It isn't strictly necessary but it does make the data format more structured and easier to understand. For example, without the `<entries>` tag in the previous blog data, it would be impossible to tell that the blog format is capable of supporting multiple `<entry>` tags but only one `<title>` and `<author>` tag. The `<entries>` tag implies that there is a collection of multiple blog entries, which gives the data more structure and makes it more obvious how the data should be used.

Q: What is the connection between XML and Ajax?

A: Ajax was once taken to be an acronym for **A**synchronous **J**avaScript **A**nd **X**ML, so XML was at one point directly tied to Ajax. That acronym is now considered passé, as the role of Ajax has widened to not always require XML as part of the equation. But the reality is that XML still forms the basis of most Ajax applications because it provides such a great mechanism for modeling data.

As we find out later in the chapter, there is a connection between Ajax and XML in the way that JavaScript supports Ajax. JavaScript doesn't lock you into using XML as a data format for carrying out Ajax requests and responses, but it does make them much easier when handling all but the most trivial of data. So although Ajax purists may claim that XML and Ajax have no real connection to one another, in practical terms they usually go hand in hand. The old acronym still rings true most of the time even if it has fallen out of favor. We'll explore the "asynchronous" part of the acronym a bit later.

I still don't get it. How does storing data in a special format make it dynamic?

XML alone isn't dynamic but it happens to mesh quite well with both Ajax and the DOM.

XML is the data format most commonly used with Ajax, and therefore is the logical candidate for representing blog data that will be sent back and forth from server to client in the data-driven version of YouCube. It's the highly structured nature of XML that makes it so ideal for shuttling data.

And XML's similarity to HTML (XHTML) makes it possible to use the DOM to access XML data as a tree of nodes. This means you can write JavaScript code that traverses a tree of XML nodes, carefully isolating desired data, and then incorporating it into a web page dynamically. It's all these things and more that make XML a great data storage solution for building dynamic, data-driven pages.

Injecting YouCube with Ajax

With a shiny new XML blog document in hand, Ruby is ready to dynamically load it into the YouCube page with the help of Ajax.

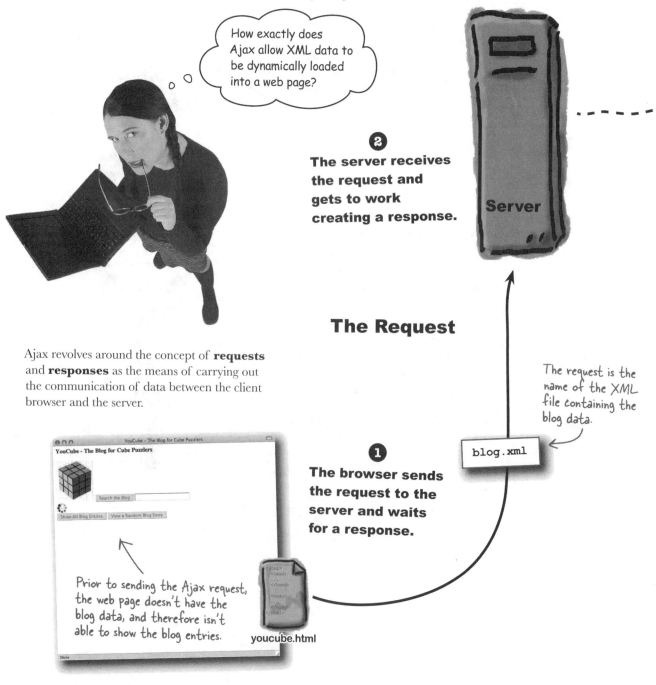

How exactly does Ajax allow XML data to be dynamically loaded into a web page?

❷
The server receives the request and gets to work creating a response.

Server

The Request

Ajax revolves around the concept of **requests** and **responses** as the means of carrying out the communication of data between the client browser and the server.

The request is the name of the XML file containing the blog data.

blog.xml

❶
The browser sends the request to the server and waits for a response.

Prior to sending the Ajax request, the web page doesn't have the blog data, and therefore isn't able to show the blog entries.

youcube.html

3

The server creates a response for the browser by packaging up the data in the blog file.

The entire contents of the XML blog file are returned in the Ajax response.

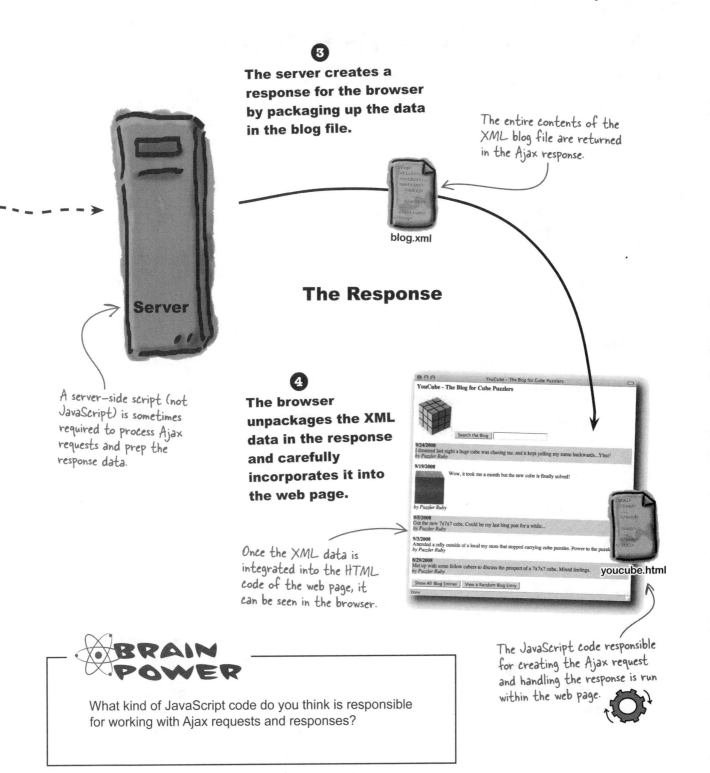

blog.xml

The Response

A server-side script (not JavaScript) is sometimes required to process Ajax requests and prep the response data.

4

The browser unpackages the XML data in the response and carefully incorporates it into the web page.

Once the XML data is integrated into the HTML code of the web page, it can be seen in the browser.

youcube.html

The JavaScript code responsible for creating the Ajax request and handling the response is run within the web page.

BRAIN POWER

What kind of JavaScript code do you think is responsible for working with Ajax requests and responses?

JavaScript to the Ajax rescue: XMLHttpRequest

JavaScript includes a built-in object called XMLHttpRequest that is used to initiate Ajax requests and handle Ajax responses. This object is fairly complex, containing several different methods and properties that work together to support Ajax.

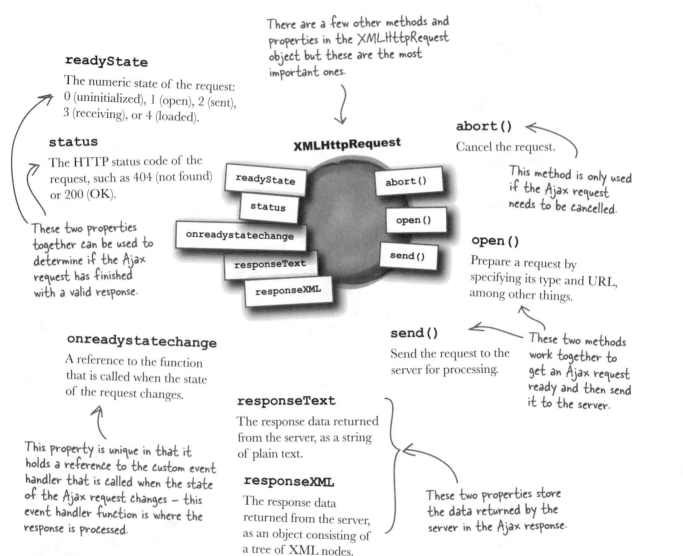

readyState

The numeric state of the request: 0 (uninitialized), 1 (open), 2 (sent), 3 (receiving), or 4 (loaded).

status

The HTTP status code of the request, such as 404 (not found) or 200 (OK).

These two properties together can be used to determine if the Ajax request has finished with a valid response.

There are a few other methods and properties in the XMLHttpRequest object but these are the most important ones.

XMLHttpRequest

readyState

status

onreadystatechange

responseText

responseXML

abort()

open()

send()

abort()

Cancel the request.

This method is only used if the Ajax request needs to be cancelled.

open()

Prepare a request by specifying its type and URL, among other things.

send()

Send the request to the server for processing.

These two methods work together to get an Ajax request ready and then send it to the server.

onreadystatechange

A reference to the function that is called when the state of the request changes.

This property is unique in that it holds a reference to the custom event handler that is called when the state of the Ajax request changes — this event handler function is where the response is processed.

responseText

The response data returned from the server, as a string of plain text.

responseXML

The response data returned from the server, as an object consisting of a tree of XML nodes.

These two properties store the data returned by the server in the Ajax response.

XMLHttpRequest is pretty complex

The XMLHttpRequest is incredibly powerful and also surprisingly flexible. But with that power and flexibility comes **complexity**, meaning that even the most basic of Ajax requests requires a fair amount of JavaScript code. This is thanks in part to browser inconsistencies, but it also doesn't help that the different options available for fine-tuning the object's behavior can be confusing when all you really need to do is quickly move some data dynamically.

The XMLHttpRequest object is powerful but also somewhat of a pain to use.

As an example, consider that the following code is necessary just to create an XMLHttpRequest object that will work across a variety of browsers:

```
var request = null;
if (window.XMLHttpRequest) {
  try {
    request = new XMLHttpRequest();
  } catch(e) {
    request = null;
  }
// Now try the ActiveX (IE) version
} else if (window.ActiveXObject) {
  try {
    request = new ActiveXObject("Msxml2.XMLHTTP");
  // Try the older ActiveX object for older versions of IE
  } catch(e) {
    try {
      request = new ActiveXObject("Microsoft.XMLHTTP");
    } catch(e) {
      request = null;
    }
  }
}
```

The code has to try a few different approaches to creating the XMLHttpRequest object because some browsers (IE) support it differently.

The try-catch statement is an advanced JavaScript error-handling mechanism that allows a script to gracefully deal with runtime errors.

 Geek Bits

The problem with creating an XMLHttpRequest object is that browsers must provide their own implementations of the object. The good news is that the methods and properties are consistent across all browsers—it's the object creation that has to factor in browser differences.

After the XMLHttpRequest object is created, it's time to set the request handler function and then open the request.

This is the custom function that is called when the server responds to the request.

```
request.onreadystatechange = handler;
request.open(type, url, true); // always asynchronous (true)
```

Opening the request gets it ready to be sent, and also determines what kind of request it is (GET or POST).

When opening a request, you must specify the type ("GET" or "POST"), as well as the server URL and whether or not the request is asynchronous. An **asynchronous request** takes place in the background without making a script wait, so pretty much all Ajax requests are asynchronous.

Of gets and posts

The **type** of an Ajax request is very important, and reflects not only what is being sent to the server, but also the **intent** of the request. One type of request, also known as a request **method**, is GET, which is used primarily to retrieve data from the server without affecting anything on the server. The other type of request, POST, typically involves sending data to the server, after which the state of the server usually changes somehow in response to the data that was sent.

The two types of requests used with Ajax are GET and POST, the same ones used when submitting HTML forms.

GET

Used for data retrieval that doesn't change anything on the server. Small amounts of data can still be sent to the server in the URL if necessary. GET is perfect for retrieving the blog data from an XML file on the server.

POST

Used to send data to the server that somehow causes a change in the state of the server, such as saving data to a database. Data can still be returned in a response. POST is ideal for a task such as dynamically adding a new blog entry to the blog using a web form.

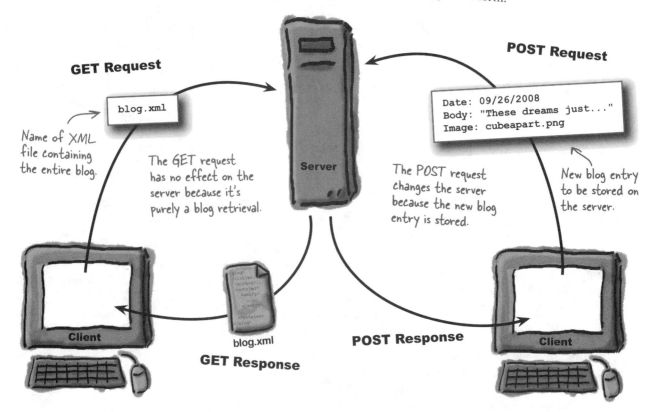

GET Request

`blog.xml`

Name of XML file containing the entire blog.

The GET request has no effect on the server because it's purely a blog retrieval.

Server

POST Request

Date: 09/26/2008
Body: "These dreams just..."
Image: cubeapart.png

The POST request changes the server because the new blog entry is stored.

New blog entry to be stored on the server.

Client

blog.xml

GET Response

POST Response

Client

Get or Post? A request with XMLHttpRequest

After deciding on a request type and specifying it when opening the request, it's finally time to send the request to the server for processing. The specific code to submit a request varies according to whether the request is a GET or a POST.

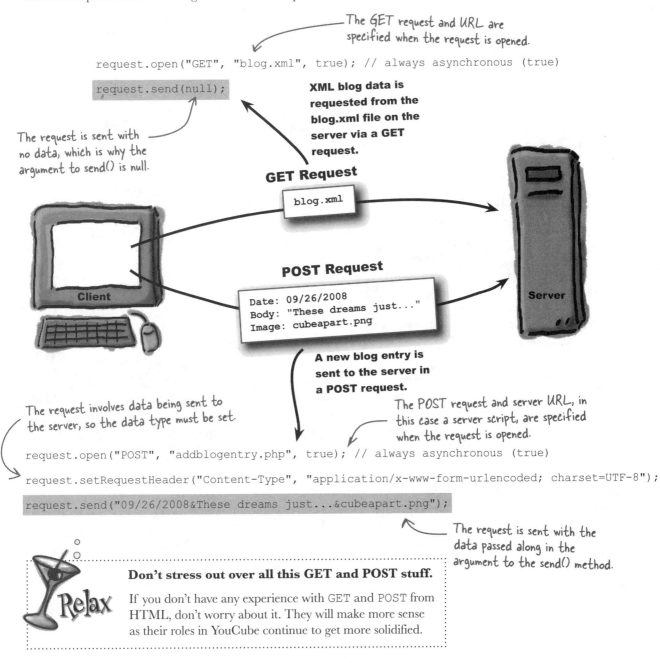

The GET request and URL are specified when the request is opened.

```
request.open("GET", "blog.xml", true); // always asynchronous (true)
request.send(null);
```

The request is sent with no data, which is why the argument to send() is null.

XML blog data is requested from the blog.xml file on the server via a GET request.

GET Request

blog.xml

Client

Server

POST Request

Date: 09/26/2008
Body: "These dreams just..."
Image: cubeapart.png

A new blog entry is sent to the server in a POST request.

The request involves data being sent to the server, so the data type must be set.

The POST request and server URL, in this case a server script, are specified when the request is opened.

```
request.open("POST", "addblogentry.php", true); // always asynchronous (true)
request.setRequestHeader("Content-Type", "application/x-www-form-urlencoded; charset=UTF-8");
request.send("09/26/2008&These dreams just...&cubeapart.png");
```

The request is sent with the data passed along in the argument to the send() method.

Don't stress out over all this GET and POST stuff.

If you don't have any experience with GET and POST from HTML, don't worry about it. They will make more sense as their roles in YouCube continue to get more solidified.

Make XMLHttpRequest less painful

Although the XMLHttpRequest object is incredibly powerful, it comes with a fairly steep learning curve, as you no doubt already realize. Not only that, but it requires a certain amount of "boilerplate" code that has to go into every Ajax application that uses it. For this reason, lots of third party libraries have been created to make it easier to use the XMLHttpRequest object. Many of these libraries extend the features of JavaScript, which is great but requires even more learning.

For this reason, a helpful strategy for YouCube is to create a minimal custom object that serves as a convenient assistant to XMLHttpRequest, allowing us to focus purely on **doing things** with Ajax, as opposed to wrestling with the XMLHttpRequest object or mastering some third party library. This custom object, AjaxRequest, takes a minimalist approach to making the XMLHttpRequest object more usable.

The custom AjaxRequest object eases the pain of making Ajax requests.

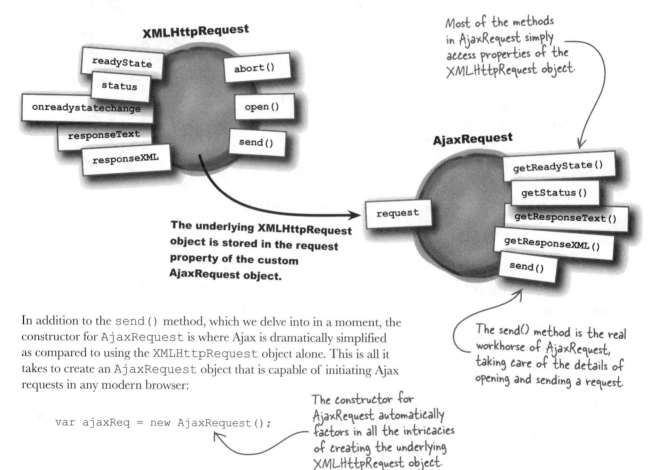

Most of the methods in AjaxRequest simply access properties of the XMLHttpRequest object.

The underlying XMLHttpRequest object is stored in the request property of the custom AjaxRequest object.

The send() method is the real workhorse of AjaxRequest, taking care of the details of opening and sending a request.

In addition to the send() method, which we delve into in a moment, the constructor for AjaxRequest is where Ajax is dramatically simplified as compared to using the XMLHttpRequest object alone. This is all it takes to create an AjaxRequest object that is capable of initiating Ajax requests in any modern browser:

```
var ajaxReq = new AjaxRequest();
```

The constructor for AjaxRequest automatically factors in all the intricacies of creating the underlying XMLHttpRequest object.

JavaScript Magnets

The custom `AjaxRequest` object wraps up the standard `XMLHttpRequest` object, providing a much simpler interface for sending Ajax requests and handling their responses. Problem is, the `send()` method of the `AjaxRequest` object is missing a few key pieces of code. Use the magnets to finish the code for the method.

```javascript
AjaxRequest.prototype.send = function(type, url, handler, postDataType, postData) {
  if (this.request != null) {
    // Kill the previous request
    this.request.abort();

    // Tack on a dummy parameter to override browser caching
    url += "?dummy=" + new Date().getTime();

    try {
      this.request.onreadystatechange = ..................... ;

      this.request.open(.................'............., true); // always asynchronous (true)

      if (type.toLowerCase() == "get") {
        // Send a GET request; no data involved

        this.request.send(..............);

      } else {
        // Send a POST request; the last argument is data

        this.request.setRequestHeader("Content-Type", ........................... );

        this.request.send(....................... );

      }
    } catch(e) {
      alert("Ajax error communicating with the server.\n" + "Details: " + e);
    }
  }
}
```

handler

url

null

type

postDataType

postData

JavaScript Magnets Solution

The custom `AjaxRequest` object wraps up the standard `XMLHttpRequest` object, providing a much simpler interface for sending Ajax requests and handling their responses. Problem is, the `send()` method of the `AjaxRequest` object is missing a few key pieces of code. Use the magnets to finish the code for the method.

The send() method sends an Ajax request with details spelled out in its arguments.

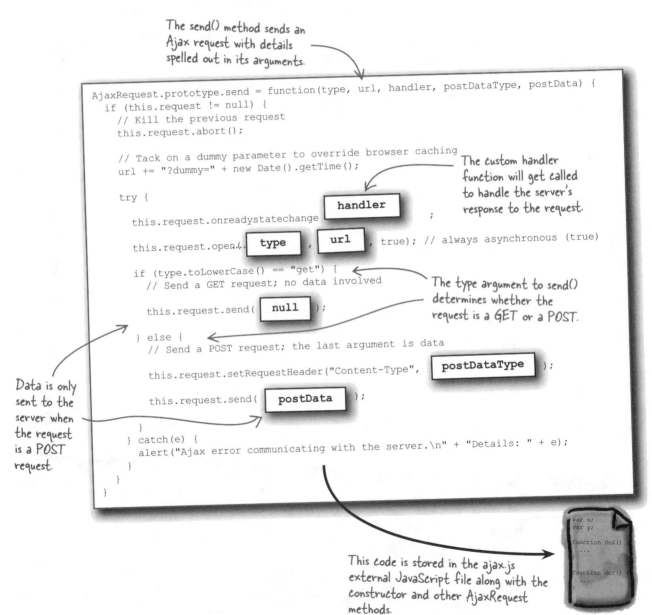

```
AjaxRequest.prototype.send = function(type, url, handler, postDataType, postData) {
  if (this.request != null) {
    // Kill the previous request
    this.request.abort();

    // Tack on a dummy parameter to override browser caching
    url += "?dummy=" + new Date().getTime();

    try {
      this.request.onreadystatechange       handler       ;

      this.request.open(..   type   ,   url   , true); // always asynchronous (true)

      if (type.toLowerCase() == "get") {
        // Send a GET request; no data involved
        this.request.send(   null   );
      } else {
        // Send a POST request; the last argument is data
        this.request.setRequestHeader("Content-Type",   postDataType   );

        this.request.send(   postData   );
      }
    } catch(e) {
      alert("Ajax error communicating with the server.\n" + "Details: " + e);
    }
  }
}
```

The custom handler function will get called to handle the server's response to the request.

The type argument to send() determines whether the request is a GET or a POST.

Data is only sent to the server when the request is a POST request.

This code is stored in the ajax.js external JavaScript file along with the constructor and other AjaxRequest methods.

ajax.js

Making sense of an Ajax request

The custom `AjaxRequest` object consists of a constructor and several methods, one of which is particularly useful. The `send()` method is used to prepare and issue an Ajax request to a server in a single call. All Ajax requests issued using `send()` are either GET or POST requests, which correspond to HTML form submission requests. The difference is that an Ajax request doesn't require a complete reload of a page.

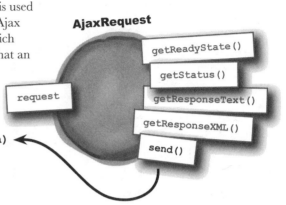

AjaxRequest

`getReadyState()`

`getStatus()`

`getResponseText()`

`getResponseXML()`

`request`

`send()`

```
send(type, url, handler, postDataType, postData)
```

type

The type of the request, GET or POST.

url

The URL of the server (blog.xml in the case of YouCube). Data can be packaged into this URL if necessary.

postDataType

The type of data being sent (only for POSTs, not required for GETs).

handler

The callback function used to handle the response.

postData

The data to be sent (only for POSTs, not required for GETs). POST data can be submitted in several different formats.

All Ajax requests involve these same pieces of information, although GET requests skip the last two arguments, which are optional. So the first three arguments to `send()` are the most important, and are sufficient for most simple Ajax requests. As an example, the following call to `send()` uses the first three arguments to request (GET) XML data from a file named movies.xml on the server:

Don't panic over the handling of requests.

We'll get to the ins and outs of how Ajax requests are handled in custom JavaScript code soon enough. For now, just understand that a **custom request handler function** must be set for a request, and that the function is called when a request is completed.

The type of request.

The URL of the requested data file.

```
ajaxReq.send("GET", "movies.xml", handleRequest);
```

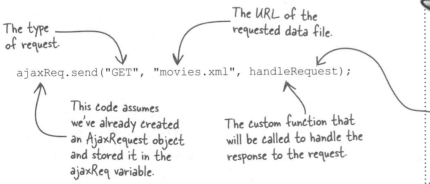

This code assumes we've already created an AjaxRequest object and stored it in the ajaxReq variable.

The custom function that will be called to handle the response to the request.

The ~~bull~~ request enters the server's court

When the `send()` method is called on an `AjaxRequest` object, an Ajax request is sent to the server, and the web page is left to go about its business while the server processes the request. This is where the asynchronous part of Ajax really shines. If the request was synchronous, the page would be frozen, unable to do anything until the server returns with a response. But since the request takes place **asynchronously**, the page isn't halted and the user experience isn't stalled.

While the server processes the request, the page is allowed to go about its own business without being stalled.

youcube.html

blog.xml

Just because the page isn't frozen while a request is being processed doesn't necessarily mean the user can actually do anything productive. It all depends on the specific page. In the case of YouCube, successfully viewing the blog is entirely dependent on getting the blog data back from the server in an Ajax response. So in this case the user experience is tied to the Ajax response.

An _asynchronous_ Ajax request takes place without freezing a page while it waits for the request to be processed by a server.

BULLET POINTS

- The `XMLHttpRequest` object is the **standard** object for carrying out Ajax requests but it can be somewhat messy to use.

- The **custom** `AjaxRequest` object serves as a convenient way to use Ajax without having to deal

- directly with `XMLHttpRequest`.

- Ajax requests always fall into one of two types, `GET` or `POST`, which is determined by the data being sent to the server, as well as how the data affects the server.

- The `send()` method of the `AjaxRequest` object

Q: **Is the** `AjaxRequest` **object necessary for carrying out Ajax requests?**

A: No. It's perfectly fine to use the `XMLHttpRequest` object directly to issue Ajax requests and handle their responses. But why would you when there is a much easier way thanks to the `AjaxRequest` object? The `AjaxRequest` object doesn't do anything earth-shattering—it's just a convenience object that helps simplify the task of using Ajax by taking care of the "busy work" involved in assembling Ajax requests.

Q: **How is an Ajax request/response any different than an HTTP request/response?**

A: HTTP requests and responses are used by web browsers to retrieve HTML web pages from web servers. Ajax requests and responses are very similar to HTTP requests and responses except for a couple of key differences: the Ajax versions can occur at any time and don't necessarily involve the delivery of HTML data. In fact, one of the huge benefits of Ajax is that it can be used to request **any** kind of data.

It's a big deal that Ajax can handle any kind of data, but it's also the size of the data that matters as much as anything. Ajax isn't limited to handling an entire page or document of data at a time. In fact, it's really geared toward the delivery of little bite-sized pieces of data. In doing so, Ajax allows a page to dynamically modify itself by requesting little chunks of data and then incorporating it into the page. And all of this happens without the page ever having to be reloaded.

Q: **So Ajax makes it possible to dynamically assemble a web page in pieces?**

A: Yes! That's the main idea behind Ajax. But it's more than just assembling a page from pieces. It's also about the **timing** of when this assembly occurs. Ajax requests and responses take place in real time, often without interrupting the usability of a page. In other words, users aren't stuck waiting for an entire page to reload when all that needs to be updated is one small section of the page. That section of the page can be loading in the "background" while someone continues to read and interact with other parts of the page.

Q: **What do** `GET` **and** `POST` **have to do with all this?**

A: `GET` and `POST` determine the specifics of how an Ajax request is handled by the server. However, they aren't any different in terms of being able to dynamically request data of any type at any time—all of the Ajax benefits apply to both request types. The main distinction between `GET` and `POST` has to do with whether or not the server undergoes a change in state based upon the data, such as storing it in a database. If so, a `POST` is in order. Otherwise, go with `GET`.

WHAT'S MY PURPOSE?

Match each Ajax-related piece of code to what it does.

`XMLHttpRequest`

Retrieves data without changing anything on the server.

`GET`

Submits an Ajax request to the server, resulting in a response.

`send()`

Sends data to the server, somehow resulting in a change on the server.

`AjaxRequest`

The standard JavaScript object that makes Ajax possible.

`POST`

The custom object used to simplify Ajax requests and responses.

✦ WHAT'S MY PURPOSE? ✦

Match each Ajax-related piece of code to what it does.

XMLHttpRequest

GET

send()

AjaxRequest

POST

Retrieves data without changing anything on the server.

Submits an Ajax request to the server, resulting in a response.

Sends data to the server, somehow resulting in a change on the server.

The standard JavaScript object that makes Ajax possible.

The custom object used to simplify Ajax requests and responses.

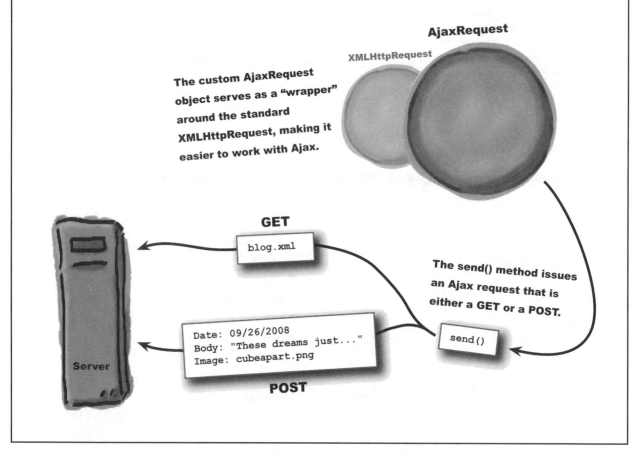

AjaxRequest

XMLHttpRequest

The custom AjaxRequest object serves as a "wrapper" around the standard XMLHttpRequest, making it easier to work with Ajax.

GET

blog.xml

The send() method issues an Ajax request that is either a GET or a POST.

Date: 09/26/2008
Body: "These dreams just..."
Image: cubeapart.png

send()

Server

POST

Interactive pages start with a request object

Regardless of how Ajax is being used or what kind of data it is attempting to access, any Ajax communication of data begins with a request. So Ruby's first task in turning YouCube into a data-driven application is to issue an Ajax request for the XML file containing the blog data.

It sounds as if I need to create an AjaxRequest object and then use it to send a request for the blog data.

1 Create an AjaxRequest object.

2 Issue a GET request to retrieve the blog.xml file from the server.

3 Handle the request... ?

Ruby still isn't sure about step 3, but she can focus on the first two steps for now.

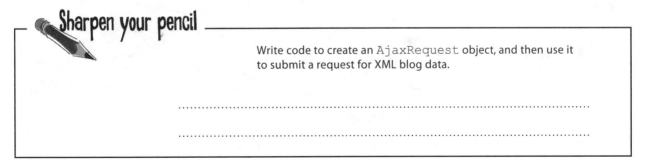

Sharpen your pencil

Write code to create an AjaxRequest object, and then use it to submit a request for XML blog data.

....

....

Sharpen your pencil Solution

Write code to create an `AjaxRequest` object, and then use it to submit a request for XML blog data.

1 `var ajaxReq = new AjaxRequest();`

2 `ajaxReq.send("GET", "blog.xml", handleRequest);`

The Ajax request is a GET request since all we're doing is retrieving data from the server.

The XML file is specified as the URL of the request.

None of this means much until we handle the response in the custom handleRequest() function.

Call me when you're done

Once an Ajax request is sent, the browser's role changes—it's not waiting for a response from the server. But because Ajax requests are typically carried out **asynchronously**, the user can continue interacting with the page while the browser waits for the response behind the scenes. In other words, the Ajax request doesn't halt the page while the request is being processed on the server. Once the request is finished being processed on the server, its response is handled in JavaScript code using a callback function, the **request handler**.

> **The client script handles the response to an Ajax request using a custom callback function.**

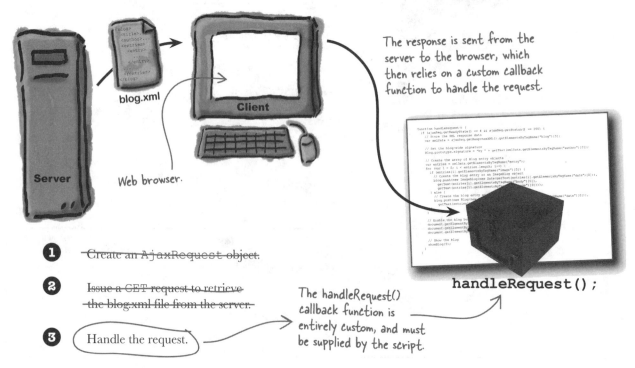

The response is sent from the server to the browser, which then relies on a custom callback function to handle the request.

blog.xml

Client

Server

Web browser.

`handleRequest();`

1 ~~Create an AjaxRequest object.~~

2 ~~Issue a GET request to retrieve the blog.xml file from the server.~~

3 Handle the request.

The handleRequest() callback function is entirely custom, and must be supplied by the script.

Handling a response...seamlessly

The custom request handler callback function, `handleRequest()` in this case, is called once an Ajax request finishes. In addition to signaling that a request has completed successfully, this function's job is to take action based upon the response data returned by the server.

> I get that the request handler is called to take care of the Ajax response, but how does it access the response data?

Methods of the AjaxRequest object have access to the Ajax response data.

The request handler function provides access to the data passed back in an Ajax response through two methods of the `AjaxRequest` object, `getResponseText()` and `getResponseXML()`.

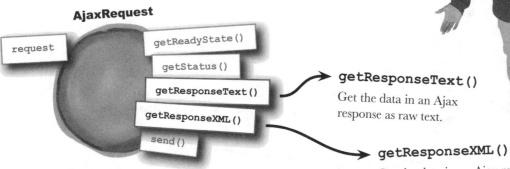

getResponseText()

Get the data in an Ajax response as raw text.

getResponseXML()

Get the data in an Ajax response as structured XML code.

Only one of these methods has access to viable data for any given response, meaning that the format of the data determines which method should be used. So `getResponseXML()` should be used if the response data is XML, in which case `getResponseText()` won't return meaningful data. The same is true in the reverse if the data is raw text, as opposed to structured XML code.

Knowing that XML code is structured a lot like HTML code, how could you access the XML blog data in the request handler?

> If XML is just a bunch of tags, then can the DOM be used to process the XML response data?

The DOM to the rescue

Ruby's puzzling skills are certainly paying off because she's dead-on with her idea of using the DOM to process XML response data. The DOM is all about manipulating HTML data as a tree of nodes. But there is nothing HTML-specific about the DOM, which means that it can also be used to work with XML as a tree of nodes. Ruby just has to think about her YouCube XML blog data in terms of **nodes**.

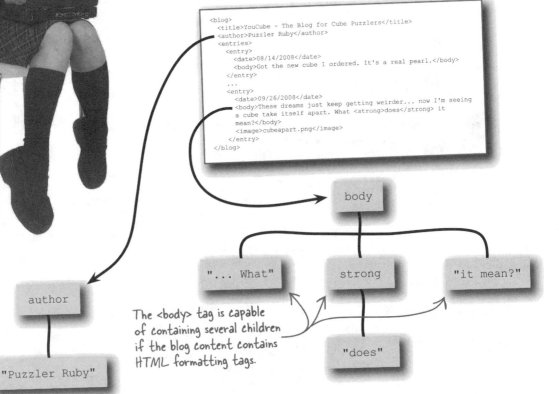

```
<blog>
  <title>YouCube - The Blog for Cube Puzzlers</title>
  <author>Puzzler Ruby</author>
  <entries>
    <entry>
      <date>08/14/2008</date>
      <body>Got the new cube I ordered. It's a real pearl.</body>
    </entry>
    ...
    <entry>
      <date>09/26/2008</date>
      <body>These dreams just keep getting weirder... now I'm seeing
      a cube take itself apart. What <strong>does</strong> it
      mean?</body>
      <image>cubeapart.png</image>
    </entry>
  </entries>
</blog>
```

body

"... What"   strong   "it mean?"

"does"

author

"Puzzler Ruby"

The <body> tag is capable
of containing several children
if the blog content contains
HTML formatting tags.

The <author> tag
contains the author name
as a child text element.

Ruby needs to be able to extract the content from nodes of XML data, which is a repetitive DOM task that is better suited to a function. There's no sense in adding a bunch of duplicate code to YouCube if it can be avoided.

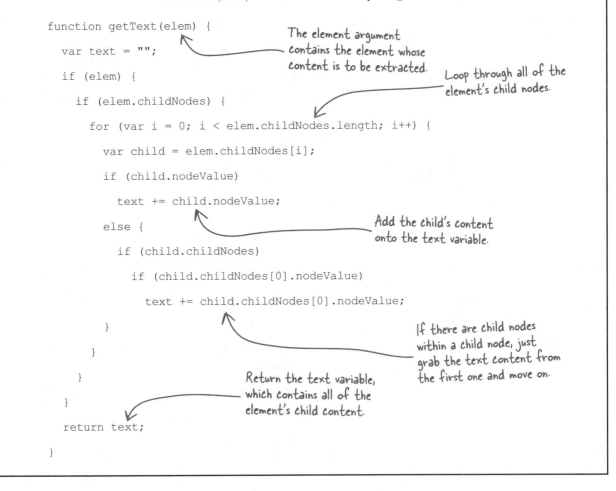

The getText() Function Up Close

The custom `getText ()` function handles the drudgery of drilling into
an element (node) in the DOM tree and pulling out all of its content.

```
function getText(elem) {
  var text = "";
  if (elem) {
    if (elem.childNodes) {
      for (var i = 0; i < elem.childNodes.length; i++) {
        var child = elem.childNodes[i];
        if (child.nodeValue)
          text += child.nodeValue;
        else {
          if (child.childNodes)
            if (child.childNodes[0].nodeValue)
              text += child.childNodes[0].nodeValue;
        }
      }
    }
  }
  return text;
}
```

The element argument contains the element whose content is to be extracted.

Loop through all of the element's child nodes.

Add the child's content onto the text variable.

If there are child nodes within a child node, just grab the text content from the first one and move on.

Return the text variable, which contains all of the element's child content.

Sharpen your pencil

Given that the XML response data has already been stored in a
variable named `xmlData`, write code to set the signature of the
YouCube blog to the name stored in the `<author>` XML tag.

Sharpen your pencil
Solution

Given that the XML response data has already been stored in a variable named `xmlData`, write code to set the signature of the YouCube blog to the name stored in the `<author>` XML tag.

`Blog.prototype.signature = "by " + getText(xmlData.getElementsByTagName("author")[0]);`

The signature is a class property, so it must be set through the prototype object of Blog.

Use the custom getText() helper function to extract the text content from the <author> tag.

There should only be one <author> tag in the XML data, so just grab the first one.

Handling Ajax Responses

This week's interview:
The handleRequest() Ajax request handler fesses up

Head First: We hear that you're pretty good at responding to Ajax requests. What does that involve?

handleRequest(): When an Ajax request goes down, I get tapped to handle the response, which often contains data sent from the server. My job is to first make sure the request was carried out OK on the server, and if that checks out, then I get to dig through the data and take care of integrating it into the web page if necessary.

Head First: So you actually get called when a request finishes?

handleRequest(): Oh yeah. In fact, I get called several times throughout the request process, but most of the time people are only interested in me doing something at the very end.

Head First: I see. And how do you know when that is?

handleRequest(): Well, the AjaxRequest object has a couple of methods I can call to check the state and status of the request to make sure it has finished without any problems.

Head First: Once that happens, how do you know what to do?

handleRequest(): Well, it's really not up to me. Remember, I'm a custom function, so I'm different in every application.

Head First: Why is that?

handleRequest(): Because different applications use response data in different ways—it's entirely application-specific. And so am I.

Head First: Wait a minute, you mean someone has to write you over again for every application?

handleRequest(): That's right. It only makes sense because a shopping cart application would process its Ajax responses very differently than a blog, for example. Ajax makes sure I get called once the server finishes with the request, and from then on everything is completely custom.

Head First: So part of building an Ajax-powered web page is creating a custom request handler?

handleRequest(): Absolutely. That's where most of the real work in an Ajax application takes place.

Head First: That's very enlightening. I appreciate it.

handleRequest(): I'm always happy to respond.

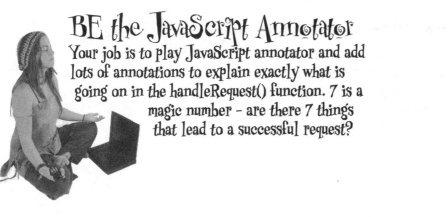

BE the JavaScript Annotator

Your job is to play JavaScript annotator and add lots of annotations to explain exactly what is going on in the handleRequest() function. 7 is a magic number - are there 7 things that lead to a successful request?

```javascript
function handleRequest() {
  if (ajaxReq.getReadyState() == 4 && ajaxReq.getStatus() == 200) {
    // Store the XML response data
    var xmlData = ajaxReq.getResponseXML().getElementsByTagName("blog")[0];

    // Set the blog-wide signature
    Blog.prototype.signature = "by " + getText(xmlData.getElementsByTagName("author")[0]);

    // Create the array of Blog entry objects
    var entries = xmlData.getElementsByTagName("entry");
    for (var i = 0; i < entries.length; i++) {
      // Create the blog entry
      blog.push(new Blog(getText(entries[i].getElementsByTagName("body")[0]),
        new Date(getText(entries[i].getElementsByTagName("date")[0])),
        getText(entries[i].getElementsByTagName("image")[0])));
    }

    // Show the blog
    showBlog(5);
  }
}
```

BE the JavaScript Annotator Solution

Your job is to play JavaScript annotator and add lots of annotations to explain exactly what is going on in the handleRequest() function. 7 is a magic number - are there 7 things that lead to a successful request?

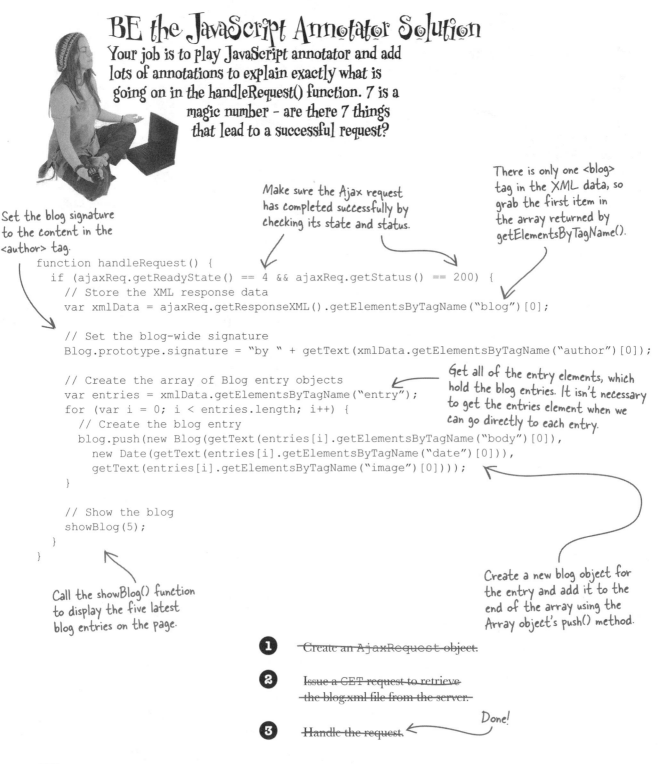

Set the blog signature to the content in the <author> tag.

Make sure the Ajax request has completed successfully by checking its state and status.

There is only one <blog> tag in the XML data, so grab the first item in the array returned by getElementsByTagName().

```javascript
function handleRequest() {
  if (ajaxReq.getReadyState() == 4 && ajaxReq.getStatus() == 200) {
    // Store the XML response data
    var xmlData = ajaxReq.getResponseXML().getElementsByTagName("blog")[0];

    // Set the blog-wide signature
    Blog.prototype.signature = "by " + getText(xmlData.getElementsByTagName("author")[0]);

    // Create the array of Blog entry objects
    var entries = xmlData.getElementsByTagName("entry");
    for (var i = 0; i < entries.length; i++) {
      // Create the blog entry
      blog.push(new Blog(getText(entries[i].getElementsByTagName("body")[0]),
        new Date(getText(entries[i].getElementsByTagName("date")[0])),
        getText(entries[i].getElementsByTagName("image")[0])));
    }

    // Show the blog
    showBlog(5);
  }
}
```

Get all of the entry elements, which hold the blog entries. It isn't necessary to get the entries element when we can go directly to each entry.

Call the showBlog() function to display the five latest blog entries on the page.

Create a new blog object for the entry and add it to the end of the array using the Array object's push() method.

1 ~~Create an AjaxRequest object.~~

2 ~~Issue a GET request to retrieve the blog.xml file from the server.~~

Done!

3 ~~Handle the request.~~

YouCube is driven by its data

Ruby is thrilled with the Ajax makeover of YouCube (it's saving her a ton of time) but she does have a nagging usability concern related to what happens on the page while the blog data is loading.

> The latest versions of the YouCube files are available at http://www.headfirstlabs.com/books/hfjs/.

> The blog really works great with the data separated out into XML code, but is there a way to let the user know the blog is busy loading? Just something to let them know that the page is working.

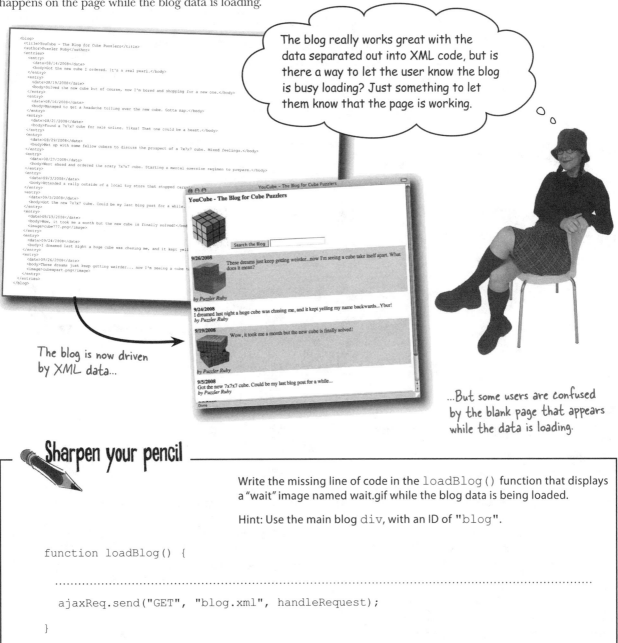

The blog is now driven by XML data...

...But some users are confused by the blank page that appears while the data is loading.

Sharpen your pencil

Write the missing line of code in the `loadBlog()` function that displays a "wait" image named wait.gif while the blog data is being loaded.

Hint: Use the main blog div, with an ID of `"blog"`.

```
function loadBlog() {

    ..................................................................................

    ajaxReq.send("GET", "blog.xml", handleRequest);

}
```

Sharpen your pencil
Solution

Write the missing line of code in the `loadBlog()` function that displays a "wait" image named wait.gif while the blog data is being loaded.

Hint: Use the main blog `div`, with an ID of `"blog"`.

```
function loadBlog() {

    document.getElementById("blog").innerHTML = "<img src='wait.gif' alt='Loading...' />";

    ajaxReq.send("GET", "blog.xml", handleRequest);

}
```

The "wait" image completely replaces the blog content while the blog data is loading.

innerHTML is easier to use than the DOM in this case since we're adding an image tag with a couple of attributes.

The animated wait.gif image is used in place of the blog entries to let the user know the blog data is loading.

wait.gif

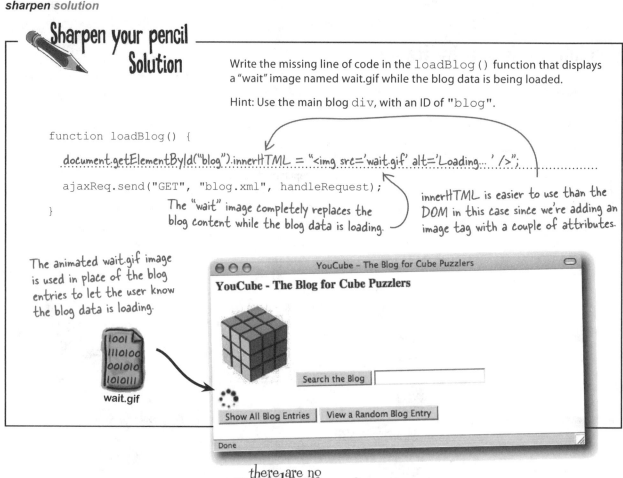

there are no
Dumb Questions

Q: The last YouCube blog entry contained an HTML `<strong>` tag. How is that possible in XML code?

A: Remember that XML code can be used to represent any kind of data. In this case, knowing that the body of a blog entry is getting injected into a web page, it is technically possible to include HTML tags that affect how the body appears on the page. In other words, the body content of a particular blog entry can contain HTML tags that are passed along as special formatting nodes in the XML code. This is a fairly tricky prospect, however, since we'd have to reconstruct the HTML formatting nodes in the HTML code for the page when injecting the XML data into the page. Instead of going down that path, the YouCube code elects to just pull the text content out of any HTML tags, leaving the formatting behind. Ruby is still free to add HTML formatting tags to blog content, possibly for a future version of YouCube, but they are ignored for formatting purposes. Their text does remain, which is a good thing.

Q: How does the ready state and status of an Ajax response work?

A: These two properties ultimately come from the `XMLHttpRequest` object, and their job is to keep track of the **state** of the request, such as (0) uninitialized or (4) loaded, as well as the **status** of the request, such as 404 (not found) or 200 (OK). It's certainly possible to track these properties closely but it's not necessary. All you need to know is that an Ajax request has completed successfully if the state is 4 (loaded) and the status is 200 (OK). That's why the `handleRequest()` function only leaps into action if both of these conditions have been met.

Dysfunctional buttons

Although the Ajax overhaul of YouCube has primarily taken place behind the scenes, out of the view of YouCube users, there is apparently a user interface issue that has come to light. More specifically, it seems the buttons on the page aren't quite working as they should.

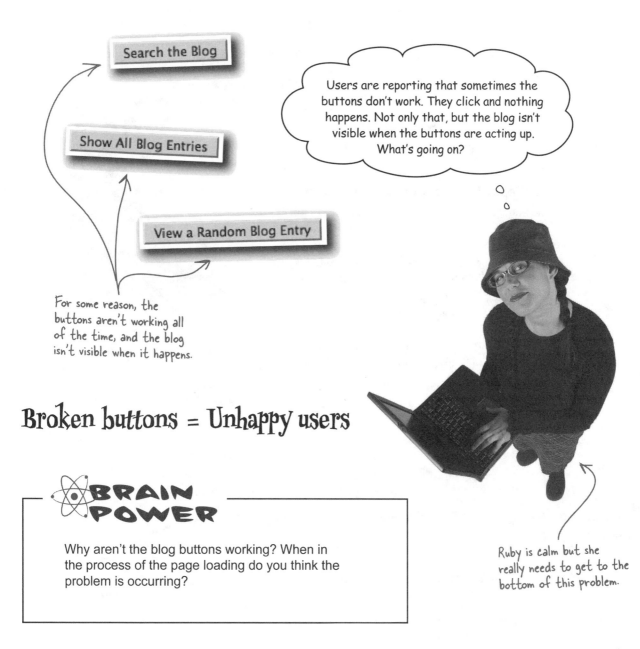

Users are reporting that sometimes the buttons don't work. They click and nothing happens. Not only that, but the blog isn't visible when the buttons are acting up. What's going on?

For some reason, the buttons aren't working all of the time, and the blog isn't visible when it happens.

Broken buttons = Unhappy users

Ruby is calm but she really needs to get to the bottom of this problem.

⚛ BRAIN POWER

Why aren't the blog buttons working? When in the process of the page loading do you think the problem is occurring?

The buttons need data

The problem with the YouCube buttons is that they are only applicable when blog data is available. And since the blog data is now loaded from an external XML file, there will be a period of time, usually very brief, where the page has no data. During this period, the buttons make no sense at all and are only confusing users.

> Can the buttons just be disabled until blog data is available?

Disabling the buttons is an excellent solution.

Disabling the buttons while the blog data is loading is a simple and elegant way to solve the button problem. Since the Ajax request to load the blog data is issued when the page first loads, the buttons can start out disabled and can be enabled in the `handleRequest()` function, which is when we know the Ajax request has finished.

To actually carry out the disabling, we need to use the `disabled` attribute of the `<input>` tag. This tag must be set to `"disabled"` in HTML code to **disable** a button. Conversely, it must be set to `false` in JavaScript code to **enable** a button element.

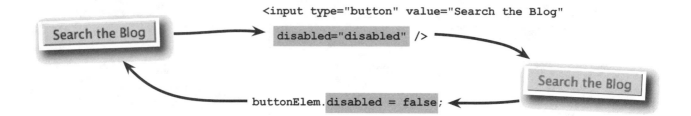

```
<input type="button" value="Search the Blog"
    disabled="disabled" />
```

```
buttonElem.disabled = false;
```

JavaScript Magnets

Use the magnets to finish the code in the YouCube page so that the blog buttons are disabled until the blog data finishes loading. You'll need to use some of these magnets more than once.

```html
<html>
  <head>
    <title>YouCube - The Blog for Cube Puzzlers</title>

    <script type="text/javascript" src="ajax.js"> </script>
    <script type="text/javascript" src="date.js"> </script>

    <script type="text/javascript">
      ...
      function handleRequest() {
        if (ajaxReq.getReadyState() == 4 && ajaxReq.getStatus() == 200) {

          ...
          // Enable the blog buttons

          document.getElementById(..................).................. = ..............;

          document.getElementById(..................).................. = ..............;

          document.getElementById(..................).................. = ..............;

          ...
        }
      }
      ...
    </script>
  </head>

  <body onload="loadBlog();">
    <h3>YouCube - The Blog for Cube Puzzlers</h3>
    <img src="cube.png" alt="YouCube" />
    <input type="button" id="search" value="Search the Blog"
              .................. = .................. onclick="searchBlog();" />
    <input type="text" id="searchtext" name="searchtext" value="" />
    <div id="blog"></div>
    <input type="button" id="showall" value="Show All Blog Entries"
              .................. = .................. onclick="showBlog();" />
    <input type="button" id="viewrandom" value="View a Random Blog Entry"
              .................. = .................. onclick="randomBlog();" />

  </body>
</html>
```

Magnets:

`true`

`"search"`

`"viewrandom"`   `disabled`   `false`   `"showall"`   `"disabled"`

JavaScript Magnets Solution

Use the magnets to finish the code in the YouCube page so that the blog buttons are disabled until the blog data finishes loading. You'll need to use some of these magnets more than once.

```html
<html>
  <head>
    <title>YouCube - The Blog for Cube Puzzlers</title>

    <script type="text/javascript" src="ajax.js"> </script>
    <script type="text/javascript" src="date.js"> </script>

    <script type="text/javascript">
      ...
      function handleRequest() {
        if (ajaxReq.getReadyState() == 4 && ajaxReq.getStatus() == 200) {
          ...
          // Enable the blog buttons

          document.getElementById( "search" ).disabled = false ;

          document.getElementById( "showall" ).disabled = false ;

          document.getElementById( "viewrandom" ).disabled = false ;

          ...
        }
      }
      ...
    </script>
  </head>

<body onload="loadBlog();">
    <h3>YouCube - The Blog for Cube Puzzlers</h3>
    <img src="cube.png" alt="YouCube" />
    <input type="button" id="search" value="Search the Blog"
      disabled = "disabled" onclick="searchBlog();" />

    <input type="text" id="searchtext" name="searchtext" value="" />
    <div id="blog"></div>
    <input type="button" id="showall" value="Show All Blog Entries"
      disabled = "disabled" onclick="showBlog();" />

    <input type="button" id="viewrandom" value="View a Random Blog Entry"
      disabled = "disabled" onclick="randomBlog();" />

  </body>
</html>
```

Time-saving web-based blog additions

YouCube is now driven by dynamic data but Ruby has yet to fully reap the reward. The true benefit of dynamic data in YouCube won't come home to her until she has the ability to use a **web-based interface** for adding blog entries. Instead of editing an XML file to add to the blog, she wants to be able to just enter a new entry on a Web page and have it saved to the server.

> I'm sick of editing files and then FTPing them to the server just to update my blog. I'd like to update YouCube from the comfort of my own browser!

Edit code + Upload files = No fun!

Ruby envisions a web page just for her that allows her to post a new blog entry by simply filling out a form. She could always be a click away from updating her blog, and all she'd need is a browser. No text editors, no FTP clients, just her cube puzzling enthusiasm.

```
●●●          YouCube – Adding to the Blog for Cube Puzzlers          ◯

YouCube - Adding to the Blog for Cube Puzzlers

Date: 10/04/2008
Body: I'm really looking forward to this puzzle party at the end of the month.
Image (optional): 
[ Add the New Blog Entry ]

Done
```

Adding a new blog entry is as easy as filling out the fields and clicking a button!

The new add blog page uses form fields for the three pieces of blog entry data.

⚛ BRAIN POWER

How could Ajax be used to add XML blog entries through a web page user interface?

Writing blog data

When thinking of a blog addition in terms of Ajax, it's possible to imagine an Ajax POST request that sends along the new blog entry data to the server, after which the server writes the data to the blog.xml file as a new blog entry. The Ajax response doesn't really need to do anything in this case since there is nothing to return.

> Hang on! How exactly does the new blog entry get written to the blog.xml file on the server? I thought JavaScript couldn't *write* files. And isn't JavaScript a **client** technology?

JavaScript isn't the answer for writing to a file on the server.

JavaScript isn't an option for writing to the blog.xml file on the server. In fact, you can't even run JavaScript code on the server. This is because JavaScript is a client technology designed to be run solely in web browsers. In this particular case JavaScript doesn't help us because we need to write a file on the server. This is not an uncommon problem, which is why server-side technologies are often used in conjunction with JavaScript.

What we need is a technology similar to JavaScript but purely for doing things on the server. There are several options out there but one comes to mind that isn't too complicated and works surprisingly well with XML data...

PHP to the rescue...this time

A scripting language called PHP offers everything we need to write blog data to an XML file on the server. The real task involved is to read the XML file, then add the new blog entry to the existing entries, and then write all of the blog entries back out to the original file. But it all goes back to receiving the new blog entry data on the server as an Ajax request from the client browser.

PHP is a scripting technology that can carry out tasks on the server.

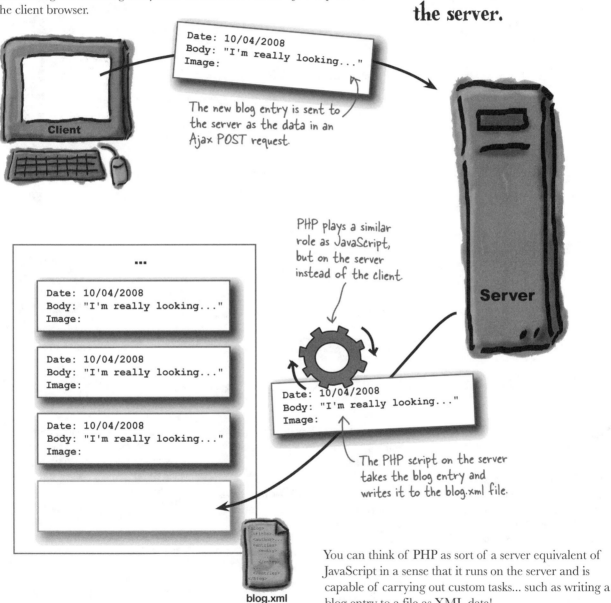

The new blog entry is sent to the server as the data in an Ajax POST request.

PHP plays a similar role as JavaScript, but on the server instead of the client.

The PHP script on the server takes the blog entry and writes it to the blog.xml file.

blog.xml

You can think of PHP as sort of a server equivalent of JavaScript in a sense that it runs on the server and is capable of carrying out custom tasks... such as writing a blog entry to a file as XML data!

Ready Bake PHP

On the server side of YouCube, a PHP script handles the details of adding a new blog entry to the XML blog data that is stored in the file blog.xml.

Load the raw XML data into the $rawBlog variable.

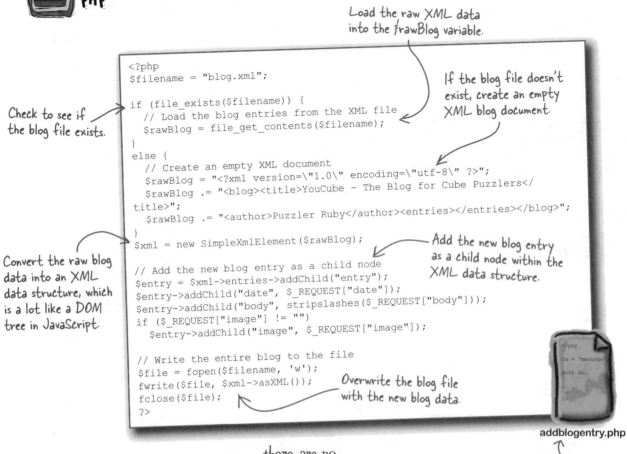

Check to see if the blog file exists.

If the blog file doesn't exist, create an empty XML blog document.

Convert the raw blog data into an XML data structure, which is a lot like a DOM tree in JavaScript.

Add the new blog entry as a child node within the XML data structure.

Overwrite the blog file with the new blog data.

```php
<?php
$filename = "blog.xml";

if (file_exists($filename)) {
  // Load the blog entries from the XML file
  $rawBlog = file_get_contents($filename);
}
else {
  // Create an empty XML document
  $rawBlog = "<?xml version=\"1.0\" encoding=\"utf-8\" ?>";
  $rawBlog .= "<blog><title>YouCube - The Blog for Cube Puzzlers</title>";
  $rawBlog .= "<author>Puzzler Ruby</author><entries></entries></blog>";
}
$xml = new SimpleXmlElement($rawBlog);

// Add the new blog entry as a child node
$entry = $xml->entries->addChild("entry");
$entry->addChild("date", $_REQUEST["date"]);
$entry->addChild("body", stripslashes($_REQUEST["body"]));
if ($_REQUEST["image"] != "")
  $entry->addChild("image", $_REQUEST["image"]);

// Write the entire blog to the file
$file = fopen($filename, 'w');
fwrite($file, $xml->asXML());
fclose($file);
?>
```

addblogentry.php

This PHP script is stored in the file addblogentry.php.

there are no Dumb Questions

Q: Do I have to use PHP to write files on the server?

A: No, not at all. There are all kinds of technologies out there for writing server scripts. You have Perl (CGI) and Java servlets to name a few, and they can do all of the same things that PHP can do. So if you're more comfortable with one of these other technologies, by all means use it to create the server-side component of your Ajax applications.

Q: Can I get away with using Ajax without having to use a program on the server at all?

A: In some cases yes but in most cases no. Keep in mind that all but the most simple Ajax requests involve the server receiving data from the client and then doing something with it, such as looking up something in a database or writing something to a file or database. The main YouCube blog page is a good example of an Ajax request that is simple enough to

not require any server scripting. Most Ajax applications aren't so lucky, so in most cases you will need to do some degree of coding on the server. The real issue is whether or not the server can just send back an entire file, as is the case with blog.xml, or if it has to somehow process data and do something with it on the server, such as write it. The good news is that the kinds of scripts required on the server for many Ajax applications are quite simple, and can often be figured out without a mastery of a server scripting technology.

PHP has needs, too

Unlike JavaScript, which is inherently supported in modern browsers, PHP support isn't always a foregone conclusion on the server. So before you go posting PHP files to your Web server, it's probably worth checking with your system administrator or Web hosting service to see if PHP is supported. If it isn't, you'll need to do all you can to get it added, or possibly find a different Web server. The PHP script for YouCube simply won't work unless PHP is supported on the server.

Running a PHP script may require some tweaks to your Web server.

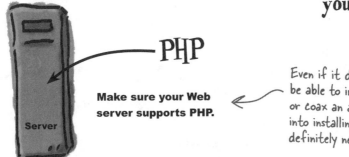

PHP

Make sure your Web server supports PHP.

Even if it doesn't, you may be able to install it yourself or coax an administrator into installing it. You'll definitely need it for Ajax!

Support for PHP on your web server is the first hurdle. The second hurdle is figuring out where to place PHP files on the server. In many cases it's OK to place PHP files in the same folder as your HTML web pages and external JavaScript files. However, some PHP installations are pickier and require PHP scripts to be stored in a special folder. Again, this is a question that can be answered by a system administrator.

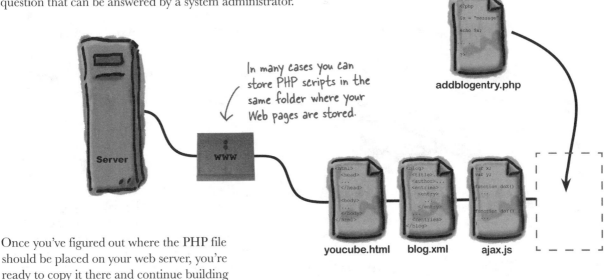

In many cases you can store PHP scripts in the same folder where your Web pages are stored.

addblogentry.php

youcube.html   **blog.xml**   **ajax.js**

Once you've figured out where the PHP file should be placed on your web server, you're ready to copy it there and continue building the YouCube blog addition web page.

Feeding data to the PHP script

With PHP working on the server and the PHP script file in place, we can more closely examine what the PHP script needs in order to write data to an XML file on the server. This will help us arrive at a design for the Ajax request that provides the server exactly what it needs to carry out the task.

The PHP script is expecting the data for a new blog entry, which we know consists of at least two pieces of information, and potentially three.

Data is fed to the PHP script through an Ajax request.

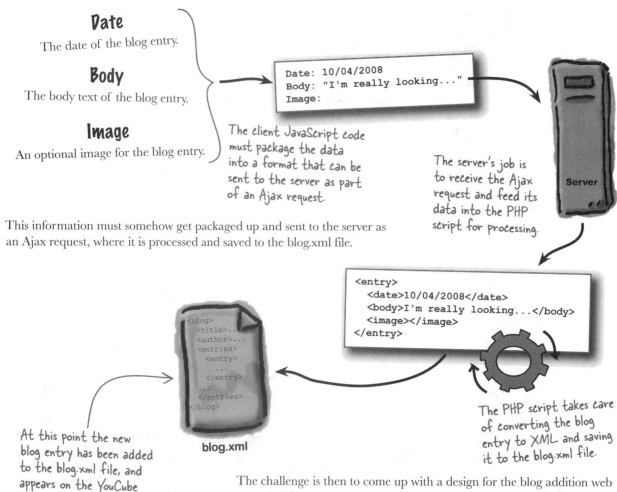

Date
The date of the blog entry.

Body
The body text of the blog entry.

Image
An optional image for the blog entry.

```
Date: 10/04/2008
Body: "I'm really looking..."
Image:
```

The client JavaScript code must package the data into a format that can be sent to the server as part of an Ajax request.

The server's job is to receive the Ajax request and feed its data into the PHP script for processing.

This information must somehow get packaged up and sent to the server as an Ajax request, where it is processed and saved to the blog.xml file.

```
<entry>
  <date>10/04/2008</date>
  <body>I'm really looking...</body>
  <image></image>
</entry>
```

The PHP script takes care of converting the blog entry to XML and saving it to the blog.xml file.

blog.xml

At this point the new blog entry has been added to the blog.xml file, and appears on the YouCube blog automatically the next time the blog page is loaded or refreshed.

The challenge is then to come up with a design for the blog addition web page that first presents a user interface for entering a new blog entry, and then gathers that information and shuttles it to the server in an Ajax request. The good news it that we don't really need to do anything in response to the request other than maybe confirming that the new blog entry has been saved successfully.

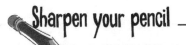

Sharpen your pencil

Sketch out the design for the YouCube blog entry addition web page, making sure to show exactly how the Ajax request and response factor into the flow of data.

Sharpen your pencil
Solution

Sketch out the design for the YouCube blog entry addition web page, making sure to show exactly how the Ajax request and response factor into the flow of data.

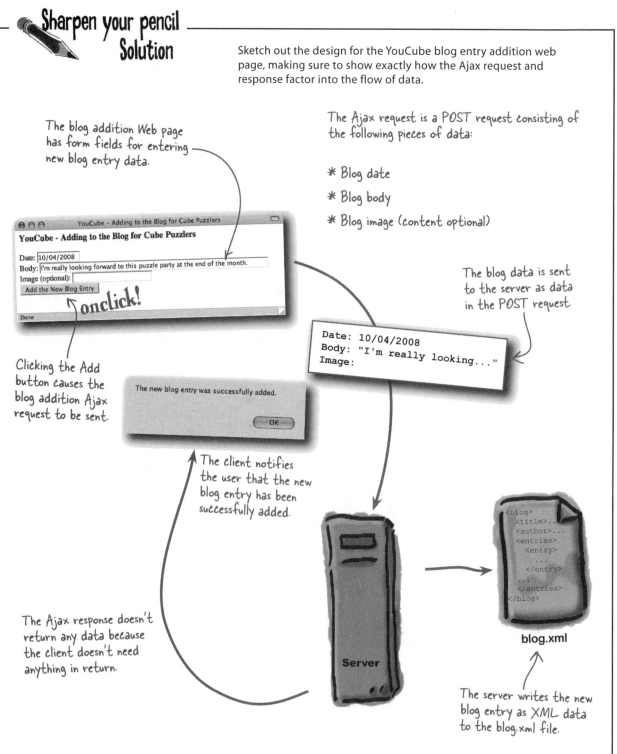

The blog addition Web page has form fields for entering new blog entry data.

Clicking the Add button causes the blog addition Ajax request to be sent.

The Ajax response doesn't return any data because the client doesn't need anything in return.

The Ajax request is a POST request consisting of the following pieces of data:

* Blog date
* Blog body
* Blog image (content optional)

The blog data is sent to the server as data in the POST request.

The client notifies the user that the new blog entry has been successfully added.

The server writes the new blog entry as XML data to the blog.xml file.

Getting it up: Posting blog data to the server

An Ajax POST request is a little more involved than a GET request because it requires sending data to the server. Although the POST request supports different ways of packaging up data for the server, the trusted technique of **URL encoding** the data fields works just fine. This technique is the same one that browsers use to pass fields of data to a server in the URL of a web page, and is distinguished by the ampersand characters (&) that are used to separate each piece of data.

```
Date: 10/04/2008
Body: "I'm really looking... "
Image:
```

```
"date=10/04/2008&body=I'm really looking forward... &image="
```

An individual piece of data consists of a name/value pair.

Each piece of data is separated from others by an ampersand.

This data format requires each piece of data to have its name and value separated by an equal sign (=), and then each name/value pair is separated from other data by an ampersand (&). The format is called URL encoded, and has its own data type that gets set as the data type of the Ajax POST request.

This is the official data type of URL encoded data, and must be specified as part of the POST request.

```
"application/x-www-form-urlencoded; charset=UTF-8"
```

With the blog entry data formatted into the URL-encoded format and the data type of the POST request, we're ready to put together the request code and send the data to the server so that it can be saved to the blog.xml file.

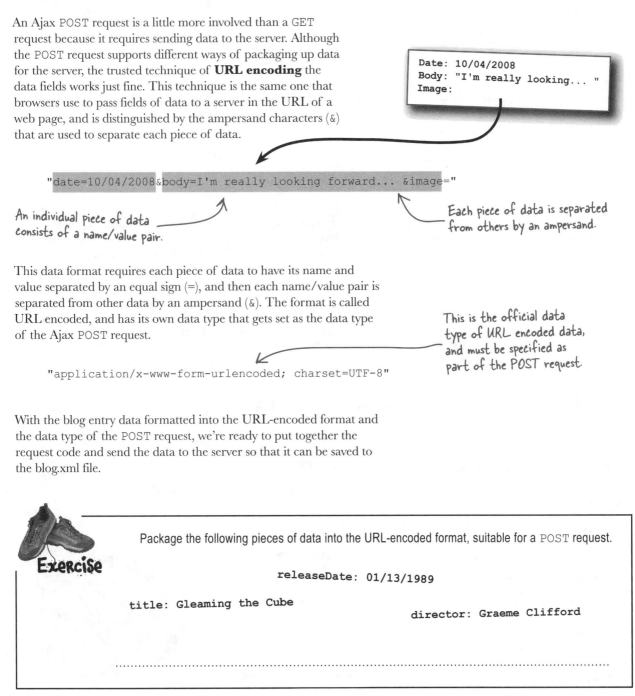

Exercise

Package the following pieces of data into the URL-encoded format, suitable for a POST request.

releaseDate: 01/13/1989

title: Gleaming the Cube

director: Graeme Clifford

....

Exercise Solution

Package the following pieces of data into the URL-encoded format, suitable for a POST request.

releaseDate: 01/13/1989

title: Gleaming the Cube

director: Graeme Clifford

"title=Gleaming the Cube&releaseDate=01/13/1989&director=Graeme Clifford"

there are no Dumb Questions

Q: If the YouCube blog addition script doesn't require any data from the server in the Ajax request, why bother handling the request at all?

A: The reason is because knowing that a request has completed is still very important. So even though we don't need the server to return any data in response to the request, we still very much need to know if and when the request has successfully completed. That's what allows the script to know when to display the alert that confirms the new blog entry addition.

Q: Could a GET request also be used in the blog addition script?

A: Yes, technically it could. It's still possible to send data along to the server in a GET request, but you have to specify it directly in the URL of the request. That's not really the problem—the problem is that GET isn't intended to be used in situations where the state of the server is changing. And in this case the state of the server is definitely changing due to it writing a new blog entry to the blog.xml file. So a POST request is the right approach if for no other reason than because it clearly indicates the intent of the communication to the server.

Q: Since it takes time for the server to process the Ajax request and save the blog entry, is there a problem if the Add button gets clicked again before the request finishes?

A: Yes, it is a problem. Each click of the Add button cancels the current Ajax request and issues a new one. Although that may very well be the goal of someone clicking it twice, the user interface would be much clearer if the option to click the button is simply removed while the request is being processed. So the code to add a new blog entry should disable the Add button while the Ajax request is taking place, and then enable it again once the request has finished. Small touches like this to the user interface of a JavaScript application can go a long way toward making it more intuitive and easier to use, resulting in happier users.

Q: What happens to the spaces in the blog data that gets formatted into a URL encoded string? That seems to sometimes be a problem with URLs.

A: The spaces don't present a problem in this case because Ajax automatically handles processing the data and making sure it gets to the server in a suitable format.

Q: Since the image is optional in the blog, does it always have to be passed along to the server when adding a new blog entry?

A: No, it doesn't have to be. But keep in mind that there's nothing wrong with sending an empty piece of data where there is no value following the equal sign in the URL encoded string, like this:

`"date=...&body=...&image="`

In this example, the image data field is still sent to the server even though it doesn't actually contain any data. This is where the PHP script on the server shines, because it is smart enough to know that the image field is empty, and therefore the new blog entry doesn't have an image.

Sharpen your pencil

Write the missing lines of code to finish the `addBlogEntry()` and `handleRequest()` functions in the YouCube blog addition script.

```
function addBlogEntry() {
  // Disable the Add button and set the status to busy

  ................................................................................

  ................................................................................


  // Send the new blog entry data as an Ajax request
  ajaxReq.send("POST", "addblogentry.php", handleRequest,
    "application/x-www-form-urlencoded; charset=UTF-8",

    ............................................................................

    ............................................................................
                                                              );
    ............................................................................
}


function handleRequest() {
  if (ajaxReq.getReadyState() == 4 && ajaxReq.getStatus() == 200) {
    // Enable the Add button and clear the status

    ............................................................................

    ............................................................................


    // Confirm the addition of the blog entry
    alert("The new blog entry was successfully added.");
  }
}
```

Sharpen your pencil
Solution

Write the missing lines of code to finish the `addBlogEntry()` and `handleRequest()` functions in the YouCube blog addition script.

The Add button is disabled while a blog entry is being saved to the server.

The status area of the page displays a "busy" message so the user knows they are waiting on something.

```
function addBlogEntry() {

    // Disable the Add button and set the status to busy
    document.getElementById("add").disabled = true;

    document.getElementById("status").innerHTML = "Adding... ";
```

This is a POST request.

A server PHP script is used to process the blog entry and save it to the blog file on the server.

```
    // Send the new blog entry data as an Ajax request
    ajaxReq.send("POST", "addblogentry.php", handleRequest,

        "application/x-www-form-urlencoded; charset=UTF-8",

        "date=" + document.getElementById("date").value +

        "&body=" + document.getElementById("body").value +

        "&image=" + document.getElementById("image").value    );

}
```

Assemble the request POST data from the date, body, and image form fields.

```
function handleRequest() {

    if (ajaxReq.getReadyState() == 4 && ajaxReq.getStatus() == 200) {

        // Enable the Add button and clear the status
        document.getElementById("add").disabled = false;

        document.getElementById("status").innerHTML = "";
```

Check to make sure the blog save request finished successfully.

```
        // Confirm the addition of the blog entry
        alert("The new blog entry was successfully added.");

    }

}
```

Enable the Add button and clear the status area now that the blog entry has finished saving.

Blogging made easy

Ruby can't believe how much of a difference it makes being able to update her blog without having to open a file, edit code, and upload the file to the server. Not only is her blog now truly data-driven, she is feeling a lot more inspired to write some new blog data!

The page confirms that the blog entry was successfully added.

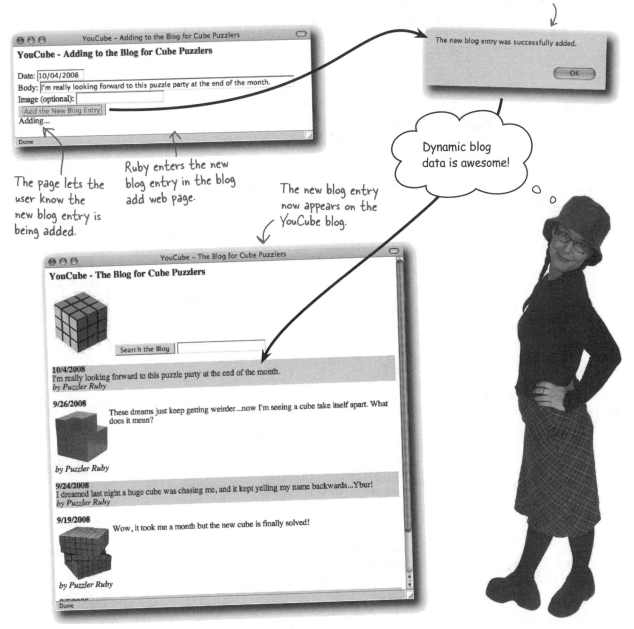

The page lets the user know the new blog entry is being added.

Ruby enters the new blog entry in the blog add web page.

The new blog entry now appears on the YouCube blog.

Dynamic blog data is awesome!

Making YouCube more, uh, usable

You don't become a third-degree cube puzzle black belt without a serious attention to detail. So it's not terribly surprising that Ruby wants to make the blog addition page absolutely perfect. And Ruby has learned that Ajax applications are known for their attention to detail when it comes to usability. So she wants to make some improvements to the usability of her new page so that it's on par with modern Web pages.

> I want to maximize my blog entry efficiency so that I can post faster, and hopefully more often.

Maximizing YouCube blog data entry

Since the vast majority of blog entries are made in the present, Ruby figures it will save her some precious keystrokes if the date field of the blog form is automatically filled with today's date. And since she is going to use the current date for most blog entries, she'd like to place the input focus on the body field of the form. That way she can start typing away on a blog entry the moment the page opens. Sure, none of these changes are absolutely critical to the blog working, and they aren't directly related to Ajax, but they dramatically improve the "feel" of the page, which is very much in the spirit of Ajax. Besides, it will help ensure that Ruby keeps the blog up to date by posting regularly.

Auto-fill this field with the current date.

Set the input focus here so that Ruby can immediately start entering blog text.

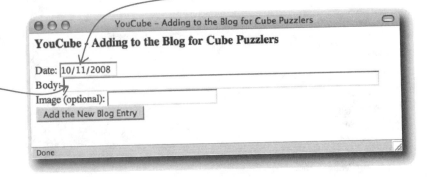

Auto-fill fields for your users

If you recall, the format of YouCube blog dates is MM/DD/YYYY, which means we need to make sure to format the current date in the auto-filled date form field to the same format. So we need some code to format the current date as MM/DD/YYYY.

> You already created a Date method that does this but it's stored in the main YouCube blog page. Is there a way to share it with the blog addition page?

Sharing common code is always a good idea to prevent duplication.

We certainly don't want any duplicate code floating around in YouCube that we have to maintain in two different places, so sharing the date-formatting code between the two pages is a great idea. And there is definitely a way to store the code in one place and then share it in any page that needs it.

How would you share the `shortFormat()` code across both YouCube pages?

Repetitive task? How about a function?

Sharing JavaScript code across multiple web pages involves breaking the code out into its own file, or module, and then importing this file into each of the pages. We've seen this done already with the `AjaxRequest` object, which is stored in the file ajax.js, and then imported with the following line of code:

The name of the JavaScript
file is set to the src attribute
of the `<script>` tag.

```
<script type="text/javascript" src="ajax.js"> </script>
```

The `shortFormat()` method of the `Date` object can accomplish a similar goal by being placed into a file named date.js, and then imported into each of the YouCube web pages.

```
Date.prototype.shortFormat = function() {
    return (this.getMonth() + 1) + "/" + this.getDate() + "/" + this.getFullYear();

}
```

The familiar `<script>` tag is used to import JavaScript code that is stored in external files.

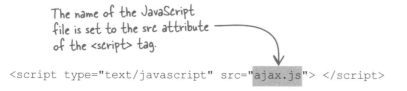

date.js

The same JavaScript code is shared in two places thanks to storing the code in an external file.

A similar `<script>` tag that was used for the Ajax code can then be used in each of the YouCube pages to import the script code stored in date.js.

```
<script type="text/javascript" src="date.js"> </script>
```

The entire contents of the
date.js file are imported with
this single `<script>` tag.

It's almost never a bad idea to break reusable JavaScript code into its own file that can be shared in more than one place.

```
<div id="blog"></div>
```

The shortFormat() method
formats blog entries in the
main YouCube page...

...and it also formats the
current date in the date field
of the blog addition page.

```
<input type="text" id="date" name="date" value="" size="10" />
```

Sharpen your pencil

Write the code for a function named initForm() that is called
in the onload event handler of the YouCube addition script. The
function must initialize the date field with the current date, and
then set the input focus to the body field.

....

....

....

....

Sharpen your pencil
Solution

Write the code for a function named `initForm()` that is called in the `onload` event handler of the YouCube addition script. The function must initialize the date field with the current date, and then set the input focus to the body field.

The date field is set to the current date.

```
function initForm() {

    document.getElementById("date").value = (new Date()).shortFormat();

    document.getElementById("body").focus();

}
```

Set the input focus to the body field.

Blog productivity soars

Ruby has finally reached utter satisfaction with the YouCube blog. Her blog is both data-driven and user-friendly thanks to Ajax and a ruthless commitment to detail that only a master puzzler could muster.

The input focus is set to the body when the page first loads.

The date is automatically set to the current date when the page opens.

I really, really love my blog!

YouCube – Adding to the Blog for Cube Puzzlers

YouCube - Adding to the Blog for Cube Puzzlers

Date: 10/11/2008
Body: Whew, I'm finally finished working on the blog script!
Image (optional):
Add the New Blog Entry

Done

YouCube - The Blog f

YouCube - The Blog f

Search the Blog

10/11/2008
Whew, I'm finally finished working on the blog script!
by Puzzler Ruby

10/4/2008
I'm really looking forward to this puzzle party at the end of the month.
by Puzzler Ruby

9/26/2008
These dreams just keep getting weirder...now I'm seeing a cube take itself apart. What does it mean?

by Puzzler Ruby

Done

 # JavaScriptcross

Are you feeling dynamic? How about some data to
go with that perky attitude? Crossword data, that is.
Get to it!

Across

2. A server scripting technology that complements JavaScript in Ajax applications.
3. The server's answer to an Ajax request.
5. This kind of function gets called when an Ajax request is finished.
8. This technology can be used to Web pages much more responsive.
9. This kind of data makes Web pages much more interesting.
10. The standard JavaScript object used to support Ajax functionality.
12. A request type that usually just requests data from the server.

Down

1. The ML in HTML stands for ...... language.
2. A request type that usually involves a state change on the server.
4. The method of the AjaxRequest object used to issue a request.
6. The custom object created to simplify the use of Ajax.
7. The X in XML stands for this.
10. This makes <blog>, <author>, and <entry> possible.
11. When an Ajax application asks the server for data.

 # JavaScriptcross Solution

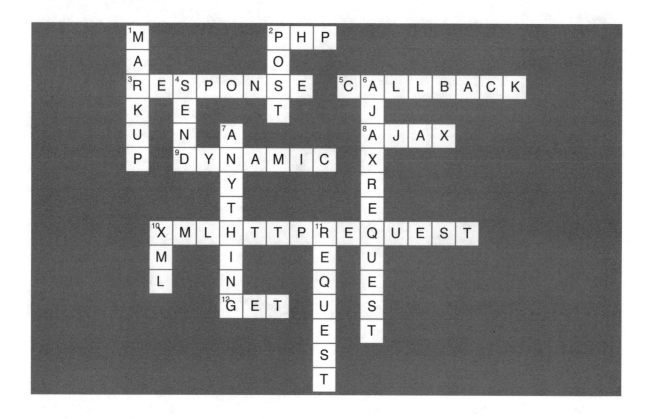

Page Bender

Fold the page vertically to line up the two brains and solve the riddle.

What has Ajax given Ruby?

— It's a meeting of the minds! ←

Ajax has given Ruby so much, it's
a hard thing to nail down. There's dynamic
data for one thing, which has made
cube blogging a lot easier. Ruby can now talk
about her cube puzzles with ease.

Where do you go from here?

Well you've made it through Head First JavaScript, and are ready to continue on your journey of creating interactive user experiences with JavaScript and beyond...but where should you go next? Here are a few things we think you might be interested in as you take your next steps building and creating applications for the wild world wide web.

> Left or right? Time for an if/else statement.

TRY the Head First JavaScript Forum

Exasperated over expressions? Overwhelmed by operators? Or are you just curious to share your latest JavaScript creation with the Head First community? Stop in for a spell at the Head First JavaScript forum at Head First Labs (***http://www.headfirstlabs.com***) and join in one of the discussions...or start a new one!

READ another book

You've got the essentials down, so get ready to dig deeper into the ins and outs of more advanced JavaScript.

JavaScript the Definitive Guide

JavaScript & DHTML Cookbook

LEARN more from other sites

Quirksmode   *www.quirksmode.org*

Unfortunately, different browsers sometimes have their own way of doing things with JavaScript. Get the scoop on JavaScript browser inconsistencies at Quirksmode.

Mozilla JavaScript Reference
http://developer.mozilla.org/en/docs/JavaScript

It won't be long at all until you're venturing off the beaten bath and need to find out more about built-in JavaScript objects. Explore every nook and cranny of JavaScript with Mozilla's online reference.

Prototype JavaScript Framework
http://www.prototypejs.org

Tempted to try a third-party library of reusable code to take JavaScript to a whole new level? Prototype is one of the best, and it's completely free!

Index

Symbols

! (negation operator) 164, 165, 218

!= (inequality operator) 163

&& (AND operator) 217

++ (increment operator) 202

-- (decrement operator) 202

< (less than operator) 164

<= (less than or equal to operator) 164

== (equality operator) 163

   versus = 164

= versus == 510, 532

> (greater than operator) 164

>= (greater than or equal to operator) 164

| | (OR operator) 218

A

action 6–7

Ajax 541

   asynchronous Ajax request 560

   connection between XML and Ajax 548

   custom callback function 564

   GET request 554–555

   handleRequest( ) 565

   Handling Ajax Responses 568

   PHP 579–584

      running scripts 581–582

   POST request 554–555, 585

   ready state and status of an Ajax response 572

   request/response 561

      YouCube project 563–564

   URL encoding 585

   XML 549

   YouCube project 550–551

AjaxRequest object 556–561

   getResponseText( ) method 565

   getResponseXML( ) method 565

   handler 559

   handleRequest( ) function 569–570

   making sense out of 559

   postData 559

   postDataType 559

   send( ) method 560

   type 559

   url 559

alert( ) function 19, 297

alert boxes 297, 314

   debugging 507–509

   empty 162

      resolving 163

   problems debugging with 515

   problems with 345

   validation 309

anonymous functions 279

apostrophes 21

   debugging 502, 532

   escape characters 511

appendChild( ) method 361

arguments 252

   altering 260

   limits 260

Array.sort( ) method 423

arrays 198

   Arrays Exposed 200

   as objects 420

   data stored in 201

   form array 293

   indexed 199, 201, 202

   mapping array to seat images 204

   mining data 199